Globalization and Animal Law

Global Trade Law Series

VOLUME 32

Globalization and Animal Law

Comparative Law, International Law and International Trade

Thomas G. Kelch

Wolters Kluwer
Law & Business

Published by:
Kluwer Law International
PO Box 316
2400 AH Alphen aan den Rijn
The Netherlands
Website: www.kluwerlaw.com

Sold and distributed in North, Central and South America by:
Aspen Publishers, Inc.
7201 McKinney Circle
Frederick, MD 21704
United States of America
Email: customer.service@aspenpublishers.com

Sold and distributed in all other countries by:
Turpin Distribution Services Ltd.
Stratton Business Park
Pegasus Drive, Biggleswade
Bedfordshire SG18 8TQ
United Kingdom
Email: kluwerlaw@turpin-distribution.com

Printed on acid-free paper.

ISBN 978-90-411-3338-0

Printed in Great Britain.

About the Author

Thomas G. Kelch is a Professor of Law at Whittier Law School in Costa Mesa California and is an attorney in the State of California. He has been teaching, writing and speaking on Animal Law issues for more than 15 years. For nine of the past ten summers he has taught a class on International and Comparative Animal Law in either Spain or France in a Whittier Law School Summer Program, and the idea for and a significant amount of what is discussed in this book was developed and planned in preparing that class. Professor Kelch has also taught and acted as an attorney in other areas of the law, including Bankruptcy, Commercial and Corporate Law. Among his publications are a number of articles on Animal Law issues, including: "Animal Experimentation and the First Amendment," 22 Western New England L. Rev. 467 (2001); "The Role of the Rational and the Emotive in a Theory of Animal Rights," 27 Boston College Env. L. Rev. 1 (1999); and "Toward a Non-Property Status for Animals," 6 N.Y.U. Env. L.J. 531 (1998).

Professor Kelch has a B.G.S. degree, with High Distinction, from the University of Michigan, a J.D., Magna Cum Laude, from the University of Michigan Law School, a Masters Degree in Philosophy from the University of California at Irvine and an M.B.A. from the University of Southern California. He also has a seemingly endless stream of rescue animals living with him in Southern California.

Table of Contents

Preface and Acknowledgments

I began researching and teaching in the area of international and comparative animal law about ten years ago when I first taught an overseas class on Animal Law at a Whittier Law School summer program in Santander, Spain, and incorporated in it issues relating to EU law, the World Trade Organization, the General Agreement on Tariffs and Trade, the Convention on International Trade in Endangered Species and other international and individual country laws. Since that first class, I have refined both the class and the materials that I use in the class, which I have now taught for the last eight years in Toulouse, France. The idea for this book arose out of teaching this class and the realization that there was really not much written about the subject of international and comparative animal law. While the genesis of the book was my teaching in Europe, the materials presented here are significantly different from those I have ever used in my class and reflect a choice of subjects of particular interest to me and, I hope, to readers.

This is not a casebook. It is not a treatise. It is not meant to provide a complete guide to comparative or international law relating to animals. It is rather meant to provide an introduction to and analysis of what I believe to be some of the more important individual country and international laws relating to the treatment of animals. In the process of analyzing these laws, I provide my thoughts on these laws and on what may be the future of these and related laws. I do not hide the fact that my personal beliefs favor the abolition of the present uses of animals in agriculture, experimentation and entertainment because, frankly, I do not think I could have written the book without revealing at least some of my feelings on these matters. On the other hand, I try to objectively present the contours and boundaries of the laws analyzed, so that those having different views are able without difficulty to develop and draw different conclusions.

In the more than two years that I worked on this book, there have been many individuals and entities that have provided aid and support in accomplishing my task. I first want to thank Whittier Law School for providing financial and other support in completing this project. I want to specifically thank Rosalie Robles, Henrietta Johnson, Jen Maniscalco and Mary James for their work on revising many drafts of the book and otherwise helping get this project done. Rosalie Robles, in particular, whose work was outstanding, spent weeks doing virtually nothing other than work on this book. Curt Jones of the Whittier Law School Library was also extremely helpful in obtaining many of the sources used in the book. I also had a great group of Research Assistants from Whittier Law School who provided much support and hard work on the book, including Kimberly Clark, Kelley Harman, Shana Newman, Juan Ortiz, Jill Schacter and Craig Smith. I want to give special thanks to my Research Assistant Kimberly Clark, who provided skilled, efficient and unparalleled hard work, suggestions and insights in completing the book. Apart from me, Ms. Clark spent more time working on this book than anyone and her dedication and intelligence proved invaluable in this project. William J. Kelch, my brother, who among other things has a degree in Veterinary Medicine, a PhD in Comparative and Experimental Medicine, and a Masters Degree in Statistics, provided me sage and insightful advice on scientific and other issues relating to animal experimentation. I also want to give special thanks to my wife, Candace Lawrence, who not only helped edit the book, but if not for the influence of her knowledge, compassion, and commitment to animal issues, I likely would never have pursued what is now my passion, Animal Law.

Chapter 1
Exploitation

I. A SHORT HISTORY OF THE RELATIONSHIP OF HUMANS AND ANIMALS

A. The Personal

As the spreading morning sunlight paints the forest floor with shifting patterns of yellow light, muffled footsteps are barely perceptible over the hill; ancient humans have awakened for the hunt. A young doe, alert, but not perceiving the quiet danger slowly cresting the rise, feeds on vegetation on the floor of the woods. Near a high and rocky precipice, she is effectively surrounded as three fur-clad men hoist stone-tipped wooden spears, and with skill honed over hundreds of similar hunts, hurl their weapons at her. Two strike the target, one in the hindquarters, the other in the chest. The doe starts, makes a groaning noise, begins to run, or rather stagger, in retreat, but her escape is short-lived, as she collapses less than 50 yards away on a bed of now bloodied leaves. Nevertheless, this contest between the hunter and hunted often ends in disappointment for the hunter; life is hard, cold, short and brutish for all in this world.

But this was a successful morning in the life of these humans in a hunter-gatherer tribe. Nothing of the doe was wasted; meat for food, skin for clothes and housing, sinew for binding and sewing and bone for tools and fashion accessories. But not without a price. Humans had not yet acquired the arrogance to kill other creatures without at least a twinge of remorse and did not yet view themselves as unique images of God atop a hierarchy, ruling other animals by Divine Right.[1]

1. The example here is one that could be drawn from the culture of Native American hunter-gatherers. Precisely what all groups of hunter-gatherer humans believed is unknown. I merely use the model of Native American culture as an example. The premise being developed, the local nature of early human relationships with animals, holds true regardless of the nature of the

There might even have been dances, prayers, rituals and ceremonies to celebrate the kill, and assuage the spirit of the doe that died on those bloody leaves.[2]

This was the world of human hunter-gatherer culture. The relationship between humans and animals was one of competition between equals, competition that was necessary in order to eke out sustenance sufficient to continue another day, week, or month; to find enough warmth to see another spring; to garner enough energy to deliver DNA to offspring who will continue the species. The luxury to conceptualize, analyze and categorize the creatures of the world in a ladder of moral supremacy where humans look down derisively on their animal ancestors did not yet exist.

In this culture, humans did not see themselves as anything other than animals, like the doe, the bear, the fish and the quail. They did not conceive of themselves as rulers of the natural world atop a hierarchy ordained by God, but as participants in the world with other animals that had skills and powers that they lacked.[3] They saw in other animals powerful spirits to be appeased so that they could continue to successfully exploit those animals. Perhaps what they really saw were pieces of themselves imprinted in their DNA from their animal predecessors.

At this point in human history, the relationship between animals and humans was personal. The hunter and the hunted were eye-to-eye. The victory of the hunter or the hunted was a personal tragedy or triumph for either one or the other. The bounty of success for the human was shared only among kin and tribe, those who could also look into the eyes of the doe. The kill was food, clothing and adornment. There was a closeness in the relationship between animals and humans so that our utilization of animals was something that we daily witnessed and touched. There was no distance, no separation, no alienation. Instead there was an intimate and personal connection, founded on desperate necessity.

Assuming that it is accurate, as is now generally accepted, that homo sapiens emerged about 200,000 years ago,[4] about 95% of human history looks something like this picture of a very personal relationship between animals and humans. But this changed.

---

culture's beliefs. In regard to the relationship between animals and humans in Native American culture: *see* David S. Johnston, *The Native American Plight: Protection and Preservation of Sacred Sites,* 8 WIDENER L. SYMP. J. 443, 447–48 (2002); Rennard Strickland, *Implementing the National Policy of Understanding, Preserving, and Safeguarding the Heritage of Indian Peoples and Native Hawaiians: Human Rights, Sacred Objects, and Cultural Patrimony*, 24 ARIZ. ST. L. J. 175, 181–82 (1992); Anastasia P. Winslow, *Sacred Standards: Honoring the Establishment Clause in Protecting Native American Sacred Sites*, 38 ARIZ. L. REV. 1291, 1297–98 (1996); J.J. Finkelstein, *The Ox that Gored*, 71 TRANS. OF AMER. PHIL. SOC. 5, 52–54 (1981).

2. For discussions of the spiritual nature of the relationship between humans and animals in Native American cultures, *see generally* COLIN G. CALLOWAY, ONE VAST WINTER COUNT 36–37 (2003); Winslow, *supra* note 1, at 1296–98.

3. *See* Johnston, *supra* note 1, at 448–49 (stating that Native Americans saw animals as superior to humans); Rod Preece and Lorna Chamberlain, ANIMAL WELFARE & HUMAN VALUES 10 (Wilfrid Laurier University Press 1993) (hereinafter "Preece and Chamberlain") (discussing how hunter gatherers felt themselves to be an intrinsic part of nature).

4. FREDERICK L. COOLIDGE & THOMAS WYNN, THE RISE OF HOMO SAPIENS 244, 247 (2009).

B. The Local

Humans are not unintelligent creatures. At some point, humans came to understand that the hunter-gatherer lifestyle was not a particularly efficient one. Perhaps there was another way. As humans came together in larger numbers, they began to kidnap and hold prisoner the wild adversaries they had formerly pursued in a gamble with low odds. In confinement, animals could be easily subdued, slaughtered and molded to the purposes of their human captors. Thus, some 9,000 to 12,000 years ago, the movement toward an agrarian society began, as humans traded their spears for spades and abandoned the hunt for the homestead.[5]

The din of the agricultural village's market began early, as did the hunt. There were sheep, chickens and goats galore shuffling in a mixture of dust and excrement. These animals were not the alert and fiery-eyed wild animals that the hunter-gatherer knew, but new breeds intentionally shaped to cooperate with their new human masters. The hungry no longer stepped silently into the wilds to find succor, but found it through trade with experts in raising and sculpting formerly wild animals into creatures both robust in physical characteristics and pliable in temperament.

There were those who created tools; those who wove; those who protected us from hostile attack; those who raised food and those who prepared it for sale. One large step forward from the hunt had been achieved; now there was trade. The struggle to eat was no longer a battle with a mysterious and wily denizen of the forest, but a struggle to acquire the economic value that could be traded for sustenance and even more. The question now became—what can I create that the shepherd and farmer will so value that I can trade it for a sheep, a goat, or a chicken?

Although in the chaos of the market one might still take dinner home alive, it was not the same as in hunter-gatherer days. Dinner was docile, it was ripe to be taken by a simple knife stroke to the throat; it was not the alert and circumspect animal that so often eluded us in the past. We created the earliest form of robot, a biological machine crafted to satisfy human desires. The animals humans used no longer had to be pursued, perhaps for days, over the top of that hill. Now they were delivered. They could be transported from village to village; herded, driven, channeled, and steered to the market to satisfy the weaver, the tool-maker and the grocer. Eventually animals were even given legal status; unfortunately for them, it was the status of property.[6]

In this culture, unless I was the farmer, I was now at least once removed from the animals that my body converted to muscle, bone and blood. My meals and

---

5. Juliet Clutton-Brock, A Natural History of Domesticated Mammals 26 (2d ed. Cambridge U. Press 1999) (using a 9,000-year figure for domestication of animals); Preece and Chamberlain, *supra* note 3, at 7 (stating that cultivation of the soil began about 12,000 years ago).
6. See Steven M. Wise, Rattling the Cage: Toward Legal Rights for Animals 23–34 (Perseus Publg. 2001). As Wise describes, Near Eastern, Mesopotamian and Israelite law provided for the ownership of animals. In addition, Cuneiform tablets speak of ownership of numerous types of domesticated animals.

clothes might come from animals similar to those the hunter-gatherer chased, but the chase was no longer mine. The animals might be brought to me from some miles away, raised in the bucolic countryside by a jolly, toothless man that I did not know very well. But I did know him. He was local. But the personal relationship between the consumer and the consumed was largely gone; it was now a matter of commerce. It was local commerce; the animals did not travel too far; but it was commerce nonetheless.[7]

C. The Global

Now the smell is a blend of diesel fumes, cow defecation and urine. The sounds are a mixture of terrified bovine groans, the slow wearing of rubber tires on concrete and the roar of an internal combustion engine burning the remnants of ancient forests. Today, animals, animal products and everything else can be trucked, sent by rail, or flown over long distances in short periods of time. Animals no longer just travel from village to village, but from country to country. Animal products, as a result of modern technologies of food preservation, can be kept and transported around the world and remain fresh. We can have *foie gras* from France, caviar from Russia, Kobe beef from Japan and more.

But the march of modern technology has not stopped at improvements in the transport of food products. As there was an industrial revolution, which changed the manufacture of industrial and consumer products, so has there been a similar revolution in the use of animals. As the industrial factory became the engine for the production of non-food products, another kind of factory was created to satisfy human desires for animal products—the "factory farm." The idea is the same as for any other factory: economies of scale can produce products in the most economically efficient manner possible. So we now have chicken farms housing as many as 125,000 hens[8] and feedlots for cattle with as many as 100,000 animals,[9] all of which is done in the smallest possible amount of space. As an example of the factory nature of modern agriculture, consider this description of the lot of pigs that are factory-farmed for their flesh:

> In some ways the lot of intensively farmed pigs—or hogs as they are known in the farming world—is the worst of all. For pigs are highly intelligent—at least as intelligent as dogs, sometimes more so. For example, a pig named Hamlet is able to move a cursor (designed for use

7. As an example, see the discussion of the closer relationship between humans and animals in Germanic culture prior to the 1930s, in Isobel Leybold-Johnson, *Lawyer Lends His Voice to the Animals* (Jan. 25, 2009), http://www.swissinfo.ch/eng/Lawyerlendshisvoicetotheanimals.html?cid=979670.
8. Karen Davis, *The Battery Hen: Her Life is Not for the Birds*, http://www.all-creatures.org/articles/egg-battery.html (last visited May 21, 2010).
9. PBS Frontline, *Interview with Michael Pollan,* http://www.pbs.org/wgbh/pages/frontline/shows/meat/interviews/pollan.html (last visited Apr. 30, 2010).

> by a chimpanzee) into different colored boxes on a computer, using his snout; a Jack Russell terrier has not learned to do similar tasks after a year. As youngsters, factory-raised pigs are kept in horribly overcrowded pens, usually on cement or slatted floors. Living in such close proximity, denied outlet for their exuberant energy, they sometimes chew off one another's tails. And so it has become the practice to cut off their tails at birth. In order that they shall put on weight as quickly as possible they are given growth hormones. When they are taken to slaughter, their legs, weak from lack of exercise, sometimes actually break as they try to support their unnaturally heavy bodies. Then they are dragged, squealing in pain. And soon they are squealing in terror. People who have experienced animal slaughterhouses have told me that pigs, very clearly, know what is about to happen, and struggle fiercely to avoid that last walk.[10]

The lives of the sows that produce pigs for consumption as meat are also quite unpleasant:

> Sows kept for breeding are confined in tiny individual stalls so narrow they cannot turn around. Deprived of all opportunity to express their natural behavior, they bite at anything they can reach. Then they give up, become listless, behave as though "in mourning," head lowered, eyes glazed. When ready to give birth, a sow must endure the torture of the farrowing hoop—a metal cage in which she must lie, unable to stand or turn over, pinned on her side so there can be no danger that she might squash a precious piglet. To a free sow her piglet is precious—precious because it is her baby. She will not lie on it. Only in a tiny pen, deprived of any chance to nurture her young in pig fashion—make a nest, lick them, shower them with porcine love—only then may she accidentally crush one. But to the industrial farmer her piglet is "precious" for its potential monetary value.[11]

The number of animals used for food is mind-numbing. For example, there are about 5.5 billion egg-laying hens on earth, about 1.5 billion in China, 284 million in the United States, and 430 million in Europe.[12] About 70%–80% of these hens are kept in battery cages.[13] Two-thirds of the hens in Europe are kept in battery cages, but in some countries, like Spain, the number is 95%.[14] The figure for

---

10. JANE GOODALL, HARVEST FOR HOPE 71 (Warner Wellness 2005).
11. *Id.* at 71–72.
12. Food & Agriculture Organization for the United Nations Regional Office for the Near East, *Iran... Iran's Egg Industry Safe: IEC Chief* TEHRAN TIMES, Nov. 10, 2005, http://agriculture-news.net/index.aspx?Type=Briefnews &ID=1853.
13. Beauty Without Cruelty, *Battery Farming and Chickens*, http://www.bwcsa.co.za/issues/animals-as-food/chickens (last visited Apr. 30, 2010).
14. Compassion in World Farming, *One Billion Eggs Now From Cage-Free Hens as Leading UK Companies Win 2009 Good Egg Awards* (2009), http://www.ciwf.org.uk/includes/documents/cm_docs/2009/n/nr4708.pdf.

battery cage hens in the United States is also 95%.[15] There are from five to ten birds in each battery cage where they have to live in a space smaller than a standard sheet of paper.[16]

Looking at further hard numbers on the use of animals in agriculture provides a stark picture of the magnitude of this animal use. For example, Table 1.1 shows worldwide figures on the number of birds of several kinds, pigs, sheep and goats used in agriculture worldwide. With the possible exception of sheep, this table shows that the number of the animals being used in agriculture is consistently increasing over time.

Table 1.2 gives worldwide statistics for other animals used in dairy and meat productions, as well as other agricultural uses. With a few exceptions, notably mules and horses, the trend in these uses of animals in agriculture is in a consistent upward trajectory. Notably, use of "Animals Live Nes," a category that includes a hodge-podge of "non-traditional" animals like deer, ostriches and antelope has increased more than 14-fold since 1961.

Consistent with this upward momentum in use of animals, the per capita consumption of animal products has sharply increased in recent history.[17] Worldwide poultry consumption more than quadrupled between 1961 and 2005.[18] Over the same period, per capita consumption of pig meat nearly doubled.[19] But consumption of some animal products has decreased, though not in the magnitude of the increases noted above. For example, consumption of bovine meat, though it has increased slightly on a per capita basis since 1961, has actually decreased by about 10% from the late 70s.[20] More detailed information on consumption of meat is set forth in Table 1.3.

As shown in Table 1.4, per capita consumption of eggs increased from 4.56 kilograms per person per year to 8.57 kilograms between 1961 and 2007; milk has gone from 74.93 kilograms per year to 84.93; cheese from 1.71 kilograms to 2.84.[21] Butter consumption on the other hand, seems to be trending downward.[22] Further detail on consumption of dairy products is set forth in Table 1.4.

Similar consistent upward trends in consumption of seafood, with a few exceptions like consumption of demersal fish and marine fish, occurred between 1961 and 2005 as shown in Table 1.5. For instance, per capita supply of freshwater fish has increased by about three and one-half times during the period 1961 to 2005, while the per capita supply of other aquatic animals has increased by 14 times.

---

15. Animal Visuals, *Fact Sheet: Battery Cages,* Feb. 12, 2009, http://www.animalvisuals.org/empathy/virtualbatterycage/.
16. *Id.*
17. *See generally,* Brian Halweil, *Meat Production Continues to Rise*, Aug. 20, 2008, at http://www.worldwatch.org/node/5443.
18. Food & Agriculture Organization of the United Nations, *FAOSTAT*, http://faostat.fao.org/ (last visited Apr. 30, 2010); [hereinafter "FAOSTAT"].
19. *Id.*
20. *Id.*
21. *Id.*
22. *Id.*

Table 1.1. Pigs, Poultry, Sheep and Goats Used for Meat, Egg Production or Breeding Purposes Globally

	Pigs	Chickens	Turkeys	Geese and Other Guinea Fowl	Ducks	Sheep	Goats
	Stocks (Head)	Stocks (1,000 Head)	Stocks (1,000 Head)	Stocks (1,000 Head)	Stocks (1,000 Head)	Stocks (Head)	Stocks (Head)
2009	941,212,507	18,554,765	548,880	357,438	1,173,438	1,071,274,348	867,968,573
2008	937,953,552	18,139,070	569,888	352,714	1,152,522	1,086,307,458	864,400,877
2007	921,935,352	17,878,616	526,499	344,776	1,132,675	1,105,610,121	836,893,906
2006	926,095,589	17,401,028	550,575	333,166	1,107,574	1,104,192,341	827,789,739
2005	907,773,192	17,001,530	511,577	321,783	1,097,735	1,091,375,497	826,905,503
2004	894,310,558	16,460,953	521,324	311,213	1,064,229	1,063,115,959	805,629,686
2003	898,653,143	16,068,220	522,615	279,292	1,026,996	1,035,154,168	784,883,268
2002	893,276,623	15,876,570	546,102	268,990	1,045,492	1,025,893,803	768,392,794
2001	884,315,893	15,083,346	543,251	241,688	987,282	1,037,143,369	756,680,628
2000	899,104,897	14,468,989	537,923	238,246	947,720	1,058,830,774	746,845,394
1999	894,355,480	13,676,484	436,742	222,639	878,706	1,055,089,037	729,954,294

Table 1.1. (cont'd)

	Pigs	*Chickens*	*Turkeys*	*Geese and Other Guinea Fowl*	*Ducks*	*Sheep*	*Goats*
	Stocks (Head)	*Stocks (1,000 Head)*	*Stocks (1,000 Head)*	*Stocks (1,000 Head)*	*Stocks (1,000 Head)*	*Stocks (Head)*	*Stocks (Head)*
1997	831,866,763	14,179,895	472,789	243,774	948,025	1,041,393,723	694,295,736
1995	899,253,754	12,967,705	452,073	231,106	804,934	1,075,580,702	672,941,531
1993	875,847,536	11,886,197	434,997	189,318	727,770	1,120,618,258	612,928,001
1991	864,726,536	11,065,372	443,274	148,001	577,009	1,184,275,962	595,506,408
1989	847,633,682	10,253,475	416,604	117,473	518,577	1,198,350,926	574,342,533
1987	835,829,784	9,558,525	397,579	101,659	495,953	1,142,089,337	522,215,805
1985	793,467,788	8,612,386	343,277	85,032	419,665	1,118,608,733	486,078,510
1975	685,650,456	5,891,056	228,195	62,776	295,153	1,047,921,744	405,451,809
1965	496,424,493	4,349,023	154,789	43,523	222,799	1,030,878,735	367,424,287
1961	406,180,364	3,883,539	204,241	36,640	193,453	994,268,736	348,726,793

Source: FAOSTAT, <http://faostat.fao.org/> (search criteria: "Production" + "Live Animals" + "World+") (last visited June 14, 2010).

Table 1.2. Animals Used for Dairy Production, Meat, Draft or Breeding Purposes Globally

	*Animals Live Nes**	*Cattle*	*Asses*	*Mules*	*Horses*	*Buffaloes*	*Camels*
	Stocks (Head)	*Stocks (Head)*	*Stocks (Head)*	*Stocks (Head)*	*Stocks (Head)*	*Stocks (Head)*	*Stocks (Head)*
2009	5,921,856	1,382,241,378	43,620,601	11,163,242	59,019,729	188,306,103	25,385,468
2008	5,775,580	1,372,379,502	43,456,406	11,168,447	58,698,885	185,292,102	25,326,309
2007	5,937,146	1,357,835,311	42,723,226	11,737,028	59,027,375	182,575,666	24,807,390
2006	6,153,552	1,359,320,243	42,432,440	11,876,728	58,833,855	179,542,934	24,392,494
2005	6,356,052	1,348,240,602	42,051,512	11,993,342	58,721,002	176,382,243	23,859,490
2004	6,679,181	1,341,991,429	41,629,415	12,242,679	57,732,548	173,786,175	23,693,667
2003	6,984,559	1,334,522,168	41,597,114	12,428,143	56,974,467	171,674,884	22,917,073
2002	5,896,344	1,323,595,701	41,818,541	12,677,411	56,189,715	168,732,181	22,458,689
2001	6,691,444	1,316,425,491	41,845,022	12,792,664	57,109,676	166,281,138	22,135,070
1999	6,052,877	1,312,717,311	41,603,156	13,059,506	57,130,516	162,276,957	21,559,705
1997	5,856,876	1,309,087,706	41,071,672	13,166,997	57,384,150	159,190,892	20,575,385
1995	5,880,185	1,326,102,261	42,821,270	14,546,121	59,214,155	158,535,500	20,515,485
1993	5,412,604	1,306,091,717	42,115,875	15,021,503	58,647,333	154,480,957	20,011,658

Table 1.2. (cont'd)

	*Animals Live Nes**	*Cattle*	*Asses*	*Mules*	*Horses*	*Buffaloes*	*Camels*
	Stocks (Head)	*Stocks (Head)*	*Stocks (Head)*	*Stocks (Head)*	*Stocks (Head)*	*Stocks (Head)*	*Stocks (Head)*
1991	5,645,840	1,298,482,910	43,987,931	14,950,552	60,663,039	150,214,579	19,324,194
1989	5,476,326	1,289,950,644	43,484,038	14,740,521	60,224,639	145,643,417	19,871,586
1987	4,672,074	1,266,575,758	42,290,334	14,387,631	60,176,776	141,762,124	19,220,163
1985	4,360,193	1,260,012,902	40,864,223	13,961,247	60,019,036	136,241,764	19,100,903
1975	1,921,945	1,187,927,592	39,732,087	13,454,827	61,983,292	113,030,110	17,107,812
1965	255,065	1,008,908,424	36,766,287	10,591,096	58,673,511	94,373,552	14,582,482
1961	415,450	942,175,069	36,958,302	10,476,736	62,161,208	88,321,807	12,926,638

Source: FAOSTAT, <http://faostat.fao.org/> (search criteria: "Production" + "Live Animals" + "World+") (last visited June 14, 2010).
* Animals Live Nes includes other animals grown for meat, eggs, skin, feathers, etc. *e.g.*, deer, ostrich and antelope.

Table 1.3. Meat Food Supply per Capita from 1961 to 2007

	Bovine Meat		*Goat and Mutton*		*Poultry*		*Pig Meat*	
	Kilograms per Person per Year	*Grams per Person per Day*	*Kilograms per Person per Year*	*Grams per Person per Day*	*Kilograms per Person per Year*	*Grams per Person per Day*	*Kilograms per Person per Year*	*Grams per Person per Day*
2007	9.59	26.27	1.89	5.19	12.62	34.58	15.05	41.24
2005	9.40	25.74	1.86	5.09	12.04	32.98	15.22	41.69
2003	9.35	25.61	1.78	4.87	11.62	31.84	15.15	41.52
2001	9.26	25.37	1.75	4.80	11.16	30.57	14.80	40.54
1999	9.62	26.36	1.76	4.82	10.53	28.85	14.98	41.04
1997	9.70	26.56	1.73	4.73	9.94	27.22	14.13	38.72
1995	9.74	26.69	1.76	4.83	9.38	25.69	13.92	38.15
1993	9.66	26.46	1.73	4.73	8.50	23.28	13.66	37.42
1991	10.22	27.99	1.74	4.77	7.92	21.71	13.05	35.74
1989	10.28	28.16	1.71	4.69	7.26	19.88	12.99	35.60
1987	10.45	28.63	1.65	4.53	6.99	19.16	12.43	34.05
1985	10.39	28.47	1.60	4.39	6.29	17.23	12.28	33.63
1983	10.31	28.25	1.59	4.37	6.11	16.75	11.72	32.11
1981	10.44	28.60	1.59	4.35	5.94	16.26	11.61	31.81

Table 1.3. (cont'd)

	Bovine Meat		*Goat and Mutton*		*Poultry*		*Pig Meat*	
	Kilograms per Person per Year	*Grams per Person per Day*	*Kilograms per Person per Year*	*Grams per Person per Day*	*Kilograms per Person per Year*	*Grams per Person per Day*	*Kilograms per Person per Year*	*Grams per Person per Day*
1979	10.70	29.31	1.53	4.20	5.54	15.19	11.33	31.05
1977	11.34	31.08	1.53	4.19	4.96	13.59	9.99	27.36
1975	11.08	30.36	1.60	4.39	4.56	12.49	10.17	27.86
1973	10.26	28.10	1.65	4.51	4.44	12.16	10.36	28.39
1971	10.47	28.69	1.77	4.85	4.14	11.34	10.20	27.94
1969	10.80	29.60	1.78	4.87	3.78	10.36	9.35	25.62
1967	10.44	28.59	1.80	4.94	3.53	9.68	9.64	26.40
1965	9.93	27.19	1.79	4.91	3.28	8.99	9.23	25.29
1963	9.93	27.20	1.86	5.10	3.03	8.29	8.72	23.88
1961	9.34	25.58	1.89	5.18	2.87	7.86	7.95	21.77

Source: FAOSTAT, <http://faostat.fao.org/> (search criteria: "Food Supply" + "Livestock and Fish Primary Equivalent" + "World+") (last visited June 16, 2010).

Table 1.4. Eggs and Dairy Food Supply per Capita from 1961 to 2007

	Eggs		Cheese		Milk		Butter		Cream	
	Kilograms per Person per Year	*Grams per Person per Day*	*Kilograms per Person per Year*	*Grams per Person per Day*	*Kilograms per Person per Year*	*Grams per Person per Day*	*Kilograms per Person per Year*	*Grams per Person per Day*	*Kilograms per Person per Year*	*Grams per Person per Day*
2007	8.57	23.48	2.84	7.77	84.93	232.68	1.32	3.60	0.43	1.17
2005	8.39	22.98	2.81	7.70	82.42	225.80	1.30	3.55	0.39	1.08
2003	8.27	22.65	2.76	7.56	79.96	219.06	1.28	3.50	0.41	1.13
2001	8.13	22.27	2.73	7.47	78.23	214.32	1.23	3.36	0.43	1.17
1999	8.00	21.92	2.63	7.21	78.36	214.69	1.17	3.20	0.43	1.18
1997	7.66	21.00	2.59	7.09	76.87	210.60	1.13	3.10	0.43	1.17
1995	7.35	20.13	2.53	6.92	76.67	210.05	1.18	3.23	0.43	1.18
1993	6.65	18.21	2.54	6.96	74.94	205.30	1.26	3.44	0.51	1.39
1991	6.54	17.91	2.65	7.26	75.16	205.92	1.35	3.70	0.63	1.72
1989	6.25	17.11	2.76	7.57	77.51	212.36	1.52	4.18	0.68	1.87
1987	6.17	16.91	2.76	7.57	78.24	214.36	1.55	4.25	0.68	1.86
1985	6.06	16.60	2.70	7.39	78.62	215.39	1.53	4.19	0.72	1.98
1983	5.65	15.49	2.61	7.14	76.34	209.16	1.53	4.19	0.67	1.83
1981	5.58	15.29	2.53	6.94	76.02	208.28	1.52	4.18	0.66	1.80

Table 1.4. (cont'd)

	Eggs		*Cheese*		*Milk*		*Butter*		*Cream*	
	Kilograms per Person per Year	*Grams per Person per Day*	*Kilograms per Person per Year*	*Grams per Person per Day*	*Kilograms per Person per Year*	*Grams per Person per Day*	*Kilograms per Person per Year*	*Grams per Person per Day*	*Kilograms per Person per Year*	*Grams per Person per Day*
1979	5.52	15.12	2.55	6.97	76.70	210.14	1.58	4.33	0.73	1.99
1977	5.34	14.63	2.43	6.65	75.57	207.05	1.55	4.26	0.67	1.85
1975	5.23	14.34	2.30	6.30	74.53	204.20	1.54	4.21	0.59	1.62
1973	5.15	14.11	2.26	6.18	73.56	201.52	1.59	4.36	0.56	1.53
1971	5.16	14.13	2.13	5.85	75.02	205.52	1.56	4.28	0.50	1.36
1969	4.96	13.57	2.05	5.62	75.94	208.05	1.66	4.54	0.48	1.31
1967	4.80	13.16	1.97	5.40	74.90	205.19	1.65	4.53	0.44	1.21
1965	4.67	12.81	1.86	5.10	73.07	200.20	1.71	4.67	0.44	1.19
1963	4.54	12.43	1.77	4.86	75.43	206.65	1.68	4.60	0.42	1.14
1961	4.56	12.50	1.71	4.67	74.93	205.30	1.70	4.64	0.40	1.10

Source: FAOSTAT, <http://faostat.fao.org/> (search criteria: "Food Supply" + "Livestock and Fish Primary Equivalent" + "World+") (last visited June 16, 2010).

Table 1.5. Fish and Seafood Food Supply per Capita from 1961 to 2007

	Freshwater Fish		Demersal Fish		Crustaceans		Cephalopods		Other Aquatic Animals		Other Marine Fish	
	Kilo-grams per Person per Year	Grams per Person per Day	Kilo-grams per Person per Year	Grams per Person per Day	Kilo-grams per Person per Year	Grams per Person per Year	Kilo-grams per Person per Day	Grams per Person per Day	Kilo-grams per Person per Year	Grams per Person per Day	Kilo-grams per Person per Year	Grams per Person per Day
2007	5.41	14.81	3.00	8.23	1.62	4.43	0.56	1.52	0.14	0.39	1.09	2.98
2005	5.16	14.14	3.05	8.36	1.53	4.18	0.52	1.43	0.14	0.39	1.13	3.10
2003	4.75	13.02	3.07	8.41	1.46	4.01	0.56	1.54	0.14	0.38	1.16	3.18
2001	4.57	12.52	2.96	8.10	1.43	3.91	0.50	1.38	0.10	0.28	1.44	3.95
1999	4.33	11.87	2.95	8.07	1.34	3.67	0.50	1.38	0.11	0.30	1.45	3.97
1997	4.02	11.03	3.17	8.69	1.27	3.47	0.47	1.29	0.11	0.30	1.54	4.21
1995	3.69	10.10	3.14	8.60	1.20	3.29	0.48	1.31	0.08	0.21	1.48	4.05
1993	3.15	8.63	2.87	7.86	1.06	2.90	0.43	1.18	0.05	0.13	1.51	4.14
1991	2.83	7.76	3.09	8.47	1.00	2.74	0.41	1.13	0.06	0.15	1.48	4.07
1989	2.78	7.62	3.37	9.24	0.95	2.59	0.51	1.39	0.05	0.13	1.65	4.51
1987	2.59	7.09	3.49	9.56	0.89	2.44	0.46	1.25	0.05	0.13	1.58	4.33
1985	2.29	6.29	3.38	9.26	0.81	2.22	0.36	0.99	0.05	0.13	1.40	3.84

Table 1.5. (cont'd)

	Freshwater Fish		*Demersal Fish*		*Crustaceans*		*Cephalopods*		*Other Aquatic Animals*		*Other Marine Fish*	
	Kilo-grams per Person per Year	*Grams per Person per Day*	*Kilo-grams per Person per Year*	*Grams per Person per Day*	*Kilo-grams per Person per Year*	*Grams per Person per Year*	*Kilo-grams per Person per Day*	*Grams per Person per Day*	*Kilo-grams per Person per Year*	*Grams per Person per Day*	*Kilo-grams per Person per Year*	*Grams per Person per Day*
1983	2.06	5.64	3.21	8.78	0.74	2.02	0.35	0.96	0.07	0.19	1.36	3.73
1981	1.89	5.19	3.32	9.09	0.75	2.04	0.31	0.84	0.03	0.09	1.47	4.02
1979	1.74	4.77	3.30	9.03	0.74	2.02	0.34	0.93	0.08	0.22	1.39	3.80
1977	1.75	4.78	3.43	9.39	0.68	1.87	0.31	0.84	0.07	0.19	1.50	4.11
1975	1.78	4.88	3.79	10.39	0.61	1.67	0.31	0.85	0.05	0.14	1.44	3.93
1973	1.80	4.93	3.81	10.43	0.62	1.71	0.28	0.77	0.08	0.22	1.42	3.89
1971	1.77	4.86	3.58	9.81	0.54	1.47	0.25	0.69	0.05	0.13	1.36	3.73
1969	1.71	4.69	3.53	9.67	0.52	1.43	0.28	0.76	0.03	0.09	1.34	3.68
1967	1.68	4.61	3.33	9.12	0.52	1.42	0.28	0.78	0.03	0.08	1.33	3.66
1965	1.68	4.60	3.07	8.41	0.48	1.32	0.26	0.70	0.02	0.04	1.22	3.34
1963	1.51	4.15	2.91	7.97	0.46	1.26	0.31	0.84	0.01	0.04	1.17	3.20
1961	1.54	4.22	2.74	7.50	0.43	1.17	0.23	0.62	0.01	0.03	1.05	2.88

Source: FAOSTAT, <http://faostat.fao.org/> (search criteria: "Food Supply" + "Livestock and Fish Primary Equivalent" + "World+") (last visited June 16, 2010).

Not surprisingly, similar upward trends can be seen in consumption in the United States of a number of animal products.[23] Overall this data shows substantial increases in consumption of animal products, and, given the trends shown by the data, one would expect these numbers to continue to increase in the future.

What all of this information indicates, is that the use of agricultural animals is trending upward,[24] thereby resulting in increased numbers of these animals and their suffering. And it does not appear that these statistical tendencies are likely to change significantly in the foreseeable future. The treatment of these animals then becomes a more serious global problem every day.

Modern technology has not limited itself to changing our relationship with food animals, however. Technology has found even more new uses for animals. We now routinely use them to scientifically test the products of modern technology. Presently, we are actually in the business of manufacturing new forms of life, including animals, through genetic engineering, and this promises to increase in the future. We use animals in movies. We transport them around the globe to languish in zoos for our "education and enjoyment" or to amuse us with their well-trained antics.

The volume of these latter uses is not as well documented as in the case of food products, but we do have some rough information. Some examples on the use of animals in science:

(a) At least 33 animals are killed every second in experiments worldwide.[25] In Great Britain alone the number is one every four seconds.[26]

(b) The number of animals used in experiments in the United States *that are covered* by the Animal Welfare Act were, for fiscal year 2007:[27]

  (i) Dogs: 72,037
  (ii) Cats: 22,687
  (iii) Primates: 69,990
  (iv) Guinea Pigs: 207,257
  (v) Hamsters: 172,498
  (vi) Rabbits: 236,511
  (vii) Farm Animals: 109,961
  (viii) Other: 136,509
  (ix) Total: 1,027,450

23. *See* USDA Economic Research Service, *Livestock, Dairy, and Poultry Outlook: Tables*, http://www.ers.usda.gov/publications/ldp/LDPTables.htm (last visited Feb. 5, 2011).
24. Halweil, *supra* note 17.
25. V.I.N., *Does Animal Testing Help Human Medicine? 33 Facts to be Considered* (VIN Newsletter), http://www.prijatelji-zivotinja.hr/index.en.php?id=366 (last visited Apr. 30, 2010). Note that rats and mice are not covered by the United States Animal Welfare Act and are not included in these statistics. In addition, 16 research facilities are not included in the data since they either did not submit reports or were late in providing the information.
26. *Id.*
27. *United States Dept. Agriculture, Animal Care Annual Report of Activities Fiscal Year 2007*, 13 (2008).

(c) Of the animals used in the United States described above, those experiencing unalleviated pain in the relevant experiment totaled 77,766 and those experiencing alleviated pain totaled 557,471.[28]

(d) Because the United States Animal Welfare Act does not cover rats and mice, there are no accurate records of the use of these animals in science in the United States, but one estimate as of 1992 was that the total number of animals used in experiments in the United States each year, including rats and mice, is 20 million.[29] Figures estimating between 17 and 22 million can be found elsewhere.[30] Yet another source estimates an even higher number of animals being used:

> More than twenty-five million vertebrate animals are used in testing in the United States each year—including monkeys, chimpanzees, beagles and other dogs, cats, rabbits, mice, birds, farm animals, and still other sentient beings. After the experiments conclude, essentially all of the animals who have survived the research are killed. When invertebrate animals are considered, the estimated number rises to as high as 100 million.[31]

(e) In Europe, where the statistics actually include the animals most often used in experiments, rats and mice, the number of animals used in 2005 was 12.1 million.[32]

(f) In Great Britain in 2008, the total number of scientific procedures on animals was 3.7 million, which was an increase of 454,000 from 2007.[33] This figure includes 1.9 million genetically modified animals, which constituted an increase in use of these animals by 160,000.[34]

If these figures are not sobering enough, further detail on the number and types of animals used in experiments is contained in Chapter 4.[35]

---

28. *Id.*
29. Phillip J. Hilts, *Use of Research Animals Falls 50% Since 1968,* Mar. 3, 1994, N.Y. Times, at A18.
30. US Congress, *Office of Technology Assessment, Alternatives to Animal Use in Research, Testing, and Education*, 214 (US Gov't Printing Off. 1986), *available at* http://govinfo.library.unt.edu/ota/Ota_3/DATA/1986/8601.PDF.
31. Stephanie Ernst, *Animal Use and Abuse Statistics: The Shocking Numbers,* Oct. 5, 2008, http://animals.change.org/blog/view/animal_use_and_abuse_ statistics_the_shocking_numbers.
32. *Fifth Report on the Statistics on the Number of Animals Used for Experimental and Other Scientific Purposes in the Member States of the European Union*, Commission of the European Communities, 8 (2007).
33. Home Office, *Statistics of Scientific Procedures on Living Animals Great Britain 2008*, 5 (Stationary Off. July 21, 2009). Note that the term "procedure" is typically used (because it sounds better?) to refer to things like surgeries, exposures to chemicals or pharmaceuticals, and other processes that are performed on animals used in experiments.
34. *Id.*
35. *See* Chapter 4, *infra* notes 401 through 407 and accompanying text, as well as Tables 4.1 and 4.2 of Chapter 4.

So what we see in our modern world is the use of animals throughout the world on an unprecedented scale. Along with this unprecedented use has come unparalleled profit and unparalleled globalized trade in animals. As a general proposition, globalization is an economic phenomenon fueled by a combination of multinational corporations, technology, treaties and avarice. As an economic phenomenon, it runs on "products." Since animals are property, they are among the innumerable products traded in the globalized economy. As a historical event, the rise of the globalized economy has made an even more profound change in the relationship between humans and other animals than the progression from hunter-gatherer to agricultural culture. Human relationships with the animals they use are now very far from being personal. Even when eating animals, we now generally do not even see the animal we eat, only parts of it. We definitely never see the animals sacrificed in experiments for the "safety" of our products. Our relationships with the animals we utilize are not even local anymore. We do not know the farmer; we never see the animals alive at the market or elsewhere. Our food and other animal products often come from the other side of the globe. Our sellers are multinational corporations, some owned by private equity firms, which generate enormous wealth from the suffering of animals, enlist the global media to promote their products and defend themselves vociferously against anyone or anything that might take action that could reduce their profits.

The extent to which we are alienated from our exploitation of animals in the globalized world is illustrated by a story told to me by one of my colleagues. One day his nine-year-old daughter asked what exactly it was that they were eating. She was told that it was chicken. She then apparently for the first time had the clear realization that she was eating what had been a live bird and was quite upset; in fact, she became a vegetarian from that moment on. We have so disengaged ourselves from our exploitation of animals that it takes a sensitive child nine years to realize what is actually going on. Do you suppose it would take a child in a hunter-gatherer society nine years to comprehend that formerly live animals were on the menu? And it is not only children who are kept in the dark. Most adults conveniently fail to think about where their meals and products come from, and it is easy to do because we have become so far removed from the actual processes that produce our food and other products. It seems that many humans do not even make their own choices about what they eat and buy; those choices are made by the global marketing machine that tells them what they want. We have effectively hired agents to do the dirty work to animals and to hide the pain, suffering and despair that is a result of that dirty work. But as any first-year law student knows, you cannot absolve yourself of responsibility by hiring an agent to act on your behalf. Given this fact, let us look at some examples of what we as humans are responsible for.

II. SOME NOT-SO-FICTIONAL LIVES

It would be rather hard today to follow the life of an animal used in agriculture or experimentation unless you were the farmer or the experimenter. Even then it might not be so easy to identify one animal among so many and follow its story, at least in the case of agricultural animals that do not have to be specifically identified and followed for scientific reasons. One thing that none of these animals will have is a name. The following are not-so-fictional stories of animals used in agriculture and experimentation. They are based on the conditions in which animals of these kinds are kept and exploited. They will also be given names.

Sandra is a hen in a battery cage hen operation. After hatching she is debeaked using a hot machine blade and has this procedure done again at about seven weeks of age.[36] When she is old enough to lay eggs, she will spend the rest of her short ten- to eighteen-month life[37] standing unnaturally in the battery cage without room to spread her wings.[38] The following description provides a good idea of what is it like being a battery cage hen:

> Step your mind into a crowded elevator, an elevator so crowded you cannot turn around without bumping into (and aggravating) your neighbor. The elevator is so crowded you are often held aloft. This is a kind of blessing as the slanted floor is made of wire which cuts into your feet.
>
> After some time, those in the elevator will lose their ability to work in the interest of the group. Some will become violent; others will go mad. A few, deprived of food and hope; will become cannibalistic.
>
> There is no respite, no relief. No elevator repairman is coming. The doors will open once, at the end of your life, for your journey to the only place worse [referring to "processing," meaning slaughter].[39]

Apart from the appalling housing conditions, Sandra will suffer from various diseases while confined in the cage, including fatty liver hemorrhagic syndrome that causes the liver to become enlarged and covered with blood clots, and osteoporosis that leads to broken bones in one of six laying hens.[40] Her neck lacks feathers and is covered with blisters from reaching for food across a "feeder fence."[41] Sandra eventually becomes a "spent hen," unable to produce eggs economically, and is tossed into a transport cage headed for the slaughterhouse. If she does not have any broken bones before this time, she likely will by the time she reaches her final destination.[42] By this time, Sandra also has abscesses oozing from her body,

---

36. *See* Davis, *supra* note 8.
37. *See id.*; SPCA New Zealand, *Battery Cages—Statistics*, http://rnzspca. org.nz/battery-cages-statistics-2 (last visited Apr. 30, 2010).
38. *See* Humane Society of the United States, *The Humane Society Cage-Free vs. Battery-Cage Eggs: Comparison of Animal Welfare in Both Methods*, Sept. 1, 2009, http://www.humanesociety.org/issues/confinement_farm/facts/cage-free_vs_battery-cage.html.
39. Jonathan Safran Foer, Eating Animals 47 (Back Bay Books, 2009).
40. *See* Davis, *supra* note 8; FreeBetty.com, *The Real Cost of Caged Eggs*, http://www.freebetty.com/cage_eggs.php (last visited Apr. 30, 2010) [hereinafter *Free Betty*]; Farm Sanctuary, *Access Farm Sanctuary Research Report The Welfare of Hens in Battery Cages,* http://www.farmsanctuary.org/ issues/factoryfarming/eggs (last visited Apr. 30, 2010).
41. Davis, *supra* note 8; *Free Betty, supra* note 40.
42. Davis, *supra* note 8.

bruises and internal hemorrhaging.[43] Sandra's life ends with her throat being slit, probably after having been stunned, hopefully unconscious, by electric shock.

The males of her species do not do so well either. The males of laying chickens are all destroyed in ways that are mind boggling in their cruelty:

> Most male layers are destroyed by being sucked through a series of pipes onto an electrified plate. Other layer chicks are destroyed in other ways, and it is impossible to call those animals more or less fortunate. Some are tossed into large plastic containers. The weak are trampled to the bottom, where they suffocate slowly. The strong suffocate slowly at the top. Others are sent fully conscious through macerators (picture a wood chipper filled with chicks).[44]

Such are the lives of billions of birds.

The life of a veal calf is not pleasant either. Red is one of these unfortunate animals. Red spends his day in a crate approximately thirty inches by seventy-two inches that is designed to inhibit proper muscle growth.[45] His diet is a milk substitute low in iron that causes anemia, resulting in the "desirable" pale flesh.[46] Due to his housing, he is dirty; Red cannot move to clean himself.[47] Red also has joint swelling because he has trouble extending his front legs and moving from a standing to a lying position and vice versa.[48] The stress of his cramped condition causes him to engage in strange behaviors like "tongue rolling" and "sham chewing."[49] After three to six months in these conditions, Red, who can barely walk because of sickness and muscle atrophy, is trucked to the slaughterhouse.

These short and gruesome lives are the lives of countless animals.

III. MORE NONFICTION: MICHAEL VICK AND HIS DOGS

This is the real story of the lives of some animals used for "entertainment" purposes: dog fighting. American football player Michael Vick ran a dog fighting operation called Bad Newz Kennels, was convicted on felony dog fighting charges and served 21 months in prison. It can be argued that he should not now be either on the street or playing in the National Football League (NFL). But from his perspective, this is all academic, because he is both out of jail and playing in the NFL. He even has the nerve to discuss be permitted to again have dogs.

43. *Id.*
44. FOER, *supra* note 39, at 48–49.
45. People for the Ethical Treatment of Animals, *Veal: A Byproduct of the Cruel Dairy Industry*, http://www.peta.org/factsheet/files/FactsheetDisplay.asp?ID=102 (last visited Apr. 30, 2010).
46. *Id.*
47. *Id.*
48. *Id.*
49. *Id.*

The dogs that he tortured and killed were not so lucky. Much has been said, written and televised about this, but it bears further reflection since dog fighting and cock-fighting have not gone away. Dog fighting is, of course, not new; in the United States, it has been entertainment and the subject of wagering since at least the early nineteenth century. While it is now illegal in all 50 states of the United States, it continues underground in the cities and in rural areas.[50] Dog fighting is a messy business, not just in the bloody contests themselves, but also as a result of the suffering and ugliness the dogs endure on a daily basis in training.[51] It is not just the fighters who suffer; there are "bait" animals utilized to evaluate the dogs' fighting skills and these animals are generally mauled or killed as a part of the "training."[52] It is reported that muzzles of bait dogs are wrapped with duct tape to preclude them from injuring dogs being trained for fighting by trying to defend themselves.[53] Another way to accomplish the same result is to grind the teeth of the bait dogs to the gums so that they cannot injure fighting dogs.[54] Cats and rabbits may also be used as bait animals for the fighters.[55]

The stories of the surviving Vick dogs have been well publicized. Of the 49 dogs recovered from Vick's property, all but one were thought able to be rehabilitated.[56] Some of the stories are good. "Cherry," thought to be a "bait dog," was so mentally damaged he was frightened of his own leash and initially refused to so much as walk.[57] Eventually after months of rehabilitation at Best Friends Animal Rehabilitation Center in Utah, Cherry became confident enough for adoption[58] and now has a permanent home.[59]

Georgia, thought to be a champion fighter,[60] had apparently been forced to breed with other dogs, likely by restraining her to a "rape stand," where dogs are restrained and forced to breed.[61] Her teeth had been pulled (so that she could not injure animals with which she was forced to breed), her jaw broken, ears cropped,

---

50. Hanna Gibson, *Dog Fighting Detailed Discussion* (Mich. St. U.C.L. 2005), http://www.animallaw.info/articles/ ddusdogfighting.htm.
51. *Id.*
52. Maryann Mott, *U.S. Dog Fighting Rings Stealing Pets for "Bait,"* Nat'l Geographic News, Feb. 18, 2004, http://news.nationalgeographic.com/news/2004/02/0218_040218_dogfighting.html.
53. *See generally,* Pet-Abuse.com, *Severely Injured Dog Left in Trash Bin,* Feb. 22, 2006, http://www.petabuse.com/cases/7414/AL/US/ (detailing the abuse of the bait dog "Lucky").
54. Fox41.com, *Trial Underway for Accused Dogfighter,* Apr. 21, 2010, http://www.fox41.com/Global/story.asp?S=12353272.
55. Mott, *supra* note 52.
56. Brigid Schulte, *Once Groomed for Fighting, Vick's Dogs Find New Lives,* The Virginian-Pilot, July 8, 2008, at A1.
57. Scott MacFarlane, *Unique Program Saves Michael Vick's Fighting Dogs; Tortured Animals Successfully Underwent Rehab,* Sept. 3, 2008, http://www.ktvu.com/news/17382977/detail.html#.
58. *Id.*
59. Kelli Perez, *Vicktory for Michael Vick Pitbull Ray,* Dec. 4, 2009, http://dogspired.com/awareness/7927/.
60. MacFarlane, *supra* note 57.
61. *Id.*

and tail broken several times.[62] Again, Best Friends managed to rehabilitate Georgia and she has become a "cutie-pie who snores, plays, always carries a bone in her mouth, and is even fighting to pass the Canine Good Citizen test."[63]

What is lost sight of in delight with these results, which are the culmination of much time and effort by many caring people, is the trail of carnage that came before these "lucky dogs" and continues into the future. Many animals were, of course, killed and maimed in bloody orgies of human depravity at Vick's operation.[64] But this is not an isolated instance. Ventures of this kind continue to operate around the world and generate considerable profits for their operators.

IV. THE PROJECT

So the world has become a vast global economic marketplace in animals controlled, in large part, by wealthy multinational corporations that exploit the economic value of animals. Animals now often travel vast distances to market or to where they are used in experiments, exhibited or fought. In this world of factory farms, big business scientific experimentation and vast "entertainment" venues using animals, like bullfights, circuses and dogfights, the conditions in which many animals are kept and the treatment they receive at our hands is often worse than deplorable, as the examples above illustrate.

So what kinds of regulations affect this global animal marketplace? What sorts of laws do various countries have regulating animals in agriculture, experimentation and other uses? What types of international treaties and conventions exist covering the treatment of animals and trade in them? It is to these subjects that I now proceed.

What is presented is not a survey of all of the laws, treaties and regulations that exist on these subjects. Rather, the goal is to look at laws that are illustrative of the various approaches taken by different countries and the international community to regulate the uses of animals. Certain laws are analyzed because they are recent, novel or reveal fundamental facts or forces at work in the relationship between animals and humans. Some are reviewed because they are not novel and represent norms in existing animal protection laws. To this end the remainder of this book is structured as follows:

– Chapter 2: This chapter briefly looks at the philosophical history of the relationship between humans and animals, and scrutinizes contemporary philosophical thought on this relationship. It also analyzes recent scientific research relating to cognitive and other abilities of animals. This research reveals animals to have cognitive and other abilities beyond what has traditionally been thought and this has profound implications for the morality

62. *Id.*
63. *Id.*
64. There is further discussion of Vick and his dog fighting operation in Chapter 5.

of actions we take with respect to animals (and, if we believe that there should be a connection between law and morality, whether these actions should be legal).

- Chapter 3: Issues relating to the global use of animals in agriculture are analyzed in this chapter. Some of the most pressing problems relating to the use of animals in agriculture are highlighted and discussed, including the use of battery cages for egg-laying hens, problems relating to factory style feedlots and animal slaughter operations, and the confinement and treatment of veal calves. The approaches taken by the EU and Sweden to these issues will be analyzed and critiqued.
- Chapter 4: This chapter is structured like Chapter 3 and will describe some of the uses of animals in science and experimentation, and differing views on the efficacy of the use of animals in science. A typology of regulatory schemes is developed and described (regulatory schemes on animal experimentation tend to fall into certain identifiable categories) and the approaches of the EU, UK, Sweden, Australia and Canada will be described and analyzed under this typology.
- Chapter 5: Animals are used in circuses, zoos, rodeos, bullfights, roadside shows and other venues for the entertainment of humans. They are often trained using methods that include beatings and other forms of violence, housed in squalid and unnatural conditions and, in some of these events, publicly tortured and killed for entertainment purposes. This chapter will analyze laws regulating the use of animals in entertainment in New Zealand, India and Austria.
- Chapter 6: Environmental and animal welfare[65] issues intersect in the area of trade in endangered species. Many species of animals around the globe

65. The promotion of "animal welfare" is sometimes derided as a concept that justifies the present treatment of animals and the meager steps presently taken to protect animals, while keeping animals legally and literally in a state of slavery. This "animal welfarism" allows the continued ownership and use of animals, but tries to improve the condition of animals by requiring that animals be treated "humanely" and not be subjected to "unnecessary" suffering. This position is thought by some to be antithetical to animals being anything other than property, is contrary to the idea of animal "rights," and is often justified by some form of utilitarianism. "Animal Welfarism" has been extensively discussed and criticized by Gary Francione in his book ANIMALS, PROPERTY, AND THE LAW at 6–7 (1995) and elsewhere. *See*, for example, Gary L. Francione, *Animals, Property and Legal Welfarism "Unnecessary" Suffering and the "Humane" Treatment of Animals*, 46 RUTGERS L. REV. 721 (1994); Gary L. Francione, *Animal Rights and Animal Welfare*, 48 RUTGERS L. REV. 397 (1996); Gary L. Francione, *Animal Rights Theory and Utilitarianism: Relative Normative Guidance*, 3 ANIMAL L. 75 (1997); Gary L. Francione, *Reflections on Animals, Property and the Law and Rain Without Thunder*, 70 LAW & CONTEMP. PROBS 9 (2007). I will nonetheless often use the term "animal welfare" when I describe laws or regulations that impact animal issues in this book simply for lack of another easily understood and commonly used term to describe these regulations. Moreover, these regulations generally are, in fact, regulations that fit within the "animal welfare" paradigm. It is my personal view, as expressed in my other writings on these subjects, that animals should be given personhood status and should have rights. But that is a debate for another day in another context. It is my goal here to discuss extant animal law, such as it is.

are endangered or threatened with extinction and it is frequently the case that the danger to these species comes in substantial part because of trade in these animals, their organs or other parts. The Convention on International Trade in Endangered Species addresses trade in endangered species, and its terms and efficacy in protecting endangered species are evaluated in this chapter.

- Chapter 7: The World Trade Organization (WTO) and the General Agreement on Tariffs and Trade (GATT) are primary mechanisms for regulation of international trade. It comes as a surprise to many to learn that the agreements and treaties relating to the WTO and the GATT have huge impacts not only on trade in animals, but also on the internal regulations that countries use to protect animal interests. This chapter examines in detail the language of the GATT relevant to animal welfare and scrutinizes, among others, the seminal GATT decisions in the *Tuna/Dolphin* and *Shrimp/Turtle* cases. This chapter concludes with recommendations on future interpretation and revision of the GATT.
- Chapter 8: Germany, Switzerland, India, Brazil and several other countries have made attempts to provide constitutional protection for the interests of animals. This chapter will review these constitutional provisions and discuss whether they can ever evolve into real tools for protection of animals and establishment of their rights, or are merely "window dressing" that will never have any real impact on the treatment of animals.
- Chapter 9: The book will conclude with closing thoughts on the state of animal law and its future in a globalized world.

To these tasks I now proceed.

Chapter 2
Morality, Science and the Law

> Moral courage is the most valuable and usually the most absent characteristic in man.
>
> George Patton

So what does moral theory have to do with global animal law issues? Well let us start by asking some questions about the treatment of animals by humans to see how moral theory relates to the human/animal relationship. Should we utilize "economical" factory farms where animals are kept in crowded, filthy and unnatural conditions to be raised for food? Should animals be subjected to painful experiments to analyze the effects and "safety" of pharmaceuticals, medical devices, cosmetics and other products, or in the study of physiology, psychology and other subjects? Should laying hens be debeaked and kept in battery cages without enough room for each hen to stand on the floor of the cage? Should geese be force-fed an unnatural diet that enlarges their livers and sickens them so the wealthy can dine on *foie gras*? Should calves be kept immobile and fed an unnatural diet so humans can eat light-colored veal? Should elephants be beaten, stabbed and confined so that they can entertain humans? More generally, should humans eat animals at all; should humans use animals for experiments at all; should humans keep and confine animals for their own amusement at all?

These are questions about the appropriate relationship between humans and animals. What this relationship should be and whether humans should exploit animals in these ways reduces to a question of morality. Is treating millions upon millions of animals in these ways morally right? If so, then we need not legislate on these topics. If not, then it is our moral duty to take appropriate legal steps to end these practices.

Morality is something on which everyone has an opinion; politicians, theologians, patrons at bars and coffeehouses all have his or her brand of morality, and often are not reticent about imparting these views to others. Morality is a part of the discipline of philosophy, an endeavor seeming to consist of ceaseless arguments which never reach denouement. While this might discourage us from even beginning down this road, believing, as did Ambrose Bierce, that philosophy is "a route of many roads leading from nowhere to nothing," to understand the relationship between humans and animals it is necessary to have a grasp of which moral theory, if any, justifies the torture and killing of other creatures on so grand a scale. To this end, I will review some of the more influential moral theories and their connection to the relationship between humans and animals.

Much of what humans believe about animals, though, including much moral thought, is based on what seems to be a misconception about the nature of non-human animals and our misconception filters into our moral perspectives on animals. As we will see, it is only fairly recently that science has begun to address issues about the true nature and capacities of our fellow creatures. So this chapter will also look at some of the recent advances in scientific knowledge about animals and we will see that this knowledge may impact how animals should fit in our moral theories.

Before doing all of this though, it is important also to consider the relationship between morality and the law. If there is no such relationship, then our discussion should end here. So we must ask, should the law reflect moral principles? We have all heard complaints that the law should not legislate morality, *i.e.*, there should not be laws against prostitution or the use of drugs, which are considered to be issues of morality. There is indeed a theory of jurisprudence that held considerable sway in the twentieth century that denies a connection between law and morality: legal positivism. To theories about the relationship of law and morality I now proceed.

I. LAW AND MORALITY

I am making a not uncontroversial assumption in my discussion of the animal law issues discussed in this book: I believe that there should be a connection between law and morality. I will not tarry here explaining the foundations of my particular moral beliefs, other than to say that they are reflected in other writings of mine and find their foundations in, among other things, compassion and empathy.[1] I believe that there are certain fundamental moral principles to which, at least in the abstract (as opposed to in practice), the vast majority of people would agree. For example, I assume that it is generally accepted that pain, suffering, fear and depression are moral negatives that should be minimized. In my view, these and similar moral principles, in turn, should be reflected in the law.

---

1. *See* Thomas G. Kelch, *The Role of the Rational and the Emotive in a Theory of Animal Rights*, 27 B.C. ENVTL. AFF. L. REV . 1 (1999); Thomas G. Kelch, *Toward a Non-Property Status for Animals*, 6 N.Y.U. ENVTL. L.J. 531 (1998). The views set forth in the former article will be touched upon later in this chapter in the discussion of feminist theories.

The jurisprudential theory of legal positivism denies a connection between law and morality. This theory has been defined as the "theory that legal rules are valid only because they are enacted by an existing political authority or accepted as binding in a given society, not because they are grounded in morality or in natural law."[2] Normatively, the legal positivist believes that law must be separate from morality.[3] The "law is not derived necessarily from fundamental moral principles, but rather is simply 'posited' by human beings and human institutions.... To the positivist, therefore, laws and legal systems satisfying certain sociological criteria count as valid laws and legal systems, regardless of their moral content."[4] As a result, legal reasoning is merely the application of the legislature's rules to specific fact situations.[5] Positivism in the early and mid-twentieth century fostered democratic ideals by removing the judiciary's power to invalidate new legislation aimed at more socially and economically progressive policies.[6] This theory of the law as the sum of the legislature's decisions eventually gave way to the advent of new technologies and the growing trend of seeking protection for moral rights underlying the Constitution.[7] That there were difficulties with the positivist view became viciously clear after the rise of Nazism which, under strict positivist analysis, created laws which were valid by legal positivism standards.

I reject legal positivism. Instead, I believe that the law should reflect fundamental moral principles that are generally accepted by people of good faith. This kind of jurisprudential theory is a type of "Natural Law" theory. Although Natural Law theories have often been propounded as derived from the divine law of God,[8] more recently such theories have been based not on divine moral law, but on other moral theories founded on reason and human nature.[9] It is not, however, my present purpose to either justify or elucidate my own "Natural Law" theory, but rather to describe various philosophical theories relating to the relationship between animals and humans that might form moral grounding for the law relating to animals. I proceed with this analysis with the understanding that there should be a connection between moral principles and the law.

2. Black's Law Dictionary 978 (9th ed. 2009).
3. Herbert Hovenkamp, *Positivism in Law & Economics*, 78 Cal. L. Rev. 815, 818 (1990).
4. Frederick Schauer, *Constitutional Positivism*, 25 Conn. L. Rev. 797, 799–800 (1993).
5. Aaron Fichtelberg, *Liberal Values in International Criminal Law: A Critique of Erdemovic,* 6 J.Int'l Crim. Just. 3 (2008).
6. *See* Phillip Soper, *Judge White and the Exercise of Judicial Power: Why Theories of Law Have Little Or Nothing to Do With Judicial Restraint*, 74 U. Colo. L. Rev. 1379, 1387 (2003).
7. *Id.*
8. Blake D. Morant, *The Teachings of Dr. Martin Luther King, Jr. and Contract Theory: An Intriguing Comparison*, 50 Ala. L. Rev. 63, 76–77 (1998).
9. *E.g.*, Black's Law Dictionary 1127 (9th ed. 2009); Harold J. Berman, *Toward an Integrative Jurisprudence: Politics, Morality, History*, 76 Cal. L. Rev. 779, 781 (1988); Phillip E. Johnson, *Some Thoughts About Natural Law*, 75 Cal. L. Rev. 217, 217–26 (1987); Morant, *supra* note 8, at 76–77.

II. PYTHAGORAS, ARISTOTLE, DESCARTES, KANT, THE MANY MORAL VIEWS OF ANIMALS AND SCIENCE

A. An Initial Taste of Philosophical History and Theory

People often think that serious discussion of the treatment of animals by humans is a relatively recent phenomenon. In fact, it is not, and most moral philosophers over the ages have taken some position on the relationship between humans and animals. One of these philosophers, the first to coin the term "philosopher" (a person attempting to find the truth, as opposed to a "sage," or a person who knows), was Pythagoras.[10]

When we think of Pythagoras, we think of the Pythagorean Theorem and geometry. There was much more to Pythagoras; indeed, some thought him to be more than a mortal man.[11] While not a great deal of detail is known about Pythagoras, one thing that we do know is that he was much concerned with the relationship between humans and other animals. Pythagoras led a school that was far more than just a school of mathematics and is perhaps better viewed as a religion.[12] Men and women were treated equally by the Pythagorean School.[13] Those in the school "enjoyed a common way of life ... [p]roperty was communal ... [e]ven mathematical discoveries were communal and by association attributed to Pythagoras ...."[14] One of the foundations of Pythagoras' teaching was a commitment to vegetarianism. He also believed in the transmigration of souls.[15] While Pythagoras had a number of reasons for his view on vegetarianism, including his belief in the transmigration of souls (which means that if you eat meat you could theoretically be eating your deceased grandmother), he also favored vegetarianism because he felt that it promoted peace.[16] He felt that those who believed it wrong to harm or kill other creatures will find killing other humans and engaging in war an abomination.[17] From Ovid, we are told this of Pythagoras' thought:

> His lips, learned indeed but not believed in this, he was the first to open in such words as these: "O mortals, do not pollute your bodies with a food so impious! You have the fruits of the earth, you have apples, bending down the

---

10. Grover W. Brunton, *Pythagoras: The First Philosopher and Discoverer of the Forty Seventh Problem of Euclid* 3 (2005), http://www.mastermason.com/Millennium382/Papers/Pythagoras.pdf.
11. *Id.* at 1.
12. G. Donald Allen, *Pythagoras and the Pythagoreans* 3 (1999), http://www.math.tamu.edu/~don.allen/masters/Greek/pythag.pdf.
13. *Id.*
14. *Id.* at 4.
15. Brunton, *supra* note 10, at 2.
16. *See* Iamblichus' Life of Pythagoras, or Pythagoric Life, 134–35 (Thomas Taylor trans., 2003) [hereinafter Iamblichus].
17. *Id.*

> branches with their weight, and grapes swelling to ripeness on the vines; you have also delicious herbs and vegetables which can be mellowed and softened by the help of fire. Nor are you without milk or honey, fragrant with the bloom of thyme. The earth, prodigal of her wealth, supplies you her kindly sustenance and offers you food without bloodshed and slaughter ... Oh, how criminal it is for flesh to be stored away in flesh, for one greedy body to grow fat by eating the body of another, for one live creature to go on living through the destruction of another living thing .... It may be that, in the first place, with the killing of wild beasts the steel was warmed and stained with blood [suggesting that violence and war in general may have roots in the treatment of animals]."[18]

In keeping with these words, when sacrifices to the gods were called for, he offered up millet, cakes, honeycombs and fumigations.[19]

The teachings of Pythagoras make clear then that the debate relating to the relationship of humans to other animals is one that has been ongoing throughout human civilization. Interestingly, it is one area of human behavior in which there has been little or no change in the 2,500 years since Pythagoras lived. So perhaps we might say that Pythagoras' views have utterly failed in turning any culture toward vegetarianism or revising our treatment of animals. Oddly, this connects to the unresolved issue of Pythagoras' death. It has been said that he was assassinated along with many of his followers; it has also been said that he was not killed in an attack on his school, but "escaped, only to die of a broken heart" because of the collapse of his efforts to change mankind.[20]

Where Pythagoras failed to sway Western thought, Aristotle succeeded, and effectively determined the relationship between humans and animals for nearly the last 2,500 years in the Western world. Teacher of Alexander the Great, keeper of a zoo and, apart from being perhaps the most influential western philosopher in history, a great systematizer and categorizer of the natural world;[21] it was in his efforts to categorize the contents of the natural world that Aristotle is said to have created what is called the "Great Chain of Being," a hierarchical structure of nature, advancing from the lowest inanimate objects, like minerals, through plants that have the gift of life, to animals, then to man and on up to the Prime Mover, God.[22] So according to Aristotle, what attributes divide the world on this linear chain? His most influential bases of dividing the natural world were

18. Ovid, Metamorphoses 369–73 (Frank Justus Miller trans., 2d ed. Harvard U. Press 1984).
19. Iamblichus, *supra* note 16, at 108–09.
20. Brunton, *supra* note 10, at 4.
21. *See* Arthur O. Lovejoy, The Great Chain of Being 56–57 (illustrated ed., Harvard U. Press 1964); Richard McKeon, *Introduction, in* Introduction to Aristotle xi-xv (Richard McKeon ed., J.A. Smith trans., Mod. Libr. 1992) (hereinafter "Aristotle").
22. *See* Lovejoy, *supra* note 21; Aristotle, *On the Soul, in* Introduction to Aristotle, *supra* note 21, at 184–89.

"powers of soul," ranging from the nutritive, possessed by plants, to the rational, a characteristic of man.[23]

While Aristotle is often alleged to have propounded this rather simplistic linear hierarchy to describe the natural world, Aristotle's actual view was more nuanced and complex. He recognized that animals differed in many ways and that with respect to one characteristic one species might be "superior" to another, while on another attribute the other species might be "superior."[24] A simple linear description of a "Chain of Being" describing the natural world, then, is not actually the invention of Aristotle, but rather an invention of the interpreters of Aristotle.[25] In any event, by the end of the Middle Ages, this interpretation of "Aristotle's" linear hierarchy shaped the Western view of the world.

The lack of any real change in the relationship between animals and humans over the last 500 years can perhaps best be laid at the feet of René Descartes. This might not be evident if one were to see him walking his dog, Monsieur Grat, along Prinsengracht Canal in Amsterdam, but he was a vivisectionist who propounded views of the nature of animals that allowed their merciless persecution. These views survive even today, although many scientists have finally decided to actually study the true nature of animals, rather than take the word of a seventeenth century philosopher.

So who was this man, Descartes? He was surely a man of considerable abilities, but he just as surely had his foibles. "Descartes may have been the first to describe the conditioned reflex, probably slept in the nude, may have been a mathematically gifted gambler, and likely smoked pot."[26] In addition, he was a member of the gentry, which probably had some impact on his world view.[27] And as it turns out, Descartes might not have had much of an attachment to Monsieur Grat after all, since he sent him to a friend in France for the purpose of introducing his breed to that country (though we are not certain what his breed was).[28]

Descartes' world was one in which science was emerging and flourishing. The fog of the Middle Ages was dissipating and the flow of information from objective efforts to understand the world was rapidly increasing. One issue that was being studied was the functioning of animal and human bodies. But how does

---

23. Aristotle, *supra* note 21, at 181–87; *see also* ARISTOTLE, THE POCKET ARISTOTLE 48–49 (Justin D. Kaplan ed., W.D. Ross Trans. 1958); THE CLASSICAL PSYCHOLOGISTS 141–43 (Benjamin Rand ed. 1912).
24. *See id.* at 186; LOVEJOY, *supra* note 21, at 55–56.
25. *See* LOVEJOY, *supra* note 21, at 59. The supposed hierarchical relationship of humans and other animals has been described as underlying the practice in some places in the Middle Ages of having trials of animals for killing, injuring, or having sex with humans. STEVEN M. WISE, RATTLING THE CAGE: TOWARD LEGAL RIGHTS FOR ANIMALS 35–38 (Perseus Publg. 2001). The reason for these trials was that events like an animal injuring or killing a human turned the divinely prescribed hierarchy upside down. *Id. See also* J.J. Finkelstein, *The Ox that Gored*, 71 TRANS. OF AMER. PHIL. SOC. 5, 27–32, 48, 64–73 (1981).
26. David Lavery, *Cogito, Ergo Sum: The Life of René Descartes by Richard Watson,* THE GA. REV. 437 (1989) (book review).
27. STEPHEN GAUKROGER, DESCARTES 24 (1995).
28. RICHARD WATSON, COGITO, ERGO SUM 167 (2002).

one determine how animal and human bodies function? With the tools at hand in Descartes' time, the mechanism was vivisection, the live dissection of animals, a practice that Descartes not only justified with his philosophical arguments, but participated in personally. He is known to have practiced vivisection on dogs (sorry Monsieur Grat!) and rabbits.[29] But how can we justify the practice of dissecting animals while they are alive; there must be a moral imperative that prevents such cruelty?

1. Animals as Automatons and Humans as the Ends of Morality

If one were to ask many philosophers why non-human animals may morally be treated in ways so wildly different from the way that humans may be treated, they would likely refer to some characteristic of humans that sets them apart from other animals, or suggest some defect of non-human animals that causes them to differ from humans. Ironically, "[o]ne of the things that sets humans apart from other animals is our perennial efforts to establish our distinctiveness from them."[30] Many such supposed distinguishing characteristics have been identified, including rationality, moral agency, self-awareness, emotion and use of language. Note, however, that in order for any such characteristic to be a basis for morally distinguishing humans from other animals, the characteristic must be morally significant. For example, I could say that humans are the only featherless bipeds, but the characteristic of being a featherless biped does not have any moral significance. While one could argue about whether the characteristics noted above, rationality and so on, are actually morally significant in the context of the treatment of non-human animals, I will assume for the purposes of this discussion that these characteristics are morally significant.

Descartes' view of the nature of animals, which has been characterized as one of the "most dramatic, aberrant and influential events in intellectual history,"[31] did not rely on any one of these characteristics. His view was, one could say, even more primitive. He is widely said to have viewed animals, including the physical instantiation of humans, as no more than unfeeling machines, without pain, without suffering.[32] But humans have something that animals do not—a soul; this is the distinguishing feature that causes humans to have feelings of pain, suffering and emotions in general. If animals, on the other hand, are nothing more than unfeeling machines without pain, without the inherent moral value of a soul, then

29. *Id.* at 167.

30. Lori Gruen, *The Morals of Animal Minds, in* THE COGNITIVE ANIMAL 437, 438 (Marc Bekoff et al. eds., 2002) [hereinafter THE COGNITIVE ANIMAL]. Note, for example, that Social Darwinists have described the evolution of humans toward civilization as a process of distinctions between humans and animals becoming more pronounced. Finkelstein, *supra* note 25, at 49.

31. Gerald Carson, MEN, BEASTS, AND GODS 38 (Charles Scribner's Sons 1972).

32. RENÉ DESCARTES, A DISCOURSE ON METHOD AND SELECTED WRITINGS 47–51 (John Veitch, trans., Am. ed. 1951); WATSON, *supra* note 28, at 12–13; *see also* TOM REGAN, THE CASE FOR ANIMAL RIGHTS 3–5 (U. Cal. Press 2004) [hereinafter REGAN].

vivisection can be justified, and the scientific research of the day, propelled by vivisection, could proceed unabated. So, Descartes' theories were indeed a boon to science.[33]

While the popular view of Descartes is that he believed animals were machines without pain, his writings are actually rather more ambiguous. It has been argued, for example, that Descartes may be interpreted not to have propounded this "monstrous" view of animals, but to have recognized animal consciousness, sensation and feeling.[34] Certain of Descartes' writings include references to animals having feelings of "anger, fear [and] hunger," or "expression[s] of... feelings," and "expressions of fear, hope and joy."[35] This sort of talk, of course, is inconsistent with the idea that animals are unfeeling machines, lacking any type of real sensation or feeling. Based on these statements, it has been argued that Descartes did not really hold the monstrous view of animals often attributed to him, but may have recognized animal pain and feelings or, at least, have been "fuzzy" in his thought on this issue.[36]

Whatever the truth about Descartes' views, the popular interpretation of Descartes as viewing animals as automatons incapable of pain, allowed the human use of animals in agriculture, experimentation and otherwise without moral concern, and is a view that held sway in the scientific community for hundreds of years. Only recently have scientists begun to see the similarities between animals and humans, and realize that many animals, with their similar physiology and brain structure, have pain and other experiences similar to those of humans.[37]

That animals have pain in much the same way as humans is now established. The common sense view that animals experience pain is well supported by both philosophical arguments and empirical facts.[38] From an evolutionary perspective, it can hardly be doubted that animals of all sorts experience pain since pain serves useful functions that contribute to the survival of species.[39] Moreover, the nervous system physiology of other animals is very similar to that of humans. For example, pain in humans is known to occur when nociceptors, a kind of sensory receptor, are stimulated at sufficient levels.[40] It has been discovered that mammals and other vertebrates have similar receptors.[41] Likewise the pain detection threshold of

---

33. WATSON, *supra* note 28, at 12–13.
34. *See* John Cottingham, *A Brute to the Brutes? Descartes' Treatment of Animals*, 53 PHIL. NO. 206, at 551 (1978).
35. *Id.* at 556–57.
36. *Id.* at 558–59.
37. For a discussion concerning scientific views on pain relating to the US Animal Welfare Act, *see* LARRY CARBONE, WHAT ANIMALS WANT 141–64 (Oxford U. Press 2004).
38. David DeGrazia & Andrew Rowan, *Pain, Suffering and Anxiety in Animals and Humans*, 12 THEORETICAL MED. & BIOETHICS 193, 193–94 (1991).
39. *See* MARC BEKOFF, ANIMALS MATTER 66–67 (Shambhala Publications, Inc. 2007) [hereinafter ANIMALS MATTER].
40. DeGrazia & Rowan, *supra* note 38, at 197; *see also* MARC BEKOFF, MINDING ANIMALS 130 (Oxford U. Press 2002) [hereinafter MINDING ANIMALS].
41. *See* DeGrazia & Rowan, *supra* note 38, at 197.

humans and other animals appears to be the same.[42] Naturally occurring opiates, endorphins, have been found in many animals, including invertebrates, which again indicates the existence of pain such as humans experience in animals also.[43] Pain may be seen then as a kind of consciousness that has developed in all animals that have nociceptor pathways.[44]

Kant took a different tack from Descartes' common-sense-bending idea that animals do not have sensations of pain in dealing with the relationship of humans and animals.[45] Kant subscribed to the view that humans have a morally practical reason (*i.e.*, are moral agents and are rational) and that this characteristic sets them apart from other animals and entitles humans alone to moral consideration.[46] Humans are the "ends" of morality and cannot be used as "means."[47] Other creatures are not entitled to moral consideration; only humans have the privilege of being owed direct moral duties. This is not to say that Kant believed that animals should be treated badly. Rather, although we do not owe direct moral duties to animals, we do owe them duties indirectly.[48] Unsurprisingly, these indirect duties arise out of moral concern for humans.[49] If we are cruel to animals, this cruelty will harden our hearts to such cruelty, making similar behavior toward other humans more likely.[50] Thus, we have a duty to treat animals well. But this duty arises not from any duty to animals, but rather through our direct moral duties to other humans.

2. The Marginal Cases Problem and Other Views of the Entities Entitled to Moral Consideration

Assume we agree that rationality or moral agency or language distinguishes humans from animals in a morally significant way. If so, then presumably we can, consistent with morality, treat animals differently from humans, perhaps in the way that we do now. Unfortunately for one taking this position, there is a perhaps insoluble problem presented by this view, often called the "marginal cases problem." This problem arises from the fact that there are many humans who Tom Regan refers to as "moral patients"; humans that do not have these supposed distinguishing characteristics of rationality, moral agency, or language.[51] For example, there are infants, people with birth defects and people who have suffered injuries that do not have one or all of these characteristics. If rationality or moral

42. *See id.*
43. *See id.* at 198.
44. *See id.* at 199.
45. *See* REGAN, *supra* note 32, at 174–85 (explaining Kant's general view on animals).
46. IMMANUEL KANT, THE METAPHYSICS OF MORALS 230–31 (Cambridge U. Press 1991).
47. *Id.*
48. *Id.* at 238.
49. *Id.*
50. *Id.*
51. *See* REGAN, *supra* note 32, at 151–56 (for a detailed examination of the marginal cases problem).

agency or language is our morally significant distinguishing factor, then these moral patients fall outside of the group entitled to moral consideration. Therefore, these entities are not entitled to moral consideration and thus can morally be treated in the way that animals are presently treated—used for food, scientific experiments, or entertainment purposes.

This is not a position that any reasonable person wants to take, but there do not seem to be any really good arguments to solve the marginal cases problem. Either these humans are due moral consideration or they are not. If they are not, because they do not meet the stated standard, then one must live with the consequences—that they can be treated as we presently treat animals. If they are, then one must come up with an explanation as to why they are entitled to moral consideration other than rationality or moral agency or language. In addition, if human moral patients are given moral consideration, then animals with characteristics similar to these human moral patients should also be given moral consideration.

One might take the position that the real morally significant factor here is being a member of a species that has one of these distinguishing characteristics. This falls into the trap, however, of being nothing more than a kind of prejudice akin to racism. The claim would be that the moral patient is a member of a group whose members generally have some distinguishing characteristic and that this characteristic morally distinguishes the entire group, even though not all members of the group have that characteristic. These same sorts of arguments based on supposed group characteristics were for centuries made to enslave humans and the application of such arguments here should be rejected as they have been in relations among groups of humans. If you claim that a characteristic distinguishes your group, at the very least you should be able to show that all members of the group, without ad hoc exceptions, have the characteristic. Moreover, you must also be able to prove that only your group has the characteristic, something that thus far I have been assuming in the present discussion. The marginal cases problem then really causes conceptual difficulties for those relying on the characteristics described above to morally distinguish humans, even if we assume that humans are the only ones with these characteristics, an assumption modern science is proving inaccurate, as we shall shortly see.

There are, however, views of the characteristic entitling a creature to moral consideration that include non-human animals. Tom Regan holds the view that those who are "subjects-of-a-life" are entitled to moral consideration. This includes entities with the following characteristics:

> To be the subject-of-a-life ... involves more than merely being alive and more than merely being conscious .... [I]ndividuals are subjects-of-a-life if they have beliefs and desires; perception, memory, and a sense of the future, including their own future; an emotional life together with feelings of pleasure and pain; preference- and welfare-interests; the ability to initiate action in pursuit of their desires and goals; a psychophysical identity

> over time; and an individual welfare in the sense that their experiental [sic] life fares well or ill for them, logically independently of their utility for others and logically independently of their being the object of anyone else's interests.[52]

Regan believes that at least all mammals over one year of age fit into this category and are entitled to moral consideration.[53] In addition, he would give the "benefit of the doubt" and thus moral consideration to certain other animals, such as those having consciousness, that have not been proven to act intentionally.[54] Precisely what animals would fit into this category is unclear. Regan bases this extension of moral consideration on the supposition that being a subject-of-a-life is *sufficient* to garner moral consideration, not a *necessary* prerequisite.[55] Thus, other animals that fall short of being the "subject of a life" are still recognized as having inherent value worthy of respect and consideration.[56]

There are also those who simply say that entities due moral consideration include all entities that are "conscious." While there is no single accepted definition of consciousness, what is typically meant is some sort of "self-consciousness," the understanding that one is an entity that continues through time and has the ability to reflect on what one has done or is doing. A distinction is sometimes made between "perceptual consciousness" and "reflective consciousness."[57] Perceptual consciousness is simply being aware of one's perceptions—the entity is aware at any particular moment that it is having a perception, but does not connect its series of perceptions into a cohesive whole. In other words, an entity with nothing but perceptual consciousness would not understand that its series of perceptions constitute a continuing, ongoing entity; it would not be aware of itself as a continuing entity. Note that an entity with nothing but perceptual consciousness would not be able to learn. How can an entity learn if it cannot connect one perception with another? For example, if we cannot connect our childhood perception of burning ourselves on the stove with any future perceptions, how can we learn not to put our hands on a hot stove?

A creature with reflective consciousness, on the other hand, is able to connect its perceptions in such a way as to be able to recognize itself as an entity continuing through time, and can remember and connect present perceptions with old ones. This type of entity, unlike one with only perceptual consciousness, can connect

---

52. REGAN, *supra* note 32, at 243.
53. *Id.* at 247.
54. *Id.* at 246.
55. *Id.* at 245.
56. *Id.* at 245–46.
57. *See generally* Mark H. Bickhard, *Consciousness and Reflective Consciousness*, 18 PHIL. PSYCHOL. 205 (2005); Gordon G. Gallup, *Do Minds Exist in Species Other Than Our Own?*, 9 NEUROSCI. & BIOBEHAVIOURAL REVS. 631, 631–41 (1985); Juan Carlos Gómez, *Embodying Meaning: Insights from Primates, Autism and Brentano,* 22 NEURAL NETWORKS 190, 190–96 (2009); Jacques Vauclair, *Categorization and Conceptual Behavior in Nonhuman Primates, in* THE COGNITIVE ANIMAL, *supra* note 30, at 239, 240–41.

past perceptions with present perceptions and thus has the ability to learn from experience. From our own experience, we can see that there are a large number of animals that appear to have this kind of consciousness. We observe many animals, particularly mammals like dogs and cats, which have the ability to learn and seem to us to have reflective consciousness. If we include these animals among those entitled to moral consideration, then we would seem to be under a moral imperative to change our behavior relating to these animals in a revolutionary way.

There are also those who identify other characteristics as the qualities that entitle an entity to moral consideration. There are those, like Jeremy Bentham, who see the experience of pain to be the morally relevant characteristic, finding that "the question is not, Can they reason? Nor, Can they talk? But, Can they suffer?"[58] In this view, any entity that can feel pain is entitled to moral consideration. Yet others say that just being a living thing is the talisman of being due moral consideration.[59] It has also been argued that it is not just animals that are entitled to moral consideration, but that entire ecosystems are of moral significance.[60]

What we see here in these different views is a gradual widening of the universe of those entitled to moral consideration. But how do these views relate to what we know of the world? Are any non-human animals rational? Do they have language? Are they really conscious? It is to these issues that I now turn.

III. DARWIN, EVOLUTION AND ANIMAL MINDS

To ask, "Do you believe in evolution?" is similar to the question, "Do you believe in gravity?," although unfortunately there are a considerable number of people who do not grasp this concept. Evolution is a scientifically established "fact" in the same way that gravity is an established scientific fact. All right, so calling something a "scientific fact" is not the proper way to speak about scientific propositions since propositions of science are characterized as "hypotheses," "theories" or "laws." And these hypotheses, theories and laws are subject to revision or replacement by new hypotheses, theories, or laws. Science is an iterative process. So it is possible that our theories relating to gravity or evolution could change or be overthrown.

The point here, however, is to note that evolution has been established in the same way that gravity has been established—via scientific method. Evolution has been established through the fossil record which tells a nearly four-billion-year story of the evolution of life on Earth, through the genetic and biochemical records

58. JEREMY BENTHAM, AN INTRODUCTION TO THE PRINCIPLES OF MORALS AND LEGISLATION 311 (Oxford Press 1907).
59. JULIAN H. FRANKLIN, ANIMAL RIGHTS AND MORAL PHILOSOPHY 78–79 (2005).
60. J. Baird Callicott, *Multicultural Environmental Ethics,* 130 DAEDALUS No. 4, at 77, 85–86, 88–89 (MIT Press 2001); J. Baird Callicott, *Review of Tom Regan, The Case for Animal Rights (1985), in* LAW AND THE ENVIRONMENT 91, 91–100 (Robert V. Percival et al. eds., Temple U. 1997); ALDO LEOPOLD, A SAND COUNTY ALMANAC 201–41 (Oxford U. Press 1966).

of life that show how all life forms are connected and through observation of evolution in organisms that reproduce so rapidly that evolution can be observed in real time.[61]

Darwinian evolution is generally viewed as a gradual process; change does not occur overnight, but results from gradual accumulations of genetic changes over periods of time more akin to the geological than the historical. Anything measurable in our lives or those of the creatures around us is generally too short for anything significant to happen in evolutionary terms.[62] The evolution of traits and characteristics is then a gradual process that typically extends over vast periods of time. There is continuity in evolution,[63] not massive shifts and splits. For example, while there is substantial debate about why hominids, unlike other apes, became bipeds, the fossil evidence reveals that hominids maintained a grasping big toe, used for tree climbing, for upward of a million years after they had evolved bipedal behavior.[64] Thus, even as new skills and characteristics develop, the old machinery may remain in place for long periods of time, not disappearing until the usefulness of the trait has long since evaporated.

One thing of great interest to Charles Darwin was the development of mental abilities in animals. This issue is crucial to those concerned with animal welfare and rights issues, since justifications for using animals in agriculture, science and entertainment are generally based on the idea that animals are markedly different from humans in their cognitive abilities, and do not experience suffering, depression or other emotions like humans. Cognitive and mental abilities, however, like other traits, do not appear overnight. The evolution of cognitive traits is gradual and there will be "no inexplicable jumps in cognitive abilities."[65] This is precisely what Darwin believed. He stated that, "[t]here is no fundamental difference between man and the higher mammals in their mental faculties" rather, "[t]he difference in

---

61. *See* John Pojeta, Jr. & Dale A. Springer, *Evolution and the Fossil Record* 3, 15, 18 (The Am. Geological Inst. & The Paleontology Soc'y 2001) *booklet available at* http://www.agiweb.org/news/evolution/; Peter R. Grant & B. Rosemary Grant, *Evolution of Character Displacement in Darwin's Finches*, 313 SCI. 224, 224–26 (2006).
62. I refer to "Darwinian evolution" because, as we know, science is an ongoing process and there are theorists that argue that evolution is not always gradual. For instance, the concept of "punctuated equilibrium" states that speciation can and often does occur in spurts and dramatic changes over shorter periods of time when a number of individuals in a species have substantial genetic mutations. The debate over whether evolution is primarily gradual or more along punctuated equilibria lines continues and some even question whether Darwin was a thorough-going gradualist. *See* MARK RIDLEY, EVOLUTION (3d ed. 2003), *available at Phylic Gradualism*, http://www.blackwellpublishing.com/ridley/a-z; NECSI, *Gradualism and Punctuated Equilibrium*, http://necsi.org/projects/evolution/evolution/grad+punct/evolution_grad+punct.html (last visited Apr. 24, 2010); Wesley R. Elsberry, *Punctuated Equilibria*, http://www.talkorigins.org/faqs/punc-eq.html (last visited Apr. 24, 2010).
63. ANIMALS MATTER, *supra* note 39, at 62.
64. John Noble Wilford, *The Transforming Leap, from Four Legs to Two, in* THE SCI. TIMES BOOK OF FOSSILS AND EVOLUTION 196–203 (Nicholas Wade ed. 1998).
65. Güven Güzeldere et al., *Darwin's Continuum and the Building Blocks of Deception in* THE COGNITIVE ANIMAL, *supra* note 30, at 353.

mind between man and the higher animals, great as it is, certainly is one of degree and not of kind."[66]

For centuries it was simply assumed that a Cartesian view of the relationship between animals and humans was an accurate one. Animals had nothing that could be called rationality or true cognitive ability; animals did not have any moral sense; animals were not self-aware; animals did not have emotions; animals did not have anything that could be called language and animals did not experience pain as we do. But Darwin's insights began the process of disproving theories that focus on how different humans are from animals. After Darwin, the focus began to change to searching for similarities between humans and other animals, not differences. It is really only in the last 50 years that serious attention has been paid to the cognitive abilities of animals in the relatively new science of cognitive ethology. As we will see, Darwin's view of animal minds has turned out to be consistent with the results of scientific inquiry into the cognitive and emotional traits of animals. In fact, the differences between humans and even "lower" animals like insects are being shown by science to be much smaller than generally thought.

IV. CALCULATING PARROTS, FORWARD LOOKING RAVENS, ABSTRACT THOUGHT IN BABOONS AND SPEAR-HUNTING CHIMPS

A. Abstract Thought and Conceptualization

Is it true that humans have allegedly morally relevant characteristics like rationality, moral agency, self-awareness and language and non-human animals do not?[67] For example, are humans the only animals that exhibit rational behavior? There is evidence that they are not. Anecdotally there are many stories of animal behavior that indicate rational, logical actions by animals. For example, Pink, a golden retriever, was lying on the beach with his guardian Mark. Mark, deaf in one ear, "didn't hear [a] pick-up truck coming down the beach, but saw Pink mov[e] out of the corner of his eye .... Pink place[d] herself in the truck's path, causing it to swerve off the course that would have taken it directly across the spot where [Mark] lay." Mark said Pink's purpose was clear, " 'her hair bristled, her jaws set

66. Charles Darwin, The Descent of Man and Selection in Relation to Sex 66, 128 (D. Appleton & Co. 2d ed. 1909).

67. Much of what is discussed in the following sections is based on animal experiments, some of which caused pain and suffering to animals. One might ask whether one should effectively sanction this activity by using the information gleaned from these experiments. This is an issue analogous to that relating to the use of Nazi experimental data from human experiments. While I understand the concerns that surround all of this and feel unease in using and describing some of these experiments, I use this data with the belief that its use will further our understanding of the true nature and abilities of animals, and will help to change the human/animal relationship for the better. One might say I am a utilitarian on this issue.

tightly and her path took her straight into the truck's path.' "[68] Or take the case of Samuri, a blind six-year-old Akita, who alerted his guardians that their 25-year-old neighbor had collapsed after suffering a stroke.[69] Or consider Peeka, the dog that alerted her guardians that someone had placed a baby child on their porch in minus twenty-nine degree temperatures.[70]

But we need not rely on such anecdotes; there is scientific evidence of rational behavior in animals. One of the more famous examples of sophisticated cognitive behavior in animals is Alex the Parrot.[71] Alex was studied by Professor Irene M. Pepperberg and mastered a number of skills in addition to being able to communicate with researchers by using English words. Among other things, he learned counting and some simple addition, the concept of "none" or "zero," as well as the concepts of "same" and "different."[72] The concepts of same or different that Alex learned related to categories of color, shape and materials, which he applied to various objects.[73] Alex was able to apply these concepts not only to the objects that he was trained with, but also to new items that he had not previously been exposed to.[74] The concepts Alex learned are very advanced, abstract concepts that had previously been thought to be beyond the ken of other animals, let alone a "lowly bird." And what better example of rational thought can there be than learning mathematical concepts, or the ideas of same and different?

As it turns out, modern science is discovering that "bird brains" of numerous kinds engage in all sorts of rational behavior previously thought to be the sole domain of humans. Ravens have been shown to plan for the future by caching food.[75] Ravens can also problem-solve. They have been shown to be able to decipher the problem of freeing food tied to the end of a string by gradually raising the food and repeatedly placing their foot on the string to slowly raise the food until it is accessible.[76] Similarly, dolphins have been shown to be able to create and

---

68. Kevin Moran, *This Dog Proves to be One Man's Best Friend with Act of Heroism*, THE HOUSTON CHRONICLE, Oct. 2, 1997 at A26.
69. Jack Boland, *Four Legged Heroes; The Purina Animal Hall of Fame Ceremony Honours 4 Deserving Doggies* THE TORONTO SUN, Apr. 25, 2006, at 7.
70. Purina Animal Hall of Fame, *Please Welcome Our 2008 Inductees*, http://www.purina.ca/about/halloffame/2008.aspx (last visited Apr. 27, 2010).
71. I will be using the terms "cognition" and "cognitive" frequently. But what do these words mean? Cognition is commonly defined as "the act or process of knowing including both awareness and judgment," WEBSTER'S UNIVERSAL ENCYCLOPEDIC DICTIONARY 348 (Barnes & Noble Books 2002). It has also been defined as "an ability to step outside the bounds of the innate" or the "capacity to perform mental operations or transformations and thus to plan or make decisions." James L. Gould, *Can Honey Bees Create Cognitive Maps? in* THE COGNITIVE ANIMAL, *supra* note 30, at 41, 41. As we will see, many types of skills are studied as elements of cognition: conceptual and abstract thought, tool usage, language usage and acquisition, etc.
72. IRENE M. PEPPERBERG, ALEX & ME 190–91 (Collins 2008) [hereinafter ALEX & ME].
73. Irene Maxine Pepperberg, *Cognitive and Communicative Abilities of Grey Parrots, in* THE COGNITIVE ANIMAL, *supra* note 30, at 247, 249–50.
74. *Id.*
75. Bernd Heinrich, *Raven Consciousness, in* THE COGNITIVE ANIMAL, *supra* note 30, at 47, 50.
76. *Id.* at 50–51.

execute simple plans, as well as recognize more complicated solutions to complex problems after observing their human educators complete the actions involved, which has been referred to as "one of the abilities that characterize[s] good human problem solvers."[77] Animals also engage in another form of rational behavior—cooperation. In a study using pairs of hyenas:

> a pair of ropes dangled from an overhead platform. If the animals pulled the ropes in unison—and only in unison—the platform would spill out food. "The first pair walked into the pen and figured it out in less than two minutes," Drea [the person conducting the study] says. "My jaw literally dropped."[78]

If it were humans accomplishing such planning and problem solving, we would undoubtedly assume that the humans were using conceptual tools like considering how long the cached food would need to last, recalling and applying past experience with falling objects and how they could be prevented from falling, etc. Do non-human animals use these conceptual tools? Are they able to develop and use abstract concepts? Are they capable of abstract thought? If we were to choose a group of animals that we think would clearly not have the ability to conceptualize because they are "too primitive" or "their brains are too small," we would probably choose insects. The trouble with this choice is that it would be wrong. There is evidence that insects, too, can use abstract concepts.

Concept comprehension can be shown by an animal's ability to solve novel problems. Bees have demonstrated the ability to solve novel problems by learning concepts to apply to these problems. First, bees are able to recognize and distinguish human letters.[79] Second, bees have been shown to successfully form even more complex concepts in several instances:

- They are able to learn that "symmetrical targets offered food while asymmetrical ones did not," and vice versa.[80]
- They learned the concepts of "same" and "different," using the well-established method of matching to sample, which teaches these concepts using a sample pattern or color, followed by either a matching pattern or color to teach "same," or a different pattern or color to teach "different." Once the bees learned these abstract concepts, they could apply them to new, never-before-seen patterns and colors.[81]

---

77. Stan A. Kuczaj II & Rachel Thames Walker, *How Do Dolphins Solve Problems? in* COMPARATIVE COGNITION 580, 594 (Edward A. Wasserman & Thomas R. Zentall eds., 2006) [hereinafter COMPARATIVE COGNITION].
78. Jeffry Kluger, *Inside the Minds of Animals,* TIME, Aug. 16, 2010, at 36, 41; *See also* Rod Preece and Lorna Chamberlain, ANIMAL WELFARE & HUMAN VALUES 42–43 (Wilfrid Laurier University Press 1993) (stating that animal engage in planning and do not act solely based on "instinct").
79. Gould, *supra* note 71, at 43.
80. *Id.*
81. *Id.* at 44.

The ability to learn the same/different concept and to recognize that different symmetries represent different things would be considered acts of cognition when performed by humans or other animals.[82] So why should we call it something else when a bee does it?

We need not confine ourselves to bees, however, to find animals that can conceptualize and use abstractions. In fact, as research into the cognitive abilities of animals proceeds, the number of animals shown to have such abilities grows apace. We have already seen some of the cognitive abilities of parrots and ravens. Other types of birds have also been shown to have quite remarkable cognitive abilities. For instance, pigeons have been shown to be able to conceptualize and engage in abstract thought.[83] Pigeons understand the concepts of same and different, and the concept of motion in connection with the sweep of the hands of a clock.[84]

How have these conceptual abilities of pigeons been revealed? As an example, in one experiment, which used photographs, pigeons learned the concepts of same and different related to four conceptual categories: the texture of the image, the features of the image, the geometric nature of the image and the type of object pictured in the image.[85] To ensure that the pigeons actually learned the concept of same/different, experimenters added a fifth category, color and gray-scale photos and the majority of pigeons succeeded also in applying the same/different concept to this new category.[86] Thus, the birds demonstrated that they had learned the concept of same/different and applied it to novel circumstances, proving that they understood same/different in an abstract way.[87] The researchers concluded, "[O]ur results suggest that pigeons may have a previously unappreciated capacity for learning and using abstract S[ame]—D[ifferent] relations among individual elements across a wide variety of stimuli (texture, feature, geometric, object, photographs) and that they can do so whether these relations are presented simultaneously or successively."[88]

It is frequently argued that abstract conceptual thought requires the ability to use language. The results in experiments with pigeons show that this is false:

> Such evidence [as described in the experiments above] strengthens the claim that pigeons may be capable of formulating rule-based concepts that give them previously undocumented behavioral flexibility in regard to identity and difference judgments, much like higher primates. Thus this integral component of intelligent behavior may be more widespread in the animal kingdom

82. *See id.*
83. *See* Howard A. Wasserman, *General Signs, in* THE COGNITIVE ANIMAL, *supra* note 30, at 175, 175–77.
84. *Id.* at 177, 180.
85. Robert G. Cook, *Same-Different Concept Formation in Pigeons, in* THE COGNITIVE ANIMAL, *supra* note 30, at 229, 231.
86. *Id.*
87. *Id.*
88. *Id.* at 233.

> than previously supposed. Furthermore, it challenges prior claims that S-D behavior and rule-based behavior more generally, are critically tied to language.[89]

These results with pigeons have been replicated.[90] Indeed, in experiments described by Robert Cook and Edward Wasserman, it was found that pigeons in fact use similar conceptual mechanisms as humans do in making these same—different distinctions.[91] Not only have pigeons been found to use the same conceptual mechanisms as humans, both pigeons and dolphins have been found to perform some conceptual tasks better than young and less gifted human beings.[92] For instance, tests with pigeons on "rotation invariance," the ability to rotate an image mentally and identify its mirror image, show that although pigeons' accuracy level is slightly lower than humans on this test, pigeons can do the rotation tests faster than any humans.[93]

One might be wondering now if there is any cognition in animals other than birds (and from what we have seen above—dolphins and bees) since so much has been discovered about pigeons, ravens and parrots. Another group of animals that has had extensive cognitive testing are primates of various types. Primates have been found to be able to use abstract concepts at very high levels of sophistication. In fact, baboons are able to categorize at the most abstract level of a five-level scale of abstraction used by researchers.[94] They were also able to use previously learned categories in same/different exercises when applied to new examples.[95] As an example of the kinds of tasks used to analyze these abilities, baboons were tested on the ability to distinguish food items from other sorts of items. In doing these tests, the baboons reached the same level of abstraction as humans, but humans used propositional reasoning (*i.e.*, language) to make the distinctions, while baboons used perceptual distinctions between the objects.[96] Again, cognitive skills are shown to exist in the absence of language.

The study of animal cognitive abilities is now advancing to analyze animal abilities to understand relations between relations, a skill more sophisticated than merely understanding same—different relations. Leading the charge in this new research is University of Iowa psychologist, Ed Wasserman: "'It's called relations between relations, and it's a basic scaffold of intelligence,' ... [l]ast year Wasserman conducted a study that proved that some animals have begun building that scaffold. In his research, baboons and—surprisingly—pigeons got the relations-between-relations

---

89. *Id.* at 234 (citations omitted).
90. *See* Robert G. Cook & Edward A. Wasserman, *Relational Discrimination Learning in Pigeons, in* COMPARATIVE COGNITION, *supra* note 77, at 307–24.
91. *See id.* at 319–22.
92. Juan D. Delius & Julia M. Delius, *Intelligences and Brains: An Evolutionary Bird's Eye View, in* COMPARATIVE COGNITION, *supra* note 77, at 555, 558–60.
93. *Id.* at 561–62.
94. Vauclair, *supra* note 57, at 240–41.
95. *Id.* at 241.
96. *Id.* at 243.

idea, correctly identifying the proper pairings [of pictures presented] with a peck or a joystick when images were flashed on a screen."[97]

In addition, what are referred to as "relational similarity" skills have been found in apes.[98] What exactly are these skills? For one, these skills are thought to be "extraordinarily pronounced in humans" and the "one thing that 'makes us smart.'"[99] Relational similarity skills are believed to underlie many important and complex cognitive functions such as reasoning, language, propositional structure and predication, inductive inference, categorization, analogy and metaphor.[100] To illustrate this type of proficiency, consider this problem: Prison is to Inmate as School is to what? If we are given these possible answers—a. fish; b. teacher; c. student; or d. parent; the correct answer is c. student.[101] This is an example of the use of relational similarity skills. Another example is the ability to see the similarity between things like a "treasure map and an island, or between a marriage and an industrial joint venture."[102] Relational similarity skills then are the ability to see how one set of objects or concepts is similar to another, even though the situational components are different.

A recent study tested this ability in children and several non-human primate species (chimpanzees, bonobos, gorillas and orangutans).[103] Unlike most previous studies, these tests did not use linguistically based methods of testing these skills, but instead focused on three dimensional pairs of objects and tested for the ability to determine how they spatially related to each other. This methodology allowed the experimenters to determine if language was necessary to develop these skills.[104] All children under four and all non-human primates were found to be capable of relational similarity skills when accompanied by at least one cognitive crutch, such as proximity or gravity.[105] Moreover, children over four, chimps and bonobos were able to demonstrate these relational similarity abilities without the benefit of any additional aiding factor.[106] This latter result suggests that, on these tasks, the skill tested evolved after the evolutionary split between orangutans and gorillas, on one hand, and chimps, bonobos and humans on the other.[107] On some tests, non-human apes performed better than all groups of children, while on other tasks (those involving reasoning by non-causal relational similarity) only children over four, chimps and bonobos were successful.[108] Young chimpanzees have also

97. Kluger, *supra* note 78, at 41.
98. *See* Daniel B. Haun & Joseph Call, *Great Apes' Capacities to Recognize Relational Similarity*, 110 COGNITION 147, 147–58 (2009).
99. *Id.* at 148.
100. *Id.* at 147–48.
101. This example was created by my research assistant Kimberly Clark.
102. Haun & Call, *supra* note 98, at 147.
103. *Id.*
104. *Id.* at 147–49, 157–58.
105. *Id.* at 156–58.
106. *Id.*
107. *Id.* at 158.
108. *Id.*

been found to perform better than adult humans on a memory test.[109] All of this demonstrates that relational similarity abilities do not require language and that certain primates have this fundamental and invaluable cognitive skill.[110]

B. THE GREATEST FORM OF FLATTERY

They say that imitation is the greatest form of flattery, but it is also a "complex skill and a demanding cognitive trait" that is very useful in social learning.[111] Research shows that dolphins are able to imitate both the vocalizations and behaviors of others:[112]

> Dolphins, as imitative generalists ... must be able to mentally represent the behaviors of others or of themselves in order to copy or reproduce those behaviors. When a dolphin imitates a human's motor acts, it must in some cases form analogies between its body image and the human body plan. For example, if the human raises a leg in the air, the dolphin will raise its tail ... and if the human waves his or her arms, the dolphin will wave its pectoral fins.[113]

This imitation requires an animal to recognize itself as an entity distinct from those around it, and further requires it to make judgments about which human body parts correspond to those of a dolphin.

Chimps imitate too. Chimps have been found to learn how to eat different foods through imitation of other chimps.[114] In fact, chimps located in different groups have been found to have different social behaviors—they may effectively have different cultures.[115] This was shown in an international study of chimp populations in Africa, where chimps were studied to determine the presence or absence of 65 different observed chimp behaviors.[116] The purpose of the study was to see whether all chimps engaged in these behaviors, or if there were cultural variations between different chimp populations in how they behave.[117] The results showed 39 variations between different chimp study sites.[118] What appears to be the case is that animals with social structures tend to have more sophisticated

---

109. Fiona MacRae, *The Chimps that Beat Humans in a Memory Test,* Dec. 4, 2007, http://www.dailymail.co.uk/news/article-499432/The-chimps-beat-humans-memory-test.html.
110. Haun & Call, *supra* note 98, at 157.
111. Louis M. Herman, *Exploring the Cognitive World of the Bottlenosed Dolphin, in* THE COGNITIVE ANIMAL, *supra* note 30, at 275, 277.
112. *Id.*
113. *Id.* at 277–78 (citations omitted).
114. Andrew Whiten, *From the Field to the Laboratory and Back Again: Culture and "Social Mind" in Primates, in* THE COGNITIVE ANIMAL, *supra* note 30, at 385, 386, 388.
115. *Id.* at 390.
116. *Id.* at 388.
117. *Id.*
118. *Id.*

mental processes that develop from social learning.[119] Some of the skills that apes possess include "some understanding of causality, some representation of the self, and some appreciation of the beliefs of others."[120] These social skills may be the foundation of what appears to be cultural behavior by chimps.

C. Planet of the Apes: Spear-Hunting Chimps

One of the traditional talismans of human superiority has always been that humans alone make and use tools, and other animals do not. Like much common wisdom about the "superiority" of humans, once there is scientific research on the issue, common wisdom turns out to be false. Chimps use stones to open nuts.[121] Bonobos have also been seen marking trails so that they can return to where they began their trip. In the wild, bonobos have been seen to split into groups and then mark their paths so that the different groups of bonobos can find each other after splitting up.[122] This indicates a number of skills, including planning for the future and using tools for marking paths. Further, researchers noted that the bonobos were deliberate in their markers rather than arbitrary, by leaving them only in places where other bonobos could foreseeably get lost unless there was some indication of where the others had gone.[123] Thus, the bonobos were not only capable of planning for the future, but also of doing so in a manner which showed rational and deliberate thought.[124] Chimps have also recently been observed doing something completely unexpected—hunting with spears. A particular group of chimps have developed the skill of finding and sharpening wooden spears, which are then used by the chimps for hunting bush babies, their primary food source.[125]

Other primates have also been observed to use tools.[126] Capuchin monkeys are considered "masters of tool use," because they have been found to "readily and spontaneously use tools in a large variety of circumstances."[127] Gorillas have also been observed using tree branches to test water depth; using tree trunks as bridges to cross swamps; using rakes to bring far flung-food within their reach; and using dipping devices to capture honey and peanut butter from logs.[128]

---

119. *See* Delius & Delius, *supra* note 92, at 565–67.
120. *Id.*
121. Tetsurp Matsuzawa, *Chimpanzee Ai and Her Son Ayumu: An Episode of Education by Master-Apprenticeship, in* The Cognitive Animal, *supra* note 30, at 189.
122. Animals Matter, *supra* note 39, at 53–54.
123. *Id.*
124. *See id.*
125. *Ape Genius* (PBS television broadcast, Feb. 19, 2008), *transcript available at* http://www.pbs.org/wgbh/nova/transcripts/3504_apegeniu.html.
126. Laurie R. Santos et al., *Domain-Specific Knowledge in Human Children and Nonhuman Primates: Artifacts and Foods, in* The Cognitive Animal, *supra* note 30, at 205, 206–07.
127. Elisabetta Visalberghi, *Insight from Capuchin Monkey Studies: Ingredients of, Recipes for, and Flaws in Capuchins' Success, in* The Cognitive Animal, *supra* note 30, at 405.
128. E.V. Lonsdorf et al., *An Experimental, Comparative Investigation of Tool Use in Chimpanzees and Gorillas*, 77 Animal Behaviour 1119, 1119–20 (2009).

And this capacity for tool use is not exclusive to primates, either. Crows and ravens use sticks as tools for various things, including digging out food from crevices and other places they cannot reach with their beaks, flushing other birds out of their nests so they can take their eggs, and caching and hiding food from competitors.[129] Rooks, a type of crow, can "reason through how to drop stones into a pitcher partly filled with water in order to raise the level high enough to drink from it."[130] Dolphins have been seen to use sponges as a kind of glove while foraging;[131] Egyptian vultures and other birds crack eggshells by repeatedly dropping stones or other objects on them;[132] crows create hooks to get food that is stored in buckets outside of their reach;[133] and fish fire off water drops at insects to knock them from perches into the water.[134] So tool use is not terribly rare in the animal world; in fact, it is common to a wide range of animals, all the way from humans to apes, to birds, to fish.

D. Problem Solving Chimps

As long ago as 1925, substantial problem-solving abilities were observed in chimps.[135] Wolfgang Köhler, a Gestalt psychologist, carried out an experiment where bananas were suspended from the ceiling of a chimpanzee's cage, out of reach of the chimpanzee.[136] The chimps were provided tools for getting the food:

> Several boxes of various sizes were scattered about the cage ... Initially the chimpanzee jumped up and down continuously trying to reach the banana. It then stayed relatively quiet for a time. After a while, the chimpanzee jumped up, piled the boxes one on top of the other, and climbed the boxes to reach the bananas.[137]

Different chimps were found to solve the problem in different ways; one chimp tried to climb up a pole it had placed under the bananas; several succeeded by stacking crates, but had trouble getting their centers of gravity right;[138] another

129. John M. Marzluff & Tony Angell, In the Company of Crows and Ravens 22, 46, 227–32, 240–45; *see generally* Thomas Bugnyar et al., *The Ontogeny of Caching in Ravens, Corvus Corax*, 74 Animal Behaviour 757, 760 (2007).
130. Kluger, *supra* note 78, at 40.
131. M. Krützen et al., *Cultural Transmission of Tool Use in Bottlenose Dolphins*, 102 Proc. of the Nat'l Acad. of Sci., U.S.A. 8939, 8939–43 (2005).
132. M.A. Panger, *Object-Use in Free-Ranging White-Faced Capuchins (Celus capucinus) in Costa Rica*, 106 Am. J. of Physical Anthropology 311, 311–21 (1998); J. Alcock, *The Evolution of the Use of Tools by Feeding Animals*, 26 Evolution 464, 464–73 (1972).
133. A.A.S. Weir, et al., *Shaping of Hooks in New Caeldonian Crows*, 297 Sci. 981 (2002).
134. Alcock, *supra* note 132.
135. Erika Cox, Psychology for A Level 554 (2001).
136. *Id.*
137. *Id.*
138. J.L. Gould & C.G. Gould, *The Animal Mind*, ¶6, http://www.pigeon.psy.tufts. edu/psych26/kohler.htm (last visited Apr. 27, 2010).

chimp put a crate under the bananas and knocked the bananas down with a pole.[139] The chimps appeared to be solving the problem via cognitive trial and error; analyzing the situation before they manipulated the tools.[140] The observed behaviors—failure, a pause, then considering the tools available, and finally, a renewed effort—appeared to involve both planning and insight to solve the problem.[141] Köhler concluded that the chimpanzees performed what he referred to as insight learning; they formed a mental representation of the entire problem, which allowed them to solve it with the use of available resources.[142]

E. Studious Primates and Logical Sea Lions: Animal Learning

As previously discussed, we now know that chimps learn by observation.[143] We also saw chimps solve problems through what appeared to be complex problem-solving techniques.[144] Studies further show that monkeys, too, have similar abilities. Researchers Laurie R. Santos, Mare D. Hauser and Elizabeth S. Spelke have found that monkeys, while looking at new tools given to them, focused on the tools' functionality, rather than their color or texture.[145] In other words, the monkeys focused on the characteristics of the tool that displayed its usefulness, rather than characteristics that did not reveal the usefulness of the item. They also discovered that the monkeys honed in on the functional characteristics of tools in the same way that humans do.[146] Additionally, it was found that monkeys, like chimps, were able to learn purely through observation of others.[147]

Monkeys have further been found to have significant math skills—they can learn to order numbers, and appear to learn math in the same way that humans do.[148] Thus, Elizabeth M. Brannon and Herbert S. Terrace, who have studied the mathematical learning skills of monkeys, have concluded that "[t]hese data provide compelling evidence that animals and humans use the same numerical comparison process."[149]

Ludwig Wittgenstein, the philosopher and logician who endeavored to reduce all of the mysteries of philosophy to issues of language, would probably be surprised to learn that the world of logicians includes sea lions. Assume the

---

139. *Id.*
140. *Id.*
141. *Id.*
142. Cox, *supra* note 135, at 554–55.
143. *See* Matsuzawa, *supra* note 121, at 189–95.
144. *See supra* notes 135 through 142 and accompanying text.
145. Santos et al., *supra* note 126, at 207.
146. *Id.*
147. *Id.* at 212.
148. Elizabeth M. Brannon & Herbert S. Terrace, *The Evolution and Ontogeny of Ordinal Numerical Ability, in* The Cognitive Animal, *supra* note 30, at 197–204.
149. *Id.* at 202.

relationship: if A then B, and if B then C. Given this, sea lions can learn if... then rules and can understand equivalence relationships like the following:

- Novel reflexive/identity: *if* A, *then* A
- Symmetrical: *If* B, *then* A and *if* C, *then* B.
- Transitive: *If* A, *then* C.[150]

Sea lions learn these relationships without the use of linguistic codes; so even the learning of logic does not require language.

> Th[us,] conceptual reorganization of information allows an animal to connect different objects, events, and individuals in structured categories on the basis of common elements or shared functions. While humans use linguistic codes to facilitate such abstract problem solving, these studies show us that some nonhuman animals that lack language are nonetheless capable of logically organizing their perceptual worlds.[151]

It is not just sea lions who have these logic skills and can understand equivalence relationships. Pigeons and dolphins are also members of the logicians' club, able to understand transitive relationships.[152] Thus, logic, an aspect of rationality, is a skill not confined only to humans.

F. THE MORAL SENSE OF "BEASTS"

Even if animals have some measure of rationality, certainly only humans are able to make moral decisions. So this characteristic can surely distinguish humans from animals and without doubt is a morally relevant characteristic. Nonetheless, like rationality, language and other mental abilities, Darwin teaches that moral sentiments evolve in stages.[153] As a result, we would expect to see other animals showing some evidence of moral sentiments, and we do. Lori Gruen has said that moral agency or moral reflection may be understood "as made up of a set of capacities," such as the ability to recognize conflicts in one's desires; to deliberate; to permit new information to change existing beliefs; to act on discovered solutions and so on.[154] Marc Bekoff and Jessica Pierce have similarly defined morality as "a suite of interrelated other-regarding behaviors that cultivate and regulate complex interactions within social groups. These behaviors relate to both well-being and harm, and norms of right and wrong attach to many of them."[155] Bekoff and Pierce go on to identify three categories of moral behavior in animals:

---

150. Ronald J. Schusterman et al., *The Cognitive Sea Lion: Meaning & Memory in the Laboratory and in Nature, in* THE COGNITIVE ANIMAL, *supra* note 30, at 217, 222–24.
151. *Id.* at 224–25.
152. *See* Delius & Delius, *supra* note 92, at 558–61.
153. Gruen, *supra* note 30, at 439.
154. *Id.*
155. MARC BEKOFF & JESSICA PIERCE, WILD JUSTICE 7 (2009).

> We envision a suite of moral behavior patterns that falls into three rough categories ... the cooperation cluster, the empathy cluster, and the justice cluster.... The cooperation cluster includes behaviors such as altruism, reciprocity, trust, punishment, and revenge. The empathy cluster includes sympathy, compassion, caring, helping, grieving, and consoling. The justice cluster includes a sense of fair play, sharing, a desire for equity, expectations about what one deserves and how one ought to be treated, indignation, retribution and spite.[156]

In other words, moral agency is not a compartmentalized characteristic composed of a single skill or ability; it is a mélange of capacities. Many philosophers fail to recognize this about moral agency. Kantians and neo-Kantians typically believe moral agency to be either altogether extant or not.[157] This leads to rejecting animals' ability to conceivably have any capacity for moral action, and derives, in part, from a simplistic belief that animals lack self-awareness which was thought by the Kantians to be a necessary requisite to moral agency.[158] This focus on the need for some single characteristic that grounds moral decisions fails to recognize the many aspects and abilities that go into the making of moral decisions, and leads researchers to ignore those same aspects and abilities in animals.[159]

Nonetheless, there is scientific evidence of moral choices by non-humans. In the 1960s, an experiment was done with rhesus monkeys, in which a monkey was placed in a compartment where it could pull a chain to get food.[160] The monkey could see into another compartment where there was another monkey. The second monkey would be given an electrical shock if the monkey with the chain pulled the chain to get food. The experiment found that, generally, the monkey with the ability to pull the chain to get the food would not do so, once he or she had discovered that pulling the chain caused a shock to the other monkey. The chain-controlling monkeys would starve themselves rather than injure the other monkeys.[161] These feelings of empathy have been found to occur in many animals, as is discussed in more detail below in the discussion of animal emotions. What follows from this is that even scientific researchers believe that they are seeing this:

> [a] startling possibility: if animals share with humans the capacity for empathy, they have in place the cornerstone of what in human society we know as morality. For among humans, the capacity to understand what another feels allows us to be compassionate, to avoid causing pain or suffering, and to act with an intention to improve the welfare of those around us. And if, indeed, animals share this cornerstone of morality, this may set in motion a

156. *Id.* at 8.
157. Gruen, *supra* note 30, at 438–40.
158. *Id.* at 438–39.
159. *Id.* at 438–40.
160. *See* Jules H. Masserman et al., *Altruistic Behavior in Rhesus Monkeys,* 121 THE AM. J. OF PSYCHIATRY 584 (1964).
161. *Id.*

> serious reappraisal of how we understand animals, how we understand morality, and how our empathy for animals can guide our behavior toward them.[162]

Empathy, which has been found to exist in many animals, can be seen as the basis of morality. If it is a foundation of morality, as many feminist moral philosophers and certain other moral philosophers maintain, then this evidence shows that humans are not the only animals capable of making moral decisions.[163]

Certain social animals have what is referred to as "social morality." Social morality, which is described as behaving fairly, can be seen in social animals in their rules of play, and in the bonds that develop within social groups.[164] In addition, social animals have been seen to learn what is right and wrong from the social group.[165] Social animals have been observed to engage in altruistic behavior to help other animals within their group. For example, in one experiment, monkeys with control over food have chosen less desirable food for themselves, in order to provide better food to others.[166] In this experiment, Capuchin monkeys were placed in contiguous chambers. One monkey had control over a lever that delivered food to both monkeys. When monkeys were given a choice between taking only undesirable food for themselves (celery) and giving nothing to another monkey, or giving another monkey desirable food (marshmallows) and taking celery for themselves, the monkeys chose the option that gave food to the other monkey.[167] Monkeys continued to choose this option even when their choice of undesirable celery for themselves, and nothing for the other monkey, was upgraded to a desirable marshmallow for themselves and nothing for the other monkey.[168] Thus, the monkeys were making a clear, altruistic choice.

Similar evidence of altruistic empathetic behavior in monkeys is revealed by observations of the behavior of Diana monkeys. An old female was unable to make a machine that took tokens and then delivered food work properly. Her mate, seeing her conundrum, picked up tokens she had dropped, put them into the machine, and let her have the food.[169] There was no evidence that the mate's behavior benefited him in any way.

The scientific evidence is that both the emotional building blocks of morality (empathy, caring and similar emotions) and actual moral behavior is exhibited by a number of types of animals. It may be that morality has evolved in different ways

---

162. Jessica Pierce, *Mice in the Sink: On the Expression of Empathy in Animals*, 5 J. OF ENVTL. PHIL. No. 1, 75–96 (2008), at 1–2 *available at* http://www.environmentalphilosophy.org/ISEEIAEPpapers/2007/Pierce.pdf (page number references are to the online pdf file).
163. *See infra* notes 279 through 290 and accompanying text.
164. *See* MINDING ANIMALS, *supra* note 40, at 129–31.
165. *Id.*
166. Venkat R. Lakshiminarayanan & Laurie R. Santos, *Capuchin Monkeys Are Sensitive to Others' Welfare*, 18 CURRENT BIOLOGY, No. 21, at R999, R999-00 (2008).
167. *Id.*
168. *Id.*
169. MINDING ANIMALS, *supra* note 40, at 102.

in different species, so that what is morality becomes species-specific.[170] It also appears that the degree of moral complexity varies from species to species.[171] But no matter what is found to be the true nature and extent of morality within the animal world, scientific evidence is now mounting that animals do exhibit the component elements necessary to be considered moral, and do sometimes exhibit moral behavior itself. Thus, another of the bastions of human superiority, the ability to be moral agents, is called into question by scientific study.

G. Mirrors, Repetitive Behavior and Self-awareness

Are animals aware of themselves as entities distinct from others around them? Or is animal consciousness just a series of disconnected sensations, with no glue that holds these sensations together as a continuing self? The debate on animal self-awareness has been a long and time-consuming one, but what is being learned relating to animal cognition, moral behavior and emotions, shows that at least some animals are self-conscious. How, for example, could a monkey engage in altruistic or empathetic behavior if it was not first aware of itself as an entity, and second, aware of the "other," the creature toward which it showed empathy?

The problem with the concept of self-awareness is that it is difficult to measure. The minds and emotions of others, humans and animals alike, are often hidden from us. How can we tell whether another animal is aware of itself as a continuing entity, distinct from others? This would seem to require entering the consciousness of another entity, which is not something we can do. Traditionally, the most popular test for determining self-awareness in other animals is the mirror test. An animal is placed in front of a mirror and is observed to determine if the animal behaves as if it recognizes itself as the creature in the mirror. If so, the animal is self-aware. If not, it is not.

There is considerable controversy about the efficacy of this test.[172] Great apes, like chimps, have "passed" this test, but many other animals, including other primates, have not.[173] Elephants, like chimps, pass the mirror test. An elephant with a yellow spot painted on its ear was placed in front of a mirror and very obviously inspected its ear to see what the yellow mark was, thereby showing that it was aware that it was looking at itself in the mirror.[174] Most recently, magpies have

---

170. Bekoff & Pierce, *supra* note 155, at 19–21.
171. *Id.*
172. *See* Marc Bekoff, & Paul W. Sherman, *Reflections on Animal Selves, in* Animal Passions and Beastly Virtues 66, 70–71 (Temple U. Press 2006) [hereinafter *Animal Selves*]; Robert W. Mitchell, *Kinesthetic-Visual Matching, Imitation, and Self Recognition in* The Cognitive Animal, *supra* note 30, at 345, 345; Gordon G. Gallup et al., *The Mirror Test, in* The Cognitive Animal, *supra* note 30, at 325–33 [hereinafter Gallup].
173. Gallup, *supra* note 172, at 325–27.
174. Benjamin L. Hart, *Large Brains and Cognition: Where do Elephants Fit In?*, 32 Neurosci. and Biobehavioral Rev. 86, 90 (2008); Joshua M. Plotnik et al., *Self-Recognition in An Asian Elephant*, 103 Proc. Nat'l Acad. Sci. No. 103, 17053–57 (2006).

passed the mirror test, the first non-mammalian species to do so.[175] But does this test really measure self-awareness? It seems that what it really tests is whether the animal understands how a mirror functions, which does not have anything to do with whether an entity is self-aware.

What would seem to be called for is some other way to determine self-awareness.[176] Researchers have been working on measuring self-awareness by other means. For instance, dolphins have been shown to be able to repeat past behaviors on command, which shows that they have a mental representation of what they have previously done, thereby showing self-awareness.[177] It has also been theorized that self-cognizance may be greatest in social species, since they "benefit most from reflecting on and revising their behavior" based upon how others respond to them.[178] Consider also, how could an animal learn anything if it did not have some concept of itself as a continuing entity? If it did not understand itself as a continuing entity, it could never relate its earlier experiences to later ones, and could therefore learn nothing.

One kind of behavior that itself shows self-awareness is deception. Intentional deception has been defined as selectively presenting or withholding information to change the perceptions of others, typically for the benefit of the deceiver.[179] Deceptive behavior shows self-awareness in animals, since animals that deceive clearly recognize and reason about the perceptions and the intentions of others, as distinct from themselves, which indicates this self-awareness.[180] For example, Rhesus monkeys who could choose between identical food containers, one of which made noise and another that did not, overwhelmingly chose the silent container when competing with human experimenters for food.[181] In other words, the monkeys silently stole the food so that the humans could not hear their activity. Similarly, Rhesus monkeys have been found to surreptitiously take food away from human competitors based upon where the humans are looking; the monkeys choose to seize the food when the humans are looking away, or when the humans' vision is blocked.[182]

But it is not only primates that engage in deceptive behavior; this phenomenon has also been observed in rodents as well. Tree squirrels, animals that cache food for future use, which is itself an indication of planning, have been shown to

175. Helmut Prior et al., *Mirror-Induced Behavior in the Magpie (Pica pica): Evidence of Self-Recognition*, 6 Pub. Libr. Sci. Bio. 1642, 1642–43 (2008).
176. *See Animal Selves, supra* note 172, at 71–72.
177. Herman, *supra* note 111, at 280.
178. *Animal Selves, supra* note 172, at 72.
179. Güzeldere et al., *supra* note 65, at 353; *see also* Laurie R. Santos et al., *Rhesus Monkeys, Macaca Mulatta, Know What Others Can and Cannot Hear,* 71 Animal Behaviour 1175, 1176 (2006) [hereinafter *Rhesus Monkeys*].
180. *See Rhesus Monkeys, supra* note 179, at 1179; Jonathan I. Flombaum & Laurie R. Santos, *Rhesus Monkeys Attribute Perceptions to Others,* 15 Current Bio 447, 447 (2005).
181. *See Rhesus Monkeys, supra* note 179, at 1177–78.
182. Flombaum & Santos, *supra* note 180, at 447–48.

deceptively cache food in order to stop the pilfering of their food caches.[183] To avoid pilfering, the squirrels dig a number of holes, and then put food into only some of the holes, so that they may mislead other animals.[184] This behavior is clearly conscious deception, which is supported by the facts that this behavior becomes more prevalent when there are other squirrels close by who may be watching the food-sequestering squirrel and this form of deception increased when the experimenters performed acts of pilferage for the squirrels to witness.[185] This skill of deception, like morality, however, is neither just present nor absent, but exists at varying levels of complexity.[186] This deceptive behavior has been traced to genetic mutation by natural selection at its most basic level (nature's deceptions such as protective coloration) and to socio-ecological development at more complex levels (where deception is manipulation of another's mental state, which requires an understanding of the other entity's mental state).[187]

Although not deceptive behavior, awareness of other minds is also shown in the distinct ways that adult bonobos play with fellow adults versus immature bonobos; the differentiated behavior reveals awareness of both their own ages and those of others, and therefore a sense of self.[188] There is also evidence that animals can determine the intentions of others, which is an ability, like deception, that has been found to have its neurological foundation in mirror neurons.[189] This ability to determine the intentions of others also indicates self-awareness.

Another example revealing that dolphins and primates have an understanding of other minds, as well as the intentions of others, is shown in the way that these animals exchange "favors." Dolphins and primates engage in petting, grooming or playing in ways that actually constitute performance of a service; thus, earning a debt to be repaid later by the other dolphin or primate. These debts are paid in the form of other useful services, such as help in protecting the young when things become dangerous or when a fight over a mate breaks out.[190] This shows not only an awareness of self as distinct from others, but also the recognition of both the self and others as continuing entities. Thus, despite the mirror test, there is substantial evidence that animals can understand, and reason and draw conclusions about the perceptions and intentions of others, which reveals qualities of self-consciousness.[191]

---

183. *See* Michael A. Steele et al., *Cache Protection Strategies of a Scatter-Hoarding Rodent: Do Tree Squirrels Engage in Behavioural Deception?*, 75 Animal Behaviour 705 (2007).
184. *Id.* at 706, 711–12.
185. *Id.* at 711–12.
186. *See* Güzeldere et al., *supra* note 65, at 353–56.
187. *Id.*
188. E. Palagi, *Sharing the Motivation to Play: The Use of Signals in Adult Bonobos*, 75 Animal Behaviour 887, 892–94 (2007).
189. Derek E. Lyons et al., *Reflections of Other Minds: How Primate Social Cognition Can Inform the Function of Mirror Neurons*, 16 Current Opinion in Neurobiology 230, 231 (2006).
190. Kathleen Maria Dudzinski et al., *A Comparison of Pectoral Fin Contact Between Two Different Wild Dolphin Populations*, 80 Behavioural Processes 182, 188–89 (2009).
191. *See* Flombaum & Santos, *supra* note 180, at 450; Palagi, *supra* note 188, at 893; *Rhesus Monkeys*, *supra* note 179, at 1176, 1180.

H. The Wise Guy Parrot and Signing Bonobos

What about language? Do animals other than humans have language? Charles Darwin believed that language evolved from natural signals used by animals.[192] It is now well established that both chickens and vervet monkeys use different natural signs, *i.e.*, alarm signals, to represent dangers of different kinds.[193] For example, chickens use different calls for predators in the air than they do for predators on the ground.[194] In addition, chickens use yet other calls to indicate the presence of food.[195] Prairie dogs have been observed to have unique alarm calls for hawks, for coyotes, for domestic dogs and for humans.[196]

Cartesians, on the other hand, take the position that humans alone are uniquely rational creatures, and "that language is the ultimate manifestation of that unique rationality."[197] According to Noam Chomsky, expounding on this theory, humans have a unique language faculty that other animals do not, and that part of this language faculty is a "universal grammar":[198]

> It is a reasonable surmise, I think, that there is no structure similar to UG [universal grammar] in nonhuman organisms and that the capacity for free, appropriate, and creative use of language as an expression of thought, with the means provided by the language faculty, is also a distinctive feature of the human species, having no significant analogue elsewhere. The neural basis for language is pretty much of a mystery, but there can be little doubt that specific neural structures and even gross organization not found in other primates (e.g., lateralization) play a fundamental role.[199]

Thus, it seems to be Chomsky's position that language ability is innate to humans, and that the neurological structures responsible for language are a sort of "language organ" which is not present in nonhuman animals.[200]

Perhaps the most telling part of the material quoted above is that, although Chomsky says the neural basis for language is "pretty much of a mystery," he has "little doubt" that humans are the only animals with the neural capacity to have language. If the neural basis for language is such a mystery, how can he possibly have "little doubt" about anything related to the neural basis for language? His position is simply an example of something that deniers of animal abilities in language, cognition and other skills frequently do—they deny as obvious that animals have certain skills, with absolutely no evidence in support of their position. This

---

192. *See* Christopher S. Evans, *Cracking the Code: Communication and Cognition in Birds, in* The Cognitive Animal, *supra* note 30, at 315.
193. *Id.* at 315–17.
194. *Id.*
195. *Id.* at 317–19.
196. Animals Matter, *supra* note 39, at 51–52.
197. Roger S. Fouts, *Apes, Darwinian Continuity, and the Law*, 10 Animal L. 99, 104–05 (2004).
198. Noam Chomsky, Reflections on Language 36–41 (1975).
199. *Id.* at 40–41.
200. *Id.*

type of non-argument has been the watermark of those who are opposed to recognizing the various abilities of animals throughout history. Aristotle created his hierarchy[201] without even rudimentary knowledge of the functioning of either human or animal bodies and brains; Descartes, while having the advantage of a greater knowledge base than that available to Aristotle, proposed that animals were machines, when he had only an extraordinarily limited knowledge of the functioning of animal or human bodies. It is only within the last forty to fifty years that any serious attempts have been made to determine the true capacities of animals; but those claiming that animals have no significant language or other skills have had no difficulty in asserting their beliefs without any evidence, as exemplified by Chomsky's statements.

Notwithstanding Chomsky, there is evidence that at least some animals do have true linguistic skills in using human language. For example, in 1966, researchers Allen and Beatrix Gardner brought a ten-month-old Chimpanzee, Washoe, to the University of Nevada, where they taught him sign language.[202] They cross-fostered (which meant fostering the chimp with a human family as though the chimp were a child of the humans) Washoe with four other chimps who were also taught sign language. Ultimately, through five years of training and cross-fostering, the chimps' language skills grew in terms of vocabulary, responses to questions, number of utterances, proportion of phrases, variety of phrases, length of phrases, complexity of phrases, and inflection.[203] In addition, all five of the chimps signed to each other, friends, strangers, each other, and also to dogs and cats.[204] It has also been determined that young chimps can learn signing from other chimps, without any human supervision or intervention.[205] "The Gardeners [also] found that vocabulary and phrase development in the cross-fostered chimpanzees [grew steadily], as in human children, and showed degrees of change and growth rather than discrete junctures."[206]

Similar experiments have been performed with bonobos by Sue Savage-Rumbaugh, who used a keyboard with symbols on it that referred to objects, activities and abstract concepts like "now" and "bad."[207] One of her bonobos, Kanzi, learned 348 symbols, and learned to combine them in regular ways in what

---

201. But recall that Aristotle actually had a more nuanced view of the relationships between humans, animals, plants and other aspects of the world than he is given credit for when people suggest that he was wedded to a strict "Great Chain of Being" linear structure of those relationships. *See supra* notes 23 through 25, and accompanying text.
202. Fouts, *supra* note 197, at 107–08.
203. *Id.* at 108.
204. *Id.*
205. Fouts et al., *Chimpanzee Signing: Darwinian Realities and Cartesian Delusions, in* The Cognitive Animal, *supra* note 30, at 285, 286–87.
206. Fouts, *supra* note 197, at 109.
207. Paul Raffaele, *Speaking Bonobo*, Smithsonian Mag. (Nov. 2006), *available at* http://www.smithsonianmag.com/science-nature/speakingbonobo.html.

is called a "proto grammar."[208] Savage-Rumbaugh also claims that Kanzi knows about 3,000 spoken English words.[209]

Dr. Irene Pepperberg studied language development in an African Grey Parrot named Alex.[210] She worked with Alex for over 22 years, during which he developed a large vocabulary and used it in a sophisticated way, roughly similar to the language use of a two-year-old child.[211] Alex could, in addition, break-up words into constituent sounds,[212] which is called "anticipatory co-articulation," one of the building blocks of language.[213] But Alex did not just use language; he made appropriate statements like "calm down" when someone seemed upset; he intentionally gave wrong answers; he deceived researchers; and he learned difficult mathematical concepts like zero and equivalence. So Alex was not just a poster-bird for animal language acquisition, but was far more profound; he showed that animal minds are much more sophisticated and complex than was previously thought or, indeed, imagined.[214]

It is one thing to recognize or even correctly use a particular word; it is quite another to understand the grammar and syntax of a language. "Semantics and syntax are considered the core attributes of any human natural language."[215] If animals were found to comprehend and utilize rules of grammar, then the idea that only humans can have language would no longer be tenable. There is substantial and growing evidence that non-human animals indeed do have and use grammar skills.

For example, in the world of birds, it is not only Alex the parrot who has been found to have profound linguistic skills: starlings have been discovered to have grammatical abilities previously thought only to exist in humans.[216] Birds are capable of what is referred to as "recursive center-embedding" of information from bird songs, "which allows for the creation of new (and grammatically correct) utterances" using new clauses within bird song "sentences."[217] An example of this recursive center-embedding would be transforming "Oedipus ruled Thebes" to "Oedipus, who killed his father, ruled Thebes."[218] Chomskian linguists believe that recursive center embedding is a unique feature of human language and is

208. *Id.*
209. *Id.*
210. *See* ALEX & ME, *supra* note 72.
211. The Alex Foundation, *Alex the African Grey Parrot and Subject of Landmark Studies of Bird Intelligence Dies at 31,* http://www.alexfoundation.org/press_release.html (last visited Apr. 27, 2010).
212. ALEX & ME, *supra* note 72, at 142.
213. *Id.*
214. *Id.* at 214–19.
215. Herman, *supra* note 111, at 278.
216. *See* T.Q. Gentner, *Neural Systems for Individual Song Recognition in Adult Birds*, 1016 ANNALS OF THE N.Y. ACAD. OF SCI. 282–302 (2004).
217. *See* Inga Kiderra, *The Birds and the B's: Challenging Chomsky, Starlings Learn 'Human Only' Syntax Patterns*, UNIV. CAL. SAN DIEGO NEWS, Apr. 26, 2006, http://ucsdnews.ucsd.edu/newsrel/soc/gentner_starling06.asp.
218. *Id.*

unique to the human language faculty.[219] The evidence of starling and other animals' use and understanding of recursive center embedding refutes this claim.[220]

Dolphins have also been found able to process both semantic and syntactic information in language.[221] "Our studies of language comprehension have revealed capabilities in the dolphin for processing both semantic and syntactic information .... The dolphin is capable of understanding that changes in word order change meaning."[222] This comprehension by dolphins occurred without explicit training.[223] Dolphins were also found capable of extracting syntactically correct phrases from within a string of words syntactically without meaning.[224] Dolphins have also been shown to understand that symbols represent objects, and understand the difference between "actual" things and mere representations of them.[225] A truly fascinating test revealed that dolphins responded to televised gestures in the same manner as if they had occurred in physical reality, and knew to use real objects in response rather than attempting to get objects from the television screen instead.[226] This experiment shows that the dolphins could understand the difference between a representational medium and the real world.[227] Not to be outdone by their fellow ocean-going mammal cousins, sea lions have also been shown to comprehend equivalence relations and syntax in the ordering of gestures made to them.[228] They can accomplish this without the use of linguistic codes, as would be used by humans.[229]

Notwithstanding all of this recently discovered evidence of animal use of language and grammar, claims that animals have learned, or can learn, language are still disputed by some in the scientific community. For example, Savage-Rumbaugh's results have been criticized by Stephen Budiansky on the grounds that bonobos generally only form sentences from symbols when they want something (like food, toys, etc.) and that they only use language when taught it, not in the wild.[230] Both of these critiques of the bonobos' abilities could be leveled at humans as well. Humans generally use language to express that they want something, do they not? Moreover, it is not entirely clear that bonobos and chimps do not use any sort of language in the wild; consider for example, the trail-marking activity of bonobos described earlier.[231] In addition, what about the chimps that taught sign language to other chimps, without any human prompting? Isn't this

219. *Id.*
220. *Id.*
221. Herman, *supra* note 111, at 278–79; Kuczaj & Walker, *supra* note 77, at 582–86.
222. Herman, *supra* note 111, at 278–79 (citations omitted).
223. *Id.* at 279.
224. *Id.*
225. *Id.* at 279–80.
226. *Id.*
227. *Id.*
228. Ronald J. Schusterman et al., *supra* note 150, at 217, 223.
229. *Id.* at 224–25.
230. Stephen Budiansky, If a Lion Could Talk 156 (The Free Press 1998).
231. *See* notes 122 through 124 and accompanying text.

effectively the use of a language "in the wild"? Whatever the true linguistic capabilities of animals, this is an area of research that is receiving attention that did not exist even 40 years ago, and the discovered abilities of animals in this area are multiplying rapidly; despite the best efforts of those who would deny them.

I. ANIMAL EMOTIONS

Based on Descartes' concept of animals as machines, we might assume that animals do not have emotions, either of a positive or negative nature. Therefore, in accordance with this theory we need not be concerned about the well-being of these "machines" since they can suffer neither depression, anxiety, happiness, or love. But, standing in dark relief against this theory, every person with any familiarity with animals has felt compelled by the obvious joy of animals in play; the unmistakable shame and regret of the punished dog and the profound depression of chained elephants, as their heads sway aimlessly back and forth. Moreover, given what we know about evolution, we expect animals to possess emotions similar to ours. This is what Darwin maintained; he believed that there is "continuity between the emotional lives of humans and other animals."[232] Darwin stated, "[t]he lower animals, like man, manifestly feel pleasure and pain, happiness and misery."[233]

It is contrary to the notion of common sense as well as our common daily observations to think that animals do not have emotions. Indeed, science now proves that animals surely do have emotions. Emotions, which are "defined as psychological phenomena that help in behavioral management and control,"[234] have typically been divided into two categories: primary and secondary. Primary emotions are fear and fight or flight reactions, and from everything we have observed, there is no doubt that animals operate under these types of emotions.[235] Secondary emotions are more sophisticated; they are emotions "that are experienced or felt, those that are evaluated and reflected on."[236] As detailed below, animals have been discovered to have these secondary emotions as well.

There are many anecdotal stories of animals showing a wide range of emotions, documented in a variety of sources. Jane Goodall described a chimp so distraught by his mother's death that he literally grieved until he caused his own death:

> Never shall I forget watching as, three days after Flo's death, Flint climbed slowly into a tall tree near the stream. He walked along one of the branches,

---

232. Marc Bekoff, *Beastly Passions in* ANIMAL PASSIONS AND BEASTLY VIRTUES 35, 35 (Temple U. Press 2006).
233. *Id.* (quoting CHARLES DARWIN, ON THE ORIGIN OF SPECIES BY MEANS OF NATURAL SELECTION 511 (Joseph Carroll ed., Broadview Press 2003)).
234. MINDING ANIMALS, *supra* note 40, at 105.
235. *Id.* at 106.
236. *Id.*

> then stopped and stood motionless, staring down at an empty nest. After about two minutes he turned away and, with the movements of an old man, climbed down, walked a few steps, then lay, wide eyes staring ahead. The nest was one which he and Flo had shared a short while before Flo died.... In the presence of his big brother [Figan], [Flint] had seemed to shake off a little of his depression. But then he suddenly left the group and raced back to the place where Flo had died and there sank into ever deeper depression.... Flint became increasingly lethargic, refused food and, with his immune system thus weakened, fell sick. The last time I saw him alive, he was hollow-eyed, gaunt and utterly depressed, huddled in the vegetation close to where Flo had died.... The last short journey he made, pausing to rest every few feet, was to the very place where Flo's body had lain. There he stayed for several hours, sometimes staring and staring into the water. He struggled on a little further, then curled up—and never moved again.[237]

Stories of elephant emotions are legion. For example, one story, told by elephant researcher Cynthia Moss, concerns a family of elephants caring for a newborn that had been born with bent legs. The mother and her other child stayed with him without food, for days, until his legs began to work properly,[238] which exhibits feelings of empathy. We have previously seen evidence of empathy in monkeys in the behavior of Diana monkeys. Additionally, you will recall the story of the old female monkey whose mate, observing her inability to cause a machine to deliver food, picked up tokens she had dropped, put them into the machine for her, and let her have the food.[239]

It is not necessary to rely on anecdotes, however, since "[c]urrent research in ethology, neurobiology, endocrinology, psychology and philosophy is providing compelling evidence that at least some animals have a wide range of emotions including fear, joy, happiness, shame, embarrassment, resentment, jealousy, rage, anger, love, pleasure, compassion, respect, relief, disgust, sadness, despair and grief."[240] This range of emotions has been found to exist in at least some vertebrates.[241] Even that ancient reptile, the iguana, appears to show signs of pleasure.[242] In fact, it may be that reptiles were the first animals to actually experience their own emotions.[243]

So how have all of these emotions been observed and determined to exist by ethologists and other researchers? Joy and happiness are shown in the play behavior of animals.[244] Grief and sorrow at losses have been observed in geese, sea lions,

237. *Id.* at 100 (quoting Jane Goodall).
238. *Id.* at 101.
239. *Id.* at 102. For an excellent discussion of acts of empathy and kindness by chimpanzees and other animals, *see* Frans de Waal, OUR INNER APE 169–214 (2005).
240. MINDING ANIMALS, *supra* note 40, at 102–03.
241. *Animal Selves, supra* note 172, at 35.
242. MINDING ANIMALS, *supra* note 40, at 107–08.
243. *See Animal Selves, supra* note 172, at 36–37.
244. MINDING ANIMALS, *supra* note 40, at 112–13.

antelope and elephants.[245] Konrad Lorenz observed that "[a] grey-lag goose that has lost its partner shows all the symptoms that [developmental psychologist] John Bowlby has described in young human children in his famous books.... the eyes sink deep in their sockets, and the individual has an overall drooping experience, literally letting the head hang."[246] Similarly, animals experiencing the loss of others have been observed to withdraw from their group, sit in the same place and stare blankly into space as though paralyzed.[247]

More positive emotions, like love, have also been observed in animals, as can be seen in courtship rituals that have been viewed in birds, whales and even fish.[248] Biologist Bernd Heinrich has observed ravens engaging in behavior he characterized as falling in love.[249] Evidently, "[t]here are common brain systems and homologous chemicals underlying love (and other emotions) that are shared among humans and [non-human] animals. The presence of these neural pathways suggests that if humans can feel romantic love, then at least some other animals must also experience this emotion."[250]

Numerous other emotions have been seen in animals. Anger has been observed in dolphins, giraffes and octopuses.[251] Embarrassment has been observed in monkeys. In one instance, a monkey who has fallen is seen looking around to see if anyone saw him fall and then, satisfied that no one saw him, struts off.[252] As was noted earlier, animals sometimes have been seen engaging in what is referred to as social morality—being fair and having empathy toward others in their community.

The evidence for feelings of empathy in animals is becoming quite extensive. Mice suffer distress when they observe another mouse in pain.[253] It has been said of this information on mice that "[t]his data confirms that empathy is an ancient capacity, probably present in all mammals."[254] Indeed, this data seems to be borne out in other species, with monkeys and apes evidencing empathy.[255] Empathy has been frequently seen in elephants, as well.[256] Empathy has also been observed in Cetaceans. Science has discovered much more than this, though, which has made the evidence for empathy in animals that much stronger; the cells important in processing emotions and, in particular, empathy, have been located and studied in Cetaceans:

245. *Id.* at 113.
246. *Id.*
247. *Animal Selves, supra* note 172, at 38.
248. *See id.* at 37; MINDING ANIMALS, *supra* note 40, at 21, 114.
249. *Animal Selves, supra* note 172, at 37.
250. MINDING ANIMALS, *supra* note 40, at 114.
251. *Id.* at 116.
252. *Id.* at 117.
253. Pierce, *supra* note 162, at 8–9. The author notes the irony of causing pain in mice to observe that mice have empathy. What should we say about the human experimenters?
254. *Id.* at 1.
255. *Id.* at 4–6.
256. *Id.* at 6–7.

> Cetacean researchers were surprised recently by the discovery of spindle cells, which were long thought to exist only in humans and other great apes, in humpback whales, fin whales, killer whales, and sperm whales in the same area of their brains as spindle cells in human brains. Spindle neurons are important in processing emotions and appear to play a role in empathy and in feelings of love. Researchers believe that spindle cells may have existed in the toothed whales for at least twice as long as in humans. It may turn out that other cetaceans—including the baleen whales, which are of a different suborder than dolphins, porpoises, and toothed whales—also have spindle cells, which would suggest that empathy is widespread among this order of animals.[257]

So, far from being unfeeling automatons, as Descartes reportedly maintained, many animals are now seen to have a full range of emotions. The very scientists whose experiments Descartes' theories made appear ethically justifiable are perhaps now coming to realize that the traditional foundation of the relationship between humans and animals is wrong.

It is worth noting that modern scientific research on animals, as well as industrial farming of animals, has traditionally been justified by a "scientific" description of what animals are like. It has long been asserted as scientific fact that animals do not have pain as we know it and do not have rich emotional lives or complex thoughts; it is therefore, the fallacious logic goes, morally acceptable to use them as raw material to test the potency of our drugs and cosmetics and to eat them after subjecting them to horrible living conditions. As it turns out, of course, the scientific description has all along been wrong. If our morality (and thus, our behavior) were guided by logic and reality, it would be a happy day for animals around the world. Unfortunately, morality, logic and reality are rarely woven together into a seamless garment.[258]

What all this means is that when we use animals for exploitative purposes, it is absolutely necessary that we acknowledge that animals feel emotions like we do—they suffer, become depressed, fall into despair, etc. And whenever we use animals in a way that stimulates these emotions, we are ultimately responsible for their suffering.

What we have found in modern science when we actually make the effort to discover the true nature and skills of other animals, is that the supposed distinctions between animals and humans that justify our use and abuse of animals do not, in actuality, exist. The idea that only humans are rational, that only humans can act in a moral way, that only humans consciously plan for the future, that only humans can use abstract concepts, that only humans learn via imitation of others, that only humans have math skills, that only humans can create and use tools, that only humans use logic, that only humans are self-aware, that only humans have language, that only humans have emotions; all of these presumed bastions of

257. *Id.* at 6.
258. *Id.* at 9.

human superiority have been burst asunder by contemporary science which is just now beginning the much needed and timely quest for the truth concerning animal cognition, emotions and other intellectual functions.

V. ANIMAL LIBERATION, ANIMAL RIGHTS AND FEMINISM

From the foregoing discussion of traditional philosophical theories and modern science concerning the relationship between humans and animals, several things become evident: those arguing in favor of the conventional use of animals in agriculture, experimentation and the like tend to focus on perceived differences between animals and humans, but long-held assumptions about these differences and the cognitive and emotional make-up of animals are now rapidly being overturned by scientific research. As a part of this evolution in thought about the human/animal relationship are modern philosophical voices that challenge traditional philosophical theories.

A. Utilitarianism

Peter Singer brought the moral issues surrounding the relationship between humans and non-human animals into modern public consciousness with his well-known 1975 book, *Animal Liberation*. Since then the animal/human relationship has become a subject of considerable philosophical and legal debate. For example, in the early 1990s, there were only a handful of law schools that taught classes on animal law in the United States; today more than 100 schools offer such classes. While there are other authors and activists who have been influential in bringing these issues to the fore, Peter Singer virtually single-handedly provided the philosophical foundation for the discussion of our relationship with animals.

Singer is a utilitarian. Utilitarianism is a philosophical theory with a rich history and some of its proponents have used utilitarian theory to promote change in the way we relate to and treat animals. The foundation of utilitarianism is the idea that there is one fundamental principle of moral philosophy, and that is "maximization of utility." In other words, when making a moral choice among several possible actions, the utilitarian will choose the path that maximizes overall utility. But what exactly is the "utility" that the utilitarians urge us to maximize?

Different utilitarian philosophers have answered this question in different ways.[259] Jeremy Bentham, for example, was what is referred to as a "hedonistic"

259. I am oversimplifying utilitarian philosophy here and am focusing just on Bentham and Singer. I do this since they are the utilitarian philosophers who are most often discussed in connection with the human/animal relationship and my purpose here is to focus on this issue. For this reason I do not survey the field of utilitarian philosophy including "rights" utilitarians, "rule" utilitarians, and so on.

utilitarian. He believed that utility can be measured by pleasure and pain; so we are to maximize pleasure in the world and minimize pain. Since Bentham believed that animals feel both pleasure and pain, their pleasure and pain is calculated in his utility quotient in exactly the same way that the pleasure and pain of humans is calculated. The pain of humans and animals counts equally for Bentham.

Singer, however, does not measure utility by pleasure and pain; rather, the measure of utility in his theory is the satisfaction of "preferences."[260] Maximization of total satisfaction of preferences in the world, then, is the basis of his utilitarian philosophy. So what exactly are "preferences," and do animals have them? While one could argue that a "preference" is a sophisticated multifaceted concept that requires the use of language and other advanced characteristics, according to Singer, preferences can be seen as "interests."[261] According to Singer, entities that are sentient, *i.e.*, able to experience suffering, are the entities that have "interests" and are entitled to have their interests considered within his utility calculation.[262] Like pleasure and pain to Bentham the preferences of all entities that can suffer count equally to Singer.

In Singer's utilitarianism then, the preferences of animals count equally with those of humans.[263] As a result, the obvious, if unspoken preferences of animals (to be free from pain, to have freedom of movement, to engage in activities according to their nature), enter the utility calculation as equal to ours. In Singer's view, if utilitarianism were properly applied, and we were to take into account the preferences of animals, our relationship with animals would be completely transformed. We would generally stop eating animals, and exploiting them for experiments and entertainment as we now do.

There are, however, a number of problems with utilitarian theory. There is, for example, the famous killing-of-innocents problem, which can be illustrated by any number of hypothetical problems including the following one:[264] Assume that a city has been victimized by a vicious serial killer. Many have been killed by this person and the city is so terrified of the killer that people stay indoors, do not engage in commerce and live in constant fear. Assume also that those in city government now know that the killer will not kill again, but there is no way to convince the populace of this fact without the trial, conviction and execution of the killer. In addition, there is a person concerning whom the city has sufficient evidence to convict for the crime; the problem is that this person is innocent. The guilty person is known to city government, but there is no way that this person could possibly be convicted of the crimes, because there is insufficient evidence.

---

260. PETER SINGER, PRACTICAL ETHICS x–xi, 12–15, 94–95, 119–34 (2d ed. Cambridge U. Press 1993) [hereinafter PRACTICAL ETHICS].
261. *See id.* at 12–15, 55–62, 119–34; REGAN, *supra* note 32, at 206.
262. PRACTICAL ETHICS, *supra* note 260, at 58–59; Peter Singer, *All Animals Are Equal, in* ANIMAL RIGHTS AND HUMAN OBLIGATIONS 148, 148–53 (Tom Regan ed., 1989).
263. PRACTICAL ETHICS, *supra* note 260, at 55–62.
264. This is based on an example that I believe I heard in a lecture, but am unsure of the ultimate source. In any event, one can fashion any number of stories to illustrate this point.

Should the city try, convict and execute the innocent person, assuming that no one would ever discover that he was wrongly convicted? If it did, there would be a huge increase in utility, according to hedonistic utilitarian theory. Commerce would begin again. The populace would return to the streets. Fear would subside. The only disutility would be to the innocent person convicted of the crime and those close to him or her. Overall, convicting and killing the innocent person will result in more pleasure (the populace's return to normalcy) than pain (the innocent person's death). Thus, the utility calculation in this case favors the seemingly highly immoral result of conviction and execution of the innocent person, since the huge amount of utility created by ending the fear caused by the serial killer far outweighs the loss of utility of the innocent person. This kind of example has often been used to illustrate that utilitarianism, since it measures moral value only under some defined utility consequence, can lead to decisions that severely impair the interests of individuals in favor of an overall increase in community utility in a way that no one feels comfortable with since they do not seem to be "moral" decisions.

Singer's preference utilitarianism seeks to solve, among others, this kind of problem with hedonistic utilitarianism. According to Singer, in the hypothetical, the innocent person would have strong preferences about the future, among them the preference to continue living; violation of these preferences would be a direct wrong to this person which would preclude killing the innocent person to satisfy the less monumental preferences of others in the city.[265] Tom Regan has pointed out that while this might be an accurate account in the case of a human with a clear vision of its future and an understanding of its mortality, it is not clear that this same thing could be said of humans with mental defects or of animals.[266] Do they have preferences about the future or a concept of mortality that would make killing them in similar circumstances wrong? It is surely not clear that animals do have these capacities, particularly a sense of mortality. In other words, Singer's theory may provide no protection at all against the killing of animals that do not have preferences about their future or an understanding of their mortality, or for that matter, humans that do not have such preferences or understanding.

Our killing of innocents story illustrates a number of other problems with utilitarian theory. The theory has an ad hoc nature. How do we measure utility and who is the arbiter of the values to be placed on the pleasure or pain, or preferences, of entities entitled to consideration? There does not seem to be any objective basis on which to assign these utility values nor is there any authority to act as arbiter of these values. Further, as has been pointed out by, among others, Tom Regan, utilitarianism views humans and animals as nothing more than vessels which contain some amount of utility, and the value of these vessels is determined solely by how much utility is contained within the vessel.[267] It is only the consequences of actions that count, not the participants in the actions. The vessels themselves,

---

265. *See* REGAN, *supra* note 32, at 206–08.
266. *Id.*
267. *Id.* at 208–11.

whether human or animal, have no inherent value.[268] No one, human or animal, has rights in this utilitarian theory. Indeed, it is because the vessel in our hypothetical, the innocent person, has no inherent value and therefore no rights, that it is even a possibility to conclude that this person should be killed. If humans (or animals) had some inherent value apart from their utility, this kind of result could never occur, because the inherent moral value of the innocent would protect him or her from untimely death.

The lack of any inherent value in humans or animals in utilitarian theory leads also to the "replaceability" problem. If one could painlessly kill an entity (either human or animal) and replace it with an entity that would experience at least as much utility as the dead entity, there then would not be any moral difficulty in this action under utilitarian theory. This idea could then be used to argue for the use of animals in agriculture (among other practices), since it could be argued that each animal killed in agricultural activity is then replaced by an animal that will experience at least as much utility as the dead one. Now one could argue that agricultural animals typically experience only negative utility, and therefore, this example is not an accurate reflection of how the theory would actually work; but, given the right situation for the animal, say it is not in a factory farm, and prior to being painlessly killed, has enjoyed a pleasant life, it does seem that the theory would allow for the replacement of one agricultural animal by another.[269] Thus, even Singer's utilitarian theory could be used to justify the use of animals in agriculture.

Perhaps the most telling criticism of utilitarianism in the context of the human/animal relationship, however, is that it seems to be the theory that is actually used by humans to determine the relationship between themselves and animals. Humans eat animals, knowing that they suffer in order to become food. Nonetheless, humans eat them, determining that their preference for eating animal flesh outweighs the suffering of the animals. Humans experiment on millions of animals annually, believing that the progress made in medicine and product safety outweighs the suffering of the animals. And so on in other areas in which animals are used by humans. Thus, perhaps the most damning indictment of utilitarianism may be seen by simply looking at the relationship between humans and animals that exists in the world, and recognizing that a form of utilitarianism is used to justify present practices.

The use of utilitarian theory in the law relating to animals is, in fact, easy to document. For example, animal cruelty laws in the United States and many other places in the world make the inflicting of "unnecessary" suffering on animals illegal, but these laws often explicitly except from their application things like the use of animals in agriculture and experimentation owing to the alleged economic, cultural and societal value realized from these activities. Meat eating is a long-standing cultural tradition and the meat industry is a huge one that creates countless jobs, generates enormous economic value and provides humans the benefit of

268. *Id.*
269. Both Singer and Regan discuss this issue at some length. *See* PRACTICAL ETHICS, *supra* note 260, at 110–34; REGAN, *supra* note 32, at 206–11.

what they believe to be tasty and nutritious food. Likewise, animal experiments pave the way for "safe" drugs and other products that also generate untold amounts of economic utility. That these agricultural and scientific arenas are exempted from application of anti-cruelty laws is a result of utility calculations that find human interests to outweigh those of animals. Thus, animal cruelty laws effectively prohibit only those activities that do not promote economic, cultural, or social utility thought to outweigh the suffering of the animals. So what we seem to see in the real world of the human/animal relationship is that the way this relationship is presently structured is a result of utilitarian calculations.

Undoubtedly a utilitarian like Singer would respond that my analysis simply shows that the utility calculation has not been properly performed by individuals and policy makers; if these people were to properly weigh the utility interests involved, the outcome would be quite different. Perhaps this is so. Nonetheless, since there is no inherent value in any entity under traditional utilitarian theory, the pleasure or preferences or interests of any individual can always be outweighed by the interests of others. There is, therefore, no safety net of inherent value or rights which can prevent certain actions, like the killing of innocents, from being considered moral in some circumstances.

B. Rights Theory

One way to avoid the problems of utilitarianism is to assign value to the vessel containing utility. What I will call "Rights Theory" does this. One proponent of this kind of theory is Tom Regan, who has written the influential book, *The Case for Animal Rights*. In this book, he argues that at least all mammals over the age of one year should be considered to have moral rights that must be respected. Exactly how does he get to this conclusion?

As discussed earlier in this chapter, Regan makes a distinction between "moral agents" and "moral patients." The former are entities that have the ability to, among other things, make moral judgments,[270] and the paradigm of such an entity would be a normal adult human being. The latter are entities that "lack the prerequisites that would enable them to control their own behavior in ways that would make them morally accountable for what they do."[271] These entities cannot do right or wrong because they are unable to bring moral principles to bear on their actions. Among the entities that are moral patients are human infants, children and the deranged. Animals are also placed in this category.

Although my discussion here greatly oversimplifies Regan's exhaustive and detailed analysis, one of Regan's main points is that moral agents have "inherent value," or a moral value not dependent upon the experiences, pleasure or preferences of the moral agent.[272] Thus, moral agents have value beyond that admitted

270. Regan, *supra* note 32, at 151–52.
271. *Id.* at 152.
272. *Id.* at 235–37.

by utilitarians—in this view the utilitarian receptacle itself is given value. This value is held by all moral agents equally, and no moral agents have more inherent value than any others.

If Regan were to stop here, we would still be essentially in the same place where Kant left us[273] but Regan does not stop here. He argues that because moral patients can be harmed in some of the same ways that moral agents can, *i.e.*, be subjected to gratuitous suffering or denied their preferences, and because we have direct duties to all entities not to harm them in these ways, moral patients, too, can be seen as having inherent moral value.[274] This inherent moral value of moral patients is held equally with moral agents; again, there are no gradations in inherent value. The group of entities that Regan believes have inherent value in this way is all mammals over one year of age.[275] In addition, he would give the "benefit of the doubt" (and thus moral consideration), to certain other animals such as those having consciousness, but who have not yet been proven to act intentionally.[276]

In this way, Regan arrives at the conclusion that both moral agents and moral patients have inherent value, and thus derives the "Respect Principle" that says that entities having inherent value are entitled to respect.[277] Then from the Respect Principle Regan derives the "Harm Principle," which asserts that entities that have inherent value should not be harmed.[278] In this way, Regan derives the right not to be harmed for both moral agents and patients—and thus for both humans and non-human animals as well. As a result, in Regan's moral world animals would have rights not to be harmed that would preclude our present uses of animals in agriculture, experimentation and entertainment. This, unlike utilitarianism, is a theory that does actually create rights in animals.

C. Feminist Theory

Feminist theory is not monolithic and there are a variety of feminist perspectives. In this section, I will describe one prominent feminist view of the human/animal relationship that I believe to be both a useful contrast to the views described above, and a useful tool in considering the present state of the human/animal relationship and the law.

This branch of feminist thought rejects both utilitarianism and what I have referred to as Rights Theory. This particular feminist view is built on an utterly different foundation and challenges the underpinnings of both of the modern philosophical theories I have thus far described. To feminists, the arguments of Singer and Regan are premised on the "Western Male" view of the world. In this

---

273. *See supra* notes 45 through 50 and accompanying text.
274. *See* Regan, *supra* note 32, at 187–89.
275. *Id.* at 247.
276. *Id.* at 246.
277. *Id.* at 248–49.
278. *Id.* at 262–63.

world view, "rational" argument is the sole method of finding truth; the world is divided into countless dualisms, each containing normative content, such as good/bad, god/man, man/woman, human/animal, etc., and the world is organized in a sort of hierarchy, not unlike Aristotle's Great Chain of Being.[279] There is no place here for emotions, sentiment, or feelings.

That there is no place for emotion in their arguments is indeed explicitly stated by both Singer and Regan who preface their arguments with the assertion that their views are based on rational argument, not on emotions or feelings or even fondness for animals.[280] In the "Western Male" world view, rationality and emotion form opposite dualities, with rationality of course considered the normative superior of the two. Emotion is to be avoided. The views of Singer and Regan, arising from this tradition, are therefore firmly rooted in the realm of rational argument, not in the realm of the emotive. Moreover, these thinkers maintain some aspects of Aristotelian hierarchy in their theories; Regan with his focus on creatures that are the "subjects of a life" or have some sort of "consciousness" and Singer with the need to have an animal that can sensibly be considered to have "preferences." To many feminists, this "Western Male" view of the world is a clinical and sterile world, divided, categorized and pigeonholed according to traditions that have roots even prior to Aristotle. This feminist view generally eschews all of this and embraces a fundamentally different picture of the world and its inhabitants.

In this feminist view, the world is conceived of holistically as a web of relationships between different humans, between humans and animals, and between humans, animals and their environment.[281] Here the very concept of dividing the world by species is called into question[282] and what is morally correct cannot be determined based solely on rational thought. Instead, the idea that moral truths can be found through rational argument is rejected in favor of a view that discovers the underpinnings of moral theory in emotions and feelings that arise only in connection with the relationships we have with the world.[283] Therefore, it is feelings of compassion, caring and empathy that ground moral truths, not cold rational arguments. Indeed, morality requires one to feel, to have emotions.[284] And one should note that scientists study morality as being grounded in emotions, so one can accurately say that this theory is consistent with the science of morality. This perspective that morality is grounded in the emotive is actually not a new one; it was, in fact, a view held by one of the more influential "Western Male" philosophers,

---

279. Marti Kheel, *The Liberation of Nature: A Circular Affair, in* BEYOND ANIMAL RIGHTS 17–18 (Josephine Donovan & Carol J. Adam eds., 1996).
280. *See* REGAN, *supra* note 32, at xlii–iii (stating that his is a purely rational endeavor, not rooted in emotions); PETER SINGER, ANIMAL LIBERATION ii–iii (1990) (stating that he is not "inordinately fond of dogs, cats or horses" and does not "love" animals).
281. Kheel, *supra* note 279, at 18–23.
282. *See* Maneesha Deckha, *The Salience of Species Difference for Feminist Theory,* 17 HASTINGS WOMEN'S L. J. 1 (2006).
283. Kheel, *supra* note 279, at 22–31.
284. *Id.* at 24–31.

David Hume. Hume believed that the mechanism of rational argument can never discern a single moral proposition.[285] Morality is grounded in feelings and emotions that are effectively "hard-wired," innate characteristics of humans.[286]

To the feminist, grounding morality in the emotive does not require that rationality be jettisoned; there is recognition instead that none of us are ever really free of emotion. It is quite impossible to be purely rational; our lives are lived in states that combine at once the emotive and the rational,[287] and rationality and emotion cannot be atomized and separated. To take any action at all in the world, one must be motivated to do so, and to be motivated is inherently to have emotion.

From this perspective is born a new way to look at the relationship between humans and animals. Our moral duties to animals evolve from appropriate feelings of compassion and empathy toward the suffering of animals, and thus require that we treat animals very differently than we do now—with compassion and empathy visible in all of our actions. But feminism does not necessarily lead to "rights" in animals. Many feminists reject the idea of rights altogether, in all contexts, because they believe that the concept of "rights" is just another artifact of the "Western Male" world view.[288] Rights, they believe, are only necessary because of the competitive and antagonistic world created by the "Western Male" world view.[289] In any society based on principles of compassion and empathy, these "rights," as shields against the overreaching of our fellow humans, would be unnecessary.[290] This feminist perspective provides a different approach for analyzing the morality of the human/animal relationship, and tells us that we should act in ways consistent with our feelings of compassion and empathy, and that our actions should always be guided by these feelings. This theory, like that of Regan, leads to a world in which animals would not be used in agriculture, experimentation and entertainment, but it arrives at this different world via a wholly distinct universe of ideas.

VI. CONCLUSIONS

Traditionally, the human/animal relationship has been viewed within the realm of moral philosophy as one of hierarchy. One or another characteristic is always said to distinguish humans from other animals, and this distinction, whether it be it the

285. David Hume, A Treatise of Human Nature 455–76 (Oxford 1978).
286. *Id.* On the issue of the relationship of morality and emotion generally, *see* Thomas G. Kelch, *The Role of the Rational and the Emotive in a Theory of Animal Rights*, 27 B.C. Envtl. Aff. L. Rev. 1, 25–34 (1999).
287. *See id.*at 28–29; *see also* Marcia Lind, *Hume and Moral Emotions, in* Identity, Character and Morality 133, 142–43 (Owen Flanagan & Amelie Oskenberg Rorty eds., 1990).
288. Josephine Donovan, *Animal Rights and Feminist Theory, in* The Feminist Care Tradition in Animal Ethics 58, 58–86 (Josephine Donovan & Carol J. Adams eds. 2007).
289. Marti Kheel, *Nature and Feminist Sensitivity, in* Tom Regan, Animal Rights and Human Obligations 261 (1989).
290. See the general discussion of the need for "rights" in the animal rights debate in Ted Benton, *Animal Rights: An Eco-Socialist View, in* Animal Rights 19, 19–41 (Robert Garner ed., 1996).

existence of a soul, or rationality, or language, enables humans to feel morally safe in their often horrifying treatment of animals. But the comfortable safety of this human position has come under spirited attack from both novel moral theories and the empirical facts. The three moral theories of utilitarianism, Rights Theory and feminism have each challenged the traditional notion that humans can morally view themselves as superior to animals and correspondingly treat animals however they please.

But perhaps even more important than these steps in the formulation of moral theories that challenge the traditional view are the facts—which are why I focus on important recent scientific discoveries relating to the cognitive and other capacities of animals. From the science of evolution we learn that the capacities of animals closely related to us are likely very similar to ours, and from the scientific data now being collected, these predictions of the science of evolution are being confirmed. Animals of many kinds, from insects to apes, are now found to have cognitive and other abilities far beyond what was previously thought possible, and which approach and, in some cases, surpass our own abilities. We find rationality in bees, language in birds and highly developed emotions in elephants, and all of these discoveries have been made in the infancy of true scientific study of the cognitive abilities of animals. And these scientific advances are even being introduced into the popular media, witness articles on the cognitive abilities of animals in the American magazine *Time*.[291] So the long-held view that humans have characteristics that morally distinguish them from animals is being challenged, not only conceptually and abstractly in the philosophical universe, but also factually and powerfully in the scientific one.

291. *See* Kluger, *supra* note 78.

Chapter 3

Animals in Agriculture

I. PIPPI LONGSTOCKING, A HORSE ON THE PORCH WITH RED RIBBONS, TORTURE AND ASTRID LINDGREN

Pippi Longstocking, the children's book character created by Swedish writer Astrid Lindgren, was remarkable in a number of ways. She lived alone in her home, named Ville Villekulla, and had been left a great deal of gold by her sailor father.[1] She was extraordinarily strong; indeed, she was stronger than any police officer.[2] She was so strong, it turns out, that she could lift a horse.[3] And lift a horse she did. With some of her gold she bought a horse that lived on her porch.[4] Whenever she wanted to have tea on the porch, she simply lifted the horse down off of the porch.[5] She braided her horse's tail into pigtails tied with red ribbons and on special occasions he might be fed cakes and sugar.[6] Not only did Pippi's horse get special treatment, but Pippi also protected other animals from abuse.[7]

Unfortunately, animals used in agriculture do not have the same kind of life as Pippi's horse. Although Pippi's horse was property; she did buy him with gold after all; he was not treated as merely an economic asset by Pippi. Rather, he was her pet and companion. Animals used in agriculture are considered property and are, indeed, treated as such, generating much gold for their often large corporate owners. In modern agricultural practices, laying hens, as

1. Astrid Lindgren, The Adventures of Pippi Longstocking 4–5 (Viking 1997).
2. *See id.* at 4.
3. *Id.*
4. *Id.*
5. *Id.* at 4–5.
6. *Id.* at 55, 93.
7. *Id.* at 133–35.

exemplified by Sandra in Chapter 1, are kept in cages where there is not even enough room for the seven or eight or more chickens in the battery cage to stand up. They live on top of each other, with nothing on the floor of their cage but wire mesh. They typically never see the light of day and live their short depressing lives entirely in these miserable conditions, producing eggs for humans. Knowing what we already know about the cognitive, linguistic and emotive characteristics of birds, one can only imagine the suffering caused to the many millions of chickens treated this way.

Similar suffering marks the loud, dirty and frightening end of life for livestock animals. Let me describe this process for a steer I will call Speckles. Prior to slaughter, Speckles embarks on a one-way trip. The first stop of the trip is the cattle feedlot, a filthy, crowded and smelly place. Assuming that Speckles gets to the feedlot without being injured in the truck ride, he is delivered into a kind of hell with as many as 100,000 animals jammed into a few hundred acres. Here he is fed food to fatten him up and in the process is exposed to the excrement that covers the ground and eventually him:

> When it [a cow or bull] gets to the feedlot, its life changes in a substantial way. It will never see any grass ever again … A feedlot is a city of cows … It's cattle pens, black earth, as far as you can see. Of course it's not really earth, you learn as you get a little closer; its manure, reaching to the horizon.
>
> [There are] 35,000, 50,000, 100,000 animals in the space of a couple of hundred acres ….
>
> ….
>
> I haven't even mentioned the smell. I mean, it is overwhelming, the smell of these places … And it's not the smell of a cow on a farm. This is the smell of the bus station men's room. It's fierce ….
>
> ….
>
> … The cows I saw on the feedlot looked sullen. I'm very concerned not to anthropomorphize them, but that was how they appeared to me. They're standing around in their manure all day long. Animals have evolved basically to avoid their feces. Natural selection discourages this, because there are parasite[s] [and] diseases. So in general, animals will stay away from that.
>
> They're forced to exist with their feces all the time. When they go to sleep, that's what they lie down in. The beds in these feedlots, you look and you say, "Oh, there's dirt. They're in dirt." And of course no grass could grow there. But you look a little closer and it is manure, as far as you can see ….[8]

After his sojourn at the feedlot, Speckles has the last trip on his transportation ticket punched and he proceeds to the slaughterhouse in a cramped truck with

8. PBS Frontline, *Interview with Michael Pollan,* http://www.pbs.org/wgbh/pages/frontline/shows/meat/interviews/pollan.html (last visted May 8, 2010).

colleagues from the feedlot. It is here that he is led, with the sound of the stun gun banging and the smell of manure and death swirling about, single file behind the other cattle, to meet the man with the stun gun. The man will approach from the front, lay the gun against his skull and fire; if Speckles is lucky it will work, and he will be unconscious. If it does not work, he will remain conscious while he is hoisted by a hind leg into the air to have his throat cut. One journalist has described the process as follows:

> One night I visit a slaughterhouse somewhere in the high plains. The slaughterhouse is one of the nation's largest. About 5,000 head of cattle enter it every day, single file, and leave in a different form ....
>
> ....
>
> For eight and a half hours, a worker called a sticker does nothing but stand in a river of blood, being drenched in blood, slitting the neck of a steer every ten seconds or so, severing its carotid artery. He uses a long knife and must hit exactly the right spot to kill the animal humanely. He hits that spot again and again. We walk up a slippery metal stairway and reach a small platform, where the production line begins. A man turns and smiles at me. He wears safety goggles and a hard hat. His face is splattered with gray matter and blood. He is the knocker, the man who welcomes cattle to the building. Cattle walk down a narrow chute and pause in front of him, blocked by a gate, and then he shoots them in the head with a captive bolt stunner—a gun attached to the ceiling by a long hose—which fires a column of compressed air that knocks the cattle unconscious. The animals keep strolling up, oblivious to what comes next, and he stands over them and shoots. For eight and a half hours, he just shoots. As I stand there, he misses a few times and shoots the same animal twice. As soon as the steer falls, a worker grabs one of its hind legs and shackles it to a chain, and the chain lifts the huge animal into the air.
>
> I watch the knocker knock cattle for a couple of minutes. The animals are powerful and strong one moment and then gone in an instant, suspended from a rail, ready to have their necks slit. A steer slips from its chain, falls to the ground, and gets its head caught in a conveyor belt. The line stops as workers struggle to free the steer, stunned but alive, from the machinery. I've seen enough.[9]

So this is how and where Speckles life ends.

Sandra and Speckles do not paint the picture that most people have of how agricultural animals are raised. Most people have a view of "Old MacDonald's farm" with smiling animals freely roaming about. That this view is wildly mistaken is made obvious in this description of the modern world of factory farming

9. Eric Schlosser, *Fast Food Nation: Meat and Potatoes,* ROLLING STONE MAGAZINE, Sept. 3, 1998, *available at* http://www.ericsecho.org/investigation2.htm.

by David Kirby in his book *Animal Factory*, which reveals what modern animal agriculture is really about—economic efficiency and profit:

> Government and industry call these massive compounds "confined [or concentrated] animal feeding operations," or CAFOs ... Chances are you have seen them from up above, while flying in an airplane: long white buildings lined up in tightly packed rows of three, four, or many more.
>
> CAFOS are where most of our animal protein—our milk, cheese, butter, yogurt, eggs, chicken, turkey, bacon, sausage, cold cuts, ribs, pork chops, and, increasingly, beef and fish—comes from these days. Old McDonald's farm—with his big red barn and clucking chicks in the yard—is quickly fading away into a romanticized past. Today MacDonald would most likely be working as a contract grower for some conglomerate, raising tens of thousands of animals inside giant enclosures according to strict instructions dictated by the company, which typically owns the livestock but is not responsible for the thousands of tons of waste left behind before the survivors are trucked off to slaughter.
>
> Large companies with kitchen-table names like Perdue, Tyson, Smithfield, Cargill, ADM, and Land O'Lakes now control much of the poultry and livestock production in the United States. They own the animals, they control the all-important processing and packing plants, they often operate their own distribution networks, and they sell an array of brands to consumers in the supermarket.[10]

So today the picture of agricultural animals raised in a pastoral setting, perhaps wandering along a clear stream surrounded by green vegetation and tended by a kindly farmer in overalls, is a myth. The truth is not pleasant; it is horrifying. In the end, Sandra, Speckles and the billions of animals like them are actually just pawns in a giant global economic juggernaut controlled by a few multinational corporations.

The author of the Pippi Longstocking books, Astrid Lindgren, worked to change the way farm animals like Sandra and Speckles were treated in her native Sweden. While she was not a vegetarian, she was appalled by the way animals were treated in agriculture and focused on trying to change the treatment of agricultural animals. Her campaign against factory farming that started in 1983 led to the "Lex Lindgren" animal welfare law, also referred to as the *Swedish Animal Protection Ordinance*.[11] Lindgren's efforts began a debate on the treatment of animals in agriculture that is ongoing in Europe.[12] Her writings, published in the Swedish newspaper *Expressen,* brought the abysmal reality of factory farmed

10. David Kirby, Animal Factory xiv (St. Martin's Press 2010).
11. Birgitta Steene, *Astrid Lindgren's Legacy*, openDemocracy, Nov. 14, 2007, http://www.opendemocracy.net/article/arts_culture/astrid_lindgren_legacy.
12. *Id.*

animals to the consciousness of the Swedish people and continued upward of three years.[13]

The Albert Schweitzer Award of the Animal Welfare Fund was given to Astrid Lindgren for her work in obtaining enactment of the *Swedish Animal Protection Ordinance*.[14] Through her efforts, the opinions of the Swedish people changed; those in agriculture began to consider ethics and consumers started demanding products be produced in humane ways.[15] Use of animals in agriculture was no longer merely a question of economics; now ethics were involved.[16] Ingvar Carlsson, Sweden's then prime minister, visited Astrid and told her that her published letters stating that, "Every pig is entitled to a happy pig life," convinced him of the correctness of her position.[17]

As we will see in this chapter, as a result of the efforts of Astrid Lindgren and others, Sweden now has a comprehensive law on factory farming practices that, among other things, prohibits the sub-therapeutic use of antibiotics, cramped housing conditions, electrical prods,[18] and unenriched battery cages.[19] The animal welfare campaign in Sweden leading to the *Swedish Animal Protection Ordinance* is described in *My Cow Wants to Have Fun* by Astrid Lindgren and Kristina Forslund.[20] Astrid "never assumed that she spoke for others, except those without a voice of their own: children and animals."[21]

II. SOURCES OF EUROPEAN LAW

The laws focused on in this section are European laws. Indeed, many recent laws and regulations focusing on the welfare of agricultural animals are European and it can effectively be argued that European countries are taking the lead on many animal welfare issues. Some European laws analyzed here and in other chapters are the laws of individual countries; others are conventions and rules created by entities like the Council of Europe or the European Union. It is necessary, then, to understand something about these European institutions.

---

13. Animal Welfare Institute, *Astrid Lindgren Establishes Foundation for Farm Animals,* 48 AWI QUARTERLY NO. 2, 7 (1999), http://www.awionline.org/ht/d/ContentDetails/i/1515 [hereinafter *AWI*].
14. *Id.*
15. *See* Michelle Jendral et al., *Alternatve Layer Hen Housing Systems in Europe* (2005), http://www.afac.ab.ca/reports/reporthenhousing.pdf.
16. *See id.* at 94–95; *see* DAVID J. MELLOR ET AL., THE SCIENCES OF ANIMAL WELFARE (4th ed. Wiley-Blackwell 2008); Gunnela Stahle, *Swedes Do it Better,* OPENDEMOCRACY, June 6, 2007, http://www.opendemocracy.net/ecology-foodwithoutfrontiers/article_428.jsp.
17. Myrna Oliver, *Astrid Lindgren, 94; Creator of Pippi Longstocking Adventures,* L.A. TIMES, Jan. 29, 2009, at B10.
18. *AWI*, *supra* note 13.
19. Stahle, *supra* note 16.
20. astridlindgren.se, *FAQ—Frequently Asked Questions,* http://www.astridlindgren.com/en/faq (last visited May 9, 2010).
21. Steene, *supra* note 11.

The Council of Europe (CE), based in Strasbourg, France, was created in 1949 to protect democracy, the rule of law and human rights.[22] It is comprised of 47 member countries and is perhaps most well known for maintaining the European Court of Human Rights, which enforces the European Convention on Human Rights that was created by the CE.[23] Our concern, however, is with several conventions that have been created by the CE and that have been very influential in European law relating to animals used in agriculture.[24]

The European Union (EU) has also created a number of directives and regulations that will be analyzed here. Since EU promulgations will be a significant focus in this chapter (and this book), it is useful to understand the structure and functioning of the EU.[25] The European Council, which is composed of the heads of state of EU member countries, sets the general policies and priorities of the EU and it just became an official EU institution under the Treaty of Lisbon in 2009.[26] The main decision-making body of the EU is the Council of the European Union (hereinafter "Council"), which is composed of representatives of the Member States of the EU.[27] The functions of the Council include passing laws, coordinating economic and other policies and priorities of the EU, and other duties specified in the treaties creating the EU, including, under the Treaty of Lisbon, a commitment to animal welfare.[28] It is important to understand that the EU was originally the European Economic Community, which focused on the economic integration of European countries under the Treaty of Rome.[29] Given this fact, it is not

22. Information relating to the history, purposes and accomplishments of the Council of Europe are set forth on their website: Council of Europe, *Council of Europe in Brief,* http://www.coe.int/aboutCoe/default.asp (last visited May 9, 2010).
23. See the following for information on the European Court of Human Rights and the European Convention on Human Rights: http://www.echr.coe.int/ECHR/EN/Header/Basic+Texts/The+Convention+and+additional+protocols/The+European+Convention+on+Human+Rights/ (last visited May 9, 2010).
24. A "convention" is, like a treaty, an agreement among states. Often conventions are created in the context of large international meetings relating to specific subjects, like global warming or animal welfare. *See* US Fish & Wildlife Service, *International Protocols, Treaties and Conventions*, 530 FW 2 (2009), *available at* http://www.fws.gov/policy/530fw2.pdf. The terms "treaty" and "convention" are often used interchangeably and the distinction between the two is not always clear, particularly in Europe. *See* US Foreign Policy Encyclopedia, *Treaties*, http://www.answers.com/topic/treaty (last visited May 9, 2010).
25. The EU website contains descriptions of how the EU works and contains documents, including directives and regulations promulgated by the EU. *See* Europa, http://europa.eu/index_en.htm (last visited May 9, 2010).
26. Europa, *The European Council—An Official Institution of the EU*, http://www.european-council.europa.eu/the-institution.aspx (last visited Jan. 30, 2011).
27. Europa, *The Council of the European Union*, http://europa.eu/institutions/inst/council/index_en.htm (last visited June 6, 2010).
28. *Id.*; *see also* Treaty of Lisbon Amending the Treaty on European Union, the Treaties Establishing the European Communities, art. 2(21), Dec. 13, 2007, 2007 O.J. (C 306) 49 [hereinafter *Treaty of Lisbon*].
29. *See generally* Europa, *Treaties and Law*, http://europa.eu/abc/treaties/index_en.htm (last visited May 9, 2010).

surprising that while the EU has now gone far beyond simply integrating and regulating economic activity, the economic role of the EU is extremely important.

Directly under the Council is the subordinate Permanent Representatives Committee (PRC), which is a group of ambassadors from each member country that prepares work for the Council, and works with the EU Commission and the civil service of the individual member countries on EU matters.[30] While the PRC has no substantive decision-making power, they can make some procedural decisions under the Council Rules of Procedure.[31]

Another important body in the EU is the EU Commission. The members of the Commission are, by agreement of the EU members, appointed for five-year terms, subject to European Parliament approval.[32] Since 2004, there has been one commissioner for each Member State. Perhaps the most important role of the Commission is the ability to propose legislation, for it is the Commission that has the sole authority to propose legislation in the EU.[33] Any such legislation is presented by the Commission to the Parliament and the Council for adoption.[34] Some of the Commission's other duties are described as follows:

> The Commission enjoys a substantial degree of independence in exercising its powers. Its job is to uphold the common interest, which means that it must not take instructions from any national EU government. As "Guardian of the Treaties," it has to ensure that the regulations and directives adopted by the Council and Parliament are being implemented in the [M]ember [S]tates. If they are not, the Commission can take the offending party to the Court of Justice to oblige it to comply with EU law.
>
> As the EU's executive arm, the Commission implements the decisions taken by the Council in areas such as the common agricultural policy. It has wide powers to manage the EU's common policies, such as research and technology, overseas aid, regional development, etc. It also manages the budget for these policies.[35]

The Commission is the executive enforcement mechanism for the treaties and laws created by the EU. The Commission also has the important role of maintaining relations with international organizations, including the WTO,[36] which we will see is extraordinarily important in international trade relations. In these trade relations,

30. P.S.R.F. Mathijsen, A Guide to European Union Law 83 (9th ed. 2007) [hereinafter Guide].
31. *Id.*
32. Europa, *How Does the EU Work?*, http://europa.eu/abc/12lessons/lesson_4/index_en.htm (last visited June 6, 2010).
33. Europa, *The European Commission,* http://europa.eu/institutions/inst/comm/index_en.htm (last visited June 6, 2010) [hereinafter *Commission*].
34. *Id.*
35. Europa, *Europe in 12 Lessons,* http://europa.eu/abc/12lessons/lesson_4/index_en.htm (last visited Aug. 26, 2010).
36. *Commission*, *supra* note 33.

the EU negotiates as a block.[37] Note that members of the Commission, unlike the Council and representatives elected to the European Parliament, do not represent the interests of their individual countries. Instead, the members of the Commission are to represent the interests of the entire EU region.[38]

Another arm of the EU is the European Parliament (hereinafter "Parliament"). Representatives to Parliament are popularly elected by the people of EU countries, and have a duty to represent the interests of their constituents.[39] The powers of the Parliament include the crucial power of being able to censure and remove the Commission; in other words, the Parliament has ultimate control over the Commission.[40] The Parliament also has the ability to put questions to the Council or the Commission, and to be consulted on and give its opinion on legislation.[41]

Probably the most important decision-making procedure involving the Parliament is what is called "co-decision." This procedure is used for most EU law-making and puts the Parliament on a level playing field with the Council in passing laws.[42] Ultimately, then, most EU legislation requires approval of the Parliament and the Council. In fact, the co-decision procedure has been expanded under the recent Treaty of Lisbon, thus increasing the role of the Parliament in the EU.[43]

Not surprisingly, there is a judicial arm of the EU which is composed of two courts. The first is the European Court of Justice (ECJ), which serves the judicial role of interpreting EU law.[44] In this role, the ECJ has actually created law relating to fundamental human rights.[45] This court is independent of the Member States and other European institutions. Procedurally, the ECJ behaves in some ways similar to European courts and in others like courts in the United States. In court proceedings in the ECJ, the Court may call witnesses, appoint experts and order document production.[46] The ECJ also has the help of "Advocates General" who are lawyers that provide analysis and advice to the members of the Court on cases pending before the body.[47] The ECJ has the power, similar to that of courts in the United States, to overrule its own earlier decisions although this rarely occurs.[48]

---

37. *Id.*
38. *Id.*
39. Europa, *The European Parliament*, http://europa.eu/institutions/inst/parliament/index_en.htm (last visited June 6, 2010).
40. *Id.*
41. *Id.*
42. *Id.*; Europa, *Decision-Making in the European Union*, http://europa.eu/institutions/decision-making/index_en.htm (last visited June 6, 2010) [hereinafter *Decision-Making*].
43. Europa, *Treaty of Lisbon—The Treaty at a Glance*, http://europa.eu/lisbon_treaty/glance/index_en.htm (last visited June 6, 2010).
44. Europa, *The Court of Justice*, http://europa.eu/institutions/inst/justice/index_en.htm (last visited June 6, 2010) [hereinafter *Court of Justice*].
45. RHONA K.M. SMITH, INTERNATIONAL HUMAN RIGHTS 103 (Oxford U. Press 3d. ed. 2007).
46. Guide, *supra* note 30, at 143–44.
47. *Court of Justice, supra* note 44.
48. Stefan Schmitz, *How Dare They? European Merger Control and the European Commission's Blocking of the Electric/Honeywell Merger*, 23 U. PA. J. INT'L ECON. L. 325, 353 n. 145 (2002).

Note that the ECJ has determined that EU law controls over the national laws of individual countries, something like the relationship between federal and state law in the United States[49] The decisions of the ECJ must ultimately be enforced, however, by the courts and other institutions of the individual Member States.[50]

The ECJ also acts as the appellate body for the General Court (GC), previously known as the European Court of First Instance.[51] The GC was formerly a court attached to the ECJ, but is now "an independent part of the Community Judicature."[52] Jurisdiction over EU matters is divided between the ECJ and GC.

What the countries of the EU have done is cede some of their sovereign power to EU institutions on economic and other issues.[53] This cession of power has resulted in a great deal of EU legislation applicable to the individual Member States. The legislation of the EU comes in two forms: "directives" and "regulations."[54] Directives are legislation of the EU that "direct" individual EU Member States to create laws consistent with the provisions of the directive.[55] This requires that each country change its law to be consistent with the directive, but each country has flexibility in the way that it complies with the directive. Each country's law may differ from other countries' laws so long as they meet the requirements of the directive. Regulations, on the other hand, are positive laws of the EU that are applicable to all Member States and must be directly followed by the states.[56] Here there is no flexibility given to the individual states. A regulation is directly enforced against all persons and states within the EU.

With these European institutions in mind, let us review some European laws relating to the use of animals in agriculture.

III. EUROPEAN LAW

Given the issues that exist relating to the use of animals in agriculture, there are at least three sorts of regulatory responses that a country might adopt. First, it could do nothing and claim that there is no need to legislate on animal issues, since their interests are already adequately provided for. Second, it could take a "rights" view

---

49. Yvonne N. Gierczyk, *The Evolution of the European Legal System: The European Court of Justice's Role in the Harmonization of Laws*, 12 ISLA J. INT'L & COMP. L. 153, 167–68 (2005).
50. *Court of Justice, supra* note 44.
51. Court of Justice for the European Union, *General Court,* http://curia.europa.eu/jcms/jcms/Jo2_7033/presentation (last visited June 8, 2010).
52. Guide, *supra* note 30, at 150.
53. Europa, *EU Institutions and Other Bodies,* http://europa.eu/institutions/index_en.htm (last visited June 6, 2010).
54. *Decision-Making, supra* note 42.
55. European Commission, *What are EU Directives?,* http://ec.europa.eu/community_law/introduction/what_directive_en.htm (last visited June 8, 2010).
56. European Commission, *What are EU Regulations?,* http://ec.europa.eu/community_law/introduction/what_regulation_en.htm (last visited June 8, 2010).

of the relationship between animals and humans, and say that humans do not have the right to injure, torture, and kill animals for use in agriculture, and that such use violates the rights of animals. Third, it could take an intermediate position and say that it is morally, economically and culturally appropriate to use animals in agriculture, but this use must be in accord with "humane" practices. This presumably means that we can still use hens to create eggs for human consumption; we can still use cattle and pigs for their flesh, and so on. We just have to do these things in a way that is consistent with rules that theoretically take the interests of the animals into consideration and avoid suffering whenever possible.

It is from this sort of intermediate vantage point that European and other countries that regulate animal welfare issues have approached the use of animals in agriculture and, for that matter, the use of animals in most all contexts. Other non-European countries, to one extent or another, often follow the first regulatory response, which is to do nothing. And there is little, if anything, that one could point to anywhere that creates a rights position on the use of agricultural animals, although we will later discuss certain bans on the uses of animals in experimentation and entertainment, as well as certain constitutional provisions passed by a few countries, which may be considered a step in this direction. Let us begin our analysis of some European laws with a document created more than 30 years ago by the CE.

A. European Convention for the Protection of Animals Kept for Farming Purposes

The European Convention for the Protection of Animals Kept for Farming Purposes (hereinafter "CE Farming Convention") was opened for signature in 1976 and was aimed at practices of "industrial stock breeding."[57] Conventions created by the CE were the first international documents setting forth ethical principles for the use of animals in agriculture, in experiments, and as pets.[58] A Standing Committee with representatives from each signatory country was created by the CE Farming Convention for the purpose of "elaboration and adoption of recommendations to the Contracting Parties containing detailed provisions for the implementation of the principles set out" in the Convention.[59] One of the 34 entities that have signed and ratified the CE Farming Convention is the European Union.[60] The CE Farming Convention, though relatively old, has been a foundation for EU

57. Council of Europe, *European Convention on the Protection of Animals Kept for Farming Purposes,* "Explanatory Report", http://conventions.coe.int/Treaty/EN/Reports/Html/087.htm. (last visited May 10, 2010) [hereinafter *CE Farming Convention Explanatory Report*].
58. Council of Europe, *Biological Safety—Use of Animals By Humans,* http://www.coe. int/t/e/legal_ affairs/legal_ co-operation/biological_safety,_use_of_animals/ (last visited May 10, 2010).
59. European Convention for the Protection of Animals kept for Farming Purposes, Arts. 8–9, Mar. 10, 1976, Europ. T.S. 087 [hereinafter *CE Farming Convention*].
60. *See* Council Decision 78/923, 1978 O.J. (L 323) 12, 12–13.

legislation and plays an important historical role in the development of European law on the use of animals in agriculture.

The CE Farming Convention, which was purportedly drafted based on ethical principles, applies to "the keeping, care and housing of animals, and in particular to animals in modern intensive stock-farming systems."[61] "Animals" are defined as "animals bred or kept for the production of food, wool, skin or fur or for other farming purposes, and modern intensive stock-farming systems shall mean systems which predominantly employ technical installations operated principally by means of automatic processes."[62] The focus of the Convention then is the use of animals in modern factory farming.

The general standard for treatment of animals under the CE Farming Convention requires that: "[a]nimals shall be housed and provided with food, water and care in a manner which—having regard to their species and to their degree of development, adaptation and domestication—is appropriate to their physiological and ethological needs in accordance with established experience and scientific knowledge."[63] It is not difficult to understand the concept of physiological needs, *i.e.*, the needs necessary for physical survival like breathing, eating, etc., but what is meant by "ethological needs"? "Ethology" is a relatively new science devoted to the study of animal behavior, usually in a natural setting, rather than the laboratory.[64] To meet ethological needs it is necessary that an animal be able to behave in a way consistent with its normal behavior in a natural setting. So to meet physiological and ethological needs, it is not only necessary to satisfy physical needs for survival, but also to meet behavioral and psychological parameters, so that an animal can live in a way consistent with its nature or telos.

Other requirements of the CE Farming Convention include rather fuzzy standards relating to freedom of movement, feeding of animals, lighting, temperature and ventilation conditions where animals are confined, and inspection requirements. These requirements can presumably be met by any number of types of regulations and the Convention does not attempt to define precisely how the standards are to be met:

> These articles set out principles relating to particularly important aspects of animal welfare. The committee endeavoured to elaborate principles which are precise enough to prevent a completely free interpretation, but wide enough to allow for different needs. The underlying idea is to avoid any unnecessary suffering or injury and to secure conditions that shall be in conformity with physiological and ethological needs of the individual animals. These provisions were conceived as guiding principles for the subsequent elaboration of

61. *CE Farming Convention, supra* note 59, at art. 1.
62. *Id.*
63. *Id.* at art. 3.
64. Consider the definitions and descriptions at: Dictionary.com, "Ethology," http://dictionary.reference.com/browse/ethology (last visited May 10, 2010); Merriam-Webster's Online Dictionary, "Ethology," http://www.merriam-webster.com/dictionary/ethology (last visited May 10, 2010).

> detailed measures in the form of recommendations of the Standing Committee provided for in Chapter II of the Convention.[65]

Although there is much vague language in the stated requirements of the Convention, apparently for purposes of flexibility, some of this language may have enormous implications for the effectiveness and interpretation of the EC Farming Convention and laws patterned after it.

The first phrase that we need to analyze in this regard is "in accordance with established experience and scientific knowledge," which is used in the general standard set forth above and in more specific standards relating to confinement of animals and lighting, ventilation and related requirements.[66] The Explanatory Notes to the Convention do not address the meaning of this phrase, but it is one that may be laden with coded meaning. Note that it indicates that standards should be consistent with "established experience." What exactly is this "established experience"? It would by default appear to be the way that we both presently and in the past have handled and cared for agricultural animals. As a result, this language could be used to argue that present uses and abuses of animals are prima facie appropriate, since they are consistent with "established experience." The same sort of argument can be used with respect to the language "established … scientific knowledge" since such established scientific knowledge has not in the past been typically cited as a reason for improving the treatment of agricultural animals (although as we have seen in the study of ethology and cognitive ethology, this may be changing and we will see that the EU is, in fact, now using modern scientific discoveries to justify new animal welfare rules). As a result, this language may potentially be used to support the status quo with respect to the treatment of agricultural animals.

Perhaps the most often used type of phrase in legislation relating to the treatment of animals is one found in several places in the Convention, exemplified by Article 6, which provides that, "[n]o animal shall be provided with food or liquid in a manner, nor shall such food or liquid contain any substance, which may cause *unnecessary suffering or injury* (emphasis added)."[67] We will see this kind of language repeatedly in laws relating to all aspects of the treatment of animals, including many EU laws in subsequent sections of this chapter, and, in fact, in virtually every piece of legislation relating to animal welfare. The phrase "unnecessary suffering or injury" or "unnecessary pain and suffering," or the like is therefore ubiquitous in legislation relating to animal treatment. What precisely does this phrase mean?

If we analyze the "unnecessary" language under its ordinary meaning, we might believe that this language really has power; any use of animals that results in injury or suffering that could in any way be avoided is prohibited. A dictionary

65. *CE Farming Convention Explanatory Report, supra* note 57, at Arts. 3–6.
66. *CE Farming Convention, supra* note 59, at Arts. 3–6.
67. *Id.* at art. 6 (emphasis added).

definition of "unnecessary" is "not essential, needed, or required."[68] Utilizing this definition, the use of animals in agriculture is itself "unnecessary," since there is no reason that we "need" to eat animals or employ products made from animals. Indeed, we could all be vegan and from a health perspective, as well as ethical and environmental ones, we would all be better off. Thus, one might think, under ordinary use of language, this phrase would end the use of animals in agriculture.

This is, of course, not the way this language has been interpreted. Instead, there is a long history of this sort of language being interpreted to effectively mean "unnecessary to accomplish any economic, cultural or other socially accepted purpose."[69] For instance, the suffering involved in the raising and keeping of hens for eggs can be justified by economic interests: the needs of the many producers, distributors, retailers and their employees involved in creating and selling eggs. Likewise, the eating of eggs is familiar, accepted, and enjoyed in most cultures and is also therefore socially acceptable. Other practices such as rodeos that cause substantial suffering to animals can also be justified under this standard, since rodeos are, for example, an integral part of the culture of the Western United States. Thus, a practice causes "unnecessary suffering" only when there is no arguable human economic, cultural, or social interest advanced by the suffering involved. The suffering must therefore be wholly gratuitous and have absolutely no redeeming economic, cultural, or social value to violate these "unnecessary" suffering standards.

The detail of the strictures of the CE Farming Convention focuses on providing general rules on the feeding, housing and other physical conditions of animals kept for farming purposes. For instance, it does not prohibit the cruel practice of keeping veal calves in continuous confinement. Rather, it states that if "an animal is continuously or regularly tethered or confined, it shall be given the space appropriate for its physiological and ethological needs ...."[70] But there is something odd about this; how is it even conceivable that the ethological needs, the natural behavior of an animal, could be met while the animal is continuously tethered or confined? What animal has such a condition as its natural situation?

Thus, the CE Farming Convention is an animal welfare convention that requires signatory countries to comply with a number of fairly vague and, one could cogently argue, lax standards in their regulation of factory farming. These standards relate to the way that animals are housed and cared for in factory farming, but do not prohibit typically accepted types of factory farming practices.

68. Encarta World English Dictionary, "Unnecessary," http://encarta.msn.com/encnet/features/dictionary/DictionaryResults.aspx?refid=1861708239 (last visited May 10, 2010).
69. *See e.g.*, Gary L. Francione, Animals, Property, and the Law 17–23 (1995); Thomas G. Kelch, *Toward a Non-Property Status for Animals,* 6 N.Y.U. Envtl. L.J. 531, 541 (1998).
70. *CE Farming Convention, supra* note 59, at art. 4.

B. European Union Directives and Regulations

Only in the last 40 to 50 years, have there been serious efforts to regulate the treatment of animals in agriculture, experimentation and entertainment. It is primarily only in the last 30 years that the EU has addressed these issues, and it has done so in a fairly comprehensive way, since there are laws relating to the treatment of animals in all three of these areas. However, even in this relatively short period of time, there have been some significant revisions of EU laws relating to the treatment of animals.

Just recently, for example, the EU ratified the Treaty of Lisbon, which went into effect on December 1, 2009. This treaty amends the Treaty on European Union and the Treaty Establishing the European Community (TEC). The TEC has now been renamed the Treaty on the Functioning of the European Union (TFEU). The important aspect of the Treaty of Lisbon for present purposes is that it recognizes animals as "sentient beings," and requires that the EU consider animal welfare in policy-making decisions in Article 6b of the TFEU which states:

> In formulating and implementing the Union's agriculture, fisheries, transport, internal market, research and technological development and space policies, the Union and the Member States shall, since animals are sentient beings, pay full regard to the requirements of animal welfare, while respecting the legislative or administrative provisions and customs of Member States relating in particular to religious rites, cultural traditions and regional heritage.[71]

Included within the term "sentient beings" are all vertebrates, as well as some invertebrates such as shellfish used in fisheries and vertebrate fish caught by fisheries.[72] Sentience here is apparently equated with the capacity for feeling pain.[73]

What this means is that the EU, in its foundational treaty, recognizes the sentience of animals, and, in making policy decisions in agriculture, fisheries, transport, internal market, research and technical development and space policies, is to "pay full regard" to animal welfare. One may well question, however, why animal concerns are only worthy of consideration in direct connection with these particular policies, or better yet, why animal welfare concerns are apparently not considered worthy of consideration outside of these policy areas. One also must wonder what may eventually befall this language when it is confronted by alternative ideals that demand respect for diverse religious, cultural and regional traditions. One can then anticipate the type of balancing of human versus animal interests that is ubiquitous in animal welfare laws, and in which the interests of humans seem inevitably to trump those of animals. Nonetheless, since the Treaty of Lisbon has only recently come into effect, we can only speculate on how it will in the end be

71. *Treaty of Lisbon, supra* note 28, at art. 2(21).
72. United Kingdom Parliament, Select Committee on the European Union, *10th Report of Session 2007–08: The Treaty of Lisbon: An Impact Assessment Vol II: Evidence*, D2 (2008), *available at* http://www.publications.parliament.uk/pa/ld200708/ldselect/ldeucom/62/62ii.pdf.
73. *Id.* at D10.

interpreted; however, the general tone of the language suggests that this treaty may ultimately be more symbolic than effective for animals' interests.

In any event, with all the recent EU legislative activity, the EU presents a unique laboratory for studying the evolution of laws relating to animal welfare. Within this laboratory we can observe the social, political and economic forces and ideas that contribute to and shape this new regulatory scheme. For this reason, as I present the chosen examples of EU legislation, I will from time to time digress and discuss the antecedents of present law and trace the path of these antecedents to the present. I will begin with an EU Council Directive concerning the treatment of animals in agriculture generally.

1. Council Directive 98/58/EC Concerning Protection of Animals Kept for Farming Purposes

The Council of the EU has created a number of directives relating to the use of animals in agriculture. The broadest of these is a directive that relates generally to protecting animals used in agriculture. The organization of this directive, Council Directive 98/58/EC Concerning the Protection of Animals Kept for Farming Purposes, reveals the structure that these directives typically take. The Directive contains the substantive standards of the law and appended to the Directive is an Annex that contains more detailed provisions that carry out the policies of the Directive. As a directive, it provides guidelines that must be followed in the laws of member countries in the treatment of animals in agriculture.

What are the purposes of this Directive? Note that EU directives and regulations typically have recital sections that describe the purposes of the legislation. In the case of Council Directive 98/58/EC (Appendix I) we see two separate strands of purpose. First, there is the purpose relating to the protection of animals that can be seen in the following language in the introduction to the directive:

> Whereas all Member States have ratified the European Convention for the Protection of Animals Kept for Farming Purposes ....
>
> Whereas the Community, as a contracting party, must give effect to the principles laid down in the Convention;
>
> Whereas those principles include the provision of housing, food, water and care appropriate to the physiological and ethological needs of the animals, in accordance with established experience and scientific knowledge;
>
> ....
>
> Whereas Declaration No 24 annexed to the Final Act of the Treaty on European Union calls on the European institutions and the Member States, when drafting and implementing Community legislation, in particular on the common agricultural policy, to pay full regard to the welfare requirements of animals ....[74]

74. Council Directive 98/58, 1998 O.J. (L 221) 23, 23.

This language shows that the Directive is aimed at meeting the requirements of the CE Farming Convention and contains language lifted directly from that convention. For example, the Directive states that meeting the "physiological and ethological" needs of animals is a fundamental principle, but also that these needs are to be met "in accordance with established experience and scientific knowledge."[75] This language was previously noted in connection with the CE Farming Convention and, at least in theory, purports to have as its purpose the protection of animals used in agriculture.

There is a second purpose for the Directive stated in its introductory language and this purpose is economic:

> Whereas differences which may distort conditions of competition interfere with the smooth running of the organisation of the market in animals;
>
> Whereas there is therefore a need to establish common minimum standards for the protection of animals kept for farming purposes in order to ensure rational development of production and to facilitate the organisation of the market in animals; whereas to that end it is appropriate to take account of animal welfare provisions already laid down in Community rules ....[76]

This recognizes that differences in animal welfare regulation between states may cause one country to have a competitive advantage over another. For example, if one country bans battery cages for laying hens and other countries do not adopt the ban, the egg producers from the country that bans battery cages will be at a competitive disadvantage, because their costs to produce eggs will exceed those of other countries. These two purposes, one, the protection of animals and two, the provision of a level competitive playing field, are not necessarily aimed at similar goals; what is beneficial for animals may not be beneficial for commerce, and if we balance human economic interests against animal interests, it is likely that human interests will prevail given the long history of human use of animals and the equally long history of little or no concern for animals.

The common language of the CE Farming Convention and Council Directive 98/58/EC goes further than the introductory language of the Directive. The Directive applies to animals kept for production of food, wool, skin or fur or other farming purposes, as is the case under the Convention. The Directive does not apply to wild animals, animals used in experiments or entertainment, or invertebrates.[77] In Article 3 of the Council Directive, we also find the requirement that owners and keepers of animals must ensure that "animals are not caused any unnecessary pain, suffering or injury." The Directive does not prohibit any particular use of animals in agriculture, but rather allows these uses so long as "unnecessary" pain and suffering do not occur, which is, as we have seen, a kind of code for allowing any use of animals so long as it is consistent with exploiting

---

75. *Id.*
76. *Id.*
77. *Id.* at art. 1.

the economic value of the animals or with exploiting animals for culturally and socially acceptable purposes.

Council Directive 98/58/EC gives specific requirements for the treatment of animals used in agriculture. The Annex to the Directive requires the following:

- Adequately trained staff to care for animals.
- Inspection of animals and equipment at least once a day.
- Veterinary care for sick or injured animals.
- Records must be kept of medical care given to animals and of the mortality of animals.
- Freedom of movement of animals must not be restricted in a way that causes unnecessary suffering or injury.
- Construction and other requirements for the housing of animals.
- Animals housed outside of buildings are to be kept protected from the elements and from predators.
- "Animals must be fed a wholesome diet which is appropriate to their age and species and which is fed to them in sufficient quantity to maintain them in good health and satisfy their nutritional needs. No animal shall be provided with food or liquid in a manner, nor shall such food or liquid contain any substance, which may cause unnecessary suffering or injury."[78]

While the Annex contains the abovementioned specific requirements, it does not address the mutilation of animals such as dehorning, branding etc., which the Directive leaves to "national provisions" which presumably means that individual countries can adopt whatever measures they see fit.[79]

What are the enforcement mechanisms for the Directive? The EU Commission is required to make a report to the Council every five years on experience under the Directive and to further make proposals based on that experience.[80] In addition, Member States are required to have inspections of agricultural facilities to ensure that they are in compliance with the Directive and they must report to the EU Commission on the results of those inspections.[81] EU Commission Decision 2006/778/EC sets rules concerning the requirements of inspections under Council Directives 98/58/EC, 91/629/EEC, 91/630/EEC and 1999/74/EC.[82] These rules require that certain categories of information described in the Annexes to the EU Commission Decision be collected and that any failures of farming facilities to comply with these requirements be reported to the Commission.[83] When necessary, veterinary experts may be dispatched by the EU Commission to make inspections of facilities in Member States to ensure compliance with the

78. *Id.* at Annex § 14.
79. *Id.* at Annex § 19.
80. *Id.* at art. 5.
81. *Id.* at art. 6.
82. Commission Decision 2006/778, 2006 (L 314) 39, 39.
83. *See id.*

Directive.[84] Member States are required to provide the veterinarians doing the inspections assistance necessary for the veterinarians to complete their inspections.[85]

In Article 10 of the Directive, we see the language that requires all member countries to bring their laws into conformance with the Directive:

> Member States shall bring into force the laws, regulations and administrative provisions, including any sanctions, necessary to comply with this Directive not later than 31 December 1999, subject to any different decision taken by the Council in the light of the report referred to in Article 8. They shall forthwith inform the Commission thereof.[86]

What we see in Council Directive 98/58/EC is a general directive aimed at the use of animals in agriculture in the EU. It is however, only one of a number of directives relating to the use of animals in agriculture. There are a number of other directives that apply to the use of specific types of animals in agriculture, like Council Directive 2008/119 relating to the protection of calves.

2. Standards for the Protection of Calves

We see in the treatment of calves an example of the historical progression of the regulation of animals in agriculture within EU legislation. Council Directive 91/629/EEC was amended a number of times by Council Regulation 806/2003/EC, Council Directive 97/2/EC and Commission Decision 97/182/EC until its recent repeal in 2008 by Council Directive 2008/119. The new Directive repeals 91/629/EC and effectively codifies it and the amendments made by the later directive, regulation and decision into a single Directive. As a result, this provides an opportunity to analyze how EU regulation of the use of certain animals in agriculture is progressing.

Looking first to the recitals of Council Directive 91/629/EEC, it is notable that the stated purposes of this Directive focus on economic issues, such as competition and the necessity of calves to agriculture. There is little mentioned here of animal treatment issues, which is notable, given that the keeping of calves is a practice in which it is agreed that there are monumental issues regarding animal treatment. Calves kept for veal are often kept confined and/or tethered for their entire lives in "veal crates," and fed an unnatural diet of milk or milk substitute so that their flesh turns out light in color, as was described in Chapter 1.

The Directive states that it "lays down the minimum standards for the protection of calves confined for rearing and fattening."[87] Given that veal calves are often kept in confined conditions, it is not surprising that the space allowed to

84. Council Directive 98/58, *supra* note 74, at art. 7.
85. *Id.*
86. *Id.* at art. 10.
87. Council Directive 91/629, art. 1, 1991 O.J. (L 340) 28, 28. The discussion of this Directive is based on its original form, not as it has been amended.

calves is a major issue addressed in the Directive. Article 3 of 91/629/EEC sets forth rules for the amount of space that animals must have if kept in groups or when housed in individual boxes or stalls. The Annex to the Directive provides further detailed provisions relating to the treatment of calves and requires the following:

- The construction and materials used to house calves must not be harmful to the animals.
- Calves cannot be kept in complete darkness and must be able to see other calves. Presumably this is in recognition of the need of animals to have a day/night routine and to satisfy in some sense the social needs of the animals.
- The animals must be inspected at least once a day.
- Veterinary treatment must be provided to injured or sick animals.[88]

One recalls that a requirement of Council Directive 98/58/EC is that animals are required to be fed a wholesome diet. Any pretence of compliance with this requirement concerning veal calves disintegrates when considering section 11 of the Annex to 91/629/EEC, which states, in part, "the requirement for a minimum quantity of dried feed containing digestible fibres does not apply to the production of veal calves for white meat."[89] This is a perfect example of the economic and cultural interests of humans outweighing any interest in the welfare of animals. It is recognized elsewhere in this Directive and in 98/58/EC that a healthy diet is necessary for healthy animals. But under Directive 91/629/EEC, where the trivial interest of humans to consume tender white meat is shoved into the equation, it is the animals' interests that are sacrificed. As we will see, however, this aspect of Council Directive 91/629/EEC has been amended to provide for better nutrition for calves.

The enforcement mechanisms of this Directive are like those of Council Directive 98/58/EC. Member States are required to carry out inspections of a "statistically representative" sample of the different farming systems used in the state.[90] It is also required that every two years a report on the results of these inspections be transmitted to the EU Commission.[91] The Commission is also empowered to do spot inspections of facilities in Member States.[92]

Unlike Council Directive 98/58/EC, Council Directive 91/629/EEC contains import restrictions. Article 8 of the Directive provides that any animal imported into Member States must be "accompanied by a certificate issued by the competent authority of that country, certifying that they have received treatment at least equivalent to that granted to animals of Community origin as provided for by this

88. *Id.* at Annex §§ 1–10.
89. *Id.* at Annex § 11.
90. *Id.* at art. 7.
91. *Id.*
92. *Id.* at art. 9.

Directive."[93] As we analyze the directives and regulations of the EU, a pattern will appear relating to import restrictions, which we will see appears to be related to the World Trade Organization (WTO), the General Agreement on Tariffs and Trade (GATT) and decisions made under GATT. At this point, we should just note that there is an international trade restriction contained in this Directive.

Council Directive 97/2/EC was the first amendment to Directive 91/629/EEC to provide more protection to calves. Its stated purposes differ in certain respects from those of its predecessor. As in Council Directive 91/629/EEC, it still indicates a focus on economic competition and regulation of markets, but it also purports to "pay full regard to welfare requirements of animals" and references an opinion of the Scientific Veterinary Committee in 1995 as a foundation for the amendments in the new regulation.[94]

Among its specific provisions, Council Directive 97/2/EC prohibits confinement of calves in individual pens after the age of eight weeks, except when a veterinarian certifies that the animal's health or behavior requires isolation.[95] The routine use of veal crates is, thus, effectively ended by this amendment.[96] This Directive also prescribes minimum space requirements for calves held in groups, and requires that individual pens be perforated to allow the calves to see and touch other calves.[97] Commission Decision 97/182/EC continues down this path by providing further protection for calves stating that owners must inspect calves kept indoors at least twice a day and outdoor calves at least once a day.[98] Calves are now to be fed at least twice a day, one more time than was required in Directive 91/629/EEC.[99] The tethering of individually housed calves is now prohibited, and tethering of outdoor calves is allowed only for short periods of time for feeding purposes.[100] Regulations pertaining to the health of calves have been modified to require that calves be given food with sufficient iron to maintain certain specified blood haemoglobin levels and be provided a minimum amount of fibrous food.[101] As a result, the exception to requiring fibrous food for white meat veal calves in Council Directive 91/629/EEC has been removed. Thus, the diet of veal calves has been addressed in a positive way, even though it weighs against the supposed interests of humans.

The latest EU Directive on the protection of calves, Council Directive 2008/119/EC, effectively codifies Council Directive 91/629/EEC and the changes made to it by Council Regulation 806/2003/EC, Council Directive 97/2/EC, and

93. *Id.* at art. 8.
94. Council Directive 97/2, recitals, 1997 O.J. (L 025) 24.
95. *Id.* at art. 1(a).
96. Stephanie J. Engelsman, *"World Leader"—At What Price? A Look at Lagging American Animal Protection Laws,* 22 PACE ENVTL. L. REV. 329, 354 (2005).
97. Council Directive 97/2, *supra* note 94, at art. 1(a)–(b); *see* Engelsman, *supra* note 96, at 354.
98. Commission Decision 97/182, art. 1, 1997 O.J. (L 076) 30–31.
99. *Id.*
100. *Id.*
101. *Id;* Engelsman, *supra* note 96, at 354.

Commission Decision 97/182/EC. It does not by itself make relevant changes to the substantive rules on the treatment of calves. One interesting aspect of the latest Directive is that it retains the provision of Directive 91/629/EEC requiring that imported animals must be certified to have received treatment at least equal to that required by EU regulations. The significance of this restriction on imports will be shown in a later discussion of the WTO and the GATT.

In this progression of EU regulations, we can observe an evolution in the law of agricultural animal protection over a relatively short period of time. While these changes do not prohibit the keeping of calves for veal production, they do at least serve to make the short lives of these unfortunate animals somewhat better than they are in many countries by prohibiting most veal crates, prohibiting most tethering and solitary confinement of calves and improving their diet. Nonetheless, the calves continue to live only short, crowded and uncomfortable lives punctuated by eventual terror, followed by slaughter.

3. Standards for the Protection of Pigs

Like the 1991 Directive on the protection of calves, Council Directive 91/630/EEC relating to the protection of pigs was amended on several occasions and ultimately repealed by Council Directive 2008/120/EC, which codifies the original and amending Directives into a single document.[102] So once again, the opportunity to observe the historical progress of EU legislation on the use of animals in agriculture is presented to us.

Council Directive 91/630/EC, like the 1991 Directive on the protection of calves, focuses in its recitals on economic issues as the purpose of the regulation. It refers to "rational development of production" and "differences [in regulation] which may distort conditions of competition."[103] Thus, while the Directive purports to be aimed at protection of animals, it also reveals a strong economic rationale.

This Directive applies to "pigs confined for rearing and fattening."[104] Like the Directive relating to calves, this provision lays out housing and space requirements for pigs in detail.[105] Also like 91/629/EEC, this Directive states that materials for and construction of housing for pigs must not be harmful to the animals, requires daily inspections of animals and equipment, and prohibits permanent darkness for pigs.[106] Pigs are to be provided a diet appropriate to their age, weight, and behavioral and physiological needs, and must be fed at least once a day.[107] Also, specific provisions are made for housing and treatment of specific types of

102. Council Directive 2008/120, 2008 O.J. (L 47), 5.
103. Council Directive 91/630, 1991, recitals, O.J. (L 340), 33, 33–34.
104. *Id.* at art. 1.
105. *Id.* at art. 3.
106. *Id.* at Annex ch. I, §§ 1, 3–6.
107. Council Directive 2008/120, *supra* note 102, at Annex ch. I § 6; Council Directive 98/58, *supra* note 74, at Annex §§ 14–17.

pigs, like boars, sows, gilts and piglets.[108] Inspections and reporting requirements by Member States and spot inspections by the EU Commission are provided for, as we have seen in other directives.[109] Also, like 91/629/EEC, this Directive provides that animals imported from non-Member States must be certified by the non-member country to have been treated at least as well as required by 91/630/EEC.[110]

As in the case of standards for veal calves, we are given an opportunity to observe the evolution of regulations relating to treatment of pigs in agriculture, since Directive 91/630/EEC has been substantively amended by Directives 2001/88/EC and 2001/93/EC. Council Directive 2001/88/EC states in its recitals that it is based on, among other things, a 1997 Scientific Veterinary Committee opinion which "concluded that pigs should benefit from an environment corresponding to their needs for exercise and investigatory behavior and the welfare of pigs appeared to be compromised by severe restrictions of space."[111] Thus, the EU purports to be relying on scientific data relating to physiological and ethological needs to determine the proper policies relating to the treatment of animals. When we further analyze the future of EU regulation, we will see that promoting scientific research on the welfare of animals and following the recommendations of the scientific community on such matters is a major goal of future EU legislation. Of course, the "scientific community" and the legislators operate from the premise that the use of animals in agriculture is something that should continue—with appropriate regulations, of course. Presumably the idea that perhaps these animals should not be used at all for food purposes was not one of the proposals ever entertained in these scientific deliberations.

Council Directive 2001/88/EC references social and economic values that must be balanced with animal welfare considerations. It states that a "balance must be kept between the various aspects to be taken into consideration, as regarding welfare including health, economic and social considerations, and also environmental impact."[112] Synthesizing this statement with the concept that we are to follow the best scientific knowledge on these issues, the EU doctrine on animal welfare in agriculture appears to maintain that we are to follow the latest scientific knowledge on animal welfare tempered by social and economic realities; we must therefore balance the scientifically established welfare interests of animals against human social and economic values. As Gary Francione has pointed out, in this kind of balancing act the human interests seem virtually always to prevail.[113]

In any event, the substance of Council Directive 2001/88/EC sets forth detailed space requirements for pigs kept for agricultural purposes based on the

108. Council Directive 2008/120, *supra* note 102, at Annex ch. II.
109. *Id.* at arts. 7, 9.
110. *Id.* at art. 8.
111. Council Directive 2001/88, recitals para. 4, 2001 O.J. (L 316) 1, 1.
112. *Id.* at recitals para. (6).
113. *See* Francione, *supra* note 69, at 17–23.

weight of the pigs.[114] The tethering of sows and gilts is prohibited by the Directive after January 1, 2006.[115] The traditional gestation crate for sows that keeps sows from turning around or moving in any natural manner, and which is recognized as one of the "most inhumane aspects of modern-day livestock production,"[116] is prohibited under Council Directive 2001/88/EC.[117] This is only somewhat good news for sows, however, since sows can still be confined in groups where the pens in which they are kept are of a particular size.[118] In addition, pig operations with fewer than ten sows may still keep sows in gestation crates so long as they have sufficient room to "turn around easily in their boxes."[119] The Directive further requires that feeding systems for pigs be designed so that all pigs have appropriate access to "food even when competitors for food are present."[120]

In a similar vein is Council Directive 2001/93/EC, which is also based on the Scientific Veterinary Committee opinion that forms the basis for Directive 2001/88/EC. Directive 2001/93/EC addresses other issues relating to the raising of pigs, including methods of tail docking, tooth clipping, tooth grinding and castration. It is recognized that these practices cause immediate and sometimes prolonged pain in pigs.[121] As a result, this Directive amends the Annex to Council Directive 91/630/EC and prohibits these procedures with certain exceptions. For example, while the Directive prohibits tail docking or reduction of corner teeth as a routine matter, it allows these practices where evidence of injuries to pigs exists that would presumably be remedied by these procedures.[122] These injuries to pigs would presumably be the result of pigs biting the tails of other pigs, which is a behavior that is a consequence of the crowded conditions in which the animals are kept. Castration continues to be permitted by means other than by tearing of tissue.[123] All of these procedures must be performed by a veterinarian or other properly trained person.[124] This Directive also addresses the type of areas that must be provided for pigs to lie down, requires that pigs be housed in a way that allows them to see other pigs, requires pigs to have light that mimics daylight for at least eight hours a day and requires daily feeding of all pigs.[125]

Council Directive 2008/120/EC effectively consolidates Council Directive 91/630/EEC and its subsequent amendments. Note that as in the amendments to the provisions relating to calves, the import of pigs into the EU under Directive

114. Council Directive 2001/88, *supra* note 111, at art. 1.
115. *Id.* at art. 1(3).
116. Engelsman, *supra* note 96, at 348.
117. *Id.* at 348; Council Directive 2001/88, *supra* note 111, at art. 1(4).
118. Council Directive 2001/88, *supra* note 111, at art. 1(4).
119. *Id.* at art. 1(4)(b).
120. *Id.* at art. 1(6).
121. Commission Directive 2001/93, recitals para. (4), 2001 O.J. (L 316) 36, 36.
122. *Id.* at Annex ch. 1(8).
123. *Id.*
124. *Id.*
125. *Id.* at Annex ch. 1(2)-(6).

2008/120/EC continues to require a certificate that the animals imported received treatment at least equivalent to that required by the EU.[126]

We see in this amendment process an evolution of treatment of pigs based on a mélange of explicitly considered interests: scientific, social and economic. The result is a set of detailed rules regarding the housing, feeding and medical care of pigs kept for agricultural purposes. In provisions similar to those relating to calves, we observe a progression toward more "humane" treatment of pigs. Thus, we see Council Directive 91/630/EEC amended to do away with gestation crates for sows, to prohibit the tethering of pigs and to restrict certain mutilation procedures. What is apparently never asked, however, is why we should imprison the pigs for any purposes at all. As usual, human interests appear to resolve that question without the need for any discussion.

4. Laying Hens and Chickens for Meat Production

In looking at other EU directives, we have seen varying emphases in fundamental purposes described in the recitals to the directives. In the chronologically earlier directives, such as the ones relating to pigs and calves, economic purposes appear to be in the most prominent position. In the case of the 1998 Directive relating to the protection of animals kept for farming purposes, we saw an enhanced focus on the treatment of animals. In Council Directive 1999/74/EC (Appendix II) regarding the treatment of laying hens, while there is reference made to economic issues, we see animal welfare clearly prioritized again. First, reference is made to Council Directive 98/58/EC and the principles stated in that Directive requiring consideration of the physiological and ethological needs of animals.[127] Second, the Directive makes clear that one of the main purposes behind the Directive is addressing the use of battery cages in the EU, and the need to ultimately end their use:

> The Commission report referred to in recital 2, based on an opinion from the Scientific Veterinary Committee, concludes that the welfare conditions of hens kept in current battery cages and other systems of rearing are inadequate and that certain of their needs cannot be met in such cages; the highest possible standards should therefore be introduced, in the light of various parameters to be considered in order to improve those conditions ….[128]

Here we see clear recognition that the present treatment of hens is not appropriate to their needs and should therefore be changed. This change in focus of the recitals from the 1991 Directives to the ones later in the 1990s may be the result of societal changes brought about by greater public exposure to the conditions in which battery hens live, coupled with greater recognition of the interests of animals in the late 1990s. As mentioned before, in the early 1990s there was only a handful (less than ten) of law schools in the United States offering animal law classes. Now

126. Council Directive 2008/120/EC, *supra* note 102, at art. 8.
127. Council Directive 1999/74, recitals para. (3), 1974 (L 203) 53, 53.
128. *Id.* at recitals para. (7).

there are over 100 such schools and the number is increasing all the time. This indicates that interest in and awareness of animal treatment issues has increased substantially since the early 1990s. Thus, the change in emphasis in European legislative purposes may reflect this same trend toward greater interest in issues relating to animal treatment.

Whatever the true purpose of the Directive, it does set forth a prescription for the end of traditional hen battery cages, albeit over a rather long period of time. The Directive is somewhat limited in its operation, however, since it only applies to laying hen operations of 350 or more hens and thus does not apply to the small producer.[129] Presumably, this may be because it is believed that smaller operations are not as likely to be factory farms which use battery cages. In any event, these smaller operations are still subject to the general rules on animal treatment in EU Directive 98/58/EC.

Council Directive 1999/74/EC goes on to state that it applies to what are defined as "laying hens," which are members of a particular species of chicken.[130] While the Directive has provisions we are now familiar with relating to lighting, daily inspections, etc., it also sets forth a prescription for the eventual end of traditional unenriched battery cages for hens in the EU, which it does through the mechanism of directing what kinds of hen operations can be constructed and used in the future. The Directive divides hen operations into three categories: alternative systems, unenriched cage systems and enriched cage systems.[131] Since January 1, 2002, alternative systems are the only kind of systems permitted to be built in the EU. Alternative systems require feeders and drinking troughs allowing a certain amount of space per bird, one nest per seven birds, a littered area of at least 250 cm^2 per bird, with the littered area covering at least one-third of the ground surface, and perches for the birds with a certain amount of area per bird.[132] These alternative systems do away with cages for hens; they do not, however, require that hens be raised in what one would call a "free range" farming operation. Alternative systems are essentially non-cage systems that provide more space and "amenities" for hens than typical in a cage system; no more, no less.

The provisions relating to unenriched cage systems provide that all cage systems remaining after January 1, 2003 must comply with specific space, feeding, watering and other requirements.[133] The unenriched systems do not require nesting areas or littered space for the hens and are simply battery cage systems requiring a certain amount of space per bird. Rearing of birds in these kinds of systems is prohibited after January 1, 2012.

The prohibition on unenriched cage systems does not mean that the EU has entirely prohibited cage systems. Enriched cage systems can and will continue to

129. *Id.* at art. 1.
130. *Id.* at art. 2.
131. *Id.* at chs. I–III.
132. *Id.* at ch. I.
133. *Id.* at ch. II.

be used. These systems are cage systems that provide a greater amount of space per bird than unenriched cage systems and further provide perches and litter in the cages for the hens.[134] So these "more pleasant" cage systems may continue to be used in the EU, theoretically until the end of time. It is left to individual countries to outlaw cage systems entirely, should they wish to go beyond the strictures of the EU Directives, as has occurred in Germany.[135]

The enforcement mechanisms for this Directive are somewhat different from those previously reviewed. This Directive requires that all establishments covered by the Directive must be registered with the Member States and shall be given a number so that eggs from the facility can be traced in the event there is a need to do so.[136] This registration system is also the subject of Commission Directive 2002/4/EC, which provides further-detailed rules on the registration of all production sites for eggs.[137] As we have seen in other EU legislation on agricultural animals, Member States are required to inspect these facilities to ensure that the Directive is being carried out and to report to the EU Commission on these inspections, while the EU Commission is given the authority to do its own inspections to ensure that the Directive is being followed in each Member State.[138]

It should also be noted that, unlike the directives of the early 1990s, this Directive, like Council Directive 98/58/EC, does not have any provisions relating to imported hens or eggs. Thus, these Directives only apply to EU member countries, and therefore do not have international trade implications.

A Directive similar to Council Directive 1999/74/EC has recently been created for chickens kept for meat production. Council Directive 2007/43/EC sets forth minimum requirements for the rearing of chickens for meat production. Again, we see in the recitals a statement that animal welfare, as interpreted by the Scientific Committee on Animal Health and Animal Welfare, is a foundation of the Directive.[139] At the same time, we can also see that religious, cultural, regional, competitive and economic issues are balanced against those same animal welfare concerns.[140] Like the laying hen provisions, this Directive only applies to operations of a certain size, those with 500 or more chickens. Again, the focus here, as in the regulation of laying hens, is on housing, lighting, space and inspection requirements for chickens raised for meat production on factory farms.

Some of the particular requirements are twice daily inspections, availability of litter for the chickens and continuous access to food and water.[141] This Directive also prohibits surgical procedures performed on chickens for other than therapeutic

---

134. *Id.* at ch. III.
135. Engelsman, *supra* note 96, at 352–53.
136. Council Directive 1999/74, *supra* note 127, at art. 7.
137. Commission Directive 2002/4, art. 1, 2002 (L 30) 44, 44.
138. Council Directive 1999/74, *supra* note 127, at arts. 8–9.
139. Council Directive 2007/43, recitals paras. (1), (4), 2007 (L 182) 19, 19–20.
140. *Id.* at recitals paras. (1), (6), (10).
141. *Id.* at Annex 1, paras. 1–9.

or diagnostic purposes.[142] Having stated this rule, the Annex to the Directive goes on to authorize "beak trimming" and castration of chickens in certain circumstances.[143] "Beak trimming" is less benignly referred to as "debeaking." Debeaking is often seen as necessary in intensive farming operations because in the crowded conditions under which these chickens live, they sometimes engage in the pecking of other birds and cannibalism. So as a result of the conditions in which the chickens are kept, they behave in ways that they would not otherwise—which results in the removal of their beaks.

As a whole, what do we observe in these Directives concerning the improvement in the conditions of factory farmed chickens? These Directives address some of the issues raised by factory farming such as overcrowding; the necessity of monitoring animal health; the ability of animals to behave in natural ways; and the aberrant behavior caused by extreme overcrowding. But these provisions do not address these issues by prohibiting or fundamentally changing the systems that are used to confine chickens. Instead, what is provided is marginally more space for the animals; rather more access to litter and nests; a "natural" pattern of lighting, etc. So in analyzing these rules under the purported purposes of the directives, it seems that once again the economic interests behind the continuation of intensive farming methods are protected while some cleaning up around the edges of factory farming is performed to make the prisoners' short lives somewhat more bearable. We address the effects of factory farming, the deplorable conditions of factory farmed animals, not the cause, factory farming itself. This, we find, is the pattern of much modern animal welfare legislation.

5. The Protection of Animals During Transport

Although animals are sometimes transported for other reasons, it is frequently the case that the principal transportation many animals experience is to their slaughter. But even though slaughter is the endpoint of much animal transportation, we ironically make provisions for a "humane" last voyage. Humans have been transporting animals for millennia. There are, for example, pictographs in ancient Egyptian tombs showing herdsmen taking cattle across a crocodile-infested Nile.[144] These herdsmen used the natural behaviors of the animals to accomplish this task, calf following cow and taking advantage of the general predilection of cattle to follow each other. Long-distance transport of animals dates back to Roman times.[145]

142. *Id.* at Annex 1, para. 12.
143. *Id.*
144. Temple Grandin, Livestock Handling and Transport 65 (2007).
145. Jean Blancou & Ian Parsonson, *Historical Perspectives on Long Distance Transport of Animals,* 44 Veterinaria Italina, No. 1, 19, 19–30 (2008), *available at* http://www.izs.it/vet_italiana/2008/19_30.pdf.

The terror felt by animals in transportation processes is made clear in an 1890 account:

> A New York newspaper account contemporary with Plimsoll's investigations reported on the conditions aboard one such ship: "The cattle are tightly jammed together … mad and furious with terror and unrest. They have to stand all the time (sometimes sixteen days) they are on board. This alone is prolonged torture." In heavy weather, ships "rolled and pitched," and the "suffering beasts [were] thrown from side to side, goring each other with their horns." Another seaman was paraphrased in the same newspaper series: "A sea-sick man, he said, is one of the most pitiful things one can see, but his sufferings are nothing to those of a dumb brute. They will look at one so pleadingly and helplessly that you almost feel like crying for them. You have no idea how they are knocked about when a wave strikes the ship. Between overcrowding, the storms, and our sticks, the poor beasts have a hard time enough."[146]

This is one aspect of the treatment of animals that many people probably do not much consider; but, as this 1890 account shows, we certainly should. And while transportation methods have changed from the 1890s, long distance transport of animals resulting in similar suffering still frequently occurs.

When we consider these issues in the context of EU regulation of the transportation of animals, we again have the opportunity to scrutinize the historical progression of animal welfare regulation in the EU. We have Council Directive 91/628/EEC on the Protection of Animals during Transport and Council Regulation (EC) No. 1/2005 that replaces the earlier Directive. Council Directive 91/628/EEC applied to the transport of a list of animals including cattle, pigs, dogs, cats, birds and other vertebrates.[147] It did not apply to transport of pets by travelers and certain short distance transportation.[148]

One of the main strictures of the Directive was that only animals that are not ill or injured are to be transported.[149] Not surprisingly, this requirement did not apply to animals transported for scientific research.[150] This requirement also did not apply to transport of "animals that are slightly injured or ill whose transport would not cause unnecessary suffering."[151] Again we see the term "unnecessary suffering" which is going to be interpreted and applied by those with an economic interest in the animal being transported regardless of its condition.[152] Not

146. Encyclopedia Britannica's Advocacy for Animals, *Highways to Hell: The Long-Distance Transport of Farmed Animals,* (2008), *available at* http://advocacy.britannica.com/blog/advocacy/2008/06/highways-to-hell-the-long-distance-transport-of-farmed-animals/.
147. Council Directive 91/628, art. 1, 1991 (L 340) 17, 17–27.
148. *Id.*
149. *Id.* at art. 3(b).
150. *Id.*
151. *Id.*
152. The language "unnecessary suffering" is also used in Articles 5 and 9 of the Directive. *Id.* at art. 5.

surprisingly, the general substantive standard for transporting animals was that animals were not to be transported in a way that causes unnecessary suffering.[153] Animals that become injured or ill during transport were to be provided veterinary treatment and if necessary were to be slaughtered on an emergency basis in a way that did not cause unnecessary suffering.[154]

Transporters were regulated through registration and other requirements. Some of these requirements included maintaining properly trained staff, requiring itineraries for journeys exceeding 24 hours and providing plans for feeding and watering animals when the journey was longer than 24 hours.[155] We are at least spared the concept that ethological needs are being considered here since there are no animals whose natural behavior would include being transported to their death. Not surprisingly, there were also rules relating to the construction and condition of the means of transportation.[156]

Council Regulation (EC) No. 1/2005 purports to strengthen the protection of animals in transport as it repeals and replaces Council Directive 91/628/EEC. The new Regulation has several purposes. First, it is intended to respond to new scientific evidence relating to the welfare of animals contained in an opinion adopted by the Scientific Committee on Animal Health and Animal Welfare on March 11, 2002.[157] Second, it intends to correct differences in national rules relating to the transportation of animals under the Directive.[158] Third, this Regulation also responds to distortions of economic competition resulting from differences in national legislation on the transport of animals.[159] These latter two goals are accomplished by creating a regulation rather than a directive.

The new Regulation applies to the "transport of live vertebrate animals carried out within the Community."[160] Council Regulation (EC) No. 1/2005 does not apply to transport for non-economic purposes or to transport to and from veterinarians for veterinary treatment.[161] The main substantive standard for the transportation of animals in the Regulation is that "[n]o person shall transport animals or cause animals to be transported in a way likely to cause injury or undue suffering to them."[162] This language differs slightly from the "unnecessary" suffering language used in the earlier Directive, but it seems unlikely that "undue" suffering is meant to signal a standard different from the ubiquitous "unnecessary" language. Like the earlier Directive, the Regulation requires that animals to be transported must be "fit for the journey."[163]

153. *Id.*
154. *Id.* at art. 3(c).
155. *Id.* at arts. 3–5.
156. *Id.* at Annex § 2.
157. Council Regulation 1/2005, recitals para. (8), 2004 (L 3) 1, 1–37.
158. *Id.* at para. (10).
159. *Id.* at para. (22).
160. *Id.* at art. 1(1).
161. *Id.* at art. 1(5).
162. *Id.* at art. 3.
163. *Id.*

Some of the main points of the new Regulation relate to documenting and monitoring journeys, and education and training of personnel. Transporters are required to carry detailed documentation describing their journey, the owner of the animals and the expected duration of the journey.[164] Transporters are also required to hold authorizations from national authorities in order to act as transporters.[165] These authorizations are only to be granted to persons who can prove that they have appropriate staff and equipment to comply with the Regulation, and have had no serious infringements of legislation on the welfare of animals in the three years prior to applying for the authorization.[166] Those who handle the animals must have received training specified in the Annexes to the Regulation, and must have certificates of competence issued by the national authority.[167] For "long journeys," meaning those longer than eight hours, the means of transportation must also have been inspected and approved by national authorities,[168] and must be certified by national authorities as meeting certain design, construction and maintenance standards.[169] In addition, transporters must comply with additional regulations in order to be authorized to manage long journeys. For example, the use of navigation systems is required to monitor long journeys involving, among other animals, horses, cattle and pigs, so that there exists a record of the journey, and these records must be kept for at least three years.[170] National authorities are required to carry out checks of transporters to ensure that transporters are in compliance with the Regulation and are also required to submit annual reports on inspections carried out.[171] At border stations, national authorities are required to have official veterinarians check to determine that animals are being transported in compliance with the Regulation.[172] If it is found that animals are not being transported in compliance with the Regulation, authorities are to take any necessary action to protect the welfare of the animals, including changing drivers, repairing equipment, transferring animals to another means of transport, unloading and accommodating the animals, or where there are no other means to safeguard the welfare of the animals, to euthanize them.[173]

In the evolution of Council Directive 91/628/EEC into Council Regulation (EC) No. 1/2005, we can see the following:

- Standardization and uniformity in rules relating to animal welfare has become a major concern for the EU. This was prompted here by differences in national regulations under Council Directive 91/628/EEC and

164. *Id.* at art. 4.
165. *Id.* at art. 6.
166. *Id.* at art. 10.
167. *Id.* at art. 6.
168. *Id.* at arts. 2(m), 7.
169. *Id.* at art. 18.
170. *Id.* at art. 6(9).
171. *Id.* at arts. 15, 27.
172. *Id.* at art. 21.
173. *Id.* at art. 23.

perceived imbalances in competition caused by these varying rules. This problem is solved by creating a regulation rather than a directive to cover animal transport.
- Utilization of the latest science relating to the welfare of animals attempts to promote the best possible animal welfare rules, given the uses which animals serve.
- Training, education and certification of personnel are viewed as primary methods of assuring the welfare of animals.

What is not a part of this or any of the other regulations we have seen is any sort of ban on or change in the uses which animals serve. The farming and transport of animals continues, now under rules that purport to make agricultural animals' short horrifying lives marginally more tolerable and to make what are literally the last journeys of animals "more pleasant" for the animal. But the effort at making captive agricultural animals' lives "more pleasant" does not stop here. Once the animals have reached the end of this last trip, they also have the "benefit" of regulations relating to their slaughter.

6. Slaughter and Killing of Agricultural Animals

Some of the more oxymoronic statements one will ever encounter can be found in regulations relating to slaughter. In the United States, for example, there is the "Humane Slaughter Act." Here we have a Council Directive on "the protection of animals at the time of slaughter and killing" and a subsequent Council Regulation on "the protection of animals at the time of killing." These titles drip with irony.

The EU law on slaughter and killing again affords an opportunity to see the evolution of animal protection standards in the EU. In 1988, the EU approved the European Convention for the Protection of Animals for Slaughter.[174] Following this approval, the EU passed Council Directive 93/119/EC dealing with the protection of animals during slaughter and killing which has most recently been replaced by Council Regulation (EC) No. 1099/2009 (Appendix III). I will begin this analysis with an examination of Council Directive 93/119/EC which remains valid until December 31, 2012, and then scrutinize the changes that have been made by Council Regulation (EC) No. 1099/2009 which will become effective on January 1, 2013.

In addition to the purposes we have seen before of setting common standards to ensure economic competition and proper functioning of markets, and to spare animals "avoidable pain and suffering," Council Directive 93/119/EC introduces another purpose that is common in regulations relating to slaughter—protecting certain religious practices relating to slaughter even though these practices do not meet the normal standards for animal protection of the Directive.[175] In particular, the requirement of stunning animals prior to slaughter, one of the main

174. Council Decision 88/306, 1988 O.J. (L 137) 25, 25–26.
175. Council Directive 93/119, recitals, art. 5(2), 1993 O.J. (L 340) 21, 21–34.

"protections" of animals bound for slaughter, is dispensed with in allowing slaughter pursuant to certain religious rites.[176]

The specific requirements of this Directive lead us to some graphic language describing the actual treatment of animals revealing the brutal nature of slaughtering practices. The Directive applies to "the movement, lairaging, restraint, stunning, slaughter and killing of animals bred and kept for the production of meat, skin, fur or other products and to methods of killing animals for the purpose of disease control."[177] There is, however, much killing of animals outside of these parameters, like killing in hunting, animal experiments, and cultural and sporting events. Killing in these contexts is not covered by the Directive.[178] Again, we see that if there is some cultural, social or other benefit to humans in a particular activity, the meager protections we otherwise give to animals are sacrificed for the human interest.

As in animal transport, it is rather absurd to think about the ethological needs of animals in this context. Instead, the concern here is that "[a]nimals shall be spared any avoidable excitement, pain or suffering during movement, lairaging, restraint, stunning, slaughter or killing."[179] It is interesting to note that the typical language "unnecessary" is replaced here with "avoidable." It is not clear what this change in the ordinary animal welfare language means, but it may be in recognition of the fact that pain and suffering are unavoidable during slaughter, unlike some other contexts, and that all that can be expected here is that "avoidable" suffering, in fact, be avoided.

Common problems, like dealing with "downer" animals, ones injured in transportation, are addressed in the Directive. Traditionally, these animals, bellowing in pain, were dragged by a chain attached to one leg into the slaughterhouse to be dispatched. Under Council Directive 93/119/EC, animals are to be unloaded upon arrival at the slaughterhouse as soon as possible.[180] If it is found that animals are injured or ill, they are to be killed on the spot unless they can be moved without further suffering.[181] In this way, the Directive does away with some of the most horrifying practices relating to "downers."

The Directive goes on to prescribe a number of rules for "slaughter," which is the killing of an animal by cutting the animal's throat and letting the blood drain.[182] As an initial and overarching rule it is necessary that establishments see to it that employees have the skill to perform their tasks humanely.[183] Most animals, including cows, pigs, rabbits and poultry brought to slaughterhouses must be stunned prior to being slaughtered.[184] The purpose of this is to ensure that the

176. *Id.* at art. 5(2).
177. *Id.* at art. 1(1).
178. *Id.* at art. 1(2).
179. *Id.* at art. 3.
180. *Id.* at Annex A.
181. *Id.* at art. 12.
182. *Id.* at art. 2(7).
183. *Id.* at art. 7.
184. *Id.* at art. 5(1)(c).

animal is not conscious when it is slaughtered. Methods of stunning include the captive bolt pistol, which is a mechanism often used for large animals like cows, concussion, electronarcosis, which is electric shock typically done in "water baths" for poultry, and exposure to carbon dioxide.[185] It is after the animal is stunned that slaughter, the killing of the animal by bleeding, occurs; usually with the animal hung upside down by one leg and having its throat cut manually.

This Directive and its Annexes are quite instructive on the methods of killing used in agricultural operations. While slaughter after stunning is the usual method of killing for food animals like cows, pigs and poultry, other methods are used for other kinds of animals and for certain specified purposes described in Annex C to the Directive. For example, free bullet pistol or rifle is an approved method for certain game species. Decapitation can be used for poultry. Electrocution, gassing and killing by placing the animal in a vacuum are methods allowed in other circumstances. The killing of fur animals reveals other clever methods of producing death like drug overdoses, electrocution with cardiac arrest, exposure to chloroform and "mechanically-operated instruments which penetrate the brain."[186] The methods used for fur animals are designed so that there will be no damage to the animal's pelt.

To enforce this Directive, the Commission can send experts to inspect facilities to see that they are complying with the requirements of the Directive.[187] With respect to imported meat products, a health certificate accompanying the meat must be provided stating that the requirements of the Directive have been met.[188] The Commission is also authorized to inspect slaughterhouses in non-member countries to carry out this requirement.[189]

It is with this backdrop and 15 years experience under Council Directive 93/119/EC that Council Regulation (EC) No. 1099/2009 was passed in 2009 and codified. In the purposes of the Regulation we see some evolution in the concerns surrounding animal welfare in the killing process. Indeed, one express purpose of the Regulation is to address growing animal welfare concerns in society[190] and it is recognized that this was one of the reasons for revision of the rules on killing. To this end, one of the main objectives of the Regulation is to encourage "innovation in relation to stunning and killing techniques" to improve animal welfare at the time of killing.[191] The Regulation purports to be based, in part, on opinions and guidelines adopted by the European Food Safety Authority and the World

---

185. *Id.* at Annex C.
186. *Id.* at Annex F.
187. *Id.* at art. 14.
188. *Id.* at art. 15.
189. *Id.*
190. *See* Commission of the European Communities, *Proposal for a Council Regulation on the Protection of Animals at the Time of Killing,* "Explanatory Memorandum" (2008), *available at* http://ec.europa.eu/food/animal/welfare/slaughter/proposal_en.pdf [hereinafter Explanatory Memorandum]; Council Regulation 1099/2009, recitals para. (4), 2008 O.J. (L 303) 1, 1.
191. Explanatory Memorandum, *supra* note 190, at 3.

Organization for Animal Health.[192] Accomplishing innovation and improvement in slaughter processes is recognized to require development of techniques based on technical and scientific progress and innovation.[193] Economic concerns have not been jettisoned, however, and are a concern at the fore of this Regulation. It is noted that one of the reasons that the new rules are put in the form of a regulation, rather than a directive, is that animal protection rules have been unequally enforced in Member States resulting in competitive imbalances.[194]The Regulation intends to correct these imbalances and create a "level playing field" for slaughterhouses throughout the EU.[195]

The scope of the Regulation is consistent with that of Council Directive 93/119/EC and applies to the "killing of animals bred or kept for the production of food, wool, skin, fur or other products …."[196] It does not apply to scientific experiments, hunting activities, or cultural or sporting events.[197] The general principle underlying the Regulation relating to the treatment of animals remains the same as under the earlier directive, to spare animals "any avoidable pain, distress or suffering during" killing.[198] To accomplish this the Regulation requires that steps be taken to provide for the physical comfort and protection of animals to be killed, to protect them from injury, to handle them in a way taking into consideration natural behavior and to ensure that animals are not subject to prolonged periods without food or water.[199] Again, these rules are rather ironic; for example, as we lead animals to slaughter we are to take into consideration their natural behavior? How is the natural behavior of an animal ever going to be connected in a meaningful way to being led to death? The language, the concerns and the rules seem detached from reality. The animals are being killed; any protection provided at this point can be viewed as short-lived and pitiable.

In any event, to achieve these goals the Regulation does offer a detailed regulatory scheme for slaughter. Killing is to be performed only after stunning except in cases of religious slaughter.[200] There are also a few exceptions to the stunning requirements for operators supplying small quantities of meat and those killing animals for private domestic consumption.[201] A number of new rules are set forth relating to stunning. Regular checks are required to make certain that stunning is effectively occurring and that animals do not remain conscious after stunning.[202] In addition, the Regulation requires that all persons performing stunning and other operations in the slaughtering process have appropriate competence and are issued

192. Council Regulation 1099/2009, *supra* note 190, at recitals paras. (6)–(7).
193. *See id.*; Explanatory Memorandum, *supra* note 190, at 10.
194. Explanatory Memorandum, *supra* note 190, at 10.
195. *Id.*
196. Council Regulation 1099/2009, *supra* note 190, at art. 1.
197. *Id.*
198. *Id.* at art. 3.
199. *Id.*
200. *Id.* at art. 4.
201. *Id.* at arts. 10–11.
202. *Id.* at arts. 5, 16.

a "certificate of competence" by national authorities.[203] The manufacturers of stunning or restraint mechanisms are not free from regulation. They are required to provide instructions for the use of such equipment and the conditions under which the equipment is to be used.[204] Users of this equipment must see to it that it is "maintained and checked" and operated in accordance with the manufacturer's instructions.[205] Similarly, the new Regulation sets forth rules on the construction and layout of slaughterhouses.[206] Thus, the personnel, equipment and premises of slaughterhouses are now all subject to specific regulations.

So that operators conduct killing operations in a fashion consistent with the Regulation, it introduces the concept of "Standard Operating Procedures" (SOPs). Operators of slaughterhouses are required to create and implement SOPs consistent with Article 3 of the Regulation which sets forth the substantive requirements for how animals are to be protected during the slaughter process.[207] These SOPs must be followed in the killing operation and shall be made available to the competent governmental authority on request.

Another major change from Directive 93/119/EC is the requirement that all slaughterhouses must have a person designated as an animal welfare officer holding a certificate of competence.[208] This person is "responsible for ensuring compliance with the rules laid down" in the Regulation, is to report directly to the operator of the slaughterhouse and must be in a position to require personnel at the slaughterhouse to take remedial actions necessary to ensure compliance with the Regulation.[209] The precise duties of the animal welfare officer are to be described in the SOPs of the slaughterhouse.[210] There is no requirement of an animal welfare officer for slaughterhouses killing less than 1,000 livestock "units" or 150,000 poultry "units" per year.[211]

The mass killings of livestock and poultry as a result of mad cow disease and bird flu did not go unnoticed in the EU. Special provisions relating to depopulation operations are contained in Council Regulation (EC) No. 1099/2009. These provisions require that action plans be put in place by the relevant governmental authorities of Member States to ensure compliance with the rules relating to killing of animals in depopulation operations.[212] However, the Regulation also provides that derogations from the requirements of the Regulation can be granted by national governments to protect human health or slow down the progression of disease.[213]

---

203. *Id.* at art. 7.
204. *Id.* at art. 8.
205. *Id.* at art. 9.
206. *Id.* at art. 14.
207. *Id.* at art. 6.
208. *Id.* at art. 17.
209. *Id.* at art. 17(1)–(2).
210. *Id.* at art. 17(3).
211. *Id.* at art. 14(6).
212. *Id.* at art. 18.
213. *Id.*

Another new requirement of the Regulation is that each Member State must establish a "reference centre" or network for the purpose of aiding slaughterhouses in complying with animal welfare requirements.[214] These centres or networks are to, among other things, accredit bodies that issue certificates of competency under the Regulation, provide scientific and technical expertise relating to approval of slaughterhouses, assess new stunning methods and opine on good practices in the industry.[215]

National authorities may enforce the Regulation by requiring amendments of SOPs, increasing monitoring requirements, withdrawing certificates of competence, and suspending or withdrawing any delegation of power to an entity empowered to issue certificates of competence.[216] Member States are also required to create penalties for violations of the Regulation that are "effective, proportionate and dissuasive."[217] They may also maintain rules stricter than those set forth in the Regulation.[218]

What can we learn from the historical progression of Council Directive 93/119/EC to Council Regulation (EC) No. 1099/2009? There are a number of emphases in the new Regulation that differ from or expand on what was in Council Directive 93/119/EC and are consistent with what we have seen in Council Regulation (EC) No. 1/2005 on the transport of animals:

- *Standardization*: There are several aspects of the Regulation that evidence a movement toward standardization of animal welfare concerns and protections. First, the fact that the new rules are set forth as a regulation rather than a directive shows that the EU wants to achieve consistent rules governing animal welfare in the context of killing and slaughter. This desire for standardization was born from the fact that the use of directives to regulate these matters was not working given the uneven enforcement of Directive 93/119/EC. Second, the Regulation dictates standardization of another kind—animal welfare SOPs in slaughterhouses. This intends to ensure that the Regulation is complied with and that all personnel are aware of the sanctioned methods of killing.
- *Education and Training*: One of the main focuses of the Regulation is education and training of personnel. This can be seen from the requirement of certificates of competence and the creation of reference centres or networks as repositories of information on methods of slaughter.
- *Science as the Foundation of Proper Practices*: Much of the impetus for the changes in the rules relating to slaughter came from technological and scientific advances. This focus on science and the use of science to establish proper practices is also evident in the newly required national reference centres or networks.

214. *Id.* at recitals paras. 52–53, art. 20.
215. *Id.*
216. *Id.* at art. 22.
217. *Id.* at art. 23.
218. *Id.* at art. 26.

Whether this focus on standardization, training and science will in the future lead to continuing "advances" in animal welfare in the context of slaughter can only be known as time passes. Nonetheless, it is hard not to feel the biting irony and logical paradox of melding the humane with the intentional annihilation of millions of creatures.

So this ends our analysis of the regulatory scheme for agricultural animals in the EU. We have seen regulation of the general welfare of these animals from cradle (for calves) to grave (slaughter). What we have observed is a scheme that purports to avoid unnecessary suffering within a process of factory farming which by its very nature results in massive amounts of suffering. What is really happening is that given human desires to eat animals and use animal products, and given the huge economic interests lurking behind and promoting these desires, the regulatory scheme engages in a dance purporting to protect the interests of animals while at the same time recognizing and protecting the human economic and other interests involved. But in this balancing we see a scheme where human interests invariably appear to outweigh those of the animals. Indeed, if the animal interests prevailed, there would be only one regulation—abolition.

But before going on to look at Swedish law on agricultural animals, which is an example of a law thought to be quite favorable to the interests of animals, there is one other aspect of animal agricultural products to consider. What happens to the products at the retail level? Do we regulate the way they are presented to the public?

7. Labeling and Marketing Standards

Marketing of animal products sometimes trumpets the humane treatment of the animals that produced, or indeed are, the products in the package. Sometimes marketing brags about the environmentally ethical and conscientious way that the product was produced. We see this in claims that eggs are "free range" or "cage free," or that products are "organic" or "dolphin-safe." But what do these terms actually mean? If there is no regulation of the meaning of these terms, their true meaning is left up to the whim of the marketer or seller. Is there any regulation of the truth of these claims that may impact consumer decisions on which products to buy?

One example of a regulation relating to labeling issues is Commission Regulation (EC) No. 589/2008 concerning the marketing of eggs in the EU.[219] Note that this is a regulation, not a directive. As a result, this law is directly applicable to all Member States in the EU and the citizens of those states; there is no flexibility for individual states to fashion their own rules. The labeling of eggs as to method of production in the EU is an issue that has followed what can only be characterized as a complicated, circuitous and tortured path with a number of

219. Commission Regulation 589/2008, arts. 7(1)(a), 10(1)(g), 10(3), 13(1), 15–16, 2008 O.J. (L 163) 6, (EC).

regulations and directives having been passed on this issue over the past 20 years.[220]

The journey to the present state of EU law on egg labeling basically began with Council Regulation (EEC) No. 1907/90 which provided that egg producers could identify the type of farming method used, whether barn raised or free range.[221] This scheme was not effective in providing useful information for consumers because there was no requirement that battery cage raised eggs be identified.[222] Paragraph (2) of the recitals to Council Regulation (EC) No. 5/2001, whose amendment to Council Regulation (EEC) No. 1907/90, in conjunction with Commission Regulation (EC) No. 2295/2003, which initiated the EU mandatory egg labeling scheme, clearly states its purpose to change this:

> The Commission has undertaken to propose an amendment to the marketing standards and to make it compulsory to indicate the farming method on eggs and packs so that consumers are not liable to be misled. To that end, clear and unambiguous compulsory labeling is the only way of ensuring that the consumer is able to make an informed choice between the various classes of egg on the basis of the farming method.

The terms that could be used in the labeling of eggs, were defined in Article 13 and Annexes II and III of Commission Regulation (EEC) No. 2295/2003.[223]

This set of rules on egg labeling was further amended by Council Regulation (EC) No. 1028/2006 which repealed Council Regulation (EEC) No. 1907/90.[224] Council Regulation 1028/2006 was then simultaneously repealed and incorporated in Council Regulation (EC) No. 1234/2007.[225] The end of the long road to the present rules on farming method egg labeling and the latest regulation on the subject, Council Regulation (EC) No. 589/2008, effectively requires, along with

---

220. *See, e.g.,* Council Regulation 2771/75, 1975 O.J. (L 282) 72 (allowing for marketing standards to be created); Council Regulation 1907/90, 1990 O.J. (L 173) 5 (creating certain marketing standards); Council Regulation 5/2001, 2001 O.J. (L 2) 1 (amending Council Regulation 1907/90 to make the labeling of egg shells compulsory); Commission Regulation 2295/2003, 2003 O.J. (L 340) 16 (setting forth the criteria for the reserved terms used to label egg production methods); Commission Regulation 1651/2001, 2001 O.J. (L 220) 5 (EC); Council Regulation 1028/2006, 2006 O.J. (L 186) 1; Council Regulation 1234/2007, 2007 O.J. (L 299) 1 (repealing Council Regulation 1028/2006 while incorporating certain of its provisions); Commission Regulation 589/2008, *supra* note 219 (laying down rules to implement Council Regulation 1234/2007, including those standards not addressed or incorporated from Regulation 1028/2006); Council Regulation 1274/91, 1991 O.J. (L 121) 11–24 (repealed by Commission regulation 2295/2003).
221. *See* Council Regulation 1907/90, *supra* note 220, arts. 7, 10 (prior to amendment by Council Regulation 5/2001); *Response by Compassion in World Farming to DG Sanco Consultative Document on Labeling: Competitiveness, Consumer Information and Better Regulation for the EU* (2006), *available at* http://ec.europa.eu/food/food/labellingnutrition/betterregulation/docs/58.pdf [hereinafter "CWF"].
222. CWF, *supra* note 221, at 2.
223. Commission Regulation 2295/2003, *supra* note 220, at art. 13, Annexes II-III.
224. Council Regulation 1028/2006, *supra* note 220, at art 12.
225. Council Regulation 1234/2007, *supra* note 220, at recitals paras. (52), (105), art. 201.

related provisions, that producers label conventionally raised (non-organic) packs of eggs as "free range eggs," "barn eggs," or "eggs from caged hens" and provide a code on the eggs themselves that indicates the farming method used.[226] In this process of regulatory evolution, we see a developing EU animal welfare related regulatory program where results under a non-mandatory labeling regime were considered inadequate to properly inform consumers; so the labeling scheme, which has gone through a number of transformations, has been made mandatory.

Under Council Regulation (EC) No. 589/2008 and related provisions both egg packages and the egg shells themselves must be labeled. Article 12(2) of this Regulation provides that "packs containing Class A eggs shall bear on the outer surface in easily visible and clearly legible type the farming method."[227] Class B eggs (which are not generally sold to the public) are not required to be marked with farming method although they may be so marked.[228] Note that in addition to package labeling of conventionally produced eggs with the terms "free range eggs," "barn eggs," or "eggs from caged hens," organically grown eggs can simply be labeled as "organic."[229] The eggs themselves are required to be labeled with the type of farming method, but this labeling may take the form of a numeric code.[230] These numeric codes are 1 for "free range," 2 for "barn raised," 3 for "caged birds," and 0 for "organic."[231] You will find in Europe that eggs themselves are sometimes, in addition to the numeric code relating to farming method, actually marked "free range," etc. This, however, is not required.

What these terms mean is of obvious importance. "Free range eggs" are required to be produced in conditions that satisfy at least the following requirements:[232]

- Open-air runs must be continuously accessible to hens during daylight hours.
- The open-air runs must be mainly covered with vegetation and are not to "be used for other purposes except for orchards, woodland and livestock grazing if the latter is authorized by the competent authorities."
- With certain exceptions, the maximum number of hens in the open-air runs must not exceed 2,500 hens per hectare or one hen per four square meters and the runs may not extend beyond 150 meters from the building in which hens are housed.

---

226. Commission Regulation 589/2008, *supra* note 219, at art. 12(2), Annexes I-II; Council Regulation 1234/2007, *supra* note 220, at Annex XIV; Commission Directive 2002/4, *supra* note 137, at Annex; *see also* CWF, *supra* note 221, at 2; USDA. Foreign Agricultural Service, *Animal Welfare Labeling—European Commission Report* No. E49084, 2 (2009); USDA Foreign Agricultural Service, *Italy Food and Agricultural Import Regulations and Standards Country Report* No. IT4014, 14–15 (2004).
227. Commission Regulation 589/2008, *supra* note 219, at art. 12(2).
228. *Id.* at art. 12(4); *see also* Council Regulation 1234/2007, *supra* note 220, at Annex XIV.
229. Commission Regulation 589/2008, *supra* note 219, at art. 12(2); Council Regulation 2092/91, 1991 O.J. (L 198) 1, art. 2.
230. Council Regulation 1234/2007, *supra* note 220 at Annex XIV; Commission Directive 2002/4, *supra* note 137, at Annex.
231. Commission Directive 2002/4, *supra* note 137, at Annex.
232. Commission Regulation 589/2008, *supra* note 219, at Annex II(1).

"Barn eggs" must be raised in conditions that at least meet the requirements of "alternative systems" under Article 4 of Directive 1999/74/EC described earlier.[233] Eggs labeled as "eggs from caged hens" must be produced in either enriched or unenriched cage systems described in Articles 5 and 6 of Directive 1999/74/EC.[234]

Organic eggs must meet requirements specified in Council Regulation (EC) No. 834/2007 which governs organic livestock production and specifies certain animal welfare conditions for products that are sold as "organic." The recitals to this Regulation state that concern for animal welfare standards is a part of what it means to be "organically" produced: "[o]rganic stock farming should respect high animal welfare standards and meet animals' species-specific behavioral needs while animal-health management should be based on disease prevention. In this respect, particular attention should be paid to housing conditions, husbandry practices and stocking densities."[235] Specific requirements for all organic livestock production under this Regulation include providing "permanent access to open air areas, preferably pasture, whenever weather conditions and the state of the ground allow this …."[236]Other requirements for organic livestock production include that "husbandry practices, including stocking densities, and housing conditions shall ensure that the developmental, physiological and ethological needs of animals are met."[237]

So the EU, through this labyrinth of directives and regulations, has imposed a mandatory labeling scheme for egg shells and packages to give consumers an informed choice between eggs produced under different farming methods, including organic farming. One important question here is whether this labeling scheme has any impact on behavior—have consumers, given this information, made the choice to purchase eggs produced in free range conditions? There is evidence that it may have changed consumer behavior. United Kingdom statistics indicate that from 2001 to 2009 sales of free range eggs increased from 22% of those sold to 38%, while barn eggs percentage has remained the same and cage raised eggs has declined from 70% to 60%.[238] This period covers the period after 2004 when the mandatory egg labeling scheme became effective[239] and is some indication that some consumers have chosen to buy eggs labeled as "free range" once given information on farm production methods.

---

233. *Id.* at Annex II(2).
234. *Id.* at Annex II(3).
235. Council Regulation 834/2007, recitals para. (17), 2007 O.J. (L 189) 1.
236. *Id.* at art. 14(b)(iii).
237. *Id.* at art. 14(b)(ii); *see also* ThePoultrySite, *International Egg and Poultry Review,* Feb. 4, 2009, http://www.thepoultrysite.com/poultrynews/17039/international-egg-and-poultry-review.
238. Royal Society for the Prevention of Cruelty to Animals, *Briefing Note on the European Labeling System* (2010) [hereinafter *Briefing Note*]. Note that percentages described in this RSPCA document do not seem to add up, but the point is that the sales of free range eggs has increased.
239. *Id.*

Claims have been made that, notwithstanding the long road to mandatory farming method labeling of eggs, the EU Commission may be headed toward repealing this requirement. In 2009, Compassion in World Farming reported that the EU Commission was discussing doing away with the labeling requirement.[240] This claim has been denied vociferously by the EU.[241] We will need to wait for further legislative action to determine who is correct on this issue.

There are also additional recent regulations relating to the labeling of organic products. Council Regulations (EC) No. 834/2007/EC and 2008/889/EC set forth standards to be applied to persons selling, labeling and marketing products as "organic."[242] The standards govern things such as how land can be converted so that it is categorized as organic; the type of feed that must be given to animals to be considered organic; and even some provisions relating to the treatment of animals where the products of these animals are sold as organic.[243] In addition, the new regulations introduced a new mandatory label, the "Euro-Leaf," so named for its leaf-like shape, for organic products in the EU on July 1, 2010.[244]

It seems, then, that labeling is becoming a major focus of EU animal welfare regulation and there are discussions about creating yet more labeling schemes for animal products.[245] Depending on the response of consumers, labeling requirements may become a force in changing the treatment of animals in agriculture. Unfortunately, if consumers continue to insist upon the use of animal products, labeling may only have the ultimate effect of allowing some consumers to feel better about their purchases, and thus rationalize their use of animal products. In this sense, labeling may be counterproductive to a long-term goal of ending the use of animals in agriculture altogether. Animals are obviously still being used in animal welfare-labeled products. Allegedly improved conditions do not alter this fact.

C. Swedish Animal Welfare Act and Animal Welfare Ordinance

One country that has not had any difficulty in complying with the directives of the EU relating to animal issues is Sweden. Sweden first passed its Animal Welfare

240. Compassion in World Farming, *EU Egg Labeling Law Under Threat,* Apr. 7, 2009, *available at* http://www.ciwf.org.uk/news/laying_hens/eu_egg_labelling_law_under_threat.aspx.
241. British Free Range Egg Producers Associations, *EU Denies Egg Labelling Claims,* May 11, 2009, *available at* http://www.theranger.co.uk/?show=newsArticle&id=21360.
242. *See* Council Regulation 834/2007, *supra* note 235; Commission Regulation 2008/889, 2008 O.J. (L 250) 1; The Organic Trust, *New Regulations Governing the Organic Sector,* Apr. 6, 2009, http://www.organic-trust.org/news/detail/new_regulations_governing_the_organic_sector [hereinafter *Organic Trust*].
243. *Organic Trust, supra* note 242.
244. *Id.*; Press Release, Europa, New EU Labelling Rules Including New EU Logo Come Into Force on July 1 (June 30, 2010) (available at http://europa.eu/rapid/pressReleasesAction.do?reference=IP/10/861&format=HTML&aged=1&language=EN&guiLanguage=en.
245. *See* CWF, *supra* note 221; *Briefing Note, supra* note 238.

Act (hereinafter "SAWA") and Animal Welfare Ordinance (hereinafter "SAWO") in 1988 (Appendix IV).[246] This, as we have seen earlier, was championed by Astrid Lindgren. The SAWA and the SAWO create a comprehensive law relating to animals used in agriculture, science and entertainment. So let us see how this EU country has dealt with the use of animals in agriculture in a manner that is consistent with the requirements of EU law.

Swedish law originally established a governmental agency, the Animal Welfare Agency ("AWA"), which was committed to evaluating and enforcing the law relating to the treatment of animals.[247] The AWA was created because it was believed that the Swedish Board of Agriculture, which had previously overseen animal welfare legislation, was not giving animal welfare issues sufficient consideration.[248] The AWA now no longer exists and the Board of Agriculture is again in charge of much of the administration of the law and is charged with creating regulations under the law.[249] Given the original reason for creating an AWA, this development should be regarded with some concern when contemplating the evolution of Swedish animal law.

One of the first statements made in the SAWA is a general description of the way animals should be treated in agriculture and elsewhere. It states, in section 2(1) that, "[a]nimals shall be treated well and shall be protected from unnecessary suffering and disease." This then sets the standard that the SAWA and SAWO mean to achieve—humane treatment of animals and prevention of "unnecessary suffering and disease." While this latter language differs slightly from the typical "unnecessary pain and suffering" language we encounter in such statutes, its true meaning conforms to the idea discussed earlier that what, in reality, is prohibited are acts that are "unnecessary" within the context of economic, social and cultural norms of Swedish society. While the social and cultural norms of Swedish society may be more animal-friendly than those of many other countries, the Swedes still use animals for food, scientific purposes and entertainment, just as other nationalities do. That we are not really observing anything different having to do with the use of animals in Sweden is made abundantly clear when we note that section 13 of the SAWA states, "[a]nimals shall be spared unnecessary discomfort and suffering when they are taken to slaughter and when they are slaughtered."

In attempting to avoid "unnecessary suffering," what is the yardstick by which we can measure the suffering of animals, and exactly what are the needs of animals that the law is attempting to serve? We do not see references to "ethological

246. Djurskyddslagen (Svensk författningssamling [SFS] 2009: 303) (Swed.) [hereinafter AWA]; Djurskyddsförordningen (Svensk författningssamling [SFS] 2008:1501) [hereinafter AWO].

247. C. Berg & M. Hammarstrom, *The Process of Building a New Governmental Authority Based on Public Demands for Improved Animal Welfare,* 103 Livestock Sci. Issue 3, 297, 297–300 (2006).

248. *Id.* at 298.

249. The AWA and AWO refer in places too numerous to describe to the power of the Board of Agriculture to issue regulations under the AWA and AWO, and also provide that the Board of Agriculture has responsibilities in approving practices under and granting certain exceptions to the law.

needs," but in section 4(1) of the SAWA it states that "[a]nimals shall be accommodated and handled in an environment that is appropriate for animals and in such a way as to promote their health and permit natural behavior." This reference to "natural behavior" can be viewed as a reference to ethological needs, since what ethology addresses is the behavior of animals in a natural environment. For example, in another context, the social needs of foxes are addressed in SAWO section 9(a)(1) that says that "[f]oxes may only be kept in such a way as to satisfy their need to socialize with other foxes and to move, dig and otherwise occupy themselves." So the SAWA and SAWO purport, at least in certain respects, to require treatment that takes into account the natural social and other behaviors of agricultural animals.

One often hears that Sweden has done away with factory farming. Is this accurate, and if not, what steps have been taken to end intensive farming methods in Sweden? Whether or not it is accurate to say that Sweden has ended factory farming, Sweden has taken strides to provide more space and better living conditions to agricultural animals. For example, "hens for egg production may only be housed in hen-housing systems that satisfy the hens' need for nests, perches and sand baths. The accommodation shall be such as to ensure that mortality and conduct disorders remain at a low level."[250] This effectively ends the use of traditional battery cages in Sweden, but note that it is nonetheless recognized that hens will be kept in conditions that may cause "conduct disorders." This tends to belie the idea that intensive farming methods are ended; if animals were not kept in unnatural conditions, we might rightly assume that they would not experience such behavioral disorders.

Larger animals are required to be given access to the outdoors in the summer. Cattle, other than dairy cattle, must be permitted to go to pasture in the summer and, where possible, pigs must be allowed outdoors in the summer.[251] So while weather conditions in Sweden require agricultural animals to be housed inside during inclement weather, in summer they must not be confined if possible.

The housing in which animals are kept is regulated under the SAWO as well. New construction and modifications of buildings used to accommodate agricultural animals must be approved by the government.[252] Any such construction must meet requirements like providing sufficient space for "all the animals to lie down at the same time and to move freely."[253] Premises are to be designed in a manner allowing "animals to behave naturally."[254] Similarly, new technology used on animals must be approved by the Swedish Board of Agriculture.[255] In the area of such technology and its use, the Swedish law seems to send conflicting messages.

250. AWO, *supra* note 246, at § 9(1).
251. *Id.* at §§ 11–12.
252. *Id.* at § 5.
253. *Id.* at § 1(1).
254. *Id.* at § 1(2).
255. *Id.* at § 8.

The use of electric shocking devices, or cattle prods, is prohibited.[256] The dehorning of cattle is, however, allowed.[257]

Perhaps "inconsistent" is the best description of the Swedish law. While it evidences real concern for animals in allowing space to move and greater freedom for animals when conditions permit, it nonetheless continues the underlying agricultural use of animals that many see as the real crux of the animal welfare problem here. In addition, the Swedish law also continues certain practices, such as the dehorning of cattle, which are considered inhumane. However, Swedish law does meet the requirements of the EU directives and can thereby serve as one model of a law that accomplishes this goal.

IV. SYNTHESIS OF LAWS RELATING TO THE USE OF ANIMALS IN AGRICULTURE

Present laws relating to use of animals in agriculture obviously do not follow the "rights" advocate's path of prohibiting the use of animals in agriculture. Instead, what we observe is the prohibition of certain clearly inhumane practices, requirements relating to feeding and inspecting farmed animals, as well as requirements dictating certain amounts of space for animals to mitigate the wretchedly crowded and cruel conditions that plague factory farms. This is quite evident in the historic evolution of EU law on this subject which reveals progress, based on scientific knowledge, toward increasingly strict rules on animal treatment and the qualifications required of those involved in the farming of animals. In the end, we improve the conditions of the prisoners; yet we do not release them. While many applaud any moves to improve the conditions of animals in agriculture, those interested in ending altogether the use of animals in agriculture must guard against the complacency that arises when people mistakenly believe that we have addressed the plight of animals used in agriculture by virtue of the few rules that presently exist. For those committed to ending the use of animals in agriculture, the work has barely begun and it is clear that the kind of steps taken in the laws we have reviewed will not lead to the liberation of farmed animals from their bondage. Hopefully, with the help of committed activists and compassionate legislators bolder changes will be seen in the future.

---

256. *Id.* at § 15.
257. *Id.* at § 25.

Chapter 4
Animals in Science

I. USE OF ANIMALS IN SCIENCE

A monkey's surgically removed hand and a monkey skull adorned psychologist Edward Taub's desk as paper weights.[1] From these facts, only the surface insensitivity of this man, can be seen. The actual experiments that he carried out, however, show more clearly the depth of human cruelty and irrationality exhibited in the use of animals in science. In Taub's experiments at the Institute for Behavioral Research (IBF) in Maryland, he performed "deafferentation" operations severing the spinal nerves of monkeys so that they would effectively be paralyzed in one or more limbs.[2] Taub then proceeded to attempt to get the monkeys to use their deafferented limbs through the use of "noxious stimuli," like electric shock, and clamping of medical instruments on the monkeys' bodies.[3] PETA founder Alex Pacheco obtained a job at IBF and gathered and ultimately exposed evidence of not only the cruelty of the experiments performed by Taub, but also of the filth and neglect to which the animals were subjected.[4] Pacheco brought that evidence to the Maryland State Police, who raided and closed down Taub's facility based on Pacheco's evidence.[5] Although Taub was prosecuted and convicted for failing to

1. Alex Pacheco & Anna Francione, *The Silver Spring Monkeys*, in IN DEFENSE OF ANIMALS 135, 145 (Peter Singer ed., N.Y.: Basil Blackwell 1985) [hereinafter *Pacheco*].
2. *See id.* at 136; JEFFREY M. SCHWARTZ & SHARON BEGLEY, THE MIND AND THE BRAIN 134–54 (2002) [hereinafter SCHWARTZ].
3. *Pacheco, supra* note 1, at 138–39; SCHWARTZ, *supra* note 2, at 140.
4. *Pacheco, supra* note 1, at 135–44.
5. *Id.* at 141. There are many sources that describe the Silver Spring Monkey experiments and their aftermath, including a video by People for the Ethical Treatment of Animals that contains many images of the IBF operation, as well as a large number of articles, including the following: Robert Reinhold, *Fate of Monkeys, Deformed for Science, Causes Human Hurt After Six Years,* N.Y. TIMES, May 23, 1987, at 18; Neal D. Barnard et al., *NIH Research Protocol for Silver*

provide adequate veterinary care for the monkeys, his conviction was eventually overturned on appeal, on the ground that the state statute under which he was prosecuted did not apply to federally funded experiments.[6]

One nagging question remains on the subject of Taub's experiments: even if he had been successful in showing that excruciating pain can cause paralyzed limbs to come to life again, what possible use could this finding serve? If extreme pain did cause the monkeys to again move their limbs, would we then do the same thing to paralyzed humans? The answer is obvious, and thus, the experiment may rightly be deemed impractical and unnecessary, as well as inhumane and immoral. Nonetheless, Dr. Taub is considered a hero to some in the animal experimentation set. In 1997, he was awarded the American Psychological Society's highest award, which named him a William James Fellow.[7] This award was based on supposed findings about "massive cortical reorganization" which he claimed resulted, at least in part, from his Silver Spring monkey experiments.[8] Taub is also credited with "constraint-induced movement therapy" where stroke patients are forced to use limbs affected by a stroke via restraint of their useful limbs.[9] Again, according to Taub, this allegedly useful therapy resulted in part from his Silver Spring monkey experiments.[10]

As for the monkeys, the remainder of their lives after IBF did not turn out so well. Even though the National Institutes of Health, who had control of the monkeys, claimed that no further invasive research would be performed on them, most of the monkeys were nonetheless subjected to further experiments and were subsequently euthanized.[11] This is not the only example of seemingly mindless abuse of animals in medical, psychological and other animal research; others are described later in this chapter. But the magnitude and nature of the torture of animals in the name of science is not something those involved in this industry really want the public to know.

One need only consider that there were estimates in 2005 of between 115,300,000–127,000,000 animals used in experiments worldwide[12] to conclude

---

Spring Monkeys: A Case of Scientific Misconduct (pts.I–II), 2 Persps. on Med. Res. (Americans for Medical Advancement 1990), *available at* http://www.curedisease.net/reports/Perspectives/vol_2_1990/SilverSprings1.html; Associated Press, *2 Lab Monkeys Killed After Top Court Acts*, N.Y. Times, Apr. 14, 1991.

6. Taub v. State, 463 A.2d 819, 819–22 (Md. 1983).
7. Association for Psychological Science, *William James Fellow Award 1997*, "Edward Taub," http://www.psychologicalscience.org/awards/james/citations/taub.cfm (last visited May 14, 2010).
8. U. Ala. Birmingham, Dept. Psychol., *Dr. Edward Taub,* http://www.psy.uab.edu/taub.htm (last visited May 14, 2010).
9. Schwartz, *supra* note 2, at 160.
10. *Id.* at 159–61.
11. Jordan Curnutt, Animals and the Law 53–57 (2001); Schwartz, *supra* note 2, at 153–58.
12. *See* K. Taylor et al., *Estimates for Worldwide Laboratory Animal Use in 2005*, 36 ATLA 327 (2008) (calculating the worldwide number of animals used to be over 115.2 million); Andrew Knight, *127 Million Non-Human Vertebrates Used Worldwide for Scientific Purposes in 2005*,

that perhaps some of these experiments may be unnecessary and lacking in serious scientific value under any analysis. Indeed, the list of cruel, wacky and downright insane animal experiments throughout history is a long one. Here are some examples:

- One bizarre type of experiment is the creation of Siamese twins by sewing two otherwise separate animals together, which is called Parabiosis. Frequently, it is found that the newly created "twins" attack each other. Experimenters found a solution for this; they sew the animals' cheeks to their paws so that fighting is impossible. There is no scientific benefit in these experiments since it is known that what will occur in these experiments is that each animal's immune system will reject the new animal.[13]
- After cutting off their tails and blinding them, an experiment placed cats in a revolving drum to determine how long they could stay awake before dying.[14]
- The Royal Veterinary College in London performed experiments where 4 mm diameter Teflon probes were inserted in cat's vaginas until the cats screamed in pain. This experiment was repeated with 1 mm diameter needles, inserted up to 40 mm deep in the cats' vaginas.[15]
- In 1994, after making rats drunk, experimenters made rats "walk along a swaying horizontal bar." The startling result? Alcohol was found to impair rats' performance in proportion to the amount of alcohol consumed.[16]
- In another experiment, the amazing conclusion was reached that dogs with full stomachs do not eat as much as normal. As a continuation of this profound experiment, some of the dogs' throats were surgically slit, causing food eaten to fall through the slit rather than pass into the digestive system. The information gained from the experiment? It was discovered that dogs with slit throats eat longer than ones lacking slit throats.[17]
- Electrodes were attached to seven-day-old kittens in another crazy experiment where the kittens were shocked up to 700 times per day while nursing. The mother cat, after figuring out what was occurring, tried to stop the torture by trying to claw the experimenter, bite the wires delivering the shocks and flee from her kittens when they had wires attached to their legs. When the wires were removed, she would then feed and care for the kittens.[18]
- Isolation of animals in experiments has a rather long history. In one example, dogs were kept in complete isolation from birth until the age of eight

---

36 ATLA 494 (2008) (evaluating Taylor et al.'s conservative estimate of 115.2 million and calculating a more likely figure to be 127 million).

13. HANS RUESCH, SLAUGHTER OF THE INNOCENT 71 (2003).
14. *Id.* at 104.
15. DR. TONY PAGE, VIVISECTION UNVEILED 3 (1997).
16. *Id.*
17. RUESCH, *supra* note 13, at 107.
18. *Id.* at 118–19.

months. Once released from isolation it was found, oddly enough, that they behaved quite differently from dogs that had not been isolated. For example, isolated dogs often froze when pain was inflicted. Excited by these amazing results, the experimenter, Ronald Melzack, then held lit matches under the dogs' noses, chased them about with motorized toy cars delivering 1,500 volt shocks to the dogs and stabbed the dogs with dissection needles. For his trouble, Mr. Melzack was given nearly $60,000 in Federal grants by the United States government.[19]

- German experimenter Mortiz Schiff cut open dogs, sewed their intestines closed, forced sand and pebbles into their stomachs, and then poured boiling water down their throats. The purpose of this experiment? To determine how long death would take in these circumstances.[20]

This list of strange and often macabre experiments could be extended for many pages; but this is not the purpose of my stating these examples. Rather, even those who subscribe to a utilitarian view of animal experimentation, *i.e.*, that animal experiments can be justified if the alleged benefits of the experiments outweigh the suffering of animals, would find many, if not all, of the experiments described above to be troubling because of the lack of demonstrable benefit.

But the problems inherent to animal experimentation are not only confined to senseless experiments; there are also what can be called "institutional" problems with much of the animal experimentation that takes place. Some of these "institutional" problems are the following:

- Many experiments are repeated when data already exists on the issue being researched. For example, many countries require that certain drugs or products be tested on animals before they are introduced to the markets.[21] Thus, the same product may be tested in many different countries, when results are already available from tests done elsewhere.[22] In addition, when patents on drugs expire or generic drugs begin competing with an established drug, pharmaceutical companies often create a new drug, highly similar to the earlier drug, and do animal tests to validate the new nearly identical drug,[23] often as required by law. Manufacturers also frequently test products on animals to protect themselves, even if the

19. *Id.* at 131–32.
20. *Id.* at 91.
21. *See* KATZUNG & TREVOR'S PHARMACOLOGY 37 (Anthony J. Trevor et al. eds., McGraw-Hill Medical 8th ed. 2007).
22. PETA Media Center, *Government Required Animal Testing: Overview* http://www.peta.org/mc/factsheet_display.asp?ID=125 (last visited Sept. 4, 2010); Pandora Pound et al., *Where Is The Evidence That Animal Research Benefits Humans?*, 328 BMJ 514, 516–17 (2004); Peter Singer, *Experiments On Animals,* 299 BMJ 1238 (1989) [hereinafter Singer 1989].
23. *See* KAREN DAWN, THANKING THE MONKEY 222–23 (2008); Singer 1989, *supra* note 22.

constituent parts of the product have previously been tested or even if the product has been tested by others.[24]

- Inadequate review by presently existing regulatory bodies may result in needlessly repeated experiments and the approval of experiments with little or no scientific merit. For example, at the University of Washington, infant monkey isolation experiments intended to induce self-mutilation by the monkeys were approved without modification by a United States Institutional Animal Care and Use Committee ("IACUC").[25] In fact, a project of a similar nature was already underway and was unknown to the IACUC.[26] In other cases, experiments that lack scientific merit are approved. For instance:

> The Panel [of former members of United States IACUCs] cited proposals which would be considered cruel by most people and which had little scientific merit, but were approved by IACUCs anyway ... A protocol designed to teach students the effects of alcohol on short-term memory entailed forcing animals to ingest a solution of alcohol and water for up to four weeks, with this solution being the animals' only source of fluid ... Experiments were also approved in which substances were to be administered to animals until 50% of them died (the Lethal Dose 50 (LD 50 test)); cocaine was given to pigs and piglets; insects were fed on the shaven skin of rabbits; and pigs were bled to the verge of death and revived.[27]

- The failure to publish results of animal studies when they fail is also a source of repetition of experiments and has been described as "unethical."[28] Failure to publish such results can cause the failed experiment to be repeated thus wasting both animals and economic resources.
- In education, PhD candidates in study areas involving medical research, like pharmacology, toxicology, physiology and psychology are often required to participate in animal studies while in graduate school and, after graduation, many of the former students slightly modify research on which they had worked earlier and do it again since they find this an easy way to get grant money.[29] Here we have what is essentially repetition of experiments that have already been done; wasteful both economically and in terms of animals.

---

24. *See* DAWN, *supra* note 23, at 222–24; C. RAY GREEK ET AL., SACRED COWS AND GOLDEN GEESE 48, 58 (Continuum International Publishing Group, Inc. 2002).
25. Physicians Committee for Responsible Medicine, *Animal Care and Use Committees: Structural Problems Impair Usefulness,* http://www.pcrm.org/resch/anexp/IACUC.html (last visited May 15, 2010) [hereinafter PCRM Animal Care].
26. *Id.*
27. *Id.*
28. Malcom R. MacLeod et al., Letter to the Editor, *Surveying the Literature from Animal Experiments,* 331 BMJ 110 (2005).
29. GREEK ET AL., *supra* note 24, at 81.

- While it can be said that the point of PhD student research is the undertaking of new original research, are there no other ways to train PhD students in sciences like pharmacology, toxicology, physiology and psychology than through participation in animal experiments? It seems that even those who believe that animal experiments are useful and morally justifiable might be persuaded that one does not actually have to do an animal experiment in order to know how to do such an experiment. Could it not be taught by computer or other types of modeling of the process required for an experiment? Moreover, might the PhD students' time be better served doing theses on existing research in a particular area to compile all of the results that have already been obtained, so that future experiments on issues already resolved would not be necessary? As is discussed in more detail below, many scientists argue that systematic and meta-reviews of prior animal experiments could yield useful data that could reduce the number of experiments undertaken. Would this not be the most economically and ethically efficient way to proceed, assuming we believe that experimentation can be ethically permitted at all? One response that scientists might have to this is that the answer is "no." Undertaking new and original research is considered the essence of PhD education in many areas of science. But is this really necessary to accomplish the educational goals sought? Moreover, one problem with the whole concept of requiring "new and original research" is that without adequate systematic and meta-analysis of prior research, a scientist can never be sure that his or her research is "original."
- Note that there may be institutional reasons we do not want to be economically efficient here. Animal experimentation is big business. The production of animals and related products for experiments is estimated to be worth anywhere from one hundred billion to one trillion dollars worldwide per year.[30] Another multibillion dollar industry is the actual performance of animal experiments.[31] A lot of jobs, careers and fat securities portfolios would disappear if animal experimentation were ended. Thus, to try to end animal experiments or even reduce the amount of animal experimentation in the world will hit very heavy institutional headwinds in an industry with this kind of economic and political clout.

But there is more. There are those who argue that it is not clear that animal experiments do actually produce useful information. For instance, there are many well-known cases of the inefficacy of animal experiments, most of which are attempts to extrapolate from animal studies the likely effects of a substance or tool on

30. *See* GREEK ET AL., *supra* note 24, at 92–93.
31. *See* DONNA YARRI, THE ETHICS OF ANIMAL EXPERIMENTATION 14 (2005); Michael A. Budkie, *The Animal Experimentation Scandal: An Audit of the National Institutes of Health Funding of Animal Experimentation*, "Audit Findings," *available at* http://www.all-creatures.org/wlalw/report-anexp-audit.html (last visited May 31, 2010).

humans. Thalidomide was tested on animals and thereby determined safe before it was used on humans with demonstrably horrifying results.[32] Pregnant women who took the drug often had horribly deformed, limbless children as a result of the drug.[33] The Thalidomide disaster was, ironically, the impetus for making animal testing obligatory and, perhaps even more ironically, if the drug were again "assessed exclusively on its results in such tests it would still be passed today."[34] If penicillin had been tested only on guinea pigs or hamsters it never would have been provided to humans since penicillin is poisonous to guinea pigs and hamsters.[35] Similarly, aspirin fails in animal tests,[36] as does digitalis (a heart drug),[37] and insulin, which causes animal birth defects.[38] One can, of course, respond to these cases of failed animal experiments by saying that these are simply anecdotal cases of problems with animal experiments and there have been thousands of other cases where it appears that animal experiments have successfully analyzed substances.

There are nonetheless scientists and other commentators who challenge the underlying hypothesis that animal experiments can and do provide useful information. The utility of animal experiments is frequently supported by the argument that such experiments can be used as predictive models for the likely effects of substances and medical devices on humans. It is clear that this assumption is often made in arguments relating to the efficacy of animal experiments and is an assumption commonly made in the lay community. Is it true that animal experiments can be effectively used to predict human responses to substances and devices? This issue is discussed at length in a recent article written by Niall Shanks, a philosopher of science, Ray Greek, an anesthesiologist, and Jean Greek, a veterinarian (hereinafter the authors of this article will collectively be referred to as "Shanks"):

---

32. Niall Shanks et al., *Are Animal Models Predictive for Humans?* 4 PHIL., ETHICS, AND HUMAN. IN MED. (2009) 10–11 (page numbers are to online pdf publication) [hereinafter Shanks et al.]; *see* GREEK ET AL., *supra* note 24, at 44–47. There is actually some controversy about exactly when Thalidomide was first tested on animals. Some claim that it did not occur until after the drug was found to have problems. The better evidence is that the drug was tested before it was released. Ray Greek has stated, notwithstanding claims that thalidomide was not tested on animals prior to its release, that this:

> is a gross misstatement. Since animal testing was already the established protocol … [a]nd according to a German medical journal of the epoch, toxicity tests on animals were conducted on pregnant rodents and phocomelia did not occur. Is it controversial whether tests specific to teratogenicity were performed, though data from Germany suggests they were. Even Time magazine February 23, 1962, stated that thalidomide was released "after three years of animal tests". GREEK ET AL., *supra* note 24, at 44–47.

33. GREEK ET AL., *supra* note 24, at 44–47.
34. Kathy Archibald, *Animal Testing: Science or Fiction?*, http://www.gan.ca/lifestyle/animal+testing/articles+on+animal+research/index.en.html (last visited Sept. 20, 2010).
35. PIETRO CROCE, VIVISECTION OR SCIENCE 16 (1999); PAGE, *supra* note 15, at 104.
36. *See* RUESCH, *supra* note 13, at 369.
37. *Id.* at 9, 238.
38. *See* GREEK ET AL., *supra* note 24, at 48–52.

> There is an assumption that has taken on the trappings of a theory or perhaps an overarching hypothesis in the animal model community that results from experiments on animals can be directly applied to humans; that animal models are predictive. This has resulted in an unquestioned methodological approach; using animals as surrogate humans.
>
> ....
>
> When a concept such as "Animal models can predict human response" is accepted as true, it is not functioning as a hypothesis. We have referred to this as an overarching hypothesis but could have easily referred to it as an unfounded assumption. An assumption or overarching hypothesis might in fact be true but its truth must be proven.[39]

One of the main points of the analysis in Shanks is that the idea that animal experimentation models are "predictive" of human results is actually a scientific hypothesis, albeit one that has not yet been proven to be true.

What is it to say that "x" is "predictive" of "y"? Without any scientific training, most people would say that "x" is predictive of "y" if, whenever "x" is present, there is a high probability of "y." And this is, indeed, what Shanks concludes:

> If a modality such as animal testing or using animals to predict pathophysiology in human disease is said to be a predictive modality, then any data generated from said modality should have a very high probability of being true in humans. Animal models of disease and drug response fail this criterion.
>
> In medicine, even positive predictive values of .99 may be inadequate for some tests and animal models do not even roughly approximate that. Therefore, animal models are not predictors of human response.[40]

So what would a "predictive" scientific model look like? The predictive value of most medical studies in the fields of toxicology, pathophysiology and pharmacology are evaluated by statistics. Such statistics are produced by looking at the sensitivity, specificity, positive predictive value (PPV) and negative predictive value (NPV) of a test.[41] To be predictive for humans, according to Shanks, animal tests must have a PPV and a NPV in the 0.95–1.0 range.[42]

Existing data reveals that animal tests do not fall within this range. Shanks studied testing data for six drugs that had been tested on both animals and humans; what was found was that overall, these tests on animals only predicted results for humans 31% of the time:

> The animal tests were shown to have a sensitivity of 0.52 and the positive predictive value was 0.31. The sensitivity is about what one would expect from a coin toss and the PPV less. Not what is considered predictive in the

39. Shanks et al., *supra* note 32, at 18.
40. *Id.*; *see also* Pound et al., *supra* note 22, at 514.
41. Shanks et al., *supra* note 32, at 5.
42. *Id.*

scientific sense of the word. Values of this nature are more appropriately referred to as guesses.

....

[T]here is little correlation between animal and human data .... The patterns exhibited by both are what are frequently referred to as a shotgun pattern; meaning that if one fired a shotgun full of bird shot at a target one would see the same pattern. No precision and no accuracy.[43]

For example, although "rats and humans are 90% identical at the genetic level," 90% of drugs safe for animals fail in human clinical trials, resulting in a predictive power of only 10%.[44] Animals predict carcinogens in humans so ineffectively that both the EPA and the World Health Organization are forced to either over-include useful chemicals as possible carcinogens or exclude harmful chemicals from their respective carcinogen databases. Indeed, in 1980 there were approximately 1,600 chemicals known to cause cancer in mice and other rodents, but only about 15 known human carcinogens.[45] United States Secretary of Health and Human Services Mike Leavitt stated in 2007, "[c]urrently, nine out of ten experimental drugs fail in clinical studies because we cannot accurately predict how they will behave in people based on laboratory and animal studies."[46]

There are, however, questions that can be raised relating to Shanks' analysis. Scientists involved in animal experimentation do not, in fact, expect there to be anything like a one-to-one correspondence between results in animals and results in humans. The process of analyzing the characteristics and likely effects of a substance or device on humans involves an often long iterative process that proceeds through a number of steps. This process will often begin with *in silico* (computer modeling) analyses and *in vitro* (test tube) tests, and then go on to animal testing and human trials of the substance or device. In this process, scientists do not expect to get definitive results from any one test, including animal tests, and there may be a number of animal tests using different species performed on a substance or device. Nonetheless, this process creates a fund of knowledge at each stage that will inform the scientists on whether to go on to the next step of the process.

---

43. *Id.* at 6. Note that it is the positive predictive value and negative predictive value, not the sensitivity or specificity of a model, that is important in determining its predictive value as described in Shanks:

> The sensitivity of a test is the probability (measured on a scale from 0.0 to 1.0) of a positive test among people whose test should be positive ... Specificity is the probability of a negative test among people whose test should be negative .... The positive predictive value of a test is the proportion of people with positive test results who are actually positive. The negative predictive value is the proportion of people with negative test results who are actually negative ... [I]n order for a test to be useful given the demanding standards of medical practice ... it needs to be [sic] have PPV and NPV in at least the .95 to 1.0 range. *Id.* at 5.

44. *Id.* at 7 (quoting U. Sankar, citing Howard Jacob).
45. *Id.* at 12.
46. *Id.* at 4.

At the animal testing stage of this process scientists do not expect to get results predictive of human responses at the 0.95–1.00 level suggested by Shanks. Consider, for example, that even a test of a substance within a species could have a PPV or a NPV of less than the 0.95–1.00 level Shanks indicates is necessary to be "predictive" when compared to another identical test within the same species. What scientists do expect is to get evidence that is suggestive and informative about the likely effects of the substance or device. Indeed, Shanks admits that "studying animals can lead to new knowledge. This point is not in dispute."[47] It can then be argued that the "new knowledge" that is gained through animal experiments, though not predictive at the level Shanks argues is necessary, is precisely the kind of knowledge scientists expect to gain in these experiments and is valuable as a step in determining the efficacy of devices, pharmaceuticals and other substances. In other words, it can be argued that the 0.95–1.00 NPVs and PPVs required by Shanks to meet the criteria of having "predictive" value is not something that any scientist suggests is possible or achievable in animal experiments. But this does not mean that animal experiments do not provide information that is useful in the iterative process of determining the characteristics of substances and devices tested.

Nonetheless, whether Shanks is using the term "predictive" in the way scientists involved in animal experimentation would use it or not, the question remains—is the creation of the fund of knowledge obtained through animal experiments justifiable even from a utilitarian perspective of benefit to humans and other animals? The result of Shank's analysis is clear; the "predictive" value of the animal experiments studied is quite low. And this is exactly why we often need to do multiple animals tests with multiple species. Is the "suggestive and informative" evidence obtained in these types of experiments with such low predictive value for humans worth the price in animal suffering and economic resources? The fact that multiple animal tests must be performed to get any useful information actually seems to cut against continuing such tests. The price in animal suffering and gold is even higher than one might first assume as a result of the low predictive value of animal tests and the concomitant need for multiple animal tests. This should make the utilitarian in each of us squirm.

It is not only Shanks, however, that challenges the efficacy of animal experiments. Similar conclusions by scientists questioning the efficacy of animal tests can be found in other studies,[48] many of which point to methodological and other problems discovered in numerous animal tests. For example, Italian pathologist Pietro Croce has argued, in line with the Shanks thesis, that animal experimentation data "cannot be applied to humans because of the biological differences between animals and humans and because the results of animal experiments are

47. *Id.* at 9.

48. The Shanks article discusses a number of scientific analyses questioning the efficacy of animal experiments. *Id.* at 6–12.

too dependent on the type of animal model used."[49] Croce's conclusion is buttressed by some of the results discussed earlier relating to the wild variation in results that can be obtained with a particular substance when it is tested on different species. Note also, that given this fact, it is possible for experimenters to make choices of animal species used in experiments in order to obtain a desired result.

In an analysis of experimental methodology, Pablo Perel et al., compared results of six kinds of treatments in animal tests and human clinical trials, and found concordance between animal tests and human clinical trials in only three of the six.[50] This study also found that most of the animal experiments were carried out in a methodologically poor fashion, with randomization and blinding used only rarely in the experimental protocols.[51] The use of randomization and blinding in experiments is important in that "it has been shown that animal experiments carried out without either are five times more likely to report a positive treatment effect."[52] Perel is not the only author to reveal poor scientific and statistical methodology in animal experiments:

> There is evidence that poor experimental design and inappropriate statistical analysis of experimental results leads to inefficient use of animals and scientific resources in toxicological research. Previous studies of statistical methods used in other areas of biomedical research reveal similar findings. In some cases, the level of statistical expertise appears to be so low that investigators are either unaware of the potential value of obtaining statistical advice, or they are unable to obtain appropriate statistical advice because there are so few biometricians with experience in their field of interest.[53]

Other systematic reviews of animal experiments have revealed other sorts of methodological deficiencies. There have been cases where animal tests of substances have gone on simultaneously with human clinical trials.[54] Pandora Pound et al., point out the error in such a methodology: "Animal experiments can inform decisions about what treatments should be taken forward in clinical trials only if their results are valid and precise and if the animal studies are conducted before clinical trials are started."[55] So it does not make scientific sense to conduct human clinical

49. Ian Roberts et al., *Does Animal Experimentation Inform Human Healthcare? Observations from a Systematic Review of International Animal Experiments on Fluid Resuscitation,* 324 BMJ 474, 474 (2002).
50. Pablo Perel et al., *Comparison of Treatment Effects Between Animal Experiments and Clinical Trials: Systematic Review*, BMJ, doi:10.1136/bmj.39048.407928.BE (2006) [hereinafter Perel et al.].
51. *Id.* For definitions of "randomization" and "blinding," *see* Valerie J. Easton & John H. McColl, *Statistics Glossary*, http://www.stats.gla.ac.uk/steps/glossary/alphabet.html (last visited Jan. 30 2011).
52. *Id.*
53. Joanne Zurlo et al., *The Three R's: The Way Forward*, 104 ENVTL. HEALTH PERSP. NO. 8 (1996), *available at* John Hopkins University Center for Alternatives to Animal Testing, http://caat.jhsph.edu/publications/Articles/3r.html (citations omitted) [hereinafter Zurlo et al.].
54. Pound et al., *supra* note 22, at 516.
55. *Id.*

trials at the same time as animal testing. Similarly, Pound identified cases where negative results were obtained in animal experiments and yet human trials went ahead anyway.[56] In these circumstances one must ask why the animal experiments were performed at all since they were apparently ignored in proceeding with human trials.[57]

Even if one knows that a substance is harmful to animals and is likely also harmful to humans, predicting the risk presented by human exposure to the substance is problematic.[58] For example, there is evidence that mice are more sensitive to radiation than humans.[59] So how can we measure risk to humans through tests on mice? The answer would appear to be that we cannot. Overall, there is little clear evidence on how we can estimate risks to humans from animal tests.[60] This is a result of a lack of data and studies of interspecies risk comparisons.[61]

Some recent real world results also call into question the efficacy of animal experiments. For example, it has been pointed out that "[m]ost of us know that cancer, heart disease and stroke are the leading causes of death in the West. But many people would be surprised by the next biggest killer: side effects of prescription medicines." One example of this is what has been called by the Associate Safety Director of the United States Food and Drug Administration the "single greatest drug-safety catastrophe in the history of the world," the estimated 140,000 heart attacks and strokes caused by the arthritis drug Vioxx.[62] This drug appeared safe, even possibly beneficial to the heart in animal experiments.[63] And it is not just Vioxx that has had these types of problems. Drugs such as Cerestat, Maxipost, Zendra, Lotrafiban, Gavestinel, Nimodipine and Clomethiazole have passed animal studies and resulted in injuries and death to humans.[64] Indeed, it has been alleged that pharmaceutical companies overuse animal experimentation data to reduce the number of more costly human clinical trials required to ensure the safety of products.[65]

There are, of course, many scientists who believe that animal tests provide useful, "predictive" data that can then be extrapolated to humans.[66] Many scientists cite the Olson Study to claim that animal experiments are predictive of human results. This study finds a sensitivity correlation of 70% between animal and human studies, and on this basis claims that animal experiments are predictive for

56. *Id.*
57. *See id.*
58. *See* Stephen L. Brown et al., *Review of Interspecies Risk Comparisons*, 8 Regulatory Toxicology & Pharmacology 191, 191–206 (1988).
59. *Id.* at 194.
60. *See id.* at 201–04.
61. *Id.*
62. Archibald, *supra* note 34.
63. *Id.*
64. *Id.*
65. *Id*
66. Note also that these people generally earn their livelihoods from animal experiments.

humans.[67] Note first, however, that this correlation is a sensitivity correlation, not a PPV or NPV of a test, and even a PPV number at this level is not even close to what was previously described as "predictability" by Shanks.[68] Shanks has pointed to other reasons to be skeptical about the Olson Study:[69]

- It was conducted by the pharmaceutical industry.
- The report itself confesses it is "not, as a matter of fact, up to th[e] task" of measuring predictive reliability of animal models.
- Terminology again—the study invents the term "true positive concordance rate" and then relies on it in its analysis. True positive concordance rate is actually nothing more than sensitivity and this is only one of the statistical elements to be factored into measuring predictive power.
- It studies only clinical trial drugs, and leaves out scores of drugs that do not make it that far in the process.
- It creates a distinction in side effects ("major" and "lesser") but fails to count the lesser side effects.
- Even ignoring all the above points, the sensitivity correlation measured a predictive power of 70%—which is still far too low to be considered predictive for human responses.

Even scientists who are favorably inclined toward animal experiments frequently express concerns about their accuracy. Often they point to methodological and communications failures among scientists as being responsible for these concerns.[70] It has been suggested that the usefulness of animal experiments could be improved if there were better communication between animal experimenters and those doing human studies.[71] Further, it is claimed that there is a paucity of "meta" studies (a statistical methodology for compiling existing research about a given topic to focus and refine further research) on the effectiveness of animal experiments, which, if properly conducted, could improve the relevance of animal studies.[72] This meta-analysis, which effectively pools the results of a number of experiments to increase the statistical power of these studies, is a methodology that can be effectively used to reduce the number of experiments performed.

There is one kind of animal experiment that one could argue must be useful—an experiment on a particular species of animal for the benefit of that species of animal; an intra-species test. If, for example, I experimentally test a drug meant for dogs on dogs, surely I am getting useful information. While in a purely

---

67. Shanks et al., *supra* note 32, at 16.
68. *Id.*
69. *Id.* at 16–18.
70. Perel et al., *supra* note 50; *see also* Roberts et al., *supra* note 49.
71. Perel et al., *supra* note 50.
72. Roberts et al., *supra* note 49, at 476; Perel et al., *supra* note 50 (commenting on the efficacy of systematic reviews of animal research to facilitate the usefulness of this research). For a discussion of meta-analysis *see* James Neill, *Meta-Analysis: Research Methodology*, May 10, 2006, http://wilderdom.com/research/meta-analysis.html.

scientific sense this may be true, even a utilitarian would want to know that the benefit of the test justified the suffering of the dogs used in the experiment. Variation exists, both genetic and physiological, among the individual members of a species; one individual member of a species, therefore, may react differently to a substance or device than another. In the United States, to understand this principle one need look no further than one's favorite pharmaceutical TV commercial, where in a hushed and calm voice the announcer presents a sometimes eerily long list of possible side effects attendant to the product. Of course, if one performs enough intra-species experiments, one will likely discover many intra-species differences and dangers. The question remains, however: is the knowledge gained in this way worth the suffering involved?

Moreover, if one subscribes to a moral theory that recognizes an animal's right to bodily security and to be free from human imposed harm, the usefulness, or lack thereof, of animal experiments is immaterial. Animal experiments are simply never justified under this rights view, because animals, like humans, have a right not to be harmed for the benefit of others. It is only if one subscribes to or uses a theory such as utilitarianism, which decides moral issues on the basis of the consequences of an act, that this issue concerning the efficacy of animal experiments becomes relevant. With this brief introduction to animal experimentation, let us look at some regulatory schemes that have been created to control animal experiments.

II. TYPES OF ANIMAL EXPERIMENTATION REGULATORY SCHEMES

Different countries have developed varying strategies for regulating experimentation on animals. While some of these schemes combine elements of the different strategies, we can identify the following as typical strategies that have been used:

- *Direct Government Regulation and Licensing:* A number of countries have adopted schemes creating governmental agencies and bureaucracies to regulate experimentation on animals. These regulatory designs focus on government licensing and approval of experimenters and experiments. They do not rely on the experimenters themselves to police scientific procedures used.
- *Ethical Committee Approval Schemes:* Under this type of regulatory mechanism, ethical committees are required to either review or specifically approve animal experiments, after consideration of animal welfare issues. Some of the schemes use governmentally established ethical committees, while others rely on committees that the experimenters themselves are required to create. Committee schemes often grant power to the committees to control and terminate experiments, while committees in the United States under the United States Animal Welfare Act are primarily limited to reviewing experiments and advising experimenters, and cannot actually

control or terminate any experiment, although they can suspend experiments in some circumstances.

- *Self-Regulation by Experimenters:* This regulatory method relies on the experimenters to regulate themselves through procedures established by the scientific community, or suggested or required by governmental agencies. While this appears to allow the foxes to police henhouse, there are those who believe that the Australian scheme, which provides for a committee system implemented by experimenters, is perhaps the best regulatory scheme that presently exists.

In analyzing the following regulatory laws, we should keep these categories in mind, and observe how these schemes have been used and combined by different countries.

III. ANIMALS AND SCIENCE: THE REGULATORY UNIVERSE

A. THE EU REGULATORY SCHEME

1. EU Council Directive 86/609/EEC

In the area of animal experimentation, we are again able to see the process of evolution of an animal welfare regulatory scheme in the EU and some of the difficulties, social, scientific, political, and economic, that arise in attempting to pass animal-related legislation. The presently effective primary EU regulation of animal experiments is Council Directive 86/609/EEC, which is based on, and owes much of its language to, the European Convention for the Protection of Vertebrate Animals Used for Experimental and Other Scientific Purposes.[73] This Directive's days are numbered, however, since in September 2010, the European Parliament passed Council Directive 2010/63/EU which repeals Council Directive 86/609/EEC and changes in very substantial ways the regulation of animal experimentation in the EU.[74] The repeal of Council Directive 86/609/EEC will be effective

73. European Convention for the Protection of Vertebrate Animals Used for Experimental and Other Scientific Purposes, *opened for signature* Mar. 18, 1986, 170 Europ. T.S.; *see also Commission Proposal for a Directive of the European Parliament and of the Council on the Protection of Animals Used for Scientific Purposes*, COM (2008) 543 final [hereinafter Commission Proposal 543].

74. Council Directive 2010/63, 2010 O.J (L 276) 33 [hereinafter Council Directive 2010/63/EU.]; European Commission, Environment: Laboratory Animals, http://ec.europa.eu/environment/chemicals/lab_animals/home_en.htm (last visited Sept. 27, 2010) [hereinafter Laboratory Animals]; Press Release, Europa, EU Revises Laws To Better Protect Animals Used in Scientific Experiments (Sept. 9, 2010), *available at* http://europa.eu/rapid/pressReleasesAction.do?reference=IP/10/1105&format=HTML&aged=0&language=EN&guiLanguage=en [hereinafter EU Revises Laws]; Memorandum 10/398 on Questions and Answers on the New Directive for the Protection of Animals Used for Scientific Purposes (Sept. 9, 2010), *available at* http://europa.eu/rapid/

January 1 2013 (with the exception of Article 13 of the directive which will be repealed as of May 10, 2013) and EU countries will be required to adopt and publish laws conforming to the new Directive by November 10, 2012.[75] So the evolution of legislation on experimentation in the EU provides an opportunity to observe how time, as well as social, scientific, political and economic issues, have shaped a very recent piece of EU legislation on animal experimentation.

I begin this look at the development of EU law on animal experiments with presently effective Council Directive 86/609/EEC, which has as one of its stated purposes a desire to remedy disparities in Member State laws relating to animal experiments that "may affect the functioning of the common market."[76] It also states the goal of ensuring that "the number of animals used for experimental or other scientific purposes is reduced to the minimum, that such animals are adequately cared for, that no pain, suffering, distress or lasting harm are inflicted unnecessarily and ensur[ing] that, where unavoidable, these shall be kept to a minimum."[77] As we have seen many times previously, the "unnecessary pain, etc." language is used again; but what we also know is that this language effectively gives free reign to humans to do whatever they want so long as there is some human utility to be gained by the action in question. Once again, it seems that only utterly gratuitous suffering is slated for prohibition.

The Directive applies to animal experiments designed to determine the safety of foodstuffs and other products; to prevent, assess and detect disease and physiological conditions of plants, animals and humans; and to protect the natural environment for the health and welfare of humans and animals.[78] The animals that the Directive covers are live vertebrate animals including certain larval forms of vertebrates, but "excluding foetal or embryonic forms."[79] We also see that those who are regulated include the experimenters themselves, as well as breeding and supply establishments.[80]

But what is an "experiment"? This is defined as:

> [A]ny use of an animal for experimental or other scientific purposes which may cause it pain, suffering, distress or lasting harm, including any course of action intended, or liable, to result in the birth of an animal in any such condition, but excluding the least painful methods accepted in modern practice … of killing or marking an animal.[81]

---

pressReleasesAction.do?reference=MEMO/10/398&format=HTML&aged=0&language=EN&guiLanguage=en [hereinafter Q & A].

75. Council Directive 2010/63/EU, *supra* note 74 at Art. 62.
76. Council Directive 86/609, recitals, 1986 O.J (L 358) 1, 1–28 [hereinafter Council Directive 86/609].
77. *Id.*
78. *Id.* at art. 3.
79. *Id.* at art. 2(a).
80. *Id.* at arts. 7, 14–15.
81. *Id.* at art. 2(d).

Effectively, an animal becomes subject to an experiment only when it is subjected to some procedure that may cause it pain, suffering, or lasting harm. It does not cover animals that are killed so their organs, tissues, or cells may be harvested.[82] Thus, only painful animal experiments are regulated; if you are not causing pain, suffering, or lasting harm, the Directive does not apply.

With respect to experimenters, the Directive requires that all experiments be carried out by "competent authorized persons" or by persons under the control of such persons.[83] All the people who carry out, participate in or care for animals used in experiments must have "appropriate education and training."[84] Those who carry out or supervise the experiments "shall have received instruction in a scientific discipline relevant to the experimental work undertaken and … have satisfied the governmental authority that they have attained a level of training sufficient for carrying out their tasks."[85] There are two things to notice about this. First, there is a requirement that there be a governmental "authority" responsible for supervising animal experiments and the persons who conduct them. The second interesting aspect is that this requirement explicitly gives license to "scientists" to conduct experiments; if a non-scientist were to conduct the kind of experiments that are often performed by scientists they would be violating this law and likely other laws relating to cruelty to animals generally. So "scientists," those who have successfully concluded some course of training in science, are effectively exempted from laws that otherwise protect animals from cruelty and are free to do what non-scientists cannot. Thus, becoming a scientist gives a person power over animals that non-scientists do not have.

Breeding and supply establishments must be approved by or registered with the relevant governmental authority.[86] Among their other duties, breeders and suppliers must keep records of animals sold or supplied and to whom the animals are sold, and must identify animals that die in the breeding and supply establishment.[87]

So when can animals be used in experiments and what kind of animals can be used? First, the Directive imposes a general constraint that mandates that an experiment on an animal is not to be undertaken if there is a "reasonably and practically" available alternative method of obtaining the result desired.[88] Second, should an animal experiment be performed, the choice of species must be carefully considered, so that the species of animal used is the one that will be subjected to the least pain and suffering in the experiment.[89] Third, the Directive states that in choices among experiments, those experiments requiring the fewest animals

---

82. Djurförsök.info, *Facts and Numbers*, Apr. 15, 2009, http://www.djurforsok.info/english/home/factsandnumbers.4.1c39844f11d7804ba518000450.html (last visited Sept. 18, 2010) [hereinafter Djurförsök].
83. Council Directive 86/609, *supra* note 76, at art. 7.
84. *Id.* at art. 14.
85. *Id.*
86. *Id.* at art. 15.
87. *Id.* at art. 17.
88. *Id.* at art. 7(2).
89. *Id.* at art. 7(3).

should be the ones chosen.[90] Fourth, the Directive addresses the use of stray animals in experiments, which is an issue typically addressed in animal experimentation regulations. The rationale for always considering this issue in legislation is that stray animals presumably once were someone's pets. The discovery that your dog Snuffy has ended up in an animal experiment because she happened to get loose engenders great outrage. In fact, exactly this issue served as the genesis of the United States Animal Welfare Act.[91]

In this regard, Directive 86/609/EEC provides that animals must be obtained only from breeding or supply establishments, unless they are imported, and feral or stray animals are not to be used for purposes of experimentation.[92] Nonetheless, Articles 15 and 19 of the Directive provide that general or special exemptions to this rule can be granted to supplying establishments, as determined by the relevant governmental authority. Article 19, however, makes clear that general exemptions may not be given for the use of stray cats and dogs. For these species, only special exemptions can be made. So while there is a general prohibition on the use of stray animals, both general and special exemptions to this rule can be made in some circumstances.

Another issue ordinarily dealt with in experimentation regulation is the use of animals in more than one experiment, for historically the same animals have sometimes been used over and over again in painful experiments. For example, to train veterinarians to perform surgery, sometimes multiple operations are performed on a particular animal. The EU Directive answers this concern by prohibiting the use of animals "more than once in experiments entailing severe pain, distress or equivalent suffering."[93] Multiple experiments can, therefore, be performed, but only if they do not involve "severe" pain and suffering. Thus, painful experiments can be performed over and over again on individual animals so long as the pain is not deemed "severe." This leads to a question that is not addressed in the Directive: how does one determine when pain becomes "severe"?

There is another equally disturbing side to this coin: what exactly does prohibiting multiple uses of animals in experiments tacitly encourage? Obviously, it increases the overall number of animals used in painful experiments. So the question becomes is it more humane to only use animals once but use more of them? This is a seemingly insoluble problem that exists under the current EU Directive and, as we will see, other animal experimentation laws addressing this issue.

The Directive goes on to provide a number of more specific requirements for the treatment of animals in experiments:

- Animals must be provided with housing, food, water, care and freedom of movement "appropriate to their health and well-being."[94]

90. *Id.*
91. *See* Larry Carbone, What Animals Want 142 (Oxford U. Press 2004).
92. Council Directive 86/609, *supra* note 76, at art. 15.
93. *Id.* at art. 10.
94. *Id.* at art. 5(a).

- Restrictions on the ability of animals to satisfy physiological and ethological needs are to be kept at an absolute minimum.[95] The very idea of the ethological needs of an animal being met in a painful animal experiment seems absurd. What is obviously meant is that natural behavior is to be limited as little as possible in the experimental protocol.
- Daily inspections of animals are required.[96] Any defect or suffering of the animal is to be eliminated as soon as possible.[97]
- Experiments are to be designed "to avoid distress and unnecessary pain and suffering to the experimental animals."[98] In planning and designing an experiment then, the experimenter is to consider the pain and suffering that might be inflicted and attempt to minimize it through the design of the experiment.
- Experiments are to be carried out using general or local anesthesia unless anesthesia would be more traumatic than the experiment itself or where "anesthesia is incompatible with the object of the experiment."[99] When would anesthesia be incompatible with the object of an experiment? At least two types of circumstances can be identified. One is where pain is the object of the experiment. It is not infrequently the case that experiments are done on animals for the purpose of determining the effects of pain. Another circumstance is when the level of pain from some treatment is deemed important in analyzing the efficacy of the treatment.
- Experiments involving "prolonged" severe pain must be specifically authorized by the relevant governmental authority.[100] The authority is to take "appropriate judicial or administrative action if it is not satisfied that the experiment is of sufficient importance for meeting the essential needs of man or animal."[101] Presumably this "appropriate action" by the governmental authority would be to stop or limit the experiment.
- The EU Commission and Member States of the EU are to encourage research into the development and validation of alternative methods to replace all or parts of animal experiments.[102]
- Member States are free to adopt measures stricter than those set forth in the Directive.[103]

Article 13 of the Directive requires that EU Member States collect statistical information on the numbers and kinds of animals used in experiments.[104] Why is

95. *Id.* at art. 5(b).
96. *Id.* at art. 5(c).
97. *Id.* at arts. 5(d)–(e).
98. *Id.* at art. 7(4).
99. *Id.* at art. 8(2).
100. *Id.* at art. 12(2).
101. *Id.*
102. *Id.* at art. 23(1).
103. *Id.* at art. 24.
104. *Id.* at art. 13.

such information important? One of the difficulties that people concerned with animal experimentation must contend with is that there is a dearth of information available about animal experimentation that has been and is being performed. How many animals are and have been used? For what purposes? How are the experiments conducted? Those who perform animal experiments maintain that they have certain intellectual property, competitive and other concerns that restrict them from disclosing the nature of their experiments and how they are performing them. In addition, since many of these experiments, not to mention their volume, would probably not be well received by the public, these experimenters have obvious reasons for not providing information on what they are doing.[105] This problem of lack of information is very acute in the United States where the most frequently used animals, mice, rats and birds, are not regulated at all by the Animal Welfare Act, and for this reason information on experiments on them is not subject to reporting requirements.[106] It is then easy to see that the reporting of accurate information on experiments is vitally important so that concerned parties can offer this information to the public, as well as use it in their analyses of animal experiments. Directive 86/609/EEC takes a step in this direction by requiring that at least information on the number and types of animals used in experiments be collected.

The Directive also addresses a problem noted in my introduction of this subject: the problem of experiments already performed in one country and unnecessarily repeated in another to meet regulatory requirements for pharmaceutical and other products. In Article 22(1) of Council Directive 86/609/EEC, Member States are directed to "as far as possible recognize the validity of data generated by experiments carried out in the territory of another Member State unless further testing is necessary in order to protect public health and safety." To this end, member countries are required to provide information on experiments carried out in their territory.[107] In addition, the EU Commission is to establish a consultative committee to facilitate the exchange of information on animal experiments.[108] The obvious purpose here is to attempt to reduce duplicative experiments, which is stated in the recitals to Directive 86/609/EEC as one of its goals.

One can see in this Directive elements of the "3Rs," a well-known animal experimentation concept. The 3Rs, "reduce, refine and replace," began with a proposal by Charles Hume, Director of the Universities Federation for Animal

105. On how the truth about animal treatment is hidden from public scrutiny, *see* Amy B. Draeger, *More than Property: An Argument for Adoption of the Universal Declaration on Animal Welfare*, 12 DRAKE J. AGRIC. L. 277, 288 (2007); David Favre, *Integrating Animal Interests Into Our Legal System*, 10 ANIMAL L. 87, 91 (2004).

106. *See* Richard L. Crawford, *A Review of the Animal Welfare Enforcement Report Data 1973 Through 1995*, 7 ANIMAL WELFARE INFO. CENTER NEWSL. No. 2 (1996), *available at* http://www.nal.usda.gov/awic/newsletters/v7n2/7n2crawf.htm (follow "General" hyperlink).

107. Council Directive 86/609, *supra* note 76, at art. 22(2).

108. *Id.* at art. 22(3).

Welfare in 1954, and work on formulating the 3Rs was performed by W.M.S. Russell and R.L. Burch:[109]

> The Three R's originated in a proposal made in 1954 by Charles Hume, founder of the Universities Federation for Animal Welfare (UFAW)[,] that the UFAW should undertake a scientific study of humane techniques in laboratory animal experiments. The project was managed by a committee under the chairmanship of Sir Peter Medawar, the Nobel prize-winning immunologist, with William Lane-Petter, Secretary of the Research Defense Society of Great Britain, among its members. Christine Stevens, founder of the Animal Welfare Institute (AWI) in the U.S., provided financial support for the project. W.M.S. Russell, a zoologist, and R.L. Burch, a microbiologist, were appointed to carry out the work, which led to the publication of the book *The Principles of Humane Experimental Technique* in 1959.[110]

In 1999, the 3Rs were analyzed and elaborated on in the Bologna Declaration of the 3rd World Congress on Alternatives and Animal Use in the Life Sciences.[111] The 3Rs dictate that scientists attempt to *reduce* the number of animals used in experiments, to *refine* experiments so that as little pain and discomfort is inflicted on animals as necessary and to *replace* animal experiments with other methods of obtaining information where possible.[112]

Although Directive 86/609/EEC does not explicitly incorporate the 3Rs, it does advance the goals of the 3Rs in a number of ways. For instance, it dictates care in designing and carrying out experiments to insure use of a minimum number of animals, promotes causing as little suffering as possible by requiring government approval of some painful experiments and encourages discovery of alternative methods of obtaining information gained in animal experiments. In keeping with the 3Rs and based on Article 23 of Council Directive 86/609/EEC, a European Center dedicated to attempting to find and validate non-animal techniques to obtain information now obtained in animal experiments was created in 1991. This is the European Centre for the Validation of Alternative Methods (ECVAM). Its stated purposes are:[113]

- To coordinate the validation of alternative test methods at the European Union level.[114]

---

109. Zurlo et al., *supra* note 53.
110. *Id.*
111. Paula Gerber, *Scientific Experimentation on Animals: Are Australia and New Zealand Implementing the 3Rs?*, *in* ANIMAL LAW IN AUSTRALASIA 212, 214 (Peter J. Sankoff & Steven White eds., Federation Press 2009).
112. *Id.* at 213–17.
113. European Center for the Validation of Alternative Methods, http://ecvam.jrc.it/ (follow "About ECVAM" hyperlink) (last visited Aug. 13, 2010).
114. *Id.*

- To act "as a focal point for the exchange of information on the development of alternative" test methods.[115]
- To set up, maintain and manage databases on alternative procedures.[116]
- To promote dialogue between legislators, industries, scientists, "consumer organizations and animal welfare groups, with a view to the development, validation" and international recognition of alternative test methods.[117]

Some of what the ECVAM has done includes putting together a database known as DB-ALM which provides scientific knowledge on alternatives to animal testing.[118] It has also created other databases on results of testing of compounds, on studies concerning validation of new methods and on *in vitro* ("test tube," non-animal testing) toxicology labs.[119] Additionally, ECVAM evaluates and validates non-animal methods of testing compounds.[120] Thus, ECVAM has become a resource for information on non-animal testing of compounds and products, as well as the validation of non-animal testing methods.

While the 3Rs are a conceptual tool intended to promote animal welfare in science, they also contain a number of shortcomings. First, they are premised on the proposition that the use of animals in experiments is appropriate.[121] Second, the 3Rs are basically founded on utilitarian principles, which once again weigh the interests of animals against the supposed needs of humans to perform animal experiments.[122] Regardless of their propriety, however, the 3Rs have become something of a cliché in the world of animal experimentation. They are, as we will see, referenced and touted in many regulatory schemes.

How does this EU Directive fit within the typologies of animal experimentation regulatory schemes earlier discussed? Actually, it does not seem to require any single approach. This is one of the advantages (or disadvantages?) of the EU issuing directives; directives allow individual countries to meet requirements in different ways, which allows great flexibility in meeting EU requirements. Nonetheless, since Directive 86/609/EEC requires that a governmental authority approve certain actions and perform other duties, at least some aspects of a Direct Government Regulation and Licensing model are utilized here, although one could presumably create a governmental committee system to perform the role of this governmental authority. In addition, ethical committees could also be used along

115. *Id.*
116. *Id.*
117. *Id.*
118. *Id.* (follow "Activities" hyperlink).
119. *Id.*
120. *See id.*
121. Nicole Fenwick et al., *The Welfare of Animals Used in Science: How the "Three Rs" Ethic Guides Improvements,* 50 CANADIAN VETERINARY J. 523, 526 (2009) [hereinafter Fenwick].
122. *Id.* at 523–25.

with a separate governmental licensing and regulatory agency. A purely self-regulatory scheme would not be sufficient under this Directive.

2. A New EU Directive

In September 2010, after more than two years of negotiation among EU bodies and several different versions of a proposed directive, the EU Parliament created a new Directive on animal experimentation that will, at the beginning of 2013, replace Directive 86/609/EEC and will require Member States to adopt and publish laws conforming to its strictures by November 10, 2012. This new Directive changes in notable ways the regulatory scheme that has governed experimentation in the EU for nearly 25 years and reveals many of the forces at work in the EU's efforts to improve animal welfare. According to European Environment Commissioner Janez Potočnik, with the enactment and implementation of this new Directive, "[t]he European Union will soon have the highest standards of experimental animal welfare in the world."[123]

The new Directive contains extensive recitals that expose much about the scientific, social, political and economic policies underlying the EU effort to improve the conditions of animals used in experiments and reduce the need for such experiments. The Directive begins by recognizing that Article 13 of the Treaty on the Functioning of the European Union makes animal welfare an important value in the EU.[124] In furthering this value the Directive purports to be based on new scientific knowledge relating to animal welfare.[125] The EU recognizes that "[o]ur knowledge of animal welfare requirements and [] [of animals'] capacity to experience pain, suffering and distress has increased since 1986 and the research environment has also changed."[126] While replacement of the use of live animals in experiments is seen as desirable, the recitals state that "the use of live animals continues to be necessary to protect human and animal health and the environment."[127] The seemingly inconsistent recognition of the value of animals and animal welfare along with the competing alleged necessity of use of animals in painful experiments is continued in paragraph (12) of the recitals of the new Directive:

> Animals have an intrinsic value which must be respected. There are also the ethical concerns of the general public as regards the use of animals in procedures. Therefore, animals should always be treated as sentient creatures and their use in procedures should be restricted to areas which may ultimately benefit human or animal health, or the environment. The use of animals for

---

123. EU Revises Laws, *supra* note 74.
124. Council Directive 2010/63/EU, *supra* note 74, at recitals para. (2).
125. *Id.* at recitals para. (6).
126. Q & A, *supra* note 74.
127. Council Directive 2010/63/EU, *supra* note 74, at recitals para. (10).

> scientific or educational purposes should therefore only be considered where a non-animal alternative is unavailable.

Ethical concerns are said to require that "procedures that result in severe pain, suffering or distress, which is likely to be long lasting and cannot be ameliorated, should be prohibited."[128] So we see in these introductory recitals to the Directive a number of seemingly inconsistent conceptual strands purporting to motivate this new law: the intrinsic value of animals, ethical concerns of the populace, and scientific need for animal experiments to benefit both humans and animals. One might logically ask, if animals have intrinsic value that is being recognized, how can the mere fact of their utility in experiments overcome that value?

Regardless of this moral dilemma, the new Directive goes on to deal with an issue previously noted: the fact that little useful information is made available to the public on experimentation. The recitals state that the new Directive aims to "ensure that the public is informed," but at the same time intends to protect proprietary information by permitting users of animals in experiments to provide anonymous "non-technical" summaries of projects.[129]

Apart from the concerns and policies intended to protect animals, satisfy the ethical feelings of the public, and meet scientific needs, there are lurking economic worries. The recitals to the New Directive make much of competitive imbalances caused by divergent regulations in different EU states concerning animal experimentation. It is noted that disparities in the laws in Member States "are liable to constitute barriers to trade in products and substances the development of which involves experiments on animals."[130] This concern for the economic competitiveness of the animal experimentation and other industries is raised several times in the Recitals.[131] This mélange of potentially conflicting animal and economic interests is recognized by the EU in its description of the purposes of the new Directive: "[t]he main objectives are to considerably improve the welfare of animals used in scientific procedures, to ensure fair competition for the industry, and foster research activities in the European Union."[132] Thus, as we have seen in other contexts, interests of animals are again weighed in a balance that includes not only concerns about human health and welfare interests, but also economic interests. So the industries that experiment on animals and rely on experimentation in production of their products are a factor in the equation of how the EU regulates animal welfare issues in experimentation.

With this economic element in place, it is hard to see how animal experimentation could ever end. If industry concerns are at the table, then it appears virtually certain that use of animals in experimentation will continue eternally. An industry that benefits from more and more animal experimentation is unlikely to voluntarily

128. *Id.* at recitals para. (23).
129. *Id.* at recitals para. (41).
130. *Id.* at recitals para. (1).
131. *Id.* at recitals paras. (41), (44), (46).
132. Q & A, *supra* note 74.

reduce its income stream by reducing or eliminating animal experiments. So while much ink is spilled in the Recitals to the new Directive on protection of animals in experiments and reducing the number of animals used in experiments, if industry concerns are also in the mix it seems this ink might well have been saved since animal experimentation is certain to continue given a balancing of animal welfare and human economic concerns.

Let us now turn to the substantive provisions of the new Directive. In section 1(a) this Directive, unlike Council Directive 86/609/EEC, explicitly recognizes and follows the 3Rs.[133] The application of the 3Rs is further delineated in Article 4, which provides that non-animal testing strategies shall be used whenever possible. This article also requires that Member States ensure that the number of animals used is reduced to the minimum necessary and that procedures be refined to reduce pain to a minimum.

The types of animals to which the new Directive applies have been broadened. Not only are live vertebrate animals and certain larval and foetal forms of vertebrates included, but live cephalopods are also covered.[134] Recall that Council Directive 86/609 does not cover any invertebrates, like cephalopods, and does not apply to any foetal forms of vertebrates. We will see that there is trend toward covering invertebrate animals in animal experimentation legislation given that evidence now exists indicating that invertebrates experience pain. With respect to the practices to which the Directive applies, a number of practices are explicitly excluded from coverage, including non-experimental agricultural and veterinary practices, and animal husbandry practices.[135] Note also that individual states are free to maintain existing stricter animal experimentation regulations that are the law in these individual states on November 9, 2010.[136]

So what practices does the new Directive regulate? The definition of a regulated "procedure" in Article 3 of this Directive identifies a particular level of pain that must exist for an action to be considered a "procedure" covered by the legislation. It states that a "procedure" is the use of an animal for scientific or educational purposes that may cause pain or distress at a level equal to or higher than "that caused by the introduction of a needle in accordance with good veterinary practice."[137] This baseline of pain is used elsewhere in the legislation as well. How one determines that this level of pain exists is not clear; it seems only personal experience can inform such a determination. Procedures may only be carried out for certain specified purposes. These include:[138]

- basic research;
- "translational or applied research" with aims of prevention, diagnosis or treatment of diseases, detection and assessment of physiological conditions,

133. Council Directive 2010/63/EU, *supra* note 74, at art. 1(1)(a).
134. *Id.* at art. 1(3).
135. *Id.* at art. 1(5).
136. *Id.* at art. 2(1).
137. *Id.* at art. 3(1).
138. *Id.* at art. 5.

or improving the welfare and production conditions of animals reared for agricultural purposes;
- testing of drugs, foodstuffs and other substances;
- protection of the environment and preservation of species;
- higher education; and
- forensic inquiries.

A "project" is defined in Article 3(2) as a program of work with a scientific objective involving "one or more procedures." As we will see, it is "projects" that are subject to mandatory evaluation and authorization.

In provisions that represent a growing trend in animal experimentation legislation, the use of primates is, depending on species, either specially controlled or banned. Article 8 provides that non-human primates are not to be used in procedures except in the case of basic research, certain research on detection or prevention of debilitating or potentially life threatening human diseases, drug, food or substance testing, or research aimed at protection of the species in question. This research on non-human primates can only be undertaken when the purpose of the experiment cannot be achieved by use of any other species.[139] Certain specified types of non-human primates not born or bred in captivity are not permitted to be used in basic research and great apes are not to be used in procedures at all, with the exception that they may be used when essential to the preservation of the species in question or relating to an "unexpected outbreak of a life-threatening or debilitating condition in humans" provided the purpose of the experiment cannot be met with the use of any other species.[140] So use of those species most closely related to humans is restricted and in the case of great apes is banned except in certain extraordinary circumstances.

This movement toward prohibitions on use of certain animals closely related to humans ratchets back speciesism[141] one level. Now regulators are taking the position that use of animals closely related to humans should be prohibited or greatly restricted. This species-specific type of rule is one that we also will see in special restrictions on the use of pet animals like dogs and cats in other animal experimentation legislation. As an example from the new Directive, note that Articles 31 and 32 have special informational, identification and marking requirements for dogs and cats. In the new Directive though it is not just animals we like, such as dogs and cats, that get some special treatment, but also those genetically close to humans. So, as an animal, being in the good graces of humans or within close genetic proximity is sometimes rewarded. The ultimate result, however, may be bad news for other, less vaunted species, whose numbers among those used in experiments may increase as a result of this human largess.

---

139. *Id.* at art. 8(1)(b).
140. *Id.* at arts. 8(2), 8(3), 55(2). Language quoted is from Article 55(2).
141. "Speciesism" is a term that has been used by Peter Singer and others to describe the differential and discriminatory treatment that humans participate in and allow relating to members of other species.

While government authorities may grant exceptions where no purpose bred animals (those bred strictly for use in experiments) can achieve the purpose of the procedure, wild animals are not to be used in procedures.[142] Similarly, with certain exceptions, feral and stray animals are not permitted to be used in experiments.[143] Endangered species, with a few exceptions, also cannot be used in animal experiments.[144] As a general rule animals to be used in experiments are to be animals bred for such purposes.[145] With respect to non-human primates, however, use of animals not bred in captivity or from self-sustaining colonies will be permitted for certain periods of time (defined by species) specified in Annex II to the new Directive.[146]

Regulation of actual experiments begins with the requirement that procedures are not to be carried out on a live animal if the result sought can be obtained by a method recognized in EU legislation that does not require use of a live animal.[147] In further homage to the 3Rs, procedures are to be chosen that use the least number of animals and cause the least amount of pain.[148] Experiments involving "death as an endpoint," *i.e.*, those where death is the known and expected outcome of the procedure, are to be avoided; and where death is inevitable, experiments are to be designed to use as few animals as possible and the duration of pain in the experiment is to be kept to a minimum.[149]

Unless "inappropriate," anesthesia or analgesics are to be used in procedures causing pain.[150] Whether use of anesthesia is appropriate depends on whether administering the anesthesia would be more traumatic than the procedure itself and whether anesthesia is incompatible with the purpose of the experiment.[151] The latter would be the case, of course, where the experiment studies pain or where the level of pain in the procedure is an element of the experiment that needs to be measured.

In a change from Council Directive 86/609/EEC, the new Directive requires that Member States classify all procedures on a pain scale of "non-recovery," "mild," "moderate," or "severe." This effort at classifying pain is a new concept in EU legislation. The classification scheme is used in a number of contexts in the Directive, including Articles 15 and 55, which provide that procedures involving "severe" and long-lasting pain that cannot be alleviated are not to be performed unless specifically authorized by a member country "for exceptional and scientifically justifiable reasons."[152] The other side of this coin is that procedures

142. Council Directive 2010/63/EU, *supra* note 74 at art. 9.
143. *Id.* at art. 11.
144. *Id.* at art. 7(1).
145. *Id.* at art. 10(1).
146. *Id.* at art. 10(1), Annex II.
147. *Id.* at art. 13(1).
148. *Id.* at art. 13(2).
149. *Id.* at art. 13(3).
150. *Id.* at art. 14(1).
151. *Id.* at art. 14(2).
152. *Id.* at art. 15(2), 55(3). Quoted material is from Section 55(3).

involving severe pain can be performed so long as they do not involve long-lasting and unalleviated pain.

These pain categories for procedures are defined in Annex VIII. "Non-recovery" procedures are those done under anesthesia where the animal will not recover consciousness.[153] Procedures classified as "mild" are those where the animals "are likely to experience short-term mild pain ... as well as procedures with no significant impairment of the well-being or general condition of the animals ...."[154] Procedures classified as "moderate" are ones where the animals "are likely to experience short-term moderate pain ... as well as procedures ... likely to cause moderate impairment of the well-being or general condition of the animals."[155] "Severe" procedures are those where "the animals are likely to experience severe pain ... or long lasting moderate pain ..." and procedures "likely to cause severe impairment of the well-being or general condition of the animals ...."[156] The classifications are to be applied "based upon the most severe effects likely to be experienced by an individual animal after applying all appropriate refinement techniques."[157]

At this point one might think that this classification scheme really does not tell us much, particularly given that each of the pain classifications is defined using the word being defined. "Moderate" procedures are defined using the word "moderate"; "severe" using "severe," etc. Section III of Annex VIII, however, does add some substance to the pain category scheme by describing example procedures that fit within each pain level classification. In this section of the Annex, "mild" procedures include administering anesthesia, applying telemetry devices, MRI imaging and feeding a modified diet expected to cause "mild clinical abnormality."[158] "Moderate" procedures include irradiation or chemotherapy with a sub-lethal dose, creating genetically modified animals by surgical procedures and surgery under anesthesia with post-surgical pain.[159] "Severe" procedures include toxicity testing with death as an end point of the procedure, irradiation or chemotherapy with death as an end point and inescapable electric shock intended to produce learned helplessness.[160] These descriptions provide some substance to otherwise circular definitions and should give those making these decisions some guidance in applying the pain level categories.

Reuse of animals in experiments is handled in a way similar to Council Directive 86/609/EEC in that reuse is allowed in procedures classified as "mild" or "moderate," where the animal's general level of health has been restored.[161] In

153. *Id.* at Annex VIII § I.
154. *Id.*
155. *Id.*
156. *Id.*
157. *Id.* at Annex VIII § II.
158. *Id.* at Annex VIII § III.
159. *Id.*
160. *Id.*
161. *Id.* at art. 16(1).

other words, animals are not to be reused in experiments involving severe pain. In exceptional circumstances, however, exceptions can be made to allow an animal to be reused in a severe class procedure so long as the animal has not been previously used in more than one severe level experiment.[162] One difference in the new law is that the pain level descriptions in the new Directive have been given substance by the definitions described above. Now there is some description of what "severe" pain is.

In an apparent effort to efficiently use animals that are killed in experiments, Article 18 of the new Directive states that Member States are to facilitate the sharing of organs and tissues of animals killed. Rehoming of animals is allowed but not required, as is return of animals to a suitable habitat or husbandry system.[163]

The new Directive creates a number of requirements for persons and institutions breeding, supplying or using experimental animals. For example, all breeders of experimental animals, suppliers of these animals and "users" (those performing "procedures") must be authorized and registered with the relevant governmental authority with responsibility relating to animal experimentation.[164] This authorization can only be granted if the person and the institution involved are in compliance with the requirements of the Directive.[165] Suspension or withdrawal of this authorization or other appropriate action is to be taken if a breeder, supplier, or user no longer is in compliance with the Directive.[166]

There must be at least one person at each breeding, supply, or user establishment responsible for animal welfare, and education and training of personnel at the facility.[167] Among the responsibilities of the designated person or persons carrying out these tasks is the responsibility to make sure that any "unnecessary pain, suffering, distress or lasting harm that is being inflicted on an animal ... is stopped."[168] The responsible person or persons also must make sure that projects are carried out in accordance with project authorizations obtained for experimental projects.[169] Each establishment that engages in breeding, supply, or use of experimental animals must also have a designated veterinarian or other qualified expert.[170] Personnel must be adequately trained and those involved in designing experimental procedures and projects must have received instruction in the scientific discipline relevant to the project undertaken.[171]

162. *Id.* at art. 16(2).
163. *Id.* at art. 19.
164. *Id.* at art. 20(1).
165. *Id.*
166. *Id.* at art. 21(1).
167. *Id.* at art. 24(1).
168. *Id.* at art. 24(2).
169. *Id.*
170. *Id.* at art. 25.
171. *Id.* at art. 23(2).

Construction and design of facilities and equipment must be suited to the animals being housed.[172] The requirements for the housing and other facilities for animals used in animal experiments are set forth in detailed rules in Annex III to the new Directive. The rules in this Annex include requirements for the ventilation, lighting and temperature of facilities, as well as species-specific rules for the sizes of enclosures for animals and some rules for animal care.

Further specific rules relating to the care and accommodation of animals are provided in Article 33 of the new Directive. This article requires that animals be provided with accommodations, food, water and other care "appropriate to their health and well-being." In an irony that we saw earlier in Council Directive 86/609/EEC, Article 33 also provides that restrictions on the ability of animals to meet their ethological needs are to be kept to a minimum. Strictures in the new Directive mandate daily checks of animals and require that any unnecessary pain and suffering is to be eliminated as rapidly as possible.

Member States are required to carry out regular inspections of breeders, suppliers and users to establish that these facilities are following the rules contained in the Directive.[173] At least one-third of all facilities in each state must be inspected annually and all facilities housing primates must be inspected once a year. To make sure that facilities are not just dressing up their operations for planned inspections, "an appropriate portion of the inspections shall be carried out without prior warning."[174] While the Directive is quite specific about requiring that one-third of facilities be inspected each year, the number required to be unannounced is left ambiguous.

One of the major changes in the new Directive is the requirement that each breeder, supplier and user must set up what is called an "Animal Welfare Body."[175] The Directive is not very detailed about the membership of this body, but does state that it must include at least the designated person responsible for the animal welfare standards described above and, in the case of a user of experimental animals, a scientific member.[176] There is no requirement that any lay or outside animal welfare representative be a part of this Animal Welfare Body. The body is, however, to "receive input" from the designated veterinarian or qualified expert at the facility.[177] The Animal Welfare Body is to serve a largely advisory role at the establishment, with duties including:[178]

- Advise staff on animal welfare issues and the 3Rs.
- Establish internal operating procedures relating to monitoring and reporting on the welfare of animals.

172. *Id.* at art. 22.
173. *Id.* at art. 34.
174. *Id.* at art. 34(4).
175. *Id.* at art. 26(1).
176. *Id.* at art. 26(2).
177. *Id.*
178. *Id.* at art. 27(1). Article 26(3) provides that small breeders, suppliers and users may use means other than an Animal Welfare Body to fulfill these tasks.

- Monitor projects with a view to identifying elements that further the 3Rs.
- "Advise on rehoming schemes."

The general intent is that the Animal Welfare Body will "foster a climate of care and ensure a systematic application of the current Three Rs methods and techniques as well as ensure the uptake of the new, emerging ones."[179]

Perhaps the most important aspect and the real regulatory substance of an animal experimentation regulatory scheme are its rules relating to approval of experimental projects. The new EU Directive contains rules mandating that all experimental projects be authorized by the "competent authority" of the Member State that has responsibility for implementing the Directive and that no project can be carried out without a favorable project evaluation by this authority.[180] This competent authority must be designated by each Member State under Article 59(1) of the Directive. While one would expect that this competent authority would be some governmental body, this is not necessarily the case. Article 59 of the new Directive states that "bodies other than public authorities" may be designated to implement "specific tasks laid down" in the Directive in certain circumstances. These circumstances are that the non-public body must have appropriate expertise to undertake the task and not have any conflict of interest concerning the performance of the task in question.[181] So tasks required of the "competent authority" can be performed by private entities.

Project authorizations required by section 36 of the Directive are to occur only after an application for approval of the project is submitted.[182] This application is to include a non-technical summary of the project as well as detailed information on the project described in Annex VI to the Directive, including information on how the 3Rs have been applied to the project.[183] The non-technical project summary is to be anonymous, is not to identify the user or its personnel and is to be presented in a way that safeguards intellectual property and confidentiality.[184] Changes to projects that may negatively impact animal welfare require amendment or renewal of a project authorization and are subject to the need for a further positive project authorization by the competent authority.[185] Project authorizations can be granted for periods not exceeding five years.[186]

The evaluation of the project under these procedures must verify that the project is justified from a scientific or educational perspective or is required by law; that the "purposes of the project justify using animals"; and that the project design results in procedures being performed in the most humane and

179. Q & A, *supra* note 74.
180. Council Directive 2010/63/EU, *supra* note 74, at arts. 36, 59.
181. *Id.* at art. 59(1).
182. *Id.* at art. 37(1).
183. *Id.*
184. *Id.* at art. 43(1).
185. *Id.* at art. 44.
186. *Id.* at art. 40(3).

environmentally sensible manner possible.[187] The project evaluation must also include, among other things:[188]

- Analysis of the objectives of the project and its scientific or educational benefits.
- Assessment of compliance with the 3Rs.
- Assignment of pain classifications for the procedure.
- A harm-benefit analysis to determine if the projected pain and suffering is ethically justified given the expected benefit to be gained by humans, animals or the environment.[189] Here we see a utilitarian type calculation of harms and benefits based on the suffering of animals expected to occur in the project, and the human and other benefits to be gained through the project.

It is said that this project evaluation process, including the mandatory ethical analysis, "forms the core of project authorization and should ensure the implementation of" the 3Rs.[190] All of this is to be done while safeguarding the intellectual property and confidential information of those on whose behalf the experiment is undertaken.[191] Retrospective analyses of experiments are also to be performed when determined appropriate by the competent authority.[192] All projects involving non-human primates and those involving "severe" pain are to go through such a retrospective analysis.[193]

Simplified administrative procedures for authorizations are permitted for projects not using non-human primates that are classified as "non-recovery," "mild," or "moderate."[194] The application procedure is truncated in the simplified administrative procedure requiring only basic information about the user, persons responsible for the project and the places where the project will be undertaken.[195] Note that penalties for violations of these and the other requirements of Member State provisions created under the new Directive are to be "effective, proportionate and dissuasive."[196]

To attempt to address the duplication of experiments as a result of regulatory requirements in the many Member States, Article 46 states that "[e]ach Member State shall accept data from other Member States that are generated by procedures recognized by the legislation of the Union, unless further procedures need to be carried out regarding that data for the protection of public health, safety or the environment." This presumably means to require that testing done under this and other EU legislation be recognized by all Member States. It is believed that "[t]he

187. *Id.* at art. 38(1).
188. *Id.* at art. 38(2).
189. *See also id.* at recitals para. (39).
190. *Id.* at recitals para. (38).
191. *Id.* at art. 38(4).
192. *Id.* at arts. 38(2)(f), 39.
193. *Id.* at art. 39(2).
194. *Id.* at art. 42(1).
195. *Id.* at art. 42(2).
196. *Id.* at art. 60.

duplication of experiments will be significantly reduced by the sharing of non-confidential data derived from experiments and through systematic ethical evaluation assessing the project proposals."[197]

Replacement of animal experiments is also promoted by the creation of a Union Reference Laboratory to promote and validate alternatives to animal testing, act as an information exchange on alternative methods and maintain databases on alternative approaches to accomplishing the scientific objectives sought in animal experiments.[198] This laboratory is to be referred to as the European Centre for the Validation of Alternative Methods, an organization that has existed to coordinate validation of alternative approaches to animal testing since 1991,[199] and which is discussed above. The newly designated laboratory is to "continue the work so far carried out by the [ECVAM]."[200] Member States are also required to create a national committee on protection of animals used in science to advise competent authorities on matters relating to the care and use of animals in procedures.[201] Acknowledging that the science relating to the use of animals in experimentation advances over time, Article 50 of the Directive provides that the EU Commission may adopt certain modifications to, among others, the Annex on pain classifications.

It is interesting and informative to observe some of the provisions that existed in the proposals that led to the new Directive and did not make it into the final version of the law. The initial proposal that ultimately led to this new Directive was the Proposal for a Directive of the European Parliament and of the Council on the Protection of Animals Used for Scientific Purposes, COM (2008) 543 Final (2008) (hereinafter "Commission Proposal 543"). The Commission created Commission Proposal 543 and sent it to the EU Parliament. The Parliament could have approved the Directive and sent it on to the EU Council as written, but instead the Parliament refused to approve it in the form presented by the Commission. The Parliament proposed a number of revisions to the proposal. So we have two historical sources to compare with the new legislation that actually passed the EU Parliament.

One difference between Commission Proposal 543 and the new Directive is that the former covered more invertebrate animals than does the legislation that was passed by Parliament. In addition to Cephalapods, Commission Proposal 543 covered Cyclostomes and Decapod Crustaceans, while the Parliamentary version covered Cephalopods and Decapod Crustaceans.[202] Unlike the new Directive both Commission Proposal 543 and the Parliamentary proposal required that each

197. Q & A, *supra* note 74.
198. Council Directive 2010/63/EU, *supra* note 74 at art. 48, Annex VII.
199. *Id.* at recitals para. (47).
200. EU Revises Laws, *supra*, note 74.
201. Council Directive 2010/63/EU, *supra* note 74, at art. 49.
202. Commission Proposal 543, *supra* note 73, at art. 2; European Parliament Legislative Resolution of May 5, 2009 on the Proposal for a Directive of the European Parliament and of the Council on the Protection of Animals Used for Scientific Purposes, EUR. PARL. DOC. P6_TA (2009) 0343, art. 2(2) (2009) [hereinafter Parliament Resolution].

institution participating in experiments, or breeding or supplying animals for experiments have an Ethical Review Body.[203] While these proposed Ethical Review Bodies are fundamentally the same in terms of structure and duties as the Animal Welfare Bodies under the new Directive, the name Ethical Review Body did give a different impression of their duties. Note also that the Parliamentary version required that there be a member on the Ethical Review Body "with expertise in the application of the principles of replacement, reduction and refinement."[204] Commission Proposal 543 also required an annual review of experiments by the Ethical Review Body to determine whether projects needed to be submitted to the government agency overseeing animal experiments for amendment or renewal.[205] Thus, while the new Directive has made a number of not insubstantial changes from Commission Directive 86/609/EEC, it does not go quite as far in some respects as the proposals that preceded the new Directive.

It has, in fact, been argued that there were some potentially sinister reasons for some of the changes made to the initial proposed Directive. Industry and economic concerns may have resulted in changes unfavorable to animal welfare concerns:

> When the draft Directive was first proposed by the Commission in 2008, there were concerns in the sector that a number of its provisions would overly hinder research and place unworkable administrative burdens on the industry. Since then, the more controversial provisions have been diluted or removed altogether...
>
> The text as it presently stands represents a compromise between researchers and animal welfare campaigners as it recognizes that the use of animals in scientific procedures remains essential, whilst seeking to improve and harmonize animal welfare standards.[206]

I suppose that we should not be particularly surprised that the law is the result of compromise and that aspects of the original proposal were jettisoned for economic and political purposes. This is the nature of the political process.

In any event, some of the major changes that are wrought by the new Directive that was born of this compromise are the following:

- Animals covered under the new law include certain invertebrates.
- The use of primates in experiments is limited and great apes are not to be used except in only a very few extraordinary circumstances.

---

203. Commission Proposal 543, *supra* note 73, at art. 25; Parliament Resolution, *supra* note 202, at art. 27; European Economic and Social Committee, *Opinion on the Proposal for a Directive of the European Parliament and of the Council on the Protection of Animals Used for Scientific Purposes*, NAT/422 § 3.4.1 (2009).
204. Parliament Resolution, *supra* note 202, at art. 27(2).
205. Commission Proposal 543, *supra* note 73, at art. 26.
206. Janet Knowles, *Revised Protection for Animals for Scientific Purposes,* EVERSHEDS, June 15, 2010, https://www.eversheds.com/uk/Home/Articles/index1.page?ArticleID=templatedata/Eversheds/articles/data/en/Healthcare/Revised_protection_for_animals_used_for_scientific_purposes.

- A classification scheme for levels of pain and suffering has been created that is used to determine the types of experiments that will be allowed, the levels of scrutiny to which these experiments will be subjected and when reuse of animals will be permitted.
- Member States are now required to designate a Competent Authority to regulate animal experimentation and administer an approval and evaluation mechanism for animal experiments.
- Establishments that breed, supply or use animals must designate a person responsible for animal welfare at the institution, and must create an Animal Welfare Body. This latter entity performs largely advisory functions relating to animal welfare at the establishment.
- All animal experiments must be approved by a competent authority designated by the Member State government.
- The evaluation process for approval of animal experiments requires an ethical evaluation balancing the human, animal or environmental benefits of the experiment against the pain and suffering to be experienced by animals in the experiment.

Some of these concepts are novel, while others have been tried before. This institutionalizes in the EU what is basically a Direct Government Regulation and Licensing scheme, while in some sense also suggesting a committee type structure for the Animal Welfare Bodies created by regulated institutions. The efforts at classifying pain levels and regulating based on this classification system is a new idea for the EU. The restrictions on uses of primates and apes in the new Directive is, as we will see in the laws of other countries, a trend in modern animal experimentation legislation. Ethical evaluations are also now typical in regulatory schemes.

While one important stated intent of the new Directive is to reduce the number of animals used in experiments through explicit application of the 3Rs, "[t]he actual reduction in the number of animals used in experiments as a direct result of the new [D]irective is difficult to quantify."[207] One must, nonetheless, wonder about the real likelihood that there will be meaningful reduction in the use of animals in experiments when one recalls that one of the purposes of the new Directive is to promote the competitiveness of the EU animal experimentation industry. Increasing competitiveness and other economic concerns would seem to be at odds with the purpose of reducing the use of animals in testing, although, one aspect of "competiveness" that one could cite as being consistent with the reduction of the number of animals used in experiments is the development of alternative methods of testing. And alternative methods of testing is a focus of the new Directive. So in this sense at least the reduction of animal use and competiveness can coexist.

207. Q & A, *supra* note 74.

3. Cosmetics Testing

That millions of animals die so that humans can preen themselves is perhaps one of the most infuriating aspects of the use of animals. While one can make what might pass for rational arguments for the use of animals in agriculture or the testing of seemingly life-saving medicines, the idea that animals die so that one's complexion can be a bit rosier serves as a pinnacle of both vanity and cruelty alike. Nonetheless, these products are still tested on animals. The EU, as of 2009, unlike most other political subdivisions, including the United States, no longer allows the use of animals for the testing of cosmetics.[208]

4. The Future of Animal Welfare in the EU

As we have seen, the EU has taken a number of steps to attempt to improve the welfare of animals in agriculture and experimentation. Will it continue to produce yet more stringent regulations to provide further protection for animals? There is some reason to believe that it will. The EU Commission has developed an Action Plan on the protection of animals for the period 2006–10.[209] This Action Plan has influenced the new provisions relating to agricultural animals reviewed in the last chapter as well as the new EU animal experimentation regulations discussed above. Following are the stated objectives of the Action Plan:[210]

- "Continue to promote high animal welfare standards in the EU and at the International Level."[211]
- Continued support for the 3Rs in animal experimentation.
- Promote a more consistent and coordinated approach to animal protection issues "taking into account aspects such as the socio-economic impact of any new measures (emphasis omitted)."[212]
- Better focus the direction of animal welfare policies for the future.
- Coordinate current resources in light of future goals.

---

208. Commission to the European Parliament and Council, *Report on the Development, Validation and Legal Acceptance of Alternative Methods to Animal Tests in the Field of Cosmetics (2008)*, 3–4, COM(2010) 480 final (Sept. 16, 2010); *see also* Stephanie J. Engelsman, *"World Leader"— At What Price? A Look at Lagging American Animal Protection Laws*, 22 PACE ENVTL. L. REV. 329, 355–56 (2005) [hereinafter Engelsman]; Avril Stephens, *Animal Rights Slam EU Testing Ban*, CNN.COM, Nov. 7, 2002, at http://edition.cnn.com/2002/WORLD/europe/11/07/eu.cosmetics/ (last visited June 16, 2010).
209. *Communication from the Commission to the European Parliament and the Council on a Community Action Plan on the Protection and Welfare of Animals 2006–2010* COM (2006) 13 final.
210. *Id.* at 2–3.
211. *Id.*
212. *Id.* at 3 (emphasis omitted).

With respect to particular areas for action to be taken, the EU Commission identifies the following:[213]

- Upgrade current Minimum Standards for animal welfare and protection.
- Promote policy-oriented scientific research on animal protection and promote the 3Rs.
- Standardize indicators for determining animal welfare in husbandry practices.
- Inform animal keepers and handlers, as well as the public, on animal welfare issues.
- Continue to work internationally to raise awareness of animal issues, create a better consensus among countries on these issues and investigate trade opportunities in animal friendly systems of production.

There has been some EU action in the recent past that can be interpreted as following the admonitions of the Action Plan. For example, Council Regulation (EC) No. 1/2005 relating to animal transportation can be seen as incorporating some Action Plan ideas, even though it was created before the stated 2006 commencement of the Action Plan. Some of the goals of the regulation, like standardization and uniformity of rules in the EU states, are in line with the Action Plan, which calls for consistent and coordinated policies, and the standardization of animal practices. Council Regulation (EC) No. 1099/2009 on animal slaughter is one passed within the period covered by the Action Plan, and can also be viewed as incorporating a number of its goals. It purports to strengthen animal protection in the process of slaughter by providing better physical comfort and protection for animals, *i.e.*, better rules on providing food and water, etc. Since it is in the form of a regulation rather than a directive, it also promotes the standardization and uniformity goals of the Action Plan. This standardization and uniformity also contains an economic aspect, and is intended, once again, to correct competitive imbalances caused by non-uniform laws in EU countries. Standardization of practices is also addressed in the introduction of Standard Operating Procedures in slaughterhouses. Keeping operators and employees aware of animal welfare issues is accomplished by the establishment of national reference centres or networks. So Council Regulation (EC) No. 1099/2009 does follow recommendations made in the Action Plan.

The new EU experimentation Directive also contains elements consistent with the Action Plan. As urged by the Action Plan, it explicitly recognizes and follows the 3Rs. The Directive contains many new provisions intended to improve the welfare of animals in animal experiments as directed by the Action Plan. Through the new EU Reference Laboratory known as the ECVAM, policy oriented research is to be carried out on alternative testing methods. This Laboratory also serves as an informational resource for those involved in the animal experimentation

213. *Id.* at 3–4.

industry. Moreover, the history of the new Directive indicates that it was designed to meet the requirements of the Action Plan.[214]

While the hortatory statements of the Action Plan may sound good, and actions taken in the last few years may be consistent with its goals, whether they will ultimately translate into real and significant benefit to animals remains to be seen. There are several cautionary notes that need be sounded. For example, much emphasis is placed on considering the socio-economic impact of animal protection measures in the Action Plan. While one presumes that policy makers do not ignore such concerns when legislating, still economic and social issues can often effectively be used to staunch progress in the protection of animals. Moreover, the Action Plan notes that budgetary and economic considerations must also be taken into account in future actions.[215] Since steps toward animal protection generally cost the government and others money, this raises concerns about the true impact on animal protection that this or any other action plan is likely to have if these concerns are at the fore in decision-making.

That economic issues are of concern to the EU with respect to broadening animal protection rules is also shown in the recent EU communication on animal welfare legislation in other countries.[216] While this communication predicts that the trend of increasing animal welfare legislation in the EU will continue, it also recognizes that these steps result in increased costs for EU producers, and could put them at a competitive disadvantage when compared to other countries' producers.[217] It is also recognized that competitive distortions as a result of different countries having varying animal welfare standards could ultimately undermine steps to protect animals.[218] The path to addressing these competitive distortions is, however, not easy to see. The Commission points to consumer demand for better animal treatment; international dialogue; bilateral agreements; and labeling schemes to make consumers aware of animal treatment issues as possible means of promoting animal welfare and tackling competitive distortions resulting from contrasting animal welfare schemes in different countries.[219] But if consumers' budgets do not allow the luxury of paying more for products they believe are ethically produced, the competitive pressures on the EU may inhibit further progress on animal welfare issues in Europe.

Perhaps the aspect of the Action Plan that most makes it unlikely to result in anything more than superficial changes on the edges of animal welfare is that the Plan continues to consider animals as property; to accept as morally and legally correct the use of animals for food, science and other purposes; and to weigh the

214. Commission Proposal 543, *supra* note 73, at 6 (in the Explanatory Memorandum portion of the legislative proposal).
215. *Id.* at 5, 8–9, 12.
216. *Communication from the Commission to the Council and the European Parliament on Animal Welfare Legislation on Farmed Animals in Third Countries and the Implications for the EU*, COM 2002/626 (2002).
217. *Id.* at 2, 15.
218. *Id.* at 3.
219. *Id.* at 3–4.

interests of rightholder humans against those of non-rightholder animals. It does not take any real or significant steps on a path that would change the assumed hierarchy that allows animals to be used for all of these purposes.

One organization that might be useful in promoting better international standards for animal treatment in the EU and the rest of the world is the World Organization for Animal Health, also known as the Office International Des Epizooties (hereinafter "OIE"), which recently resolved that it would incorporate animal welfare considerations into its major functions.[220] As a part of this mandate on animal treatment, the OIE will be working to, among other things, develop guidelines leading to better animal welfare practices, promote education on animal welfare issues and maintain informational databases on animal welfare information.[221] As a part of this effort, on May 27, 2010, the OIE, with contributions from the EU, "adopted the first international standards for the '[u]se of animals in research and education ....' "[222] So the work of the OIE has recently produced results.

Will the EU continue to strengthen its animal welfare standards? The EU, at least in its public pronouncements, purports to be committed to pursuing continued improvements in animal welfare standards. Its legislative agenda and results do signal that the EU does take animal welfare seriously and it can probably be said with confidence that the EU is at the forefront of international efforts to improve the welfare of animals. Nonetheless, for those who wish to see the abolition of the use of animals in agriculture, experimentation and other areas, there is continuing frustration with the general underlying premise in all of these efforts that these uses of animals are morally justified and that our focus should be on making the lives of the animals used more pleasant, not on ending their use. From a practical perspective one must also be concerned about whether economic and competitive pressures will ultimately stagnate real progress. But this will only become known through the passage of time.

B. United Kingdom Regulation of Animal Experiments

United Kingdom law on animal experiments has a history going back to 1876[223] and is now contained in the Scientific Procedures Act of 1986 (SPA) which, like the Swedish law discussed in the next section, is one that is designed to, and presumably does comply with, the requirements of EU Council Directive 86/609/EEC. We will see how the use of a Directive by the EU has allowed these two countries to approach the animal experimentation issue with quite different regulatory provisions.

220. International Committee of the OIE, *Resolution No. XIV, Animal Welfare Mandate of the OIE* (2002).
221. *Id.*
222. Laboratory Animals, *supra* note 74.
223. Gerald Carson, Men, Beasts, and Gods 195 (Charles Scribner's Sons 1972).

Animals covered by the SPA are living vertebrates and invertebrate octopuses after they become able to feed independently.[224] The procedures regulated under the SPA are "any experimental or other scientific procedure applied to a protected animal which may have the effect of causing that animal pain, suffering, distress or lasting harm."[225] This language, not surprisingly, is much the same language that we saw in Council Directive 86/609/EEC. The SPA goes on to state that the administration of any analgesic or anesthetic to treat the animal for pain is disregarded when determining if a procedure is covered by the Act.[226] Ringing, tagging, or marking of animals is not covered if the procedure "causes only momentary pain or distress and no lasting harm."[227] Recognized agricultural, animal husbandry, or veterinary practices are also not covered.[228]

The main thrust of the SPA is contained in section 3, which provides a three-part licensing process for animal experiments. It states that no one can conduct a regulated procedure on animals unless each of the following requirements are met:[229]

- The person performing the procedure has a personal license from the Secretary of State allowing him or her to perform a regulated procedure.
- The project under which the procedure is performed is licensed by the Secretary of State.
- The facility where the procedure is carried out is a place specified in the personal and project licenses. The establishments in which projects are to be carried out must be approved in a certificate issued by the Secretary of State.[230]

The focus in granting personal licenses to experimenters is on the applicant's education, training and competence.[231] The regulation of project licenses is more detailed. In order for a project to be approved it must be undertaken for at least one of a group of broadly specified purposes:[232]

- Prevention, diagnosis or treatment of disease in man, animals or plants.
- Analysis of physiological conditions of man, animals or plants.
- Protection of human or animal health and welfare, or protection of the environment.
- Advancement of behavioral or biological sciences.

---

224. United Kingdom Scientific Procedures Act, 1986 § 1(1) [hereinafter SPA]; Animals (Scientific Procedures) Act (Amendment) Order 1993/2103, art. 3; Marla K. Conley, *Caring for Dolphins, Otters, and Octopuses: Speciesism in the Regulation of Zoos,* 15 ANIMAL L. 237, 259 (2009).
225. SPA, *supra* note 224, at § 2(1).
226. *Id.* at § 2(4).
227. *Id.* at § 2(5).
228. *Id.* at § 2(8).
229. *Id.* at § 3.
230. This latter requirement is set forth in SPA § 6.
231. *Id.* at § 4.
232. *Id.* at § 5(3).

- Training other than in primary or secondary schools.
- Forensic inquiries.
- Breeding of animals for scientific purposes.

Along with meeting at least one of these specified purposes, the project must be analyzed under a substantive standard that weighs the "likely adverse effects on the animals concerned against the benefit likely to accrue as a result of the programme to be specified in the licence."[233] Again we are presented with the familiar weighing of human against animal interests.

Additional requirements for issuance of a project license include that a project will not be approved if it can possibly be achieved without the use of animals,[234] that it must use as few animals as possible, and that it must use animals with the lowest sensitivity to pain possible and cause the least suffering to animals required to produce "satisfactory results."[235] Cats, dogs, primates, or equidae are not to be used unless the Secretary of State is convinced that no other species is suitable for the project.[236] Here again are species-specific limitations on experimentation.

The SPA has a number of explicit requirements for the care of animals in experiments. Facilities in which animal experiments are conducted shall be in a condition to ensure that "the environment, housing, freedom of movement, food, water and care provided ... are appropriate for the animal's health and well-being."[237] In addition, restrictions on the ability of animals to satisfy physiological and ethological needs are to be kept to an "absolute minimum."[238] It is, of course, difficult to imagine a condition more contrary to any animal's ethological needs than being subjected to painful experiments. Nonetheless, the idea is that the animal should be kept in conditions as close to the animal's ethological needs as possible, within the context of the experiment. This context, however, is in fact likely to be wildly divergent from the animal's ethological norm. In any event, to enforce these rules relating to the conditions of experimental animals, daily inspections of the animals' conditions are required.[239]

The SPA follows quite literally EU Council Directive 86/609/EEC on the use of anesthetics for painful experiments. It states, in Schedule 2A of the SPA, that all experiments are to be carried out with the use of general or local anesthesia. There are of course, exceptions to this rule. The requirement is lifted if the anesthetic would cause more trauma than the experiment, and where it would be incompatible with the purpose of the experiment, *i.e.*, where the pain of the animal is relevant to the experiment.

---

233. *Id.* at § 5(4).
234. *Id.* at § 5(5)(a) contained in The Animals (Scientific Procedures) Act 1986 (Amendment) Regulations 1998, 1998/1974, art. 3 [hereinafter 1998 amendment].
235. *Id.* at § 5(5)(b) (in 1998 amendment).
236. *Id.* at § 5(6).
237. *Id.* at § 6B(a) (in 1998 amendment).
238. *Id.* at § 6B(b) (in 1998 amendment).
239. *Id.* at § 6B(c) (in 1998 amendment).

The SPA does not stop at regulating experimenters, their projects and facilities; it also regulates those who breed and supply animals for experiments.[240] Like establishments where experiments are performed, those breeding or supplying animals for experiments must have a certificate from the Secretary of State relating to the facility in which they carry on their activity.[241]

What about the ubiquitous issues of the use of strays and reuse of animals in experiments? Use of stray dogs or cats is resolved in the expected way in section 10(3) of the SPA which provides that these animals cannot be used unless the Secretary of State grants an exception which is only to be granted if no other suitable animal for the purpose of the project can be obtained. Similar protection is provided in the same section for a group of animals including primates, ferrets, gerbils and a number of other animals listed in Schedule 2 to the SPA.[242] However, for those species other than cats and dogs, the condition that no other animal can be obtained suitable for the experiment for an exception to be granted does not apply. Endangered and wild animals are also generally not permitted to be used in experiments.[243]

Reuse of animals is the subject of detailed regulation in the SPA. If an animal has been used for a procedure that has caused "severe" pain or distress, then the animal may not be used for any more procedures that will involve severe pain or distress.[244] There are, however, circumstances in which reuse can be authorized by the Secretary of State where there has not been severe pain or distress in a previous procedure.[245] Here we revisit the question triggered by the use of this same "severe" pain or distress language as in EU Council Directive 86/609/EEC: what exactly is meant by "severe" pain or distress?

More detail is added to the meaning of the SPA on these reuse issues in a guidance publication on the "Use, Continued Use and Reuse of Animals" by the Animals Scientific Procedures Division of the Home Office Science and Research Group (hereinafter "ASP").[246] While the ASP has created a detailed document describing its rules on use, continued use and reuse of animals, it does not define what is meant by "severe" pain or distress.[247] What this document does do, however, is reveal that the concept of "reuse" of an animal in an experiment is not as crystalline as it might seem, and in actuality means something different from what one might assume. "Use" of an animal for the purposes of the SPA is:

---

240. *Id.* at § 7.
241. *Id.*
242. *Id.* at § 10(3)(b).
243. *Id.* at § 10(3)(c) contained in The Animals (Scientific Procedures) Act (Amendment) Regulations 1993, 1993/2102, art. 2.
244. *Id.* at § 14(1) (in 1998 amendment).
245. *Id.* at §14 (2)–(3) (in 1998 amendment).
246. Animals Scientific Procedures Division of the Home Office Science and Research Group, *Animals (Scientific Procedures) Act of 1986: Use, Continued Use and Reuse of Animals* (2008), *available at* http://www.homeoffice.gov.uk/publications/science/769901/licences/project-licences/use-of-animals?view=Binary.
247. *See id.*

> The "use" of a protected animal under project licence authorities extends from the time the first regulated procedure is applied to the animal up to the time when the observations, or the collection of data (or other products) for a particular scientific purpose (usually a single experiment or test), are completed.[248]

"Continued use" of an animal is:

> [T]he use of an animal in a series of regulated procedures for a particular scientific purpose extending over more than one project licence protocol (and often over more than one project licence). The use of the same animal must be essential in order to achieve the objectives of the second or subsequent protocols. It is not necessary that all of the protocols are on the same project licence for continued use to apply. The arrangement helps minimise duplication of information, and avoids undue repetition and over-complex licence authorities.[249]
>
> "Reuse" of an animal is "a term used where, after completion of one series of regulated procedures, an animal is used again in the same or a different protocol, where a *previously unused animal* would have equally sufficed to meet the objectives of the second and subsequent use (emphasis in original)."[250]

Looking at these definitions together, it is clear that "use" of an animal does not mean the use of an animal in a single procedure or act that causes pain or suffering, as one might naively assume, but rather use of the animal *for a particular scientific purpose*. In other words, a number of painful actions can be taken with respect to an animal without constituting "reuse" of the animal, unless a "series" of regulated procedures has already been performed on the animal and a previously unused animal would do just as well in the new procedure. The deciding factor is the supposed *scientific need to use the same animal*, not whether that animal has been subjected to a painful procedure in the past. This is made even clearer by reading the definition of "continued use" which makes clear that a single animal may be subjected to many painful "procedures" in a single "use." So "use" and "reuse" in this context have different meanings than one might originally assume from reading the SPA alone. But the use of language in odd ways in the context of the regulation of animals should not surprise anyone, given the special meaning of "necessary" and similar words that we have previously encountered. In any event, given these definitions, the ASP tells us that "continued use" or "reuse" of animals requires the approval of the Secretary of State.

A provision in the SPA that we have not previously encountered is a prohibition on live exhibition to the general public of any regulated procedure

248. *Id.* at 3 (citations omitted).
249. *Id.* (citations omitted).
250. *Id.* (emphasis in original).

under the SPA.[251] This does not prohibit the filming of procedures for later broadcast.[252] There are a number of possible reasons for a provision like this. It could be to protect the public from seeing what is done to animals in experiments, but then this could be discovered from the later broadcast of the event. Another reason could be to protect the experimenters from the frequently unexpected events that often occur on live TV; remember, it is only live broadcast that is affected here. Given, however, that the animal experimentation industry intentionally exists in a shadow world where information is fiercely protected and where there is pervasive fear of exposure of what the industry actually does, one must always be concerned about limitations on dissemination of information. The public has a right to know what occurs in this industry and, at the moment, the public has little to no information.

So how are all of these pieces of the SPA enforced? There are inspectors with medical or veterinary qualifications appointed by the Secretary of State, who visit places where regulated experiments take place and report to the Secretary any violations of the SPA that they have observed.[253] The Secretary of State has the power to suspend or revoke licenses of any person whenever it appears to the Secretary that it would be "appropriate to do so," among other reasons.[254] In addition to this power of the Secretary of State, violations of licensing requirements, carrying out procedures not in accordance with a license or violation of the general animal cruelty provisions of the UK Protection of Animals Act of 1911 can lead to up to two years in prison.[255] Lesser offenses are also specified, which can lead to a fine. Interestingly, the Criminal Justice Act 2003 (c. 44) removed a possible three-month prison term for these latter offenses.[256] One other surprising aspect of this set of consequences is that violating the rules on multiple use of animals is placed in this lesser offences category.[257] So the enforcement mechanism for this law includes both administrative actions that can result in the loss or suspension of a license, and criminal liability of varying stringency, depending on the type of offense committed.

It so far appears then that the SPA is a pure Direct Government Regulation and Licensing regulatory scheme. But as it turns out, there is also a committee involved in the United Kingdom law. This is the "Animal Procedures Committee" (APC), created in section 19 of the SPA. This committee, however, is not the type of committee referred to in the typology of Ethical Committee Approval Schemes described earlier. The APC is instead a committee formed to advise the Secretary of State on matters relating to the SPA.[258] In advising the Secretary, the APC is to

251. SPA, *supra* note 224, at § 16(1).
252. United Kingdom Secretary of State, *Guidance on the Operation of the Animals (Scientific Procedures) Act 1986*, § 2.89 (2000).
253. SPA, *supra* note 224, at § 18.
254. *Id.* at § 11–13.
255. *Id.* at § 22(1).
256. *Id.* at § 22(3).
257. *Id.*
258. *Id.* at § 20(1).

consider the "legitimate requirements of science and industry and [] the protection of animals against avoidable suffering and unnecessary use in scientific procedures."[259] This standard is in line with the general standard of section 5(4) of the SPA which requires the Secretary of State to weigh the adverse affects on animals of any given project against the benefit likely to occur as a result of the experiment. What we have then is a utilitarian cost/benefit type of analysis, attempting to balance the supposed human interests in experiments against the pain and suffering of animals. The interests of the animal experimentation industry are made quite explicit in the charge of the APC that it is to take into account the "requirements" of the industry. The interests of animals, one can only suppose, will once again take a back seat to the alleged human and industry interests in this process.

That the above is the case appears to be supported by statistics on the use of animals in experiments in the United Kingdom, which indicate that the number of animals being used in the United Kingdom for experiments has been increasing, not decreasing, as is described in Table 4.2 discussed later in this chapter.[260] Thus, notwithstanding the SPA, the use of animals is not declining after all, which suggests that the SPA is not achieving the effect of reducing the amount of animal experimentation in the United Kingdom, but to the contrary, is serving the animal experimentation industry quite well. One might attempt to cast this in a different light, of course, *i.e.*, that human needs for animal experiments are ever increasing, even though the aims of the SPA are genuinely to reduce the use and suffering of animals in experiments. Whatever the reason for the increase in the use of animals in experiments in the United Kingdom, to the extent the stated purpose of the law is to reduce the number of animal experiments and the number of animals used in those experiments, the goal is clearly not being reached.

So after consideration of its utilitarian stance and lack of apparent impact on reduction of the use of animals, what can be said about the SPA as a regulatory mechanism? The United Kingdom law, despite its advisory APC, is effectively a pure Direct Government Regulation and Licensing regulatory scheme. There is a government bureaucracy established for licensing those involved in animal experiments, the projects of those experimenters and the facilities where projects are carried out. This bureaucracy has procedures for approving licenses and cost/benefit substantive standards for making decisions on licenses. Even if one were satisfied with the procedures and standards applied, the use of such a bureaucracy to regulate animal experiments can only function effectively if it is properly staffed and funded. And if this were the case one might expect that the number of experiments and animals used would decline.

That this entire game involving the modern human/animal relationship in experimentation is ultimately rigged in favor of the experimenters and against animals can be seen from a United Kingdom law that protects animal research

259. *Id.* at § 20(2).
260. *See infra* notes 401 through 404, and accompanying text.

organizations from interference by animal activists. This law makes it a crime to commit a crime or tortuous act with the intent of harming an animal research organization or intimidating people involved in animal experiments.[261] This offense carries a prison term of up to five years and a potential fine.[262] Compare this to the maximum two-year term for any form of torture or mayhem in dealing with animals committed in violation of the SPA, and exactly where the thumb is planted on the scales of justice in this case becomes obvious.

C. The Swedish Animal Welfare Act and Animal Welfare Ordinance

The Swedes have not only been at the forefront of animal welfare regulation relating to farmed animals, but also concerning animals used in experiments. These latter regulations are contained in the same documents as the agricultural animal provisions, the Swedish Animal Welfare Act (SAWA) and Swedish Animal Welfare Ordinance (SAWO) (Appendix IV).[263] As we will see, Swedish law on animal experimentation provides an example of a combination of several of the regulatory scheme typologies identified at the outset of this chapter.

The first thing we need to know is what is regulated by Swedish law. "Animal experiments" are the use of animals for scientific research, diagnosis of disease, development and manufacture of pharmaceuticals and chemicals, teaching, where there is the risk of suffering to the animal, and similar purposes.[264] It also includes the production of genetically modified animals. This definition is broader than the one in EU Council Directive 86/609/EEC, which focuses on painful procedures. The Swedish definition includes any use of animals for scientific research, etc. and includes the killing of animals for use of their organs, tissues, or cells.[265]

"Laboratory animals" are defined as those "used in animal experiments or … bred, kept or supplied for animal experiments."[266] This definition has considerable breadth according to the Swedish Board of Agriculture:

> Laboratory animals are animals that are bred for or used in animal experiments. This includes everything from laboratory rats to wild animals outfitted with radio transmitters.
>
> Embryos, semen and eggs are viewed as laboratory animals if they are meant to develop into living animals and used in animal experiments. If, on

261. Serious Organised Crime and Police Act, 2005, c. 15, §§ 145–149 (U.K.).
262. *Id.* at § 147.
263. Djurskyddslagen (Svensk författningssamling [SFS] 2009: 303) (Swed.) [hereinafter AWA]; Djurskyddsförordningen (Svensk författningssamling [SFS] 2008:1501) (Swed.) [herein after AWO].
264. AWA, *supra* note 263, at § 1c.
265. Djurförsök, *supra* note 82.
266. AWA, *supra* note 263, at § 1b.

the other hand, they are not to develop into living animals, they are classed as animal products.

Animals used in education in a way that does not expose them to the risk of suffering are not considered laboratory animals, but are instead classed as education animals. This may for instance encompass animals used at agricultural schools.[267]

There are several interesting aspects of the concept of "laboratory animals" in this definition: it applies to some aspects of wildlife study, such as those captured, outfitted with radio transmitters and released for tracking the animal's activities.[268] Animals used in education are covered only when there is risk of suffering. What this presumably means is that animals kept in classrooms only for observational purposes are not covered. One might query, however, whether simply keeping an animal captive in an enclosure for observation might not cause suffering to the animal? It would seem so, but this suffering does not appear to have been intended to be included by the authors of the law, so we see "suffering" implicitly defined not to include being held captive.

If one wants to conduct an animal experiment in Sweden, what are the requirements? SAWA section 19a provides that government permission is required "before laboratory animals can be used, bred, kept or supplied." This requires obtaining a license from the government for performing experiments on animals, breeding them for experiments, supplying animals for experiments and housing such animals.[269] So initially we can see that there is a governmental entity that oversees the use of animals in experiments. Guidance as to when animal experiments are permitted is provided in section 19 of the SAWA which provides:

Animal experiments may only take place provided that

1. the purpose of the activity cannot be attained by any other satisfactory method that does not entail the use of animals;
2. as few animals as possible are used;
3. the activity is organized in such a way as not to subject the animals to greater suffering than is absolutely necessary; and
4. no animals other than animals bred for the purpose are used in the activity.[270]

This set of provisions expresses the 3Rs. If alternative methods to an animal experiment exist, animals are not to be used—so replacements are to be pursued. Also, in any experiment using animals, the fewest possible are to be used,

267. Jordbruksverket, (Swedish Board of Agriculture) *Definition of Animal Experiments and Laboratory Animals*, http://www.sjv.se/swedishboardofagriculture/engelskasidor/animals/laboratoryanimals/definitions.4.6621c2fb1231eb917e680002832.html (last visited May 25, 2010) [hereinafter Jordbruksverket].
268. *See id.*
269. *Id.* at *Licenses for Laboratory Animals.*
270. AWA, *supra* note 263, at § 19.

reflecting the reduction principle of the 3Rs. Refinement of practices is shown in the requirement that experiments are to be structured in a way to ensure that animals are not subjected to greater suffering than is "absolutely necessary."

We have seen the language "unnecessary suffering" and similar phrases before. The language of this particular provision, however, requires that the experiment be "organized" so that there be no more suffering than "absolutely necessary." One could view this as requiring a more strict level of scrutiny of suffering than is required under language which uses only the term "unnecessary" or the like. The difficulty is, of course, how can we ever know if there actually exists some higher level of scrutiny in the process? The "organizing" of the experimental activity is done in the design of the experiment, and while we will see that experiments are subject to analysis by both a governmental agency and Ethical Committee, it would nonetheless be hard to determine if these entities are actually applying a higher standard than would be the case without the "absolutely necessary" verbiage. We do not have a baseline against which to measure such decisions to determine if the language really makes a difference. If we are going to allow experiments at all, determinations of the "necessity" of suffering reside in a fuzzy and inexact world where we must analyze the extent of the suffering of animals and what is "necessary" or "absolutely necessary" may be impossible to distinguish. The only way to give terms of this kind real meaning would be to have benchmarks or standards under which animal suffering can truly be measured, like the pain level classifications in the new EU Directive on animal experiments discussed above.

The approval process for experiments in the Swedish law involves two steps: first, it is necessary to obtain a permit under section 40 of the SAWO from the Swedish Board of Agriculture (SBA).[271] Such permits are required for animal experiments using mammals, birds, reptiles, amphibians, fish and cyclostomes.[272] When making a decision whether to issue such a permit, "special attention" is to be paid to the qualifications of the applicant and the condition of the premises on which the activity is to be carried out.[273] The second level of approval required is approval by an Ethical Committee created under the SAWA and SAWO.[274] These committees are distributed around Sweden on a geographic basis, and there are to be at least six of these committees created by the SBA under section 42 of the SAWO. There are actually seven such committees divided by counties.[275]

The composition of the committees is of obvious relevance to how they function and make decisions. These Ethical Committees must have a Chair and one or more Vice Chairs appointed by the SBA.[276] The committees are to include "laypeople, research workers and representatives of the personnel who handle

271. *Id.* at § 19a; AWO, *supra* note 263, at § 40(1).
272. AWO, *supra* note 263, at § 40(1).
273. AWA, *supra* note 263, at § 19a(2).
274. *Id.* at § 21; AWO, *supra* note 263, at § 41(1).
275. Jordbruksverket, *supra* note 267, at *Ethical Evaluation of Animal Experiments.*
276. AWO, *supra* note 263, at § 43.

laboratory animals."[277] The number of members of the committees is not to exceed 14.[278] In fact, these committees do have 14 members each.[279] Half of the members of these Ethical Committees must be laypersons, while laypersons representing animal welfare organizations must be less than half of the lay members of the committees.[280] What is clear here is an explicit stacking of the committees against animal welfare advocates. Given the structure of these committees, it is clear that half of the committee members will be from the experimentation industry, the other half lay persons, but less than half of these lay persons may be animal welfare advocates. In so structuring these committees the continuation of animal experiments is assured, because there will never be a committee that says "no" to all experiments or, as we will see shortly, to any significant number of experiments. Moreover, half of each committee will be effectively controlled by experimenters, so persuading only one lay member of the appropriateness of an experiment will be necessary to approve an experiment. Thus, animal experiments are sure to continue, ironically as an "ethical" matter, by virtue of these "ethics committees."

The standards applied to approvals of experiments by Ethical Committees are set forth in section 21 of the SAWA and require the committee to "weigh the importance of the experiment against the suffering of the animal" and the committee cannot approve an experiment if it is not considered important to the "public interest." Even though these committees appear structured to result in easy approval of experiments, the committees do have actual approval power over experiments and can deny applications. Their decisions are binding, but a Committee decision can be appealed to administrative courts,[281] which contrasts with committees created under the Animal Welfare Act in the United States, in that these latter committees have primarily an advisory role; they cannot prevent any experiment from taking place nor can they dictate the protocol used in an experiment.

So what actually occurs in these ethical reviews? According to Olle Bergman, of the approximately 1,700 applications received a year, more than 95% are approved.[282] If the applications were being seriously reviewed, one might expect a lower approval rate. It is claimed, however, that there are other reasons for the high approval rate:

> "We thoroughly review each case, regardless of whether it is simple or complex. If anything is unclear, we turn to the applicant and request additional information," says Mats Sjöquist, scientific representative on the Ethical Committee on Animal Experiments in Uppsala ....

277. *Id.* at § 43(1).
278. *Id.* at § 44(1).
279. Olle Bergman, *Swedish Law Requires Ethical Review of All Animal Experiments*, http://www.djurforsok.info/english/home/regulations/swedishlawrequiresethicalreviewofallanimalexperiments.4.1c39844f11d7804ba518000170.html (last visited May 25, 2010).
280. AWO, *supra* note 263, at § 43(3).
281. AWA, *supra* note 263, at § 38; *see also* Jordbruksverket, *supra* note 267, at *Ethical Evaluation of Animal Experiments*.
282. Bergman, *supra* note 279.

> By the time that the applications are placed on the committee's meeting agenda, most of the uncertainties have been clarified. In part, this explains why so few applications are rejected.[283]

The suggestion here is that applications are very thoroughly vetted, and that by the time an application actually reaches the Committee any ethical issues have typically been addressed and already resolved. Note, however, that this view of the process is from the perspective of those who are involved in the process.

One of the emphases of the Swedish law is on the training and qualifications of personnel involved in animal experiments. In any experiment conducted under the SAWA there must be a supervisor approved by the SBA, a veterinarian and personnel sufficient in number and training for the experiment.[284] The supervisor and veterinarian are responsible for ensuring that experimental activity is conducted in compliance with Swedish law.[285] The criteria for approval by the SBA of an experiment supervisor are the following:

- The Supervisor must have knowledge relevant to the experiments and the ability to monitor and influence them.
- Normally, the supervisor must work at the facility, but this is not required.
- They must have the ability to get to the facility quickly if required.
- At least two years experience with laboratory animals is required.[286]

In certain specialized areas, such as medical research and development, and biological research and development, further detailed educational requirements are also imposed.[287] Those under the supervisor, *i.e.*, anyone handling, caring for or taking part in the experiment must have familiarity with Swedish legislation on the use of animals in experiments, the ability to care for and handle the animals, an understanding of animal anatomy, nutrition, and disease, and the capacity to determine if animals are suffering.[288] Behind these requirements is presumably the idea that if people involved in experiments are well trained and understand the law relating to experiments, the suffering of animals will be reduced, and experiments will be properly conducted, thereby avoiding the necessity of performing the experiments again.

Not only do those involved in experiments have to meet certain requirements, but facilities used for experiments are subject to regulation as well. New construction of facilities for animal experiments must be approved by the SBA.[289] In addition, modification of existing facilities in a way that has a significant impact on animal health or welfare must be approved.[290] Approvals of facilities focus on

283. *Id.*
284. AWA, *supra* note 263, at § 20(1).
285. *Id.* at § 20(2).
286. Jordbruksverket, *supra* note 267, at *Veterinarian and Approved Supervisor*.
287. *Id.*
288. *Id.* at *Licenses for Laboratory Animals*.
289. AWO, *supra* note 263, at § 55.
290. *Id.*

*Table 4.1. Animals Used Per Annum in Sweden for Scientific Purposes**

*Year***	*European Definition*	*Swedish Definition, Excluding Fish Samples*	*Fish Samples*	*Swedish Definition, including Fish Samples*
2007	524,764	1,034,465	6,096,188	7,130,653
2006	532,685	758,213	6,653,651	7,411,864
2005	505,681	1,273,277	6,356,105	7,629,382
2004	446,936	1,005,480	7,065,550	8,071,030
2003	518,053	520,000	9,500,000	10,020,000
2002	281,184	481,000	---	---
2001	269,710	439,000	---	---
2000	288,800	402,500	---	---
1999	324,067	552,000	---	---
1998	300,704	493,000	---	---
1997	266,685	435,000	---	---
1996	286,012	718,000	---	---
1995	331,201	558,000	---	---
1990	338,343	494,000	---	---
1985	---	519,000	---	---
1982	---	488,500	---	---

*This table is arranged based on different definitions of "laboratory animal" used in keeping these statistics. The sources of this data described below, state that the "European Union" definition includes those animals actually used in some scientific procedure, whereas the Swedish definition includes all animals used in experiments and those "bred, kept or supplied" for experimental purposes. *See* Djurförsök.info, *Facts and Numbers*, http://www.djurforsok.info/english/home/facts andnumbers. 4.1c39844f11d7804ba518000450.html (last visited Apr. 15, 2009).
**For statistics for years 2004–2007, *see* Djurforsok.info, *How Many Animals Are Used in Research in Sweden?*, http://www.djurforsok.info/english/home/factsandnumbers/howmanyanimalsareusedinr esearchinsweden.4.1c39844f11d7804ba518000979.html (last visited June 14, 2010); for all other years, *see* Forska Utan Djurförsök *Animal Experiments*, http://www.forskautandjurforsok.se/in-english/animal-experiments/ (last visited June 14, 2010).

animal welfare issues and providing environments where the animals can behave in a natural fashion.[291] Special facilities ensuring that animals cannot come into

291. Jordbruksverket, *supra* note 267, *Licenses for Laboratory Animals*.

contact with the outside environment are required of locations producing or using genetically modified animals.[292]

If this Swedish law is having a real impact, one might reasonably expect to see the number of experiments decline over time. Nonetheless, this is not what Swedish statistics show as indicated in Table 4.1. While there have been some recent declines in use of animals when fish samples are included in the figures, the numbers under the European Union definition of "laboratory animal" and the Swedish definition of "laboratory animal" show an upward trend in the use of animals in experiments over time.

So what is learned from the Swedish approach to animal experimentation? First, note that the combined government permit process and Ethical Committee review makes the Swedish law a hybrid of the Direct Government Regulation and Licensing typology and the Ethical Committee Approval typology and illustrates how these different approaches can be combined. Here they have been combined to provide a two-tiered approval process. Second, the Ethical Committee review process is effectively structured to ensure the continuation of animal experiments, since the committees are stacked against animal advocates. As a practical matter, the maximum percentage of committee members that will be from animal welfare groups is less than 25%. Further, the evidence indicates that these Ethical Committees generally do not consider the ultimate question of whether the experiments should be performed at all; instead they focus on technical issues relating to the experiments.[293] Third, it is difficult to discern in the data relating to animal experiments in Sweden that this process is resulting in real change in the number and nature of animal experiments.

In sum, while the SAWA and SAWO contain what may appear to be substantial governmental regulation and substantive restrictions on animal experimentation, it appears that it is business as usual in the animal experimentation community, with experiments still continuing unchecked. A cynical view of this is that the regulation of experiments really just provides "cover" for the experimenters by providing them the ability to claim that they are highly regulated and required to minimize suffering to animals, all the while continuing to experiment in greater volume. A less cynical view, but one that might be difficult to establish from available statistics, is that the regulations are actually having an impact. Perhaps the number of experiments has not decreased because there are more products and devices that are deemed to require testing as time goes by, and it may also be that the substantive requirements of the law do make the experimenters at least consider, grapple with and address issues of pain that, without the regulations, they might well easily ignore.

On one somewhat heartening note, the SBA has exempted all great apes and nine species of gibbons from research programs, thereby prohibiting their use in experiments.[294] Here again, we see a move in the direction of species-specific

292. *Id.*
293. This issue is discussed in detail *infra* notes 393 through 401 and accompanying text.
294. Engelsman, *supra* note 208, at 359–60.

prohibitions that appear to be becoming quite popular in the area of experimentation and, as we will see later, in the use of animals in entertainment. But a nagging question about those species-specific bans on use of animals is whether such bans simply cause other animals to be used in experiments, thereby not actually causing a reduction in the number or severity of experiments.

D. Australian Code of Practice for the Care and Use of Animals for Scientific Purposes

In Australia, each state or territory has regulations on animal experiments and requires some sort of approval of experiments.[295] The foundation of these rules is the Australian National Health and Medical Research Council's Code of Practice for the Care and Use of Animals for Scientific Purposes (hereinafter "Australian Code").[296] The Australian Code is produced by a large group of entities including the National Health and Medical Research Council, the Commonwealth Scientific and Industrial Research Organization, the Australian Research Council, the Australian Vice-Chancellors' Committee, state and territory governments in Australia and certain animal welfare organizations.[297] This code sets forth detailed rules on animal experimentation and is lauded by some as one of the best, if not the best, set of rules on animal experimentation in existence.

The Australian Code is broad in its application. It applies to non-human vertebrates as well as cephalopods.[298] The inclusion of at least some non-vertebrates in its coverage is historically somewhat unusual in experimentation legislation, although as we have seen in the new EU Directive and the United Kingdom SPA, coverage of some invertebrates seems to be the current trend. Another rather unusual feature of the Australian Code is that it applies to wildlife studies, which it also considers to be "experiments."[299] This recognizes that even simple observa-

---

295. Act Now.com.au, *No, This Is Not An Issue Page About Peter Rabbit Doing His Final Modern History Exam,* Animal Testing, Feb. 2, 2009, http://www.actnow.com.au/Issues/Animal_testing.aspx [hereinafter Act Now]; Gerber, *supra* note 111, at 223; New South Wales Department of Primary Industries, *The Australian Code of Practice for the Care and Use of Animals for Scientific Purposes (Factsheet 8)* (2005), *available at* http://www.dpi.nsw.gov.au/agriculture/ livestock/animal-welfare/research-teaching/factsheets/awfact08 (last visited June 18, 2010) [hereinafter Factsheet 8]; The UFAW Handbook on the Care and Management of Laboratory and Other Research Animals 119 (Robert Hubrecht & James Kirkwood eds., Wiley-Blackwell 8th ed. 2010). The form of the state and territory regulation of animal experiments will be discussed in more detail below.

296. National Health and Medical Research Council,*Australian Code of Practice for the Care and Use of Animals for Scientific Purposes*, app. 2 (7th ed. 2004) [hereinafter Australian Code]; *see also*, Act Now, *supra* note 295.

297. Australian Code, *supra* note 296, at ii; *see also* Factsheet 8, *supra* note 295.

298. Australian Code, *supra* note 296, at *Definitions of Terms Used in the Context of the Code.*

299. *Id.* at § 5.

tional studies of wildlife may be detrimental to wildlife due to potential interference with natural behavior.[300]

In the more typical case of laboratory experiments, the Australian Code mandates that animals used in experiments "must be suitable for the scientific purpose taking into account their biological characteristics ...."[301] One type of animal is given special treatment as we have observed in other laws: primates. It is believed that the use of primates raises "[s]pecial ethical and welfare concerns,"[302] presumably because of the close evolutionary relationship between other primates and humans. With respect to these animals, investigators (defined as a person using animals for scientific purposes)[303] must take "special care" to justify the use of these species in experiments.[304] Notice how this provision so clearly expresses human hierarchical thought. Not only do we see humans as superior animals in some grand hierarchical scheme, but we distinguish between species of animals by virtue of how closely related these animals are to humans—special concern must be shown to primates due to the closeness of their relationship to humans and their presumably "more human" characteristics.

The Australian Code applies generally to scientific and teaching activities involving the use of animals.[305] A "scientific activity" is one required to achieve a "scientific purpose," which is defined as "all [] purposes which aim to acquire, develop or demonstrate knowledge or techniques in any area of science ...."[306] Similarly "teaching" is "developing, imparting or demonstrating knowledge or techniques in any area of science."[307] In undertaking these activities, the Australian Code explicitly adopts as guiding principles the 3Rs.[308]

The use of animals in scientific and teaching activities is permitted only "when they are essential" to one or more of the following:[309]

- Obtaining information relevant to the understanding of humans or animals.
- Maintaining or improving animal or human health and welfare.
- Improving animal management or production.
- Obtaining information relating to the natural environment.
- Reaching educational objectives.

Notice that among what might appear to be entirely laudatory objectives in a utilitarian sense, is an economically motivated one, improvement of the management or production of animals.

300. *Id.* at § 5.1.2.
301. *Id.* at § 1.14; *see also* § 3.1.8.
302. *Id.* at § 3.3.79.
303. *Id.* at *Definitions of Terms Used in the Context of the Code.*
304. *Id.* at § 3.3.79.
305. *Id.* at § 1.1.
306. *Id.* at *Definitions of Terms Used in the Context of the Code.*
307. *Id.*
308. *Id.* at § 1.
309. *Id.* at § 1.1.

The obligations of what are referred to as Investigators (experimenters) and Teachers (educators) are not merely hortatory in the Australian Code; to use animals for experimental or teaching purposes requires that an Investigator or Teacher obtain written approval of the project from an Animal Ethics Committee (AEC) formed under the Code.[310] Requests for approval of projects are in the form of proposals to the AEC and "must be sufficient to satisfy the AEC that the proposed use of animals is justified by weighing the predicted scientific or educational value of the proposal against the potential impact on the welfare of the animals."[311] The information required in proposals and its manner of presentation is described in detail in section 2.2.16 of the Australian Code. The information required includes a description of the project and its benefits, detailed information on how the 3Rs have been followed in the decision to perform the project, and a justification of the project weighing the scientific value of the project against its impact on animals.[312]

The AEC must consider and approve all proposals before they can be carried out.[313] To obtain approval, in addition to the weighing of the scientific value of the project against the impact on animals noted above, the project must also be found to meet all of the requirements of the Code. The process of AEC deliberation on animal experiments is meant to achieve consensus.[314] If consensus cannot be reached, the AEC is to explore ways to have the proposal changed to reach consensus.[315] If consensus is still not possible, the AEC can then make its decision on a majority vote.[316] Once an experiment is approved, it is subject to annual review.[317] The Investigator is required to submit an annual report and the AEC is required to review that report.[318] The AEC is then to determine whether the project should be continued, suspended, modified, or discontinued.[319] Completed projects are also subject to reporting requirements that demand provision of information on whether the aims of the project were reached, how many animals were used, whether the well-being of the animals was maintained at the level anticipated, and conclusions concerning how future projects could be modified to reduce animal welfare impacts.[320]

Again, the composition of the ethical committees is crucial. AECs must be formed by the institutions that carry out experiments.[321] Institutions or persons infrequently using animals for scientific purposes can access AECs formed by others.[322]

---

310. *Id.* at §§ 1.3, 1.6, 3.1.4.
311. *Id.* at § 2.2.15 (citations omitted).
312. *Id.* at § 2.2.16.
313. *Id.* at §§ 2.2.18, 2.2.20.
314. *Id.* at § 2.2.22.
315. *Id.*
316. *Id.*
317. *Id.* at §§ 2.2.37–2.2.39.
318. *Id.*
319. *Id.* at § 2.2.38.
320. *Id.* at § 2.2.39.
321. *Id.* at § 2.1.1.
322. *Id.* at § 2.1.1(i).

The committees must have at least four persons that include one person in each of the following categories: a veterinarian, a person with recent experience in animal use in science or teaching, a person committed to animal welfare, and a person independent of the institution, who has not been involved in use of animals in science or teaching and who does not meet the requirements of any other of the categories.[323] This latter requirement prevents the fourth member from being a person committed to animal welfare. If the committee has more than four members, at least one-third of the members must be either from the animal welfare or independent categories.[324] Like the Swedish committee system, we once more see that the committee appears stacked in favor of those involved in and supportive of experimentation.

In addition to approval of proposals, AECs are responsible for setting up and monitoring guidelines for the care of animals used in experiments at the institution.[325] To accomplish this, the AECs are obligated to establish and document standard operating procedures which insure compliance with the Australian Code.[326] These procedures are to govern the operation of the AEC and its monitoring activities.[327] AECs also have their own reporting requirements; they are required to submit an annual report to their governing institution concerning the number and types of projects assessed, the physical facilities of the institution, activities related to the educational needs of personnel and any matters that may affect the ability of the institution to comply with the Australian Code.[328]

One might then reasonably ask, how are the AECs policed? As can be gleaned from the previous discussion, the Australian AEC system is primarily a system of self-regulation. Each institution sets up a committee and presumably follows the rules of the Australian Code in approving and monitoring experiments. As a policing mechanism for this system it is "recommended" in the Australian Code that each institution having an AEC be subject to a formal external review of the operation of its AEC at least every three years.[329] This review is to be conducted by a qualified team external to the institution and is intended to verify that the institution is protecting the welfare of animals as required by the Australian Code. Some of the things to be reviewed by the external review team include determining that the welfare of animals is being properly managed, that the 3Rs are being implemented, that the AEC is meeting its obligations under the Code, that the AEC is communicating effectively within the institution, and that the AEC is given support sufficient to meet its obligations.[330]

In addition to obligations of persons involved in animal experiments, the Australian Code sets forth a number of obligations of Teachers. As we have seen,

---

323. *Id.* at § 2.2.2.
324. *Id.* at § 2.2.7.
325. *Id.* at § 2.2.1.
326. *Id.* at § 2.2.10.
327. *Id.*
328. *Id.* at § 2.2.40.
329. *Id.* at app. 1.
330. *Id.*

Investigators are required to obtain approval for projects from the AEC, must report to the AEC annually and cannot continue with their experiments if they do not meet reporting obligations.[331] Teachers are subject to the same general obligations relating to proposals, which include describing the proposed use of animals and following the 3Rs.[332] Proposals by Teachers must also indicate the number of students that will be involved in the activity, the number of animals to be used, how often each animal will be used and how the academic success of the project will be measured.[333] The Teacher, like the supervisor of an animal experiment, has responsibility for the care of animals in his or her charge.[334] Certain procedures, like surgery or the introduction of diseases to animals, are not to be performed by Teachers in schools or colleges.[335]

How does the Australian Code deal with the issue of repeated use of animals in experiments? Repeated use of animals is generally not permitted without AEC approval.[336] It is recognized, however, that repeated use of animals reduces the overall number of animals ultimately used and for this reason the AEC can approve reuse of animals taking into account the following factors:[337]

- The pain, distress and long term impact of the previous procedure on the animal.
- The total time of use of the animal.
- The pain and distress involved in the additional procedure or procedures.
- Whether the animal has fully recovered from the prior procedure.

The Australian Code explicitly recognizes the advantages of reuse of animals, since it reduces the number of animals that must be used. Nonetheless, reuse is subject to AEC approval, and the AEC must take into account the pain and distress that would be inflicted on the animal to be reused in determining whether or not to allow reuse.

With respect to pain and distress, the Code requires that all steps possible be taken by Investigators and Teachers to avoid or minimize pain and distress.[338] Animals must also be monitored to determine levels of pain and distress, and any such pain or distress must be alleviated promptly.[339] The obligation to alleviate pain takes precedence over continuing or finishing the project.[340] This can be directly contrasted with the approach of EU Council Directive 86/609/EEC, which allows unalleviated pain when necessary to attain the "object of the experiment."[341]

331. *Id.* at §§ 2.2.18, 2.2.20, 2.2.37.
332. *Id.* at §§ 3.1.1, 6.
333. *Id.* at § 6.3.1.
334. *Id.* at §§ 3.1.1, 6.2.1.
335. *Id.* at § 6.4.3.
336. *Id.* at § 3.3.11.
337. *Id.*
338. *Id.* at § 3.3.5.
339. *Id.*
340. *Id.* at § 3.3.10.
341. *See supra* note 99 and accompanying text.

So the Australian Code purports to put pain in the primary position when analyzing whether or not to allow the continuation of experiments, even to the apparent detriment of the "scientific purpose" of the experiment, unlike other regulatory schemes we have seen.

There are a number of aspects of the Australian system that present fascinating contrasts to the other regulatory schemes we have seen. First, notice that Australia's scheme is primarily a self-regulatory system with some state and territory government regulatory overlay. All schemes previously examined are national governmental regulatory schemes. (EU Directive 86/609/EEC, of course, requires Member States to have laws which follow its strictures as will the new EU Directive effective in 2013.) While the state and territory regulatory systems in Australia vary in certain aspects, all eight major Australian states and territories have incorporated the Australian Code into their laws.[342] Each of these states and territories also requires some authorization or licensing of persons involved in animal experiments.[343] Most Australian states also have government monitoring of animal experiments to ensure compliance with the Australian Code and state laws.[344] Some states have provisions in addition to those in the Australian Code. For example, in Queensland skin and eye irritancy tests, LD50 or similar tests, and testing of cosmetics or sunscreen products on animals is prohibited, although the government can grant exceptions to this prohibition.[345] Thus, if nothing else, there is some variety to regulations in Australia, since unlike the other countries so far discussed, Australian animal experimentation laws are not national, but at the state and territory level.

Second, consistent with the self-regulatory foundation of the Australian scheme, the committees in the Australian system are constituted at the level of the experimenting institution, while the Swedish committees are geographically formed government-appointed committees, unconnected with experimenting institutions. The institutional basis of the Australian committees is similar to the Institutional Animal Care and Use Committees which are required under the United States Animal Welfare Act and which are also formed within individual

342. Gerber, *supra* note 111, at 223.

343. *See e.g.*, Animal Research Review Panel & Industry & Investment New South Wales—Animal Welfare Branch, *Other Australian Legislation*, http://www.animalethics.org.au/legislation/other-australian-legislation (last visited May 31, 2010); *see also, e.g.*, Animal Research Act 1985 § 2A (N.S.W.); Queensland Government, Department of Employment, Economic Development & Innovation, *Animal Ethics and Using Animals for Scientific Purposes*, http://www.dpi.qld.gov.au/27_9907.htm (last visited Feb. 2, 2011) [hereinafter Queensland Government Use of Animals]; Queensland Government Department of Primary Industries, *Monitoring Program for the Scientific Use Code*, *available at* http://www.dpi.qld.gov.au/documents/AnimalIndustries_AnimalWelfareAndEthics/MonitoringProgram-ForTheScientific-UseCode.pdf (last visited Feb. 2, 2011) [hereinafter *Monitoring Program for the Scientific Use Code*]; Animal Ethics Infolink, *Other Australian Legislation*, http://www.animalethics.org.au/legislation/other-australian-legislation (last visited Feb. 2, 2011) [hereinafter *Other Australian Legislation*].

344. *See Monitoring Program for the Scientific Use Code, supra* note 343; *Other Australian Legislation, supra* note 343.

345. Queensland Government Use of Animals, *supra* note 343.

experimenting institutions.[346] The difference between the Australian and United States committee systems is that the Australian AECs actually have power to deny approval of experiments and experimental protocols, while their United States counterparts largely have only advisory authority.

Third, note that when one has an essentially self-regulatory system, the system is only going to be as efficient as are its self-regulators. Yes, it is true that all of the major Australian states and territories have some regulations of their own on animal experiments, but they do rely in major part on the Australian Code. Whether such a regulatory structure will actually result in outcomes favorable for animals is dependent on the integrity of the self-regulators and those who monitor the self-regulatory system. One could say that there is a strong element of blind faith behind this kind of self-regulatory mechanism.

As an essentially self-policed committee arrangement with an overlay of state and territory laws, the Australian model is a combination of the Direct Government Regulation and Licensing typology and the Ethical Committee Approval typology described earlier. The extent of governmental involvement in this system is, however, substantially less than in the Swedish system. In Sweden, there is regulation by two sets of governmental authorities: the permit process of the SBA and ethical review by the local committees appointed by the SBA. In Australia, the system is, with local state variations, a private institution committee system with state and territory governmental institutions licensing experimenters and, in some cases, monitoring them. The Canadian system we will now analyze is even more of a true self-regulatory system than that of Australia.

E. THE CANADIAN COUNCIL ON ANIMAL CARE GUIDELINES

While the Australian institutional committee system is essentially self-regulatory in its structure, it has been incorporated in the laws of the major Australian states and territories and is, therefore, required to be followed by these governments. The Canadian system is a self-regulatory institutional committee system similar to that of Australia, but is a more "pure" self-regulatory system that is not officially made a part of Canadian national or provincial law, with some exceptions discussed below. The Canadian Council on Animal Care (CCAC) has created this committee process for analyzing and approving animal experiments. The CCAC describes itself as follows:

> The CCAC was incorporated as a non-profit, autonomous and independent body in 1982.
>
> The CCAC is mostly funded by public monies through the Canadian Institutes of Health Research [] and the Natural Sciences and Engineering

346. United States Animal Welfare Act, 7 U.S.C. §§ 2132(n), 2143(b) (2008).

> Research Council [] with additional contributions from federal science-based departments and private institutions.[347]

National law does not require the committee process which is described by the CCAC *Guide to the Care and Use of Experimental Animals* (hereinafter "Guide"),[348] but it has been described as a de facto requirement for experimenters, since funding agencies require approval by these committees.[349] While there are national criminal laws relating to cruelty to animals, it is provincial law that covers animal experiments. Seven provinces, Alberta, Manitoba, Saskatchewan, Ontario, New Brunswick, Nova Scotia and Prince Edward Island, all have laws on animal experimentation, and all of these provinces, other than Ontario, incorporate the CCAC Guidelines into their law.[350]

The Guide itself is a formidable document which has two volumes and many hundreds of pages. In the first volume are general provisions on the use of animals in experiments, while the second volume focuses on the use of particular kinds of animals.[351] Note that general guidance on the meaning and intent of the Guide are set forth in the *Terms of Reference for Animal Care Committees* published by the CCAC.[352] There are also a number of other voluminous CCAC publications on procurement of animals used in science; the use of fish in research; the design of laboratory animal facilities; and the care and use of wildlife and other related subjects.[353] In addition, adherence to the 3Rs in animal experimentation in Canada is called for by the CCAC document, *Ethics of Animal Investigation*.[354] One rather unusual aspect of the Canadian regulation is that the use of stray and donated animals is not prohibited.[355]

---

347. Canadian Council on Animal Care (CCAC), *History and Funding*, http://www.ccac.ca/en_/about/history_funding (last visited Mar. 3, 2011).

348. CCAC, *Guide to the Care and Use of Experimental Animals Vol. 1*, (Ernest D. Olfert et al., eds., Canadian Council on Animal Care 1993), *available at* http://www.ccac.ca/en/CCAC_Programs/Guidelines_Policies/PDFs/ExperimentalAnimals_GDL.pdf [hereinafter Guide].

349. PCRM Animal Care, *supra* note 25. Note, however, that private institutions not receiving this kind of funding may indeed not be inspected under this committee system as is more fully discussed at *infra* note 389 and accompanying text. *See* David Sztybel, *The Canadian Council on Animal Care's Code of Ethics: A Critical Evaluation*, MED. RESEARCH MODERNIZATION COMMITTEE, *available at* http://www.mrmcmed.org/DavidSztybel.html (last visited Feb. 2, 2011).

350. CCAC, *Legislation in Canada Related to Experimental Animals*, http://www.ccac.ca/en/CCAC_Programs/ETCC/Module01/11.html (last visited June 3, 2010).

351. CCAC, *List of CCAC Guidelines, available at* http://www.ccac.ca/en/CCAC_Programs/Guidelines_Policies/GDLINES/Guidelis.htm (last visited May 31, 2010) [hereinafter CCAC List]; Guide, *supra* note 348.

352. *See* CACC, *Terms of Reference for Animal Care Committees* (2006), *available at* http://www.ccac.ca/en/CCAC_Programs/Guidelines_Policies/PDFs/TOR_2006_en.pdf, [hereinafter TOR].

353. *See* CCAC List, *supra* note 351 (listing documents on animal experimentation currently in place in Canada).

354. CCAC, *Ethics of Animal Investigation (1989)*, http://www.ccac.ca/en/CCAC_Programs/Guidelines_Policies/POLICIES/ETHICS.HTM (last visited May 31, 2010).

355. *See* Guide, *supra* note 348, at 83 (discussing the legal use of stray and donated animals).

The Canadian System, like those of Sweden and Australia, requires that all animal experiments be approved through a committee system. These Animal Care Committees (ACC or ACCs) are to be created at each institution that carries on animal experiments and are to be composed of members holding no less than two-year and not more than four-year terms, renewable up to a maximum of eight years.[356] Composition of the ACCs can vary based on the needs of the particular institution, but should include:[357]

- Scientists or teachers experienced in animal care and use not actively using animals while on the ACC.
- A veterinarian.
- An institutional member whose normal activities have not involved animal use.
- One or more (preferably more than one) person representing community interests. (Note that it is not required that this person have any animal welfare credentials or background.)
- Technical staff representation.
- Student representation when the institution is a University.
- The ACC Coordinator, which is a required position at each institution, but this coordinator may be part-time.
- The Animal Facilities Manager.

The Veterinarian, ACC Coordinator and Animal Facilities Manager who are required to be on the committee are not subject to the term limit rules described above.[358]

No research testing or teaching program may be commenced without prior ACC approval of a written protocol.[359] The written protocol submitted to an ACC must include a rather long list of information on the experiment, including information on how experimenters have considered the 3Rs prior to presenting their protocol.[360] The institution must also provide an appeal mechanism for projects that are not approved.[361]

The general standard for the use of animals in experiments is that:

> [t]here must be a reasonable expectation that studies involving animals will: a) increase understanding of structures and processes underlying behaviour; b) increase understanding of the particular animal species used in the experiment; or c) result eventually in benefits to the health and welfare of humans or other animals.[362]

---

356. *Id.* at 28.
357. *Id.* at 28–29; TOR, *supra* note 352, at 2–3.
358. Guide, *supra* note 348, at 28.
359. *Id.* at 30; TOR, *supra* note 352, at 4–5.
360. Guide, *supra* note 348, at 31; TOR, *supra* note 352, at 4–7.
361. Guide, *supra* note 348, at 33.
362. *Id.* at 245.

This requirement links with the obligation of animal researchers to submit a written protocol revealing that the project has scientific merit, ordinarily shown through independent peer review of the project, and also the obligation of the ACC to find that such merit exists.[363] In the "reasonable expectation" language, again we see the use of, to put a positive spin on it, flexible language or, to put a negative spin on it, ambiguous language, like the "unnecessary pain and suffering" phrase that we have seen before. This "reasonable expectations" concept seems to be one that can be molded, stretched or interpreted in virtually any manner one chooses. Surely, even those performing some of the bizarre experiments described earlier in this chapter proffered some semblance of a scientific basis for their experiments; but would any logical person view them as having a "reasonable expectation of yielding useful information" in any objective sense? What seems to be reasonable and what often passes for science appear frequently to inhabit different universes. Let's not forget that Edward Taub of Silver Spring monkey fame was presented with an award for his strange forays into animal experimentation.

In addition to the approval of protocols, the ACC has a number of substantive animal care responsibilities including:[364]

- Ensuring appropriate care for animals and availability of veterinary care.
- Making sure that unnecessary pain or distress is avoided.
- Making certain that anesthesia or analgesia are used for painful experiments, except where there is a scientifically justified reason for not using them which is approved by the ACC. This is similar to what we have seen in other regulatory schemes that allow for pain and suffering where it is a part of the experimental purpose.
- Ensuring that the animal experimentation establishment has standard operating procedures for all activities involving animals.

Post-approval monitoring procedures for each institution's animal use protocols are also required and the ACC must periodically review those procedures.[365] It is also an obligation of the ACC to visit experimentation facilities at least once a year.[366] In addition, the experimental protocols are to be reviewed yearly and new protocols are required of all projects after a maximum of three renewals.[367]

On an ongoing basis, the ACC must have the authority to:[368]

- Stop any objectionable procedure if unnecessary pain or distress is being experienced by an animal.
- Immediately stop any animal use that diverges from the approved use.
- Euthanize an animal humanely if the animal is experiencing pain and distress not part of the protocol and this pain or distress cannot be alleviated.

363. *Id.* at 30, 32; *see also* TOR, *supra* note 352, at 7.
364. Guide, *supra* note 348, at 33–34; TOR, *supra* note 352, at 9–10.
365. Guide, *supra* note 348, at 29, 35.
366. *Id.* at 35.
367. *Id.* at 33; *see also* TOR, *supra* note 352, at 8–9.
368. Guide, *supra* note 348, at 29.

The foregoing provides only an outline of the obligations of the ACCs; there is considerably more detail on the responsibilities of the ACCs in the voluminous Guide.

The ACCs themselves are subject to assessment by CCAC Panels composed on average of three scientific members and one animal welfare member.[369] Along with a director, this means the panels are generally made up of five members.[370] These Panels do periodic assessments of local ACCs, typically on a three-year basis.[371] In addition to regular scheduled visits, the Panels can make special or unannounced visits.[372] As with other groups we have seen in animal experimentation operations, these panels are skewed toward animal experimenters and those sympathetic to animal research. Presumably this imbalance leads to a generally favorable attitude by these panels toward the experiments and experimenter community, which is clearly borne out by the fact that experiments continue apace.

The Guide also regulates, as do the laws of other countries we have seen (to one extent or another), the facilities where experiments are performed and animals are housed. With respect to facilities, the Guide provides many recommendations concerning the design, construction, and environment maintained in animal experimentation facilities.[373] The statements about design are stated as things that "should" be done, revealing that these are only recommendations rather than strict rules.[374] There are many other aspects of animal care and use that are the subject of recommendations and requirements in the Guide, including:

- Recommendations for facilities and environments for specific types of animals used in experiments.[375]
- "General principles" relating to maintaining the social and behavioral requirements of animals.[376]
- Standards for experimental animal surgery.[377]
- Control of pain.[378]
- Use of anesthesia.[379]
- Euthanasia.[380]
- Use of animals in psychology.[381]
- Use of animals in neurobiological research.[382]

---

369. *Id.* at 19–20.
370. *See* Canadian Federation of Humane Societies, *Who's Watching*?, http://cfhs.ca/research/who_s_watching/ (2009).
371. Guide, *supra* note 348, at 19.
372. *Id.* at 19–21.
373. *Id.* at 44–51.
374. *Id.*
375. *Id.* at 65–93.
376. *Id.* at 94–151.
377. *Id.* at 179–86.
378. *Id.* at 187–205.
379. *Id.* at 206–21.
380. *Id.* at 222–39.
381. *Id.* at 240–49.
382. *Id.* at 250–52.

The Canadian system also has fairly detailed rules on the use of animals in pre-University schools. This aspect of experimental and educational animal use is governed primarily by the Youth Science Foundation Canada, which incorporates the requirements of the Guide.[383] In science fair projects, for example, vertebrate animals are generally not to be used with the following four exceptions: mere observation of animals is permitted in zoos, on farms and in the wild, behavioral experiments with positive rewards are allowed when the animals will not be stressed, projects involving animal experimentation may be conducted under the supervision of research personnel at a university, hospital, or governmental agency, and observation of embryos is permitted.[384]

So what can be said of the Canadian system as governed by the Guide? One thing that can be observed is that the Guide and its related documents are long and detailed, which does not necessarily mean that they are truly beneficial, or even a step in the right direction. The Guide is a mélange of recommendations and requirements containing various hortatory statements and discussions; indeed, it is sometimes difficult to determine where the recommendations leave off and the real requirements begin, and it is equally difficult to determine why experimenters would feel compelled to actually follow the recommendations when they are only suggestions, which are not enforced in any measure. Perhaps the most conscientious of experimenters will assiduously adhere to every recommendation of the Guide, but it would certainly be fanciful to assume that all will.

Like the other regulatory schemes we have seen, the Canadian system continues to allow nearly any kind of animal experiment, including "burning, freezing, fracturing, staging predator-prey encounters, electrical shocking, inducing of extremely high or low temperatures, and striking or beating of unanaesthetized animals … so long as an external review is obtained."[385] And these reviews, moreover, are effectively conducted by other researchers or research interests that are both predisposed to favor virtually any kind of experiment at all, and may have their own conflicts of interest, given their personal interests in animal experimentation.[386] Remember that in the Canadian ACC system, there does not even exist a requirement that animal welfare interests be represented on the committees (although there is an Animal Welfare person on CCAC Panels that review the ACCs); all that is necessary is that there be a representative of community interests. This contrasts with the other committee systems that we have seen which do at least have a requirement of animal welfare interest representation. So the Canadian scheme can be viewed as even more heavily weighted toward the interests of the experimenters than are the Australian or Swedish systems.

As we have seen, language relating to animal welfare can generally be manipulated in a way that allows humans to do whatever they feel is in their best interests.

---

383. Id. at 26–27; Youth Science Canada, *Use of Animals in Research,* http://www.ysf.ca/files/PDF/governance/policy/en/4.1.2_Animals.pdf (last visited Feb. 9, 2010) [hereinafter YSFC].
384. YSFC, *supra* note 383, at § 8.1–8.2.
385. Sztybel, *supra* note 349.
386. *See id.*

We have seen that the ever-present "unnecessary" pain or suffering language is tantamount to having carte blanche to engage in any economically, socially, or culturally acceptable behavior concerning animals. There is language of this sort in the Guide; for example, experiments are allowed so long as there is a "reasonable expectation of benefit to humans." This language, in addition to being vague, has also been characterized as the "lowest standard of justification"[387] that could be used, because just about anything could be found acceptable under this standard. Other language is used that is equally indeterminate, such as the gentle admonition to experimenters to use "best efforts" to find alternatives to use of animals.[388] Language that allows such wobbling in potential interpretation gives experimenters wide latitude in satisfying themselves and others that they have eagerly complied with the requirements and recommendations of the Guide.

Moreover, any system that is effectively self-regulating raises suspicion; it creates the proverbial fox in the henhouse scenario. How can anyone rationally expect that those who would obviously prefer to be left alone, perhaps because they do not want the light of day to shine on their enterprise, are going to conscientiously regulate their own behavior under purely voluntary guidelines? Moreover, although the Guide purports to be applicable to all who conduct experiments in Canada, privately funded operations may not be inspected at all under this system.[389]

If it could be established, however, that the use of animals has declined over time under this scheme, then perhaps one could argue that it has, despite some questionable elements, nonetheless achieved some success. This is indeed what the Guide claims: "As a result, although the research community is growing, the numbers of experimental animals has, to date, steadily declined …."[390] This statement is, to say the least, puzzling, since the CCAC statistical data on its own website appears to contradict this statement. For example, these statistics show that the total animals used in experiments in Canada has increased from 1,756,416 in 1996 to 2,272,815 in 2008.[391] So again we see that, despite the CACC self-regulatory system, animal experimentation has been trending upward, not downward. We have now seen this pattern so often that one almost begins to think that perhaps it is not despite these regulatory schemes that animal experimentation is increasing, but because of them.

387. *Id.*
388. *Id.*
389. *Id.*
390. Guide, *supra* note 348, at 19.
391. CCAC, *Annual Surreys of Animal Use,* http://www.ccac.ca/en_/publications/audf/stats-aud (last visited Mar. 3, 2011).

IV. CONCLUSIONS, ALTERNATIVES AND A GLANCE TOWARD THE FUTURE

It is evident that there are many ways to approach the issue of regulating animal experimentation. We have seen that each of the typologies discussed earlier have been used by different countries and that these different methodologies can be combined in various fashions. The United Kingdom follows most closely the Direct Government Regulation and Licensing type system. In Sweden and Australia we see mixed systems combining aspects of the Direct Government Regulation and Licensing type with the Ethical Committee Approval scheme, but these two systems also have a number of distinctions. The governmental regulation in Australia is done at the state and territory level, while in Sweden it is the national government that is involved. Also, the level of government involvement in Australia is limited basically to requiring that the AEC committee system be followed by institutions. In Sweden, the committees themselves are created by the government and there is a separate government licensing regulatory mechanism. So these regulatory schemes not only vary in type, but also in their intensity.

But are any of these regulatory mechanisms working? Well, there is licensing in the United Kingdom, licensing and committee approvals in Sweden, and committee approvals in Australia and Canada; so to this extent, they are working. But consider, for instance, that in 2003 approximately 99% of the experiments reviewed by Ethics Committees in Sweden were approved. Only 22 of 1733 cases were rejected.[392] It could be argued that the experiments and their protocols were approved because they were all so well done and so clearly necessary for the advancement of human knowledge, and human and animal welfare. But the truth likely lies elsewhere.

In an ongoing study of Animal Ethics Committees in Sweden, it was found that different members of committees viewed the "ethical" issue involved in their work in diverse ways. There were some scientist members of the committees who actually saw the ethical issue as being one of promoting the use of animals in experiments, since in their view it is ethically required to use animals in research for the benefit of humans.[393] Even one non-scientist member of a committee is quoted as saying "I don't care about the animals at all, I just care for humans."[394] This perspective, of course, is quite contrary to the purposes of these committees, the charge of which is to look at animal experiments from an ethical perspective and to consider the interests of animals in this analysis. In the case of these particular committee members, the entire process has been turned on its head.

If these were the only views expressed by committee members, then even a supporter of these committee regulatory processes would have to admit to utter

---

392. Malin Ideland, *In the Name of Science? How Members of Animal Ethics Committees Talk about Ethics* 1, 2 (2007), *available at* http://dspace.mah.se/bitstream/2043/4524/1/In_the_name_of_Science.muep.pdf.

393. *Id.* at 4–5.

394. *Id.* at 5.

and complete failure. The Swedish study, however, found that a majority of committee members did view the ethical issue as pertaining to the welfare of the animals.[395] This was the case generally for even the scientist members of these committees. Nonetheless, it seemed that the ethical issues discussed by the committees were not typically about the ethics of the particular experiment itself; or of animal experiments in general; but only of specific aspects of the way the experiment was to be performed, such as what was the appropriate "end-point" (the time the animal will be killed) for the experiment.[396] The underlying ethical issue, that of performing the experiment at all, which committee members appear to view purely as a utilitarian cost/benefit analysis, did not occupy the committees' time.[397] Why would this be? One reason is that the scientists dominated the interpretation of the issues in the committee meetings.[398] The experiments are, after all, science. In addition, there is great pressure to reach consensus on these committees. Concerning the underlying ethical issues of the value of the experiments themselves, there is little likelihood that consensus could ever be reached, so the members instead concentrate on issues that they can easily reach consensus on: safe, technical scientific questions.[399]

What all this indicates is that while committees meet and deliberate, they may not even focus on the underlying issues of the ethical appropriateness of animal experiments generally or even of the particular experiment being proposed, but instead deliberate on technical details of the experiments, which would explain the extremely small number of experiments that are rejected. It does not seem as though experiments are being rejected in any significant numbers under any of the regulatory systems we have reviewed. As the statistics set forth in Table 4.2 show, the use of animals in experiments continues generally on an upward trajectory, notwithstanding the regulations that have been applied.[400]

Not only are the number of animals used in experiments increasing, but there is evidence that the number of painful experiments continues to rise.[401] The following has been said on this subject about animal experiments in the United Kingdom:

> The annual UK Government statistics have revealed another appalling surge in animal experimentation during 2008. It is the seventh yearly increase in succession and the highest figure since the current system began in 1986. In 2008, 3,656,080 million experiments took place in British labs, an increase of 454,499 (14%) on 2007. The number of animals used also rose abruptly to 3,583,223 (some animals are used in more than one experiment, hence the difference in figures between the number of experiments and the number of

395. *Id.* at 6.
396. *Id.* at 8.
397. *Id.* at 4–9.
398. *Id.* at 8.
399. *Id.* at 9.
400. *See* Gerber, *supra* note 111, at 228.
401. *Id.* at 218.

Table 4.2. National Statistics of Animals Used in Scientific Procedures from 1999 to 2008

	Australia[a]	*Canada*[b]	*United Kingdom*[c]	*Sweden*[d]	*United States*[e]	*New Zealand*[f]
2008	N/A	2,272,815	3,583,223	N/A	N/A	341,520
2007	11,482,441	2,054,909	3,125,826	524,764	1,027,450	246,667
2006	6,893,020	2,535,989	2,946,624	532,685	1,012,713	318,489
2005	4,862,198	2,316,285	2,812,850	505,681	1,177,566	263,214
2004	6,489,005	2,307,232	2,778,692	446,936	1,101,958	246,122
2003	N/A	2,489,219	2,721,599	518,053	1,188,469	320,911
2002	N/A	2,103,135	1,817,485	281,184	1,137,718	263,684
2001	N/A	2,136,329	2,567,713	269,710	N/A	318,583
2000	N/A	1,954,059	2,642,993	288,800	N/A	324,395
1999	N/A	1,746,606	1,905,462	324,067	N/A	249,272

Information used in the table was obtained from the following sources:

[a] Humane Research Australia, *Statistics—Animal Use in Research & Teaching, Australia,* http://www.aahr.org.au/statistics.html (last visited Feb. 2, 2011). These numbers include aquatic species. The 2006 figure excludes statistics for Northern Territory and Australian Capital Territory; including these statistics would bring the national statistic to approximately 7.4 million. The 2007 figure excludes Queensland, Northern Territory, so the approximate national total is estimated to be more than 12 million.

[b] *See* Canadian Council on Animal Care, *Facts and Figures*, http://www.ccac.ca/en/Publications/New_Facts_Figures/table01/table01_index.htm (last visited June 13, 2010).

[c] Annual reports regarding animal use in the United Kingdom are compiled by the Home Office, *available at* http://tna.europarchive.org/20100413151426/http://scienceandresearch.homeoffice.gov.uk/animal-research/publications-and-reference/statistics/index.html (last visited June 14, 2010).

[d] Forska Utan Djurförsök (The Swedish Fund for Research Without Animal Experiments), *Animal Experiments* http://www.forskautandjurforsok.se/in-english/animal-experiments/ (last visited June 14, 2010); Djurforsok.info, *How Many Animals Are Used in Research in Sweden?*, http://www.djurforsok.info/english/home/factsandnumbers/howmanyanimalsareusedinresearchinsweden.4.1c39844f11d7804ba518000979.html (last visited June 14, 2010). The figures used are based on the European definition of "animal," not the Swedish definition.

[e] Figures for use of animals covered by the United States Animal Welfare Act are reported each fiscal year by the Animal and Plant Health Inspection Service, *available at* http://www.aphis.usda.gov/animal_welfare/index.shtml. (last visited June 18, 2010). Note that the most often used animals in experiments, rats and mice, are not covered by these statistics.

[f] Animal use statistics are contained in an annual report prepared by the National Animal Ethics Advisory Committee, *available at* http://www.biosecurity.govt.nz/regs/animal-welfare/naeac/annual-reports (last visited June 13, 2010).

animals used). By law, the Home Office only counts those experiments that are likely "to cause pain, suffering, distress or lasting harm."[402]

Notwithstanding that all the regulatory systems discussed in this chapter in one way or another either codify or follow the 3Rs, "reduction" does not really seem to be occurring.[403] It could be that this is because scientists do not really focus on reduction, but instead focus more intently on refinement, with a goal of trying to reduce suffering in the experiments.[404]

Yet another worry on the issue of animal experimentation in Europe is the Registration, Evaluation, Authorisation and Restriction of Chemicals (REACH) legislation which will require safety testing of all chemicals sold in the EU by 2018.[405] REACH is expected to result in a "deluge of animal tests" to comply with this legislation.[406] So a real reduction in European animal testing does not seem to be on the horizon; the future would appear instead to hold a large increase in animal testing for the claimed purpose of benefiting human health and safety.

It is important to note in our examination of animal experimentation, that there are advances in science that, if only the will to end animal suffering existed, might substitute for the use of many animals in experiments. There are *in vitro* systems, where cell tissue cultures and organs are used in experiments rather than living animals.[407] These *in vitro* tests can be very accurate and useful: "A ten year international study proved that human cell culture tests are more accurate and yield more useful information about toxic mechanisms than traditional animal tests."[408] This, of course, raises the question of where the cells, tissue and organs are obtained if animal cells, tissue, or organs are to be used in such tests. If animal cells, tissue, or organs are going to be used in *in vitro* research, obviously the organs and cells must come from animals. So even *in vitro* research on animal cells or organs requires use of animals. For some experiments, lower organisms such as bacteria, fungi and plants can be used in lieu of animals.[409] Additionally the use of vertebrates at early stages of development could bypass the use of adult sentient animals.[410] Mathematical and computer models may be used to replace animals in

402. Uncaged, *Animal Experimentation—The Facts*, http://www.uncaged.co.uk/vivisect.htm (last visited June 1, 2010).
403. Gerber, *supra* note 111, at 213, 215, 217–18, 224, 228.
404. *Id.* at 217.
405. Alison Abbott, *European Research Animal Use Holds Steady*, Oct. 10, 2010, *available at* http://www.nature.com/news/2010/101007/full/news.2010.524.html.
406. *Id.*
407. *Id.* at 216–17; Darian M. Ibrahim, *Reduce, Refine, Replace: The Failure of the Three R's and the Future of Animal Experimentation,* 2006 U. Chi. Legal F 195, 199 (2006); Dale Jamieson, Morality's Progress 125 (2002).
408. Archibald, *supra* note 34.
409. Gerber, *supra* note 111, at 216–17; Ibrahim, *supra* note 407, at 199.
410. *See* Gerber, *supra* note 111, at 216–17; *see generally* Ani B. Satz, *Would Rosa Parks Wear Fur? Toward a Nondiscrimination Approach to Animal Welfare*, 1 J. Animal L. & Ethics 139, 158 (2006).

some circumstances.[411] But one of the most efficient ways to reduce the number of animals used in experiments is a simple one, albeit one that does not get nearly enough consideration; the rampant use of animals for unnecessary experiments could be reduced by the simple sharing of information on experiments so that experiments do not become redundant.[412] There are also moves toward trying to replicate biological systems through what are essentially plastic chips with cells from different organs connected together with fluid exchange pathways.[413] So there are existing alternatives to animal testing that are accepted in the scientific community and, even in the view of this community, can replace certain animal experiments. Increased efforts to find alternatives to animal tests could result in new techniques and technologies that could replace more animal experiments.

So what might progress look like and how might it be achieved in the future? It is highly unlikely that everyone will suddenly come to the conclusion that animal experiments are morally wrong and scientifically unsound. But the truth about animal experimentation, which includes gruesome and preposterous experiments that are done and redone in endless repetition, and information on the questionable efficacy of animal experiments, are all messages that must be disseminated to a widespread public. Perhaps, even more than with respect to the treatment of agricultural animals, I believe that the general public, if it actually knew what was occurring daily in animal labs, would bring pressure to change the present system. In the case of agricultural animals, the selfishness of "I need to eat hamburgers" may be too much for many to overcome. But in the case of animal experimentation, the immediate self-interest is much lower and the milieu is much more abstract than the craving for familiar food, particularly if one understands that the intended benefit of the experiments may well be chimerical. So not surprisingly, some change may yet come through education.

Since we have not seen a reduction in the number of animals being used in experiments, what sorts of regulations might result in fewer animals being used? If we had rules that prohibited certain kinds of experiments or prohibited the use of certain types of animals in experiments, perhaps the number of experiments might start to decrease. For example, LD50 tests could be prohibited, or experiments that have as their "scientific" purpose only determining the impact of pain could be made illegal. New Zealand, for example, similar to the EU in its new Directive on animal experiments, has prohibited the use of great apes in experiments, unless the experiment would benefit the animal in question or its species.[414] Unfortunately, whether this regulation will aid in reducing animal experiments in

411. *See* Gerber, *supra* note 111, at 216–17; Ibrahim, *supra* note 407, at 199; JAMIESON, *supra* note 407, at 125.
412. *See* Gerber, *supra* note 111, at 214–17; About Animal Testing, *Rapid Information Sharing to Reduce Animal Tests,* http://www.aboutanimaltesting.co.uk/rapid-information-sharing-reduce-animal-tests.html (last visited June 10, 2010).
413. *See* Hurel Corporation, *Technology: Overview,* http://www.hurelcorp.com/overview.php (last visited May 31, 2010) (for examples of the work being conducted in this field); *see* Jamil El-Ali et al., *Cells on Chips,* 442 NATURE 403 (2006).
414. Gerber, *supra* note 111, at 221–22.

New Zealand cannot be determined, since there were no great apes being used in experiments in New Zealand at the time the law was created.[415] We have also seen similar species-restrictive moves in laws and regulations of the United Kingdom and Australia, though none of these, of course, are outright prohibitions on the use of animals in experimentation. Whether these actions result in reductions in the use of animals will only be able to be assessed in the future, but the danger of these species-specific prohibitions is that they may just cause other species of animals to be used instead and thereby not result in any overall reduction in experimental use of animals.

The development of alternatives to animal testing, like some of those mentioned previously, may aid in bringing about an end to animal testing. Organizations like the ECVAM in Europe may help move the scientific community in this direction. At our present technological stage, however, alternatives to animal testing do not seem likely to replace a substantial part of current animal experimentation. That this is the case is confirmed by the statistics that show increases in the use of animals in experiments notwithstanding efforts to find alternatives.

Whatever the future holds and whatever the proper strategy for change may be, it is crucial that the public know what is really going on, which is perhaps encapsulated in the following:

> Dr. Hoggan, the English physiologist, related an incident he had witnessed in Claude Bernard's laboratory. A small mongrel dog, whose hind quarters were paralyzed as a result of an operation, had been removed from the operating table and left on the floor. He started dragging himself painfully toward a retriever that had been blinded a few days earlier for another experiment and was kept under observation. Its eyes had begun to putrefy. The blind dog managed to pick itself up, tottered toward the half-paralyzed little mongrel and wagged its tail.
>
> Nobody else in that lab seemed to notice the scene, which prompted Dr. Hoggan to write: "The pathetic gesture of mutual sympathy put the human race to shame."[416]

---

415. *Id.* at 222.
416. Ruesch, *supra* note 13, at 53.

Chapter 5
Animals in Entertainment

I. ZOOS, CIRCUSES AND OTHER EXHIBITIONS

She was forty and an experienced trainer.[1] There were differing descriptions of what happened. Apparently she was stroking the killer whale's head when she was pulled into the water and spectators "saw all the thrashing and the bubbles and him pushing her with his nose."[2] Some said the whale grabbed her by the waist and dragged her under.[3] Others said that she was grabbed by the hair.[4] However it happened, Dawn Brancheau was dead.

This was not the first time that the killer whale Tillikum had been caught swimming with drowned humans under suspicious circumstances. He had drowned one of his trainers in a 1991 incident.[5] A man who apparently had snuck into the park after hours or had hidden in the park after it closed was found naked and drowned on the back of Tillikum in 1999.[6] So, one has to wonder, how did SeaWorld imagine that something like this would not happen again? Why would they continue to expose their employees and the public to an animal that had repeatedly killed humans?

The likely answer, not surprisingly, is money. SeaWorld Florida is owned by The Blackstone Group, a huge private equity firm, which is involved in, among

---

1. Jane Sutton, *Orca Kills Trainer at Florida's Seaworld* [sic], Feb. 25, 2010, http://www.reuters.com/article/idUSTRE61N6GS20100225.
2. John Couwels & Brian Todd, *SeaWorld Trainer Killed by Killer Whale*, Feb. 25, 2010, http://www.cnn.com/2010/US/02/24/killer.whale.trainer.death/index.html (quoting Paula Gillespie, a bystander).
3. Sutton, *supra* note 1.
4. Ed Pilkington, *Killer Whale Tilikum [sic]to Be Spared After Drowning Trainer by Ponytail*, Feb. 25, 2010, http://www.guardian.co.uk/world/2010/feb/25/killer-whale-tilikum-drowned-trainer-hair.
5. Sutton, *supra* note 1.
6. Couwels & Todd, *supra* note 2; Sutton, *supra* note 1.

other things, private equity transactions, real estate, and what they call "credit and marketable alternatives," including funds of hedge funds.[7] In short, they are big operators in the financial world. They recently finalized the purchase of Busch Entertainment Corporation, which includes in its assets SeaWorld, from Anheuser-Busch InBev.[8] The press release describing the purchase states that "the purchase price is comprised of a cash payment of USD 2.3 billion and a right to participate in Blackstone's return on its initial investment capped at USD 400 million. Busch Entertainment Corporation is now known as SeaWorld Parks & Entertainment."[9] Given these facts, one can assume that SeaWorld generates a lot of money, unless, of course, Blackstone is foolish in its investments.

Blackstone's SeaWorld has created a fantasy environment in which children and adults can experience the delight of performing whales, dolphins and sea lions, and people pay considerable sums to participate in this dream world for a few hours; but sometimes the fantasy turns brutal, as it did for Dawn Brancheau. This is not the only time that exhibitions of this kind have gone wrong; there have been other reported incidents of killer whales attacking and injuring humans,[10] perhaps as many as 24 such incidents.[11] Killer whales are highly social animals who live in social groups of varying sizes,[12] and these individual groups form their own special cultures. Some pods of whales live off fish; some cannot stand fish and live off of marine mammals; some stay in particular areas; some travel extensively.[13] In their vocalizations, different groups use different dialects, different languages.[14] Given the nature of killer whales, it should hardly come as a surprise to anyone that keeping such an animal, which can weigh up to 22,000 pounds and is accustomed to travelling up to one hundred miles a day in the wild, in what amounts to a bathtub, might result in neurotic or other dangerous behavior.[15] There were, in fact, reports that the whales involved in the Brancheau incident were not following instructions just prior to the drowning.[16] But can anyone blame these intelligent, social, but nevertheless, still wild animals, forced to live in these conditions, for behaving in ways dangerous to humans? The play of a 22,000 pound

7. The Blackstone Group, http://www.blackstone.com/cps/rde/xchg/bxcom/hs/Home.htm (last visited June 16, 2010) (follow "Our Businesses" hyperlink).
8. The Blackstone Group, *Anheuser-Busch InBev and Blackstone Announce Completion of Sale of Busch Entertainment Corporation,* Dec. 1, 2009, http://www.blackstone.com/cps/rde/xchg/bxcom/hs/news_pressrelease_6207.htm.
9. *Id.*
10. *See* Humane Society of the United States, *SeaWorld Attack Reaffirms Whale of a Truth: Captive Orcas Can be Dangerous*, July 28, 2004, http://www.freerepublic.com/focus/f-chat/2458732/posts.
11. Matt Walker, *Killer Whales: What to Do with Captive Orcas?*, Feb. 25, 2010, http://news.bbc.co.uk/earth/hi/earth_news/newsid_8536000/8536184.stm.
12. Orca Free, *How They Live*, http://orcafree.org/how.html (last visited May 18, 2010).
13. *Id.*
14. *Id.*
15. Elizabeth Landau, *Biologists: Killer Whales "Neurotic" in Captivity*, Feb. 25, 2010,http://www.cnn.com/2010/US/02/25/whales.seaworld.death/index.html.
16. *Id.*

animal can surely be hazardous for any human in close proximity. But there is money to be made in this perverse fantasy world; and so it goes on.

Danger to humans from captive animals comes not just from marine predators kept in what literally amount to bathtubs. There is another large animal that has been involved in even more incidents leading to injury and death for humans than killer whales. Elephants have been involved in a large number of events causing death or injury too, and often those injuries are to children, those for whom the cartoon world of happy dancing animals has been fashioned so that they might persuade their parents to spend money there.[17] Keeping such large animals, accustomed to exercise and traveling of long distances, nearly immobilized, causes a disturbing amount of what are referred to as "stereotypic behaviors" that are not observed in these animals in the wild.[18] One example of this kind of behavior is the incessant rocking of the head by elephants, which we often see in captive elephants and one that I remember from visits to the zoo when I was a child.[19] The behavior of elephants sometimes becomes violent when they are startled in their unnatural and confined surroundings.[20] Indeed, the recognition of the difficulties and dangers of confining elephants has led to studies aiming to determine the factors most likely to result in captive elephant "well-being."[21]

So Blackstone and others make money while the spectators are amused and entertained; but this entertainment is not without its costs, and not only for people like Dawn Brancheau. The animals themselves suffer greatly in places like SeaWorld, circuses and other "amusement parks." Just a few examples:

- *Coney Island*: Since 1992, some 26 elephants or more have died under the care of Ringling Brothers Circus, some from foot diseases caused by the elephants being made to stand on hard floors for long hours and forced to spend the majority of their time chained by their feet.[22]
- *Disney's Wild Animal Kingdom*: Here 31 animals died of neglect and negligence even before the park opened, "including two West African crowned cranes who were run over by safari trucks, four cheetah cubs who swallowed a toxin found in antifreeze, and two Oriental small-clawed

17. People for the Ethical Treatment of Animals, *Elephant Incidents in the United States* (2009), http://www.circuses.com/pdfs/Elephant_Incident_List-US.pdf [hereinafter *Elephant Incidents*].
18. *See* T.M. Gruber, et al., *Variation in Stereotypic Behavior Related to Restraint in Circus Elephants*, 19 Zoo Biology 209, 209–10 (2000).
19. *See* Letter from Joyce Poole, Director Research & Conservation, Elephant Voices, to Los Angeles City Council (Nov. 24, 2008), *available at* http://www.elephantvoices.org/multimedia-resources/document-download-center/cat_view/71-statements-a-testimonies-.html [hereinafter *Poole*].
20. *See Elephant Incidents, supra* note 17.
21. *See* Gruber, *supra* note 18, at 217–20; Lisa Kane et al., *Optimal Conditions for Captive Elelphants: A Report by the Coalition for Captive Elephant Well-Being* (2005); Lisa Kane et al., *Best Practices by the Coalition for Captive Elephant Well-Being* (2005).
22. Helping Animals, *Deadly Destinations*, http://www.helpinganimals.com/travel_feat_deadlydest.asp (last visited May 18, 2010).

otters who ate poisonous seeds from loquat trees planted in their exhibit."[23]

- *SeaWorld (again)*: Between 1986 and 2008, 21 orcas died in captivity with SeaWorld.[24]
- *Six Flags Discovery Kingdom*: Here they use old fashioned training methods, *i.e.*, beatings of elephants with bullhooks (rods with sharp metal hooks attached to the end).[25] They also apparently routinely mishandle animals and fail to give proper veterinary care.[26]
- *Six Flags Wild Safari*: Abysmally:

> In one three-month period, 26 animals died at Six Flags Wild Safari. The causes of death ranged from neck and skull fractures to hypothermia, tetanus, pneumonia and drowning. While drive-through wildlife parks give the impression that they're "sanctuaries," Six Flags Wild Safari has sold "surplus" baboons to biomedical researchers and exotic hoofed animals to hunting ranches.[27]

Regardless of the real cost in the lives and well-being of both humans and animals, in the end animal exhibitions like SeaWorld and Ringling Brothers are all about profit and the creation of a fantastical environment for the amusement of humans. Unlike the amusement parks of the world, zoos have at least a colorable argument that they are doing something worthwhile. They are, after all, not typically there to make money; they are public educational projects. Of course, they display animals and usually charge admission for this privilege, but they also make efforts to breed and study animals that are endangered, which it can be argued is of real benefit to humans and animals. There is reason to doubt the veracity of this rationalization, however. For example, elephants breed quite well in the wild, as well as in captive breeding programs in their range states.[28] So the captive elephant breeding programs in places like the United States are, like the circus business, actually about money. As elephant expert Joyce Poole notes: "[c]aptive breeding [in North America] is about maintaining elephants in North America and is pure business."[29] Moreover, you do not need a zoo with thousands of animals, many of which are not endangered, but are merely imprisoned, to create a captive breeding program for endangered animals, assuming this is necessary, practical, or appropriate.

There are other arguments used to justify zoos, perhaps the most popular of which is that zoos educate the public about animals and this knowledge is valuable not only to humans, but also ultimately for animals. But is it really educational to

23. *Id.*
24. *Id.*
25. *Id.*
26. *Id.*
27. *Id.*
28. *Poole, supra* note 19.
29. *Id.*

show animals in unnatural conditions, behaving in unnatural and sometimes dangerous ways? Joyce Poole comments on this issue: "Nevertheless, it is not educational to allow children to believe that elephants are healthy and thriving in insufficient space, when science overwhelmingly shows they are not. Exhibiting elephants that display abnormal behavior caused by cramped conditions is animal abuse. You don't have to be an elephant expert to see that—kids comment on it all the time."[30] Moreover, there are clearly many ways other than zoos to educate the public about animals; you only have to look at the program guide for your cable or satellite television if you are in doubt.

Regardless of the ultimate utility of any of these activities, my intention here is to analyze some of the sorts of regulations that exist in relation to these animal entertainment enterprises. Not unlike rules on the use of animals in science, there are a number of different approaches taken to the regulation of circuses and other animal performances by different countries. With respect to circuses and similar exhibitions, some countries provide standards for the care of animals held, while others have moved to one extent or another to ban the use of animals in circuses. With respect to zoos though, the ordinary regulatory response is to regulate, not to impose bans. We will look at this range of regulatory mechanisms by analyzing legislation from New Zealand, India and Austria.

II. THE REGULATION OF CIRCUSES AND SIMILAR ANIMAL PERFORMANCES

A. NEW ZEALAND

1. Circuses

New Zealand has a general law, The Animal Welfare Act 1999 (hereinafter "NZAWA"), relating to the welfare of animals that creates mandatory rules on cruelty to animals, use of animals in experiments, hunting, prohibition of animal fighting and other issues. This law is supplemented by a number of "Animal Welfare Codes" propounded by the National Animal Welfare Advisory Committee (NAWAC), a committee created for, among other purposes, drafting these codes.[31] One of these codes is the Animal Welfare (Circuses) Code of Welfare 2005 (hereinafter "Circus Code"). This Code does not purport to ban the use of any type of animal in circuses, but rather provides rules for the care and treatment of animals used in circuses.

---

30. *Id.*
31. New Zealand Animal Welfare Act 1999 §§ 56–61, 68–79 (2008) [hereinafter *NZAWA*]. For a general critique of New Zealand's Animal Welfare Act, *see* Peter Sankoff, *Five Years of the "New" Animal Welfare Regime: Lessons Learned from New Zealand's Decision to Modernize Its Animal Welfare Legislation*, 11 ANIMAL LAW 7 (2005).

The rules set forth in the New Zealand codes are structured in a tiered way. "Minimum Standards" are set forth in the codes, using the mandatory language "must."[32] These standards have two sorts of legal effects under the NZAWA. First, a violation of these minimum standards is not itself a criminal offense, but rather constitutes evidence of a violation of the NZAWA.[33] Second, compliance with a minimum standard can be used as a defense to an alleged violation of the NZAWA,[34] thus causing the Codes to effectively "trump" the NZAWA.[35] The somewhat unusual impact of the Codes and their relationship to the NZAWA is described by the New Zealand Ministry of Agriculture and Forestry as follows:

> Codes of welfare have a particular legal status under the Animal Welfare Act. Breach of the minimum standards in a code is not an offence. Rather, any prosecutions will be for failure to meet the obligations in the Act relating to the care of an animal or for ill-treatment of an animal. Failure to adhere to the minimum standards set out in a code will, however, be able to be used as evidence to support a prosecution.
>
> Compliance with a relevant code of welfare is a defense where a person is charged with an offence under the Act. Such persons have the opportunity to argue and present evidence that their standard of care or conduct equaled or exceeded that specified in a relevant minimum standard.[36]

Another regulatory tier, "Good Practice," is an undefined term in the NZAWA, but in the Circus Code the NAWAC takes it to mean:

> a standard of care that has a general level of acceptance among knowledgeable practitioners and experts in the field; is based on good sense and sound judgment; is practical and thorough; has robust experimental or scientific foundations; and prevents unreasonable or unnecessary harm to, or promotes the interests of, the animals to which it is applied. Good practice also takes account of the evolution of attitudes about animals and their care.[37]

So Good Practices are common-sense, scientifically founded good practices that are generally accepted in the field, but failing to follow them is not a violation of New Zealand law. Sometimes, however, these practices are incorporated in mandatory requirements of the codes.[38] "Recommended Best Practices" are recommendations

---

32. Animal Welfare (Circuses) Code of Welfare 2005 § 1.8.1 (N.Z.) [hereinafter *Circus Code*].
33. *Id.* at § 1.2; Sankoff, *supra* note 31, at 15.
34. *Circus Code, supra* note 32, at § 1.2; Sankoff, *supra* note 31, at 15.
35. Sankoff, *supra* note 31, at 15–16.
36. Ministry of Agric. & Forestry, Guidelines for Drafting Codes of Welfare: MAF Information Paper No. 36, § 2.1 (Ministry of Agric. & Forestry 2001) available at http://www.biosecurity.govt.nz/animal-welfare/codes/codesofwelfare-guidelines.pdf.
37. *Circus Code, supra* note 32, at § 1.8.1.
38. *Id.* at §§ 1.8.1, 2(1).

made in the codes, but are not mandatory and failure to follow these best practices is not a violation of the NZAWA.[39] These practices are defined as:

> [t]he best practice agreed at a particular time, following consideration of scientific information, accumulated experience and public submissions on the code. It is usually a higher standard of practice than the minimum standard, except where the minimum standard is best practice. It is a practice that can be varied as new information comes to light.[40]

The codes of New Zealand, then, have the somewhat unusual structure of setting forth both minimum requirements and recommended practices, and they also frequently explain within the codes the reasons for the rules set forth in the law. Another unusual aspect of these Codes is that many of them may have actually been written by industry representatives.[41]

The substantive rules of the Circus Code start with the requirement that owners or persons in charge of animals live up to a number of fundamental duties, which include ensuring that the "physical, health and behavioral needs of the animals are met in a manner that is in accordance with both good practice and scientific knowledge."[42] Ill and injured animals must also be provided with treatment to alleviate "unreasonable or unnecessary pain or distress."[43] As we have seen many times before, the standard for treatment of animals is that we allow whatever might be deemed "necessary" to continue to allow the exploitation of animals in just about any manner thought up by humans. It is actually just gratuitous suffering that we prohibit.

There are also Minimum Standards provided for the acquisition, holding, transfer and breeding of animals. Animals are not to be acquired if it is likely that they will have to live in solitude.[44] The idea then is that animals are to be collected as if we were populating Noah's Ark; in pairs so that animals have companionship.[45] Animals kept without companions of the same species are to have companions of other compatible species.[46] Animals showing signs of distress, as indicated by an inability to adapt to circus life, are not to be held in circuses.[47] Animals are also to have access to an area in which they can avoid contact with their audience, the public.[48] As noted earlier, the Circus Code does not ban or limit the types of animals that can be kept in circuses, and certain types of wild animals are the subject of separate requirements for their care, based on species.[49]

39. *Id.* at §§ 1.2, 1.8.1.
40. *Id.* at §§ 1.8.1.
41. Sankoff, *supra* note 31, at 17.
42. *Circus Code, supra* note 32, at § 2(1).
43. *Id.*
44. *Id.* at Minimum Standard No. 1(b).
45. *Id.* at Minimum Standard No. 1(c).
46. *Id.* at Minimum Standard No. 1(d).
47. *Id.* at Minimum Standard No. 1(e).
48. *Id.* at Minimum Standard No. 2(b).
49. *Id.* at Minimum Standard Nos. 8–10.

Animals must be checked on a daily basis for health problems and must have access to veterinary treatment.[50] Since animals are often transported by circuses, standards are also provided for proper and safe transport of animals.[51] There are also rules on the provision of adequate food, nutrition and water, rules on the size and nature of shelters for animals and rules relating to exercise and behavioral stimulation for animals.[52] With respect to exercise, animals are to be given access to exercise areas for at least eight hours a day.[53] Similarly, toys, climbing elements, furniture and the like are to be provided to encourage normal behavior.[54] For lions, elephants and primates, issues relating to housing, restraint (in the case of elephants, meaning chains and tethers), and exercise are separately dealt with in specific Minimum Standards.[55]

Proper training of personnel is a high priority in the Circus Code; there must be sufficient staff with "the appropriate ability, knowledge and professional competence so as to ensure that the health and welfare of the animals is maintained in accordance with the minimum standards listed in [the] code."[56] Training on the normal range of behavior of the species cared for by the personnel is to be provided.[57]

Training of animals, which as we have seen can be brutal, is to be performed under the Circus Code based on positive reinforcement.[58] Food deprivation is not to be used and implements of training are not to be utilized in any way so as to cause unnecessary distress or injury.[59] Interestingly, electric prods fit within the category of proper equipment for use with circus animals, but "only in situations where the animal's handler is at risk."[60] It is difficult to perceive electric prods as "positive reinforcement" and it is also hard to comprehend when a handler is not at risk when dealing with wild animals like elephants and big cats. One can only wonder how a handler would interpret this, and how often these tools are actually used.

But even these Minimum Standards are subject to various exceptions; the NAWAC has the power to recommend standards that do not meet minimum requirements of the NZAWA.[61] What exactly is the reason that these more lax standards are permitted? The Code itself says it best, "in making this recommendation [for a more lax standard] the NAWAC must have regard to, among other things, the feasibility and practicality of effecting a transition from current practices and any adverse effects that may result from such a transition, *and the economic effects of any transition from current practices to new practices* (emphasis

50. *Id.* at Minimum Standard No. 11.
51. *Id.* at Minimum Standard No. 12.
52. *Id.* at Minimum Standard Nos. 4–6.
53. *Id.* at Minimum Standard No. 6(c).
54. *Id.* at Minimum Standard No. 6(d).
55. *Id.* at Minimum Standard Nos. 8–10.
56. *Id.* at Minimum Standard No. 3(a).
57. *Id.* at Minimum Standard No. 3(b).
58. *Id.* at Minimum Standard No. 7.
59. *Id.*
60. *Id.*
61. *Id.* at § 8.3, note; *NZAWA, supra* note 31, at § 73(3).

added)."[62] Thus, the economic impact of better treatment of animals is made an explicit foundation for allowing failures to comply with even the most minimal of standards.

So how is the NZAWA enforced? The law provides for inspectors who have the power to enter premises, vehicles and the like to ensure that the provisions of the Act and the Circus Code are being followed.[63] What happens if a violation of the law is found? Violations of Minimum Standards in any of the New Zealand Animal Welfare Codes may be used as evidence to support a prosecution under the NZAWA.[64] In addition, New Zealand law has just recently changed to increase penalties for animal welfare criminal violations.

Prior to July 6, 2010, offenses under the NZAWA were divided into two types: the first type were willful violations that required proof of intent, and the second type were ones where proof of intent was not required, along with some other lesser offenses.[65] Prior to the recent revisions to the NZAWA, the willful offenses carried maximum criminal penalties of up to a NZD 50,000 fine and three years in prison for individuals, and up to a NZD 250,000 fine for corporations.[66] The second group of lesser offenses had penalties of up to a NZD 25,000 fine and six months in prison for individuals, and up to a NZD 125,000 fine for corporations.[67] While these penalties were not mere slaps on the wrist, New Zealand has recently passed legislation increasing the penalties for offenses and creating a third, middle form of offense, "reckless ill treatment" of animals.[68] Under this legislation, for willful offenses the penalties are increased to up to a NZD 100,000 fine and up to five years imprisonment for individuals, and fines of up to NZD 500,000 for corporations.[69] The new "reckless ill-treatment" violations carry fines of up to NZD 75,000 and up to three years in prison for individuals, and fines of up to NZD 350,000 for corporations.[70] The non-willful and lesser offense category also sees an increase in criminal penalties, with fines of up to NZD 50,000 and up to one year in prison for individuals, and fines up to NZD 250,000 for corporations.[71] New Zealand, then, has moved toward taking even more seriously violations of animal welfare criminal laws and has imposed relatively long prison terms and large fines for violations of animal welfare legislation.

---

62. *Circus Code, supra* note 32, at § 8.3, note (emphasis added).
63. *Id.* at app. I(4). Similar provisions on inspections exist under the other Animal Welfare Codes discussed below.
64. *See e.g., id.* at § 1.2.
65. *NZAWA, supra* note 31, at §§ 29, 31, 34–35, former §§ 28, 37; *see also* Animal Welfare Amendment Act, 2010 (N.Z.) *available at* http://www.legislation.govt.nz/bill/government/2010/0118/latest/whole.html [hereinafter *AWAA*].
66. *NZAWA, supra* note 31, at former § 28.
67. *Id.* at former § 37.
68. *AWAA, supra* note 65, at §§ 5–6.
69. *Id.* at § 5.
70. *Id.*
71. *Id.* at § 6.

Whatever the enforcement mechanisms, the New Zealand law on circuses seems laissez-faire with respect to allowing the use of wild animals. What the Circus Code does provide are standards and requirements for the handling, training, housing and care of circus animals, as well as requirements for the training of circus personnel. But these rules are based ultimately on the familiar proviso that owners must avoid "unnecessary" pain and suffering or the like. And, of course, economic issues can once again trump even minimum requirements for proper care for animals. So the New Zealand scheme is one that preserves the status quo—allowing the fantastic spectacle of a circus with wild animals—while tinkering around the edges of circus practices by requiring space, exercise, wholesome food and positive reinforcement training. An encouraging note, however, is that three districts in New Zealand have recently banned the use of exotic animals in circuses on council land.[72] Perhaps this movement toward outright bans on uses of animals in New Zealand circuses will proceed successfully in the future.

2. Rodeos

New Zealand has a Code of Welfare designed to address the treatment of animals in rodeos known as the Animal Welfare (Rodeos) Code of Welfare 2003 (hereinafter "Rodeo Code", reprinted in Appendix V), which is interesting in several senses. First, rodeos are often justified based on their importance in American culture:

> Rodeo proponents claim this "sport" should be preserved as an American tradition that harkens back to the frontier days of the Old West, when cowboys tamed wild beasts with brute strength and cunning. What they fail to acknowledge is that rodeos harm animals who [sic] are forced to "perform" in a competition that is essentially a display of human domination over other species.[73]

This tradition managed to find its way to Australia and New Zealand where rodeos are also staged. [74] The second interesting fact about the regulation of rodeos is that New Zealand has a set of comprehensive legal regulations for rodeos, but the United States does not.[75]

---

72. Animal Defenders International, *Worldwide Circus Bans*, http://www.ad-international.org/animals_in_entertainment/go.php?id=281&si=1&ssi=10 (last visited June 16, 2010) [hereinafter *ADI Worldwide Circus Bans*].
73. In Defense of Animals, *Rodeo Facts*, www.idausa.org/facts/rodeos.html (last visited May 18, 2010) [hereinafter *IDA*].
74. There is a rodeo riders association in New Zealand called the New Zealand Rodeo Cowboys Association. *See* New Zealand Rodeo Cowboys Association, http://www.rodeonz.co.nz/ (last visited May 18, 2010).
75. The US, like New Zealand, has a rodeo cowboy association called the Professional Rodeo Cowboy Association and they do have their own animal welfare rules. *See* Professional Rodeo Cowboy Association, http://www.prorodeo.com/animal_welfare.aspx?xu=3 (last visited June 16, 2010).

If you knew nothing at all about rodeos and attended one, you would probably wonder where all the wild and fierce animals used in the rodeos come from. The fact is that they are not wild and fierce, but are generally domesticated and gentle. They have been forced to be wild and fierce through provocation or the infliction of pain:

> Their wild behavior in rodeo events is artificially induced by painful or irritating provocation like tail twisting or shocks from electric prods. For example, rodeo proponents claim that broncos naturally buck, but this is patently false. The reality is that horses won't buck unless handlers tighten a leather "flank strap" just below the rib cage. If you've ever been pinched in the sensitive nerve area around your abdomen, you may understand why a horse would instinctively buck in a hopeless attempt to escape the pressure. The strap is pulled so tightly that horses used in rodeos frequently exhibit open sores on their flanks caused by agitation from the strap. While the flank strap itself causes pain, the wild bucking that it induces can cause severe injuries and even fatalities. Several American cities, including Pittsburgh, Pa., have in effect banned rodeos by outlawing the use of the flank strap because it is so cruel.[76]

Similar cruel practices occur in other rodeo events. In calf roping, the animals are routinely thrown to the ground with such force as to stun the animals so that it is easier to tie their legs.[77] In Defense of Animals describes how television deals with this cruelty in rodeo broadcasts: "During these broadcasts on channels like ESPN, the camera always cuts away from the calf before he is thrown to the ground in order to spare the home audience the sight of such brutality. Even many cowboys agree that calf roping is inhumane."[78]

All of these practices result in many and frequent injuries to animals. "Because of the aggressive nature of rodeo events, animals commonly suffer serious injuries, such as torn ligaments, broken bones, fractured horns, internal bleeding, and even severed spinal cords or tracheas."[79] So this so-called "sport" is really just the terrorizing and torture of animals.

Nonetheless, the Rodeo Code begins from the premise that rodeos are an appropriate and legal activity. This Code contains the same general rules and requirements concerning the treatment of animals that we have seen in the Circus Code, *i.e.*, an obligation to secure the physical, health and behavioral needs of animals, and to insure that any ill or injured animal receives veterinary care.[80]

---

76. *IDA, supra* note 73 (citations omitted).
77. *Id.*
78. *Id.*
79. *Id.*
80. Animal Welfare (Rodeos) Code of Welfare 2003 §2 (N.Z.) [hereinafter *Rodeo Code*]. The *Rodeo Code* has been severely criticized by the Royal New Zealand SPCA, which has argued that rodeos should be banned altogether and condemns the *Rodeo Code* as "simply rubber-stamping the continuance of rodeos without addressing key animal welfare concerns, including practices which result in pain, fear and distress." Press Release, Royal N.Z. Socy. for the

As in the Circus Code, the owner or person in charge is responsible for caring for the animals. But who is "in charge" at a rodeo where the animals are handled by many people, including the contestants? The Rodeo Code provides that the organizer of the rodeo "has overall responsibility for the welfare of the animals" in the rodeo.[81] The organizer is then given certain specific obligations, like:

- Ensuring that a veterinarian is contracted for to provide care for animals during the rodeo.[82]
- Assuring that no "undue or injurious force is used to encourage any animal to participate in a rodeo event."[83] It is interesting the language used—getting the animal to "participate" in the event, as if it is voluntary.
- It is recommended in a "best practices" provision that records be kept of injuries to animals. But as a "best practice," it is not required.[84]

Also, while the contestant is using an animal, the contestant is considered the "person in charge" and is responsible for the animal.[85]

The Rodeo Code also includes a requirement that an "Animal Welfare Officer" be appointed for and present at all rodeos.[86] This person "has direct responsibility for the welfare of animals" in the rodeo and is to work with the organizer and the veterinarian to assure the welfare of the animals.[87] In one of a number of aspects of the Rodeo Code that has been criticized by the Royal New Zealand SPCA, Minimum Standard 5 provides that "unless called away to an emergency," a veterinarian is required to be in attendance at all rodeos, and this veterinarian must examine all animals before the rodeo to determine that the animals are "fit to compete."[88] It is further required that injured animals receive treatment as soon as possible.[89]

In addition, there are rules on the animals that can legally be used in rodeos and how often they can be used. For example, it is required that horses used be of a certain age, and that cattle cannot be used more than three times a day in events.[90] There are also regulations relating to the condition of the arena, the gear used by contestants and the use of electric prods for the purported purpose of

---

Prevention of Cruelty to Animals, *SPCA Condemns Weak New Rodeo Code,* Dec. 5, 2003, *available at* http://www.kiwisecure.co.nz/rnzspca/news/archive.html (hereinafter *SPCA Press Release*).

81. *Rodeo Code, supra* note 80, at § 4.1.
82. *Id.* at Minimum Standard No. 2(b)(vi).
83. *Id.* at Minimum Standard No. 2(b)(ii).
84. *Id.* at § 4.1.
85. *Id.* at § 4.3.
86. *Id.* at Minimum Standard No. 3(a).
87. *Id.* at § 4.2.
88. *Id.* at Minimum Standard No. 5. The Royal New Zealand SPCA is very critical of, among other things, allowing veterinarians to be called away from a rodeo for an emergency. *SPCA Press Release, supra* note 80.
89. *Rodeo Code, supra* note 80, at Minimum Standard No. 8(a).
90. *Id.* at Minimum Standard No. 9.

ensuring the welfare of the animals.[91] One of the countless ironies relating to the so-called protection of the welfare of animals is the bizarre contradiction of creating welfare rules relating to the use of electric prods. But thankfully, electric prods are specifically prohibited from being used "simply to harass an animal" in the Rodeo Code.[92]

There are Minimum Standards set in the Rodeo Code for specific events; for instance, saddle bronc riding requires saddles to be placed and fitted properly, and the saddle must fit in a particular way on the animal.[93] Bareback bronc riding requires that pads be used on the horses and that the judges and animal welfare officer approve these pads.[94] Other standards are set for roping events, bull riding, steer wrestling, and calf and sheep riding.[95]

What we see in the New Zealand law is a fairly comprehensive set of rules to be followed in the care and handling of animals in rodeos. Under this law, an activity that inherently causes stress and injuries to animals is still permitted, but rules are set to try to keep the torture to a minimum. Why do you suppose we allow these events to continue? There is, as usual, the priority of money; rodeos generate income for those who arrange the events. There is also the element of protection of "cultural" traditions (even though the traditional culture of rodeos does not emanate from New Zealand). But if cultural traditions in New Zealand are an appropriate defense for the ill treatment of animals, it might be appropriate, then, for Italians to bring back events in the Roman Coliseum, where "as many as five thousand"[96] animals were tortured and killed in a single day, as a Roman "cultural revival." I doubt that anyone would suggest this, but the cultural argument in favor of rodeos does not differ in basis from the Roman hypothetical; the cultural foundation for rodeos just happens to be one that developed more recently. If "cultural" tradition is the reason for these orgies of cruelty, then perhaps what is needed is a spotlight trained on these practices, with the intention of educating audiences as to the nature of the entertainment they have chosen. The real question here ought not to be, how can we torture these rodeo animals more "humanely," but why do we do it at all?

What is found in the New Zealand approach to circuses and rodeos is a regulatory regime which allows these entertainment activities to proceed, but with a set of rules regulating the use of animals within the activities. These rules once again follow the ubiquitous references to preventing "unnecessary" suffering and the like; but we know that in the denotative sense, none of these activities are really necessary at all; they are just things that humans, not animals, choose to do. So humans do them under the surface gloss of rules that purport to protect the welfare

91. *Id.* at Minimum Standard Nos. 10–12.
92. *Id.* at Minimum Standard No. 12(b)(iii).
93. *Id.* at Minimum Standard No. 13.
94. *Id.* at Minimum Standard 14.
95. *Id.* at Minimum Standards 15–18.
96. Roman Coliseum, *Tourist Guide to the Roman Coliseum,* http://www.roman-colosseum.info/colosseum/tourist-guide-roman-colosseum.htm (last visited May 18, 2010).

of the animals, but the animals continue to suffer needlessly, and without any sort of "necessity" at all.

B. India

India has a culture and history unlike that of Western countries. Among other things, it is the birthplace of the Jain religion, which practices non-violence toward all creatures and contains other tenets that require the compassionate treatment of animals. As we will see in a later chapter, this vision of non-violence and compassion is actually written into the Constitution of India, so it is not surprising to find that India has a number of laws purporting to protect animals. One of these laws is the Prevention of Cruelty to Animals Act, 1960 (PCAA). This law has a typical general animal cruelty provision that prevents, among other things, subjecting animals to "unnecessary pain or suffering."[97] This language is seen frequently in Indian animal regulations, as well as in those of other countries, as we have already discussed. The penalties for violating this aspect of the PCAA are, however, quite minor; a fine of not less than INR 10, but up to INR 50 (a little more than USD 1) for the first offense, and potential imprisonment of up to three months upon a second offense, should it occur within three years of the first.[98] Given that many countries and states within countries punish animal cruelty of various kinds as felonies or serious offenses, this seems a somewhat lax criminal punishment.

Another general provision of this law states: "For the promotion of animal welfare generally and for the purpose of protecting animals from being subjected to unnecessary pain and suffering, in particular, there shall be established by the Central Government ..." an Animal Board of India.[99] This Board has, among others, the duty to keep the laws relating to animals under constant study, to advise the Central Government on animal issues, to encourage rescue shelters for animals, and to educate on the humane treatment of animals.[100] Thus, India has a specific agency charged with the protection of the welfare of animals.

The portion of the PCAA relevant to circuses begins, in section 21, by defining "exhibit" as the showing of animals at "any entertainment to which the public are admitted through sale of tickets" and "train" as the training of animals "for the purpose of any such exhibition." The PCAA goes on to regulate the exhibition and training of animals by making such activities illegal unless the exhibitor or trainer is registered with the government.[101] This is similar to the provisions used in many other countries with respect to licensing of those who perform animal experiments;

97. The Prevention of Cruelty to Animals Act, 1960, No. 59, Acts of Parliament, 1960, § 11 [hereinafter *PCAA*], *reprinted in* Maneka Gandhi et al., Animal Laws of India 7 (3d ed. 2006) [hereinafter Gandhi].
98. *Id.*
99. *Id.* at § 4(1).
100. *Id.* at § 9.
101. *Id.* at § 22.

the idea is to regulate and control those involved in the use of animals through a bureaucratic licensing process.

If the exhibition or training is "accompanied by unnecessary pain or suffering" of animals, a police or other authorized officer can make a complaint to a magistrate, requesting that the court prohibit or condition the exhibition or training of the animals.[102] This need for judicial intervention to control the activities of exhibitors and trainers, however, seems a rather cumbersome enforcement mechanism. Another problem with this scheme is that the penalties for violations appear fairly lax; for example, violation of the registration rules is punishable by a fine of up to INR 500 or three months in prison, or both.[103] Courts may also order an animal forfeited for any violation of the PCAA, and persons violating the Act can also be prohibited from having custody of any animal whatsoever.[104]

Like New Zealand law, India has detailed rules relating to animals used in entertainment outside of the general provisions of the PCAA. These rules are set forth in The Performing Animals (Registration) Rules, 1973 (hereinafter "PAR 1973"). These rules define a "performing animal" as "any animal which is used at, or for the purpose of any entertainment to which the public are admitted through sale of tickets."[105] PAR 1973 also prescribes the form and place for the filing of registration requests for exhibitors and trainers of animals.[106]

PAR 1973 has been supplemented with new rules relating to animal performances, including the use of animals in films, in The Performing Animals (Registration) Rules, 2001 (hereinafter "PAR 2001"). PAR 2001 does not replace PAR 1973, but in the event of any conflict, PAR 2001 controls.[107] PAR 2001 changes the definition of "performing animal" to mean "an animal which is used at or for the purpose of any entertainment including a film or equine event to which the public are admitted."[108] Like PAR 1973, PAR 2001 requires registration of any person exhibiting or training animals.[109] For the use of animals in films, prior notification to the government of such use is required.[110]

In granting registrations under PAR 2001, the government "may" impose restrictions on the grant of registrations relating to, among other things, provision of veterinary care for the animals, the feeding of the animals, conditions to protect the animals from unnecessary pain and suffering, prohibition of animal fighting

---

102. *Id.* at § 24(1).
103. *Id.* at § 26.
104. *Id.* at § 29.
105. The Performing Animals Rules, 1973 § 2(b), *reprinted in* GANDHI, *supra* note 97, at 33 [hereinafter *PAR 1973*].
106. *Id.* at §§ 3–5.
107. *See* The Performing Animals (Registration) Rules, 2001, *reprinted in* GANDHI, *supra* note 97, at 39 [hereinafter *PAR 2001*]. The two sets of rules, *PAR 1973* and *PAR 2001* coexist. In the event of a conflict of *PAR 1973* and *PAR 2001*, the new rules apply. Provisions found in *PAR 1973*, but not the new rules, continue to be effective.
108. *Id.* at § 2.
109. *Id.* at § 3.
110. *Id.* at § 7.

and many other possible conditions on the exhibition of animals described in section 8 of PAR 2001.[111] Note that this aspect of the rules has recently been diluted; it originally stated that the government "shall" impose the restrictions noted in section 8; this language has been replaced with "may," thereby making the conditions discretionary in the governmental authority. In any event, the Indian law on use of animals in exhibitions creates a bureaucratic system of registration under which certain conditions may be imposed by the government.

But India has not stopped with just a registration scheme; unlike New Zealand, India has, pursuant to the PCAA, banned the training and exhibition of bears, monkeys, tigers, lions and panthers.[112] This ban was challenged by the Indian Circus Federation and the All India Circus Employees Union in *Balakrishnan, et al. v. Union of India*.[113] The Court in *Balakshrinan* made clear what was at stake in the case by providing a description of some traditional wild animal training techniques from the book by famed animal trainer Alfred Court, *Wild Circus Animals*, from which I quote the following brutal passages directly:

- "If [an animal] does attack, the animal must at once be given a severe enough correction for him to realize from the first encounter that he is not the stronger. Sometimes, indeed, it is a life-struggle, to the death."[114]
- Even when undesired behavior can be prevented without harming the animals, the animals still receive beatings: "[t]he lasso held him back and he failed to reach [another tiger]. He immediately received four or five lashes."[115]
- Unsurprisingly, these attempts to train wild animals to behave in ways wholly unnatural to them, often results in injury and death: "I had seized one of the heavy stools and I flung it with all my strength at the beast's head. The bear caught it on the skull just as the beast tore Kovack's thigh with its claws. Once more it went sprawling, knocked out, and Kovack was able to shelter [sic] at the back of the cage … I clenched my hand round the club and struck at the head with all my strength … The bear had been struck where I had aimed, above the nostrils and between the eyes. Blood flowed from its mouth, its paws stiffened in a last convulsion and it collapsed."[116]
- Indeed such deaths and injuries are so expected they were routinely taken into account as a matter of course: "I had twenty-six animals, which gave me an adequate margin; in training I should eliminate the disappointing

111. *Id.* at § 8.
112. *See Balakrishnan et al. v. Union of India*, No. 155/1999, (Kerala H.C. June 6, 2000), *available at* http://www.elaw.org/node/1831 [hereinafter *Balakshrinan*].
113. *Id.* at 2.
114. Alfred Court, Wild Circus Animals 60 (London: Burke 1954).
115. *Id.* at 67.
116. *Id.* at 89–90.

ones and there would be a replacement if an animal was killed or badly crippled."[117]

- "It was my turn to be brutal, terribly brutal and brutal I was. All the clubs I had left in the cage were broken one by one on the tiger's head, lashes came down like an avalanche, each cutting deep into the tiger's shining coat."[118]

When reading these appalling descriptions, one has to wonder what kind of creature is capable of actually doing these things; surely not someone that we typically refer to as "human"; but this is indeed what humans do.

A number of arguments were made in the *Balakrishnan* case by those challenging the ban on exhibiting and training the five specified types of wild animals. One complaint was that it was inappropriate for the government to have banned the exhibition and training of these animals by circuses, but to not have banned similar exhibitions by zoos. The court disposed of this argument by saying that circuses have only an economic purpose, to make money for the owners of the circus.[119] Zoos, according to the court, have other purposes—the conservation of species and the education of the public about wild animals.[120] Moreover, zoos do not engage in the training of animals and display of animals in performances.[121] So zoos and circuses, by this logic, cannot be equated.

Another argument made was that constitutionally protected rights to practice one's chosen profession were trampled upon by the ban.[122] To this the court responded by saying that the provisions protecting the carrying on of trades and businesses in Article 19(1)(g) of the Indian Constitution:

> do not permit the carrying on of an activity whether commercial or otherwise, if it results in infliction of unnecessary pain and suffering on the specified animals. No person has any right, much less a fundamental right to carry on a trade or business which results in infliction of unnecessary pain or suffering nor a right to carry on a trade or business in an activity which has been declared by law as an offense. Neither the owners nor the employees of circus [sic] have a fundamental right to carry on trade or business in training and exhibiting endangered animals as the said trade is of such an obnoxious and pernicious activity geared towards entertainment which cannot be taken in the interest of the general public to be a trade or business in the sense in which it is used in Article 19(1)(g) of the Constitution of India.[123]

117. *Id.* at 90.
118. *Id.* at 60.
119. *Balakrishnan, supra* note 112, at 13–14 (citing to pages from available word document).
120. *Id.*
121. *Id.*
122. *Id.* at 16–18.
123. *Id.* at 14–18.

The court went on to find that the prohibition on exhibition of these wild animals was in the public interest and was consistent with the moral rules of the Constitution of India, which spells out the duty of all citizens to treat animals with compassion, and requires the government to protect the environment and wildlife.[124] In its concluding remarks the court made what may be the strongest pro-animal rights statement of any court in the world:

> Though not homosapiens,[] [animals] are also beings entitled to dignified existence and humane treatment sans cruelty and torture. In many respects, they comport better than humans, they kill to eat and eat to live and not live to eat as some of us do, they do not practice deception, fraud, or falsehood and malpractices as humans do … All animals except the very lowest exhibit some degree of intelligent behaviour, ranging from learned responses to complex reasoning. Many believe that the lives of humans and animals are equally valuable and that their interests should count equally. Their contribution to the health of humans is invaluable … nearly every advance in health care and combating human diseases has been based on animal research. Animals also provide models for the study of human diseases. New drugs are tested on animals to help determine their potentials for causing cancer or other disease … Therefore, it is not only our fundamental duty to show compassion to our animal friends, but also to recognise and protect their rights … If humans are entitled to fundamental rights, why not animals? In our considered opinion, legal rights shall not be the exclusive preserve of the humans which [*sic*] has to be extended beyond people thereby dismantling the thick legal wall with humans all on one side and all non-human animals on the other side. While the law currently protects wildlife and endangered species from extinction, animals are denied rights, an anachronism which must necessarily change.[125]

The opinion is not, however, completely good news for animals; the court recognizes, as noted earlier, that use of animals in zoos is justified by the conservation and educational aspects of this use, and the court in the quoted passage also seems to recognize the legitimacy of the use of animals in experiments for the benefit of humans. The statements by the court arguing that animals should be considered to have rights while at the same time apparently acknowledging the propriety of confining animals in zoos and using animals in experiments are difficult, if not impossible, to reconcile.

So what we find in the Indian law is not a complete ban on use of animals in circuses, but a ban on the use of some animals in circuses. A court decision upholding this ban has made far-reaching statements declaring animals rightholders, notwithstanding the court's seemingly inconsistent recognition that animals can still appropriately be confined and exhibited at zoos and used in experiments. Nonetheless, India has taken a step further than New Zealand by doing more than

124. *Id.* at 16–18.
125. *Id.* at 17–18.

just regulate the use of animals in circuses; India has imposed a ban on the use of some wild animals in exhibitions. We will now see a country that has taken yet a further step; the banning of the use of any wild animals in circuses.

C. Austria

In 2005, Austria banned the use of any wild animals in exhibitions in section 27(1) of the Austrian Animal Protection Act (hereinafter "APA") which states: "[s]pecies of wild animal [sic] habitat animals are not allowed to be kept in circuses, variety show institutions and similar facilities."[126] This ban does not apply to domestic animals; these animals can still be used in circuses. Nonetheless, all use of animals in circuses and similar exhibitions must be approved by the Austrian government.[127] The APA also provides that the Federal Minister for Health and Women is to create minimum standards for the care of animals kept for performances and the training of personnel that care for them.[128] These provisions are part of what is one of the strongest anti-cruelty laws in the world, which includes strictures forbidding hen battery cages, prohibiting the docking of dogs' ears, and prohibiting some types of restraints for dogs, including the use of choke collars.[129]

The Austrian ban on wild animals in circuses has generated considerable controversy and now even litigation. The European Circus Association submitted a complaint to the EU Commission in May 2005, claiming that the ban on use of wild animals in circuses violated Article 49 of the EU Treaty, which states, "[w]ithin the framework of the provisions set out below, restrictions on freedom to provide services within the Community shall be prohibited in respect of nationals of Member States who are established in a State of the Community other than that of the person for whom the services are intended."[130] It was alleged that this ban violated circuses' rights under the EU Treaty to freely provide services within the community. Apparently, the "services" being referred to are the services of providing entertainment including wild animals.

Initially the EU Commission agreed with the challenge and began infringement proceedings against Austria, alleging that there was a violation of Article 49.[131] After discussions with Austrian officials, however, the Commission determined that

126. Federal Act on the Protection of Animals [Animal Protection Act—TSchG], Federal Law Gazette I No. 118/2004, § 27(1) (Austria).

127. *Id.* at §§ 27(3), (4).

128. *Id.* at § 27(2).

129. *See Austria Pushes Europe Towards a Firm Stance for Animal Rights*, Grand Rapids Press, May 30, 2004, at A14.

130. Treaty of Amsterdam Amending the Treaty on European Union, the Treaties Establishing the European Communities and Certain Related Acts, Oct. 2, 1997, 1997 O. J. (C 340) 1, art. 49.

131. The European Ombudsman, *Commission Has to Properly Examine Austrian Ban on Wild Animals In Circuses*, (press release no. 14-2009) June 29, 2009, http://www.ombudsman.europa.eu/press/release.faces/en/4135/html.bookmark [hereinafter *Ombudsman Press Release 14-2009*].

issues relating to the treatment of wild animals in exhibitions should be left up to individual states to determine.[132]

At about the same time as the submission of the complaint to the EU Commission, the European Circus Association (ECA) also submitted a complaint to the European Ombudsman.[133] The EU Ombudsman is a person elected by the EU Parliament to investigate complaints of maladministration by EU bodies:

> The European Ombudsman investigates complaints about maladministration in the institutions and bodies of the European Union (EU). The institutions include, among others, the European Commission, the Council of the EU and the European Parliament. The European Medicines Agency and the European Foundation for the Improvement of Living and Working Conditions are examples of Union bodies that he can investigate. Only the Court of Justice, the Court of First Instance, and the Civil Service Tribunal acting in their judicial role do not fall within his jurisdiction.[134]

Complaints can be made to the Ombudsman by citizens or residents of the EU.[135]

Ultimately, the Ombudsman concluded that the Commission had not properly determined that the infringement proceeding should not go forward, and should either proceed with the infringement proceeding or elucidate valid reasons for abandoning the infringement proceeding.[136] In response, the Commission stated that it believed that it had provided an adequate explanation for its decision not to proceed with the infringement proceeding and again reiterated its position that issues relating to circuses should be determined on a state by state basis.[137] Having now heard "no" as the answer to its challenge on several occasions, the ECA filed a lawsuit in October 2009, challenging the Commission decision to not proceed with an infringement action against the Austrian ban on use of wild animals in circuses.[138] This lawsuit challenges not only the wild animal ban by Austria, but also a similar ban in the City of Luxembourg.[139] Thus, this rather long story of the

---

132. *Id.*; The European Ombudsman, P. Nikiforos Diamandouros, *Draft Recommendation of the European Ombudsman in His Inquiry into Complaint 3307/2006/(PB)JMA Against the European Commission,* June 3, 2009, *available at* http://www.ombudsman. europa.eu/cases/ draftrecommendation.faces/en/4068/html.bookmark [hereinafter *Draft Recommendation*].
133. *Ombudsman Press Release 14-2009, supra* note 131.
134. The European Ombudsman, *The European Ombudsman — At a Glance*, http://www. ombudsman.europa.eu/atyourservice/ataglance.faces (follow "What does he do?" hyperlink) (last visited May 19, 2010) .
135. *Id.* (follow "Who can complain and how?" hyperlink).
136. *Draft Recommendation, supra* note 132.
137. European Commission, *Opinion of The Commission on the European Ombudsman's Draft Recommendation-Complaint by the European Circus Association (ECA), ref. 3307/2006/(PB) JMA* 3, Sept. 19, 2009, *available at* http://www.vier-pfoten.at/website/uploads/090918_ CommissionReplytoOmbudsman.pdf.
138. PR Newswire, *European Circus Association; European Circus Association Challenges Performing Animal Bans*, http://www.prnewswire.com/news-releases/european-circus-association-challenges-performing-animal-bans-62319582.html (last visited Feb. 2, 2011).
139. *Id.*

challenge to the wild animal ban continues, and it appears that it will continue until there are no avenues left for challenging it. For the time being, at least, the ban remains and its final disposition now lay in the courts.

So we see a number of approaches that have been used relating to perhaps the most controversial and tragic use of animals in circuses—the exhibition and training of wild animals. New Zealand sets forth rules relating to the treatment of animals in circuses, but does not ban the use of any type of animal. India has taken the step of banning the use of certain wild animals; but Austria has taken one further stride and has banned the use of all wild animals. As we will see later, Bolivia has gone even one step further.

III. THE REGULATION OF ZOOS

A. New Zealand

New Zealand regulates zoos under the Animal Welfare (Zoos) Code of Welfare 2005 (hereinafter "Zoo Code"). A "zoo" is defined as "a site on which animals are kept for public exhibition, education, conservation, research or entertainment ...."[140] Like the Circus Code, this has the Minimum Standards, Good Practices and Recommended Best Practices categories for stating requirements and recommendations.[141] It also has the same general standards for the owner or person in charge with respect to ensuring the health and well-being of the animals.[142]

The other standards for care of animals are similar as well to aspects of the Circus Code. For example, animals are to be handled by persons with adequate training and zoos are not to show animals that do not adapt to exhibition.[143] Daily inspections of animals are required unless such an inspection would adversely affect the animals or there are other circumstances that would cause the inspection to have an impact on the welfare of the animals.[144] Food, water and proper nutrition are to be provided.[145]

There are special provisions relating to providing proper hygiene for the animals. Facilities are required to be kept clean and effluent is not permitted to accumulate in the animal enclosures.[146] The physical facilities are required to be constructed in a way that is safe for the animals, and proper heating and other environmental conditions are to be provided.[147]

---

140. Animal Welfare (Zoos) Code of Welfare 2005 § 1.9 (N.Z.) [hereinafter *Zoo Code*].
141. *Id.* at § 1.8.1.
142. *Id.* at § 2(1).
143. *Id.* at Minimum Standard Nos. 1, 3.
144. *Id.* at Minimum Standard No. 2.
145. *Id.* at Minimum Standard No. 6.
146. *Id.* at Minimum Standard No. 4.
147. *Id.* at Minimum Standard Nos. 9, 10.

Breeding of animals is also regulated. "The breeding of animals must be managed so as to prevent overpopulation or overcrowding resulting in unnecessary pain and distress."[148] This regulation can be viewed as recognizing the idea that zoos are of benefit to many animals as places where endangered species can be bred and therefore sustained. This provision makes sure that breeding, however, does not have the effect of overcrowding the facilities.

Note that the Zoo Code explicitly recognizes that animals engage in unnatural behaviors in zoos. Indeed, these abnormal behaviors are described in section 6.1 of the Zoo Code:

> Animals in zoos may have their behaviour restricted by their environment and/or their management. In such circumstances, provision for the animals to remain physically active and psychologically stimulated is crucial to their health and well-being. The intelligence of some animals, e.g. primates, also means that they need constant stimulation or sources of mental stimuli otherwise they become bored and frustrated and may display abnormal behaviour patterns or stereotypic behaviours. These may include excessive grooming, hair pulling, repetitive pacing, running, jumping, rocking, social withdrawal, self-mutilation or infanticide.[149]

To address these issues, the Zoo Code requires that a behavioral and environmental program be created for each species held at the zoo.[150] This standard requires, among other things, that the environment, facilities and provisions for exercise must allow for "normal patterns of behavior."[151] But how can we even begin to talk about normal patterns of behavior for these animals when we are addressing huge elephants kept in enclosures, or cheetahs that routinely run very long distances kept confined in small areas? How can these animals ever experience normal patterns of behavior?

Another rather odd provision is one that requires that a veterinarian be consulted "as soon as possible" whenever any of a number of severe conditions are seen, including when an animal is in a coma.[152] If someone who is supposedly monitoring animals actually has to be told this, then that staff member is obviously not properly trained, or is completely devoid of compassion.

The rules concerning physical facilities contain some interesting provisions relating to the placement of animals in zoos. It is necessary to provide adequate space so that all animals can have isolation if desired and to provide nesting and bedding areas.[153] In addition, because it would obviously be rather disconcerting for a gazelle to be housed next to lions, the Zoo Code provides that animals are to

148. *Id.* at Minimum Standard No. 5.
149. *Id.* at § 6.1.
150. *Id.* at Minimum Standard No. 11.
151. *Id.*
152. *Id.* at Minimum Standard No. 13(b).
153. *Id.* at Minimum Standard No. 7(f).

be out of range of predator animals or territorial animals if this would cause distress.[154]

So what do we observe from these provisions? They do not really seem to do much to change the situation of zoo animals. Of course, the conditions of the animals are subject to certain Minimum Standards that are not the law in numerous other countries, but many of these provisions are vague and it is unclear exactly what the provisions mean in any particular case. For example, what are "adequate quantities of food and nutrients," or what is meant by "[t]he method of containment must not cause harm to the animals" or that "enclosures … must be maintained in a condition that minimizes harm or injury to animals …"?[155] Rules like these may just be palliatives to convince us that provision is actually being made for the well-being of the animals. But in reality is it actually possible to take wild animals, place them in, for them, completely unnatural environments, and then expect that the animals are going to act naturally and not suffer severe physical, social and psychological difficulties? Ultimately, one could argue that all these provisions do is place a stamp of government approval on zoos, and once again facilitate complacency in humans, who are being lulled into a false belief that animals in zoos are content in their confinement.

B. India

India has a set of comprehensive regulations on the keeping of animals in zoos in The Wild Life (Protection) Act, 1972 (hereinafter "WLA"). This law is generally intended to work to protect the diverse and varied wildlife of India.[156] Zoos are considered to be any establishment where animals are kept for public exhibition and includes zoos, circuses and rescue centers.[157]As a part of the regulatory scheme relating to zoos, the law creates a Central Zoo Authority (hereinafter "Authority").[158] The role of the Authority is to, among other things:[159]

- Stipulate the minimum requirements for the upkeep, housing and veterinary care of zoo animals.
- "Recognise" or derecognize zoos—this is essentially a zoo licensing procedure.
- Coordinate the acquisition of animals used in zoos.
- Coordinate captive breeding programs and provide other technical assistance for zoos including organizing the training of zoo staff.

---

154. *Id.*
155. *Id.* at Minimum Standard Nos. 6, 7, 9.
156. The Wild Life (Protection) Act, 1972, Introduction, *reprinted in* Gandhi, *supra* note 97, at 121 [hereinafter *WLA*].
157. *Id.* at § 2(39).
158. *Id.* at § 38A.
159. *Id.* at § 38C.

So what is created by the Indian law is a bureaucracy that requires zoos be "recognized" by the Authority and requires the permission of the Authority for the acquisition and transfer of animals.[160] Decisions to recognize zoos are to be made after taking into account the interests of protection and conservation of wildlife,[161] and these decisions are made under detailed rules set forth in The Recognition of Zoo Rules, 1992 (hereinafter "Zoo Rules"). Recall that these regulations apply not only to what we typically think of as zoos, but also to circuses and rescue organizations;[162] so all organizations of these kinds are subject to these regulations.

The Zoo Rules divide zoos into four categories based on the size of the zoo: large, with more than 750 animals exhibited; medium, with 500–750 animals; small, with 200–499 animals; and mini, with less than 200 animals.[163] Regulations in the rules differ based upon the size of the zoo. For example, staffing at zoos is specified in the rules, and large zoos, not surprisingly, are required to have more veterinary personnel on site than smaller operations.[164] The educational role of zoos is also codified in the rules—every enclosure at a zoo is to have scientific information on the animals and the zoo is to provide brochures or other information to visitors.[165]

There are specific strictures relating to the treatment of animals in the Zoo Rules. The rules prohibit cruelty to any zoo animals as proscribed by the PCAA.[166] The rules also provide that animals are generally not to be chained or tethered, or exhibited when ill or infirm, and animals are to be provided a clean and healthy environment.[167] Zoos are required to be closed at least one day a week, presumably to give the animals a break from crowds and being constantly observed.[168] Animals are required to be provided wholesome food, animals must be checked for health problems on a daily basis and veterinary facilities must meet certain physical requirements.[169] A fascinating rule is that animals are generally to be provided with a mate and are not to be kept without a mate for a period of more than a year without "valid reason."[170] In addition, there are rules dictating the physical conditions of zoos, including fencing, the providing of green belts, limitations on the amount of area at the zoo dedicated to buildings, the type of housing required for animals and so on.[171]

---

160. *Id.* at §§ 38H–38I.
161. *Id.* at § 38H(4).
162. *Id.* at § 2(39).
163. The Recognition of Zoo Rules, 1992 § 9, *reprinted in* GANDHI, *supra* note 97, at 228 [hereinafter the *Zoo Rules*].
164. *Id.* at §§ 10(12)–(14).
165. *Id.* at §§ 10(45)–(46).
166. *Id.* at § 10(3A).
167. *Id.* at §§ 10(5)–(7), (9).
168. *See id.* at § 10(7).
169. *Id.* at §§ 10(21)–(35).
170. *Id.* at §§ 10(37), (38).
171. *Id.* at §§ 10(8), (10), (15)–(20).

What is created here is a fairly comprehensive set of regulations of zoos, including regulation of staffing, physical and building layout, and animal feeding, care, monitoring and treatment, with the underlying concept of creating a positive impression of zoos. Zoos are meant to be seen as havens in which endangered animals can potentially be captive-bred to preserve species, and in addition, regulation of the acquisition of these wild animals presumably is meant to further the protection of wild populations from otherwise certain decline. Moreover, education of the public about wild animals is recognized as an important value embedded within the regulations. But the underlying idea of all of these regulations is that this type of use of animals is appropriate.

IV. MICHAEL VICK AND SORDID TALE OF DOG FIGHTING

Animal fighting is banned in most countries; New Zealand, for example, bans animal fighting,[172] but dog fighting is legal in Japan[173] and in Afghanistan it is now quite popular.[174] Interestingly, dog fighting was banned under the Taliban and violations of the ban were punished by death.[175] Since the fall of the Taliban, however, dog fighting has made a comeback in Afghanistan.[176] Regardless of its legal status, we know that it continues to take place around the globe. In the United States, for example, one would have had to have been asleep for the last few years to not have heard about football player Michael Vick and his dog fighting operation, Bad Newz Kennels. (In Chapter One, reference was made to Michael Vick's operation and the dogs that survived the mayhem.)

But let us look in a bit more detail at what happened at Bad Newz Kennels. Vick is a man with what appears to be a very demented sense of humor. To illustrate, at least twice Vick forced his family pets into the fighting ring with trained fighting pit bulls, which resulted in critical injuries to the animals.[177] Vick and his co-conspirators "thought it was funny to watch the pit bull dogs belonging to Bad Newz Kennels' injure or kill the other dogs."[178] Consider these other fun-filled activities of Vick and his cohorts: after lying to authorities, Vick finally admitted to personally aiding in the killing of between six to eight dogs whose performances were bad or who refused to fight when tested.[179] He, of course, only made

172. *NZAWA, supra* note 31, at § 31.
173. Don Huebscher, *Animal Cruelty a Touchy Issue for High Court*, THE LEADER-TELEGRAM (EAU CLAIRE, WIS.), Oct. 13, 2009 at Commentary.
174. Thane Burnett, *Dogs of War*, THE OTTAWA SUN, Feb. 2, 2010, at 23.
175. *Id.*
176. *Id.*
177. United States Dept. of Agriculture Office of Inspector General-Investigations, *Bad Newz Kennels Smithfield, Virginia* 4, File number: HY-3330-0018 (Aug. 28, 2008) [hereinafter *USDA Investigation*].
178. *Id.*
179. *Id.*

this admission after failing a polygraph test questioning whether or not he had participated in the killings.[180]

And what creativity he devised in the methods of killing! Some dogs were electrocuted;[181] some were shot to death, one with a .22 caliber handgun after losing a fight.[182] A red pit bull found its pathetic end by being repeatedly slammed to the ground, until its back or neck were broken.[183] Some were killed by strangulation, hung from a "nylon cord over a 2 × 4 that was nailed to two trees."[184] "One dog that did not die from hanging was taken down and drowned in a 5 gallon bucket of water."[185] In another case, Vick and a pal "took down one of the dogs that would not die from hanging and tossed the dog to the side. [They] later hung the same dog until it died."[186] Some dogs were drowned, "a process that took two people to hold the animal's legs while the dog's head was held under water" in a five-gallon bucket.[187]

Vick and his friends appeared to get an "adrenaline high" when killing dogs, and they must have been high quite a lot of the time during "Bad Newz" heyday,[188] for all dogs that lost fights were ultimately killed. A witness stated that "[t]he dog that won the fight was the only dog that was allowed to live."[189] When dogs were killed, it was at the order of Vick, who vetoed finding new homes for dogs that did not test or perform well: "[o]n occasion, [Purnell Peace, a co-conspirator] would want to give away a dog that would not fight. However, Vick stated 'they got to go,' meaning they needed to be killed."[190] Dead bodies were "stacked in the bed of [an] ATV" and buried in mass graves (typically four dogs per grave).[191] When federal agents searched the Vick premises the remains of 19 dogs were discovered.[192] Autopsies revealed deaths consistent with "hanging, drowning, and being slammed to death."[193]

Training and dog fights were carried on in three sheds on Vicks' property and were painted black. These sheds were called "the black hole."[194] Fighting dogs were housed in these sheds, while dogs too young to fight, bait dogs, and others

180. Associated Press, *USDA: Vick Found Dogfighting "Funny to Watch"*, Nov. 21, 2008, http://nbcsports.msnbc.com/id/27850103/.
181. *USDA Investigation, supra* note 177, at 5.
182. *Id.*
183. *Id.* at 4.
184. *Id.*
185. *Id.* at 10.
186. *Id.* at 11.
187. *Id.* at 4; Rhonda Cook, *Report: Michael Vick Got "Adrenaline" Rush While Killing Dogs*, Jan. 9, 2010, http://www.ajc.com/sports/atlanta-falcons/report-michael-vick-got-271212.html.
188. Cook, *supra* note 187.
189. *Id.*
190. *USDA Investigation, supra* note 177, at 9.
191. *Id.* at 6–7, 14.
192. *Id.* at 7.
193. *Id.* at 8.
194. *Id.* at 13.

were chained to automobile axles in the woods.[195] Live chickens and rabbits were utilized as bait for dogs being trained on tread mills.[196] Spring bars that the dogs hung from with their teeth clamped to rubber rings were employed to strengthen the dogs' jaws.[197] "The water in the [dog's] bowls [was] speckled with algae. Females were strapped into a 'rape stand' so the dogs could breed without injuring each other."[198]

Dog fighting is indeed not pretty. But agricultural, experimental and exhibition uses of animals are not pretty either. Why do we ban dog fights and not these other activities? Of course, there is money to be made in dog fighting, but the money does not even begin to rival that earned by McDonalds, or SeaWorld, for that matter. And where does the blood money go? Dog fighting is not something in which the upper classes typically show much interest; it is an activity that occurs mostly for the entertainment of the lower economic classes. Apparently it does not fit well with mainstream culture. So the prohibition on this activity affects those with relatively little political clout, does not attack mainstream culture because the activity is not favored by mainstream culture in the first place, and does not form a significant part of the economy. In this context, it would seem that the sensitivities of humans to the suffering of animals in forced battle have, in most countries, overridden any economic or cultural attachment to the practice. The human interests in continuing the practice appear nugatory to most, and so the interests of the animals, and of the humans who are horrified by these activities, in this particular instance prevail.

And what of Michael Vick? He spent eight months in prison[199] and is now playing football for the Philadelphia Eagles. And I have chastised India for seemingly lax punishments....

V. THE RANGE OF REGULATION OF ANIMALS AS ENTERTAINMENT

In the regulatory mechanisms reviewed in this chapter we see a number of types of legal responses to issues relating to animals kept for entertainment purposes. These can be categorized as follows:

- *Animal Welfare Rules*: Each scheme, whether regulating zoos, circuses, rodeos or other activities, provides standards for the treatment of animals where animals are permitted to be used and exhibited. These rules parrot the language typically seen in animal welfare regulations—the prohibition

195. Jim Gorant, *What Happened to Michael Vick's Dogs...* Dec. 23, 2008, http://sportsillustrated.cnn.com/2008/magazine/12/22/vick.dogs/index.html.
196. *USDA Investigation, supra* note 177, at 10.
197. Gorant, *supra* note 195.
198. *Id.*
199. Rick Reilly, *Mike Vick Went Bankrupt Sitting in Prison, How did that Happen?,* http://sports.espn.go.com/espnmag/story?id=3726426 (last visited May 20, 2010).

of "unnecessary" suffering or the like. Again, what is "necessary" is measured against the supposed benefits to humans from these activities, economic, cultural, educational, environmental and pure "entertainment." In the context of zoos, it is these kinds of regulations that predominate. They are also the only form of regulation of circuses and other exhibitions in some countries.

- *Bans on the Use of Certain Animals:* In circuses and certain other exhibitions, some countries have taken the step of placing outright bans on the use of certain types of animals. We see this in the bans on certain wild animals in India and the outright ban on wild animals in Austria. This movement toward bans on the use of animals in circuses is, indeed, gaining momentum. Portugal has recently banned individuals, circuses and unauthorized facilities from the keeping a long list of wild animals, including primates, bears and wild cats, and prohibits the purchase of a number of types of wild animals, including primates, elephants and a number of wild cats.[200] In addition, circuses are prohibited by Portuguese law from breeding animals.[201] As of July 1, 2010, Bolivia has banned the use of all animals in circuses, including domestic animals.[202] The list of countries that ban the use of some or all animals in circuses is growing and the countries with some sort of ban include: Austria, Belgium, Bolivia, Croatia, Czech Republic, Denmark, Estonia, Finland, Greece, India, Israel, Italy, Malta, Poland, Singapore, Slovakia, Spain and Sweden.[203] Thus, we see a rapidly emerging and serious movement toward bans on the use of animals in circuses in many countries and continents.
- *Prohibitions on Behavior:* In some countries, certain types of uses of animals for entertainment purposes are subject to outright bans, and in this category would be the ban on animal fighting in most countries. In this context demonstrable human benefit is difficult to determine, although one could argue that an economic benefit could be found in the wagering and other economic activity surrounding animal fighting; but the fact that it is a popular pastime with only a small segment of world population makes this economic benefit pale when pitted against general public revulsion at such events. One could also argue, however, that it is the sensibilities of humans, and not necessarily the interests of animals at all, that results in the bans on animal fighting and other aberrant behaviors relating to animals.

---

200. ENDCAP, *Portugal Bans the Keeping of Certain Wild Animals*, http://www.endcaptivity.org/index.php?option=content&task=view&id=30 (last visited May 21, 2010).
201. *Id.*
202. *See* Associated Press, *Bolivia Bans All Circus Animals*, Sept. 3, 2009, http://www.huffingtonpost.com/2009/08/03/bolivia-bans-all-circus-a_n_250303.html.
203. *ADI Worldwide Circus Bans, supra* note 72; *see also*, ENDCAP, *Circuses*, http://www.endcaptivity.org/index.php?option=content&task=view&id=20 (last visited Apr. 22, 2010); Peter Singer, *Free Tilly and Other Circus Animals*, The Japan Times Online, Mar. 10, 2010, *available at* http://search.japantimes.co.jp/cgi-bin/eo20100311a1.html.

So the regulation of animals in entertainment provides a good illustration of the way that humans typically deal with the human/animal relationship in the law. The varied interests of humans, economic, cultural, educational and others, are weighed against the interests of animals. But whenever there is any conceivable benefit to any significant human population, the interests of animals are not potent enough to carry the weight necessary to end what is demonstrable and often monumental animal suffering. What we do instead is try to protect the welfare of animals by "minimizing" their suffering to what is deemed "necessary"; that is, what is necessary in order to carry out the desires of humans, and not at all necessary to animals.

Still, some regulations on the use of animals in entertainment may also illustrate real movement away from the pure "welfarist" model of regulation of uses of animals. The movement toward bans on uses of animals in Austria, Bolivia, India and other countries exhibit a step in a different direction. Here it can be argued that, notwithstanding the human economic benefit of use of wild animals in circuses, there is the will in these countries to end the confinement and torturous training of wild animals for circuses and other performances. Thus, at least in the area of the use of animals in entertainment, we see true bans on the use of certain animals, and also bans on certain behaviors, like animal fighting. So in this realm of the law we see movement in a direction away from mere protection of the welfare of animals as used by humans; we see the prohibition of certain uses of and activities relating to animals which has the effect of actually ending the abuse of some animals in these entertainment spectacles.

This phenomenon tells us that at least some profitable economic activities involving the use of animals can, in fact, be halted. A cynical way to view this is to say that it is axiomatic that the economic profitability of circuses and similar types of entertainment will continue with or without the use of animals[204] so the economic cost to humans of a ban on use of animals is low relating to these activities. A less cynical view might be that application of pressure by animal protection groups, as well as continued public education on the treatment of animals, has ultimately resulted in some prohibitions of otherwise economically profitable uses of animals. The true test of our cynicism may, however, lie in the more pervasive uses of animals in agriculture and experimentation, both uses of animals that are extremely lucrative and rely completely on the use of animals. To see bans and prohibitions on uses of animals in these areas might move even the most skeptical of us away from cynicism. It would be nice to be offered that opportunity.

---

204. There are, however, businesses that would necessarily end as a result of a ban on use of animals in entertainment; operations like SeaWorld are examples.

Chapter 6
CITES

I. THE STORY OF CORAL

Corals appear to be mundane creatures; to look at "hard corals" is to peer at what seems to be a rock. They do not dart about, excite us with adorable behavior or have winning roles in movies, except perhaps as a backdrop to undersea adventures. In the context of international trade, however, corals pose an illustrative example of the workings of the Convention on International Trade in Endangered Species (CITES, reprinted in Appendix VI). Moreover, as it turns out, corals are extremely important creatures in world ecology and their plight may have serious implications for all of us.

So what are corals? Corals, which are in the same taxonomic group as sea anemones and jellyfish, are invertebrate animals.[1] Individual corals are called "polyps."[2] Most corals live in colonies of hundreds of thousands of polyps that are genetically identical, since polyps can grow copies of themselves, which is referred to as "budding."[3] They are divided into two types, hard and soft corals. Hard corals are the ones that create reefs[4] by extracting calcium from seawater and creating a hardened calcium carbonate structure which is used for their own protection and to promote their growth.[5] Coral reefs are the largest living structures

---

1. Marjorie Mulhall, *Saving the Rainforests of the Sea: An Analysis of International Efforts to Conserve Coral Reefs*, 19 DUKE ENVTL. L. & POL'Y F. 321, 324 (2009).
2. *Id.* at 324.
3. *Id.; see also* Tim Wijgerde, *Coral Reproduction—Part I: Biology*, CORAL SCI. (2009).
4. Mulhall, *supra* note 1, at 324; *see also* Collette Wabnitz et al., *From Ocean to Aquarium: The Global Trade in Marine Ornamental Species*, 22 (UNEP World Conservation Monitoring Centre 2003) [hereinafter Wabnitz et al.].
5. Mulhall, *supra* note 1, at 324.

in the world and are the only ones visible from space.[6] Soft corals do not create reefs.

As noted above, coral can reproduce by budding, which produces identical individuals,[7] but is not a good reproductive strategy for long-term survival. To obtain a diversity of genetic combinations, sexual reproduction is required. Corals have a number of sexual reproduction strategies; some are hermaphroditic, some species have males and females which exist separately and some can change their sex, referred to as "sequential hermaphroditism."

One fascinating type of coral reproduction performed by many coral species is called "broadcast spawning." These corals expel huge numbers of eggs and sperm into the water and the few that combine and survive become larvae that develop into adult corals.[8] Now this may not sound very intriguing, but there is something very odd about it—many of the corals perform this broadcast spawning in a synchronized way, around the time of the full moon, during only a few months of the year.[9] Explanations for this phenomenon and its timing vary and in fact the reasons may vary from species to species. For instance, it has been suggested that the timing of broadcast spawning by Acoropora reef corals in Moorea, French Polynesia, may be due to reduced tides at the specific times of this spawning, which may increase fertilization rates.[10] However, with respect to scleractinian corals in the Dampier Archipelago in Australia, it has been suggested that the timing of spawning, coinciding with reduced tides and the presence of a poleward flowing current, may be an adaptation to increase dispersal of the corals.[11]

Whatever the reason for this "Wolfman" reproductive scheme of corals, corals are species that are of incalculable ecological value. The reefs created by corals worldwide total about 284,300 square kilometers, or half the size of France[12] and are home to perhaps one-fourth of all marine species.[13] Estimates of the total number of species within reefs run from one to nine million.[14] More than 4,000 species of fish alone reside in these coral reefs[15] and coral reefs are rivaled only by tropical rain forests in ecological diversity.[16] Because of the

---

6. *Id.*
7. *See supra* note 3 and accompanying text.
8. *Id.*; James Guest, *How Reefs Respond to Mass Coral Spawning*, 320 Sci. 621, 621 (2008).
9. *See* Guest, *supra* note 8, at 621; A. Carroll et al., *Sexual Reproduction of Acropora Reef Corals at Moorea, French Polynesia*, 25 Coral Reefs 93, 93–95 (2005) [hereinafter Carroll].
10. Carroll, *supra* note 9, at 96.
11. *See* C.J. Simpson, *Mass Spawning of Scleractinian Corals in the Dampier Archipelago and the Implications for Management of Coral Reefs in Western Australia*, Bulletin 244 (Dept. Conservation & Env't, Perth, Western Australia 1985).
12. Mary Gray Davidson, *Protecting Coral Reefs: The Principal National and International Legal Instruments*, 26 Harv. Envtl. L. Rev. 499, 501 (2002).
13. *Id.*
14. *Id.* at 502.
15. *Id.*; Wabnitz et al., *supra* note 4, at 9.
16. Davidson, *supra* note 12, at 502.

importance of these ecosystems, 2008 was named the International Year of the Reef.[17]

Unfortunately, these rich ecosystems are being destroyed at a rapid rate. Estimates vary, but some contend that up to 60% of existing coral reefs may be gone by 2030; some estimates are even more pessimistic and contend that reefs in their present form may not survive past 2020.[18] The causes of destruction of reefs are pollution, sedimentation from human activity, overfishing and climate change.[19] Climate change affects reefs since increases in water temperature can kill corals.[20] Mining of reefs for limestone and dead coral to be used in jewelry, aquariums and decorative items is also a threat to the reefs.[21]

But our concern here is about trade in both live coral specimens for aquariums and dead specimens for decoration and jewelry. Worldwide, 140 species of coral are traded.[22] "According to CITES data, the global live coral trade rose steadily from 1997 to 1999, with 934,463 live pieces and 1,142,242 live pieces being traded worldwide respectively in those years. The trade decreased to 942,661 pieces in 2001."[23] Indonesia provides 95% of the world's coral and the United States imports 98% of the live coral, in addition to 85% of the world's dead coral.[24] This trade in live coral turns out to be extraordinarily wasteful, since many species of coral do not do well in captivity and die in very short periods of time, causing the collector to have to buy yet more coral.[25] Of live coral traded, 99% of it is wild coral and only .3% is captive-bred or ranched, while the remainder is non-captive bred or ranched.[26]

Corals, of course, are not the only wild animals traded in the world economy. Global trade in endangered species is the second most common reason for the decline in species, second only to habitat loss.[27] This trade in endangered species is thought to be valued at between five and seventeen billion dollars per year.[28] It is in this context that the main international treaty on trade in endangered species, CITES, attempts to regulate this robust trade.

17. Mulhall, *supra* note 1, at 321.
18. Davidson, *supra* note 12, at 504–05.
19. *Id.* at 505.
20. Mulhall, *supra* note 1, at 327–29.
21. *Id.* at 329.
22. This and other detailed trade information relating to corals and other marine ornamental species can be found in Wabnitz et al., *supra* note 4, at 7–8, 18–32.
23. *Id.* at 22.
24. Davidson, *supra* note 12, at 534–35.
25. Wabnitz et al., *supra* note 4, at 45–46.
26. *See id.* at 50.
27. Christine Fuchs, *Convention on International Trade in Endangered Species of Wild Fauna and Flora (CITES)—Conservation Efforts Undermine the Legality Principle*, 9 GERMAN L.J. 1565, 1568 (2008).
28. Saskia Young, *Contemporary Issues of the Convention on International Trade in Endangered Species of Wild Fauna and Flora (CITES) and the Debate Over Sustainable Use*, 14 COLO. J. INT'L ENVTL L. & POL'Y 167, 168 (2003).

II. THE CITES REGULATORY SCHEME

Although we will see that this may not mean too much, "CITES is acknowledged as one of the most successful international environmental treaties in the world."[29] While it is only one of many international agreements purporting to protect species and nature,[30] it may be the most well known of these agreements. CITES was established in 1973 and went into effect in 1975.[31] The convention now has 175 parties.[32] In its Preamble, CITES states that its purpose is to protect and preserve the world's wild fauna and flora now and for the future.[33] This purpose is reflected in a primary concern for the preservation of species,[34] but the Convention recognizes "the ever-growing value of wild fauna and flora from aesthetic, scientific, cultural, recreational and economic points of view."[35] What this tells us, in line with much of what we have seen previously within the context of other uses of animals, is that the economic value of animals is an ever-present concern in the regulation of the use of animals. As such, CITES does not prohibit trade in endangered species, but "strives to coordinate trade in species that may become endangered."[36] The purposes of CITES are not accomplished with a centralized international enforcement scheme; rather, each individual state is charged with primary responsibility for protecting its fauna and flora under the Convention.[37]

The body of the Convention regulates the import and export of flora and fauna. The level of regulation of trade in a specimen of flora or fauna depends on the location of its species within the three appendices to CITES where species of flora and fauna are listed. So CITES effectively operates at the level of "species," as species are generally what are listed in the appendices.[38] More specifically, the Convention regulates trade in "specimens" of members of regulated species, which are, in addition to a whole animal, "any readily recognizable part or derivative thereof."[39] This means that CITES does not just regulate trade in complete

---

29. Fuchs, *supra* note 27, at 1565.
30. See the listing of international agreements on these issues in ELIZABETH R. DESOMBRE, GLOBAL ENVIRONMENTAL INSTITUTIONS 46 (2006).
31. Wabnitz et al., *supra* note 4, at 15; Elisabeth M. McOmber, *Problems in Enforcement of the Convention on International Trade in Endangered Species*, 27 BROOK. J. INT'L L. 673, 674 (2002).
32. Convention on International Trade in Endangered Species of Wild Fauna and Flora, *Member Countries*, http://www.cites.org/eng/disc/parties/index.shtml. (last visited May 23, 2010).
33. Convention on International Trade in Endangered Species of Wild Fauna and Flora, pmbl., Mar. 3, 1973, http://www.cites.org/eng/disc/text.shtml#texttop [hereinafter CITES]; Fuchs, *supra* note 27, at 1565.
34. Fuchs, *supra* note 27, at 1567.
35. CITES, *supra* note 33, at pmbl.
36. Fuchs, *supra* note 27, at 1567.
37. CITES, *supra* note 33, at pmbl.; WORLD WILDLIFE FUND, INTERNATIONAL WILDLIFE TRADE xi, 4–5 (Ginette Hemley ed., 1994) [hereinafter WWF].
38. CITES, *supra* note 33, at arts. I(a), II.
39. *Id.* at art. 1(b).

examples of a species, but parts of an animal as well, such as ivory, shells, fur, etc. A similar definition exists for specimens of plants.[40]

There are three tiers of Appendices to CITES:[41]

(1) Appendix I: Species threatened with extinction.
(2) Appendix II: Species "not necessarily now threatened with extinction [that] may become so unless trade in specimens of such species is subject to strict regulation" and those other species that must be regulated in order to control the trade in species that may become threatened with extinction.[42] To use the example of corals again, while there are a few coral species listed in Appendix III,[43] Appendix II is where most corals covered by CITES are listed.[44] In this context, one immediately confronts a potential problem with "species" forming the basis of the listing of these animals. Coral "species" are very hard to identify and can only be identified by experts. As such, coral shipments are only listed by genus, not species, and issuing export or import permits at the "genus level may lead to certain species being driven to extinction through overcollection."[45] So the species-level listing can present problems for identifying animals that are listed under CITES, particularly those that are difficult to identify, like corals. A potential remedy for this would be to allow the blanket identification of ecosystems, or areas from which specimens originate to serve as bases for regulating under CITES. There are also circumstances where groups of animals can be listed as described below.[46]
(3) Appendix III: This Appendix lists those species protected from exploitation under a member's laws that need international cooperation for their protection.[47]

These appendices contain about 5,000 fauna and 28,000 flora.[48] While the primary level of listing plants and animals in CITES is by species, sometimes entire groups of animals are permitted to be listed, such as groups of corals, primates, cetaceans, etc.[49]

---

40. *Id.*
41. Fuchs, *supra* note 27, at 1569–74; *see also* Young, *supra* note 28, at 170.
42. CITES, *supra* note 33, at art. II(2).
43. *See id.* at app. III; CITES, *Notification to the Parties No. 2008/027* (Apr. 2, 2008).
44. *See* CITES *supra* note 33, at app. II; *see also* Davidson, *supra* note 12, at 542.
45. Wabnitz et al., *supra* note 4, at 15.
46. See *infra* note 49, and accompanying text.
47. CITES, *supra* note 33, at art. II(3).
48. Fuchs, *supra* note 27, at 1569.
49. Higher taxa, such as orders and families may be listed in Appendix II if they meet criteria stated in Annex 3 to CITES, pursuant to Resolution Conference 9.24 (Rev. CoP14) subsection (f). Convention on International Trade in Endangered Species of Wild Fauna and Flora, *Resolution Conf. 9.24 (Rev. CoP14),* "Annex 3", http://www.cites.org/eng/res/09/09-24R14.shtml (last visited May 23, 2010)*; see also* Fuchs, *supra* note 27, at 1569.

One of the main functions of CITES as an organization, as will be discussed in more detail below, is amending the Appendices from time to time. These amendments can be very politically charged undertakings; *e.g.*, attempts by industrialized nations to place animals like elephants in the Appendices were considered a kind of "cultural imperialism" by countries inhabited by these animals.[50] Another contentious issue is "split listing"—whether a species can be listed on more than one appendix at a time.[51] The issue here is whether, for example, one population of a species in one location can be listed in Appendix I and another population put on a different list due to differences in circumstances at the different locations. This type of split listing is now allowed.[52] For example, Eastern African Elephants are listed in Appendix I, while Southern African Elephants are in Appendix II.[53]

So what does it mean for a species to be listed in one of these appendices? There is a tiered system of regulation under CITES for export and import of species on these different lists. Export of Appendix I animals requires an export permit to be issued by the country of origin.[54] Such an export permit can only be granted if authorities of the state determine that export of the animal or plant in question will not be detrimental to the survival of the species.[55] Precisely what is meant by the "non-detriment" finding required for Appendix I species, however, is not clear:

> The parameters for non-detriment findings, an important means to control trade[,] are not specified in the Convention or in any resolution currently in effect. The nearest to a specification is a recommendation concerning the role of Scientific Authorities [created by states under CITES] that "the findings and advice of the Scientific Authority of the country of export be based on the scientific review of available information on the population status, distribution, population trend, harvest and other biological and ecological factors, as appropriate, and trade information relating to the species concerned."[56]

It is also required that the authorities find that the animals or plants were not obtained in contravention of the state's laws for protection of flora and fauna.[57] In addition, export of Appendix I species requires that living specimens "be prepared and shipped to [] minimize the risk of injury, damage to health or cruel treatment."[58]

50. Fuchs, *supra* note 27, at 1577.
51. *Id.* at 1577–78; McOmber, *supra* note 31, at 695–96.
52. Fuchs, *supra* note 27, at 1577–78; McOmber, *supra* note 31, at 695–96.
53. Fuchs, *supra* note 27, at 1577–78; McOmber, *supra* note 31, at 695–96.
54. CITES, *supra* note 33, at art. III(2) ; Fuchs, *supra* note 27, at 1581; Young, *supra* note 28, at 170.
55. CITES, *supra* note 33, at art. III(2). On this issue, *see also* Wabnitz et al., *supra* note 4, at 15.
56. Rosalind Reeve, Policing International Trade in Endangered Species 30 (2002).
57. CITES, *supra* note 33, at art. III(2).
58. *Id.*

The state authority must also be satisfied that an import permit has been issued for the animals or plants.[59]

The import of flora or fauna listed in Appendix I requires both an import permit and either a certificate of re-export or an export permit.[60] An import permit can only be granted if state authorities determine that the import is for purposes not detrimental to the survival of the species, the recipient will care for the specimen properly and the specimen will not be used for primarily commercial purposes.[61] What an Appendix I listing accomplishes is to effectively limit trade in such species to certain hunting trophies and specimens which are primarily used for educational or scientific functions.[62]

Import of animals and plants listed in Appendix I from the sea is treated somewhat differently from land species. Since someone bringing an animal from the sea to a particular country will necessarily not have an export or import certificate, it is necessary for persons intending to bring specimens from the sea to obtain a prior certificate from the state into which the specimen is to be imported.[63] This type of certificate is to be granted, not surprisingly, only if the state determines that import of the specimen will not be detrimental to the survival of the species; that the specimen will be properly cared for; and that the specimen is not to be primarily used for commercial purposes.[64] These are the same requirements we saw previously for import of Appendix I species not coming from the sea.

For the export of Appendix II species, an export permit granted under the same circumstances as for Appendix I species is mandatory, but an import permit is not required.[65] Note that it is necessary that there be a "Scientific Authority" established in each Member State which, among other things, "monitors exports and advises [limiting] the granting of permits if necessary."[66] For bringing into a state Appendix II specimens from the sea, a prior grant of a certificate is necessary with requirements generally the same as for export permits for other Appendix II specimens, but without the requirement that the state authorities be satisfied that the specimen was not obtained in contravention of the laws of the state for protection of fauna and flora.[67] This is presumably because specimens from the sea will often not be caught in the territorial waters of the country where the flora or fauna is brought to land, and also because of the requirement of prior authorization from the state authorities, which presumably means the authorities are already satisfied that no violation of the law is occurring.

---

59. *Id.*
60. *Id.* at art. III(3).
61. CITES, *supra* note 33, at art. III(3); *see* Fuchs, *supra* note 27, at 1581–82; Young, *supra* note 28, at 170.
62. Fuchs, *supra* note 27, at 1582; *see also* DeSombre, *supra* note 30, at 47.
63. CITES, *supra* note 33, at art. III(5).
64. *Id.*
65. *Id.* at art. IV(2); *see* Fuchs, *supra* note 27, at 1582.
66. Fuchs, *supra* note 27, at 1582.
67. CITES, *supra* note 33, at art. IV(6).

The import of Appendix II species necessitates only presentation of the export permit or re-export certificate.[68] Note that captive-bred Appendix I species are treated as Appendix II species for the purposes of CITES, so long as the exporting country certifies the captive-bred status.[69] In these cases, only a certificate to this effect is required.[70]

Export of Appendix III species understandably has the loosest strictures. What is required for export from a state that has listed a species in Appendix III is an export permit for the plants or animals.[71] This permit will only be granted if the state authority is satisfied that the specimen was not obtained in contravention of the laws of that state and that the specimen will be shipped properly.[72] Import requires presentation of a certificate of origin and, where imported from a state where the species is listed as an Appendix III species, an export permit.[73]

Not all countries are members of CITES; therefore the issue of how member countries are to deal with non-member countries with respect to species covered by CITES becomes a pivotal one. CITES itself states that members can accept permits and certificates from non-member countries if the permits and certificates substantially conform to the requirements of the convention.[74] More detail has been added to this requirement by resolution of the Conference of the Parties that created CITES. By resolution, the Conference of the Parties has determined that documents can be accepted for import of specimens if the non-member state is included in a list of non-member countries compiled by the Secretariat or after consultation with the Secretariat.[75] In addition, for "Appendix I and II species[, there] must also [be] certificates stating that the competent scientific institution in the non-party state has made a non-detriment finding, and that the specimens were not illegally obtained."[76] Acceptance of wild specimens of Appendix I species from non-member countries is allowed only in cases of conservation or animal welfare and requires consultation with the Secretariat.[77]

As with virtually any set of legal rules, there are exceptions to the mandates of CITES. These exceptions are created to provide flexibility in the system of regulation.[78] One exemption under CITES is for specimens that were obtained before the provisions of CITES applied to the species in question.[79] Note that this can be an important exception, since species are regularly being added to the

---

68. CITES, *supra* note 33, at art. IV(4); Fuchs, *supra* note 27, at 1582.
69. CITES, *supra* note 33, at art. VII(4); Young, *supra* note 28, at 181.
70. CITES, *supra* note 33, at art. VII(5).
71. CITES, *supra* note 33, at art. V(2); Fuchs, *supra* note 27, at 1582.
72. CITES, *supra* note 33, at art. V(2).
73. CITES, *supra* note 33, at art. V(3); Fuchs, *supra* note 27, at 1582.
74. CITES, *supra* note 33, at art. X.
75. CITES, Conf. 9.5 (Rev. CoP14), *Trade with States Not Party to the Convention* (2007), *available at* http://www.cites.org/eng/res/all/09/E09-05R14.pdf [hereinafter Conf. 9.5].
76. *Id.*; Fuchs, *supra* note 27, at 1584.
77. Conf. 9.5, *supra* note 75; Fuchs, *supra* note 27, at 1584.
78. Reeve, *supra* note 56, at 35.
79. CITES, *supra* note 33, at art. VII(2).

Appendices. In addition, specimens held as personal or household effects are exempt from CITES.[80] CITES also does not cover non-commercial loans, donations or exchanges of specimens between scientists or scientific institutions.[81] It is further possible for individual states to grant waivers for traveling exhibitions.[82] States can also make "reservations" for newly added species that exempt them from the strictures of CITES for that species, in which case the state is treated as a non-member state with respect to that species.[83] General reservations are not allowed; only reservations on the basis of individual species are permitted.[84]

Ultimately, any regulatory scheme is only going to be as successful as its enforcement mechanism. In the case of CITES, implementation and enforcement are primarily the responsibility of individual Member States[85] and this ultimately requires Member States to penalize trade in contravention of CITES.[86] The imposition of criminal penalties for violations of CITES can, however, be problematic. Because the Appendices change from time to time, what is criminal at a particular point in time may not be well known—so one could potentially be criminally liable under regulations that are constantly in flux and are often difficult to understand.[87] Given the fact that CITES Appendices are periodically changed, this is a problem endemic to the listing system of the regulatory scheme. In another aspect of the enforcement scheme, the CITES rules further compel "confiscation or return to the state of export of [] specimens" violating CITES.[88]

Moreover, member countries are required to provide reports on their activities under CITES. An annual report must be submitted by each member to the CITES organization on permits granted, exporters and importers in the state, the states with whom the member is trading, and the numbers and types of specimens traded.[89] Biennial reports are also required on legislative and administrative actions taken by each Member State for enforcement of CITES.[90] These reports are extraordinarily important for monitoring of compliance with and enforcement of CITES.[91] Nonetheless, there is widespread noncompliance with the reporting requirements.[92]

Although the enforcement mechanism of CITES relies primarily on individual country enforcement, CITES is not without its own teeth; CITES can recommend

80. *Id.* at art. VII(3).
81. *Id.* at art. VII(6).
82. *Id.* at art. VII(7).
83. *Id.* at art. XXIII.
84. *Id.*
85. *Id.* at art. VIII; WWF, *supra* note 37, at xi, 4–5.
86. CITES, *supra* note 33, at art.VIII(1); *see* Fuchs, *supra* note 27, at 1583.
87. *See* Fuchs, *supra* note 27, at 1590–95.
88. CITES, *supra* note 33, at art. VIII(1); *see also* Fuchs, *supra* note 27, at 1583; WWF, *supra* note 37, at 5.
89. CITES, *supra* note 33, at art. VIII(7); Fuchs, *supra* note 27, at 1585.
90. CITES, *supra* note 33, at art. VIII(7); Fuchs, *supra* note 27, at 1585.
91. Reeve, *supra* note 56, at 62–88; Desombre, *supra* note 30, at 48–49.
92. Reeve, *supra* note 56, at 64–68.

sanctions against violators. The main sanction is trade suspension,[93] and as of July 27, 2009, there were 25 countries subject to recommendations of trade suspensions.[94] Another means of enforcing the convention is the "Significant Trade Review" process.[95] In this process, the Animals and Plants Committees of CITES review trade in selected species and determine if parties are complying with their obligations relating to these species.[96] If a state is not complying with its obligations, this can lead, as a final measure, to the suspension of trade with the offending member in the affected species.[97]

III. CITES AS AN ORGANIZATION

As the foregoing discussion of the CITES regulatory mechanism indicates, CITES has an organizational structure. CITES can be broadly described as "a treaty regime."[98] Technically, CITES is not an international organization, but is:

> an association of states established by and based upon a treaty that pursues common aims, and which has organs that fulfill functions. Typically, international organizations are founded with a generally and vaguely termed framework treaty which is then dynamically concretized by treaty bodies. Executive tasks are carried out by a Secretariat. Both aspects are also true of CITES.[99]

The main decision-making body under CITES is the Conference of the Parties (CP), which meets every two years.[100] Although the CP prefers to function by consensus, it may adopt measures by two-thirds majority vote.[101] The main function of the CP is to periodically amend CITES and the Appendices.[102] In addition to the CP, CITES organizational structures include a Secretariat,[103] a Standing Committee, and also technical committees, one relating to plants and the other to animals.[104] The Secretariat role is filled by the United Nations Environment Programme (UNEP).[105]

---

93. *See* Convention on International Trade in Endangered Species, *Countries Currently Subject to a Recommendation to Suspend Trade*, http://www.cites.org/eng/news/sundry/trade_suspension.shtml (last visited May 23, 2010) [hereinafter *CITES Recommendations*]; *see also* DESOMBRE, *supra* note 30, at 49; Fuchs, *supra* note 27, at 1586; REEVE, *supra* note 56, at 93–133.
94. *CITES Recommendations, supra* note 93.
95. For a detailed discussion of this process, *see* REEVE, *supra* note 56, at 159–88.
96. Convention on International Trade in Endangered Species, *Conf. 12.8 (Rev. CoP13)* (2004).
97. *Id*; Fuchs, *supra* note 27, at 1587; *see* REEVE, *supra* note 56, at 162–66.
98. Fuchs, *supra* note 27, at 1587.
99. *Id.* at 1570 (citations omitted).
100. CITES, *supra* note 33, at art. XI.
101. CITES, *supra* note 33, at arts. XV, XVII; Fuchs, *supra* note 27, at 1576.
102. *See* Fuchs, *supra* note 27, at 1569.
103. CITES, *supra* note 33, art. XII.
104. Fuchs, *supra* note 27, at 1570–73.
105. DESOMBRE, *supra* note 30, at 48; REEVE, *supra* note 56, at 43.

So how are the all-important Appendices to CITES amended? Note first that for a species to be listed in Appendices I or II, the CP must approve the listing; on the other hand, individual countries can designate species to be listed on Appendix III, since the Appendix III category is based on domestic regulation of a particular species. The impetus for changes to the appendices comes from CITES members: "Any party [to CITES] may propose an amendment to Appendix I or II for consideration at the next [CP] meeting."[106] As noted earlier, these changes can be adopted by the CP by a two-thirds vote.[107] While the criteria used to determine if a change to the Appendices should occur have evolved over time, the present rules are contained in what are referred to as the Fort Lauderdale Criteria for Appendix I species. These criteria call for an Appendix I listing of a population of a species illustrated not to be sustainable if:[108]

- there is a small wild population;
- the area of distribution of the wild population is restricted;
- whether in an observed or predicted manner, the number of individual specimens has been reduced; or
- the current status of the species makes it likely that the species will fulfill one or more of the criteria listed above, unless it is listed in Appendix I.

The idea of these criteria is to create a scientific and objectively based set of criteria.[109] As mentioned earlier, one of the more contentious listing issues has now been resolved and it is possible for species to be "split listed" thus allowing parties to propose such listing schemes and permitting the CP to approve them.[110]

For an example of this amendment process, we can analyze what occurred in 2010 at the CITES meeting. A number of fairly high profile species were the subject of proposals at the 2010 meeting. For instance, the United States proposed that polar bears be included in Appendix I, while in a proposal going the other direction, Tanzania and Zambia wanted their elephant populations to be transferred from Appendix I to Appendix II,[111] and proposals were made to add several shark species to Appendix II, to ban commercial trade in Atlantic bluefin tuna and the United States renewed its attempt to place red and pink corals in Appendix II.[112]

The results of these proposals were disappointing to many; while the Tanzanian and Zambian proposal on opening up trade in ivory and downgrading their elephant populations was defeated, the proposals on polar bears, sharks and

106. CITES, *supra* note 33, at art. XV(1)(a).
107. *Id.* at art. XV(2)(j).
108. Young, *supra* note 28, at 177.
109. *Id.* at 177–78.
110. *Id.*
111. Humane Society International, *CITES 2010 Species Proposal Highlights*, http://www.hsus.org/hsi/policy_and_trade/treaties/convention_on_international_trade_in_endangered_species/2009/cites_proposals_021810.html (last visited May 23, 2010).
112. Humane Society International, *News About CITES 2010*, http://www.hsi.org/news/news/2010/02/ (last visited Feb. 4, 2011).

bluefin tuna also failed.[113] According to one commentator, the reasons were economic and political:

> Other groups that were pushing for a ban say that their efforts failed simply because the trade in bluefin tuna and shark fins generate far too much money. The bluefin sushi market is worth billions in Japan, and the shark fin soup market in China is considered a lucrative business.[114]

Similarly, observers from the scientific community interpreted these decisions of the CP as politics and economics trumping science.[115]

With respect to red and pink corals, the parade of "no" responses to proposals continued:

> But delegates declined to adopt a proposal offered by the United States and Sweden that would have regulated, for the first time, red and pink corals that are targeted for the jewelry, home decor and homeopathic medicine market. The 31 species that would have received new protections are taken primarily from the Mediterranean and are used in the production of high-end jewelry in European countries such as Italy and Croatia, as well as cheaper decorations and souvenirs in Taiwan and China.[116]

The costs to us all of decisions like this and the reasons for the decisions were described as follows in the Washington Post:

> Environmentalists and scientists argue that corals, which are living animals and seriously threatened by rising carbon dioxide emissions that are warming the ocean and making it more acidic, cannot afford the added pressure of a commercial harvest. Nearly 30 percent of the world's tropical coral species have disappeared since 1980, mainly because of warming, and an even larger percentage may have disappeared by the end of the last century. As coral species have struggled, the harvest has declined sharply, dropping from 450 tons annually in the 1970s to 50 tons a year today, according to the advocacy group Oceana.
>
> David Allison, Oceana's senior campaign director, said Sunday's vote demonstrated that "vanity has once again trumped conservation."
>
> "It's really shameful," Allison said in an interview from Doha, adding that the convention has lost sight of its original mission. "It's not about, How do you use trade to effectively bring about rational market management?"

---

113. Nick Clark, *Little Celebration as CITES Ends*, Mar. 26, 2010, http://english.aljazeera.net/focus/wildlifesos/2010/03/2010325185143794333.html.
114. *Id.*
115. *Id.*
116. Juliet Eilperin, *Nations Reject Coral Protections at Wildlife Conservation Conference*, WASH. POST, Mar. 22, 2010, http://www.washingtonpost.com/wp-dyn/content/article/2010/03/21/AR2010032101204.html.

> The countries that traditionally lobby for use of marine resources—Japan, Iceland, Libya and Tunisia—spoke out against protection, arguing that it would jeopardize fishing jobs.
>
> "Corals are the building blocks of many ocean ecosystems, and the science is clear: They are at great risk," said Dawn Martin, president of SeaWeb. "And now, since action was not taken at CITES, red and pink coral populations will continue to decline at an alarming rate."[117]

So the peril to corals and the innumerable species that reside in reefs is likely to continue because of human economic interests.

As in other realms of exploitation of animals, we see the supposed interests of humans overshadowing the interests of animals. The 2010 CITES meeting thus "underscored nations' unwillingness to forgo immediate economic gains from exploiting natural resources, even when these activities are putting plants and animals under intense pressure."[118] One could also reasonably conclude that the short-term economic and political interests of humans are overshadowing even the long-term interests of humans, which includes having a functioning global ecology. CITES may be becoming nothing more than a brightly harnessed show pony in an international economic game of ecological exploitation.

IV. THE EFFECTIVENESS OF CITES

Illegal trade in wildlife, notwithstanding the strictures of CITES, is still big business; global illegal trade in wildlife is estimated at between USD 5 and 10 billion a year, and only arms and drugs produce more illicit trade money.[119] Some estimates put the illegal trade at an even higher level, perhaps more than USD 20 billion annually.[120] In the face of this enormous trade is a CITES organization with average funding from 2001 to 2005 of USD 5.5 million, and even counting external funding contributions, its funding still does not exceed USD 10 million.[121] So while CITES has been lauded as one of the most successful international treaties in history, there are obvious holes in the protection it provides. Apart from the apparent economic takeover of CITES species listings made evident by the 2010 CITES Conference, and the obvious lack of funding, what other lapses are there in the CITES regulatory structure?

One of the problems with CITES is the fact that enforcement of the treaty is essentially left to individual member countries. Different countries, however, have different motivations and approaches concerning trade in wild animals. These

117. *Id.*
118. *Id.*
119. Fuchs, *supra* note 27, at 1588.
120. Liana Sun Wyler & Pervage A. Sheikh, *Report for Congress: Illegal Trade in Wildlife: Threats and U.S. Policy* 2 (Congressional Research Service, 2008).
121. Reeve, *supra* note 56, at 55, 272.

differing motivations on endangered species protection lead to myriad domestic protection laws and enforcement efforts; poor nations may see endangered species as a major asset of their economy, while wealthy nations may see these animals as sacrosanct icons that should never be driven from their habitat or killed for any amount of money.[122] In fact, many member countries have not even enacted legislation required by CITES.[123] So the inherent unevenness of the CITES regulatory scheme because of its individual state enforcement mechanism results in a wide variety of laws and enforcement schemes that may not necessarily carry out the goals of the CITES regime.

That "[e]nforcement is the Achilles' heel of CITES"[124] can be seen from a number of examples. For instance, quotas for trade in certain species, which are not specifically provided for in CITES but have nonetheless been regularly used,[125] are often exceeded.[126] That enforcement mechanisms are not always successful can also be seen in the case of corals. Sometimes coral is taken from places where it is illegal to collect coral, but is then exported with the false statement that it was collected in a country where collecting coral is legal.[127] The same occurs with other species. These difficulties can be attributed to the lack of central enforcement authority in the CITES Secretariat, or elsewhere.[128] Again the individual state enforcement scheme leaves the foxes to guard the henhouse. Proposals have been made to try to remedy these issues of member compliance with CITES by creating a Compliance Committee, but thus far such a committee has not been formed.[129]

Along with difficulties in enforcement caused by the diffuse CITES enforcement mechanism, there is also a lack of coordination among the entities actually involved in enforcement:

> Despite advances in the last decade, lack of coordination and cooperation between governmental, inter-governmental and non-governmental organizations—between national CITES authorities and enforcement agencies; between national agencies and international organizations (Interpol, WCO and the CITES Secretariat); between national agencies on a regional basis across borders; and between all of them and NGOs—is a recurring issue.[130]

Just listing the entities involved in the process makes clear the difficulties of coordination. But the coordination and organizational difficulties do not end here;

---

122. *See* Young, *supra* note 28, at 174–76.
123. Reeve, *supra* note 56, at 246.
124. *Id.* at 249.
125. *Id.* at 36.
126. Fuchs, *supra* note 27, at 1588.
127. Mulhall, *supra* note 1, at 343–44.
128. Young, *supra* note 28, at 174.
129. Reeve, *supra* note 56, at 268.
130. *Id.* at 254.

there has been notable unease in relations between UNEP, the Secretariat and others in the CITES organization itself.[131]

Another difficulty is that CITES only applies to "readily recognizable" specimens of endangered species, their parts and derivatives. But there is no definition of "readily recognizable" and the term itself is ambiguous.[132] Again it is left up to individual members to define the meaning of this term, which can create potential abuse, or at the very least, poor interpretation.[133]

An additional set of problems surround reservations, exemptions and the fact that non-member countries operate outside the system. The allowance of reservations that permit countries to reserve the right to trade in identified Appendix I species provides an explicit exit from CITES for countries wishing to continue trade in animals that have already been determined to be endangered.[134] While it has been argued that reservations have actually "not played a major role in undermining the objectives of the agreement … there certainly are some instances in which it has prevented or delayed species protection efforts."[135] Exemptions are allowed, as discussed earlier, and a number of them are frequently abused, like the exemptions for artificially propagated or captive-bred specimens, personal and household goods, animals expropriated from the wild prior to the species being listed in an Appendix and so on.[136] Moreover, allowing trade with non-parties to CITES has allowed these parties to become monopolists in trade in endangered species.[137] This problem is so severe that it is estimated that 30% of all wildlife trade is with non-parties to CITES.[138]

As discussed previously, there are also sometimes difficulties in getting species listed under CITES, which can arise from both political and economic pressures. The United States, for instance, tried to get pink and red corals placed in Appendix II. Most artists and traders in these corals are in Italy and there was opposition based on economic concerns from these groups, which ultimately halted the listing.[139] Indeed, it has been observed that listing decisions are becoming more and more economic decisions, not scientific ones.[140] The intrusion of economic and political perspectives into these decisions is the case even with the new and supposedly scientifically based Fort Lauderdale Criteria for determining listing decisions.[141]

Moreover, the focus on "species" as the criteria for listing designations presents its own set of difficulties, which can be seen quite clearly in the case of

---

131. *Id.* at 259.
132. See McOmber, *supra* note 31, at 690–93.
133. *See* Young, *supra* note 28, at 182.
134. CITES, *supra* note 33, at art. XXIII; *see also* Desombre, *supra* note 30, at 50–51.
135. Desombre, *supra* note 30, at 51.
136. *See* Reeve, *supra* note 56, at 35; Young, *supra* note 28, at 180–81.
137. Young, *supra* note 28, at 179.
138. *Id.*
139. Mulhall, *supra* note 1, at 344.
140. *Id.* at 345.
141. *See* Young, *supra* note 28, at 188.

corals. Corals themselves create ecosystems; indeed, they form one of the most fertile types of ecosystems in the world. Ecosystems are relationships of innumerable species, climatic conditions and other variables that result in a symbiosis. CITES does not allow for the protection of ecosystems like those created in coral reefs and the lack of this sort of protection may make the existing regulations deficient in protecting species intended to be protected.[142]

This is not to say that CITES is completely ineffectual; changes in consumer demand away from Appendix I species and the substitution of captive-bred animals for wild animals have been cited as successes of CITES.[143] These successes may help wild members of these particular species, but do nothing for the non-Appendix I animals which are substituted for wild Appendix I animals, or for the farmed animals which are substituted for wild ones. As a result, these animals are still exploited, and for those opposed to this kind of exploitation in its entirety, the replacement of one sort of exploitation for another can hardly be hailed as a success.

The overall results of the CITES treaty have been described as follows:

> Overall, CITES has had mixed success in its efforts to protect species through trade restrictions. It faces an inherently difficult task, involving thousands of protected species … at multiple points of export, with border inspections conducted by those untrained in taxonomy and with too many inspections to carry out, and many opportunities to transport species across borders undetected.[144]

In the end, CITES is an agreement that accepts the legitimacy of trade in animals, including those that are endangered, and this necessarily legitimizes the exploitation of all these animals.

The fundamental debate presently surrounding CITES centers on whether these rare animals and plants should be economically exploited in a way that theoretically maintains the various rare species, the "sustainable use" position, or the preservationist position that wishes to prohibit all trade in protected species.[145] Unlike the "sustainable use" position, the preservationist position places value on the species themselves and wishes to end the use of these animals entirely. "Sustainable use," on the other hand, is really just a pleasant name for continued economic exploitation of wild animals by maintaining sufficient numbers of endangered species to ensure their continued exploitation. And if this was not in itself a sufficient problem with the sustainable use concept, how do we arrive at the level of use considered "sustainable"? The truth is that we really do not often have the scientific information necessary to answer these kinds of questions.[146] So what we have in sustainable use theory is open economic exploitation

142. *See* Mulhall, *supra* note 1, at 345.
143. Fuchs, *supra* note 27, at 1589–90.
144. DeSombre, *supra* note 30, at 51.
145. Young, *supra* note 28, at 182–86.
146. *Id.*

of animals, coupled with oftentimes unknown or unknowable scientific issues of the "sustainability" of present practices. Notwithstanding the difficulties with this theory, sustainable use is the view that seems to be prevailing.[147]

That this (or worse) is the case, is obvious from the 2010 CITES Conference, which has been called by some not the "Doha Conference," but the "No-ha Conference,"[148] given its rejections for economic reasons of proposals to list numerous scientifically well-established cases of species in peril. So once again, we see the interests of humans, whether economic, cultural, political, religious, or social, easily outweighing the interests of animals and, in the end, the long-term interests of humans, as reflected by the ever-increasing destruction of our natural environment.

V. THE TALE OF THE TIGER

The example that I have been primarily using to illustrate how CITES works has been that of corals; there are, of course, many other species that are listed in CITES. I would like to end this chapter by providing, as an example to provoke thought and reveal the economic and trade realities at work in the CITES regulatory universe, the very sad case of tigers. It is a depressing irony that while 2010 was the Year of the Tiger in China, it is the use of tiger parts in traditional Chinese medicine that may cause the extinction of wild tigers entirely:[149]

> On [14] February [2010], China's 1.3 billion people will ring in the new lunar Year of the Tiger. As the spotlight turns on the dangerously endangered animal, at the heart of the matter is the continuing demand in China for tiger parts which are an ingredient in a variety of traditional Chinese medicines. It is this demand that fuels the poaching of the tiger in neighbouring India, home to the largest number of wild tigers in the world.
>
> Although Beijing officially banned trade of tiger parts in 1993, Chinese demand has remained untamed, fed by poachers and international smugglers. The result for the tiger in China itself has been catastrophic. In January, WWF China's director for conservation of bio diversity, Zhu Chunquan, warned of a "high risk" that the 50 odd remaining wild tigers in the country would soon disappear altogether in the absence of "urgent measures."[150]

---

147. *Id.* at 182–84.
148. Eilperin, *supra* note 116.
149. Pallavi Aiyar, *Help*! BUS. STANDARD, Feb. 13, 2010, at 1, 2010 WLNR 3026572; *see also* Julie Santagelo, *Evading Extinction: A 21st Century Survey of the Legal Challenges to Wild Siberian Tiger Conservation,* 1 J. ANIMAL L. 109, 110 (2005).
150. Aiyar, *supra* note 149.

The numbers of Indian tigers is also dropping rapidly due to poaching.[151] Tiger pelts can go for USD 20,000 and paws for USD 1,000.[152]

One proposed solution, which seems to be becoming a popular one for dealing with the possible extinction of animals that are being poached in the wild, is to legalize the trade in tigers and similarly endangered species.[153] In this way, the theory goes, these animals can be raised on farms and they or their parts can be sold legally thereby reducing the economic incentive to poach wild populations.[154] The idea then is to extend the "farming" of animals to wild species, creating yet another type of economic exploitation of animals. Here we take wild animals and keep them in very unnatural and typically horrifying conditions so that humans can use them in practices that have no proven scientific value at all like the use of tiger parts for medicinal purposes.

In the following quote, one can see the potential results of this kind of "solution" and the conditions of these "farmed" wild animals:

> In a shabby "wildlife park" in remote China, an incredible 1,500 tigers—half the entire number left in the wild—are bred in squalor and destined to become part of a sinister trade …
>
> Behind rusted bars, a skeletal male tiger lies panting on the filthy concrete floor of his cage, covered in sores and untreated wounds. Its once-fearsome body is so emaciated, it is little more than a pitiful pile of fur and bones.
>
> "No lack of materials. We have hundreds of dead tigers in our freezer" Death is surely a matter of days away and will be a welcome release. Wardens at the wildlife park in southwest China say, indifferently, they do not expect it to see the Year of the Tiger, which began last Sunday. "What can we do?" a female park official asks a small huddle of visitors with a sigh and a casual shrug. "He's dying, of course, but we have to keep feeding him until he does. It's against the law to kill tigers."
>
> Instead, it seems, they die slowly of neglect. In row after row of foul, cramped cages, more tigers lie alone, crippled and dying. One is hunched up against the side of its cage with its neck grotesquely deformed. Another, blinded in one eye, lies motionless.[155]

The reasons for the trade in these animals and the sad spectacles created with them highlight the horror of trade in wild animals, farmed or not:

---

151. *Id.*; Milan Dalal, *Tiger, Tiger, Flickering Light*, 31 B.C. Int'l & Comp. L. Rev. 103, 106–07 (2008); The Statesman, *Indian Tigers Face Poaching Threat from China*, Statesman, Feb. 25, 2010, 2010 WLNR 4008891 [hereinafter *The Statesman*].
152. Andrew Jacobs, *Tiger Farms in China Feed Thirst for Parts*, Deseret News, Feb. 14, 2010, at A18.
153. *See* Aiyar, *supra* note 149; Ananth Krishnan, *China Considers Legalising Tiger Trade to Curb Poaching*, Hindu, Feb. 14, 2010, at 16.
154. *See* Aiyar, *supra* note 149.
155. Richard Jones, *Exposed Dark Secret of the Tiger Farm*, Mail on Sunday, Feb. 21, 2010, 2010 WLNR 3667741.

> Tigers have been used in Chinese traditional medicine for centuries. Their eyeballs are used to treat epilepsy, their bile to stop convulsions, their whiskers to sooth toothache and their penises as a potent sexual tonic.
>
> The most valuable parts, however, are the bones, which are used to make wine that is said to cure rheumatism and arthritis, and to prolong life.
>
> ...
>
> Twice a day, a few relatively tame tigers are put on leashes and led out to amuse small groups of visitors. For the equivalent of £1.50 a time, parents and their children get the opportunity to feed strips of beef to a scrawny, under-nourished young tiger in the care of a park keeper who, with no sense of irony, tells them the tiger is a "symbol of power in the animal kingdom."
>
> ...
>
> Welfare expert David Neale from Animals Asia said after inspecting the park: "These animals are kept in appalling conditions and it is clear that many of them are suffering from malnutrition. And if what the public can see is so appalling, can you imagine what the conditions are like for the tigers hidden from view?"[156]

Apart from the evident dreadfulness of these practices, it is by no means settled that this "tiger farming" will aid wild populations.[157] And all of this is happening in the face of CITES. What this tells us is that CITES is not operating in a particularly effective manner in helping preserve wild tigers. This is due to the fact that, among other things, CITES "is widely and openly violated in China and Taiwan."[158] There are further difficulties in remedying the failures of implementation because of lack of funds and political insecurity.[159] The lack of a standardized import/export permit system has also been cited as a cause of difficulties in protecting tigers.[160] And as noted in the last section, the personal and household effects exception is abused in this context as in others.[161]

So CITES, heralded as one of the most successful international environmental treaties, is not without problems; ones that do not admit of simple solutions or, perhaps, any solutions at all, so long as the economic exploitation of these wild animals as property is permitted to continue. CITES does not prohibit trade; it tries to regulate it. But as long as there are economic incentives to fail to enforce it, to violate it, to make reservations to its application, I fear the wild tiger and other species will soon find their places in natural history museums alongside the dodo and the passenger pigeon.

---

156. *Id.*
157. *See* Dept. of the Interior, Office of the Secretary, *U.S. Leads Effort to Protect Wild Tigers from Poaching, Successfully Rallies Support for Resolution on Tiger Farms,* June 13, 2007, 2007 WL 1700894; *see also The Statesman, supra* note 151.
158. *See* Dalal, *supra* note 151, at 106–07.
159. Santagelo, *supra* note 149, at 119.
160. *Id.*
161. *Id.*

Chapter 7
The WTO and GATT

I. INTERNATIONAL TRADE AND REGULATION OF THE TREATMENT OF ANIMALS

When I began studying international and comparative law in the context of animal issues, I envisioned my task as analysis of treaties and laws of various countries and discovery of the mechanisms used around the world to regulate the treatment of animals. Certainly this is a project worthy of effort and in fact is done elsewhere in this book. To my surprise, however, I found that there was an aspect of international law that had an unexpected and crucial impact on animal welfare law throughout the world: the World Trade Organization (WTO) and the General Agreement on Tariffs and Trade (GATT, portions of which are reprinted in Appendix VII). These bastions of international trade law, I found, have had enormous impact not just on what you would expect, trade between countries, but they have profound implications for the regulation of animal welfare within countries.

As it turns out, the GATT has been interpreted as being unfavorable to the improvement of conditions of animals the world over, and can be seen, from economic and other perspectives, to encourage practices that are hostile to animal welfare, not only in terms of international trade policy, but also in terms of domestic regulations as well. This need not be the case, however. With proper analysis and perhaps some amendments, the GATT can be a mechanism that not only rationally regulates trade, but also permits advances in animal protection. Understanding the history of the WTO and GATT is the first step in comprehending the present state of international trade law relating to animals and preparing for the future.

II. HISTORY

As the thunder, fire and smoke of World War II slowly receded into the noxious fog of history, a wisp of hope for a future without war was thought to lay in the promotion of trade. Surely, if the economic fortunes of nations became intertwined; if the poorest of countries could advance economically; if the know-how and efficiency of the developed world could be shared with the undeveloped; armed conflict would become less likely. It was within this context that a number of distinct but connected agreements and institutions were negotiated in the aftermath of the second Great War in little more than 20 years. Among these agreements was the Charter for the International Trade Organization (ITO) which was to be the Constitution for international trade.[1] The GATT Treaty was intended to be an interim measure to bridge the post-war period before the implementation of the ITO.[2]

The ITO never happened. President Truman did not submit the ITO Charter to the United States Senate. The United States Congress thus failed to ratify the Charter.[3] As a result, the GATT, signed in 1947, developed into its own institution.[4] This development occurred through eight rounds of negotiations that saw changes in tariffs and agreements on a broad range of trade issues, including subsidies, import licensing and technical barriers to trade.[5] Nonetheless, the GATT institutional structure was thought not to be sufficient to handle the many trade agreements that had been reached, or to deal adequately with trade disputes.[6]

These institutional deficiencies led in the Uruguay Round of negotiations to the creation of the WTO in the *Marrakesh Agreement Establishing the World Trade Organization* in 1995.[7] The GATT was made an Annex to the WTO Agreement and was determined in the Uruguay Round to include, among other things, the "decisions" of the parties to the GATT since 1947.[8] The original purposes of the GATT were to raise worldwide standards of living, ensure full employment and optimize use of the world's resources.[9] To these purposes the WTO Agreement added the objectives of regulation of trade in services, not just goods, sustainable development, and aiding the development of developing countries.[10] The functions that the WTO is intended to undertake are to implement international trade agreements, operate as a negotiating forum for international trade issues, settle trade disputes among nations, aid developing countries and provide coherence and consistency in international trade through, among other things, cooperation with other international institutions.[11]

---

1. Raj Bhala, Modern GATT Law xii (2005).
2. *Id.*
3. *Id.*
4. Petros C. Mavroidis, The General Agreement on Tariffs and Trade 3, 5–6 (2005).
5. *See id.* at 6–9.
6. World Trade Organization Secretariat, Guide to the Uruguay Round Agreements 1 (1999) [hereinafter Guide].
7. *Id.* at 1–2.
8. Mavroidis, *supra* note 4, at 11–12.
9. Guide, *supra* note 6, at 3.
10. *Id.* at 3–5.
11. *Id.* at 3–5, 15–17.

The WTO is headed by the Ministerial Conference which is composed of the Member States.[12] This body meets at least every two years and has the power to decide all matters relating to the various WTO agreements.[13] When the Ministerial Conference is not in session, the General Council, composed of representatives of all Member States, performs the duties of the Ministerial Conference and also acts as the Dispute Settlement Body and the Trade Policy Review Body.[14] In addition to the General Council, there are three subsidiary councils on Trade in Goods, Trade in Services and Trade-Related Aspects of Intellectual Property Rights that carry out functions stated in the WTO Agreement or as assigned by the General Council.[15] In addition to these councils, there are a number of committees of the WTO that deal with diverse trade issues.[16]

Membership in the WTO can be obtained in two ways, through being an original member of the GATT of 1947 or by accession.[17] The accession method requires that all other members of the WTO agree to accession and typically involves protracted negotiations.[18] Decision-making in the WTO is usually by consensus.[19] Votes do occur, however, with a majority vote of Member States required on most matters, but with supermajorities required on other issues.[20]

One of the main reasons for the creation of the WTO was to establish a better dispute resolution process and an institutional structure for international trade disputes.[21] The lack of an efficacious dispute resolution process and institutional structure was one of the main complaints made about the GATT.[22] The first step in the present WTO dispute resolution process is to try to get parties to resolve disputes through negotiations.[23] Failing this, a panel of three to five persons, all with expertise in international trade issues, is formed to review the facts and relevant law, and to submit a panel report.[24] Any state dissatisfied with a panel report can appeal to three members of a seven-member Appellate Body.[25] The ultimate decision making body, however, is the Dispute Settlement Body, which is the General Council acting in the capacity of Dispute Settlement Body ("DSB").[26]

---

12. For an excellent description of the WTO structure on which this discussion is largely based, *see* GUIDE, *supra* note 6, at 6–30.
13. *Id.* at 6.
14. *Id.*
15. *Id.* at 7.
16. *Id.* at 7–8.
17. *Id.* at 11–13.
18. *See id.*
19. *Id.* at 13–15.
20. *Id.*
21. *See id.* at 1–2, 17–18.
22. *See id.* at 1–2, 17–19.
23. *See id.* at 19–20. The dispute settlement process is set forth in the Uruguay Round Understanding on Rules and Procedures Governing the Settlement of Disputes, contained in Annex 2 to the Marrakesh Agreement Establishing the World Trade Organization.
24. GUIDE, *supra* note 6, at 21.
25. *Id.* at 22.
26. *Id.* at 6, 20–23.

The DSB decides whether to adopt or reject reports of the panels and the Appellate Body.[27]

Assuming a dispute goes through the WTO dispute settlement process and a violation of trade law is found, it can be resolved in four ways.[28] The dispute can be settled through further negotiations between the parties;[29] the offending law can be withdrawn by the country found in violation of the trade law in question;[30] the offending country can provide compensation to the aggrieved state; or, as a last resort, the aggrieved state can retaliate against the offending country.[31] The latter remedy of retaliation allows the aggrieved country to take discriminatory trade actions against the offending state.[32]

This institutional structure of the WTO and the dispute settlement process were major accomplishments in international trade regulation. Indeed, the dispute settlement process has been referred to as the "crown jewel" of the WTO system.[33] Having briefly described the WTO structure, it is now time to look to the substance of the GATT treaty and analyze its implications for the regulation of animal welfare issues.

Relevant to this are the issues of whether the pre-1994 "decisions" that are a part of GATT include the adoption of prior Panel Reports under GATT and what precedential effect these Reports have. As noted earlier, the GATT as Annex to the WTO Agreement included prior "decisions" under GATT. So there are several foundational questions here for GATT jurisprudence. Are adopted Panel Reports under GATT included within these "decisions"? What is the impact of these Reports on future GATT jurisprudence? As it turns out, decisions adopted by the contracting parties to GATT have been found not to be "decisions" that became a part of GATT in 1994.[34] Nonetheless, adopted GATT Reports, while not in the strict sense binding *stare decisis* precedent, provide "guidance" to the WTO.[35] Even unadopted decisions may have some effect as "guidance" for future decisions.[36]

---

27. *Id.* at 23.
28. *Id.* at 23–24.
29. *Id.*
30. *Id.*
31. *Id.*
32. *Id.*
33. Press Release, WTO, WTO Disputes Reach 400 Mark (Nov. 6, 2009), *available at* http://www.wto.org/english/news_e/pres09_e/pr578_e.htm.
34. MAVROIDIS, *supra* note 4, at 11–15.
35. *Id.*
36. Robert House, *The Appellate Body Rulings in the Shrimp/Turtle Case: A New Legal Baseline for the Trade and Environment Debate,* 27 COLUM. J ENVTL. L. 491, 516, 517 (2002); *see also* Panel Report, *Argentina—Measures Affecting Imports of Footwear, Textiles, Apparel, and Other Items*, WT/DS56/R (Nov. 25, 1997) and cases cited therein.

III. GATT AND ANIMAL WELFARE

Seattle, Wednesday, December 1, 1999: tear gas wafts through the wet gloomy air. Phalanxes of protesters in dolphin costumes and turtle suits, some decorated with water-proof paint, battle with police officers and turn downtown Seattle into a chaotic war zone.[37] The protesters, estimated at 50,000, were "met by troops and tanks[,] [t]ear gas, 'flash bombs,' and rubber bullets."[38] Police cars were vandalized; "Barbie Kills" was sprayed on a toy store window.[39] Police and National Guard units became so numerous they marched with "boots clicking rhythmically on the rain-soaked streets."[40] Protesters who refused to disperse "were summarily handcuffed ... and dragged off to waiting buses."[41] Others marched down Third Street, yelling, "[o]ur streets, our world!" before being met with a fog of tear gas.[42] The fleeing crowd was pursued by the police, who fired rubber bullets and concussion grenades as the protesters retreated.[43] In all, about 600 people were arrested during the protest, on charges including assault, assault on a police officer, malicious mischief, property damage, burglary, graffiti painting and looting.[44]

So why all the anger at the WTO? Some of the protesters were anarchists, protesting against government generally, but others were concerned about the impact of international trade on a wide range of issues. These issues ranged from the environment, to labor regulation, to animal welfare.[45] Some were concerned with the use of sweat-shop labor,[46] others were concerned with the environment and the perceived assault by the WTO on environmental regulations in the *Tuna/ Dolphin* and *Shrimp/Turtle* cases that are discussed in detail below.[47] Still others were angry that European regulations on leghold traps were not enforced for fear

37. *See* Jonathan Peterson, *WTO Summit in Seattle; Activists Bring Turtles' Cause to WTO Fishbowl*, L.A. TIMES, Dec. 3, 1999, at A1.
38. *The Battle in Seattle is the Largest Since the Rallies Against the Vietnam War*, http://oikos.org/ecology/wtocan.htm (last visited May 26, 2010) [hereinafter *Battle in Seattle*].
39. CNN.com, *Curfew in Effect as Seattle Struggles to Control WTO Protests: WTO Says Violence Did Not Stop Negotiations*, Nov. 30, 1999, *available at* http://www.cnn.com/US/9911/30/wto.04/index.html.
40. Kim Murphy, *WTO Summit: Protest in Seattle; 400 Jailed as Police Occupy Seattle Streets*, L.A. TIMES, Dec. 2, 1999, at A1.
41. *Id.*
42. *Id.*
43. *Id.*
44. *See 240 WTO Protest Cases are Dropped*, L.A. TIMES, Jan. 5, 2000, at A4; Seattle P.D., *After Action Report World Trade Organization Ministerial Conference Seattle, Washington, Nov. 29–Dec. 3, 1999* 42 (2000).
45. *See* Elaine Bernard, *A Short Guide to the WTO, The Millennium Round and the Rumble in Seattle*, GLOBAL POLICY FORUM, Nov. 29, 1999, *available at* http://www.globalpolicy.org/socecon/bwi-wto/wto/1999/seattle9.htm; Tom Hayden, *The Battle in Seattle: What Was That All About?*, WASH. POST, Dec. 5, 1999, at B09; Peterson, *supra* note 37.
46. *See* Bernard, *supra* note 45.
47. *See* Peterson, *supra* note 37.

of violating the GATT Treaty.[48] The primary targets of the protesters on many of these issues were international trade decisions that prohibited sovereign nations from regulating "Process or Production Methods," or the way that things are made or created; for it is these kinds of regulations that protect laborers, the environment and animal welfare.

The issues under GATT relevant to animal welfare have arisen under a relatively few provisions of the treaty. The fundamental cornerstone of the GATT is the "most favored nation" provision of Article I, which requires that "any advantage, favour, privilege or immunity granted by any contracting party to any product originating in or destined for any other country shall be accorded immediately and unconditionally to the like product" of any country that is a party to GATT.[49] What this means is that all WTO members must give to all other members the most favorable treatment that they give to any other country concerning their treatment of like products. The purpose of this provision is to prohibit discrimination against products originating from or destined for other member countries.

One of the most significant articles for animal welfare issues is Article III. Among other things, this article contains the Rule of National Treatment, which prohibits the use of taxes and regulations for the purpose of affording protection to domestic production of goods.[50] A general statement of this principle is contained in Article III:1, which states that:

> internal taxes and other internal charges, and laws, regulations and requirements affecting the internal sale ... and internal quantitative regulations requiring the mixture, processing or use of products in specified amounts, or proportions should not be applied to imported or domestic products so as to afford protection to domestic production.

Thus, the general principle is to prohibit discrimination against imported products.

This National Treatment concept is even more clearly reflected in Article III:4, which states, in part:

> The products of the territory of any contracting party imported into the territory of any other contracting party shall be accorded treatment no less favorable than that accorded to like products of national origin in respect of all laws, regulations and requirements affecting their internal sale, offering for sale, purchase, transportation, distribution or use.

There are two aspects of Article III:4 that require amplification for present purposes. The first is that it applies to treatment of "like products," a term that is used in many places in the GATT.[51] The second notable feature of Article III:4 is

---

48. *Battle in Seattle*, *supra* note 38.
49. General Agreement on Tariffs and Trade 1994, Apr. 15, 1994, art. 1, 33 I.L.M. 1153 (1994) [hereinafter GATT].
50. *Id.* at art. III.
51. BHALA, *supra* note 1, at 3–4; GATT, *supra* note 49, at arts. I:1, II:2, III:2, III:4, VI:1, IX:1, XI:2(c), XIII:1, XVI:4, XIX:1. *See also* the discussion in Appellate Body Report, *European*

that it requires that imported products be given treatment "no less favorable" than domestic products—the substance of the "National Treatment" obligation. Treatment of imported goods must then be at least equal to that of domestic goods. It is these two aspects of Article III:4 that we need to explore in detail.

A. The "Likeness" of Products

The concept of "likeness" is one with obscure boundaries. Every tangible thing in the universe is "like" all others in certain respects; they are all, for example, composed of atoms, which in turn are composed of electrons, protons and neutrons, etc. Where then do we draw the line between like and unlike products for purposes of Article III:4? While one might fear at this point being led into some incomprehensible Wittgensteinian linguistic morass populated by "duck-rabbits" and the like, we do have some guidance from Appellate Body Reports on the concept of likeness.

In *Japan Alcoholic Beverages* the Appellate Body, using the analogy of an accordion, tells us that "likeness" is to be determined on a case-by-case basis, and may change meaning in the different places it is used in the GATT.[52] In this case the Appellate Body determined that:

> [T]here can be no one precise and absolute definition of what is "like." The concept of "likeness" is a relative one that evokes the image of an accordion. The accordion of "likeness" stretches and squeezes in different places as different provisions of the WTO Agreement are applied. The width of the accordion in any one of those places must be determined by the particular provision in which the term "like" is encountered as well as by the context and the circumstances that prevail in any given case to which that provision may apply.[53]

As a result, the concept of likeness may change from Article I to Article III:2 to Article III:4 and so on.

That the concept of likeness may change from one use to another in the GATT, however, still does not tell us what it means in any particular context. The *Border Tax Adjustments* case, as followed and supplemented by cases dealing with Article III:4 like the *EC Asbestos* case, has helped answer this question by describing four criteria to be used in analyzing the concept of "likeness":

(i) The properties, nature and qualities of the product.
(ii) End-uses of the product.

Communities—Measures Affecting Asbestos and Asbestos-Containing Products, ¶88, WT/DS135/AB/R (Mar. 12, 2001) [hereinafter *EC Asbestos*].

52. Appellate Body Report, *Japan—Taxes on Alcoholic Beverages*, H(1)(a), WT/DS8/AB/R (Oct. 4, 1996) [hereinafter *Japan—Taxes*] *see also* Bhala, *supra* note 1, at 10.

53. *Japan—Taxes, supra* note 52, at H(1)(a).

(iii) Consumer tastes and habits.
(iv) Tariff classification of the products.[54]

These criteria, however, are not meant to be an exclusive list of factors that can be reviewed, but are just tools to be used in a case-by-case analysis of the "likeness" issue.[55] There is no magic formula to the definition, such as meeting two factors or three factors makes products "like." While the properties, nature and qualities of products are very important and tariff classification alone should not determine the issue, the process of determining likeness depends on a case-specific analysis of each fact situation under all of the four *Border Tax/EC Asbestos* factors.[56]

As an example, consider the *EC Asbestos* analysis of the "likeness" issue. In this case, a French Decree banned the import of chrysotile asbestos fibers, but allowed import and use of similar polyvinyl alcohol fibers and glass fibers. The Decree also banned cement products using asbestos fibers. Canada objected to the ban on asbestos products as a violation of Article III:4, claiming that all these types of fibers are "like" and must be treated the same. Thus, the issue in *EC Asbestos* was whether chrysotile asbestos fibers are "like" polyvinyl alcohol fibers and glass fibers under this Article. The Appellate Body noted that there is no one definition of "like" for the purposes of GATT and supported this assertion by noting that the language of Article III:2 refers not just to "like" products as does Article III:4, but also to "competitive or substitutable products," which indicates that the scope of likeness in the two subsections must differ.[57] If they did not, according to the Appellate Body, the scope of the two provisions would be entirely different and would allow countries to practice trade discrimination by structuring regulations to fit within one of the subsections, like a non-fiscal regulation under Article III:4, that would not be allowed as a fiscal regulation under Article III:2:

> [W]e recognize that the relationship between these two provisions is important, because there is no sharp distinction between fiscal regulation, covered by Article III:2, and non-fiscal regulation, covered by Article III:4. Both forms of regulation can often be used to achieve the same ends. It would be incongruous if, due to a significant difference in the product scope of these two provisions, Members were prevented from using one form of regulation—for instance, fiscal—to protect domestic production of certain products, but were able to use another form of regulation—for instance, non-fiscal—to achieve those ends. This would frustrate a consistent application of the "general principle" in Article III:1. For these reasons, we conclude that the scope of "like" in Article III:4 is broader than the scope of "like" in Article III:2, first sentence.[58]

54. *EC Asbestos, supra* note 51, at ¶85; *see* BHALA *supra* note 1, at 18 (quoting *EC Asbestos*).
55. BHALA, *supra* note 1, at 18 (*quoting EC Asbestos).*
56. *EC Asbestos, supra* note 51, at ¶¶101–102; *see* BHALA *supra* note 1, at 25–28.
57. *EC Asbestos, supra* note 51, at ¶¶93–96.
58. *Id.* at ¶99.

So we see the stretching and squeezing of the accordion in the different definitions of likeness in two closely related articles, Articles III:2 and III:4. The Appellate Body went on to say that interpretation of Article III:4 likeness requires looking at the principle behind Article III, which is that countries need to "ensure 'equality of competitive conditions'" for domestic and imported goods.[59] Likeness is then ultimately a determination about the nature and extent of the competitive relationship between products.[60]

To complete the analysis of likeness and the competitive relationship between the products, the Appellate Body determined that the four-factor test of likeness needed to be applied to determine if the different types of fibers were "like." In applying these factors, the Appellate Body found that the Panel decision on this issue had not properly applied the factors, since it had only considered one of the factors, not all of them. The Appellate Body also amplified the meaning of these four factors.

The properties, nature and quality factor was said to require a determination of the physical properties of the product. It was error for the Panel to reduce this criteria to just an analysis of the ultimate "end uses" of the product; the focus should have been on the physical properties of the product.[61] With respect to these physical properties, the Appellate Body found a number of characteristics of asbestos fibers to be relevant, including molecular structure, chemical composition and fibrillation capacity. Physical characteristics also included a "defining aspect" relating to asbestos, the health risks of asbestos fibers.[62] In response to the argument that including health risks as a part of the "likeness" analysis nullified the Article XX(b) exception that allows Members of the WTO to have regulations relating to human health, the Appellate Body found that Articles III and XX were independent provisions and that reviewing human health issues under Article III:4 would not necessarily mean that a regulation might not be found inconsistent with Article III:4, but nonetheless protected by the exception of Article XX(b).[63] Thus, the Appellate Body defined the physical characteristics factor to be a broad one encompassing an expansive range of physical properties, including health concerns, and concluded that asbestos fibers physically differed from polyvinyl alcohol fibers and glass fibers on this factor.[64]

In analyzing the second and third factors relating to end uses and consumer tastes, the Appellate Body stated that these factors are critical in determining the competitive relationship between products and are a crucial aspect of Article III.[65] These factors become even more important where, as in the case of asbestos fibers on one hand and polyvinyl alcohol fibers and glass fibers on the other, the physical

59. *Id.* at ¶98.
60. *Id.*
61. *Id.* at ¶¶110–12.
62. *Id.* at ¶114.
63. *Id.* at ¶115.
64. *Id.* at ¶¶126, 134–141.
65. *Id.* at ¶¶117–18.

characteristics of the products differ greatly. In looking at the end uses of products in the "likeness" analysis, it is necessary to look not only at cases where the end uses of the products coincide, but also at cases where the end uses differ.[66]

The Panel in *EC Asbestos* declined to make findings on the third criteria, consumer tastes and habits, on the grounds that analysis of this criteria would not yield "clear results."[67] The Appellate Body found this to be error and stated that it would rarely be the case that "likeness" analysis would produce "clear results" and all of the factors needed to be analyzed regardless of whether "clear results" would be forthcoming.[68] The tariff classification factor, again not considered by the Panel, was determined by the Appellate Body to support the "unlikeness" of the fiber products, since asbestos fibers were classified differently from polyvinyl alcohol, cellulose and glass fibers for tariff purposes.[69] Ultimately, the Appellate Body found asbestos fibers to not be "like" polyvinyl alcohol and glass fibers.[70] With respect to the cement products aspect of the *EC Asbestos* Report, however, the tariff classification of cement products were all the same, regardless of the fibers contained in those products. The Appellate Body, nonetheless, did not find this factor determinative and found cement products using asbestos fibers not to be "like" cement products using other fibers.[71]

Through the use of a combination of metaphor and objective analysis of physical and other empirically verifiable characteristics, the Appellate Body of the WTO has provided a fairly clear picture of how "likeness" problems in the GATT and, in particular Article III, are to be solved. This solution has two fundamental elements; first, "likeness" is not a unified concept in the GATT; its meaning may change from article to article, and section to section; second, "likeness" is fundamentally about the competitive relationship of products, and is to be analyzed under a non-exclusive set of four factors on a case-by-case basis. All of these factors should be reviewed to make a likeness determination.

B. The National Treatment Obligation

The essence of the National Treatment obligation is that it requires non-discrimination with respect to foreign products. It has been stated that this obligation requires that internal regulations that apply to foreign and domestic like products be identical.[72] This national treatment obligation applies to three sorts of regulations: fiscal measures under Article III:2, non-fiscal measures in Article III:4 and regulations about the mixture, processing, or use of products under Articles III:1, 5 and 7.

66. *Id.* at ¶119.
67. *Id.* at ¶120.
68. *Id.*
69. *Id.* at ¶¶124–26.
70. *Id.* at ¶¶125–126.
71. *Id.* at ¶¶147–148.
72. Mavroidis, *supra* note 4, at 127–28.

While all these provisions can impact regulations relating to animal welfare, the one most likely to be applicable to typical animal welfare regulations and laws is Article III:4. Although taxes and product mixture rules certainly could impact animal welfare issues, the most likely form of regulation of animal welfare issues is "laws, regulations and requirements affecting their [the products'] internal sale, offering for sale, purchase, transportation, distribution or use" covered by Article III:4.

The language used to express the National Treatment Rule in Article III:4 is that products of foreign origin must be "accorded treatment no less favorable" than that accorded domestic products of a like nature. It has been said that this principle, founded on non-discrimination against imported products, may be even more important than the Most Favored Nation Principle.[73] What the National Treatment Rule requires is equality of opportunity and equality of competitive conditions with respect to internal domestic regulations.[74] Once products have cleared customs, the rule mandates equal conditions of competition for imported and domestic products.[75] While this rule dictates a level playing field for imported goods, it does not require any particular volume of imports, just equal conditions of competition.[76] This obligation applies not only to national governments, but also to state and local authorities.[77]

There are two aspects of Article III:4 that require explication here. First, for an obligation to arise under this part of Article III, it is necessary that there be a "law, regulation or requirement" that affects the "internal sale, offering for sale, purchase, transportation, distribution or use" of a product. If there is no such law, regulation, or requirement, it does not apply. This issue was considered in the *Canada Foreign Investment Review* matter wherein a GATT Panel considered a Canadian law that stated that the proposed acquisition or establishment of a business by a foreigner had to be reviewed by the government under a five-factor test.[78] This law did not require any promises or undertakings by foreign entities in order to acquire a business or do business in Canada, but it was typically the case that in order to do business in Canada, foreign entities would make promises to the Canadian government explaining how they would run the business and source their products.[79] Canada argued that since the law did not require any foreign entity to make any promises or undertakings in order to complete an acquisition or do business in Canada, there was no law, regulation, or requirement of the Canadian government making Article III:4 applicable to this law. The Panel rejected this argument, stating that regardless of whether the law itself required

73. Bhala, *supra* note 1, at 95.
74. *Id.* at 100.
75. *Id.* at 100–01.
76. *Id.* at 101–02, 105.
77. *Id.* at 102.
78. Panel Report, *Canada Foreign Investment Review Act,* L/5504-30S/140 (*adopted* Feb. 7, 1984) [hereinafter *Canada Investment*].
79. *Id.* at ¶¶2.3–2.9; Bhala, *supra* note 1, at 137–40.

these promises or undertakings, once such a promise or undertaking was entered into, it did become a legally enforceable "requirement" under Canadian law.[80] It was also determined that the term "requirement" was intended to be broadly construed under Article III:4 and thus embraces any measure affecting imports, even if the law does not directly address international trade.[81]

The second important aspect of Article III:4 is its substance: what does it mean to provide "less favorable treatment" to imported products? The *EC Asbestos* Appellate Body decision states that "less favorable treatment" expresses the general principle of Article III:1, that internal regulations should not be applied in a way to protect domestic production.[82] In showing "less favorable treatment," it is unnecessary to show actual trade impact from the measure; the issue is whether the regulation changes the conditions of competition between like products.[83]

Perhaps the best illustration of the application of this provision involves the Appellate Body decision in *Korea—Measures Affecting Imports of Fresh, Chilled and Frozen Beef* (hereinafter "*Korean Beef*").[84] In *Korean Beef*, a Korean law created a two-tiered distribution scheme for foreign and domestic beef, which required, among other things, that small retailers decide between selling foreign or domestic beef. These retailers could not sell both, which substantially reduced the number of outlets for sale of foreign beef in Korea. While the Panel Report in this case found that any regulation that made a distinction based on national origin violated Article III:4, the Appellate Body took a more nuanced approach, stating that differential treatment of foreign and domestic products alone did not violate this provision.[85] What was necessary to find a violation of Article III:4 was differential treatment which affected the "conditions of competition."[86] The Appellate Body found that this occurred here, since the law cut off access to normal distribution channels for imported beef.[87] The fact that ultimately the number of outlets selling foreign and domestic beef was determined by the private choice of retailers was irrelevant to whether there was a violation of Article III, since it was the Korean law that required that retailers make that choice.[88] Thus, the substantive focus of Article III:4 is equality of conditions of internal competition relating to foreign and domestic products. It is not differential treatment of foreign and domestic products alone that violates Article III:4, rather it is differential treatment that results in unequal conditions of competition. Thus, identity of treatment, as

80. *Canada Investment, supra* note 78, at ¶¶5.4–5.6; BHALA, *supra* note 1, at 141–42.
81. *See Canada Investment, supra* note 78, at ¶¶5.7–5.12; BHALA, *supra* note 1, at 143.
82. MAVROIDIS, *supra* note 4, at 168.
83. *Id.* at 169–75.
84. *Korea—Measures Affecting Imports of Fresh, Chilled and Frozen Beef,* WT/DS161/AB/R, WT/DS169/AB/ (Dec. 11, 2000) [hereinafter *Korean Beef*].
85. *Id.* at ¶141–148.
86. *Id.* at ¶¶139–48; BHALA, *supra* note 1, at 149–52.
87. *Korean Beef, supra* note 84, at ¶145.
88. *Id.* at ¶146.

suggested by Petros Mavroidis, is not precisely what is required by Article III,[89] it is a level competitive playing field that is required.

The National Treatment Rule is one focused on competition. What Article III:4 prohibits are laws, regulations and requirements that make the playing field unequal with respect to the ability to compete. It does not guaranty foreign products a particular volume of sales or equality in every respect; it requires only the ability to compete on an equal basis with domestic products.

C. The Process or Production Method Problem

We found that Article III allows countries to impose taxes and regulations in an even-handed way to domestic and imported products. In the abstract then, it would seem that a country could impose non-discriminatory animal welfare regulations to both domestic and imported products. For example, we could prohibit the raising of chickens in battery cages for the production of eggs inside our country and could similarly prohibit the importation of eggs from chickens raised in battery cages from other countries. Unfortunately, the reality may be otherwise as a result of the "process or production method" issue.

What Article III:4 states is that imported "products … shall be accorded treatment no less favorable than that accorded to like products of national origin …" This language was interpreted in the *Tuna/Dolphin I* case,[90] which was not ultimately adopted under the GATT, but is nonetheless one of the more influential GATT Panel decisions relating to environmental law.[91] *Tuna/Dolphin I* deals with the United States Marine Mammal Protection Act (MMPA) which regulates fishing for tuna and effectively prohibits the use of purse seine nets to catch tuna since this method of fishing results in high rates of dolphin mortality. The tuna of other countries was subject to embargo by the United States under the MMPA if the other countries did not use comparable methods of fishing to the United States fleet or had an overall dolphin kill rate that exceeded 1.25 times the kill rate of the United States fishing industry in a particular year. Note that it was impossible for other countries to know this kill rate since it was based on *this year's* kill rate, which cannot be known until the future.

Certain countries were determined by the United States to not be in compliance with the MMPA and were placed under an embargo. One of these countries was Mexico, which challenged the embargo under GATT. Mexico argued that the embargo was a quantitative restriction in violation of Article XI of the GATT,

89. *See* Mavroidis, *supra* note 4, at 127–29.

90. *United States—Restrictions on Imports of Tuna* DS21/R—39S/155 (Sept. 3, 1991) [hereinafter *Tuna/Dolphin I*]. This was not the only Tuna-Dolphin decision; there was a later decision that also was never adopted under the GATT often referred to as *Tuna Dolphin II. United States—Restrictions on Imports of Tuna,* DS29/R (June 16, 1994) [hereinafter *Tuna/Dolphin II*].

91. Recall that even GATT Panel Reports that were not adopted can be used as some "guidance" under the WTO scheme. *See supra* notes 35 through 36 and accompanying text.

while the United States argued that the MMPA provisions in question were permitted internal regulations of domestic and imported products under Article III:4. The Panel sided with Mexico. It stated that what Article III allows is the regulation of "products":

> The text of Article III:1 refers to the application to imported or domestic *products* of "laws, regulations and requirements affecting the internal sale... of *products*" and "internal quantitative regulations requiring the mixture, processing or use of *products*"; it sets forth the principle that such regulations on *products* not be applied so as to afford protection to domestic production. Article III:4 refers solely to laws, regulations and requirements affecting the internal sale, etc. of *products*. This suggests that Article III covers only measures affecting products as such. Furthermore, the text of the Note Ad Article III refers to a measure "which applies to an imported *product* and to the like domestic *product* and is collected or enforced in the case of the imported *product* at the time or point of importation." This suggests that this Note covers only measures applied to imported products that are of the same nature as those applied to the domestic products, such as a prohibition on importation of a product which enforces at the border an internal prohibition applied to both imported and like domestic products (emphasis original).[92]

The repeated use of the term "product" in the text of Article III and the Note led the Panel to conclude that what can be regulated under Article III is the "product as such," effectively its physical form, not the process of its creation or its method of production.[93] This same distinction between "product as such" and "process or production method" is also made in a later unadopted *Tuna/Dolphin* decision involving the same United States Statute, typically referred to as *Tuna/Dolphin II*.[94] Therefore, internal regulations relating to the "process or production method" (hereinafter "PPM") of a product cannot be properly imposed on imported products.

Thus, a distinction is being made between regulating the physical instantiation of the product and its method of production. What this means is that a country can regulate the product's physical make-up under Article III:4, but it cannot regulate the way that the product was made. A country can properly say that all automobiles sold within its borders must have seat belts (a physical characteristic), but cannot say that the seat belts have to be installed by a particular production method (the PPM). Or in our example of battery cage eggs, a country can regulate the size of eggs sold in the country, but not the way the eggs were produced, *i.e.*, by use of battery cages for the hens.

92. *Tuna Dolphin I, supra* note 90, at ¶5.11 (emphasis in original).
93. *Id.* at ¶¶5.13–5.14. The Panel actually went on after the materials quoted above and quoted even more of Article III emphasizing the use of the term "product." *See id.* at ¶5.12.
94. *Tuna/Dolphin II, supra* note 90, at ¶5.9.

This product/PPM distinction is perhaps the most important and potentially damaging interpretation of the GATT that has occurred in regard to animal welfare issues. But is product/PPM a good or workable distinction? First, no such distinction is made in Article III.[95] Second, the PPM concept was simply manufactured by the GATT Panel in the *Tuna/Dolphin* cases, decisions that were ultimately never adopted under the GATT.[96] So there is reason to think that this distinction is a mistaken one.

In addition, is it the case that what we mean by "product" is truly limited to its physical characteristics and does not extend to the way in which it was produced? For example, if it were the case that a particular drug could be made either by use of human blood, which we happen to know is often obtained in ways that exploit humans, or synthetically, which involves no exploitation, would we not see the exploitation of humans as a part of the human blood version of the "product"? Is this not also the case with respect to eggs produced in battery cages? One can also think of "products" that are so closely identified with their method of production that the two cannot really be separated. For example, with respect to products made from recycled materials, the process of production and the product itself can be seen as the same thing.[97]

As an analogy, consider the scientific information obtained by the Nazis through gruesome experiments on people. Is this information, though perhaps more scientifically relevant than any other information we have on these subjects, not itself utterly tainted by its means of production? Do we not see the "product" here, and the information gained, as fundamentally flawed because of the way it was created? Similarly, if we know that a certain product is produced through the torture of animals, is the means by which it is produced not a part of the product? The point here is that it is not obvious that the way a product is created is not a part of the "product" itself. Instead, it seems that there are instances in which the method of production becomes a fundamental characteristic of the product itself.

Moreover, if consumer tastes are to be considered in trade issues, as the case law indicates, then the way products are produced should be considered in determining whether the products are "like" products that must be treated similarly under Article III.[98] It is also worth noting that there are treaties and WTO agreements that explicitly refer to and permit the use of PPM regulations. Among these are the World Charter for Nature, which was approved by the UN General Assembly in 1982, that calls on governments to establish standards for products and manufacturing processes that may have adverse impacts on nature, as well as the WTO Agreement on Agriculture that provides that payments under certain

95. For a discussion of problems with the PPM idea, *see* Peter Stevenson, *The World Trade Organization Rules: A Legal Analysis of Their Adverse Impact on Animal Welfare*, 8 ANIMAL L. 107, 120–22, 134–35 (2002).

96. *See id.* at 120.

97. Steve Charnovitz, *The Law of Environmental "PPMS" in the WTO: Debunking the Myth of Illegality*, 27 YALE J. INT'L L. 59, 66 (2002) [hereinafter Charnovitz 2002].

98. Stevenson, *supra* note 95, at 120–21.

agricultural programs are dependent upon meeting certain conditions, such as conditions relating to production methods or inputs.[99] A number of other WTO agreements recognize the validity of PPMs, including the Agreement on the Application of Sanitary and Phytosanitary Measures, the Agreement on Technical Barriers to Trade and the Agreement on Trade—Related Aspects of Intellectual Property Rights.[100]

The GATT Panel in *Tuna Dolphin I* created the product/PPM distinction in Article III of the GATT; it is not mandated by the language of Article III or by any of its prior case law. Allowing only regulation of the product itself, effectively its physical characteristics, makes regulating animal welfare issues as internal regulations under Article III problematic. It is virtually always going to be the case that animal welfare regulations will relate to process or production methods. The obvious example is that of the battery cage. If, as postulated above, a country banned battery cages in its territory and banned the import of eggs produced in battery cages, it would be regulating a PPM, not the product itself.

This product/PPM distinction has, in fact, had a direct impact on European Union law.[101] In 1991, the EU banned the use of leghold traps in the EU and banned the import of pelts of certain animals if they were caught in leghold traps.[102] The EU determined not to enforce this measure against a number of countries and instead entered into feeble agreements on this issue with those countries, fearing that the leghold trap ban as a PPM regulation would not be valid under the GATT.[103] Similar fears led to dilution of the EU ban on animal-tested cosmetics.[104] Also, recall from the discussion in Chapter 3 of the EU laws on the use of animals in agriculture that many of the laws of the early 1990s had import restrictions requiring that imported animals and products comply with the same welfare and other rules as required in the EU. Laws of the EU during the mid-1990s, however, presumably due to fear of violating GATT, did not have these import restrictions. Again it seems the EU was fearful of the PPM issue. The EU has apparently become more confident recently, perhaps as a result of the *Shrimp/Turtle* case discussed below, since it has begun reinserting these import restrictions. In any event, the impact of the GATT and international trade law on animal welfare is not merely theoretical, it is actual. And the impact that it has had is negative.

99. Charnovitz 2002, *supra* note 97, at 61.
100. *Id.* at 61–62.
101. See the extended discussion of this issue in Stevenson, *supra* note 95.
102. Council Regulation 3254/91, 1991 O. J. (L 308) 1, 1–4.
103. *See* Stevenson, *supra* note 95, at 108–09; European Commission, *Implementation of Humane Trapping Standard in the EU*, http://ec.europa.eu/environment/biodiversity/animal_welfare/hts/index_en.htm (last visited May 25, 2010); Global Action Network, *Fur Trade*, http://www.gan.ca/campaigns/fur+trade/factsheets/index.en.html (last visited May 25, 2010).
104. Stevenson, *supra* note 95, at 108–09.

D. QUANTITATIVE RESTRICTIONS

Another issue that may arise relating to animal welfare and environmental regulations in international trade is whether a regulation that results in an embargo or similar restriction on imports from a particular country or source is a prohibited quantitative restriction under Article XI of the GATT. The language of Article XI:1 places restrictions on quotas and other measures that act as quantitative restrictions on imports and exports:

> No prohibitions or restrictions other than duties, taxes or other charges, whether made effective through quotas, import or export licenses or other measures, shall be instituted or maintained by any contracting party on the importation of any product of the territory of any other contracting party or on the exportation or sale for export of any product destined for the territory of any other contracting party.[105]

This section prohibits import or export prohibitions in the form of quotas, licensing requirements or other measures, but allows duties, taxes or other charges to be collected on imported or exported products.

This expresses the "tariffication" goal of the GATT. It is the ultimate goal of the GATT that there be no restrictions on trade other than duties and other charges, although this goal has not yet been met.[106] In other words, the only restriction on imports or exports is to be monetary charges or tariffs expressed at bound rates known to and applicable to all parties.[107]

There are exceptions to application of the restrictions of Article XI:1. The second section of Article XI provides that section 1 does not extend to export prohibitions to prevent shortages of foodstuffs or other critical products; to import or export restrictions necessary for application of standards or regulations on classification, marketing, or grading of commodities; or to certain import restrictions on agricultural or fisheries products necessary to the enforcement of certain enumerated types of governmental measures.[108]

Article XI becomes relevant to animal welfare regulations in international trade when an enforcement mechanism for an animal welfare regulation is a quantitative restriction on imports, such as an embargo, or on exports, an export ban. In such a case it will be argued by the party whose import or export of a product is restricted that Article XI prohibits such a restriction. The country imposing the restriction will argue that the regulation fits an exception to Article XI, is a permitted internal regulation under Article III or falls under one of the general exemptions of Article XX of the GATT. As we will observe below in a further discussion of *Tuna/Dolphin I*, it was argued in that case that the

105. GATT, *supra* note 49, at art. XI:1.
106. *WTO Analytical Index,* ¶340 (WTO 2003).
107. *Id.*
108. GATT, *supra* note 49, at art. XI:2.

United States embargo on Mexican Tuna was a quantitative restriction violating Article XI of GATT.

E. The Exceptions to the Substantive Provisions of GATT

As with virtually any legal rule, there are exceptions to the substantive provisions of the GATT discussed above. These exceptions are provided in Article XX of the GATT. There are three exceptions of potential relevance to animal welfare issues set forth in Article XX, the relevant portions of which provide:

> Subject to the requirement that such measures are not applied in a manner which would constitute a means of arbitrary or unjustifiable discrimination between countries where the same conditions prevail, or a disguised restriction on international trade, nothing in this Agreement shall be construed to prevent the adoption or enforcement by any contracting party of measures:
>
> (a) Necessary to protect public morals;
> (b) Necessary to protect human, animal or plant life or health;
> ....
> (g) Relating to the conservation of exhaustible natural resources if such measures are made effective in conjunction with restrictions on domestic production or consumption....

Analysis of Article XX is typically divided into two parts: examination of the specific substantive exceptions embodied in the lettered paragraphs, and scrutiny of the chapeau, the introductory language of the article.

Of these specific exceptions, one might conclude that the "protection of public morals" exception would be the most significant relating to animal welfare. After all, are animal welfare regulations not based on a moral imperative that animals are morally entitled to humane treatment? There are other treaties and international laws that include morals-based provisions, and these provisions have been interpreted to cover matters of animal cruelty and welfare.[109] It has also been asserted that international trade should have a moral baseline that cannot be crossed.

> Many commentators have expressed the idea that international trade should have a moral baseline. Ambassador Edward A. Laing views "humanitarianism" as "arguably meriting the status of legitimate discrimination" under GATT Article XX(a). Economist Richard N. Cooper contends that "[s]urely the international community cannot, and should not be able to, force a country

109. Steve Charnovitz, *The Moral Exception in Trade Policy*, 38 Va. J. Int'l L . 689, 710–18 (1998) [hereinafter Charnovitz 1998].

to purchase products the production of which offends the sensibilities of its citizenry." Peter Druker sees the need for "moral, legal and economic rules that are accepted and enforced throughout the global economy."[110]

Thus, it is likely that the policies underlying animal welfare regulations do fit within the public morals exception of Article XX. This has been stated without reservation by Steve Charnovitz, the Director of the Yale University Global Environment and Trade Study, in his comment that the policies behind the EU leghold trap ban would "surely" fit within the exception.[111] There are those, however, who would challenge this view, asserting that countries should not be able to unilaterally impose their values on other countries.[112] At this point in the history of the WTO, the issue of whether the public morals exception can be used to protect animal welfare regulations under the WTO regime is an open question, since the vitality of the exception in this context has not yet been decided.

It is also still not clear that the Article XX(b) exception relating to protecting "human, animal or plant life or health" applies to animal welfare regulations. Again, in the abstract, it would seem that application of this exception to regulation of animal welfare would be obvious; a ban on battery cages protects animal life and health because animals raised in less crowded conditions and more in line with their ethological needs are likely to be healthier, thereby resulting in fewer deaths and diseases for chickens, and also likely benefiting human health. The potential animal and human toll that can be caused by intensive agricultural methods has frequently been illustrated in recent history. In the past decade, there have been scares relating to "Mad Cow Disease" in the United Kingdom and other countries, and the Avian Flu Epidemic in the Far East. Nonetheless, it is not clear that Article XX(b) applies to animal welfare regulations except to the extent such regulations are necessary to prevent the spread of disease, and therefore to ensure greater safety to human food products.[113] This issue, like that of the public morals exception, has not been clearly decided under the GATT, and therefore, remains a significant open question.

The Article XX(g) exception relating to the conservation of exhaustible natural resources has been found to apply to environmental regulations relating to conservation of endangered species, as will be discussed below relating to the *Shrimp/Turtle* case. Its usefulness may however be limited to protection of wild animals, since it may be difficult to argue that conservation of natural resources extends beyond animals in the natural environment, to include domestic animals

110. *Id.* at 732 (quoting Edward A. Laing, *Equal Access/Non-Discrimination and Legitimate Discrimination in International Economic Law,* 14 WIS. INT'L L. J. 246, 332 (1996)); RICHARD N. COOPER, ENVIRONMENT AND RESOURCE POLICIES FOR THE WORLD ECONOMY 30 (1994); Peter F. Druker, *The Global Economy and the Nation State*, 76 FOREIGN AFF. 159, 169 (1997).

111. Charnovitz 1998, *supra* note 109, at 737.

112. *Id.* at 733.

113. Edward M. Thomas, *Playing Chicken at the WTO: Defending an Animal Welfare-Based Trade Restriction Under GATT's Moral Exception,* 34 B.C. ENVTL. AFF. L. REV. 605, 618 (2007).

used in agriculture, experimentation, or entertainment. Indeed it has been argued that this exception does not apply at all to regulations that are solely founded on animal welfare concerns.[114] Nonetheless, it is possible that this exception may at least apply to the regulation of animal experimentation on animals taken from the wild.

To understand the implications of these exceptions for animal welfare regulations it is necessary to further delve into the way these provisions have been interpreted in practice under the GATT. There are two major decisions under GATT that contain implications for animal welfare regulation, the *Tuna/Dolphin* and *Shrimp/Turtle* cases, a discussion of which follows.

1. The *Tuna Dolphin I* Interpretation of Article XX Exceptions

As discussed above,[115] in *Tuna/Dolphin I* the United States placed an embargo on tuna imported from Mexico, based on that country's failure to comply with the Marine Mammal Protection Act's requirements relating to methods of catching tuna and the dolphin kill rate of the Mexican fishing fleet. The Panel in *Tuna/Dolphin I* determined that this regulation of the United States was an embargo in violation of Article XI of the GATT, not a proper internal regulation under Article III, as the United States contended. Such a determination does not necessarily end the inquiry under GATT, however, since violations of otherwise applicable provisions of the GATT can be justified under any of the exceptions of Article XX.

In *Tuna/Dolphin I*, the United States argued that the exceptions in Article XX(b) on protection of animal life and health, and Article XX(g) on protection of exhaustible resources justified the MMPA provisions complained of by Mexico. In interpreting these claims of exception, the Panel began by stating that the exceptions of Article XX are to be narrowly construed.

> The Panel recalled that previous panels had established that Article XX is a limited and conditional exception from obligations under other provisions of the General Agreement, and not a positive rule establishing obligations in itself. Therefore, the practice of panels has been to interpret Article XX narrowly, to place the burden on the party invoking Article XX to justify its invocation ...[116]

There are three aspects to the Panel's quoted statement: first, the Panel seems to be saying that the Article XX exceptions differ from the other provisions in the GATT, in that other provisions are "positive rules" establishing obligations, while the exceptions are limited and conditional provisions of some lesser worth. The substantive, non-Article XX provisions of the GATT are given more weight

114. *Id.* at 619.
115. *See supra* notes 90 through 94 and accompanying text.
116. *Tuna/Dolphin I, supra* note 90, at ¶5.22.

and deference than the exceptions in Article XX.[117] Second, the exceptions are to be interpreted narrowly. Third, the burden of proof relating to claims of Article XX exceptions is on the party claiming the exception.

There are a number of difficulties with the Panel's analysis. Note that the language of Article XX in particular and of the GATT in general does not make a distinction between "substantive" provisions and "mere exceptions," as does the Panel.[118] There is no reason not to provide equal dignity to the provisions of GATT that state positive rules for trade issues and the exceptions to these rules that permit GATT Members to implement policies important to their people notwithstanding the trade rules. While free trade is an important value under GATT, it should also be recognized that the ability of Members to enact laws consistent with local values and culture is also an important value that is embodied in Article XX. Moreover, nowhere in the GATT is it stated that the Article XX exceptions are to be interpreted narrowly and the cases that are cited by the Panel for this proposition do not in fact state that these exceptions are to be interpreted narrowly.[119] Thus, the idea of narrow interpretation of Article XX is a concept invented by the Panel in *Tuna/Dolphin I*.

In analyzing the claim of exemption by the United States under Articles XX (b) and (g) for its actions under the MMPA, the Panel was influenced by the extraterritorial effect of the United States law. In analyzing the Article XX(b) issues, the Panel saw the main issue as whether this exception allows measures to protect human, animal or plant life or health outside the jurisdiction of the regulating party.[120] After reviewing the history of the Article XX(b) exception, the Panel concluded:

> [T]he record indicates that the concerns of the drafters of Article XX(b) focused on the use of sanitary measures to safeguard life or health of humans, animals or plants within the jurisdiction of the importing country.... The Panel considered that if the broad interpretation of Article XX(b) suggested by the United States were accepted, each contracting party could unilaterally determine the life or health protection policies from which other contracting parties could not deviate without jeopardizing their rights under the General Agreement. The General Agreement would then no longer constitute a multilateral framework for trade among all contracting parties but would provide legal security only in respect of trade between a limited number of contracting parties with identical internal regulations.[121]

The concern of the Panel was that if this regulation requiring certain methods of fishing were to be accepted, the effect would be that countries like the United States could dictate the domestic policies of other countries by refusing to allow

117. Thomas, *supra* note 113, at 617.
118. *See id.* at 635.
119. Charnovitz 1998, *supra* note 109, at 720.
120. *Tuna/Dolphin I, supra* note 90, at ¶5.25.
121. *Id.* at ¶¶5.26–5.27.

imports of goods not manufactured or created in the manner dictated by the regulating party. Ultimately, that would turn GATT into a small "trading club" of countries with identical internal laws. This same concept was used by the Panel in analyzing the applicability of the Article XX(g) exception to the MMPA regulation. Here the Panel found that Article XX(g) was intended to allow regulation of exhaustible resources within the jurisdiction of the regulating party, not to allow imposition of one county's natural resource policies on other countries. The Panel was worried that "if the extrajurisdictional interpretation of Article XX(g) suggested by the United States were accepted, each contracting party could unilaterally determine the conservation policies from which other contracting parties could not deviate without jeopardizing their rights under the General Agreement."[122] As a result, according to the *Tuna/Dolphin I* Panel, regulations cannot be justified under Article XX(b) or (g) if they have the extraterritorial affect of determining the policies of other Member States. This same idea was reiterated in *Tuna/Dolphin II*.[123] Thus, states cannot regulate under Article XX(b) or (g) if the effect of that regulation would be to impose the policies of the regulating state on the other country.

Note also that Article XX(b) allows measures "necessary" to protect human, animal and plant life or health. What is the meaning of "necessary" in this context? The Panel determined that necessity demands that a party exhaust all options "reasonably available to it" to achieve its policies through regulations consistent with the GATT.[124] Contracting parties under GATT must, then, try every existing option consistent with GATT before taking steps that violate any substantive provision of the GATT and purportedly fall within the Article XX(b) exception. One step that the Panel particularly noted as important was to attempt to negotiate cooperative agreements with other parties before taking steps such as imposing an embargo.[125]

When looked at in conjunction with the earlier discussion of PPMs, what is economically compelled by *Tuna Dolphin I* is that countries enter into a race to the bottom on animal welfare and environmental regulations. Under *Tuna/Dolphin I*, any country that enacts strict PPM animal welfare regulations internally cannot restrict imports of products that do not live up to its regulations, since such a restriction would, among other things, be to apply the country's regulations extraterritorially in violation of GATT. PPM regulations will almost invariably cost domestic producers money, which is evident in the case of battery cages. For example, raising chickens outside of battery cages will ultimately require more space, monitoring, etc., all of which are costly. Thus, imposition of an internal ban on battery cages will impose a cost on domestic producers. If imports of eggs from producers not complying with the ban on battery cages cannot be prohibited under GATT, then foreign producers will have an advantage in their cost of production over domestic producers. Imposing such a disadvantage on domestic producers is

122. *Id.* at ¶5.32.
123. *Tuna/Dolphin II, supra* note 90, at ¶5.26.
124. *Tuna/Dolphin I, supra* note 90, at ¶5.28.
125. *Id.*

unlikely to be politically or economically tenable. As a result, the *Tuna Dolphin I* decision has the effect of discouraging regulation of animal welfare and tends to give advantage to the producers and countries that have the most lax (or even non-existent) animal welfare regulations, since production free of regulation will generally be the most cost-effective method of production. This same logic applies to environmental regulations as well. So while the *Tuna Dolphin I* Panel purported to be concerned about a country imposing its laws extraterritorially, the result of the Panel decision is to effectively impose on all states the worst possible environmental and animal welfare regulations in order for each country's domestic industry to remain economically competitive.

Even though *Tuna/Dolphin I* was never adopted as a decision under the GATT it has been very influential in GATT jurisprudence relating to environmental regulations and international trade, and the interpretation of Article XX.[126] Fortunately, the case law on interpretation of Article XX in the context of animal-related regulations does not end here. The *Shrimp/Turtle* case added another layer to interpretation of Article XX in a context relevant to animal welfare regulation.

2. The *Shrimp/Turtle* Interpretation of Article XX

Several of the issues considered in the *Tuna/Dolphin I* case were revisited in *Shrimp/Turtle*, which involved a United States' law intended to protect endangered sea turtles by banning imports of shrimp from countries using fishing technology that might adversely affect sea turtles.[127] This ban did not, however, apply to nations certified under this law. A certification could be obtained by a nation if it showed that sea turtles do not occur in the waters where the nation's fleet fishes, or that the nation only harvests shrimp by means that pose no danger to turtles, or that the nation has a regulatory program comparable to that of the United States and that the nation's incidental rate of taking turtles is comparable to that of the United States' fleet.[128] A number of nations subjected to a ban under this law requested that a Panel be appointed under GATT to review this prohibition. A Report was subsequently issued by the Panel which found that the United States' measures did not fall within any exception of Article XX, and this Report was appealed to the WTO Appellate Body.

One controversial aspect of *Tuna/Dolphin I* was discussed again in *Shrimp/Turtle*. In the former case, it was stated by the Panel that it was inappropriate for a Member to impose its environmental or other regulations unilaterally on another

126. The difficulties between the United States and Mexico relating to tuna are ongoing. There is a WTO Panel presently considering an argument by Mexico that it is improperly being denied the ability to market their tuna as "dolphin safe" in the United States. It is expected that a final report will be issued in February 2011. World Trade Organization, *United States—Measures Concerning the Importation, Marketing and Sale of Tuna and Tuna Products* WT/DS381 (Dec. 14, 2009).

127. Appellate Body Report, *United States—Import Prohibition of Certain Shrimp and Shrimp Products*, ¶3, WT/DS58/AB/R (Oct. 12, 1998) [hereinafter *Shrimp/Turtle*].

128. *Id.* at ¶¶3–4.

party. Environmental and similar measures could not be imposed extraterritorially. The *Shrimp/Turtle* case backs off from this idea, and recognizes that it may simply be an unavoidable aspect of the Article XX exceptions that policies of one country will in fact be imposed on other countries. That is what the exceptions are meant to allow. The Appellate Body states that "conditioning access to a Member's domestic market on whether exporting Members comply with, or adopt, a policy or policies unilaterally prescribed by the importing Member may, to some degree, be a common aspect of measures falling within the scope of one or another of the exceptions (a) to (j) of Article XX."[129] Thus, the impediment to environmental and animal welfare regulation imposed by the concept that internal regulations cannot be enforced in a way that effectively requires other nations to adopt the policies of the regulation in question appears to have been removed by the Appellate Body in *Shrimp/Turtle*.[130] Imposition of one country's policies on another is a necessary result of the Article XX exceptions.

Much of the Appellate Body's Report addresses procedural issues about how Article XX issues are to be decided. The Appellate Body found many deficiencies in the Panel's analysis, starting with the fact that the Panel focused on the design of the United States' law, as opposed to its application.[131] Appropriate analysis under Article XX requires examination not just of the content of the measure, but of the way that the measure is applied according to the Appellate Body.[132] In other words, Article XX analysis requires looking at the way the measure is actually used and enforced by the country.

The Appellate Body also criticized the Panel for analyzing the measure under the chapeau[133] of Article XX prior to determining whether the measure fit within one of the specific exceptions of Article XX. According to the Appellate Body, Article XX analysis must proceed in the following fashion:

(1) Determination of whether the measure meets one of the specific substantive exceptions in Article XX.
(2) Determination of whether the measure constitutes arbitrary or unjustifiable discrimination between countries where the same conditions prevail or is a disguised restriction on international trade under the chapeau of Article XX.[134]

This stepwise analysis proposed by the Appellate Body is consistent with the stepwise analysis of Article XX used in the *US Gasoline* case.[135]

129. *Id* at ¶121.
130. *See* Thomas, *supra* note 113, at 626–28.
131. *Shrimp/Turtle, supra* note 127, at ¶¶115–116.
132. *Id.*
133. For those unfamiliar with use of this terminology or the French language, the "chapeau" of a provision is its introductory language; in this case the language prior to the list of specific exceptions in Article XX.
134. *Id.* at ¶¶115–22.
135. *See* Appellate Body Report, *United States—Standards for Reformulated and Conventional Gasoline,* WT/DS2/AB/R (May 20, 1996); Thomas, *supra* note 113, at 620–21.

The Appellate Body then goes on to add detail to each of the two levels of analysis with respect to the Article XX(g) exception relating to conservation of exhaustible resources claimed by the United States. The Appellate Body first disposed of the argument that "exhaustible natural resources" do not include living things and determined that although living things were renewable in the sense that they reproduced, they were also exhaustible since they could become extinct.[136] More important, the Appellate Body determined that the language of Article XX(g) was not to be interpreted as static as of the time it was written, but was to evolve along with the times, and include modern knowledge and concerns relating to the environment.[137] Taking this knowledge and these concerns into consideration leads to the conclusion that "natural resources" include living things.[138]

The language of Article XX(g) requires that a measure "relate to" conservation of natural resources. The Appellate Body found that this means there must be a relationship between the policy behind the measure, here the protection of sea turtles, and the requirements of the measure itself.[139] The Appellate Body found that there was such a relationship in this case. It found that the import ban prohibiting imports of shrimp from countries not using technology to protect turtles related to the policy of protecting sea turtles, and thus met this portion of the two-step analysis required under Article XX.[140]

The Appellate Body then went on to analyze the import ban under the chapeau. The Appellate Body began by rejecting the argument of the United States that the requirements of the chapeau are met whenever there is a relationship between the policy behind the measure and the regulation imposed by the measure. The Appellate Body recognized that accepting this argument would mean that every time a measure fit within the language of an exception in Article XX it would automatically meet the requirements of the chapeau.[141]

Instead, according to the Appellate Body, analysis under the chapeau requires consideration of three issues. These three issues are whether the measure as applied constitutes:[142]

(1) arbitrary discrimination between countries where the same conditions prevail;
(2) unjustifiable discrimination between countries where the same conditions prevail; or
(3) a disguised restriction on international trade.

The Appellate Body then added a three-part test for determining whether there was arbitrary or unjustifiable discrimination requiring that first, there must be

136. *Shrimp/Turtle, supra* note 127, at ¶128.
137. *Id.* at ¶¶128–30.
138. *Id.*
139. *Id.* at ¶¶135–136.
140. *Id.* at ¶¶138–42.
141. *Id.* at ¶149.
142. *Id.* at ¶150.

discrimination; second, the discrimination must be arbitrary or unjustifiable; and third, the discrimination must occur between countries where the same conditions prevail.[143]

After delineating these laundry lists of requirements of the chapeau, the Appellate Body goes on to state a number of general principles underlying the chapeau. It states, based on the *US Gasoline* case, that prevention of abuse of the Article XX exceptions is the goal of the chapeau.[144] The Appellate Body further concludes that the chapeau requires a balancing of the interests of Members to assert exceptions under Article XX based on important policy interests against the substantive free trade rights of other Members:

> Turning to the chapeau of Article XX, we consider that it embodies the recognition on the part of WTO Members of the need to maintain a balance of rights and obligations between the right of a Member to invoke one or another of the exceptions of Article XX, specified in paragraphs (a) to (j), on the one hand, and the substantive rights of the other Members under the GATT 1994, on the other hand. Exercise by one Member of its right to invoke an exception, such as Article XX(g), if abused or misused, will, to that extent, erode or render naught the substantive treaty rights in, for example, Article XI:1, of other Members. Similarly, because the GATT itself makes available the exceptions of Article XX, in recognition of the legitimate nature of the policies and interests there embodied, the right to invoke one of those exceptions is not to be rendered illusory. The same concept may be expressed from a slightly different angle of vision, thus, a balance must be struck between the *right* of a Member to invoke an exception under Article XX and the *duty* of that same Member to respect the treaty rights of other Members (emphasis in original).[145]

To this is added by the Appellate Body that the chapeau is an expression of good faith requiring Members to act reasonably in their dealings affected by trade treaties, including the GATT.[146] So ultimately the Article XX exceptions come down to a balancing of the good faith interests of the party asserting a strong policy interest in a regulation and the good faith interests of the offended party to conduct free trade under the "substantive" provisions of the GATT.

The Appellate Body then goes on to analyze the regulation of shrimp fishing by the United States within these parameters. In so doing, it concludes that the measure constitutes unjustifiable discrimination between countries where the same conditions prevail.[147] In coming to this conclusion, the Appellate Body asserts that the regulation effectively requires that all other countries adopt the

143. *Id.*
144. *Id.* at ¶151.
145. *Id.* at ¶156 (emphasis in original).
146. *Id.* at ¶¶156–58.
147. *Id.* at ¶161–176.

same policy as that imposed on United States shrimp trawlers.[148] While the law itself may have been intended to provide flexibility in application of its standards, in practice the Appellate Body found there to be a total lack of flexibility. The guidelines used by the United States Secretary of State under the measure amounted to requiring all other countries, regardless of different conditions that might exist in different countries, to follow a regime identical to that of United States shrimp trawlers.[149]

It was also determined that the United States had acted arbitrarily and unjustifiably in its failure to engage in serious negotiations with some GATT Members prior to the imposition of the trade ban, while undertaking serious negotiations with other Members.[150] In other words, there was differential treatment of countries in negotiations without justification. This illustrates one of the most important aspects of application of Article XX exceptions under the GATT; the WTO and the GATT mean to encourage negotiation and agreement as the fundamental tools of solving international trade disputes. As a result, the failure to engage in serious negotiations with adverse parties on trade issues will, as it did in *Shrimp/Turtle*, result in a jaundiced eye being cast by a WTO Panel or Appellate Body on an Article XX claim.

Another important aspect of the *Shrimp/Turtle* case is the assertion by the Appellate Body that "Article X:3 of the GATT 1994 establishes certain minimum standards for transparency and procedural fairness in the administration of trade regulations which, in our view, are not met here."[151] By not having a certification process that provided transparency and predictability, the United States violated the requirement for some minimum level of Due Process under GATT.[152] Note, however, that the whole idea that Due Process is a part of Article X:3 or any other provision of GATT is not entirely clear from the language of the treaty and has been questioned.[153]

Although *Shrimp/Turtle* resulted in an environmental regulatory scheme being found contrary to GATT, it nonetheless provides a better platform for allowing environmental and animal welfare regulations than appeared to be the case after the *Tuna/Dolphin* cases. *Shrimp/Turtle* recognizes that a measure can impose the policies of one Member on other GATT Members yet still be consistent with trade obligations under GATT. Indeed, as *Shrimp/Turtle* recognizes, the exceptions of Article XX would be ineffective and nugatory were there no ability to effectively impose on other Members important internal policies protected

148. *Id.*
149. *Id.* at ¶¶162–64.
150. *Id.* at ¶¶166, 167, 170–72.
151. *Id.* at ¶185.
152. *Id.* at ¶¶180–84.
153. *See* Timothy M. Reif & Julie Eckert, *Courage You Can't Understand: How to Achieve the Right Balance Between Shaping and Policing Commerce in Disputes Before the World Trade Organization,* 42 COL. J. TRANS. L. 657, 695–96 (2004) (noting that the language of the GATT does not include Due Process language and that adding Due Process ideas to the GATT may make environmental regulations more difficult).

under Article XX. The price to be paid by the regulating party for the ability to impose such a measure on others is even-handedness, openness to negotiation and Due Process. If a Member wishes to impose a regulation in the environmental or animal welfare areas, the path to success is through the following:

- The regulation must apply to domestic entities.
- It must be applied to others in a non-discriminatory manner.
- The party imposing the regulation must be open to negotiate with all other Members on an equal basis relating to the regulation.
- Any certification or other processes involved in the measure must comply with certain minimum standards of Due Process.

Thus, while the *Tuna/Dolphin* cases could be seen as closing and locking the door on any extraterritorial aspects of animal welfare regulation, *Shrimp/Turtle* opens this door to well-crafted regulations enforced in an impartial manner.

IV. THE OIE: INTERNATIONAL REGULATION OF ANIMAL WELFARE

It would be easy at this point to view the WTO/GATT regime as one inimical to the advancement of the interests of animals in international trade. But perhaps the situation is not quite that desperate. Under the WTO Agreement on the Application of Sanitary and Phytosanitary Measures (hereinafter "SPS"), to which members of the WTO are bound, the World Organization for Animal Health (hereinafter "OIE") is charged with creating standards for animal health and welfare.[154] Historically, the OIE has focused on issues relating to disease prevention and sanitary standards for animals and animal products in international trade.[155] The OIE Strategic Plan of 2001–05, however, identified animal protection as a priority of the organization and the OIE has begun creating international standards of animal welfare.[156]

The Terrestrial Animal Health Code of the OIE (hereinafter "Code") now includes a number of provisions relating to animal welfare. In creating these provisions a distinction we have not previously encountered is made between the "treatment of animals" and "animal welfare." The "treatment of animals" is said to relate to "animal care, animal husbandry and humane treatment," while "animal welfare" is described as, among other things, the "state of the animal" and "how an animal

154. *See* OIE, *International Standards*, http://www.oie.int/international-standard-setting/overview/ (last visited Feb. 4, 2011).
155. *See Id.* (discussing the Terrestrial and Aquatic Animal Health Codes).
156. OIE, *The OIE's Objectives and Achievements in Animal Welfare*, http://www.oie.int/eng/bien_etre/en_introduction.htm (last visited June 13, 2010) [hereinafter Objectives and Achievements].

is coping with the conditions in which it lives (emphasis omitted)."[157] The animal welfare provisions themselves start with a set of "guiding principles":

> [t]hat the internationally recognised "five freedoms" (freedom from hunger, thirst and malnutrition; freedom from fear and distress; freedom from physical and thermal discomfort; freedom from pain, injury and disease; and freedom to express normal patterns of behaviour) provide valuable guidance in animal welfare (emphasis omitted)."[158] These guiding principles of the Code go on to state that the 3Rs: "provide valuable guidance for the use of animals in science (emphasis omitted).[159]

The more specific provisions on animal welfare in the Code are stated as recommendations typically using "should" language.[160] These recommendations cover the transport of animals by sea, land and air, the slaughter of animals, the killing of animals for disease control and the management of stray animals.[161] The content of the recommendations are in line with the kinds of provisions that we have seen in legislation relating to the keeping of agricultural animals. For example, there are recommendations concerning the training of personnel, the planning of journeys transporting animals, the design and conditions of facilities for transport and slaughter of animals, the control of diseases in animals and the manner in which loading, unloading, stunning and slaughter of animals should be carried out.[162]

It is not intended, however, that the OIE standards will end here: "Notwithstanding the progress [in OIE animal welfare standards] made to date, there are still many challenges and the OIE is progressing [sic] the development of standards and recommendations in new areas of importance to animal welfare."[163] The OIE is, for example, convening working groups on laboratory animal welfare, and animal welfare and livestock production systems.[164] It is anticipated that new chapters of the Code will be created by these groups, with the first chapters expected to be on beef cattle and broiler chicken production systems.[165]

So under the SPS of the WTO the OIE has begun a fledgling effort to create international standards of animal welfare relating to the trade in animals. While these standards are in the form of recommendations, it can perhaps be seen as the dawn of international recognition of the interests of animals in international trade. But the path to progress is likely to be slow and it may never reach goals set

157. OIE, Terrestrial Animal Health Code 2009 §7.1.1 (Dec. 23, 2009), http://www.oie.int/eng/normes/mcode/en_chapitre_1.7.1.htm (last visited June 13, 2010).
158. *Id.* at §7.1.2(2).
159. *Id.* at §7.1.2(3).
160. *See id.* at §§7.2–7.7.
161. *Id.*
162. *Id.*
163. Objectives and Achievements, *supra* note 156.
164. *Id.*
165. *Id.*

by those who would like to see the end of the use of animals in agriculture, experimentation and entertainment. But at least not all connected to the WTO and animals is completely bleak.

V. THE FUTURE OF THE WTO AND ANIMAL LAW

Those who are committed to improving the conditions and status of animals have not only domestic battles to wage, but also have the WTO and the GATT to contend with when trying to accomplish change. We have found that there are a number of ways the WTO and the GATT work against regulations favorable to animal interests. They can interfere with efforts to create domestic laws to protect animals because laws created to apply to all producers of items sold in a country may not be able to be applied to imported items. An additional problem not noted previously is that the WTO and the GATT may be at odds with other international treaties and agreements relating to protection of animals. For instance, it may be that trade restrictions, quotas and permit requirements of the Convention on International Trade in Endangered Species discussed in an earlier chapter may conflict with the WTO and the GATT as presently interpreted.[166]

Overall, perhaps the most unfavorable concept arising from the GATT is the product/PPM distinction; if a nation wishes to create a regulation favorable to the treatment of animals, like a domestic ban on battery cages and a similar regulation preventing the import of eggs raised in battery cages, this regulation will likely not be seen as a proper internal regulation under Article III:4. Even though domestic and foreign producers are treated in precisely the same way under this regulation, *i.e.*, they are required to produce eggs outside of battery cages, the foreign producers cannot be subjected to this regulation since it constitutes a regulation of the process or production method for eggs, not a regulation of the product itself, the eggs. The economic impact of this is, of course, a negative one on the regulating nation, since its producers will be economically disadvantaged as compared to foreign producers, who can use more cost-effective factory farming techniques not available to domestic producers. The economic results of the PPM concept thus discourage regulations that would improve the conditions of factory farmed animals in countries favorably disposed to such regulations. The ultimate economic result of the PPM concept is to promote a race to the bottom for animal welfare and environmental regulation, since the nations with the most minimal animal welfare and environmental regulations will gain economic advantages in trade over other more highly regulated nations.

One might respond to this by claiming that even if a regulation is categorized as a PPM and is not permitted under Article III, it still may be justified under some exception under Article XX. This in fact is quite true, but it is not necessarily

166. Rosalind Reeve, Policing International Trade in Endangered Species 311–12 (2002).

heartening; the language of the Article XX exceptions, though argued by many to apply to animal welfare regulations and, at least in the *Shrimp/Turtle* case, actually found to be applicable to some environmental regulations, may not be found to apply to regulations aimed at protecting animals from the kind of treatment they receive in factory farms, animal experiments, circuses and exhibitions, and the like. Moreover, the case law indicates that the exceptions of Article XX are to be narrowly interpreted. Further, the two major cases in the area have found environmental regulatory schemes to not be compliant with the GATT, although at least the *Shrimp/Turtle* case did find one of the exceptions of Article XX to apply to an environmental measure. Thus, there are numerous impediments to animal welfare measures under the present interpretation of the GATT which discourage nations from enacting and implementing such regulations, as is proven by the behavior of the EU on the leghold trap ban and the ban on animal-tested cosmetics.

It is not necessary, however, to throw up our hands in despair and shrink from suggesting ways to respond to the current state of GATT law; the foundations of the arguments that favor present GATT jurisprudence on these issues are very weak, and nations should not cower in the face of these arguments. The product/PPM distinction does not have a basis in the language of the GATT and is essentially the invention of the Panel Report in *Tuna/Dolphin I*. Similarly, the narrow interpretation of Article XX exceptions and their "second class" GATT provision status also derive from the *Tuna/Dolphin I* Panel Report, and do not find support in the language of the GATT. Thus, much of the trouble with GATT law as it relates to animal issues finds its genesis in a Panel decision that was never even adopted under the GATT. As a result, very good arguments can be advanced to reverse or modify the current state of interpretation of the GATT on these issues.[167]

Another way to approach this issue more directly is by adding a new exception to Article XX that would cover regulations to protect animal welfare.[168] An exception could be provided for measures "relating to protection of domestic and wild animals." This simple language would make clear the broad scope of the provision and would, it is to be hoped, avoid interpretive problems. The use of "relating to" rather than "necessary to" as used in Articles XX(a) and (b), escapes the restrictive interpretation that has been given to the latter phrase. Indeed it would make sense to revise present Article XX(a) and (b) to replace the "necessary" language with "relating to" language.[169]

Recall as well that the OIE has embarked on a program of creating international animal welfare standards. While these are presented as recommendations, the OIE efforts relating to animal protection are ongoing. This "foot in the door" in the

---

167. On arguments against the present status of GATT jurisprudence, *See generally* Thomas, *supra* note 113, at 635–37; and Stevenson, *supra* note 95, at 135–37.

168. Stevenson, *supra* note 95, at 135–36, discusses adding an animal welfare provision to existing Article XX(b) which is one way to approach this issue. I propose a separate provision to make clear that this is intended to be a real change from present practice.

169. *See* Stevenson, *supra* note 95, at 135 (proposing that Articles XX(a) and (b) be revised to use the language "relating to" rather than "necessary to").

realm of international regulation of animal welfare should not be ignored or trivialized. Once through the door, we may see gradual and expanding awareness and regulation of animal issues on an international level.

Countries with a commitment to protecting animals should continue to advance the interests of animals and enforce laws relating to the protection of animals. By pressing forward with these regulations, the interpretive mistakes of the past may be corrected and the way cleared for recognition of the increased importance of animal interests in international trade. Ultimately, through the efforts of activists, law-makers and consumers, the time may one day arrive when the exploitation of animals in international trade ends.

Chapter 8
Constitutional Protection for Animals

I. CONSTITUTIONAL PROTECTION FOR ANIMALS?

If Aristotle's "Great Chain of Being" concerned laws, constitutions would be worshiped as God. Constitutions act as the thrones of human law, enshrining the mechanisms of governments, the fundamental principles of nations and the rights of peoples. All other law must lie prostrate before the constitution and either bow or be damned. Constitutions are where absolute monarchies end and republics begin; constitutions are where fundamental rights are born and injustices die. The 13th Amendment to the United States Constitution, for instance, is where the stain of slavery was blotted but never really eradicated. Of all laws, constitutions are made of the most solid substance, arising from the deepest feelings of a nation, difficult to change, nearly immutable. Or at least this is the theory.

It is true that rights and principles of law fundamental to just governance and fairness can be and are found in other places—statutes, court decisions and even administrative rules. But the most solid ground on which one can stand is a constitution. The ideal world for an animal rights advocate would be one in which rights of animals are enshrined within a constitution; animals would thereby have constitutional rights to life, bodily liberty and to live consistently within their ethological needs and telos. Recently a number of countries have created constitutional provisions that relate to the interests of animals, but do not go so far as to create what we would term "rights." Are these truly steps in the direction of creating real rights for animals or are they merely typical animal welfare provisions? We have seen that statutory provisions, such as those that prohibit "unnecessary" suffering, are interpreted so that the overriding interests and desires of humans to eat, experiment on and entertain themselves with animals are protected; meanwhile, a faint nod is given to the interests of animals. Are these constitutional provisions different? This chapter will focus on this and other questions on the constitutional provisions that have been created relating to animals in Germany, Switzerland, India and Brazil. We will also discuss what the future may hold for such provisions.

II. GERMANY

A. History and Culture

My father's family has German origins. (Well, actually, they were supposedly from Alsace-Lorraine, but they were from the German-speaking contingent of this now French region.) So I am quite familiar with German food, which my father insisted on having served at least occasionally. Sauerbraten, a German pot roast of beef (it is sometimes made with other meats), served with fluffy potato dumplings, was frequent fare in the Kelch household. Less frequently there were things like Sultz, which I was always told was "blood pudding," but which from recipes I have seen, seems to be a concoction made with the bones of pigs and leftover pieces of meat.[1] Then there was Leber-Klösse, liver dumplings, which seemed like disgusting grey blobs floating in putrid water. Or how about pickled pig's feet? These latter three dishes were ones that no one in my family would touch except for my father; but nonetheless, he demanded them, so he ate them alone.

So why the detour into German cuisine? Germany features, from my experience, a rather meat-centered cuisine. Beyond the dishes noted above, it is hard to go anywhere in Germany without tripping over some sort of sausage. So on the face of it, one would not expect Germany to be a country or a culture concerned about the treatment of animals; nonetheless, it is. This culture of concern for animals in

1. The Valentine Cookbook, *Gram's Soltz (Sultz) and Liver Dumplings*, Aug. 27, 2007, *available at* http://www.valentine-design.com/cookbook/2007/08/grams-soltz-sultz-and-liver-dumplings.html. The following description of Sultz from The Valentine Cookbook gives some sense of the carnage that goes into this dish:

> When Gram made this it was always something of an event. Her brother George would come by and bring hot rye bread from Meisel's Bakery. We would sit on her front porch on the big swing and the glider and eat the soltz with rye bread, mustard, sliced onions and cold beer. It is a sort of pickled meat that is really delicious. Those old German's [sic] used up everything so soltz was a way of using up the meat scraps left on bones. Later people added extra meat— Jim Auman (who is married to Aunt Mary's daughter Snooky) added chopped up turkey to his. Gram used to say that the only part of a pig you couldn't use was the squeak. Place 5–6 lbs. of meaty bones in a large kettle, cover with water, and bring to a boil. Simmer 2–3 hours until the meat is falling off the bones. Remove meat and strain the broth well. Measure it and add an equal amount of cider vinegar. Salt and pepper to taste (best if you use a fair amount of pepper). Let the meat cool a bit and remove it from the bones discarding all the fine bones and gristle. Grind the meat and add extra if you like. Add an onion. Place it back in the broth. Simmer for 5 minutes in the vinegar broth until the onion is cooked.

Germany goes back several hundred years to before Germany was even a unified country:

> While most of Europe was developing the democratic national structures that persist today, Germany remained a collection of independent kingdoms well into the nineteenth century. Though democracies may have difficulty enacting only moderately popular social policies such as animal protection, German monarchs were capable of outlawing cruel practices toward animals by simple decree. Kaiser Joseph II, for example, outlawed the baiting of animals for public entertainment in 1789, and countless other directives regarding both domestic and wild animals were enacted in the German lands as far back as 1417. German romanticism, including the works of Goethe, had a marked influence on the awareness of nature and the sensibilities of the German people. In particular, the philosopher, Schopenhauer, is credited with having engaged German-speaking lands in an ethical debate about interactions with nonhuman animals in the early 1800s. By 1871, when Germany united as one nation, its culture had already been significantly influenced by these and other social movements that contributed to the developing European humane movement. While Germany is not credited as the first country to have enacted national anti-cruelty laws, Germany already had more success in developing socially pervasive humane attitudes by the late [nineteenth] century than its neighboring European democracies.[2]

Though not the first country with animal protection laws, Germany did create a general law protecting animals that was ultimately enacted under the Nazi regime in 1933.[3] There is indeed sad irony in this. But the German legal protection of animals did not end there. After World War II, Germany continued to expand animal welfare laws resulting finally in the modern German animal protection law known as the "Tierschutzgesetz" (hereinafter the "Tierschutzgesetz")[4] Even outside this law, there are provisions having to do with the status of animals. For example, the German Civil Code states that "[a]nimals are not things. They are protected by special laws. Laws pertaining to physical objects apply to them only so far as there is no special regulation concerning them."[5] While this classic doublespeak negates what it seems to posit by providing that animals are not things, but despite this, the laws that apply to things still apply to animals; it does, at least, give voice to the idea that animals are somehow distinct from other forms of property.

The Tierschutzgesetz itself contains a foundational rule that sounds very familiar to those conversant with animal law; one cannot "injure or cause the

2. Kate M. Nattrass, "... *Und Die Tiere" Constitutional Protection for Germany's Animals*, 10 ANIMAL L. 283, 285–86 (2004) (citations omitted).
3. *Id.* at 286.
4. *Id.* at 287–88.
5. *Id.* at 288 (quoting from the Bügerlichen Gesetzbuch, the German Civil Code, at § 90a).

suffering of an animal without sound reason."[6] This makes it illegal to kill a vertebrate animal without "sound reason," and also precludes cosmetic tail docking and certain other procedures.[7] "Without sound reason" is really just a synonym for that old saw "unnecessary," and as a result, it should not be surprising that German law recognizes a very long list of "sound reasons" for injuring or killing animals—killing and injuring for food, hunting, animal experimentation and so on—all the "normal" human uses of animals.[8]

Another failing of this law is that its strictures can be overcome by what are referred to as "basic rights" of humans engrained in the German Constitution.[9] What this meant (prior to the addition of animal protection language to the German Constitution) was that whenever an animal protection provision of the Tierschutzgesetz conflicted with "basic rights" of humans in the German Constitution, the animal protection provisions became invalid.[10] These basic rights potentially protect doing all manner of cruel things to animals. Some basic rights that might conflict with animal protection provisions of German law are:

– The right to pursue a chosen profession.[11]
– The right to artistic expression.[12]
– Freedom to do research.[13]
– Freedom of religion.[14]

How do these basic rights interact with animal protection law in Germany? The freedom to practice one's profession may preclude restrictions on how farmers can treat farm animals,[15] and freedom of artistic expression has been specifically found to override the strictures of the Tierschutzgesetz in a case involving rather bizarre cruelty:

> In a case brought to the circuit court of Kassel, an artist was charged with animal cruelty [for violation of a provision of the Tierschutzgesetz]. The artist had bound a bird in a glue-like substance made of egg yolk and ground sausage in order to represent how humans are often mishandled in modern society. The bird, unable to fly, was forced to hobble about the exhibit in obvious distress. While the Kassel court agreed that the bird had suffered and

6. *Id.*
7. *Id.* at 288–89.
8. *Id.*
9. *Id.* at 292.
10. *Id.* at 290.
11. *Id.* at 292–93.
12. *Id.* at 293–94.
13. *Id.* at 294.
14. *See generally*, Claudia E. Haupt, *Free Exercise of Religion and Animal Protection: A Comparative Perspective on Ritual Slaughter*, 39 GEO. WASH. INT'L L. REV. 839 (2007) [hereinafter Haupt 2007].
15. Nattrass, *supra* note 2, at 292–93.

experienced pain, it ruled that the constitutionally protected freedom of artistic expression took precedence over the animal protection law.[16]

Similarly, freedom of research has been found to protect animal experimenters from prosecution for violation of the Tierschutzgesetz.[17] Thus, the conflict between alleged human rights and the protection of animals was quite explicit prior to the amendment to the German Constitution to include protection of animals. So what was the genesis of this constitutional provision?

B. The Creation and Content of a Constitutional Amendment on Animal Treatment

The process of amending the German Constitution to include a provision relating to animals was a fairly long one, with efforts to make the Tierschutzgesetz stronger through the creation of a constitutional provision protecting animals beginning in the 1980s.[18] It was thought by some that concern for the protection of animals was on the decline in Germany prior to the constitutional amendment, because the priority given to human basic rights was being used to undermine the protections of the Tierschutzgesetz.[19] Political wrangling kept the animal treatment amendment from being enacted for a considerable time; so in frustration, a number of individual German states created their own constitutional provisions relating to animals.[20]

Ultimately it was public reaction to a court decision that propelled the animal protection language into the German Constitution; the court case involved a Sunni Muslim butcher who had been denied a Tierschutzgesetz-required permit by the State of Hessia to perform ritual slaughter without the stunning of the animal. Given recent German history, as well as the fact that religious ritual slaughter is practiced by both Jews and Muslims, this is a very sensitive issue in Germany. The applicant claimed that the denial of the permit infringed on his constitutional rights to practice his religion and his profession.[21] The German Supreme Court agreed with the butcher, saying that denial of the permit did violate his right to practice his religion and his profession (hereinafter, this case will be referred to as the “Slaughter Decision”).[22]

This decision resulted in considerable public outrage in Germany, where many people feel that, notwithstanding history, ritual slaughter is still just animal

16. *Id.* at 293–94.
17. *Id.* at 294.
18. *Id.* at 294–95.
19. Haupt 2007, *supra* note 14, at 870.
20. Nattrass, *supra* note 2, at 294–300.
21. *Id.* at 301–02.
22. *Id.*

cruelty.[23] This public dissatisfaction was felt by both politicians and political parties, and on May 15, 2002, Article 20a of the German Constitution was amended to add the words "und die tiere" ("and the animals").[24] Article 20a of the German Constitution now states: "The state, aware of its responsibility for present and future generations, shall protect the natural resources of life and the animals within the framework of the constitutional order through the legislature and, in accordance with the law and principles of justice, the executive and judiciary."[25] The language "and the animals" was grafted onto a previously existing article of the Constitution that was aimed at environmental issues. But what does it really mean?

Examining the language literally, a number of things can be surmised; by virtue of this amendment, the state recognizes a responsibility to present and future generations. In accordance with this responsibility, the state "shall" protect natural resources, meaning the environment, "and the animals." The term "animals" is used without limitation and is not restricted to species of animals, but applies to individual animals.[26] The "state" is bound by this provision, which includes the legislative, judicial and executive branches of government.

Is this a mechanism for real change in the treatment of animals or an ethereal linguistic flourish that leaves us right where we began, in a world where animal welfare is always unfavorably balanced against the desires of humans? One thing is clear: this provision does not create rights in animals;[27] rights are reserved in the German Constitution only for humans.[28] One conceptual tool for measuring the implications of a constitutional provision such as this is a four-part categorization of constitutional provisions discussed by Professor Jose L. Fernandez relating to whether the provisions are self-executing and enforceable.[29] The four categories are:[30]

(1) Non-Mandatory: These provisions do not create any duty or obligation. These are typically stated in the form "the state 'may' do X."
(2) Mandatory/Non-Prohibitory: Provisions of this kind create rights, duties or obligations, but do not prohibit any particular act. These are not always self-executing. Whether these are self-executing will depend on factors such as:

---

23. *See* Nattrass, *supra* note 2, at 301–02; *See also* Claudia E. Haupt, *The Nature and Effects of Constitutional State Objectives: Assessing the German Basic Law's Animal Protection Clause*, 16 ANIMAL L. 213, 220 (2010) [hereinafter Haupt 2010].
24. Nattrass, *supra* note 2, at 302; *see also* Haupt 2010 *supra* note 23, at 220.
25. Haupt 2010, *supra* note 23, at 14–15 (quoting Article 20a of the German Constitution).
26. Nattrass, *supra* note 2, at 299.
27. *See id.* at 302; Haupt 2010, *supra* note 23, at 225–26.
28. Nattrass, *supra* note 2, at 302.
29. Jose L. Fernandez, *State Constitutions, Environmental Rights Provisions, and the Doctrine of Self-Execution: A Political Question?,* 17 HARV. ENVTL. L. REV. 333, 341–53 (1993) (citing 16 C.J.S. Constitutional Law §§46–48 (1984)); *see also* John C. Tucker, *Constitutional Codification of an Environmental Ethic,* 52 FLA. L. REV. 299, 316–17 (2000).
30. Tucker, *supra* note 29, at 316–17.

> [W]hether the provision provides sufficient detail and process to be susceptible to judicial enforcement. A key question is what happens if a legislature fails to act on a mandatory provision that is not self-executing. Generally, state courts are unwilling to order legislatures to act because of separation of powers principles.[31]

(3) Mandatory/Prohibitory: This kind of provision creates rights, duties or obligations and prohibits certain acts. An example of this would be a constitutional article that prohibits the legislature from abrogating the peoples' right of free speech. These are generally self-executing and will be enforced by courts.
(4) Mixed: These combine characteristics of more than one of the above categories.

The amendment to the German Constitution to protect animals would appear to be of the mandatory/non prohibitory type, creating a state objective of protection of animals which is binding on the legislative, judicial and executive branches, but which does not prohibit any particular conduct. Whether it is self-executing or not is an issue that can be debated, although the obligation to "protect animals" is rather vague and might be argued not to be self-executing for that reason.

What amended Article 20a clearly does is declare that protection of animals is a goal and objective of the state.[32] This provision has been described as follows by Claudia Haupt:

> Structurally, the nature of the provision sets it apart from rights and liberties and from organizational elements of constitutional design as state objectives are considered constitutional provisions of a separate category. The normative value of including state objectives in constitutions has been much debated, not least in connection with the constitution writing efforts of the 1990s.[33]

Statements of objectives in constitutions are not rare, nor are they always of such recent vintage. Recall that the United States Constitution states in its Preamble that it is created "in Order to form a more perfect Union, establish Justice, insure domestic Tranquility, provide for the common defense, promote the general Welfare, and secure the Blessings of Liberty to ourselves and our Posterity …."[34]

But as an objective of the state, what exactly does it mean substantively to the government that must follow it? One idea from Kate Nattrass on the impact of Article 20a is that while it will not guarantee victory for those pushing for animal protection, it does at least create a constitutional mechanism by which "the interests of animals to remain unharmed can be weighed evenly against the

31. *Id.* at 317.
32. Nattrass, *supra* note 2, at 302; Haupt 2010, *supra* note 23, at 214–15, 225–26.
33. Haupt 2010, *supra* note 23, at 214–15.
34. U.S. CONST. pmbl.

interests of humans."[35] This idea that Article 20a leads to something like equality of consideration of human and animal interests is echoed by Claudia Haupt:

> State objectives and other constitutional provisions, including the fundamental rights, are of the same constitutional rank and in case of conflict between state objectives and fundamental rights, neither take precedence. Rather, conflicts between constitutional provisions have to be resolved by determining in each individual case which provision prevails, applying the proportionality principle. In balancing the constitutional provisions, each must be given [maximum effect] ... The introduction of animal protection into the Basic Law therefore demands improving the role of animal protection in the legal system, but it does not demand the primacy of animal protection.[36]

But this idea of "even" or "equal" consideration of human and animal interests is nonetheless problematic, because it is presumably weighing the interests of humans, who already have rights guaranteed by the German Constitution, against the interests of non-rightholding animals. How can a weighing of interests, given this imbalance of power, ever be equal or fair?

Indeed, the current situation in Germany includes the unabated killing and torture of animals in agriculture and experimentation. Knowing this fact, how can one say that the interests of animals are being weighed "equally" against those of humans, when humans are guaranteed by law not to be tortured or killed.

While true "equal" weighing of animal and human interests is not borne out by the facts, might Article 20a ever actually result in more serious and favorable consideration of animal interests, thereby resulting in true gains in the movement toward the end of exploitation of animals? One desirable aspect of objectives statements in constitutions is that they may be useful in designing the future framework for political and other choices by the legislative, judicial and executive branches of government.[37] The legislature must act in a way conforming to the state objective;[38] nonetheless, the legislature has great discretion in determining how and when to use the objective.[39] As a practical matter, what this provision means for the German legislature has been argued to be the following by Claudia Haupt:[40]

- The legislature cannot lower existing animal protection standards.
- Impacts on animals of all legislation must be considered and alternatives must be chosen if a negative impact on animals is foreseen.
- Even proactive animal friendly legislation may be required where harm to animals can be foreseen.

35. Nattrass, *supra* note 2, at 303, 312.
36. Haupt 2010, *supra* note 23, at 229–30 (citations omitted).
37. *See id.* at 224.
38. *Id.* at 226–27.
39. *Id.*
40. *Id.* at 229.

The judicial and executive branches will also be impacted by amended Article 20a. For instance, the constitutional provision may guide interpretation of legislation and administrative rules in the courts.[41] Administrative agencies will need to interpret regulations in line with the objective of animal protection and implement legislation in light of the constitutional status of the interests of animals.[42] As an example, administrative agencies evaluating whether the use of animals in teaching may be permitted will now be required to look at alternatives and the teacher will have the burden of showing that the teaching objective cannot be reached without the use of animals.[43] In the past, a student who objected on the basis of conscience from participating in classroom activities involving the use of animals had the burden of showing alternative teaching methods to the use of animals.[44]

Kate Nattrass argues that placement of "and the animals" in the constitution can lead to more serious consideration of the interests of animals in Germany, so that the protected constitutional "basic rights" of humans might be subject to greater constraints:

> While the basic rights outlined in the constitution "bind the legislature, the executive, and the judiciary as inalienable rights," they can be constrained by certain laws or by other constitutional rights. For instance, the Supreme Court found that environmental protection, under Article 20a of the German Constitution (enacted prior to the animal amendment) constrained the freedom of art when exercising that freedom was environmentally harmful. Animal protection can have a similar effect on basic rights if they interfere with the ethical basis of the animal protection law. In the case against the artist who bound a bird in glue, it is likely that the decision would be reversed as a result of the animal protection amendment. The right to practice one's profession might be equally limited, if the profession involves a serious compromise of the animal protection standards.[45]

If that is true, things like the "art" described earlier, as well as the Slaughter Decision of the German Supreme Court, might be reversed by virtue of the constitutional amendment. This could be cited as real progress. Claudia Haupt states that "[p]rior to the amendment fundamental rights not subject to a textual limitation clause generally prevailed over animal protection. After the inclusion of animal protection into the constitution, constitutionally protected interests [those of humans and of animals as provided in Article 20a] must be reconciled in case of a conflict."[46] Nonetheless, Nattrass believes that there is a substantial possibility

41. Haupt 2010, *supra* note 23, at 225–26.
42. *Id.* at 229; Haupt 2007, *supra* note 14, at 870.
43. Haupt 2010, *supra* note 23, at 251–53.
44. *Id.*
45. Nattrass, *supra* note 2, at 303–04 (quoting art. I ¶3 of the German Constitution) (citations omitted).
46. Haupt 2010, *supra* note 23, at 215–16.

that even with the change in the German Constitution, the Slaughter Decision may not be impacted.[47]

There is reason to think that this is true. Though Article 20a was amended only recently, there is a case interpreting the animal protection language in the context of the religious slaughter exception in the Tierschutzgesetz which was the impetus for enactment of the animal protection provision. A German Federal Administrative Court, considering the same Sunni butcher who started the Article 20a animals amendment in serious motion, held that the religious slaughter exception to stunning in the Tierschutzgesetz is constitutional even after the enactment of Article 20a.[48] The effect of this decision has been described as follows:

> It [] found the constitutionality of the exemption provision unaffected by the introduction of the animal protection clause. The Federal Administrative Court, though, did not uphold the state administrative court's heightened standard of proof. The animal protection state objective does not prohibit granting exemptions from the stunning requirement since the intended goal of the state objective was not to award one-sided preference to animal protection. However, there is a shift in assessing the constitutionality of the exemption provision: Previously, the question was whether the general prohibition of slaughter without prior stunning with a possible exemption was an inappropriate limitation of the fundamental rights of the individual seeking an exemption; now it must conversely be asked whether granting permission to slaughter without prior stunning is compatible with animal protection. The court asserted that it is primarily up to the legislature to reconcile countervailing constitutional interests. Thus, the religious slaughter exemption has continuing effect. Like the state administrative court, the Federal Administrative Court found that the legislative intent on this issue was not modified by the state objective. A different assessment would lead to a precedence of animal protection that is not intended by the constitution nor by the legislature and that would lead to an elimination of the protection of religious freedom.[49]

What is effectively happening in this decision is the balancing of fundamental human rights against the animal protection objective of Art. 20a.[50] Thus, the battle of balancing interests of animals against those of humans continues even after placement of the animal protection objective in the German Constitution, and on one issue on which it has now been interpreted, the result remains the same as it was prior to the enactment. How this balancing will occur in other areas, such as animal experiments, is as yet unclear.[51] Recall that it has been suggested that the balancing of human and animal interests will now be on an "even" or "equal"

47. Nattrass, *supra* note 2, at 304–05.
48. Haupt 2010, *supra* note 23, at 240–44.
49. *Id.* at 243.
50. Haupt 2007, *supra* note 14, at 871.
51. *See* Haupt 2010, *supra* note 23, at 246–51.

basis; but oddly, so far the result that had occurred in the past has not been changed by this new kind of balancing. Human interests continue to prevail over animal interests.

There are other contexts in which change is expected as a result of Article 20a. Kate Nattrass asserts that criminal prosecutions have in fact been affected by the amendment, in that at least one criminal penalty since the date of enactment was substantially greater than what had occurred prior to new Article 20a.[52] In addition, Nattrass claims that there may now be changes relating to the use of animals in agriculture as a result of Article 20a; for instance, profit motive alone may lose its place as a "reasonable cause" for inflicting suffering on animals.[53] Greater constraints on the basic right of pursuing one's profession as a result of Article 20a may also embolden legislators to strengthen regulation of the use of animals in agriculture.[54] Nattrass believes that the animal experimentation community will likely see the least impact as a result of this amendment, although she states that governmental regulatory bodies may now review experiments not only concerning "technical formalities" of the experiments, but may consider more seriously the ethical aspects of the experiment and possible alternatives.[55]

Perhaps the most valuable change that could occur for animal advocates would be to have access to the courts to assert the interests of individual animals. It is possible that, while this amendment does not itself result in standing for any group to represent the interests of animals, the legislature may feel compelled to create standing for such groups based on the new provision.[56] This actually occurred in the case of the original environmental objective language in the German Constitution. Environmental groups were given standing in German courts via legislation some years after the environmental language was placed in the German Constitution.[57]

So it seems that the optimistic view of the impact of Article 20a's "and the animals" language is that it may motivate legislators, administrative agencies and judges to consider animal issues more carefully; another way of interpreting it is to say that there may be a bit more weight, this time on the animals' side of the scale, in policy decisions and interpretation of law. As Haupt sees it:

> The addition of the "three words, 'und die Tiere,' did not give any rights to animals in Germany." Indeed, the clause neither grants animals a fundamental right to life nor does it prohibit slaughter, animal experimentation or other uses of animals. Rather, the clause removed the disproportionality between unlimited constitutional rights [of humans] and animal protection and eliminated any doubts regarding the constitutionality of the Animal Protection Act with respect to fundamental rights without limitation clauses. In the future,

52. Nattrass, *supra* note 2, at 304.
53. *Id.* at 306.
54. *See id.* at 306–07.
55. *Id.* at 307–08.
56. Haupt 2010, *supra* note 23, at 231–37.
57. *Id.* at 233.

> the administrative agencies and the courts must give greater weight to animal protection especially in the area of unlimited liberty rights. Further, the legislature is now generally mandated to optimize the goal of animal protection and make laws to that effect.
>
> The intent of the constitutional amendment, however, was to strengthen animal protection in the weighing process.[58]

This constitutional provision is of recent vintage and so its true impact will have to await the passage of time and evolution of interpretation. Nonetheless, given that it does not create rights; does not change the property status of animals; does not prohibit any of the present uses of animals in agriculture, experimentation, trade, or entertainment; and continues to weigh the interests of animals and humans so that the interests of humans are necessarily paramount as right holders; it does not seem that it is presently a mechanism for substantial change. It leaves our world, with the exception of the three words "and the animals" placed in a somewhat ambiguous context, just as it was before; a hierarchy where the desires of humans to eat, perform science on and be entertained by animals continue to be fulfilled unabated. Perhaps, however, the fact that animal interests are now part of the German Constitution is a first step that will lead to others, and these future steps may lead to true advances which will end presently permitted practices.

III. SWITZERLAND

It would be hard to argue that Switzerland is not a unique country. This small and perennially neutral country, which is set in gorgeous mountains and whose people speak three languages seems somehow both impossible and necessary. Given the distinctiveness of Switzerland, it is not hard to grasp that it was the first country in Europe to include animal protection within its constitution.[59] The Swiss Constitution has been said to recognize the inherent worth of animals[60] and to acknowledge that animals are "beings,"[61] accomplishments obtained through the dedicated work of committed activists:

> If its constitution is to be believed, no one takes animal rights as seriously as Switzerland. The concept of animal rights has been enshrined in the nation's basic law since 1992, a worldwide first.
>
> Shortly thereafter, Canton Zurich took a further huge step for "animal kind" and established a position for a lawyer to protect animal rights. This

58. *Id.* at 256–57.
59. *See* Haupt 2007, *supra* note 14, at 877.
60. Stephanie J. Engelsman, *"World Leader"—At What Price? A Look at Lagging American Animal Protection Laws,* 22 PACE ENVTL. L. REV. 329, 361 (2005).
61. Lauren Magnotti, *Pawing Open the Courthouse Door: Why Animals' Interests Should Matter When Courts Grant Standing,* 80 ST. JOHN'S L. REV. 445, 490 (2006).

> public official is the best friend of man's best friends when it comes to criminal cases involving animal abuse.
>
> Recently, the position was filled by Antoine Goetschel, who actively worked to enshrine the dignity and rights of animals in the Swiss Constitution in 1992.[62]

Similar sentiments are heard from Antoine Goetschel himself: "I had the honour of helping change the Swiss [C]onstitution in 1992. Switzerland is now the only place worldwide which protects animals' dignity both in the constitution and in legislation. It encourages other states to look at Swiss solutions more closely."[63]

The most general provision in the Swiss Constitution relating to animals is Article 80 which provides:[64]

> (1) The Confederation shall legislate on the protection of animals.
> (2) It shall in particular regulate:
> (a) the keeping and care of animals;
> (b) experiments on animals and procedures carried out on living animals;
> (c) the use of animals;
> (d) the importation of animals and animal products;
> (e) the trade in animals and the transportation of animals;
> (f) the slaughter of animals.
> (3) The enforcement of the regulations shall be the responsibility of the cantons, except where the law reserves this to the Confederation.

Again, this is a mandatory/non-prohibitory provision which requires the legislature to adopt rules that relate to the use and care of animals, but does not prohibit any particular action.[65]

The Swiss Constitution contains a number of other provisions relating to animals, including Article 120 which states, in part:

> The Confederation shall legislate on the use of reproductive and genetic material from animals, plants and other organisms. In doing so, it shall take account of the dignity of living beings as well as the safety of human beings, animals and the environment, and shall protect the genetic diversity of animal and plant species.[66]

---

62. Faryal Mirza, *Helping Animals Speak Up: Switzerland Was the First Country to Give Constitutional Rights to Animals, and So It Seems Fitting that it is Home to the World's One and Only Animal Lawyer,* SWISS NEWS, *available at* http://www.thefreelibrary.com/Helping+animals+speak+up%3A+Switzerland+was+the+first+country+to+give...-a0187622149, (last visited May 25, 2010).
63. Isobel Leybold-Johnson, *Lawyer Lends His Voice to the Animals,* Jan. 25, 2009, http://www.swissinfo.ch/eng/Lawyer_lends_his_voice_to_the_animals.html?cid=979670.
64. Constitution Federal de la Confédération Suisse [Cst] [Constitution] Apr. 18, 1999, SR 101, art. 80 (Switz.) [hereinafter Swiss Constitution].
65. *Id.*
66. *Id.* at art. 120(2).

Within the typology of constitutional provisions discussed earlier, this provision would also appear to be a mandatory/non-prohibitory provision, for it requires the legislature to legislate in a way consistent with the dignity of living beings in the context of the use of reproductive and genetic material from animals and plants; it does not, however, prohibit any particular conduct.[67]

There are additional provisions in the Swiss Constitution that refer to protection of animals, including ones relating to legislation on the use of animals in agriculture and the protection of nature.[68] So what the Swiss Constitution does do is state very clearly that protection of animals is a required subject of regulation. As a consequence, one would expect this to result in legislation to protect animals, and indeed, there has been considerable legislative activity in Switzerland, some of which has been created by referenda. For instance, the Swiss Civil Code now includes a provision created by referendum in 2002, stating that "Animals are not things"; nonetheless the same section also states that measures that apply to things also apply to animals.[69] Since animals are no longer considered "things," this attempts to make clear that provisions that previously applied to animals as things now apply to animals even though they are not now things. This is the same sort of doublespeak on this issue that we have seen before in the German Civil Code. Notwithstanding this provision and those previously discussed in the Swiss Constitution, animals are still used in agriculture, experimentation and entertainment in Switzerland just as they were before; so how are they really not things? The world, including Switzerland, continues to behave as if they are no more than "things."

Apart from this Swiss Civil Code provision there are a number of other areas that have been the subject of legislation consistent with the Swiss Constitutional admonitions. In what can be seen as a family law issue, when there is a dispute in a divorce as to who owns an animal, the court is to grant exclusive ownership to the party who offers the best situation for the animal.[70] Judges are also authorized to take into account the emotional value of a companion animal when such an animal is killed or injured.[71] In 2008, the Swiss Parliament passed legislation requiring educational courses for dog owners and courses for fisherman to teach them to reduce pain to fish caught in angling.[72] In addition, Swiss law now

---

67. *See* Fernandez, *supra* note 29, at 343–45.
68. Swiss Constitution, *supra* note 64, at arts. 78, 104.
69. Code Civil Suisse [Cc] [Civil Code] Oct. 4, 2002, art. 641a (Switz.).
70. *Id.* at art. 651a(1); Swiss Federal Department of Justice and Police, *The Status of Animals*, Oct. 4, 2002 http://www.ejpd.admin.ch/ejpd/en/home/themen/gesellschaft/ref_gesetzgebung/ref_abgeschlossene_projekte0/ref_tiere.html.
71. Code des Obligations Suisse [Co] [Code of Obligations] Oct. 4, 2002, art. 43, al. 1bis (Switz.).
72. Michael Baggot, *Swiss Grant Rights to Animals, Consider the Same for Plants—Liberalize Abortion Laws,* LifeSiteNews.com, Apr. 28, 2008, *available at* http://www.lifesitenews.com/ldn/2008/apr/08042808.html; Bojan Pancevski, *New Swiss Law Protects Rights of "Social" Animals*, Timesonline, http://www.timesonline.co.uk/tol/news/world/europe/article3818457.ece (last visited May 26, 2010).

provides that "social animals," including goldfish, horses and guinea pigs, must be kept in twos, or at least have access to others of their own kind, or else the owner can be determined to be abusing the animal.[73] Farmers are also now prohibited from tethering horses, sheep and goats, and pigs and cows cannot be maintained in areas with hard floors.[74] Switzerland has abandoned proposals to allow ritual slaughter.[75] In one failure for animal interests, a referendum on giving standing to animals which stated "domestic creatures [have] the constitutional right to be represented by human lawyers in court"[76] went down in defeat on March 7, 2010.[77] On April 12, 2010, new legislation was created relating to genetically modified animals and animals used in experimentation.[78] Taking a step further than we have seen elsewhere, a Swiss Federal Government Ethics Committee on non-human biotechnology is looking into the issue of "plant dignity" and the protection of plant dignity.[79]

Switzerland has thus created a great deal of legislation on animal protection issues, a great deal of which relates to species favored by humans. There are, however, other aspects of the Swiss relationship with animals that are puzzling, including the burgeoning trade in cat fur, which explains "a total absence of stray cats" in Switzerland, as well as the reported disappearances of cats in French border areas.[80] So what does all this mean and what is the significance of these constitutional provisions in the Swiss approach to animal issues?

The provisions of the Swiss Constitution, similar to those in Germany, can be seen as a foundation, a starting point and perhaps even a catalyst for attempts to change the human/animal relationship. These constitutional provisions require legislators to legislate on animal protection issues and there has, indeed, been substantial legislative activity on these issues in Switzerland. In addition, the enshrinement of animal interests within the constitution may be seen as giving immediate legitimacy to legislative proposals and public referenda addressing these issues. So perhaps we can see the as yet unmet expectations of future legislative activity arising from enactment of the German Constitutional provision actually occurring (though sometimes successfully and sometimes not) in Swiss animal regulation legislation pursuant to the Swiss Constitution. But given, for example, the long struggle for civil rights and the rights of women in the United States, the objective of freeing animals from the hand of human exploitation may

73. Pancevski, *supra* note 72.
74. *Id.*
75. Haupt 2007, *supra* note 14, at 877–78.
76. Wesley J. Smith, *When Animals Sue*, National Review Online, Mar. 3, 2010, http://article.nationalreview.com/426742/when-animals-sue/wesley-j-smith.
77. World Radio Switzerland, *Voters Reject Pension Cuts, Animal Lawyers,* Mar. 7, 2010, *available at* http://worldradio.ch/wrs/news/switzerland/sunday-march-7-vote-results.shtml?18205.
78. *See* Confédération Suisse, *La Nouvelle Législation Sur la Protection des Animaux*, http://www.bvet.admin.ch/themen/tierschutz/02443/index.html?lang=fr (last visited Oct. 27, 2010).
79. Baggot, *supra* note 72.
80. Pancevski, *supra* note 72.

be a long, long time in coming, even with the benefit of some constitutional recognition of the interests of animals as we see in Switzerland.

A. India

India has a history and culture quite different from those of the Western European countries on which we have concentrated in this chapter. It should not be surprising then that the constitutional approach to animal issues comes from a very different direction in India. The Indian Constitution creates a duty for all citizens of India to have "compassion" for animals: "It shall be the duty of every citizen of India—... to have compassion for living creatures."[81] It also "contains a directive which encourages the prohibition of slaughtering cows."[82] This, of course, is in line with Hindu beliefs relating to cattle.

So what do these constitutional provisions mean in the real world of the law? The compassion provision creates a mandatory duty for every citizen, including those in the government, to behave in a compassionate way toward animals; but neither this duty created in citizens nor the directive on cows prohibit or require any particular conduct. One obvious question is how any very general duty like this mandated duty of compassion could be utilized or enforced? While enforcement in the daily lives of citizens of such a vague duty would seem difficult, if not impossible, the use of the provision in making and bolstering arguments relating to legislation and other laws would seem much more promising. So like the German and Swiss Constitutional provisions, these Indian provisions can at least be used to promote the interests of animals in interpretation of the law and in creation of legislation.

The Indian Constitution, however, goes further than just admonishing its citizens to be compassionate. It also provides access to the courts for those representing the interests of animals. Article 32 of the Indian Constitution effectively grants standing to representatives of animals to bring matters before Indian courts on behalf of animals. This has been recognized in Indian case law, which recognizes the public's right to sue for violations of constitutional provisions:

> In 1981, it was held that: "any member of the public having sufficient interest can maintain an action for public injury arising from breach of public duty or from violation of some provision of the constitution or the law and seek enforcement of such public duty and observance of such constitutional or legal provision. This is absolutely essential for maintaining the rule of law ..." (1981 (4) SCALE 1988 S.P. Gupta V. U.O.I).[83]

81. India Const., art. 51(A)(g).
82. M. Varn Chandola, *Dissecting American Animal Protection Law: Healing the Wounds with Animal Rights and Eastern Enlightenment*, 8 Wis. Envtl. L.J. 3, 28 (2002); *see* India Const., *supra* note 81, at art. 48.
83. Amy Mansfield, *India's Legal Doolittle,* New Zealand Lawyer, June 13, 2008, *available at* http://www.voiceless.org.au/About_Us/Voiceless_in_Print_2008/India_s_Legal_Doolittle.html (quoting Raj Panjwani).

In addition, the constitution protects freedoms of conscience, speech, and life and liberty which we have previously seen can be important in certain contexts involving the treatment of animals.[84]

As in the case of Switzerland, it can be argued that this constitutional provision has had an impact on legislation and, in addition, the behavior of courts. In fact, we have previously seen the use of the compassion provision in arguments made in the *Balakrishnan, et al. v. Union of India* case upholding the ban on use of certain wild animals in circuses in India.[85] Recall that the Indian government banned the use of bears, monkeys, tigers and panthers as performing animals and this ban was challenged in a case where the court ruled that the ban was valid and constitutional:

> The Court ruled that no person has a right to carry on a trade which results in infliction of unnecessary pain and suffering on animals; that exhibiting endangered animals for entertainment was such an obnoxious and pernicious activity which could not fall within the meaning of the word "trade"; that the government ban on the use of the animals in question under the PCA (Notification dt. 14.10.1998) was to enforce the fundamental duty to have compassion, and its impact on the right to trade was merely incidental; and that the right to life includes livelihood, but could not extend to a trade which is injurious to public interest or has an insidious effect on public morals. Obiter, the Court said, "It is not only our fundamental duty to show compassion to our animal friends but also to recognize and protect their rights." (High Court of Kerala: K.R. Nair Vs. U.O.I. O.P. No. 155 of 1999. Decided on June 6, 2000.)[86]

Note as well that it has also been held by an Indian Court that, based on the right to freedom of conscience in the constitution, manufacturers have an obligation to label all relevant products with a symbol indicating whether there are any animal products in the product being sold.[87] So it seems that animal protection interests can arise from several places in the Indian constitutional scheme.

In India, then, a constitutional duty has been created for all Indian citizens to show compassion for animals. While this rather vague duty harbors substantial difficulty, if not impossibility, of enforcement in many contexts, it does create a mandatory/non-prohibitory duty in all Indian citizens and has been successfully used in judicial arguments and opinions to protect the interests of animals. Moreover, it can also be the basis for creating legislation favorable to animal interests.

---

84. India Const., *supra* note 81, at arts. 19, 21, 25. That these sorts of human rights can impact animal treatment issues was previously made evident in the conflict in Germany relating to religious slaughter and the use of animals in art. *See supra* notes 21 to 49 and accompanying text.
85. *See* Ch. 5, *supra* notes 112–125 and accompanying text.
86. Mansfield, *supra* note 83.
87. *Id.*

Unfortunately, as we have seen in the case of other constitutional attempts at enshrining the interests of animals, the abuse of animals in India continues without interruption. Substantial "institutional exploitation of animals, which is in some areas comparable to or even worse than seen in the West" continues in India.[88] "India is a nation that is largely committed to the principle of non-violence, says [Raj] Panjwani. 'It also has possibly the largest vegetarian population. Despite this, animals in India continue to suffer enormously and in staggering numbers even though the Constitution mandates [in Article 51 A(g)] that every citizen have compassion towards all living creatures.'"[89] So the Indian Constitution contains language that sounds impressive and has had some success in protecting animals, but does not at this point in history appear to have much changed the lives of most animals in India.

B. BRAZIL

There is another type of constitutional provision that has recently become in vogue and may have implications for the treatment of animals; these are constitutional strictures relating to the environment. Provisions relating to the environment have been added to the constitutions of some 130 countries, including Argentina, Azerbaijan, Belarus, Cameroon, Croatia, East Timor, Ethiopia, France, Germany, India, Iraq, Macedonia and Panama.[90] Another country that has such a provision is Brazil. Article 225 of the Brazilian Constitution states, in part:

> All have the right to an ecologically balanced environment, which is an asset of common use and essential to a healthy quality of life, and both the Government and the community shall have the duty to defend and preserve it for present and future generations.
>
> Paragraph 1—In order to ensure the effectiveness of this right, it is incumbent upon the Government to:
>
> ...
>
> (VII) protect the fauna and the flora, with prohibition, in the manner prescribed by law, of all practices which represent a risk to their ecological function, cause the extinction of species or subject animals to cruelty.[91]

The language relating to cruelty to animals in Article 225(1)(VII) was added in 1998.[92]

---

88. Chandola, *supra* note 82, at 26.
89. Mansfield, *supra* note 83.
90. James R. May, *Constituting Fundamental Environmental Rights Worldwide*, 23 PACE ENVTL. L. REV. 113, 129, app. A (2006).
91. Constituição Federal (Brazil) *available at* Political Database of the Americas, *Federative Republic of Brazil Constitution, 1988 Constitution, with 1996 Reforms in English*, art. 225, http://pdba.georgetown.edu/Constitutions/Brazil/english96.html.
92. Lane Azvedo Clayton, *Overview of Brazil's Legal Structure for Animal Issues*, ANIMAL LEGAL HIST. CENTER (2003), *available at* http://www.animallaw.info/nonus/articles/ovbrazil.htm.

This article creates duties in both the government and the "community." These entities have the obligation to protect and preserve for present and future generations an ecologically balanced environment. In addition, the government has the duty to protect the flora and fauna from practices that might cause the extinction of species or subject animals to cruelty. In the constitutional typology we have been applying, this provision may differ from the others we have seen and may be viewed as a mandatory/prohibitory provision.[93] Notice that it includes the language "with prohibition," which indicates that practices contrary to the admonitions in the Constitution are prohibited. Again, however, as we have seen in other constitutional provisions on animal issues, this provision may present interpretive difficulties. For instance, it is difficult to imagine precisely how a prohibition on things that pose a risk to the "ecological function" of flora and fauna might be interpreted, nonetheless enforced. Notwithstanding such interpretive difficulties, however, courts in Brazil have used the anti-cruelty rule in this constitutional provision to prohibit practices like cock fighting and the Ox Feast, which involves chasing oxen through the streets while beating them with various weapons.[94] So its prohibitory character does seem to have some force.

Unfortunately, however, "[r]egardless [of the constitutional provision], animal exploitation is a very profitable industry worldwide and it is not different in Brazil."[95] That this is the case may be seen in the reality of animals in Brazil. As in other countries, Brazilian law provides that domestic animals are property.[96] Concomitant to this is that slaughter of and experimentation on this property is not prohibited by the Brazilian Constitution, notwithstanding the requirement to not treat animals cruelly.[97] The requirement to protect against animal cruelty is thought only to prohibit "unnecessary" suffering,[98] a concept seen throughout animal law.

Despite the lack of real restrictions on behavior prohibiting "normal" human conduct relating to animals, Brazil has taken a major step on the issue of standing. A judicial decision in the state of Bahia has determined that a chimpanzee can be a plaintiff in a court case where the interests of the chimp are represented by human surrogates.[99] The creation of judicial standing for the interests of animals is without question an enormous accomplishment should the implications of this case carry over into the future. In addition, Article 225 of the Brazilian Constitution clearly supplies one more legal argument in the quiver of animal rights advocates and the "abolitionist" movement in Brazil, which hopes to end all human subjugation of animals.[100]

93. *See* Fernandez, *supra* note 29, at 341–53.
94. Clayton, *supra* note 92.
95. *Id.*
96. *Id.*
97. *See* Heron Jose de Santana Gordilho, *Wildlife and the Brazilian Abolitionist Movement*, 5 J. ANIMAL L. 71, 81 (2009).
98. *Id.* at 82.
99. *Id.*
100. *See id.* at 82–89.

What the Brazilian constitutional provisions reveal is that there is another strand of recent constitutional activity relevant to animals, which is constitutional provisions relating to the environment. These provisions, one would assume, are typically drafted to protect the natural environment and wild animals; but the Brazilian example goes further than just protecting wild flora and fauna, and purports to protect all animals from cruelty at all times. Unfortunately, most of the same practices that existed before the present constitutional provision, like animal experimentation, slaughter and so on, continue in Brazil notwithstanding the purported constitutional protection afforded by the Brazilian Constitution.

IV. THE ROLE OF CONSTITUTIONS IN THE ANIMAL LAW

One common feature of these constitutional provisions is that they have been created for the most part by countries that have deep cultural predilections toward concern for animals. In India, this predilection stems from a long religious and cultural history of concern for animals over millennia. Germany and Switzerland also have cultural traditions of concern for animals, but these have developed more recently. Brazil, with its vast environmental resources, has also developed a constitutional environmental ethic that includes protection of animals.

Though the provisions themselves differ in significant ways, they are generally of a mandatory/non-prohibitory nature,[101] thus creating duties in the legislature and others to enact legislation or to behave in a recommended way, the latter being the case in the Indian Constitution. The one constitutional scheme that may possibly be seen as going further to create a mandatory/prohibitory measure that actually does prohibit certain conduct with respect to animals is that of Brazil. But what none of them ultimately do, from the perspective of proponents of animal rights and the abolition of exploitation of animals, is prohibit present uses of animals in agriculture, experimentation, or entertainment.

Similarly, they do not create any true rights in animals. Perhaps the closest to creating rights for animals is the Indian Constitution, where there is case law language derived from the constitution indicating that animals do have rights. Although merely stating that animals have rights does not make it so, the additional aspect of the Indian Constitution allowing representatives to assert the interests of animals in court does create a ready-made mechanism for the interests of animals, both collectively and individually, to be considered by the judiciary. We do not, however, see the required constitutional compassion carried out in practice in India in any systematic way, and the treatment of animals in India is still quite bad. So notwithstanding these initial forays into including animal protection provisions in constitutions, the abuse of animals continues in agriculture,

101. *See* Fernandez, *supra* note 29, at 343–49.

experimentation and entertainment in the countries having constitutional provisions.

What can we expect in the future? It is unlikely that placing animal-related provisions in constitutions will end at this stage; other countries, including Portugal and Italy, have debated, but as yet have not passed, constitutional provisions relating to the treatment of animals. Indeed, the few constitutional provisions discussed here may be the beginning of a trend toward inclusion of such provisions in constitutions. The disappointing truth, however, is that thus far it is hard to see that they have caused much impact in the real world, and so it is easy to view them as hortatory statements that mask the continued torture, slaughter and abuse of animals. But I think that ultimately they can further change in the human/animal relationship by providing both a foundation for arguing for legal transformations that prohibit present uses of animals, as well as a vital motivating force and impetus for change. Whether these constitutional tools will lead to substantial and important modifications to the status quo is a question largely unanswered at this time based on the relatively recent enactment of these provisions. It is possible though that they are a step in the direction of actual change in the treatment of animals and, if the human race manages to last long enough, perhaps even one day will lead to legal rights for animals.

Chapter 9

Past, Present and Future

I. FROM THE PERSONAL TO THE GLOBAL

In Chapter 1, I discussed some of the ways the relationship between humans and animals has changed over the course of history. What we noticed was that this relationship and the uses made of animals by humans have progressed away from relationships and uses that closely connect most humans to animals. We have moved through history away from having the personal relationships we experienced with animals in hunter-gatherer societies, to ever more attenuated relationships in agrarian societies and more recently, in the global economy.

In the world of the hunter-gatherer, the animals humans ordinarily encountered and used were wild ones that most humans typically saw, captured, touched, skinned, dressed, or prepared. Animals and humans were face to face. In what I called the "local" world, an agrarian society, most humans took a step back in their relationship with the animals they used. While on occasion they might have obtained a live animal for use as food, this animal was usually not a wild one that they had pursued and caught, but rather one that had been tamed, genetically modified and husbanded for profit by someone else. But at this point in human history it was also possible to patronize restaurants and have others do the dirty work of butchering and preparing animal products, and this is therefore what some people did for income. In this world, though, humans still had a fairly close relationship with the animals they ate or otherwise used. Commerce was generally local, and the animals humans ate were from just down the road or from the market in the square. It would be difficult, if not impossible, to not know in this particular slice of human history that one was actually eating a part of a cow when enjoying a steak.

In more recent history, however, most humans have taken a giant leap, not just a further step, away from the animals they use. As I discussed in Chapter 1, for example, in the present globalized economy, it is possible for an intelligent and sensitive child of nine to not fully comprehend that they are eating a dead animal when that is what they are systematically fed. We accomplish this marvelous feat of deception in a number of ways. The animals we eat, experiment on and use for entertainment are generally quite distant from us in our day-to-day lives. We do not interact with them at all and, except in the case of animals used for entertainment purposes, do not even see the animal while it is alive. Indeed, given the treatment to which many animals are subjected in the globalized world, it is in the interest of the industries involved in animal use that the public does not see the torture and carnage that occurs. We also hide ugly reality by giving innocuous names to animal food like "beef" or "veal" which conceal the true nature of the food and the processes by which it is made. So in this globalized economy, considerable distance is maintained between humans and their use of animals, and numerous linguistic and other barriers have been deliberately constructed to further separate humans from the reality of their use of animals.

This alteration of the relationship between humans and animals from an initially personal one to a currently global one has distanced and alienated humans from animals in a number of identifiable ways. The most obvious way is geographic: there is a historical progression of greater and greater distances between humans and the sources of their food and the other activities done on their behalf with animals. The animals that most people in the developed world eat are those that have been factory farmed in huge operations generally isolated from most humans' experience. In entertainment, there are circuses that travel across continents to perform and exhibitions, aquariums and "safaris" for which people travel thousands of miles, while the cruel training and confinement practices that result in the shows they enthusiastically applaud occurs far from their sight. Animal experimentation is tucked discretely behind locked doors, often on an industrial street or rural road where people rarely venture.

Another way humans are separated from their use of animals related to this geographic distance is what one might describe as "perceptual distance." This perceptual distance is caused by the fact that typically people are not likely to observe what is done to animals to transform them to food, or to provide pharmaceuticals, cosmetics or even animal shows, like SeaWorld or Ringling Brothers Circus.[1] There are good reasons for the existence of this perceptual distance. The political and economic interests behind factory farming, animal experimentation and animal entertainment do not, for obvious reasons, want what they are doing in secret to be seen. So they construct a perceptual wall, protected by the law, between their operations and the public to ensure that the conditions of factory-farmed animals and of animals used in experiments and entertainment are not revealed to the public. Slaughterhouses, feedlots and factory egg operations are generally kept out of view of most of the public. Animal experiments are done

1. In the case of animal use in entertainment, the customers obviously see and sometimes even interact in one way or another with the animals used, but the manner in which the animals were obtained, housed and trained is hidden from view.

behind closed doors in untraveled areas. The training of circus animals and their day-to-day lives are hidden somewhere outside the walls of the circus tent.

And the law supports this by creating strictures which prevent the public from learning about the atrocities performed on animals on their behalf and presumably for their benefit. Trespassing on the premises of slaughterhouses, feedlots, animal experimentation labs and other locations where these atrocities occur will land you in jail. Not only this, but in the United States and other places there are laws that protect animal experimenters from "harassment." Worse yet, violators of laws of this kind are often branded as "terrorists." Try to get information on animal experiments? Forget it. Intellectual property, trade secrets and other laws protect the industry from having to reveal much meaningful information as we observed in the new European Directive on animal experimentation. These laws can also be used to protect the practices of those who use animals in agriculture and entertainment. Methods of operation, experimental procedures, training methods and other processes may all be protected by these laws. As a result, we observe that human society has formalized in the law the perceptual distance between humans and animals; it is not just a coincidence of how these industries have historically developed; it is something that has been consciously created and fostered by the political and economic interests behind animal use industries for the purpose of keeping people from knowing the often horrifying practices and conditions that are the trademark of these industries.

Further examples lend additional support to the concept that maintaining perceptual distance between humans and the reality of their use of animals is a result of deliberate efforts by the economic and other interests that profit from animal use, including politicians. Some industries want to show off what they do. One of these industries is the beer industry. For example, Busch Gardens in Tampa Bay, Florida is a large amusement park, which features, by the way, wild animals in, among other things, an "Endangered Species Safari," as well as what are called "Experiences" involving tigers, elephants and orangutans.[2] This amusement park was purposely created as a monument to the Busch product and is effectively a marketing tool in addition to a presumably money making entertainment operation. Other examples across the Atlantic include the "Heineken Experience" in Amsterdam, a much less tawdry museum about the making of beer, and the Guinness Storehouse in Dublin, which showcases the history of Guinness products and features a "gravity bar." Thankfully, the latter two operations have nothing to do with animals. So some beer manufacturers manage to come up with marketing experiences for consumers that do not exploit animals, but Busch is not among them.

Imagine, if you will, a world where the meat industry creatively pushes its product as the beer industry has done. What would we think of something like "Smithfield Foods Meatland," an amusement park themed upon the business of

2. Busch Gardens, http://www.buschgardens.com/Bgt/Explore/UpClose.aspx?id=740 (last visited Sept. 2, 2010). It is interesting (ironic) that this beer company could not manage to put together an entertainment park with marketing overtones without using animals.

Smithfield Foods, a major United States meat producer that calls itself a "global food company" producing among other things, pork and turkey products.[3] Such an amusement park might provide rides like "The Conveyor" which would take you on a ride in which you are suspended upside down by one leg with knives suddenly appearing to slash at your throat. Or perhaps the "Blackbox," which would simulate a turkey production facility where you are stuffed into a poorly lit room of immense proportions with thousands of other people for perhaps four hours with no room to move around or a restroom. Would you like to visit such a place and enjoy these "rides"? Obviously not. So unlike beer companies, Smithfield Foods is unlikely to create an amusement park describing its business and it is quite improbable that anyone would wish to pay for this experience or the stark and frightening education that it would provide.

The point is that factory farming and slaughtering of animals, as well as torturing them in experiments or training, is wildly unpleasant under any circumstances, and anyone in the business of doing these things is not going to allow the public to see and know what they are doing if they can avoid it. But the public is not without any responsibility for the existence of the perceptual wall between people and their use of animals. The saying "ignorance is bliss" is not an empty platitude;[4] it is a thread that is woven through most people's lives in numerous areas of supposed concern, such as poverty, famine, environmental degradation and, of course, the treatment of animals. It is convenient for humans, so long as we are not impoverished or starving, living on a toxic waste site or incessantly faced with the suffering of animals in agriculture and other uses, to not see or concern ourselves with the plight of others. It is possible for us, who are not directly experiencing these things, to emotionally and psychologically bury any possible concerns about these practices, so long as they are kept at a distance.

I know this from personal experience. For a substantial part of my life I ate meat and enjoyed it. It is not that I didn't know what I was eating or that there were undoubtedly horrible consequences for animals because of my choices. All of this I certainly knew. And it is not that I didn't care. In fact, I recall that in the back of my mind as an adult meat eater there was always a feeling that what I was doing was wrong. It was convenient and easy for me ignore what I knew was happening because I never had to experience it. I left what I knew to be the facts in the back of my mind for years before actually bringing them to the fore and addressing them. So the perceptual distance between humans and the treatment of animals in a global civilization is not built just by corporate interests trying to protect their businesses; we consciously take advantage of that distance by erecting our own perceptual curtains as a defense to experiencing all the unpleasantness visited on animals in the world. We choose not to see what is really happening; so some of

3. Smithfield Foods, http://www.smithfieldfoods.com/our_company/about_us.aspx (last visited June 27, 2010).
4. On the "blissful" unawareness of Americans about the origins of their food, see David Kirby, Animal Factory 405 (St. Martin's Press 2010).

the bricks in the perceptual wall between humans and their treatment of animals are laid by us.

One result of this perceptual distance between humans and the fates of animals that is illustrated by my personal example is the realization that there is also a "psychological distance" between humans and animals in a globalized world economy. A result of not perceiving what happens to animals in our world is that most humans do not participate emotionally or psychologically in the use of animals anymore. Humans are emotionally and psychologically insulated from their own animal use. In hunter-gatherer societies, we either killed, skinned, dressed, or prepared the bounty of a successful hunt. Or, at the very least, we observed some or all of these things occurring. Similarly, even in the local agrarian world, at some point in my day I would likely observe activities of these kinds. In these societies we were exposed to the practices surrounding the use of animals and had no choice other than to react to and emotionally process them. Here "seeing is emotional connection."

But in a globalized world, most of us have no emotional or psychological involvement in the uses that we make of animals.[5] We do not need to feel the hopelessness of cattle crowded into a filthy, stinking feedlot, to experience the terror and struggling of pigs as they take their final walk into the slaughterhouse, or to empathize with convulsing rats used in LD50 tests. If there actually were such a place as Smithfield Foods Meatland or an animal experimentation amusement park, perhaps called Taub's World of Deafferentation, I think that the world of agricultural and experimental animals might be substantially different or it might not even exist at all. If the public actually knew and were to experience the conditions of these animals, I believe that the public would at least demand changes in the legal status quo, if not the end of some of these practices.

As I have stated before, the impact of public knowledge on the law in these areas might be greater in the area of animal experimentation and entertainment than in agriculture. For instance, a great deal of animal experimentation can be cogently shown to be repetitive and scientifically unnecessary, and the public might find it easy to say that these practices should end. Similarly, do we really need dancing elephants? These are things on which many would agree. On the other hand, to persuade people to stop eating meat or even to pay more for agricultural products so that animals in agriculture will just be treated better is likely to be a rather more difficult sale to the public, since here, unlike in the areas of animal experiments or entertainment, we see immediate and demonstrable benefit to our own selfish interests relating to what we like to eat. Indeed, we see it about three times a day. But nonetheless, education and dissemination of information on

---

5. I am not the only one to note this. It has been said, for example, that "[i]t can be argued, indeed, that as modern man knows less and less of the forests, the stream margins and meadows, or the psyches of the commonest farm animals, our sensitivity to the world of nature is probably less than it has ever been in recorded history." Gerald Carson, MEN, BEASTS, AND GODS 139 (Charles Scribner's Sons 1972).

all of these subjects is something that is certainly worth the effort. Some of us are surely able to be moved by the facts.

These geographic, perceptual and psychological walls I have described create the structure on which what I will call "moral distance" is placed. Because most people are separated by a sea of geographic, perceptual and psychological distance from their use of animals, it is easy for them to not even comprehend that moral issues exist here, or to rationalize that animals are treated well in farming and experimentation, or to think that there are strict regulations on the way animals are treated in these uses, or to find some other manufactured moral imperative to justify their uses of animals as morally sound. For example, not knowing the facts, people can structure their moral world with propositions like, "it is moral to eat meat because animal welfare is well guarded in the production of meat." This kind of thought process is encouraged by a traditional "Old McDonald's Farm" view of the world which tells us that farming is done in a peaceful pastoral setting with happy animals wandering carefree around green pastures. If you do not make an effort to inform yourself of what is really happening in the world, it is a view that is easy to adopt. A lack of knowledge about and involvement in the way animals are actually treated to provide meat, cosmetics, pharmaceuticals and other products, not to mention entertainment, creates the moral distance that allows many people to make what are really uninformed moral choices.

And these views about the uses of animals are naturally and unsurprisingly encouraged by those in the industries that use animals. For instance, fast food giants like McDonalds, Kentucky Fried Chicken and others, tout their animal welfare standards. There is, however, a more sinister side to the information propounded by the economic interests involved in animal use than this kind of self-congratulation and marketing; those who vigorously argue for the present factory farming, experimental and other uses of animals often characterize those opposed to the use of animals as being "against" humans. Those who are opposed to the use of animals want to prevent the creation of life saving drugs and plan to change the worlds' diet to an unnatural and unhealthy vegetarian one. Here we witness dualism at work: the human/animal dualism is raised and is presented from the perspective of opposition of human and animal interests; there is something irreconcilable between the interests of animals and those of humans.[6]

This fabricated human/animal battle is, of course, not actually the case since, for example, a vegetarian or vegan lifestyle proves to be healthier than the typical meat eater's lifestyle:

> [c]hoosing a nonvegetarian lifestyle has a significant health and medical cost. The total direct medical costs in the United States attributable to meat consumption were estimated to be $30–60 billion a year, based upon the higher

6. The issue of dualism is discussed in Chapter 2 in connection with Feminist philosophy.

prevalence of hypertension, heart disease, cancer, diabetes, gallstones, obesity and food-borne illness among omnivores compared with vegetarians.[7]

This is not just the ranting of a group of vegetarian nuts. In fact, "[o]ver 200 studies have revealed that a regular consumption of fruits and vegetables provides significant protection against cancer at many sites."[8] A British study found consumption of fresh fruit resulted in a 24% decrease in heart disease mortalities and a 32% decrease in cerebrovascular disease.[9] Another study shows that lifelong vegetarians have a whopping 57% lower incidence of coronary disease.[10] Fruit and vegetable consumption also has been shown to reduce the incidence of stroke and eating nuts and whole grains is associated with lower diabetes rates.[11] Just a few other health benefits of a vegan lifestyle from a list that I could extend far beyond what I include here: lower cholesterol, lower blood pressure, lower levels of breast cancer, prevention of cataracts and macular degeneration, alleviation of arthritis, preventing osteoporosis, reducing weight and so on.[12] To place a bottom line on this, on average, vegetarians live from three to six years longer than their meat-eating counterparts.[13]

And this is not even to mention the monumental negative environmental impact of the use of animals in agriculture in terms of air and water pollution, and land use. Meat eating contributes substantially to greenhouse gases; massive amounts of pollution are caused by the excrement flowing from factory farms; and about one-third of the land on earth is committed to raising meat. Jonathan Safran Foer, in his recent book, *Eating Animals* states that the "$140 billion-plus a year industry that occupies nearly a third of the land on the planet[] [and] shapes ocean ecosystems [] may well determine the future of the earth's climate."[14] Here are just some of the negative environmental impacts of the agricultural use of animals:[15]

– Animal waste produced yearly by farming operations in the United States is more than one ton for every resident and animal feeding operations create 100 times the waste of all of the sewage treatment plants in the country. This animal waste is typically kept in what are called "lagoons." But do not envision anything involving a tropical paradise or Brooke Shields. These lagoons are nothing but "digging a hole and putting crap in it."[16]

---

7. *Health Benefits of Vegetarian Diets*, http://www.vegetarian-nutrition.info/updates/vegetarian_diets_health_benefits.php (last visited Oct. 13, 2010) (emphasis omitted).
8. *Id.*
9. *Id.*
10. *Id.*
11. *Id.*
12. *57 Health Benefits of Going Vegan*, http://www.nursingdegree.net/blog/19/57-health-benefits-of-going-vegan/ (last visited Oct. 13, 2010).
13. *Id.*
14. Jonathan Safran Foer, Eating Animals 32 (Back Bay Books 2009).
15. Kirby, *supra* note 4, at xv, 69, 72, 73.
16. *Id.* at 69.

- Human waste is treated to kill pathogens; not so with animal waste. To make matters worse, consider that hog manure has from "ten to one hundred times more concentrated pathogens than human waste."[17]
- This manure can also contain things like heavy metals, antibiotics, drug resistant bacteria and hormones that can cause human health problems as well as endanger wildlife.
- The largest source of well water contamination in the United States is agricultural waste.
- Feedlot odors have been found to include 170 different chemicals many of which cause numerous types of human diseases.
- Agricultural animals used for meat create massive amounts of greenhouse gases. The precise level of greenhouse gases produced by these animals is, however, subject to some dispute. According to a 2006 United Nations report, livestock accounts for about 18% of all greenhouse gas emissions in the world, more than the amount created by transportation.[18] This figure is now the subject of controversy and the United Nations has indicated that the report was "flawed."[19] Nonetheless, no one disputes that the greenhouse gases produced by agricultural animals used for meat is very substantial. For example, animal manure constitutes 7.4% of all greenhouse gases in the United States.[20]
- Gases from these operations can also create "nitrogen rain" and can contribute to acid rains that damages wildlife habitats and the environment generally.[21] These gases can change cloud chemistry resulting in acid mists that have been seen in Europe.

To sum this up, we can turn to the Pew Commission on Industrial Farm Animal Production which is a project of The Pew Charitable Trusts and the Johns Hopkins Bloomberg School of Public Health which created an extensive report on factory farming called *Putting Meat on the Table: Industrial Farm Animal Production in America*.[22] In a press release relating to this report the Pew Commission simply states that factory farming poses "unacceptable risks to public health, the environment, and the welfare of animals."[23]

It should also be pointed out that there is a very definite connection between violence against animals and violence against humans. Indeed, serial killers almost

---

17. *Id.* at xv.
18. Simon Fairlie, *A Load of Hot Air?*, GUARDIAN, Jan. 30, 2008, http://www.sustdev.org/index.php?option=com_content&task=view&id=2412&Itemid=34.
19. *Id.*
20. KIRBY, *supra* note 4, at 73.
21. *Id.* at 72–73.
22. Pew Commission on Industrial Farm Animal Production, *Putting Meat on the Table: Industrial Farm Animal Production in America* (2008), *available at* http://www.ncifap.org/bin/e/j/PCIFAPFin.pdf.
23. KIRBY, *supra* note 4, at 405 (quoting a Press Release from the Pew Commission).

always have begun their violence on animals.[24] Those who abuse animals are five times as likely to commit violent crimes as those who have not abused animals.[25] So there really is not a battle between those who support humans and those who support animals. The interests of humans and animals actually coincide.

These facts actually provide important support for the feminist perspective on these issues; this entire dualistic phantom of a battle between the interests of humans and animals can be viewed as nothing but an artifact of the constant conflict engendered by a male-dominated culture which views relationships in the world as incessantly in conflict. But we observe quite the contrary. As can be seen from just the few facts stated above, there is a real alignment between the interests of animals and the interests of humans in terms of health, the environment and crime. And who do you suppose would be arguing contrary to all of this? Could it be other than the economic interests that promote the present milieu?

In the same way, it is often said by those involved in the experimentation community that following the views of those opposed to animal experimentation will negatively impact the health of humans. But again, even animal experimentation which could be argued to be useful in creating life saving drugs or protecting us from dangerous chemicals is extraordinarily wasteful given the enormous economic resources expended in repetitive and ill-designed experimentation. And in the case of animals in entertainment, it simply does not seem possible that most people would support this industry if they knew of the cruelty and suffering behind the pleasant façade of performing elephants and acrobatic killer whales. But accurate information on the treatment of animals in these industries is not widely disseminated. The picture of animal welfare and animal rights advocates as "nuts" and terrorists is a far more prevalent image presented to the public. This image allows people to dismiss those who oppose the use of animals in agriculture, experimentation and entertainment as radical crackpots, and to ignore the facts and arguments presented by animal advocates. So a lack of accurate information and reasoned discourse about animal treatment issues contributes to a moral distance from issues relating to animals which allows most of the public to feel comfortable in their ignorant bliss about the moral decisions they make concerning animals or to comfortably ignore the moral issue altogether.

Perhaps the most fundamental reason that we find ourselves so separated from our true relationship with animals is that we have hired agents to perform the "dirty work" that must be performed to "process" animals for our use. It is easy to maintain moral distance in our relationship with animals because we do not actually have to perform the acts necessary to put food in our refrigerators, or pharmaceuticals in our medicine cabinet, or trained seals on our stages; we have agents who perform these acts. Think of the moral dilemma in which many people would be placed if, when they ordered chicken at a restaurant, they were presented with a

---

24. *See Animal Cruelty Points to Potential Violence Against Humans*, http://www.sniksnak.com/ac/connection.html (last visited Oct. 13, 2010).
25. *Cruelty Connections*, http://www.pet-abuse.com/pages/abuse_connection.php (last visited Oct. 13, 2010).

live chicken and a knife, and were told that they would need to slaughter it to have their meal. How many people would do it? I suspect that few would. But the person who orders the chicken is just as responsible for its slaughter whether they do it themselves or they hire an agent to do it. Again, any first-year law student or, for that matter, people in general recognize that one is responsible for what one's agent does. Notwithstanding this fact though, it is easy to ignore the moral implications of your acts if you do not have the opportunity to experience them yourself and can insert an anonymous third person to perform the morally problematic act.

So what we are presented with in our globalized world is a seemingly impenetrable gulf between most humans and the animals they use, and this gulf separates humans physically, emotionally, psychologically and morally from their uses of animals. And notice too that as the distance between humans and their uses of animals increases, as the alienation of humans from their uses of animals mounts, the level of exploitation of animals increases. As we have been transformed from hunter-gatherers to farmers, to cogs in a global economy, the volume and speed of animal exploitation has increased.

So how can this gulf be crossed and the distance and alienation between humans and their uses of animals be spanned so that we realize what we are doing and can address the real moral issues that we have created? It is obvious that we will never go back to a local or personal sort of relationship with animals, so one important way forward is with education of the public on what our uses of animals actually entail. To educate, however, requires accurate and complete information. Though obtaining correct information is indispensible in this effort, it is frequently difficult since information often does not exist or, even if it does, it may be proprietary or otherwise protected from disclosure. And in this effort toward education, animal activists are opposed by multi-billion dollar industries whose obvious interest is to protect against dissemination of this information. So education of the public on these issues is not only of great importance, but is also a daunting, but I continue to hope, not insurmountable task.

II. GLOBAL REGULATION OF THE TREATMENT OF ANIMALS

A. The Nature of the Regulations

It cannot be denied that the economic world has become globally intertwined and the speed and volume of communication, transport and business activity has increased exponentially over a relatively short period of time. In this ever accelerating world, the use of animals has, like many other activities, not surprisingly also increased substantially. Given this, what legal approaches are being followed to regulate this ever escalating use of animals?

One thing that is evident from review of the regulations of different countries and other entities is that laws purporting to protect animals are generally of relatively recent vintage, beginning only about 200 years ago, with most regulation of animal issues occurring in the last 50 or so years. The movement toward regulation of the treatment of animals began in individual countries or, in some cases, even municipalities, but the treatment of animals has now become an issue discussed and, in a few instances, regulated on a global basis.

What we have discovered about the nature of these regulations is that as a general rule we require that animals used for human benefit not be subjected to "unnecessary" pain or suffering, or some standard to this effect. To this end, the regulations that we see purport to protect the welfare of animals by mandating that animals used be provided with things like housing constructed in a certain fashion, space sufficient for certain minimal levels of movement, proper and healthy exercise, feeding and nutrition, veterinary care and pain management, appropriate use of equipment, transportation guidelines and supposedly "humane" methods of slaughter. So the regulations that we generally see are those which effectively make the prisoners' lives and deaths somewhat more bearable. We do not often see the exploitative practices ended; we only see them continued in allegedly more pleasant forms.

On occasion, however, we actually do observe the end of certain exploitive practices altogether. This we have seen in the recent bans on use of certain types of animals in experiments and on use of certain animals in entertainment.

B. Moral Theory and Global Regulation of the Use of Animals

Peter Singer has been remarkably successful in bringing issues of animal treatment to public consciousness beginning with his 1970s book, *Animal Liberation*. His brand of utilitarianism would require most of us to radically change our behavior and reevaluate our lifestyles. It is ironic then to observe that in nearly all of the laws one encounters relating to the treatment of animals, the policies and strictures of these laws purport to be based on what can be characterized as utilitarian analysis.

For instance, the EU Directives and Regulations we have reviewed almost universally state as their foundations the balancing of economic and competitive concerns against interests of animal welfare. In the area of regulation of animal experiments, we see provisions that require a weighing of the likely value of the experiment against the suffering to be inflicted on animals in the experiment. And whether explicit or not, in regulating the use of animals in agriculture we observe the weighing of human culinary, cultural and historical values against the harm inflicted on animals.

So if we were to attach any moral theory to the present regulation of animal use on earth it would be the utilitarian theory that seems to fit. This is not to say that utilitarians like Peter Singer would agree with the results of the weighing of interests reflected in these laws; I suspect that they would find many reasons to reject the purported analysis that underlies these laws. One might say that the interests of animals were not given appropriate weight, or that the value to humans of the activities involved was greatly overemphasized. Nonetheless, the analysis underlying these laws is, at least in procedure, utilitarian in nature. And this once again reveals one of the problems noted in Chapter 2 about utilitarianism: there is no objective way to measure "utility" in any particular case and so there is an ad hoc nature to the theory. One can argue that another person's utility calculation is faulty, but one cannot prove it.

Finding feminist moral theory in the regulation of animal use is a difficult task. While one suspects that some of the laws created to protect animals are at least in part based on compassion, empathy and caring, finding this explicitly stated is a rarity. Nonetheless, we do see in the Indian Constitution, *e.g.*, an explicit duty in citizens to be compassionate toward animals. Also laws that purport to recognize the "inherent" or other value of animals may be seen as giving a nod to feminist views on compassion and empathy. But there is surely no systematic consideration of feminist theory in the construction of animal treatment regulations.

Another moral theory that we do not find expressed, or at least very rarely, is "rights theory" of the kind espoused by Tom Regan. We simply do not presently view animals as beings who are entitled to rights. Even provisions placed in constitutions to protect animals or recognize their "inherent" value do not go so far. It is possible, however, that this may be changing, since it can be argued that the movement toward banning the uses of certain animals in a number of contexts is one that attacks the property status of animals and can be viewed as a step toward granting rights to at least some animals. This we see in bans on the use of some, or in the case of Bolivia, all animals in circuses and in bans on experimenting on certain types of animals. If the use of an animal in a particular context is prohibited, one can contend that its status as property in this context has been altered and it has therefore been granted a right to be free of a particular category of oppression. Everyone subject to the law has a duty to refrain from the activity in question, regardless of how humanely it might be done.

Of course, the concept of what a "right" actually entails is a thorny one and it could be contended that laws of these kinds do not yet rise to the level of creating rights. A prohibition on one type of oppression, such as being used in a circus, does not necessarily prohibit other sorts of oppression. For example, presumably a cow in Bolivia can still be used for food or the production of milk; it just cannot be used in a circus. Can so incomplete and restricted a protection of bodily security be termed a "right"? We could also ask how the right is to be enforced; can an animal enforce this right? Moreover, with respect to laws that prohibit the use of some kinds of animals and not others, in what sense can we say that progress has been made in animal rights if the prohibition simply results in other types of animals being used?

In this regard, the ideas of Gary Francione on incremental legislative action which can be considered to effectively move in the direction of ending the property status of animals and creating animal rights are useful in addressing the efficacy of these measures. In his book *Rain Without Thunder*, he proposed a set of criteria for incremental change which moves toward abolition of the use of animals, rather than simply promoting the "welfare" of animals that are continued to be kept and used as property.[26] These criteria are outlined in an article he wrote after *Rain Without Thunder* where he identifies the issue as the following:

> In order for incremental change to be a step in the direction of abolition rather than marching in place within the property paradigm, it is necessary to identify measures that explicitly and progressively recognize that nonhumans have more than extrinsic or conditional value alone .... The idea [in *Rain Without Thunder*] was to identify regulations that, although not abolishing property status altogether, went well beyond the efficient exploitation of traditional welfare and rejected the status of animals as commodities through the explicit recognition that nonhumans have inherent value and interests that must be protected irrespective of economic consequences ...[27]

He then proposes the following as criteria to be followed in identifying actions that can be seen as attacking the property status of animals and recognizing the inherent value of animals:

> Briefly summarized, these criteria involve prohibitions of significant institutional activities, as opposed to traditional welfarist regulation requiring "humane" treatment or relatively minor prohibitions. For example, a prohibition on the use of any leghold trap is to be preferred over a requirement that any trapping be done "humanely." or with the use of a "padded" leghold trap. A prohibition on the use of any animals in a particular type of experiment is to be preferred over a requirement of an animal-care committee to monitor the treatment of animals used in experiments ....
>
> Moreover, the incremental change must protect interests beyond those necessary in order to exploit the animal in an efficient way ... and should be explicitly promoted as recognizing that nonhumans have interests that are not tradable or able to be ignored merely because humans will benefit from doing so. These criteria together involve the recognition that animals have interests apart from those necessary to protect in order to exploit them, and value that is not exclusively extrinsic or conditional. Finally animal advocates should never be in a position of promoting an alternative, more "humane" or "better" form of exploitation, or substituting one species for another. Any incremental legislative or regulatory measure ought to be accompanied by an unrelenting and clear call for the abolition of all institutionalized exploitation.[28]

Francione goes on to identify several measures that he believes would meet these criteria, including "a prohibition on the use animals in a particular sort of experiment, such as a ban on the use of all animals in psychological experiments" or a ban on the "use of one species of animal ... if it were not based on any supposed moral

26. Gary L. Francione, Rain Without Thunder 190–219 (Temple University Press 1996).
27. Gary L. Francione, *Reflections on Animals, Property, and the Law and Rain without Thunder*, 70 WTR Law & Contemp. Probs. 9, 45 (2007).
28. *Id.* at 45–46.

superiority of that particular species or if no other species were proposed as an alternative."[29] Since the bans on uses of various animals in circuses is not based on the moral superiority of those animals, the bans appear to meet these criteria, assuming that no other animals are intended to be used as replacements. In the case of Bolivia, at least, this is clearly met. On the issue of the emerging bans on uses of apes in experimentation, these bans do not seem to meet the criteria, because they are based on the close relationship of apes to humans and, thus, on a form of moral superiority. It is also not clear whether the bans will result in other animals being used in place of apes and these bans sometimes allow exceptions for experiments on apes in certain circumstances.

Having said all of this though, regardless of whether the measures meet a particular set of criteria, I think it difficult to deny that these steps toward prohibition are at the very least nascent strides in challenging the property status of animals, are moving toward ending certain sorts of exploitation of animals and, perhaps, ultimately even the recognition of rights in animals. If we came to a time when the collected individual prohibitions on uses of animals encompassed all uses of animals, then we could confidently say that animals had rights. So this slow shuffling toward prohibitions of certain uses of animals may be a hopeful sign for similar and broader bans in the future.

C. Global Economic Marketplace for Animals

There are a number of forces that shape the regulation of the uses of animals in our global marketplace. We have seen that as technology and culture have changed so have our uses of animals. In the globalized economy, given that animals are property, our uses of animals have developed primarily into economic activities and it is the economic interests behind these activities that are, in my view, the primary forces which now drive how animals are used in the world. These economic activities are not generally run by small local producers, as was the case in earlier agrarian societies; rather, much of the exploitation of animals today is in the control of giant, often multinational, corporations. While we might see occasional oases where the use of animals does not seem to be driven by the massive economic inertia of multinational corporations, even in small operations we see factory-like conditions and much money to be made in businesses like the many puppy mills in the United States. And in sales of other animals like corals and other wild animals, areas where smaller businesses exist, there are still substantial and influential economic interests here—witness the rejection of the listing of pink and red coral under Appendix II of CITES in 2010 as a result of economic pressure.

In numerous areas of animal use the economic power of those involved in the exploitation of animals is quite evident; the food industry includes enormous multinational corporations involved in producing, distributing and retailing animal

29. *Id.*

products. A great deal of meat production is done by large corporations like the American companies Smithfield Foods, Tyson Foods, Cargill and Swift & Co. The United States meat packing industry is notoriously concentrated in just a few large corporations.[30] As an example, in the United States, two percent of United States livestock facilities raise 40% of all animals.[31] This industry concentration has even led to protests by farmers over the low prices being paid by these giant corporations for meat and other agricultural products.[32] This meat industry concentration is not just an American phenomenon; there has, *e.g.*, been considerable recent concern about these issues in the Philippines.[33]

It is not just that the meat production industry is concentrated in a few hands. There is also vertical integration of these industries.[34] These large corporations do not just raise and slaughter agricultural animals. They also have distribution networks for their products and their own retail brands.[35] They have the animal product food industry in their control from top to bottom. This was recognized in the Pew Report discussed earlier which called for more market competition in the industry.[36]

Most people would probably be amazed that not only do these mega-agricultural corporations have concentrated and integrated control over the meat industry, they also get government subsidies to do it. For instance, over $35 billion in animal feed subsidies were paid to factory farming operations in the United States between 1997 and 2005.[37] Millions have also been paid to these corporations by the government for anti-pollution activities.[38] Government subsidies are not the only way that the true economic costs of the use of animals in agriculture are being paid unknowingly by the public. Environmental costs and other externalities exist that are not included in the price of animal products:

> According to critics, the CAFO [factory farming] model appears to be efficient, but that is only because important costs "are not reflected in either the cost of the production system or its products, but are instead paid for by the public in other ways." Such "externalities" might include declining property values, the public health costs of pollution, the cost of fighting infections, and the cost of cleanup of spills and other environmental disasters.[39]

---

30. Kirby, *supra* note 4, at xiv; *see also* Tom Philpott, *If Deals Go Through, Three Firms Will Own 90 Percent of the U.S. Beef Market*, Mar. 5, 2008, http://www.grist.org/article/meat-wagon-beef-behemoth/.
31. Kirby, *supra* note 4.
32. Meat Industry Internet News Service, *Canadian Farmers Protest Low Commodity Prices*, http://www.spcnetwork.com/mii/1999/990708.htm (last visited Aug. 23, 2010).
33. MeatIndustry.com, *PAMPI: Meat Processors Wary as Monopoly Looms*, July 10, 2010, http://www.meatindustry.org/asia/pampi-meat-processors-wary-as-monopoly-looms—1172010/.
34. Kirby, *supra* note 4, at xiv.
35. *Id.*
36. *See id.* at 410.
37. *Id.* at 403.
38. *Id.*
39. *Id.* at 408.

So while the true costs of the agricultural animal industry are hidden from the public, the industry makes billions, not just from sales of products, but from taxpayers who subsidize these giant multinational companies.

This economic power of the meat industry translates into a lot of marketing money spent on media coverage to promote their products. And so these products are relentlessly promoted, regardless of resultant animal treatment or health implications. The continuation, or actually, the expansion of the exploitation of animals, is in the economic interest of these entities. In fact, there are legal fiduciary duties in those running these corporations to maximize their profit which, of course, means the continuation and expansion of present practices. It is interesting too how cleverly these products are promoted in different places in the world. In France in the summer of 2010, for example, McDonalds had an advertising campaign which loudly touted that McDonalds' food products in France were produced in France. The buns, the meat, the potatoes: all from France. Here is a commercial play on a well-known national pride and a belief about French food and products (which is often accurate in my experience) that French products are superior to those of, for example, the United States, where McDonalds was born. But notice who is cynically making this pitch founded on French national pride—an American corporation.

It is not just the meat packing industry that is concentrated. Control of the media that the meat industry so deftly uses is itself concentrated in a few large corporate hands. This is very obvious in the United States, where the vast majority of what is referred to as "news" programming, is concentrated in about four entities. So not only do we have industry concentration relating to the meat industry, we have concentration in just a few hands of the means by which we now communicate on national and international levels—the media. The implications of this are not insubstantial. If you have very large moneyed interests in control of the food industry promoting their products through a very small number of media operations, getting messages to the public that are inconsistent with the message of the meat industry is likely to be difficult or impossible. As noted earlier, the industry clearly does not want information about animal treatment in their businesses to be disseminated to the public. Since they are not coincidentally large advertisers in the media, which is also concentrated, media companies are not likely to be welcoming to programming, or for that matter advertising, that is contrary to the meat industry sales line.

There are indeed examples of ads favorable to animal rights positions that have been rejected in the media. Perhaps the most famous was the proposed PETA Super Bowl ad on vegetarianism that was rejected by NBC on the grounds that it was rather too sexually explicit.[40] It cannot be denied that the ad is sexually suggestive, but I suspect that one could find a great deal of similarly sexually suggestive material in NBC's programming that made the cut, including Super Bowl

---

40. *PETA's Super Bowl Commercial Nixed by NBC*, L.A. TIMES, Jan. 28, 2010, http://latimesblogs.latimes.com/unleashed/2009/01/peta-superbowl.html.

ads. Other examples of rejected animal-related ads can be found in other countries. For instance, a proposed Belgian railway station ad by the animal rights group GAIA, which took an obvious position against *foie gras*, was rejected on the ground that political or philosophical ads are not accepted.[41] In Canada, another PETA ad featuring Pamela Anderson was rejected.[42] What was Ms. Anderson's reaction? In an interview with *Us Magazine,* the star is quoted to have said: "In a [] [place] that is known for its exotic dancing and for being progressive and edgy, how sad that a woman would be banned from using her own body in a political protest over the suffering of cows and chickens."[43] There are, of course, always reasons offered for these rejections of pro-animal ads, but it is difficult not to suspect that the real reasons for rejections are the content of the ads and a sycophantic pandering to the global industries that provide so much support for the media.

At the other end of the spectrum, the populace is bombarded with ads for meat products and not infrequently the spokesperson for the product is some cutesy representation of the product itself, like "amusing" animal characters Charlie the Tuna hawking tuna or the Foster Farms Chickens speaking for Foster Farms, a poultry producer in the Western United States. The list of advertisements for products that are tested on animals is quite long as well, including the many pharmaceuticals and other remedies pitched in various media. But the opportunity to buy media time to point out how these products are created or to encounter programming on animal treatment issues, even on "Animal Planet," is something often difficult to accomplish.

I do not mean to say that there are never messages in the media from animal organizations. In the United States, one frequently sees advertisements from "mainstream" animal groups, like humane societies, asking for support to care for abandoned and abused pets. But this is something that virtually no one is likely to be opposed to and there are few economic interests that are benefited by the abuse of companion animals, other than perhaps puppy mills and those who benefit from them; but puppy mills are not the targets of these ads. So it is easy for the media to accept this kind of advertising; there is no downside.

But it is not just the meat industry that wields enormous economic power over the treatment of animals and the public's knowledge about the treatment of animals. Animal experimentation, which is historically a relatively recent industrial use of animals, results in billions of dollars for those producing animals for experiments as well as those performing the experiments. In entertainment, there are operations like SeaWorld and large circuses like Ringling Brothers in the United States, which generate healthy profits for their owners. So in observing the big picture of global animal issues, it is evident that the economic forces that exploit animals are large, secretive about their operations and have huge influence

41. Best Rejected Advertising, http://www.bestrejectedadvertising.com/html/?page=print&type=banned&id=78 (last visited Sept. 10 2010).
42. Daily Contributor, *Pamela Anderson's PETA Ad Rejected in Canada*, July 15, 2010, http://dailycontributor.com/pamela-andersons-peta-ad-rejected-in-canada/17112/.
43. *Id.*

over the messages that appear in mass media. And I hardly need mention that the economic power of animal industries dwarfs the resources of animal advocacy organizations.

We also see that the law provides cover for these corporate interests. We have seen, for example, that intellectual property issues color the information that is made available about animal experimentation. Other laws, like trespassing laws, prevent people from observing what actually goes on in factory farming operations and slaughterhouses. So the force of law, as well as the power of government to enforce it, also creates barriers to truth. The end result of this is that the global economic cabal behind uses of animals in agriculture, experimentation and entertainment, due to their economic power, their control of the media and their protection under governmentally enforced property, trespassing, intellectual property and other laws, are extremely successful in hiding what they do from the public.

Not surprisingly, the economic power of the forces behind the industrial uses of animals gives them power over the political system. In his book *Animal Factory*, David Kirby describes how activists against factory farming were ignored by policy-makers, while meat industry corporate interests had access to the reigns of political power:

> Agribusiness leaders have political contacts and access to government uncharacteristic of the average citizen," the authors wrote. Activists like Karen and groups like FARM that tried to take on agribusiness were not taken seriously by state officials. "When individual concerns and complaints are taken to the state level," the report said, "they are regarded as being scientifically unfounded and emotional in nature.[44]

So it is not just economic and media power that is in the hands of the meat industry, but also the political power that goes along with this economic and media power. The meat industry controls government puppets who ignore the people who are supposed to be their constituents.

It is true that economic forces are not the only ones at work in determining how humans treat animals; we see cultural, social and religious forces at work here as well. Rodeos, though traditionally money making operations, are alleged to have great cultural significance. Travelling circuses can also be argued to have historical and cultural relevance. The influence of religion in practices relating to animals is most clearly evident in the traditional religious slaughter rules that arise in the Jewish and Moslem faiths and are codified in many laws. But due to the nature of the modern media and the economic forces at work, even these cultural and religious aspects of our relationship with animals are influenced by the economic powers that underlie the agriculture, experimentation and entertainment industries. A discussion of the animal treatment issues involved in cultural and religious practices is likely going to be just as difficult, if not more difficult, to have placed in the media as an advertisement on factory farming. So while there

44. Kirby, *supra* note 4, at 74 (quoting a report by University of Iowa Professor Kendall Thu).

are still cultural, social and religious forces behind aspects of our relationship with animals, it seems that the modern human/animal relationship has become a predominantly economic one.

This can be seen in the historical progression of human uses of animals. For hunter-gatherers, the value of an animal was not really economic; it was a matter of life or death for the human, a matter of sustenance. In agrarian societies, exchanges for value of animals were introduced into the equation, but in this world the sellers of agricultural goods were many and their economic power similarly diffuse. Today, in the global economy, there is concentration of economic power in the industries that produce and use animals in only a very few dominant entities; so the economic power that controls the use of animals is no longer diffuse, but is concentrated and massive.

Given that history shows an ever-increasing concentration of economic power in industries related to animals, what does this portend for the future of animal treatment? It is difficult to see the globalization of the world economy and the increased concentration of economic and media power in fewer and fewer entities to be a favorable development for animal interests. The information most people are exposed to is controlled by a few large corporate interests and is distributed through a media that has an economic interest in promoting those large corporate interests who are their advertisers and who support them. The political and ethical agenda is largely written by these large economic interests and disseminating the truth about these industries is likely to become ever more difficult if recent historical trends continue. So promoting animal interests, at least in the mass media, may become more and more impeded.

On the other hand, one could argue that with greater concentration of economic, media and lobbying power, the number of entities that activists need to concentrate on is reduced. It is also somewhat heartening that much of the progress that we have seen in EU legislation has occurred even while globalization and the concentration of economic power have been progressing. But note that this is, it seems, largely a European phenomenon; one can see nearly the opposite in the United States where there has been little if any real progress in regulating animals in agriculture or experimentation during this period, at least at the federal level.

Another way to view this is that one can foresee the distance between humans and their uses of animals continuing to expand by virtue of the economic and mass media realities we now face. If this perspective is accurate and if history is a trustworthy guide, continued separation and alienation of humans from the animals they use will lead to continued and, indeed, increased exploitation of animals. So steps to combat this separation and alienation should be at the fore for those who are committed to ending the exploitation of animals.

It is claimed in John 8:32 that Jesus said "[a]nd you will know the truth and the truth will set you free." Similarly, we might say that the truth can set animals free; it is my fervent belief that if people knew what was done to animals, much of our present behavior would change. I think this is particularly true in the case of animal experimentation and entertainment uses of animals, for here the interests of humans in using animals in these ways are often not immediately evident and much of the use of these animals is so clearly unnecessary that it is likely to be recognized as such by a large proportion of people who are exposed to the facts. For example, the incessant repetition of experiments under government regulatory schemes and in academia is a fact that, if disseminated, I believe would result in widespread calls for action.

The use of animals in agriculture may be harder to crack because people are very attached to their food habits, and eating is an event that necessarily occurs several times a day. I have heard on numerous occasions the statement "I could not go without a steak" or "I could never live without seafood." These statements are obviously not true, since all of us could beneficially live on a diet different from the one most of us have (which is obvious from rising obesity rates and the diseases attendant to obesity), but these statements point out how well-cemented food preferences are in our lifestyles. To change the habits of people in their food preferences is not an easy task. In addition, although the economic forces at work in animal experimentation and entertainment are huge, the food industry is even larger and the messages it sends are both incessant and powerful. Behind Charlie the Tuna trying to sell himself into a can of tuna and goofy chickens promoting chicken products are hidden the vast unpleasantness of animal production that very few people are allowed to or want to see. This industry is generally located where few people live and certainly not in areas where the politically powerful live—they would not tolerate it. The slogan "meat stinks" is not an empty slogan; so meat processing plants are placed, whenever possible, where their stench will not be noticed.

This then requires that education, even in the face of economic and mass media realities, must be a primary focus of those who wish to see animals treated with empathy and compassion, and as creatures with inherent value. Given the disparities of economic power between the many industries involved and the relatively few animal activists who oppose them, not to mention the barriers that make access to the media difficult for animal activists, perhaps the best strategies for education are local ones. For example, educational programs at elementary schools, secondary schools and universities can fulfill these local educational roles. Information on animal issues distributed at farmers' markets and other events can be aimed both at children and their parents. Even seemingly small things, like promoting "meatless Mondays," community gardens and school salad bars can serve educational purposes favorable to animals. And remember that education can occur in very informal ways—the way that we behave and interact with people and animals on a daily basis can inform the public on animal issues.

The Internet is an obvious place to provide information, but its usefulness is, it seems, limited since on the Internet you generally need to be looking for something specific in order to find it. So those who will absorb animal-related information on the Internet are those who are already looking for it, which is not necessarily a bad thing, but the biggest target audience must be people who are not already inclined to find and accept information relating to the human/animal relationship.

III. THE FUTURE

I have always been interested in animals. At one time in my youth I wanted to be a herpetologist, at another a wildlife biologist. I always felt that animals were much like me; I did not see them in the way that apparently many people do, as creatures without pain, feelings, emotions, or worth. And ironically I felt this way even while I was a meat-eater. Now, my initial childhood feelings are being borne out in science. We now know that animals have pain as we do, have a wide range of cognitive skills and in some cases exceed our own, have linguistic abilities, have a full range of emotions including despair, depression, fear, grief and empathy, and even have the constituents required for moral behavior. Even though I now feel somehow vindicated by science, the innocent thoughts on these subjects I had in my youth still wander in and out of my mind.

My introduction to the meaning of the concept of animals as property was as a child of about nine. I lived in a suburb of Detroit that had a good bit of rural land; behind my house there were woods, a creek and a farm; so there was considerable opportunity for me to experience local wildlife. One day I was walking down a dead-end street toward the woods when I came across a group of other children, some of whom I knew and some whom I didn't. One boy, whom I did know, was riding a bike around in circles and the others were watching with some excitement. Then I discovered what the excitement was about. Tied around the spokes of the bike was a nearly dead baby snake that was being pummeled by the spinning of the wheel on the front forks of the bicycle. I asked the boy driving the bike, "Why are you doing that?" He seemed somewhat astonished at my question and responded, pointing to another boy whom I did not know, "He told me to." I was not satisfied with this answer and questioned why this was a good reason to be killing the snake. He then said, "Well, it's his snake." The snake by now was likely dead. I felt helpless; there was nothing that I could do. It was, after all, the boy's snake; his capture of it made it "his" under the law. Since the snake was his property, he could request that his agent, the pilot of the bike, do with it what he wished.

This was my baptism in the status of animals as property, but I did not then understand all of the implications. In this story, though, are all of the elements that illustrate the property status of animals and the economic forces that control and explain the torture and killing of billions of animals like the poor baby snake. We have the owner of the snake, who has the right to use his property in the way he pleases,[45] who then employs an agent, the bike-riding boy, to carry out his desires; the agent then gets "paid" through whatever satisfaction he received by being the ringmaster of this little circus. The consumers of the service (entertainment?) here are the on-looking boys who vicariously take in the scene created by the boy on the bike, who can also be seen as their agent in carrying out the desired act for their consumption.

---

45. I understand that the acts of the children might be argued to violate animal cruelty laws, but for the sake of my analogy, I will assume, that like the economic forces that own agricultural and other animals, the law protects the children's acts.

In this sad story that lingers so many years later in my mind are all of the legal aspects of human use of animals relevant to the present discussion, and the story illustrates the forces that drive these uses. In the present economic milieu, large corporations own and control the use of animals in our society, and they exercise this control through human agents to raise, slaughter, experiment on, or provide entertainment with animals. The customers of these corporations are, of course, the humans who consume the animal products. So in an event that appears to have nothing to do with the place of animals in a globalized economy, the story of a dead baby snake, we can see all of the elements of our globalized economy relating to animals in microcosm; animals are property, are without legal rights, and can therefore be exploited by humans.

But there is also a non-economic side to this story. Does the story of the snake tell us something about humans and how difficult the struggle to end exploitation of animals will be? Is it simply human nature to be violent and will human exploitation of animals always continue because of the essential nature of humans? Even if "human nature" is not an impediment, are the economic and other forces too overwhelming, like the force that the concept of property had on the boy with the bike? I find it hard to be optimistic considering all of the powerful economic and other forces which are arrayed to support our present laws and practices.

On the other hand, I know that there are those who will passionately continue to pursue change in the relationship between humans and animals, even if ultimately they die disappointed in the progress of human behavior toward animals like Pythagoras. But I hope that this will not be the case. I feel that if the ghost of Pythagoras appeared with the baby snake, his message to those who wish to change the legal status of animals would be to carry on with the struggle to change attitudes, behaviors and laws. In the laws that exist today, we cannot deny some progress from Pythagoras' time to ours and should hope to see continued improvements, though perhaps not necessarily within our sight now, in the future. The poet Emily Dickinson may have summed this up best:

> If I can stop one heart from breaking,
> I shall not live in vain;
> If I can ease one life the aching,
> Or cool one pain,
> Or help one fainting robin
> Unto his nest again,
> I shall not live in vain.[46]

46. Emily Dickinson, *Not in Vain, in* ONE HUNDRED AND ONE FAMOUS POEMS 30, 30 (Roy Cook ed., 1993). Use of this poem was suggested by my research assistant, Kimberly Clark.

APPENDICES

The following materials were selected to be included in this Appendix for several reasons. The selected laws of the European Union are provided to give examples of laws relating to the treatment of animals in agriculture, while the provisions of the Animal Welfare Act and Animal Welfare Ordinance of Sweden are included as examples relating to agriculture as well as an example of a comprehensive law on animal experimentation. The New Zealand Code relating to rodeos is included to show, among other things, the structure and form of the New Zealand codes. The text of the Convention on International Trade in Endangered Species of Wild Fauna and Flora and portions of the General Agreement on Tariffs and Trade are included for easy reference for the chapters that focus on these international agreements. I want to thank the European Union, Sweden, New Zealand, CITES and the WTO for their kind permission to use these materials in this book.

Appendix I

Council Directive 98/58, 1998 O.J. (L 221), Concerning the Protection of Animals Kept for Farming Purposes (Only European Union legislation printed in the paper edition of the Official Journal of the European Union is deemed authentic)*

Council Directive 98/58/EC of 20 July 1998 concerning the protection of animals kept for farming purposes

Official Journal L 221 , 08/08/1998 P. 0023-0027

COUNCIL DIRECTIVE 98/58/EC of 20 July 1998 concerning the protection of animals kept for farming purposes

THE COUNCIL OF THE EUROPEAN UNION,

Having regard to the Treaty establishing the European Community, and in particular Article 43 thereof,

Having regard to the proposal from the Commission,[1]

Having regard to the opinion of the European Parliament,[2]

Having regard to the opinion of the Economic and Social Committee,[3]

Whereas all Member States have ratified the European Convention for the Protection of Animals Kept for Farming Purposes (hereinafter called 'the Convention'); whereas the Community has also approved this Convention by Decision 78/923/EEC[4] and has deposited its instrument of approval;

Whereas the Community, as a contracting party, must give effect to the principles laid down in the Convention;

Whereas those principles include the provision of housing, food, water and care appropriate to the physiological and ethological needs of the animals, in accordance with established experience and scientific knowledge;

Whereas it is also necessary for the Community to make further provision for the uniform application of the Convention and its recommendations and for specific rules concerning the application of this Directive;

* *Source*: <http://eur-lex.europa.eu/LexUriServ/LexUriServ.do?uri=OJ:L:1998:221:0023:0027:EN:PDF> (last visited Oct. 8, 2010).

1. OJ C 156, 23. 6. 1992, p. 11.
2. OJ C 337, 21. 12. 1992, p. 225.
3. OJ C 332, 16. 12. 1992, p. 22.
4. OJ L 323, 17. 11. 1978, p. 12.

Whereas the European Parliament, in its resolution of 20 February 1987 on animal welfare policy[5] called on the Commission to make proposals for Community rules covering general aspects of the rearing of livestock;

Whereas Declaration No 24 annexed to the Final Act of the Treaty on European Union calls on the European institutions and the Member States, when drafting and implementing Community legislation, in particular on the common agricultural policy, to pay full regard to the welfare requirements of animals;

Whereas differences which may distort conditions of competition interfere with the smooth running of the organisation of the market in animals;

Whereas there is therefore a need to establish common minimum standards for the protection of animals kept for farming purposes in order to ensure rational development of production and to facilitate the organisation of the market in animals; whereas to that end it is appropriate to take account of animal welfare provisions already laid down in Community rules;

Whereas a comparative examination of animal welfare provisions applicable in the Community and in certain non-member countries together with an appraisal thereof should be undertaken with a view to determining the nature of future Community initiatives aimed at eliminating distortions of competition,

HAS ADOPTED THIS DIRECTIVE:

Article 1

1. This Directive lays down minimum standards for the protection of animals bred or kept for farming purposes.
2. It shall not apply to:
   (a) animals living in the wild;
   (b) animals intended for use in competitions, shows, cultural or sporting events or activities;
   (c) experimental or laboratory animals;
   (d) any invertebrate animal.
3. This Directive shall apply without prejudice to specific Community rules laid down elsewhere, and in particular to Directives 88/166/EEC,[6] 91/629/EEC[7] and 91/630/EEC,[8] which shall continue to apply.

---

5. OJ C 76, 23. 3. 1987, p. 185.
6. Council Directive 88/166/EEC of 7 March 1998 complying with the judgment of the Court of Justice in Case 131–86, (annulment of Council Directive 86/113/EEC of 25 March 1986 laying down minimum standards for the protection of laying hens kept in battery cages) (OJ L 74 19. 3. 1988, p. 83).
7. Council Directive 91/629/EEC of 19 November 1991 laying down minimum standards for the protection of calves (OJ L 340, 11. 12. 1991, p. 28). Directive as last amended by Directive 97/2/EC (OJ L 25, 28. 1. 1997, p. 24).
8. Council Directive 91/630/EEC of 19 November 1991 laying down minimum standards for the protection of pigs (OJ L 340, 11. 12. 1991, p. 33).

Article 2

For the purposes of this Directive the following definitions shall apply:
1. 'animal': any animal (including fish, reptiles or amphibians) bred or kept for the production of food, wool, skin or fur or for other farming purposes;
2. 'owner' or 'keeper': any natural or legal person or persons responsible for or in charge of animals whether on a permanent or temporary basis;
3. 'competent authority': the competent authority within the meaning of Article 2(6) of Council Directive 90/425/EEC of 26 June 1990 concerning veterinary and zootechnical checks applicable in intra-Community trade in certain live animals and products with a view to the completion of the internal market.[9]

Article 3

Member States shall make provision to ensure that the owners or keepers take all reasonable steps to ensure the welfare of animals under their care and to ensure that those animals are not caused any unnecessary pain, suffering or injury.

Article 4

Members States shall ensure that the conditions under which animals (other than fish, reptiles or amphibians) are bred or kept, having regard to their species and to their degree of development, adaptation and domestication, and to their physiological and ethological needs in accordance with established experience and scientific knowledge, comply with the provisions set out in the Annex.

Article 5

1. The Commission shall submit to the Council any proposals which may be necessary for the uniform application of the European Convention for the Protection of Animals Kept for Farming Purposes and, on the basis of a scientific evaluation, any recommendations made under this Convention and any other appropriate specific rules.
2. In addition, every five years and for the first time five years after the date of entry into force of this Directive, the Commission, on the basis of experience acquired since the implementation of this Directive, in particular concerning the measures referred to in paragraph 1 and technical and scientific developments, shall submit to the Council a report, accompanied by any appropriate proposals taking into account the report's conclusions.
3. The Council shall act by qualified majority on these proposals.

---

9. OJ L 224, 18. 8. 1990, p. 29. Directive as last amended by Directive 92/118/EEC (OJ L 62, 15. 3. 1993, p. 49).

Article 6

1. Member States shall ensure that inspections are carried out by the competent authority to check compliance with the provisions of this Directive. Such inspections may be carried out at the same time as checks for other purposes.
2. From a date to be determined in accordance with the procedure laid down in paragraph 3, Member States shall submit to the Commission reports on the inspections required under paragraph 1. The Commission shall submit summaries of those reports to the Standing Veterinary Committee.
3. The Commission shall before 1 July 1999, in accordance with the procedure laid down in Article 9 submit proposals with a view to harmonising:
   (a) the inspections required under paragraph 1;
   (b) the format, content and frequency of submission of the reports referred to in paragraph 2.

Article 7

1. Whenever uniform application of the requirements of this Directive renders it necessary, veterinary experts from the Commission may, in conjunction with the competent authorities;
   (a) verify that the Member States are complying with the said requirements;
   (b) make on-the-spot checks to ensure that the checks are carried out in accordance with this Directive.
2. A Member State in whose territory an inspection is made shall provide the veterinary experts from the Commission with any assistance they may require in the performance of their tasks. The outcome of the checks made must be discussed with the competent authority of the Member State concerned before a final report is drawn up and circulated.
3. The competent authority of the Member State concerned shall take any measures which may be necessary to take account of the results of the check.
4. Detailed rules for the application of this Article shall be adopted, where necessary, in accordance with the procedure laid down in Article 9.

Article 8

1. Before 30 June 1999 the Commission shall submit to the Council a report on:
   - the comparison between animal welfare provisions in the Community and in non-member countries which supply the Community,
   - the scope for obtaining wider international acceptance of the welfare principles laid down in this Directive, and
   - the extent to which Community objectives in relation to animal welfare may be liable to be undermined as a result of competition from non-member countries which do not apply equivalent standards.
2. The report referred to in paragraph 1 shall be accompanied by any necessary proposals with the aim of eliminating distortions of competition.

Article 9

1. Where the procedure laid down in this Article is to be followed, the matter shall be referred without delay to the Standing Veterinary Committee set up by Directive 68/361/EEC,[10] hereinafter referred to as 'the Committee', by its chairman acting either on his own initiative or at the request of a Member State.
2. The representative of the Commission shall submit to the Committee a draft of the measures to be taken. The Committee shall deliver its opinion on the draft within a time limit which the chairman may lay down according to the urgency of the matter. The opinion shall be delivered by the majority laid down in Article 148(2) of the Treaty in the case of decisions which the Council is required to adopt on a proposal from the Commission. The votes of the representatives of the Member States within the Committee shall be weighted in the manner set out in that Article. The chairman shall not vote.
3. (a) The Commission shall adopt the measures envisaged if they are in accordance with the opinion of the Committee.
   (b) If the measures envisaged are not in accordance with the opinion of the Committee, or if no opinion is delivered, the Commission shall without delay submit to the Council a proposal relating to the measures to be taken. The Council shall act by qualified majority.
   If, on the expiry of a period of three months from the date of referral to the Council, the Council has not acted, the Commission shall adopt the proposed measures and implement them immediately, save where the Council has decided against the said measures by a simple majority.

Article 10

1. Member States shall bring into force the laws, regulations and administrative provisions, including any sanctions, necessary to comply with this Directive not later than 31 December 1999, subject to any different decision taken by the Council in the light of the report referred to in Article 8. They shall forthwith inform the Commission thereof.
   When Member States adopt these measures, they shall contain a reference to this Directive or shall be accompanied by such reference on the occasion of their official publication. The methods of making such reference shall be laid down by Member States.
2. However, after 31 December 1999, Member States may, in compliance with the general rules of the Treaty, maintain or apply within their territories stricter provisions for the protection of animals kept for farming purposes than those laid down in this Directive. They shall inform the Commission of any such measures.
3. Member States shall communicate to the Commission the texts of the main provisions of national law which they adopt in the field governed by this Directive.

---

10. OJ L 255, 18. 10. 1968, p. 23.

Article 11

This Directive shall enter into force on the day of its publication in the Official Journal of the European Communities.

Article 12

This Directive is addressed to the Member States.
Done at Brussels, 20 July 1998.
For the Council
The President
W. MOLTERER

ANNEX

Staffing

1. Animals shall be cared for by a sufficient number of staff who possess the appropriate ability, knowledge and professional competence.

Inspection

2. All animals kept in husbandry systems in which their welfare depends on frequent human attention shall be inspected at least once a day. Animals in other systems shall be inspected at intervals sufficient to avoid any suffering.
3. Adequate lighting (fixed or portable) shall be available to enable the animals to be thoroughly inspected at any time.
4. Any animal which appears to be ill or injured must be cared for appropriately without delay and, where an animal does not respond to such care, veterinary advice must be obtained as soon as possible. Where necessary sick or injured animals shall be isolated in suitable accommodation with, where appropriate, dry comfortable bedding.

Record keeping

5. The owner or keeper of the animals shall maintain a record of any medicinal treatment given and of the number of mortalities found to each inspection. Where equivalent information is required to be kept for other purposes, this shall also suffice for the purposes of this Directive.
6. These records shall be retained for a period of at least three years and shall be made available to the competent authority when carrying out an inspection or when otherwise requested.

Freedom of movement

7. The freedom of movement of an animal, having regard to its species and in accordance with established experience and scientific knowledge, must not be restricted in such a way as to cause it unnecessary suffering or injury.

Where an animal is continuously or regularly tethered or confined, it must be given the space appropriate to its physiological and ethological needs in accordance with established experience and scientific knowledge.

Buildings and accommodation

8. Materials to be used for the construction of accommodation, and in particular for the construction of pens an equipment with which the animals may come into contact, must not be harmful to the animals and must be capable of being throughly cleaned and disinfected.
9. Accommodation and fittings for securing animals shall be constructed and maintained so that there are no sharp edges or protrusions likely to cause injury to the animals.
10. Air circulation, dust levels, temperature, relative air humidity and gas concentrations must be kept within limits which are not harmful to the animals.
11. Animals kept in buildings must not be kept either in permanent darkness or without an appropriate period of rest from artificial lighting. Where the natural light available is insufficient to meet the physiological and ethological needs of the animals, appropriate artificial lighting must be provided.

Animals not kept in buildings

12. Animals not kept in buildings shall where necessary and possible be given protection from adverse weather conditions, predators and risks to their health.

Automatic or mechanical equipment

13. All automated or mechanical equipment essential for the health and well-being of the animals must be inspected at least once daily. Where defects are discovered, these must be rectified immediately, or if this is impossible, appropriate steps must be taken to safeguard the health and well-being of the animals.

    Where the health and well-being of the animals is dependent on an artificial ventilation system, provision must be made for an appropriate backup system to guarantee sufficient air renewal to preserve the health and well-being of the animals in the event of failure of the system, and an alarm system must be provided to give warning of breakdown. The alarm system must be tested regularly.

Feed, water and other substances

14. Animals must be fed a wholesome diet which is appropriate to their age and species and which is fed to them in sufficient quantity to maintain them in good health and satisfy their nutritional needs. No animal shall be provided with food or liquid in a manner, nor shall such food or liquid contain any substance, which may cause unnecessary suffering or injury.
15. All animals must have access to feed at intervals appropriate to their physiological needs.

16. All animals must have access to a suitable water supply or be able to satisfy their fluid intake needs by other means.
17. Feeding and watering equipment must be designed, constructed and placed so that contamination of food and water and the harmful effects of competition between the animals are minimised.
18. No other substance, with the exception of those given for therapeutic, or prophylactic purposes or for the purposes of zootechnical treatment as defined in Article 1(2)(c) of Directive 96/22/EEC,[11] must be administered to an animal unless it has been demonstrated by scientific studies of animal welfare or established experience that the effect of that substance is not detrimental to the health or welfare of the animal.

Mutilations

19. Pending the adoption of specific provisions concerning mutilations in accordance with the procedure laid down in Article 5, and without prejudice to Directive 91/630/EEC, relevant national provisions shall apply in accordance with the general rules of the Treaty.

Breeding procedures

20. Natural or artificial breeding or breeding procedures which case or are likely to cause suffering or injury to any of the animals concerned must not be practised. This provision shall not preclude the use of certain procedures likely to cause minimal or momentary suffering or injury, or which might necessitate interventions which would not cause lasting injury, where these are allowed by national provisions.
21. No animal shall be kept for farming purposes unless it can reasonably be expected, on the basis of its genotype or phenotype, that it can be kept without detrimental effect on its health or welfare.

---

11. Council Directive 96/22/EC of 29 April 1996 concerning the prohibition on the use in stockfarming of certain substances having a hormonal or thyrostatic action and of beta-agonists (OJ L 125, 23. 5. 1996, p. 3).

Appendix II

Council Directive 1999/74 (L 203), Laying Down Minimum Standards for the Protection of Laying Hens, (last visited Oct. 8, 2010) (Only European Union legislation printed in the paper edition of the Official Journal of the European Union is deemed authentic)*

Council Directive 1999/74/EC of 19 July 1999 laying down minimum standards for the protection of laying hens

Official Journal L 203 , 03/08/1999 P. 0053-0057

COUNCIL DIRECTIVE 1999/74/EC

of 19 July 1999

laying down minimum standards for the protection of laying hens

THE COUNCIL OF THE EUROPEAN UNION,

Having regard to the Treaty establishing the European Community, and in particular Article 37 thereof,

Having regard to the proposal from the Commission,[1]

Having regard to the opinion of the European Parliament,[2]

Having regard to the opinion of the Economic and Social Committee,[3]

Whereas:

(1) On 7 March 1988 the Council adopted Directive 88/166/EEC[4] complying with the judgment of the Court of Justice in Case 131/86 (annulment of Council Directive 86/113/EEC of 25 March 1986 laying down minimum standards for the protection of laying hens kept in battery cages);

(2) Article 9 of Directive 88/166/EEC requires the Commission to submit, before 1 January 1993, a report on scientific developments regarding the welfare of hens under various systems of rearing and on the provisions in the Annex to the Directive, accompanied by any appropriate adjustment proposals;

(3) Council Directive 98/58/EC of 20 July 1998 concerning the protection of animals kept for farming purposes,[5] drawn up on the basis of the European Convention for the Protection of Animals kept for Farming Purposes, lays down Community provisions designed to give effect to the principles laid down in the Convention, which include the provision of housing, food,

---

* *Source*: <http://eur-lex.europa.eu/LexUriServ/LexUriServ.do?uri=OJ:L:1999:203:0053:0057:EN:PDF>.

1. OJ C 157, 4.6.1999, p. 8.
2. OJ C 128, 7.5.1999, p. 78.
3. OJ C 101, 12.4.1999.
4. OJ L 74, 19.3.1988, p. 83.
5. OJ L 221, 8.8.1998, p. 23.

water and care appropriate to the physiological and ethological needs of the animals;

(4) In 1995 the Standing Committee of the European Convention for the Protection of Animals kept for Farming Purposes adopted a detailed recommendation, which includes laying hens;

(5) The protection of laying hens is a matter of Community competence;

(6) Differences which may distort conditions of competition interfere with the smooth running of the organisation of the market in animals and animal products;

(7) The Commission report referred to in recital 2, based on an opinion from the Scientific Veterinary Committee, concludes that the welfare conditions of hens kept in current battery cages and in other systems of rearing are inadequate and that certain of their needs cannot be met in such cages; the highest possible standards should therefore be introduced, in the light of various parameters to be considered in order to improve those conditions;

(8) However, for a period to be determined, the use of unenriched cage systems may be continued under certain conditions, including improved structural and space requirements;

(9) A balance must be kept between the various aspects to be taken into consideration, as regards both welfare and health, economic and social considerations, and also environmental impact;

(10) It is appropriate, while studies on the welfare of laying hens in various systems of rearing are carried out, to adopt provisions that allow the Member States to choose the most appropriate system or systems;

(11) The Commission must submit a new report together with appropriate proposals that take account of that report;

(12) Directive 88/166/EEC should therefore be repealed and replaced,

HAS ADOPTED THIS DIRECTIVE:

Article 1

1. This Directive lays down minimum standards for the protection of laying hens.
2. This Directive shall not apply to:
   - establishments with fewer than 350 laying hens,
   - establishments rearing breeding laying hens.

   Such establishments shall, however, continue to be subject to the relevant requirements of Directive 98/58/EC.

Article 2

1. The definitions in Article 2 of Directive 98/58/EC shall apply where necessary.
2. In addition, the following definitions shall apply for the purpose of this Directive:

(a) "laying hens" means: hens of the species Gallus gallus which have reached laying maturity and are kept for production of eggs not intended for hatching;
(b) "nest" means: a separate space for egg laying, the floor components of which may not include wire mesh that can come into contact with the birds, for an individual hen or for a group of hens (group nest);
(c) "litter" means: any friable material enabling the hens to satisfy their ethological needs;
(d) "usable area" means: an area at least 30 cm wide with a floor slope not exceeding 14%, with headroom of at least 45 cm. Nesting areas shall not be regarded as usable areas.

Article 3

According to the system or systems adopted by the Member States, they shall ensure that the owners and holders of laying hens apply not only the relevant provisions of Directive 98/58/EC and of the Annex to this Directive but also the requirements specific to each of the systems referred to below, namely:

(a) either the provisions laid down in Chapter I as regards alternative systems;
(b) or the provisions laid down in Chapter II as regards unenriched cage systems;
(c) or the provisions of Chapter III concerning enriched cages.

CHAPTER I
Provisions applicable to alternative systems

Article 4

1. Member States shall ensure that from 1 January 2002 all newly built or rebuilt systems of production referred to in this chapter and all such systems of production brought into use for the first time comply at least with the requirements below.

1. All systems must be equipped in such a way that all laying hens have:
   (a) either linear feeders providing at least 10 cm per bird or circular feeders providing at least 4 cm per bird;
   (b) either continuous drinking troughs providing 2,5 cm per hen or circular drinking troughs providing 1 cm per hen.
   In addition, where nipple drinkers or cups are used, there shall be at least one nipple drinker or cup for every 10 hens. Where drinking points are plumbed in, at least two cups or two nipple drinkers shall be within reach of each hen;
   (c) at least one nest for every seven hens. If group nests are used, there must be at least 1 m2 of nest space for a maximum of 120 hens;
   (d) adequate perches, without sharp edges and providing at least 15 cm per hen. Perches must not be mounted above the litter and the horizontal distance between perches must be at least 30 cm and the horizontal distance between the perch and the wall must be at least 20 cm;

(e) at least 250 cm2 of littered area per hen, the litter occupying at least one third of the ground surface.

2. The floors of installations must be constructed so as to support adequately each of the forward-facing claws of each foot.
3. In addition to the provisions laid down in points 1 and 2,

(a) if systems of rearing are used where the laying hens can move freely between different levels,

(i) there shall be no more than four levels;

(ii) the headroom between the levels must be at least 45 cm;

(iii) the drinking and feeding facilities must be distributed in such a way as to provide equal access for all hens;

(iv) the levels must be so arranged as to prevent droppings falling on the levels below.

(b) If laying hens have access to open runs:

(i) there must be several popholes giving direct access to the outer area, at least 35 cm high and 40 cm wide and extending along the entire length of the building; in any case, a total opening of 2 m must be available per group of 1000 hens;

(ii) open runs must be:

- of an area appropriate to the stocking density and to the nature of the ground, in order to prevent any contamination;
- equipped with shelter from inclement weather and predators and, if necessary, appropriate drinking troughs.

4. The stocking density must not exceed nine laying hens per m2 usable area. However, where the usable area corresponds to the available ground surface, Member States may, until 31 December 2011, authorise a stocking density of 12 hens per m2 of available area for those establishments applying this system on 3 August 1999.

2. Member States shall ensure that the minimum requirements laid down in paragraph 1 apply to all alternative systems from 1 January 2007.

CHAPTER II
Provisions applicable to rearing in unenriched cage systems

Article 5

1. Member States shall ensure that from 1 January 2003 all cage systems referred to in this chapter comply at least with the following requirements:

1. at least 550 cm2 per hen of cage area, measured in a horizontal plane, which may be used without restriction, in particular not including non-waste

deflection plates liable to restrict the area available, must be provided for each laying hen;
2. a feed trough which may be used without restriction must be provided. Its length must be at least 10 cm multiplied by the number of hens in the cage;
3. unless nipple drinkers or drinking cups are provided, each cage must have a continuous drinking channel of the same length as the feed trough mentioned in point 2. Where drinking points are plumbed in, at least two nipple drinkers or two cups must be within reach of each cage;
4. cages must be at least 40 cm high over at least 65% of the cage area and not less than 35 cm at any point;
5. floors of cages must be constructed so as to support adequately each of the forward-facing claws of each foot. Floor slope must not exceed 14% or 8%. In the case of floors using other than rectangular wire mesh, Member States may permit steeper slopes;
6. cages shall be fitted with suitable claw-shortening devices.

2. Member States shall ensure that rearing in the cages referred to in this chapter is prohibited with effect from 1 January 2012. In addition, with effect from 1 January 2003 no cages such as referred to in this chapter may be built or brought into service for the first time.

CHAPTER III
Provisions applicable to rearing in enriched cages

Article 6

Member States shall ensure that after 1 January 2002 all the cages referred to in this chapter comply at least with the following requirements:

1. laying hens must have:
   (a) at least 750 cm2 of cage area per hen, 600 cm2 of which shall be usable; the height of the cage other than that above the usable area shall be at least 20 cm at every point and no cage shall have a total area that is less than 2000 cm2;
   (b) a nest;
   (c) litter such that pecking and scratching are possible;
   (d) appropriate perches allowing at least 15 cm per hen;
2. a feed trough which may be used without restriction must be provided. Its length must be at least 12 cm multiplied by the number of hens in the cage;
3. each cage must have a drinking system appropriate to the size of the group; where nipple drinkers are provided, at least two nipple drinkers or two cups must be within the reach of each hen;
4. to facilitate inspection, installation and depopulation of hens there must be a minimum aisle width of 90 cm between tiers of cages and a space of at least 35 cm must be allowed between the floor of the building and the bottom tier of cages;
5. cages must be fitted with suitable claw-shortening devices.

CHAPTER IV
Final provisions

Article 7

Member States shall ensure that the establishments covered by the scope of this Directive are registered by the competent authority and given a distinguishing number which will be the medium for tracing eggs placed on the market for human consumption.

The arrangements for implementing this Article shall be determined before 1 January 2002 in accordance with the procedure laid down in Article 11.

Article 8

1. Member States shall take the necessary measures to ensure that the competent authority carries out inspections to monitor compliance with the provisions of this Directive. These inspections may be carried out on the occasion of checks made for other purposes.
2. From a date to be determined in accordance with the procedure provided for in Article 11, Member States shall report to the Commission on the inspections carried out in accordance with paragraph 1. The Commission shall submit summaries of these reports to the Standing Veterinary Committee.
3. Before 1 January 2002 the Commission shall, in accordance with the procedure laid down in Article 11, submit proposals for harmonisation of the following:
   (a) the inspections referred to in paragraph 1;
   (b) the form and content of the reports referred to in paragraph 2 and the frequency with which they are to be submitted.

Article 9

1. Whenever uniform application of the requirements of this Directive renders it necessary, veterinary experts from the Commission may, in conjunction with the competent authorities:
   (a) verify that the Member States are complying with the said requirements;
   (b) make on-the-spot checks to ensure that the inspections are carried out in accordance with this Directive.
2. A Member State in whose territory an inspection is made shall provide the veterinary experts from the Commission with any assistance they may require for the performance of their tasks. The outcome of the checks made must be discussed with the competent authority of the Member State concerned before a final report is drawn up and circulated.
3. The competent authority of the Member State concerned shall take any measures which may prove necessary to take account of the results of the checks.

4. Detailed rules for the application of this Article shall be adopted, if necessary, in accordance with the procedure laid down in Article 11.

Article 10

Not later than 1 January 2005 the Commission shall submit to the Council a report, drawn up on the basis of an opinion from the Scientific Veterinary Committee, on the various systems of rearing laying hens, and in particular on those covered by this Directive, taking account both of pathological, zootechnical, physiological, and ethological aspects of the various systems and of their health and environmental impact.

That report shall also be drawn up on the basis of a study of the socio-economic implications of the various systems and their effects on the Community's economic partners.

In addition, it shall be accompanied by appropriate proposals taking into account the conclusions of the report and the outcome of the World Trade Organisation negotiations.

The Council shall act by a qualified majority on these proposals within 12 months of their submission.

Article 11

1. Where the procedure laid down in this Article is to be followed, the matter shall be referred without delay to the Standing Veterinary Committee set up by Decision 68/361/EEC,[6] hereinafter referred to as "the committee", by its chairman acting either on his own initiative or at the request of a Member State.
2. The representative of the Commission shall submit to the committee a draft of the measures to be taken. The committee shall deliver its opinion on the draft within a time limit which the chairman may lay down according to the urgency of the matter. The opinion shall be delivered by the majority laid down in Article 205(2) of the Treaty in the case of decisions which the Council is required to adopt on a proposal from the Commission. The votes of the representatives of the Member States within the committee shall be weighted in the manner set out in that Article. The chairman shall not vote.
3. (a) The Commission shall adopt the measures envisaged if they are in accordance with the opinion of the committee.
   (b) If the measures envisaged are not in accordance with the opinion of the committee, or if no opinion is delivered, the Commission shall without delay submit to the Council a proposal relating to the measures to be taken. The Council shall act by qualified majority.
   If, on the expiry of a period of three months from the date of referral to the Council, the Council has not acted, the Commission shall adopt the

---

6. OJ L 255, 18.10.1968, p. 23.

proposed measures and implement them immediately, save where the Council has decided against the said measures by a simple majority.

Article 12

Directive 88/166/EEC is hereby repealed with effect from 1 January 2003.

Article 13

1. Member States shall bring into force the laws, regulations and administrative provisions, including any penalties, necessary to comply with this Directive not later than 1 January 2002. They shall forthwith inform the Commission thereof. When Member States adopt these measures, they shall contain a reference to this Directive or shall be accompanied by such reference on the occasion of their official publication. The methods of making such reference shall be laid down by Member States.
2. The Member States may, while respecting the general rules laid down in the Treaty, maintain or apply within their territories provisions for the protection of laying hens which are more stringent than those envisaged by this Directive. They shall inform the Commission of any measure taken to that end.
3. Member States shall communicate to the Commission the text of the main provisions of national law which they adopt in the field covered by this Directive.

Article 14

This Directive shall enter into force on the day of its publication in the Official Journal of the European Communities.

Article 15

This Directive is addressed to the Member States.
Done at Brussels, 19 July 1999.
For the Council
The President
K. HEMILÄ

ANNEX

In addition to the relevant provisions of the Annex to Directive 98/58/EC, the following requirements apply:

1. All hens must be inspected by the owner or the person responsible for the hens at least once a day.
2. The sound level shall be minimised. Constant or sudden noise shall be avoided. Ventilation fans, feeding machinery or other equipment shall be constructed,

placed, operated and maintained in such a way that they cause the least possible noise.

3. All buildings shall have light levels sufficient to allow all hens to see one another and be seen clearly, to investigate their surroundings visually and to show normal levels of activity. Where there is natural light, light apertures must be arranged in such a way that light is distributed evenly within the accommodation.
   After the first days of conditioning, the lighting regime shall be such as to prevent health and behavioural problems. Accordingly it must follow a 24-hour rhythm and include an adequate uninterrupted period of darkness lasting, by way of indication, about one third of the day, so that the hens may rest and to avoid problems such as immunodepression and ocular anomalies. A period of twilight of sufficient duration ought to be provided when the light is dimmed so that the hens may settle down without disturbance or injury.
4. Those parts of buildings, equipment or utensils which are in contact with the hens shall be thoroughly cleansed and disinfected regularly and in any case every time depopulation is carried out and before a new batch of hens is brought in. While the cages are occupied, the surfaces and all equipment shall be kept satisfactorily clean.
   Droppings must be removed as often as necessary and dead hens must be removed every day.
5. Cages must be suitably equipped to prevent hens escaping.
6. Accommodation comprising two or more tiers of cages must have devices or appropriate measures must be taken to allow inspection of all tiers without difficulty and facilitate the removal of hens.
7. The design and dimensions of the cage door must be such that an adult hen can be removed without undergoing unnecessary suffering or sustaining injury.
8. Without prejudice to the provisions of point 19 of the Annex to Directive 98/58/EC, all mutilation shall be prohibited.
   In order to prevent feather pecking and cannibalism, however, the Member States may authorise beak trimming provided it is carried out by qualified staff on chickens that are less than 10 days old and intended for laying.

Appendix III

Council Regulation 1099/2009, pmbl. ¶4, 2008 O.J. (L 303), On the Protection of Animals at the Time of Killing (Only European Union legislation printed in the paper edition of the Official Journal of the European Union is deemed authentic.)*

Council Regulation (EC) No. 1099/2009 of 24 September 2009 on the protection of animals at the time of killing Text with EEA relevance

Official Journal L 303 , 18/11/2009 P. 0001-0030

Council Regulation (EC) No 1099/2009 of 24 September 2009 on the protection of animals at the time of killing

(Text with EEA relevance)

THE COUNCIL OF THE EUROPEAN UNION,

Having regard to the Treaty establishing the European Community, and in particular Article 37 thereof,

Having regard to the proposal from the Commission,

Having regard to the Opinion of the European Parliament,[1]

Having regard to the Opinion of the European Economic and Social Committee,[2]

After consultation of the Committee of the Regions,

Whereas:

(1) Council Directive 93/119/EC of 22 December 1993 on the protection of animals at the time of slaughter or killing[3] establishes common minimum rules for the protection of animals at the time of slaughter or killing in the Community. That Directive has not been substantially amended since its adoption.

(2) Killing animals may induce pain, distress, fear or other forms of suffering to the animals even under the best available technical conditions. Certain operations related to the killing may be stressful and any stunning technique presents certain drawbacks. Business operators or any person involved in the killing of animals should take the necessary measures to avoid pain and minimise the distress and suffering of animals during the slaughtering or killing process, taking into account the best practices in the field and the methods permitted under this Regulation. Therefore, pain, distress or suffering should be considered as avoidable when business operators or any person involved in the killing of animals breach one of the requirements of this Regulation or use permitted

* *Source:* <http://eur-lex.europa.eu/LexUriServ/LexUriServ.do?uri=OJ:L:2009:303:0001:0030:EN:PDF> (last visited Oct. 8, 2010).

1. Opinion of 6 May 2009 (not yet published in the Official Journal).
2. Opinion of 25 February 2009 (not yet published in the Official Journal).
3. OJ L 340, 31.12.1993, p. 21.

practices without reflecting the state of the art, thereby inducing by negligence or intention, pain, distress or suffering to the animals.

(3) The protection of animals at the time of slaughter or killing has been covered by Community law since 1974, and was substantively reinforced by Directive 93/119/EC. However, large discrepancies have been observed between the Member States in implementing that Directive and major welfare concerns and differences susceptible to affect competitiveness between business operators have been pointed out.

(4) Animal welfare is a Community value that is enshrined in the Protocol (No 33) on protection and welfare of animals annexed to the Treaty establishing the European Community (Protocol (No 33)). The protection of animals at the time of slaughter or killing is a matter of public concern that affects consumer attitudes towards agricultural products. In addition, improving the protection of animals at the time of slaughter contributes to higher meat quality and indirectly has a positive impact on occupational safety in slaughterhouses.

(5) National law concerning the protection of animals at the time of slaughter or killing has an impact on competition and, accordingly, on the operation of the internal market in products of animal origin included in Annex I to the Treaty establishing the European Community. It is necessary to establish common rules in order to ensure the rational development of the internal market in those products.

(6) The European Food Safety Authority (EFSA), established by Regulation (EC) No 178/2002 of the European Parliament and of the Council of 28 January 2002 laying down the general principles and requirements of food law, establishing the European Food Safety Authority and laying down procedures in matters of food safety,[4] has adopted two opinions on the welfare aspects of the main systems of stunning and killing of certain species of animals, namely on the welfare aspects of the main systems of stunning and killing the main commercial species of animals, in 2004, and on the welfare aspects of the main systems of stunning and killing applied to commercially farmed deer, goats, rabbits, ostriches, ducks, geese and quail, in 2006. Community law in this area should be updated to take into account those scientific opinions. Recommendations to phase out the use of carbon dioxide for pigs and the use of waterbath stunners for poultry are not included in this Regulation because the impact assessment revealed that such recommendations were not economically viable at present in the EU. However, it is important to continue this discussion in the future. To this end, the Commission should prepare and submit to the European Parliament and to the Council a report on the various stunning methods for poultry, and in particular multiple-bird waterbath stunners. Furthermore, other recommendations should be excluded from this Regulation because they refer to

4. OJ L 31, 1.2.2002, p. 1.

technical parameters that should be part of implementing measures or Community guidelines. Recommendations on farm fish are not included in this Regulation because there is a need for further scientific opinion and economic evaluation in this field.

(7) In 2007, the World Organisation for Animal Health (OIE) adopted the Terrestrial Animal Health Code which includes guidelines for the slaughter of animals and for the killing of animals for disease control purposes. Those international guidelines contain recommendations concerning the handling, restraining, stunning and bleeding of animals in slaughterhouses and the killing of animals in cases of outbreak of contagious diseases. Those international standards should also be taken into account in this Regulation.

(8) Since the adoption of Directive 93/119/EC, Community food safety legislation applicable to slaughterhouses has been profoundly amended by the adoption of Regulation (EC) No 852/2004 of the European Parliament and of the Council of 29 April 2004 on hygiene of foodstuffs[5] and Regulation (EC) No 853/2004 of the European Parliament and of the Council of 29 April 2004 laying down specific hygiene rules for food of animal origin.[6] Those Regulations emphasise the responsibility of food business operators to ensure food safety. Slaughterhouses are also subject to a pre-approval procedure whereby the construction, layout and equipment are examined by the competent authority to ensure that they comply with the corresponding technical rules on food safety. Animal welfare concerns should be better integrated into slaughterhouses, their construction and layout, as well as the equipment used therein.

(9) Official controls in the food chain have also been reorganised by the adoption of Regulation (EC) No 882/2004 of the European Parliament and of the Council of 29 April 2004 on official controls performed to ensure the verification of compliance with feed and food law, animal health and animal welfare rules[7] and Regulation (EC) No 854/2004 of the European Parliament and of the Council of 29 April 2004 laying down specific rules for the organisation of official controls on products of animal origin intended for human consumption.[8]

(10) Conditions under which animals kept for farming purposes are killed have a direct or indirect impact on the market for food, feed or other products and on the competitiveness of the business operators concerned. Therefore, such killing operations should be covered by Community law. However, traditionally farmed species such as horses, donkeys, cattle, sheep, goats or pigs can also be kept for other purposes, such as, for example, pets, animals for shows, work purposes, or sports. Where the killing of animals of such species produces food or other products, those operations should fall within the

5. OJ L 139, 30.4.2004, p. 1.
6. OJ L 139, 30.4.2004, p. 55.
7. OJ L 191, 28.5.2004, p. 1.
8. OJ L 226, 25.6.2004, p. 83.

scope of this Regulation. Consequently, the killing of wild or stray animals for population control purposes should not fall within the scope of this Regulation.

(11) Fish present substantial physiological differences from terrestrial animals and farmed fish are slaughtered and killed in a very different context, in particular as regards the inspection process. Furthermore, research on the stunning of fish is far less developed than for other farmed species. Separate standards should be established on the protection of fish at killing. Therefore, provisions applicable to fish should, at present, be limited to the key principle. Further initiatives by the Community should be based on a scientific risk assessment for the slaughter and killing of fish performed by EFSA and taking into account the social, economic and administrative implications.

(12) It is an ethical duty to kill productive animals which are in severe pain where there is no economically viable way to alleviate such pain. In most cases, animals can be killed respecting proper welfare conditions. However, under exceptional circumstances, such as accidents in remote locations, where competent personnel and equipment cannot reach the animals, complying with optimal welfare rules could prolong their suffering. In the interest of the animals it is, therefore, appropriate to exclude emergency killing from the application of certain provisions of this Regulation.

(13) Occasionally animals can be dangerous for human beings, possibly putting human life at risk, inflicting serious injuries or transmitting deadly diseases. Preventing those risks is usually performed through the proper restraining of animals but it may also be necessary to kill dangerous animals to end such risks in certain circumstances. Under those circumstances, the killing cannot always be performed under the best welfare conditions due to the emergency. Therefore, it is necessary to derogate from the obligation to stun or immediately kill the animals in those cases.

(14) Hunting or recreational fishing activities take place in a context where conditions of killing are very different from the ones used for farmed animals and hunting is subject to specific legislation. It is therefore appropriate to exclude killings taking place during hunting or recreational fishing from the scope of this Regulation.

(15) Protocol No (33) underlines the need to respect the legislative or administrative provisions and customs of the Member States relating, in particular, to religious rites, cultural traditions and regional heritage when formulating and implementing the Community's policies on, inter alia, agriculture and the internal market. It is therefore appropriate to exclude from the scope of this Regulation cultural events, where compliance with animal welfare requirements would adversely affect the very nature of the event concerned.

(16) In addition, cultural traditions refer to an inherited, established, or customary pattern of thought, action or behaviour which includes in fact the concept of something transmitted by, or acquired from, a predecessor. They contribute to fostering long-standing social links between generations. Provided that

those activities do not affect the market of products of animal origin and are not motivated by production purposes, it is appropriate to exclude the killing of animals taking place during those events from the scope of this Regulation.

(17) The slaughter of poultry, rabbits and hares for private domestic consumption is not performed on a scale likely to affect the competitiveness of commercial slaughterhouses. Similarly, the necessary efforts required from public authorities to detect and control such operations would not be proportionate to the potential problems to be solved. It is, therefore, appropriate to exclude those operations from the scope of this Regulation.

(18) Derogation from stunning in case of religious slaughter taking place in slaughterhouses was granted by Directive 93/119/EC. Since Community provisions applicable to religious slaughter have been transposed differently depending on national contexts and considering that national rules take into account dimensions that go beyond the purpose of this Regulation, it is important that derogation from stunning animals prior to slaughter should be maintained, leaving, however, a certain level of subsidiarity to each Member State. As a consequence, this Regulation respects the freedom of religion and the right to manifest religion or belief in worship, teaching, practice and observance, as enshrined in Article 10 of the Charter of Fundamental Rights of the European Union.

(19) There is sufficient scientific evidence to demonstrate that vertebrate animals are sentient beings which should therefore fall within the scope of this Regulation. Reptiles and amphibians, however, are not animals commonly farmed in the Community and it would not, therefore, be appropriate or proportionate to include them within its scope.

(20) Many killing methods are painful for animals. Stunning is therefore necessary to induce a lack of consciousness and sensibility before, or at the same time as, the animals are killed. Measuring the lack of consciousness and sensibility of an animal is complex and needs to be performed under scientifically approved methodology. Monitoring through indicators, however, should be carried out to evaluate the efficiency of the procedure under practical conditions.

(21) Monitoring stunning efficiency is mainly based on the evaluation of consciousness and sensibility of the animals. The consciousness of an animal is essentially its ability to feel emotions and control its voluntary mobility. Despite some exceptions, such as electro-immobilisations or other provoked paralysis, an animal can be presumed to be unconscious when it loses its natural standing position, is not awake and does not show signs of positive or negative emotions such as fear or excitement. Sensibility of an animal is essentially its ability to feel pain. In general, an animal can be presumed to be insensitive when it does not show any reflexes or reactions to stimulus such as sound, odour, light or physical contact.

(22) New stunning methods are regularly developed and proposed on the market in order to face the new challenges of the farming and meat industry.

It is, therefore, important to authorise the Commission to approve new stunning methods while keeping a uniform and high level of protection for animals.

(23) Community guidelines are a useful tool to provide business operators and competent authorities with specific information on the parameters to be used in order to ensure a high level of protection for animals while keeping a level playing field for business operators. It is, therefore, necessary to authorise the Commission to draw up such guidelines.

(24) Depending on how they are used during the slaughtering or killing process, some stunning methods can lead to death while avoiding pain and minimising distress or suffering for the animals. Other stunning methods may not lead to death and the animals may recover their consciousness or sensibility during subsequent painful procedures. Such methods should, therefore, be completed by other techniques that lead to certain death before the recovery of the animals. It is, therefore, essential to specify which stunning methods need to be completed by a killing method.

(25) The conditions under which animals are stunned and the results of such stunning vary in practice due to many factors. Regular assessment of the outcome of stunning should therefore be made. For that purpose, business operators should establish a representative sample to check the efficiency of their stunning practices, taking into account the homogeneity of the group of animals, and other critical factors, such as the equipment used and the personnel involved.

(26) Some stunning protocols may prove to be sufficiently reliable to irreversibly kill the animals in all circumstances if specific key parameters are applied. In such cases, the need for checks for stunning would appear unnecessary and disproportionate. It is therefore appropriate to provide for the possibility to grant derogations from the obligations regarding checks on stunning when there is sufficient scientific evidence that a given stunning protocol provides for irreversible death to all animals under certain commercial conditions.

(27) The welfare of animals is largely influenced by the daily management of the operations, and reliable results can only be obtained if business operators develop monitoring tools to evaluate their effects. Standard operating procedures should therefore be developed at all stages of the production cycle and should be risk-based. They should include clear objectives, responsible persons, modus operandi, measurable criteria, as well as monitoring and recording procedures. Key parameters set out for each stunning method should be specified in a way ensuring proper stunning of all animals submitted to the process.

(28) Well trained and skilled personnel improve the conditions under which animals are treated. Competence with regards to animal welfare implies knowledge of the basic behavioural patterns and the needs of the species concerned as well as signs of consciousness and sensibility. It also includes technical expertise with regard to the stunning equipment used. Personnel carrying out certain slaughter operations and people supervising the seasonal killing of

fur animals should therefore be required to have a certificate of competence relevant to the operations they perform. Requiring a certificate of competence for other personnel killing animals would, however, be disproportionate to the aims pursued.

(29) Personnel with several years of experience may be presumed to have a certain level of expertise. A transitional provision regarding the certificate of competence requirements should therefore be provided for in this Regulation with regards to such personnel.

(30) Stunning equipment is developed and designed to be efficient in a specific context. Manufacturers should therefore provide detailed instructions to users concerning the conditions under which equipment should be used and maintained to ensure optimal welfare for the animals.

(31) In order to ensure efficiency, stunning and restraining equipment should be properly maintained. Equipment that is used intensively may require the replacement of certain parts and even equipment occasionally used may decrease in efficiency due to corrosion or other environmental factors. Similarly, some equipment also needs to be accurately calibrated. Business operators or any person involved in the killing of animals should therefore implement maintenance procedures for that equipment.

(32) Restraining animals is necessary for the safety of operators and the proper application of some stunning techniques. However, restraining is likely to create distress to the animals and should therefore be applied for as short a period as possible.

(33) Animals may suffer when stunning procedures fail. This Regulation should therefore provide for appropriate back-up stunning equipment to be available to minimise pain, distress or suffering to the animals.

(34) The scale of the slaughtering of poultry, rabbits and hares for the direct supply of small quantities of meat to the final consumer or to local retail establishments supplying such meat directly to the final consumer as fresh meat, varies from one Member State to the other due to the national rules governing this activity in accordance with Article 1(3)(d) and 4 of Regulation (EC) No 853/2004. It is, however, important to ensure that certain minimum animal welfare requirements apply also to those activities.

(35) With regard to the slaughter of certain categories of animals, other than poultry, rabbits and hares, for private domestic consumption, certain minimum Community requirements such as prior stunning as well as national rules exist already. Therefore, it is appropriate to ensure that minimum animal welfare rules are established also in this Regulation.

(36) Regulation (EC) No 854/2004 provides for a list of establishments from which imports into the Community of specified products of animal origin are permitted. The general requirements and the additional requirements applicable to slaughterhouses laid down in this Regulation should be taken into account for the purposes of that list.

(37) The Community seeks to promote high welfare standards in animal livestock populations worldwide, particularly in relation to trade. It supports the

specific standards and recommendations on animal welfare of the OIE, including on the slaughter of animals. Such standards and recommendations should be taken into account when equivalency with Community requirements under this Regulation needs to be established for the purpose of imports.

(38) Guides to good practice drawn up by organisations of business operators are valuable instruments to help business operators comply with certain requirements laid down in this Regulation, such as, for instance, the development and implementation of standard operating procedures.

(39) Slaughterhouses and the equipment used therein are designed for particular categories of animals and capacities. Where those capacities are exceeded or the equipment is used for purposes for which it was not designed, it has a negative impact on the welfare of animals. Information on these aspects should therefore be communicated to the competent authorities and should be part of the approval procedure for slaughterhouses.

(40) Mobile slaughterhouses reduce the need for animals to be transported over long distances and therefore may contribute to safeguarding animal welfare. However, technical constraints for mobile slaughterhouses differ from fixed slaughterhouses and technical rules may need to be consequently adapted. Therefore, this Regulation should provide for the possibility to establish derogations exempting mobile slaughterhouses from the requirements on layout, construction and equipment of slaughterhouses. Pending the adoption of such derogations, it is appropriate to allow Member States to establish or maintain national rules regarding mobile slaughterhouses.

(41) Scientific and technical progress is regularly made with regard to the construction, layout and equipment of slaughterhouses. It is therefore important to authorise the Commission to amend the requirements applicable to the construction, layout and equipment of slaughterhouses while keeping a uniform and high level of protection for animals.

(42) Community guidelines are useful to provide business operators and the competent authorities with specific information on the construction, layout and equipment of slaughterhouses in order to ensure a high level of protection for animals, while maintaining a level playing field for business operators. It is therefore necessary to authorise the Commission to adopt such guidelines.

(43) Slaughter without stunning requires an accurate cut of the throat with a sharp knife to minimise suffering. In addition, animals that are not mechanically restrained after the cut are likely to endure a slower bleeding process and, thereby, prolonged unnecessary suffering. Animals of bovine, ovine and caprine species are the most common species slaughtered under this procedure. Therefore, ruminants slaughtered without stunning should be individually and mechanically restrained.

(44) Science and technical progress are regularly made with regard to the handling and restraining of animals at slaughterhouses. It is therefore important to authorise the Commission to amend the requirements applicable to the

handling and restraining of animals before slaughter while keeping a uniform and high level of protection for animals.

(45) Community guidelines are useful to provide business operators and competent authorities with specific information on the handling and restraining of animals before slaughter in order to ensure a high level of protection for the animals, while maintaining a level playing field for business operators. It is therefore necessary to authorise the Commission to adopt such guidelines.

(46) The experience gained in some Member States has shown that the appointment of a specifically qualified person as an animal welfare officer to coordinate and follow up the implementation of animal welfare operating procedures in slaughterhouses has provided positive welfare benefits. This measure should therefore be applied throughout the Community. The animal welfare officer should have sufficient authority and technical competence to provide relevant guidance to slaughter line personnel.

(47) Small slaughterhouses predominantly involved in the direct sale of food to the final consumer do not require a complex system of management to implement the general principles of this Regulation. The requirement to have an animal welfare officer in place would therefore be disproportionate to the objectives pursued in those cases and this Regulation should provide for a derogation from that requirement for such slaughterhouses.

(48) Depopulation often involves crisis management with parallel priorities, such as animal health, public health, environment, or animal welfare. Whilst it is important that animal welfare rules are complied with at all stages in the process of depopulation, it may occur that under exceptional circumstances compliance with those rules may put human health at risk or may significantly slow down the process of eradication of a disease, thereby exposing more animals to sickness and death.

(49) Accordingly, the competent authorities should be permitted to derogate from certain provisions of this Regulation on a case-by-case basis where the animal health situation requires the emergency killing of animals and/or when no suitable alternatives are available to provide optimum welfare for them. Such derogations should not, however, be a substitute for proper planning. To this end, the level of planning should be increased and animal welfare properly integrated into contingency plans for contagious diseases.

(50) For the purpose of animal disease notification procedures, information on outbreaks of diseases in accordance with Directive 82/894/EEC of 21 December 1982 on the notification of animal diseases within the Community[9] is notified through the Animal Disease Notification System (ADNS). At present, ADNS does not provide specific information on animal welfare but may be developed in the future to do so. As a consequence, a derogation from the reporting obligation on animal welfare in case of depopulation should be foreseen in order to envisage the further development of ADNS.

9. OJ L 378, 31.12.1982, p. 58.

(51) Modern stunning and restraining equipment is increasingly complex and sophisticated, requiring specific expertise and analysis. Member States should therefore ensure that sufficient scientific support is made available to the competent authority, to which officials could refer when equipment or methods for stunning animals need to be assessed.

(52) The efficiency of each stunning method is based on the control of key parameters and its regular evaluation. Developing guides to good practice on operating and monitoring procedures for use when killing animals is important in providing proper guidance on animal welfare for business operators. The evaluation of such guides requires scientific knowledge, practical experience and compromise among stakeholders. A reference centre or network in each Member State should therefore perform this task in cooperation with the relevant interested parties.

(53) The delivery of certificates of competence should be provided in a uniform manner. Bodies or entities issuing certificates of competence should therefore be accredited according to consistent standards which should be assessed scientifically. Accordingly, the entity providing scientific support in conformity with Article 20 should provide, where necessary, its opinion on the capacity and suitability of bodies or entities issuing certificates of competence.

(54) Regulation (EC) No 882/2004 provides for certain action to be taken by the competent authority in case of non-compliance, in particular with regard to welfare rules. Accordingly, it is only necessary to provide for the additional action to be taken that is specific to this Regulation.

(55) Regulation (EC) No 178/2002 provides that EFSA shall promote the networking of organisations operating in the field within the Authority's missions so as to facilitate scientific cooperation, the exchange of information, the development and implementation of joint projects, as well as the exchange of expertise and best practices in the field of food law.

(56) The delivery of certificates of competence and training courses should be provided in a uniform manner. This Regulation should therefore set out the obligations of the Member States in this respect and the modalities under which certificates of competence are to be granted, suspended or withdrawn.

(57) European citizens expect a minimum of welfare rules to be respected during the slaughter of animals. In certain areas, attitudes towards animals also depend on national perceptions and there is a demand in some Member States to maintain or adopt more extensive animal welfare rules than those agreed upon at Community level. In the interest of the animals and provided that it does not affect the functioning of the internal market, it is appropriate to allow Member States certain flexibility to maintain or, in certain specific fields, adopt more extensive national rules.

It is important to ensure that such national rules are not used by Member States in a way to prejudice the correct functioning of the internal market.

(58) In some areas within the scope of this Regulation, the Council needs further scientific, social and economic information before establishing detailed rules, in particular, in the case of farmed fish and concerning the restraint by inversion of cattle. As a consequence, it is necessary that the Commission provide this information to the Council before proposing any amendment in those areas of this Regulation.

(59) The layout, construction and equipment of slaughterhouses require long-term planning and investment. Accordingly, this Regulation should provide for an appropriate transitional period to take into account the necessary time to allow the industry to adapt to the corresponding requirements set out in this Regulation. During that period, the requirements of Directive 93/119/EC that are applicable to the layout, construction and equipment of slaughterhouses should continue to apply.

(60) Member States should lay down rules on penalties applicable to infringements of the provisions of this Regulation and ensure that they are implemented. Those penalties should be effective, proportionate and dissuasive.

(61) Since the objective of this Regulation, namely to ensure a harmonised approach with regard to animal welfare standards at the time of killing, cannot be sufficiently achieved by the Member States and can therefore, by reason of the scale and effects of this Regulation, be better achieved at Community level, the Community may adopt measures, in accordance with the principle of subsidiarity as set out in Article 5 of the Treaty. In accordance with the principle of proportionality, as set out in that Article, it is necessary and appropriate for the achievement of that objective to lay down specific rules for the killing of animals for the production of food, wool, skin, fur or other products, and for related operations. This Regulation does not go beyond what is necessary in order to achieve that objective.

(62) The measures necessary for the implementation of this Regulation should be adopted in accordance with Council Decision 1999/468/EC of 28 June 1999 laying down the procedures for the exercise of implementing powers conferred on the Commission,[10]

HAS ADOPTED THIS REGULATION:

CHAPTER I
SUBJECT MATTER, SCOPE AND DEFINITIONS

Article 1
Subject matter and scope

1. This Regulation lays down rules for the killing of animals bred or kept for the production of food, wool, skin, fur or other products as well as the killing of animals for the purpose of depopulation and for related operations.

10. OJ L 184, 17.7.1999, p. 23.

However as regards fish, only the requirements laid down in Article 3(1) shall apply.

2. Chapter II, except for Article 3(1) and (2) thereof, Chapter III and Chapter IV except for Article 19 thereof, shall not apply in case of emergency killing outside of a slaughterhouse or where compliance with those provisions would result in an immediate and serious risk for human health or safety.
3. This Regulation shall not apply:
   (a) where animals are killed:
      (i) during scientific experiments carried out under the supervision of a competent authority;
      (ii) during hunting or recreational fishing activities;
      (iii) during cultural or sporting events;
   (b) to poultry, rabbits and hares slaughtered outside of a slaughterhouse by their owner for his/her private domestic consumption.

Article 2
Definitions

For the purposes of this Regulation, the following definitions shall apply:

(a) "killing" means any intentionally induced process which causes the death of an animal;
(b) "related operations" means operations such as handling, lairaging, restraining, stunning and bleeding of animals taking place in the context and at the location where they are to be killed;
(c) "animal" means any vertebrate animal, excluding reptiles and amphibians;
(d) "emergency killing" means the killing of animals which are injured or have a disease associated with severe pain or suffering and where there is no other practical possibility to alleviate this pain or suffering;
(e) "lairaging" means keeping animals in stalls, pens, covered areas or fields associated with or part of slaughterhouse operations;
(f) "stunning" means any intentionally induced process which causes loss of consciousness and sensibility without pain, including any process resulting in instantaneous death;
(g) "religious rite" means a series of acts related to the slaughter of animals and prescribed by a religion;
(h) "cultural or sporting events" means events which are essentially and predominantly related to long established cultural traditions or sporting activities, including racing or other forms of competitions, where there is no production of meat or other animal products or where that production is marginal compared to the event as such and not economically significant;
(i) "standard operating procedures" means a set of written instructions aimed at achieving uniformity of the performance of a specific function or standard;
(j) "slaughtering" means the killing of animals intended for human consumption;

(k) "slaughterhouse" means any establishment used for slaughtering terrestrial animals which falls within the scope of Regulation (EC) No 853/2004;
(l) "business operator" means any natural or legal person having under its control an undertaking carrying out the killing of animals or any related operations falling within the scope of this Regulation;
(m) "fur animals" means animals of the mammal species primarily reared for the production of fur such as minks, polecats, foxes, raccoons, coypu and chinchillas;
(n) "depopulation" means the process of killing animals for public health, animal health, animal welfare or environmental reasons under the supervision of the competent authority;
(o) "poultry" means farmed birds, including birds that are not considered to be domestic birds but which are farmed as domestic animals, with the exception of ratites;
(p) "restraint" means the application to an animal of any procedure designed to restrict its movements sparing any avoidable pain, fear or agitation in order to facilitate effective stunning and killing;
(q) "competent authority" means the central authority of a Member State competent to ensure compliance with the requirements of this Regulation or any other authority to which that central authority has delegated that competence;
(r) "pithing" means the laceration of the central nervous tissue and spinal cord by means of an elongated rod-shaped instrument introduced into the cranial cavity.

CHAPTER II
GENERAL REQUIREMENTS

Article 3
General requirements for killing and related operations

1. Animals shall be spared any avoidable pain, distress or suffering during their killing and related operations.
2. For the purposes of paragraph 1, business operators shall, in particular, take the necessary measures to ensure that animals:
   (a) are provided with physical comfort and protection, in particular by being kept clean in adequate thermal conditions and prevented from falling or slipping;
   (b) are protected from injury;
   (c) are handled and housed taking into consideration their normal behaviour;
   (d) do not show signs of avoidable pain or fear or exhibit abnormal behaviour;
   (e) do not suffer from prolonged withdrawal of feed or water;
   (f) are prevented from avoidable interaction with other animals that could harm their welfare.
3. Facilities used for killing and related operations shall be designed, constructed, maintained and operated so as to ensure compliance with the obligations set out in paragraphs 1 and 2 under the expected conditions of activity of the facility throughout the year.

Article 4
Stunning methods

1. Animals shall only be killed after stunning in accordance with the methods and specific requirements related to the application of those methods set out in Annex I. The loss of consciousness and sensibility shall be maintained until the death of the animal.
   The methods referred to in Annex I which do not result in instantaneous death (hereinafter referred to as simple stunning) shall be followed as quickly as possible by a procedure ensuring death such as bleeding, pithing, electrocution or prolonged exposure to anoxia.
2. Annex I may be amended to take account of scientific and technical progress on the basis of an opinion of EFSA and in accordance with the procedure referred to in Article 25(2).
   Any such amendments shall ensure a level of animal welfare at least equivalent to that ensured by the existing methods.
3. Community guidelines concerning the methods set out in Annex I may be adopted in accordance with the procedure referred to in Article 25(2).
4. In the case of animals subject to particular methods of slaughter prescribed by religious rites, the requirements of paragraph 1 shall not apply provided that the slaughter takes place in a slaughterhouse.

Article 5
Checks on stunning

1. Business operators shall ensure that persons responsible for stunning or other nominated staff carry out regular checks to ensure that the animals do not present any signs of consciousness or sensibility in the period between the end of the stunning process and death.
   Those checks shall be carried out on a sufficiently representative sample of animals and their frequency shall be established taking into account the outcome of previous checks and any factors which may affect the efficiency of the stunning process.
   When the outcome of the checks indicates that an animal is not properly stunned, the person in charge of stunning shall immediately take the appropriate measures as specified in the standard operating procedures drawn up in accordance with Article 6(2).
2. Where, for the purpose of Article 4(4), animals are killed without prior stunning, persons responsible for slaughtering shall carry out systematic checks to ensure that the animals do not present any signs of consciousness or sensibility before being released from restraint and do not present any sign of life before undergoing dressing or scalding.
3. For the purpose of paragraphs 1 and 2, business operators may use checking procedures as described in the guides to good practice referred to in Article 13.

4. Where appropriate, in order to take account of the high level of reliability of certain stunning methods and on the basis of an opinion of EFSA, derogations from the requirements laid down in paragraph 1 may be adopted in accordance with the procedure referred to in Article 25(2).

Article 6
Standard operating procedures

1. Business operators shall plan in advance the killing of animals and related operations and shall carry them out in accordance with standard operating procedures.
2. Business operators shall draw up and implement such standard operating procedures to ensure that killing and related operations are carried out in accordance with Article 3(1).
   As regards stunning, the standard operating procedures shall:
   (a) take into account the manufacturers' recommendations;
   (b) define for each stunning method used, on the basis of available scientific evidence, the key parameters set out in Chapter I of Annex I ensuring their effectiveness to stun the animals;
   (c) specify the measures to be taken when the checks referred to in Article 5 indicate that an animal is not properly stunned or, in the case of animals slaughtered in accordance with Article 4(4), that the animal still presents signs of life.
3. For the purpose of paragraph 2 of this Article, a business operator may use standard operating procedures as described in the guides to good practice referred to in Article 13.
4. Business operators shall make available to the competent authority their standard operating procedures upon request.

Article 7
Level and certificate of competence

1. Killing and related operations shall only be carried out by persons with the appropriate level of competence to do so without causing the animals any avoidable pain, distress or suffering.
2. Business operators shall ensure that the following slaughter operations are only carried out by persons holding a certificate of competence for such operations, as provided for in Article 21, demonstrating their ability to carry them out in accordance with the rules laid down in this Regulation:
   (a) the handling and care of animals before they are restrained;
   (b) the restraint of animals for the purpose of stunning or killing;
   (c) the stunning of animals;
   (d) the assessment of effective stunning;
   (e) the shackling or hoisting of live animals;
   (f) the bleeding of live animals;
   (g) the slaughtering in accordance with Article 4(4).

3. Without prejudice to the obligation set out in paragraph 1 of this Article, the killing of fur animals shall be carried out in the presence and under the direct supervision of a person holding a certificate of competence as referred to in Article 21 issued for all the operations carried out under his supervision. Business operators of fur farms shall notify the competent authority in advance when animals are to be killed.

Article 8
Instructions for the use of restraining and stunning equipment

Products marketed or advertised as restraining or stunning equipment shall only be sold when accompanied by appropriate instructions concerning their use in a manner which ensures optimal conditions for the welfare of animals. Those instructions shall also be made publicly available by the manufacturers via the Internet.
Those instructions shall in particular specify:
(a) the species, categories, quantities and/or weights of animals for which the equipment is intended to be used;
(b) the recommended parameters corresponding to the different circumstances of use, including the key parameters set out in Chapter I of Annex I;
(c) for stunning equipment, a method for monitoring the efficiency of the equipment as regards compliance with the rules laid down in this Regulation;
(d) the recommendations for maintenance and, where necessary, calibration of the stunning equipment.

Article 9
Use of restraining and stunning equipment

1. Business operators shall ensure that all equipment used for restraining or stunning animals is maintained and checked in accordance with the manufacturers' instructions by persons specifically trained for that purpose.
   Business operators shall draw up a record of maintenance. They shall keep those records for at least one year and shall make them available to the competent authority upon request.
2. Business operators shall ensure that during stunning operations appropriate back-up equipment is immediately available on the spot and is used in the case of failure of the stunning equipment initially used. The back-up method may differ from that first used.
3. Business operators shall ensure that animals are not placed in restraining equipment, including head restraints, until the person in charge of stunning or bleeding is ready to stun or bleed them as quickly as possible.

Article 10
Private domestic consumption

Only the requirements of Articles 3(1), 4 (1) and 7(1) shall apply to the slaughtering of animals, other than poultry, rabbits and hares, and the related operations outside of a slaughterhouse by their owner or by a person under the responsibility and supervision of the owner, for private domestic consumption.

However, also the requirements laid down in Article 15(3) and in points 1.8 to 1.11, 3.1 and, in as far as it refers to simple stunning, point 3.2 of Annex III shall apply to the slaughtering of animals, other than poultry, rabbits, hares, pigs, sheep and goats, outside of a slaughterhouse by their owner or by a person under the responsibility and supervision of the owner for private domestic consumption.

Article 11
Direct supply of small quantities of poultry, rabbits and hares

1. Only the requirements of Articles 3(1), 4(1) and 7(1) shall apply to the slaughtering of poultry, rabbits and hares on the farm for the purpose of directly supplying small quantities of meat by the producer to the final consumer or to local retail establishments supplying such meat directly to the final consumer as fresh meat, provided that the number of animals slaughtered on the farm does not exceed the maximum number of animals to be established in accordance with the procedure referred to in Article 25(2).
2. The requirements laid down in Chapters II and III of this Regulation shall apply to the slaughtering of such animals when their number exceeds the maximum number referred to in paragraph 1 of this Article.

Article 12
Imports from third countries

The requirements laid down in Chapters II and III of this Regulation shall apply for the purposes of Article 12(2)(a) of Regulation (EC) No 854/2004.

The health certificate accompanying meat imported from third countries shall be supplemented by an attestation certifying that requirements at least equivalent to those laid down in Chapters II and III of this Regulation have been met.

Article 13
Development and dissemination of guides to good practice

1. Member States shall encourage the development and dissemination of guides to good practice to facilitate the implementation of this Regulation.
2. When such guides to good practice are drawn up, they shall be developed and disseminated by organisations of business operators:
   (a) in consultation with representatives of non governmental organisations, competent authorities and other interested parties;

(b) having regard to scientific opinions as referred to in Article 20(1)(c).

3. The competent authority shall assess guides to good practice in order to ensure that they have been developed in accordance with paragraph 2 and that they are consistent with existing Community guidelines.
4. Where organisations of business operators fail to submit guides to good practice, the competent authority may develop and publish its own guides to good practice.
5. Member States shall forward to the Commission all guides to good practice validated by the competent authority. The Commission shall set up and run a registration system for such guides and make it available to Member States.

CHAPTER III
ADDITIONAL REQUIREMENTS APPLICABLE TO SLAUGHTERHOUSES

Article 14
Layout, construction and equipment of slaughterhouses

1. Business operators shall ensure that the layout and construction of slaughterhouses and the equipment used therein comply with the rules set out in Annex II.
2. For the purposes of this Regulation, business operators shall, when requested, submit to the competent authority referred to in Article 4 of Regulation (EC) No. 853/2004 for each slaughterhouse at least the following:
   (a) the maximum number of animals per hour for each slaughter line;
   (b) the categories of animals and weights for which the restraining or stunning equipment available may be used;
   (c) the maximum capacity for each lairage area.

   The competent authority shall assess the information submitted by the operator in accordance with the first subparagraph when approving the slaughterhouse.
3. The following may be adopted in accordance with the procedure referred to in Article 25(2):
   (a) derogations from the rules set out in Annex II for mobile slaughterhouses;
   (b) amendments necessary to adapt Annex II to take account of scientific and technical progress.

   Pending the adoption of derogations referred to in point (a) of the first subparagraph, the Member States may establish or maintain national rules applying to mobile slaughterhouses.
4. Community guidelines for the implementation of paragraph 2 of this Article and Annex II may be adopted in accordance with the procedure referred to in Article 25(2).

Article 15
Handling and restraining operations at slaughterhouses

1. Business operators shall ensure that the operational rules for slaughterhouses set out in Annex III are complied with.
2. Business operators shall ensure that all animals that are killed in accordance with Article 4(4) without prior stunning are individually restrained; ruminants shall be mechanically restrained.

Systems restraining bovine animals by inversion or any unnatural position shall not be used except in the case of animals slaughtered in accordance with Article 4(4) and provided that they are fitted with a device that restricts both the lateral and vertical movement of the head of the animal and are adjustable to be adapted to the size of the animal.

3. The following methods of restraint shall be prohibited:
   (a) suspending or hoisting conscious animals;
   (b) mechanical clamping or tying of the legs or feet of animals;
   (c) severing the spinal cord, such as by the use of a puntilla or dagger;
   (d) the use of electric currents to immobilise the animal that do not stun or kill it under controlled circumstances, in particular, any electric current application that does not span the brain.

   However, points (a) and (b) shall not apply to the shackles used for poultry.
4. To take account of scientific and technical progress, including an opinion of EFSA; Annex III may be amended in accordance with the procedure referred to in Article 25(2).
5. Community guidelines for the implementation of the rules set out in Annex III may be adopted in accordance with the procedure referred to in Article 25(2).

Article 16
Monitoring procedures at slaughterhouses

1. For the purposes of Article 5, business operators shall put in place and implement appropriate monitoring procedures in slaughterhouses.
2. The monitoring procedures referred to in paragraph 1 of this Article shall describe the way the checks referred to in Article 5 have to be carried out and shall include at least the following:
   (a) the name of the persons responsible for the monitoring procedure;
   (b) indicators designed to detect signs of unconsciousness and consciousness or sensibility in the animals; indicators designed to detect the absence of signs of life in the animals slaughtered in accordance with Article 4(4);
   (c) criteria for determining whether the results shown by the indicators referred to in point (b) are satisfactory;
   (d) the circumstances and/or the time when the monitoring must take place;
   (e) the number of animals in each sample to be checked during the monitoring;
   (f) appropriate procedures to ensure that in the event that the criteria referred to in point (c) are not met, the stunning or killing operations are reviewed

in order to identify the causes of any shortcomings and the necessary changes to be made to those operations.

3. Business operators shall put in place a specific monitoring procedure for each slaughter line.
4. The frequency of the checks shall take into account the main risk factors, such as changes regarding the types or the size of animals slaughtered or personnel working patterns and shall be established so as to ensure results with a high level of confidence.
5. For the purpose of paragraphs 1 to 4 of this Article, business operators may use monitoring procedures as described in the guides to good practice referred to in Article 13.
6. Community guidelines concerning monitoring procedures in slaughterhouses may be adopted in accordance with the procedure referred to in Article 25(2).

Article 17
Animal welfare officer

1. Business operators shall designate an animal welfare officer for each slaughterhouse to assist them in ensuring compliance with the rules laid down in this Regulation.
2. The animal welfare officer shall be under the direct authority of the business operator and shall report directly to him or her on matters relating to the welfare of the animals. He or she shall be in a position to require that the slaughterhouse personnel carry out any remedial actions necessary to ensure compliance with the rules laid down in this Regulation.
3. The responsibilities of the animal welfare officer shall be set out in the standard operating procedures of the slaughterhouse and effectively brought to the attention of the personnel concerned.
4. The animal welfare officer shall hold a certificate of competence as referred to in Article 21, issued for all the operations taking place in the slaughterhouses for which he or she is responsible.
5. The animal welfare officer shall keep a record of the action taken to improve animal welfare in the slaughterhouse in which he/she carries out his/her tasks. This record shall be kept for at least one year and shall be made available to the competent authority upon request.
6. Paragraphs 1 to 5 shall not apply to slaughterhouses slaughtering less than 1000 livestock units of mammals or 150000 birds or rabbits per year.
   For the purpose of the first subparagraph, "livestock unit" means a standard measurement unit that allows the aggregation of the various categories of livestock in order to enable them to be compared.
   When applying the first subparagraph, Member States shall use the following conversion rates:
   (a) adult bovine animals within the meaning of Council Regulation (EC) No. 1234/2007 of 22 October 2007 establishing a common organisation of

agricultural markets and on specific provisions for certain agricultural products (Single CMO Regulation)[11] and equidae: 1 livestock unit;
(b) other bovine animals: 0,50 livestock unit;
(c) pigs with a live weight of over 100 kg: 0,20 livestock unit;
(d) other pigs: 0,15 livestock unit;
(e) sheep and goats: 0,10 livestock unit;
(f) lambs, kids and piglets of less than 15 kg live weight: 0,05 livestock unit.

CHAPTER IV
DEPOPULATION AND EMERGENCY KILLING

Article 18
Depopulation

1. The competent authority responsible for a depopulation operation shall establish an action plan to ensure compliance with the rules laid down in this Regulation, before the commencement of the operation.
   In particular, the stunning and killing methods planned and the corresponding standard operating procedures for ensuring compliance with the rules laid down in this Regulation shall be included in the contingency plans required under Community law on animal health, on the basis of the hypothesis established in the contingency plan concerning the size and the location of suspected outbreaks.
2. The competent authority shall:
   (a) ensure that such operations are carried out in accordance with the action plan referred to in paragraph 1;
   (b) take any appropriate action to safeguard the welfare of the animals in the best available conditions.
3. For the purposes of this Article and in exceptional circumstances, the competent authority may grant derogations from one or more of the provisions of this Regulation where it considers that compliance is likely to affect human health or significantly slow down the process of eradication of a disease.
4. By 30 June each year, the competent authority referred to in paragraph 1 shall transmit to the Commission a report on the depopulation operations carried out during the previous year and make it publicly available via the Internet.
   With regards to each depopulation operation, that report shall include, in particular:
   (a) the reasons for the depopulation;
   (b) the number and the species of animals killed;
   (c) the stunning and killing methods used;

11. OJ L 299, 16.11.2007, p. 1.

(d) a description of the difficulties encountered and, where appropriate, solutions found to alleviate or minimise the suffering of the animals concerned;
(e) any derogation granted in accordance with paragraph 3.

5. Community guidelines for the drawing up and implementation of depopulation action plans may be adopted in accordance with the procedure referred to in Article 25(2).
6. Where appropriate, in order to take account of the information collected by the ADNS, a derogation from the reporting obligation laid down in paragraph 4 of this Article may be adopted in accordance with the procedure referred to in Article 25(2).

Article 19
Emergency killing

In the case of emergency killing, the keeper of the animals concerned shall take all the necessary measures to kill the animal as soon as possible.

CHAPTER V
COMPETENT AUTHORITY

Article 20
Scientific support

1. Each Member State shall ensure that sufficient independent scientific support is available to assist the competent authorities, upon their request, by providing:
   (a) scientific and technical expertise relating to the approval of slaughterhouses as referred to in Article 14(2) and the development of new stunning methods;
   (b) scientific opinions on the instructions provided by manufacturers on the use and maintenance of restraining and stunning equipment;
   (c) scientific opinions on guides to good practice developed within its territory for the purposes of this Regulation;
   (d) recommendations for the purposes of this Regulation, in particular in relation to inspections and audits;
   (e) opinions on the capacity and suitability of separate bodies and entities to fulfil the requirements laid down in Article 21(2).
2. Scientific support may be provided via a network, subject to all the tasks listed in paragraph 1 being performed with respect to all the relevant activities taking place in the Member States concerned.
   For this purpose, each Member State shall identify a single contact point and make it publicly available via the Internet. Such contact point shall be responsible for sharing technical and scientific information and best practices regarding the implementation of this Regulation with its counterparts and the Commission.

Article 21
Certificate of competence

1. For the purposes of Article 7, Member States shall designate the competent authority responsible for:
   (a) ensuring that training courses are available for personnel involved in killing and related operations;
   (b) delivering certificates of competence attesting the passing of an independent final examination; the subjects of this examination shall be relevant for the categories of animals concerned and correspond to the operations referred to in Article 7(2) and (3), and to the subjects set out in Annex IV;
   (c) approving training programmes of the courses referred to in point (a) and the content and modalities of the examination referred in point (b).
2. The competent authority may delegate the final examination and the issuance of the certificate of competence to a separate body or entity which:
   (a) has the expertise, staff and equipment necessary to do so;
   (b) is independent and free from any conflict of interest as regards the final examination and the issuance of the certificates of competence.

   The competent authority may also delegate the organisation of the training courses to a separate body or entity which has the expertise, staff and equipment necessary to do so. The details of bodies and entities to which such tasks have been delegated shall be made publicly available by the competent authority via the Internet.
3. Certificates of competence shall indicate for which categories of animals, type of equipment and for which of the operations listed in Article 7(2) or (3) the certificate is valid.
4. Member States shall recognise certificates of competence issued in another Member State.
5. The competent authority may issue temporary certificates of competence provided that:
   (a) the applicant is registered in one of the training courses referred to in paragraph 1(a);
   (b) the applicant is to work in the presence and under the direct supervision of another person who holds a certificate of competence issued for the specific activity to be undertaken;
   (c) the validity of the temporary certificate does not exceed three months; and
   (d) the applicant provides a written declaration stating that he/she has not previously been issued another temporary certificate of competence of the same scope or demonstrates to the satisfaction of the competent authority that he/she was unable to take the final examination.
6. Without prejudice to a decision by a judicial authority or by a competent authority prohibiting the handling of animals, certificates of competence, including a temporary certificate of competence, shall only be issued if the applicant provides a written declaration stating that he/she has committed no serious infringement of Community law and/or national law on the protection

of animals in the three years preceding the date of application for such a certificate.

7. Member States may recognise qualifications obtained for other purposes as equivalent to certificates of competence for the purposes of this Regulation provided that they have been obtained under conditions equivalent to those laid down in this Article. The competent authority shall make publicly available and keep up to date, via the Internet, a list of qualifications recognised as equivalent to the certificate of competence.
8. Community guidelines for the application of paragraph 1 of this Article may be adopted in accordance with the procedure referred to in Article 25(2).

CHAPTER VI
NON-COMPLIANCE, PENALTIES AND IMPLEMENTING POWERS

Article 22
Non-compliance

1. For the purpose of Article 54 of Regulation (EC) No 882/2004, the competent authority may in particular:
   (a) require business operators to amend their standard operating procedures and, in particular, slow down or stop production;
   (b) require business operators to increase the frequency of the checks referred to in Article 5 and amend the monitoring procedures referred to in Article 16;
   (c) suspend or withdraw certificates of competence issued under this Regulation from a person who no longer shows sufficient competence, knowledge or awareness of his/her tasks to carry out the operations for which the certificate was issued;
   (d) suspend or withdraw the delegation of power referred to in Article 21(2);
   (e) require the amendment of the instructions referred to in Article 8 with due regard to the scientific opinions provided pursuant to Article 20(1)(b).
2. When a competent authority suspends or withdraws a certificate of competence, it shall inform the granting competent authority of its decision.

Article 23
Penalties

The Member States shall lay down the rules on penalties applicable to infringements of this Regulation and shall take all measures necessary to ensure that they are implemented. The penalties provided for must be effective, proportionate and dissuasive. The Member States shall notify those provisions to the Commission by 1 January 2013 and shall notify it without delay of any subsequent amendment affecting them.

Article 24
Implementing rules

Any detailed rules necessary for the implementation of this Regulation may be adopted in accordance with the procedure referred to in Article 25(2).

Article 25
Committee procedure

1. The Commission shall be assisted by the Standing Committee on the Food Chain and Animal Health, established by Article 58 of Regulation (EC) No. 178/2002.
2. Where reference is made to this paragraph, Articles 5 and 7 of Decision 1999/468/EC shall apply.

The period referred to in Article 5(6) of Decision 1999/468/EC shall be set at three months.

CHAPTER VII
FINAL PROVISIONS

Article 26
Stricter national rules

1. This Regulation shall not prevent Member States from maintaining any national rules aimed at ensuring more extensive protection of animals at the time of killing in force at the time of entry into force of this Regulation.

   Before 1 January 2013, Member States shall inform the Commission about such national rules. The Commission shall bring them to the attention of the other Member States.
2. Member States may adopt national rules aimed at ensuring more extensive protection of animals at the time of killing than those contained in this Regulation in relation to the following fields:
   (a) the killing and related operations of animals outside of a slaughterhouse;
   (b) the slaughtering and related operations of farmed game as defined in point 1.6 of Annex I to Regulation (EC) No 853/2004, including reindeer;
   (c) the slaughtering and related operations of animals in accordance with Article 4(4).

   Member States shall notify the Commission of any such national rules. The Commission shall bring them to the attention of the other Member States.
3. Where, on the basis of new scientific evidence, a Member State deems it necessary to take measures aimed at ensuring more extensive protection of animals at the time of killing in relation to the methods of stunning referred to in

Annex I, it shall notify the Commission of the envisaged measures. The Commission shall bring them to the attention of the other Member States.

The Commission shall put the matter before the Committee referred to in Article 25(1) within 1 month of the notification and shall, on the basis of an opinion of EFSA and in accordance with the procedure referred to in Article 25(2), approve or reject the national measures involved.

Where the Commission deems it appropriate, it may, on the basis of the approved national measures, propose amendments to Annex I in accordance with Article 4(2).

4. A Member State shall not prohibit or impede the putting into circulation within its territory of products of animal origin derived from animals that have been killed in another Member State on the grounds that the animals concerned have not been killed in accordance with its national rules aimed at a more extensive protection of animals at the time of killing.

Article 27
Reporting

1. No later than 8 December 2014, the Commission shall submit to the European Parliament and to the Council a report on the possibility of introducing certain requirements regarding the protection of fish at the time of killing taking into account animal welfare aspects as well as the socioeconomic and environmental impacts. This report shall, if appropriate, be accompanied by legislative proposals with a view to amending this Regulation, by including specific rules regarding the protection of fish at the time of killing.

   Pending the adoption of these measures, Member States may maintain or adopt national rules regarding the protection of fish at the time of slaughter or killing and shall inform the Commission thereof.
2. No later than 8 December 2012, the Commission shall submit to the European Parliament and to the Council a report on systems restraining bovine animals by inversion or any unnatural position. This report shall be based on the results of a scientific study comparing these systems to the ones maintaining bovines in the upright position and shall take into account animal welfare aspects as well as the socioeconomic implications, including their acceptability by the religious communities and the safety of operators. This report shall, if appropriate, be accompanied by legislative proposals with a view to amending this Regulation concerning the systems restraining bovine animals by inversion or any unnatural position.
3. No later than 8 December 2013, the Commission shall submit to the European Parliament and to the Council a report on the various stunning methods for poultry, and in particular multiple-bird waterbath stunners, taking into account animal welfare aspects, as well as the socioeconomic and environmental impacts.

Article 28
Repeal

1. Directive 93/119/EEC is repealed.
   However, for the purpose of Article 29(1) of this Regulation, the following provisions of Directive 93/119/EEC shall continue to apply:
   (a) Annex A:
      (i) paragraph 1 of Section I;
      (ii) paragraph 1 and the second sentence of paragraph 3 and paragraphs 6, 7, 8 and the first sentence of paragraph 9 of Section II;
   (b) Annex C, paragraphs 3.A.2, the first subparagraph of 3.B.1, 3.B.2, 3.B.4 and paragraphs 4.2 and 4.3 of Section II.
2. References to the repealed Directive shall be construed as references to this Regulation.

Article 29
Transitional provisions

1. Until 8 December 2019, Article 14(1) shall only apply to new slaughterhouses or to any new layout, construction or equipment covered by the rules set out in Annex II which have not entered into operation before 1 January 2013.
2. Until 8 December 2015, Member States may provide for certificates of competence, as referred to in Article 21, to be issued by way of a simplified procedure to persons demonstrating relevant professional experience of at least three years.

Article 30
Entry into force

This Regulation shall enter into force on the 20th day following its publication in the Official Journal of the European Union.
It shall apply from 1 January 2013.
This Regulation shall be binding in its entirety and directly applicable in all Member States.
Done at Brussels, 24 September 2009.
For the Council
The President
M. Olofsson

ANNEX I
LIST OF STUNNING METHODS AND RELATED SPECIFICATIONS (AS REFERRED TO IN ARTICLE 4)

CHAPTER I
Methods

Table 1—Mechanical methods

No	*Name*	*Description*	*Conditions of use*	*Key parameters*	*Specific requirements for certain methods —Chapter II of this Annex*
1	Penetrative captive bolt device	Severe and irreversible damage of the brain provoked by the shock and the penetration of a captive bolt. Simple stunning.	All species. Slaughter, depopulation and other situations.	Position and direction of the shot. Appropriate velocity, exit length and diameter of bolt according to animal size and species. Maximum stun to stick/kill interval(s).	Not applicable.

2	Non-penetrative captive bolt device	Severe damage of the brain by the shock of a captive bolt without penetration. Simple stunning.	Ruminants, poultry, rabbits and hares. Slaughter only for ruminants. Slaughter, depopulation and other situations for poultry, rabbits and hares.	Position and direction of the shot. Appropriate velocity, diameter and shape of bolt according to animal size and species. Strength of the cartridge used. Maximum stun to stick/kill interval(s).	Point 1.
3	Firearm with free projectile	Severe and irreversible damage of the brain provoked by the shock and the penetration of one or more projectiles.	All species. Slaughter, depopulation and other situations.	Position of the shot. Power and calibre of the cartridge. Type of projectile.	Not applicable.
4	Maceration	Immediate crushing of the entire animal.	Chicks up to 72 hours and egg embryos. All situations other than slaughter.	Maximum size of the batch to be introduced. Distance between the blades and speed of rotation. Measure to prevent overloading.	Point 2.

Table 1 (cont'd)

No	*Name*	*Description*	*Conditions of use*	*Key parameters*	*Specific requirements for certain methods —Chapter II of this Annex*
5	Cervical dislocation	Manual or mechanical stretching and twist of the neck provoking cerebral ischemia.	Poultry up to 5 kg live weight. Slaughter, depopulation and other situations.	Not applicable.	Point 3.
6	Percussive blow to the head	Firm and accurate blow to the head provoking severe damage to the brain.	Piglets, lambs, kids, rabbits, hares, fur animals and poultry up to 5 kg live weight. Slaughter, depopulation and other situations.	Force and location of the blow.	Point 3.

Table 2—Electrical methods

No	*Name*	*Description*	*Conditions of use*	*Key parameters*	*Specific requirements of Chapter II of this Annex*
1	Head-only electrical stunning	Exposure of the brain to a current generating a generalised epileptic form on the electro-encephalogram (EEG). Simple stunning.	All species. Slaughter, depopulation and other situations.	Minimum current (A or mA). Minimum voltage (V). Maximum frequency (Hz). Minimum time of exposure. Maximum stun-to-stick/kill interval(s). Frequency of calibration of the equipment. Optimisation of the current flow. Prevention of electrical shocks before stunning. Position and contact surface area of electrodes.	Point 4.

Table 2 (cont'd)

No	*Name*	*Description*	*Conditions of use*	*Key parameters*	*Specific requirements of Chapter II of this Annex*
2	Head-to-Body electrical stunning	Exposure of the body to a current generating at the same time a generalised epileptic form on the EEG and the fibrillation or the stopping of the heart. Simple stunning in case of slaughter.	All species. Slaughter, depopulation and other situations.	Minimum current (A or mA). Minimum voltage (V). Maximum frequency (Hz). Minimum time of exposure. Frequency of calibration of the equipment. Optimisation of the current flow. Prevention of electrical shocks before stunning. Position and contact surface area of electrodes. Maximum stun-to-stick interval(s), in case of simple stunning(s).	Point 5.

3	Electrical waterbath	Exposure of the entire body to a current generating a generalised epileptic form on the EEG and possibly the fibrillation or the stopping of the heart through a waterbath. Simple stunning except where frequency is equal to or less than 50 Hz.	Poultry. Slaughter, depopulation and other situations.	Minimum current (A or mA). Minimum voltage (V). Maximum frequency (Hz). Frequency of calibration of the equipment. Prevention of electrical shocks before stunning. Minimising pain at shackling. Optimisation of current flow. Maximum shackle duration before the waterbath. Minimum time of exposure for each animal. Immersion of the birds up to the base of the wings. Maximum stun-to-stick/kill interval(s) for frequency over 50 Hz(s).	Point 6.

Table 3—Gas methods

No	*Name*	*Description*	*Conditions of use*	*Key parameters*	*Specific requirements of Chapter II of this Annex*
1	Carbon dioxide at high concentration	Direct or progressive exposure of conscious animals to a gas mixture containing more than 40% carbon dioxide. The method may be used in pits, tunnels, containers or building previously sealed. Simple stunning in case of slaughter of pigs.	Pigs, mustelids, chinchillas, poultry except ducks and geese. Slaughter only for pigs. Other situations than slaughter for poultry mustelids, chinchillas, pigs.	Carbon dioxide concentration. Duration of exposure. Maximum stun-to-stick interval(s) in case of simple stunning. Quality of the gas. Temperature of the gas.	Point 7. Point 8.
2	Carbon dioxide in two phases	Successive exposure of conscious animals to a gas mixture containing up to 40% of carbon dioxide, followed when animals have lost consciousness, by a higher concentration of carbon dioxide.	Poultry Slaughter, depopulation and other situations	Carbon dioxide concentration. Duration of exposure. Quality of the gas. Temperature of the gas.	Not applicable.

3	Carbon dioxide associated with inert gases	Direct or progressive exposure of conscious animals to a gas mixture containing up to 40% of carbon dioxide associated with inert gases leading to anoxia. The method may be used in pits, bags, tunnels, containers or in buildings previously sealed. Simple stunning for pigs if the duration of exposure to at least 30% of carbon dioxide is of less than 7 minutes. Simple stunning for poultry if the overall duration of exposure to at least 30% of carbon dioxide is of less than 3 minutes.	Pigs and poultry. Slaughter, depopulation and other situations.	Carbon dioxide concentration. Duration of exposure. Maximum stun-to-stick/kill interval(s) in case of simple stunning. Quality of the gas. Temperature of the gas. Oxygen concentration.	Point 8.

Table 3 (cont'd)

No	*Name*	*Description*	*Conditions of use*	*Key parameters*	*Specific requirements of Chapter II of this Annex*
4	Inert gases	Direct or progressive exposure of conscious animals to a inert gas mixture such as Argon or Nitrogen leading to anoxia. The method may be used in pits, bags, tunnels, containers or in buildings previously sealed. Simple stunning in case of the slaughter of pigs. Simple stunning for poultry if the duration of exposure to anoxia is of less than 3 minutes.	Pigs and poultry. Slaughter, depopulation and other situations.	Oxygen concentration. Duration of exposure. Quality of the gas. Maximum stun-to-stick/kill interval(s) in case of simple stunning. Temperature of the gas.	Point 8.

5	Carbon monoxide (pure source)	Exposure of conscious animals to a gas mixture containing more than 4% of carbon monoxide.	Fur animals, poultry and piglets. Other situations than slaughter.	Quality of the gas. Carbon monoxide concentration. Duration of exposure. Temperature of the gas.	Points 9.1, 9.2 and 9.3.
6	Carbon monoxide associated with other gases	Exposure of conscious animals to a gas mixture containing more than 1% of carbon monoxide associated with other toxic gases.	Fur animals, poultry and piglets. Other situations than slaughter.	Carbon monoxide concentration. Duration of exposure. Temperature of the gas. Filtration of the gas produced from engine.	Point 9.

Table 4—Other methods

No	*Name*	*Description*	*Conditions of use*	*Key parameters*	*Specific requirements of Chapter II of this Annex*
1	Lethal injection	Loss of consciousness and sensibility followed by irreversible death induced by the injection of veterinary medicines.	All species. Other situations than slaughter.	Type of injection. Using approved medicines.	Not applicable.

CHAPTER II
Specific requirements for certain methods

1. Non-penetrative captive bolt device
   When using this method business operators shall pay attention to avoid the fracture of the skull.
   This method shall only be used for ruminants of less than 10 kg of live weight.
2. Maceration
   This method shall provide instantaneous maceration and immediate death of the animals. The apparatus shall contain rapidly rotating mechanically operated killing blades or expanded polystyrene projections. The capacity of the apparatus shall be sufficient to ensure that all animals are killed instantaneously, even if they are handled in a large number.
3. Cervical dislocation and percussive blow to the head
   These methods shall not be used as routine methods but only where there are no other methods available for stunning.
   These methods shall not be used in slaughterhouses except as a back-up method for stunning.
   No person shall kill by manual cervical dislocation or percussive blow to the head more than seventy animals per day.
   Manual cervical dislocation shall not be used on animals of more than three kg live weight.
4. Head-only electrical stunning

4.1. When using head-only electrical stunning, electrodes shall span the brain of the animal and be adapted to its size.

4.2. Head-only electrical stunning shall be carried out in accordance with the minimum currents set out in Table 1.

Table 1—Minimum currents for head-only electrical stunning

Category of animals	Bovine animals of 6 months or older	Bovine animals less than 6 months	Animals of ovine and caprine species	Animals of porcine species	Chicken	Turkeys
Minimum current	1,28 A	1,25 A	1,00 A	1,30 A	240 mA	400 mA

5. Head-to-body electrical stunning

5.1. Animals of the ovine, caprine and porcine species.
The minimum currents for head-to-body electrical stunning shall be 1 ampere for sheep and goats and 1,30 amperes for pigs.

5.2. Foxes
Electrodes shall be applied to the mouth and rectum with a current of a minimum value of 0,3 amperes and a minimum voltage of 110 volts for at least three seconds.
5.3. Chinchillas
Electrodes shall be applied ear to tail with a current of a minimum value of 0,57 amperes for at least 60 seconds.
6. Electrical waterbath stunning of poultry
6.1. Animals shall not be shackled if they are too small for the waterbath stunner or if shackling is likely to induce or increase the pain suffered (such as visibly injured animals). In these cases, they shall be killed by an alternative method.
6.2. Shackles shall be wet before live birds are shackled and exposed to the current. Birds shall be hung by both legs.
6.3. For animals referred to in Table 2, waterbath stunning shall be carried out in accordance with the minimum currents laid down therein, and animals shall be exposed to that current for a minimum duration of at least four seconds.

Table 2—Electrical requirements for waterbath stunning equipment (average values per animal)

Frequency (Hz)	*Chickens*	*Turkeys*	*Ducks and geese*	*Quails*
< 200 Hz	100 mA	250 mA	130 mA	45 mA
From 200 to 400 Hz	150 mA	400 mA	Not permitted	Not permitted
From 400 to 1500 Hz	200 mA	400 mA	Not permitted	Not permitted

7. Carbon dioxide at high concentration
In the case of pigs, mustelids and chinchillas, the minimum concentration of 80% of carbon dioxide shall be used.
8. Carbon dioxide, use of inert gases or a combination of those gas mixtures
Under no circumstances shall gases enter into the chamber or the location where animals are to be stunned and killed in a way that it could create burns or excitement by freezing or lack of humidity.
9. Carbon monoxide (pure source or associated with other gases)
9.1. Animals shall be kept under visual supervision at all times.
9.2. They shall be introduced one by one, and it shall be ensured that before the next animal is introduced the previous one is unconscious or dead.
9.3. Animals shall remain in the chamber until they are dead.

9.4. Gas produced by an engine specially adapted for the purpose of killing of animals may be used provided that the person responsible for killing has previously verified that the gas used:
(a) has been suitably cooled;
(b) has been sufficiently filtered;
(c) is free from any irritant component or gas.
The engine shall be tested every year before the killing of animals takes place.

9.5. Animals shall not be placed in the chamber until the minimum concentration of carbon monoxide has been reached.

ANNEX II
LAYOUT, CONSTRUCTION AND EQUIPMENT OF SLAUGHTERHOUSES
(AS REFERRED TO IN ARTICLE 14)

1. All lairage facilities

1.1. Ventilation systems shall be designed, constructed and maintained so that the welfare of the animals is constantly ensured, taking into account the expected range of weather conditions.

1.2. Where mechanical means of ventilation are required, provision shall be made for an alarm and emergency back-up facilities in the event of breakdown.

1.3. Lairage facilities shall be designed and constructed so as to minimise the risk of injuries to the animals and the occurrence of sudden noises.

1.4. Lairage facilities shall be designed and constructed so as to facilitate the inspection of the animals. Adequate fixed or portable lighting shall be provided to enable the inspection of animals at any time.

2. Lairage facilities for animals not delivered in containers

2.1. Pens, passageways and races shall be designed and constructed to allow:
(a) the animals to move freely in the required direction using their behavioural characteristics and without distraction;
(b) pigs or sheep to walk side by side, except in the case of races leading to the restraining equipment.

2.2. Ramps and bridges shall be equipped with lateral protection to ensure that animals cannot fall off.

2.3. The water supply system in pens shall be designed, constructed and maintained so as to allow all animals at all times access to clean water without being injured or limited in their movements.

2.4. When a waiting pen is used, it shall be constructed with a level floor and solid sides, between the holding pens and the race leading to the point of stunning and designed so that animals cannot be trapped or trampled.

2.5. Floors shall be built and maintained in such a way as to minimise the risk of animals slipping, falling or injuring their feet.

2.6. Where slaughterhouses have field lairages without natural shelter or shade, appropriate protection from adverse weather conditions shall be provided.

In the absence of such protection, these lairages shall not be used under adverse weather conditions. In the absence of a natural source of water, drinking facilities shall be provided.

3. Restraining equipment and facilities

3.1. Restraining equipment and facilities shall be designed, built and maintained to:
   (a) optimise the application of the stunning or killing method;
   (b) prevent injury or contusions to the animals;
   (c) minimise struggle and vocalisation when animals are restrained;
   (d) minimise the time of restraint.

3.2. For animals of bovine species, restraining boxes used in conjunction with a pneumatic captive bolt shall be fitted with a device that restricts both the lateral and vertical movement of the head of the animal.

4. Electrical stunning equipment (except waterbath stunning equipment)

4.1. Electrical stunning equipment shall be fitted with a device which displays and records the details of the electrical key parameters for each animal stunned. The device shall be placed so as to be clearly visible to the personnel and shall give a clearly visible and audible warning if the duration of exposure falls below the required level. These records shall be kept for at least one year.

4.2. Automatic electrical stunning equipment associated to a restrainer shall deliver a constant current.

5. Waterbath stunning equipment

5.1. Shackle lines shall be designed and positioned in such a way that birds suspended on them are clear of any obstruction and that disturbance to the animals is reduced to a minimum.

5.2. Shackle lines shall be designed in such a way that birds suspended on them will not remain hung conscious longer than one minute. However ducks, geese and turkeys shall not remain hung conscious longer than two minutes.

5.3. The whole length of the shackle line up to the point of entry into the scald tank shall be easily accessible in case animals have to be removed from the slaughter line.

5.4. The size and shape of the metal shackles shall be appropriate to the size of the legs of poultry to be slaughtered so that electrical contact can be secured without causing pain.

5.5. Waterbath stunning equipment shall be equipped with an electrically insulated entry ramp and designed and maintained so as to prevent overflow of water at the entrance.

5.6. The waterbath shall be designed in such a way that the level of immersion of the birds can be easily adapted.

5.7. The electrodes in waterbath stunning equipment shall extend the full length of the waterbath. The waterbath shall be designed and maintained in such a way that when the shackles pass over the water they are in continuous contact with the earthed rubbing bar.

5.8. A system in contact with the breast of the birds shall be built from the point of shackling until the birds enter the waterbath stunner in order to calm them down.

5.9. Access to the waterbath stunning equipment shall be available to allow the bleeding of birds that have been stunned and remain in the waterbath as a result of a breakdown or delay in the line.

5.10. Waterbath stunning equipment shall be fitted with a device which displays and records the details of the electrical key parameters used. These records shall be kept for at least one year.

6. Gas stunning equipment for pigs and poultry

6.1. Gas stunners, including conveyor belts, shall be designed and built to:
(a) optimise the application of stunning by gas;
(b) prevent injury or contusions to the animals;
(c) minimise struggle and vocalisation when animals are restrained.

6.2. The gas stunner shall be equipped to measure continuously, display and record the gas concentration and the time of exposure, and to give a clearly visible and audible warning if the concentration of gas falls below the required level. The device shall be placed so as to be clearly visible to the personnel. These records shall be kept for at least one year.

6.3. The gas stunner shall be designed in a manner that, even at the maximum permitted throughput, the animals are able to lie down without being stacked on each other.

ANNEX III
OPERATIONAL RULES FOR SLAUGHTERHOUSES (AS REFERRED TO IN ARTICLE 15)

1. The arrival, moving and handling of animals

1.1. The welfare conditions of each consignment of animals shall be systematically assessed by the animal welfare officer or a person reporting directly to the animal welfare officer upon arrival in order to identify the priorities, in particular by determining which animals have specific welfare needs and the corresponding measures to be taken.

1.2. Animals shall be unloaded as quickly as possible after arrival and subsequently slaughtered without undue delay.
Mammals, except rabbits and hares, which are not taken directly upon arrival to the place of slaughter, shall be lairaged.
Animals which have not been slaughtered within 12 hours of their arrival shall be fed, and subsequently given moderate amounts of food at appropriate intervals. In such cases, the animals shall be provided an appropriate amount of bedding or equivalent material which guarantees a level of comfort appropriate to the species and the number of animals concerned. This material shall guarantee an efficient drainage or ensure adequate absorption of urine and faeces.

1.3. Containers in which animals are transported shall be kept in good order, handled with care, in particular if they have a perforated or flexible bottom, and:
(a) shall not be thrown, dropped, or knocked over;
(b) where possible, shall be loaded and unloaded horizontally and mechanically;
Whenever possible animals shall be unloaded individually.

1.4. When containers are put one on top of the other, the necessary precautions shall be taken:
(a) to limit urine and faeces falling on the animals placed underneath;
(b) to ensure stability of the containers;
(c) to ensure that ventilation is not impeded.

1.5. For the purpose of slaughter, unweaned animals, lactating dairy animals, females having given birth during the journey or animals delivered in containers shall be given priority over other types of animal. If this is not possible, arrangements shall be made so as to relieve them from their suffering, in particular by:
(a) milking dairy animals at intervals of not more than 12 hours;
(b) providing appropriate conditions for suckling and the welfare of the newborn animal in the case of a female having given birth;
(c) providing water in the case of animals delivered in containers.

1.6. Mammals, except rabbits and hares, which are not taken directly to the place of slaughter after being unloaded, shall have drinking water available to them from appropriate facilities at all times.

1.7. A steady supply of animals for stunning and killing shall be ensured in order to prevent animal handlers rushing animals from the holding pens.

1.8. It shall be prohibited to:
(a) strike or kick the animals;
(b) apply pressure to any particularly sensitive part of the body in such a way as to cause animals avoidable pain or suffering;
(c) lift or drag the animals by the head, ears, horns, legs, tail or fleece, or handle them in such a way as to cause them pain or suffering;
however, the prohibition on lifting animals by their legs shall not apply to poultry, rabbits and hares;
(d) use prods or other implements with pointed ends;
(e) twist, crush or break the tails of animals or grasp the eyes of any animal.

1.9. The use of instruments which administer electric shocks shall be avoided as far as possible. In any case, such instruments shall only be used for adult bovine animals and adult pigs which refuse to move, and only when they have room ahead of them in which to move. The shocks shall last no longer than one second, be adequately spaced and shall only be applied to the muscles of the hindquarters. Shocks shall not be used repeatedly if the animal fails to respond.

1.10. Animals shall not be tied by the horns, antlers or nose rings and their legs shall not be tied together. When animals need to be tied, ropes, tethers or other means used shall be:
(a) strong enough not to break;
(b) such as to allow the animals, if necessary, to lie down and to eat and drink;
(c) designed in such a way as to eliminate any danger of strangulation or injury, and so as to allow animals to be quickly released.

1.11. Animals which are unable to walk shall not be dragged to the place of slaughter, but shall be killed where they lie.
2. Additional rules for mammals in lairage (except for rabbits and hares)
2.1. Each animal shall have enough space to stand up, lie down and, except for cattle kept individually, turn around.
2.2. Animals shall be kept securely in the lairage and care shall be taken to prevent them from escaping and to protect them from predators.
2.3. For each pen it shall be indicated with a visible sign the date and time of arrival and, except for cattle kept individually, the maximum number of animals to be kept.
2.4. Every day that the slaughterhouse operates, before any animal arrives, isolation pens for animals that require specific care shall be prepared and kept ready for immediate use.
2.5. The condition and state of health of the animals in a lairage shall be regularly inspected by the animal welfare officer or a person having appropriate competence.
3. Bleeding of animals
3.1. Where one person is responsible for the stunning, shackling, hoisting and bleeding of animals, that person shall carry out all those operations consecutively on one animal before carrying out any of them on another animal.
3.2. In case of simple stunning or slaughter in accordance with Article 4(4), the two carotid arteries or the vessels from which they arise shall be systematically severed. Electrical stimulation shall only be performed once the unconsciousness of the animal has been verified. Further dressing or scalding shall only be performed once the absence of signs of life of the animal has been verified.
3.3. Birds shall not be slaughtered by means of automatic neck cutters unless it can be ascertained whether or not the neck cutters have effectively severed both blood vessels. When neck cutters have not been effective the bird shall be slaughtered immediately.

ANNEX IV
CORRESPONDENCE BETWEEN ACTIVITIES AND REQUIREMENTS FOR EXAMINATION OF COMPETENCE (AS REFERRED TO IN ARTICLE 21)

Slaughter operations listed in Article 7(2)	Subjects for examination of competence
All operations listed in Article 7(2)(a) to (g).	Animal behaviour, animal suffering, consciousness and sensibility, stress in animals.

(a)the handling and care of animals before they are restrained;	Practical aspects of handling and restraining animals. Knowledge of manufacturers' instructions on the type of restraint equipments used in case of mechanical restraint
(b)the restraint of animals for the purpose of stunning or killing;	
(c)the stunning of animals;	Practical aspects of stunning techniques and knowledge of manufacturers' instructions on the type of stunning equipments used. Back-up stunning and/or killing methods. Basic maintenance and cleaning of stunning and/or killing equipment.
(d)the assessment of effective stunning;	Monitoring the effectiveness of stunning. Back-up stunning and/or killing methods.
(e)the shackling or hoisting of live animals;	Practical aspects of handling and restraining animals. Monitoring the effectiveness of stunning.
(f)the bleeding of live animals;	Monitoring the effectiveness of stunning and the absence of signs of life. Back-up stunning and/or killing methods. Appropriate use and maintenance of bleeding knives.
(g)the slaughtering in accordance with Article 4(4);	Appropriate use and maintenance of bleeding knives. Monitoring the absence of signs of life.
Killing operations listed in Article 7(3)	Subjects for examination of competence
the killing of fur animals.	Practical aspects of handling and restraining animals. Practical aspects of stunning techniques and knowledge of manufacturers' instructions on stunning equipments. Back-up stunning and/or killing methods. Monitoring the effectiveness of stunning and confirmation of death. Basic maintenance and cleaning of stunning and/or killing equipment.

Appendix IV

Government of Sweden, The Animal Welfare Act and The Animal Welfare Ordinance (2009) (portions of each are reprinted below) (unofficial English translation).*

The Animal Welfare Act

The Animal Welfare Ordinance

The Animal Welfare Act The Animal Welfare Ordinance

Produced by: Ministry of Agriculture 2009

Cover photos: Elima Mwinyipembe

Art. Number: Jo 09.021

For Further information, please visit www.sweden.gov.se/agricultureStockholm Sweden, September 2009

1988:534

Consolidated text (as last amended by SFS 2009:303 of 1 January 2010)

Unofficial translation

The Animal Welfare Act

Scope of the Act

Section 1

This Act applies to the care and treatment of domestic animals and laboratory animals. It also applies to other animals if they are kept in captivity. Act (2005:1226).

EC provisions supplemented by the Act

Section 1 a

(1) The Act supplements those provisions in EC regulations (EC provisions) that fall within the scope of the Act. The Government shall promulgate the basic regulations concerned in the Swedish Code of Statutes.
(2) With regard to EC provisions that fall within the scope of several acts, the Government shall promulgate the provisions supplemented by this Act in the same manner as in subsection (1).
(3) The Government or the authority designated by the Government may issue regulations or, in individual cases, make decisions that are needed to supplement the EC provisions. Act (2006:809).

* Source: <www.sweden.gov.se/sb/d/10158/a/90310>.

Definitions

Section 1 b

"Laboratory animals" means animals that are used in animal experiments or are bred, kept or supplied for animal experiments. Act (2006:809).

Section 1 c

(1) "Animal experiments" means use of animals for:
1. scientific research;
2. diagnosis of disease;
3. the development and manufacture of pharmaceutical or chemical products;
4. teaching purposes, if the use means that the animal is killed, subjected to a surgical operation, injection or blood-letting or if the animal is caused or risks being caused suffering; and
5. other similar purposes.

(2) "Animal experiments" also means production of genetically modified animals, if gene technology, chemical or other similar methods are used. Act (2006:809).

Basic provisions concerning animal management and treatment

Section 2

(1) Animals shall be treated well and shall be protected from unnecessary suffering and disease.

(2) Animals used as laboratory animals shall not be deemed to have been subjected to unnecessary suffering or disease where such use has been approved by an ethical committee on animal experiments. Act (2005:1226).

Section 3

(1) Animals shall be given sufficient feed and water and adequate care. The feeding stuffs and water must be of good quality and appropriate for the species of animal that is being fed.

(2) Livestock buildings and other holding spaces and enclosures for animals shall provide sufficient space and shelter for the animals. Livestock buildings and other holding spaces for animals shall be kept clean.

(3) The Government or the authority designated by the Government may issue further regulations concerning:
1. feeding and watering of animals; and
2. livestock buildings and other holding spaces and enclosures for animals.

(4) Subsection (1) shall not apply to laboratory animals, unless they are kept in captivity. Act (2007:1394).

Section 3 a

(1) The Government or the authority designated by the Government may issue regulations concerning
1. compulsory prior approval of livestock buildings and other holding spaces and enclosures for animals; and
2. compulsory pre-testing of new animal management technologies.

(2) The Government may prescribe that the authority designated by the Government shall impose a special charge on persons who do not arrange for prior approval of livestock buildings or other holding spaces or enclosures for animals. The special charge shall amount to at least SEK 10 000 and at most SEK 40 000. When regulations are issued concerning the amount of the charge, account shall be taken of the complexity and scope of the prior approval procedure.

(3) The person who owned the livestock building or other holding space or enclosure for animals when a measure was taken that requires prior approval shall be liable for payment of the charge.

(4) If there are special grounds for doing so, the owner of the livestock building or other holding space or enclosure for animals may be partly or wholly exempted from paying the charge. Act (2007:1394).

Section 3 b

If a measure relating to a livestock building or other holding space or enclosure for animals that requires prior approval under regulations issued pursuant to section 3 a, subsection (1), point 1, has been taken without such approval, the authority designated by the Government shall prohibit use of the space or enclosure to house animals. A prohibition shall not, however, be ordered if the authority finds that the measure can be approved retroactively. Act (2007:1394).

Section 4

(1) Animals shall be accommodated and handled in an environment that is appropriate for animals and in such a way as to promote their health and permit natural behaviour.

(2) The Government or the authority designated by the Government may issue further regulations laying down conditions for or prohibiting certain kinds of animal management. Act (2007:362).

Section 5

(1) Animals must not be overworked.

(2) They must not be beaten or driven with implements which may hurt or otherwise injure them.

Section 6

(1) Animals must not be tied or tethered in a way that causes pain or does not allow them the necessary freedom of movement or rest or sufficient shelter from the elements.
(2) The Government or the authority designated by the Government may issue further regulations concerning the tying of animals. Act (2007:362).

Section 7

The Government or the authority designated by the Government may issue regulations concerning conditions for, or prohibitions against, sales or other transfers of ownership of animals. Act (2007:362).

Section 8

(1) The means of transport used for the transportation of animals shall be suitable for the purpose and provide shelter against heat and cold and protect the animals from shocks and abrasions and the like. To the extent necessary, the animals shall be kept separate from each other.
(2) The Government or the authority designated by the Government may issue further regulations laying down conditions for or prohibiting the transportation of animals. Act (2007:362).

Section 9

If an animal is sick, injured or in other ways, through its behaviour, shows signs of ill-health, the animal shall be given the necessary care without delay, if necessary by a veterinarian, or other measures shall be taken, unless the illness or injury is so severe that the animal must be killed immediately. Act (2003:1077).

Surgical procedures etc.

Section 10

(1) Animals must not be subjected to surgical procedures or given injections except where they are necessary for veterinary medical reasons.
(2) Subsection (1) shall not apply to surgical procedures performed or injections administered in connection with activities that have been approved by an ethical committee on animal experiments.
(3) Where special reasons exist, the Government or the authority designated by the Government may issue further regulations concerning surgical procedures performed on or injections administered to animals and regulations providing for exceptions from subsection (1). Act (2003:1076).

Section 11/Ceases to apply on 1 January 2010/

(1) A veterinarian shall be engaged when a surgical procedure is to be performed on or an injection administered to an animal. The same shall apply to other treatment for the purpose of preventing, detecting, alleviating or

curing illness or injury in an animal, if the treatment is liable to cause suffering that's not insignificant.

(2) Subsection (1) shall not apply if the treatment is so urgent that there is no time to engage the services of a veterinarian.

(3) In connection with activities that have been approved by an ethical committee on animal experiments injections may also be administered, procedures performed or other treatment given by persons who have the required training.

(4) The Government or the authority designated by the Government may issue regulations providing for exceptions from subsection (1). Act (2007:362).

Section 11/Enters into force on 1 January 2010/

(1) A veterinarian or another animal health professional as defined in the Animal Health Care Act (2009:302) shall be engaged if any of the following measures needs to be taken: a surgical 1. procedure on or administration of an injection to an animal; 2. other treatment for the purpose of preventing, detecting, alleviating or curing illness or injury in an animal, if the treatment is liable to cause suffering that is not insignificant; or 3. treatment under general anaesthesia or under a local anaesthetic injection.

(2) Subsection (1) shall not apply to urgent measures taken in order to save the animal's life or alleviate its suffering.

(3) In connection with activities that have been approved by an ethical committee on animal experiments, persons who have the required training may also administer injections and carry out surgical procedures and other treatment.

(4) The Government or the authority designated by the Government may issue regulations providing for exceptions from subsection (1). Act (2009:303).

Section 12

(1) The Government or the authority designated by the Government may issue regulations laying down conditions for or prohibiting: 1. the administration of hormones or other substances to animals in order to alter their characteristics for any purpose other than to prevent, detect, alleviate or to cure disease or symptoms of disease; or 2. breeding, the object of which is such that it may entail suffering for the animals or affect their natural behaviour.

(2) Subsection (1), point 1, shall not apply to substances that fall within the Feeding stuffs and Animal By Products Act (2006:805). Act (2007:362).

Section 12 a/Ceases to apply on 1 January 2010 by virtue of Act (2009:303)/

The Government or the authority designated by the Government may issue regulations concerning the approval of farriers. The regulations may prescribe that a charge shall be made for applications for approval. Act (2007:362).

Slaughter etc.

Section 13

Animals shall be spared unnecessary discomfort and suffering when they are taken to slaughter and when they are slaughtered.

Section 14

(1) Domestic animals shall be stunned before being bled prior to slaughter. No other measures may be taken in connection with slaughter until the animal is dead.
(2) The first sentence of subsection (1) shall not apply to animals which, owing to illness or accident, must be slaughtered immediately.
(3) The Government or the authority designated by the Government may issue further regulations providing for exemptions from the first sentence of subsection (1) with respect to poultry and rabbits. Act (2007:362).

Section 15

The Government or the authority designated by the Government may issue further regulations on the slaughter and killing of animals in other cases. Act (2007:362).

Obligation to obtain permission to keep animals in certain cases

Section 16

(1) An operating permit is required by any person who, on a professional basis or on a substantial scale: keeps, 1. breeds, supplies or sells pet animals or receives pet animals for boarding or feeding; 2. keeps, breeds, supplies or sells horses or receives horses for boarding or feeding or uses horses in a riding school business; or 3. breeds fur animals.
(2) Applications for permits shall be considered by the authority designated by the Government. This authority may also withdraw a permit that has previously been granted.
(3) When applications for permits are considered, special attention shall be paid to the question of whether the applicant can be regarded as suitable to conduct the activities and whether the premises in which the activities are to be conducted are suitable with regard to animal welfare.
(4) The Government or the authority designated by the Government may issue regulations concerning: the criteria for regarding a business as operating 1. on a substantial scale; 2. exemptions from subsection (1). Act (2008:660).

Sporting events and exhibitions involving animals

Section 17

(1) Animals must not be trained for or used in sporting events in such a way as to subject them to suffering. This shall also apply to film, video or

television productions and shows or other types of exhibition arranged for the public.

(2) The Government or the authority designated by the Government may issue further regulations concerning such use of animals. Act (2007:362).

Section 18

(1) An animal which is trained for or takes part in a sporting event in a sports arena or at a race-track must not be subjected to doping or other improper practices liable to affect the animal's performance or temperament.

(2) The Government or the authority designated by the Government may issue further regulations concerning unauthorized practices. Act (2007:362).

Animal experiments

Section 19

Animal experiments may only take place provided that

1. the purpose of the activity cannot be attained by any other satisfactory method that does not entail the use of animals;
2. as few animals as possible are used;
3. the activity is organized in such a way as not to subject the animals to greater suffering than is absolutely necessary; and
4. no animals other than animals bred for the purpose are used in the activity. Act (2005:1226).

Section 19 a

(1) Permission must be granted by the Government or the authority designated by the Government before laboratory animals can be used, bred, kept or supplied. Such permission may subsequently be withdrawn.

(2) When applications for permission are considered, special attention shall be paid to the question of whether the applicant has the qualifications required to carry on the activity in question and whether the premises in which the activity is to take place are suitable with regard to animal welfare.

(3) When applications for permission to breed laboratory animals are considered, the need for such animals shall also be taken into account. Act (2007:362).

Section 20

(1) In activities referred to in section 19 a there shall be a supervisor approved 1. by the authority designated by the Government, who shall be responsible for the activity; 2. a veterinarian who shall give advice and instructions about the conduct of the activity and assist with the treatment of the animals; and 3. personnel that is sufficient in number, and has the necessary training and skills for the activity.

(2) The supervisor and the veterinarian shall ensure that the activity is conducted in accordance with this Act and any regulations adopted in pursuance thereof.
(3) The Government or the authority designated by the Government may issue further regulations, or take decisions in individual cases, concerning the duties of supervisors and veterinarians and the training and skills of the personnel. Act (2007:362).

Section 21

(1) The use of animals in animal experiments shall be approved from an ethical perspective by an ethical committee on animal experiments before the activity commences.
(2) When examining a case the committee shall weigh the importance of the experiment against the suffering of the animal.
(3) The committee may only approve an animal experiment application if such use can be considered important in the public interest and the conditions set out in section 19, points 1–3 are fulfilled.
(4) The Government or the authority designated by the Government may issue further regulations concerning such approval, as well as regulations providing for exemption from the requirement for approval. Act (2007:362).

Section 22

(1) The Government or the authority designated by the Government may issue regulations laying down conditions for or prohibiting the breeding, keeping, supply or use of laboratory animals.
(2) The Government or the authority designated by the Government may issue regulations providing for exemptions from the provisions of this Act as regards animal experiments. Act (2007:362).

Section 23

A person who breeds, keeps, supplies or uses laboratory animals shall mark the animals and issue instructions for and make notes and submit information concerning these activities in accordance with the regulations issued by the Government or the authority designated by the Government. Act (2007:362).

Official control by the control authorities

Section 24

(1) Official control of compliance with this Act, the regulations and decisions issued pursuant to the Act, the EC provisions supplemented by the Act and the decisions issued pursuant to the EC provisions, shall be exercised by the county administrative boards and other government authorities, as determined by the Government.

(2) The authority that exercises official control shall have access to personnel trained in animal welfare to the extent needed for the authority to be able to perform its duties in a satisfactory manner. Act (2008:660).

Other responsibilities of the control authorities

Section 24 a

(1) The control authority designated by the Government shall coordinate the activities of the other control authorities and provide advice and assistance in these activities where needed.
(2) By advice and information activities and other means, the authority that exercises official control shall make it easier for individuals to fulfil their obligations under the Act, the regulations and decisions issued pursuant to the Act, the EC provisions supplemented by the Act and the decisions issued pursuant to the EC provisions. Act (2008:660).

Section 24 b

The authority that exercises official control shall work to ensure that action are taken against infringements of the Act, of the regulations or decisions issued pursuant to the Act or of the EC provisions supplemented by the Act. Act (2006:809).

Section 24 c

Repealed by Act (2008:600).

Section 24 d

Repealed by Act (2008:600).

Section 24 e

Repealed by Act (2008:600).

Section 24 f

Repealed by Act (2008:600).

Regulations concerning official control

Section 25

The Government or the authority designated by the Government may issue regulations concerning:

1. how official control shall be conducted; and
2. the obligation of a control body engaged in official control to provide information to the coordinating control authority referred to in section 24 a, subsection (1). Act (2008:660).

Section 25 a

The Government may issue regulations prescribing which provisions in Regulation (EC) No 882/2004 of the European Parliament and the Council of 29 April 2004 on official controls performed to ensure the verification of compliance with feed and food law, animal health and animal welfare rules, shall be applied when conducting official checks on animal keepers other than those holding food-producing animals. Act (2006:809).

Fees

Section 25 b

(1) The Government or the authority designated by the Government may issue regulations on the obligation to pay a fee 1. for official control under the Act, the regulations issued pursuant to the Act or the EC provisions supplemented by the Act; and 2. in matters processed under the Act, the regulations issued pursuant to the Act or the EC provisions supplemented by the Act.
(2) The Government or the authority designated by the Government may issue regulations on the calculation of fees charged by government authorities and control bodies. Act (2008:660).

Section 25 c

Repealed by Act (2008:600).

Section 25 d

Repealed by Act (2008:600).

Orders, prohibitions and remedies

Section 26

(1) Over and above what follows from the EC provisions supplemented by the Act, a control authority may issue the orders and prohibitions that are needed to ensure compliance with the Act, the regulations and decisions issued pursuant to the Act, the EC provisions supplemented by the Act and the decisions issued pursuant to the EC provisions.
(2) Orders and prohibitions under subsection (1) or under the EC provisions supplemented by the Act may be combined with a conditional fine, though not in cases referred to in section 29.
(3) If a person fails to comply with the Act, the regulations or decisions issued pursuant to the Act, the EC provisions supplemented by the Act or the decisions issued pursuant to the EC provisions, a control authority may decide on remedies at his or her expense. In urgent cases, such a decision may be issued without a preceding order. Act (2008:660).

Right to information and access etc.

Section 27

(1) To the extent needed to carry out checks, a control authority and a control body engaged in official control have a right to 1. receive information and study documents on request; and 2. receive access to areas, facilities, buildings, premises and other places where animals are kept or that are associated with the keeping of animals and there inspect the animals, conduct investigations and take samples.
(2) The provisions in subsection (1) also apply as regards EC institutions and inspectors and experts appointed by the institutions.
(3) A person who is subject to official control shall provide the assistance that is needed to allow the control to be carried out. Act (2006:809).

Assistance from a police authority

Section 27 a

The police authority shall provide the assistance that is needed for exercise of official control or enforcement of decisions under this Act, the regulations or decisions issued pursuant to the Act, the EC provisions supplemented by the Act or the decisions adopted pursuant to the EC provisions. Act (2006:809).

Exceptions for animals used in the armed forces

Section 28

The provisions in sections 24–25, 25 b, subsection (1), point 1, and sections 26–27 a shall not apply to animals used in the Swedish Armed Forces. Act (2008:660).

/Heading enters into force on 1 January 2010/

Reporting of maltreatment, etc.

Section 28 a

/Enters into force on 1 January 2010/
If, in the course of his or her professional activities, an animal health professional finds reason to believe that animals are not being kept or looked after in accordance with this Act, the regulations issued pursuant to the Act or the EC provisions supplemented by the Act, that person shall report this to the control authority. Act (2009:303).

Prohibition against having animals in care

Section 29

(1) The county administrative board shall prohibit persons to have animals, or a particular species of animal, in their care if they: fail to comply with 1. a decision taken by a control authority pursuant to section 26 which is of significant relevance to animal welfare; 2. seriously neglect the control or care of an animal; 3. maltreat an animal; 4. have been convicted of cruelty to animals pursuant to chapter 16, section 13, of the Penal Code; or 5. have

repeatedly been convicted of offences pursuant to sections 36 or 36 a or have repeatedly been the subject of decisions pursuant to section 26.

(2) No prohibition shall be imposed where the offence will manifestly not be repeated.

(3) If the person who is the subject of the prohibition is the owner of the animal, the county administrative board may also order him to dispose of it and may forbid him to procure animals, or a particular species of animal, again.

(4) The prohibition may apply for a fixed period or until further notice. Act (2006:809).

Taking charge of animals

Section 30

(1) If an animal is found so severely ill or injured that it should be killed immediately, a veterinarian or a police officer, and in urgent cases another person, may kill the animal at once.

(2) The person who has killed the animal shall immediately notify the owner or possessor of the animal to this effect. If this is not possible, the police authority shall be notified.

Section 31

The county administrative board shall decide that an animal shall be taken in charge by the police authority if:

1. the animal is gratuitously subjected to suffering and nothing is done to remedy the situation despite a request to this effect by the control authority;
2. a decision adopted pursuant to section 26, which is of significant relevance to animal welfare, is not complied with;
3. a decision adopted pursuant to section 29 is not complied with;
4. the person who has the animal in his care has been convicted of cruelty to animals pursuant to chapter 16, section 13, of the Penal Code; or the person who has the animal in his care has repeatedly
5. been convicted of offences pursuant to sections 36 or 36 a or has repeatedly been the subject of decisions pursuant to section 26. Act (2006:809).

Section 32

(1) Notwithstanding the provisions of section 31, point 1, concerning requests and remedies, the county administrative board or the police authority shall decide that an animal that is being subjected to suffering shall be taken charge of immediately if:
   1. there is deemed to be no prospect of the fault being remedied;
   2. the owner of the animal is unknown or cannot be found; or
   3. it is otherwise deemed absolutely necessary in the interests of animal welfare.

(2) If the decision has been made by the police authority, it shall be referred to the county administrative board, which shall decide without delay whether or not it shall remain in force.

(3) The police authority shall arrange for the animal to be taken charge of. Act (2008:660).

Section 33

(1) Decisions under sections 31 or 32 shall also apply to offspring to which the animal taken care of gives birth while it is being taken care of.

(2) When an animal is taken in charge, the owner shall not have access to the animal or to its offspring which has also been taken in charge without the permission of the county administrative board. Act (2003:52).

Section 34

(1) When the county administrative board decides that an animal shall be taken in charge, it shall determine whether the animal is to be sold, otherwise transferred or killed.

(2) If it proves impossible to implement the county administrative board's decision to sell or otherwise transfer an animal, the board may instead decide that the animal shall be killed.

(3) The police authority shall arrange for the animal to be sold, otherwise transferred or killed. Act (2002:550).

Section 35

(1) Expenses incurred as a result of measures taken pursuant to sections 31 or 32 may be paid in advance out of public funds.

(2) If an animal is taken in charge pursuant to sections 31 or 32, the cost of the measure shall subsequently be paid by the person against whom it was directed, unless there are special reasons to the contrary.

(3) If the police authority has arranged for the sale of an animal taken in charge, the final amount to be paid by the owner may be deducted from the purchase sum.

Penalty provisions

Section 36

(1) The penalty for offences committed deliberately or through negligence in the following cases shall be a fine or imprisonment for not more than two years:

1. offences under sections 3, 5, 6, 8–11, 13, 14, 16–19a or 21;
2. failure to comply with a rule issued pursuant to this Act; or
3. failure to comply with an order or prohibition referred to in section 29.

(2) The penalty for offences committed deliberately and in breach of an obligation that is important from the point of view of animal welfare shall be imprisonment for not more than two years.

(3) No penalties shall be imposed for minor offences.
(4) No penalties shall be imposed pursuant to this Act where the penalty for the offence provided by the Penal Code is the same or more severe. Act (2002:550).

Section 36 a

(1) A person who deliberately or through negligence infringes against the obligations, conditions or prohibitions contained in the EC provisions supplemented by the Act shall be sentenced to a fine or imprisonment for not more than two years. However, this does not apply if the infringement concerns provisions relating to exercise of official authority.
(2) The penalty for offences committed deliberately and in breach of an obligation that is important from the point of view of animal welfare shall be imprisonment for not more than two years.
(3) No penalties shall be imposed for minor offences.
(4) No penalties shall be imposed pursuant to this Act where the penalty for the offence provided by the Penal Code is the same or more severe. Act (2006:809).

Section 37

(1) If an order or prohibition on penalty of a conditional fine has been breached, a person shall not be penalised under section 36 or section 36 a for an act covered by the order or prohibition.
(2) A person who has been ordered to pay a special charge under section 3 a, subsection (2), for neglecting to arrange for prior approval of livestock buildings or other holding spaces or enclosures for animals shall not be penalised under section 36. Act (2007:1394).

Appeals etc.

Section 38

(1) Appeals against decisions issued by a central government administrative authority under this Act, under the regulations issued pursuant to the Act or under the EC provisions supplemented by the Act may be lodged with an administrative court. Leave to appeal is required for an appeal to the administrative court of appeal.
(2) Appeals against other decisions taken by a central government administrative authority may be lodged with the Government. Act (2008:660).

Section 39

The Government may issue regulations on cases in which a decision under this Act, under the regulations issued pursuant to the Act or under the EC provisions supplemented by the Act shall have immediate effect even if an appeal has been lodged against it. Act (2006:809).

Consolidated text
(as last amended by SFS 2008:1051
of 1 January 2009)
Unofficial translation

The Animal Welfare Ordinance

Introductory provision

Section 1

This Ordinance contains provisions supplementing the Animal Welfare Act (1988:534). Ordinance (2006:818).

EC provisions

Section 1 a

(1) The basic regulations in EC law that are wholly or partly supplemented by the Animal Welfare Act (1988:534) shall be specified in a Government Promulgation.
(2) With regard to provisions contained in regulations that come under the scope of more than one Act, the Promulgation shall specify which provisions are supplemented by the Animal Welfare Act.
(3) The Swedish Board of Agriculture may issue the regulations and take the decisions that are needed to supplement the EC provisions. Ordinance (2007:484).

Livestock buildings

Section 1 b

(1) Livestock buildings and other holding spaces for animals shall be sufficiently spacious to allow all the animals to lie down at the same time and to move freely.
(2) The premises shall be designed in such a way as to allow the animals to behave naturally.

Section 2

(1) Livestock buildings shall be designed in such a way as to ensure a satisfactory indoor climate. Noise shall be kept at a low level.
(2) Livestock buildings shall be fitted with windows to let in the daylight.
(3) The Swedish Board of Agriculture may issue regulations providing for exemptions from subsection (2). Ordinance (2007:484).

Section 3

The fittings in livestock buildings and other holding spaces for animals and the equipment in enclosures shall be designed in such a way as not to cause injuries or entail risks to the health of the animals. The fittings and other equipment shall not prevent the animals from behaving naturally, unnecessarily limit their freedom of movement or otherwise cause them inconvenience. Ordinance (2002:723).

Section 4

The Swedish Board of Agriculture may issue regulations concerning the size and general design of livestock buildings, other holding spaces for animals and enclosures. Ordinance (2007:484).

Prior approval of livestock buildings

Section 5

(1) Livestock buildings and other holding spaces and enclosures for horses, for animals bred or kept for the production of food, wool, hides or fur, or for animals used for teaching purposes not involving animal experiments may not be erected, extended or altered unless the livestock buildings, holding spaces or enclosures have first been approved from an animal welfare and animal health perspective. This also applies when a livestock building, other holding space or enclosure is modified in a manner that is of substantial relevance from an animal welfare or animal health perspective or when a livestock building, other holding space or enclosure that has previously been used for another purpose is taken into use or fitted out for such keeping or breeding of animals. The provisions here concerning livestock buildings, other holding spaces and enclosures also apply to parts of livestock buildings, other holding spaces and enclosures.

(2) Subsection (1) shall not apply to livestock buildings, other holding spaces and enclosures used by the Swedish Armed Forces.

(3) The Swedish Board of Agriculture may issue regulations on conditions for prior approval and on exemptions from subsection (1). Ordinance (2007:1395).

Section 6

(1) Matters relating to prior approval under section 5 shall be examined by the county administrative board. The county administrative board shall inspect livestock buildings and other holding spaces and enclosures before they are taken into use or, if more appropriate, as soon as possible afterwards.

(2) The Swedish Board of Agriculture may issue regulations concerning inspections. Ordinance (2007:1395).

Section 6 a

(1) If a person carries out a measure referred to in section 5 without the prior approval of the county administrative board, the county administrative board shall order payment of the special charge mentioned in section 3 a, subsection (2) of the Animal Welfare Act (1988:534).

(2) The special charge shall be as follows: 1. SEK 12 000 for measures relating to a new building for a relatively small number of animals using well-tried technology or a minor alteration or extension; and 2. SEK 24 000 for any other new building or for major alteration or extension.
(3) If the matter has not been taken up by the county administrative board within five years of the date when the measure was taken, no special charge may be collected. Ordinance (2007:1395).

Section 6 b

If a measure concerning a livestock building or other holding space or enclosure for animals that requires prior approval under section 5 has been taken without such approval, the county administrative board shall take a decision as referred to in section 3 b of the Animal Welfare Act (1988:534). Ordinance (2007:1395).

Pre-testing of new technologies

Section 7

(1) New animal management technologies and equipment shall be approved with regard to animal health and animal welfare before use.
(2) The Swedish Board of Agriculture may issue regulations providing for exemptions from subsection (1). Ordinance (2007:484).

Section 8

Applications for approval of new technologies shall be considered by the Swedish Board of Agriculture. Ordinance (2007:484).

Animal management

Section 8 a

The Swedish Board of Agriculture may issue regulations concerning the feeding and watering of animals. Ordinance (2007:484).

Section 9

(1) Hens for egg production may only be housed in hen-housing systems that satisfy the hens' need of nests, perches and sand-baths. The accommodation shall be such as to ensure that mortality and conduct disorders remain at a low level.
(2) The Swedish Board of Agriculture may issue further regulations concerning the accommodation of hens. Ordinance (2003:1124).

Section 9 a

(1) Foxes may only be kept in such a way as to satisfy their need to socialize with other foxes and to move, dig and otherwise occupy themselves.
(2) The Swedish Board of Agriculture may issue further regulations concerning the keeping of foxes. Ordinance (2007:484)

Section 10

Cattle kept for milk production that are older than six months shall be sent out to pasture in the summer.

Section 11

(1) Cattle, other than cattle kept for milk production, shall be sent out to pasture or otherwise allowed to graze outdoors in the summer.
(2) Subsection (1) shall not apply to animals which are younger than six months or to bulls or animals being kept in quarantine. Ordinance (1995:1225)

Section 12

Where possible, pigs kept for rearing shall be allowed outdoors during the summer.

Section 13

The Swedish Board of Agriculture may issue regulations concerning arrangements for pasture as referred to in sections 10 and 11. Ordinance (2007:484).

Section 13 a

(1) Exemptions from the provisions of sections 10 and 11 may be granted in individual cases concerning:
   1. livestock buildings taken into use after 1 July 1988, if special climatic conditions make outdoor grazing unsuitable for reasons of animal welfare or if exemptions are necessary owing to unforeseen and exceptional circumstances;
   2. livestock buildings taken into use before 1 July 1988, including livestock buildings that have subsequently been altered or extended, where special reasons exist and subject to the conditions specified in regulations issued by the Swedish Board of Agriculture.
(2) In cases referred to in subsection (1), point 1, the question of exemptions shall be considered by the Swedish Board of Agriculture. The same shall apply to cases referred to in subsection (1), point 2, if the livestock building has been altered or extended so as to increase the number of animals by more than nine adult or eighteen young animals. In other cases questions of exemption shall be considered by the county administrative board.
(3) Decisions on exemptions shall be reviewed after a certain time in accordance with regulations issued by the Swedish Board of Agriculture. Exemption decisions may be cancelled if the conditions set are not fulfilled. Ordinance (2008:1051).

Section 14

Pigs shall be housed in lounging barns.

Section 15

(1) Equipment for immobilizing pigs must not be used otherwise than as a temporary measure.
(2) Equipment or devices that give animals electric shocks for the purpose of controlling their behaviour may not be used. Nor may livestock buildings, other holding spaces for animals or enclosures be fitted out with devices of this kind.
(3) The prohibition in subsection (2) does not apply to the use of electric fences.
(4) The Swedish Board of Agriculture may issue regulations concerning:
   1. conditions for using electric fences;
   2. exemptions from the prohibition in subsection (2) concerning electric prods or electric deterrents on feed cars; and
   3. conditions for use that is permitted under regulations issued pursuant to point 2. Ordinance (2007:484).

Section 16

(1) Pens for pigs and for calves up to the age of one month shall be provided with litter bedding or similar material.
(2) Stall floors and cubicles for dairy cows shall be provided with adequate bedding of straw or similar material.

Section 17

The Swedish Board of Agriculture may issue further regulations laying down conditions for or prohibiting certain kinds of animal management. Ordinance (2007:484).

Section 18

The Swedish Board of Agriculture may issue regulations concerning the tying of animals. Ordinance (2007:484).

Section 19

It shall be prohibited to own or breed dogs which:

1. are exceptionally aggressive;
2. are irritable and bite;
3. are difficult to restrain once they have started an attack; and
4. are inclined to direct their aggression at people or other dogs. Ordinance (1997:49).

Section 19 a

Repealed by Ordinance (2002:723).

Section 20

Persons who are engaged in trade with pet animals commercially or on a large scale shall have the training or other knowledge prescribed by the Swedish Board of Agriculture. Ordinance (2007:484).

Section 21

Repealed by Ordinance (2006:818).

Section 21 a

The Swedish Board of Agriculture may issue further regulations laying down conditions for or prohibiting the sale or other transfer of animals. Ordinance (2007:484).

Transportation of animals

Section 22

Persons who transport live animals shall attend to the animals and take the necessary steps to ensure that the animals are not injured or subjected to any suffering during loading, transport and unloading.

Section 23

The Swedish Board of Agriculture may issue further regulations concerning conditions for or prohibitions against the transport of animals. Ordinance (2007:484).

Section 24

Repealed by Ordinance (1996:720).

Surgical procedures etc.

Section 25

(1) The gelding of domestic animals and dehorning of cattle and goats shall be permitted even where this is not necessary for veterinary medical reasons.
(2) Male reindeer may be gelded by persons other than veterinarians. Male pigs may be gelded by persons other than veterinarians provided that gelding takes place before the animal has attained the age of seven days. The gelding of pigs which have attained the age of seven days shall be performed under an anaesthetic.
(3) Cattle and goats shall be dehorned under an anaesthetic and the operation shall be performed by a veterinarian or a person considered suitable for this purpose by a veterinarian. Ordinance (2002:723).

Section 26

(1) The Swedish Board of Agriculture may issue further regulations concerning surgical procedures which may be performed on or injections

administered to animals where they are not necessary for veterinary medical reasons.

(2) The Swedish Board of Agriculture may issue further regulations concerning cases in which surgical procedures may be performed or injections administered by persons other than veterinarians. Ordinance (2007:484).

Section 27

The Swedish Board of Agriculture may issue detailed regulations concerning the performance of surgical procedures on and administration of injections to animals. Ordinance (2007:484).

Section 28

(1) It shall be prohibited to administer hormones or other substances to animals in order to alter their characteristics for any purpose other than to prevent, detect, cure or alleviate disease or symptoms of disease.

(2) Subsection (1) shall not apply to substances falling within the Feeding stuff and Animal By Products Act (2006:805).

(3) The Swedish Board of Agriculture may issue regulations providing for exemptions, or may in special cases grant exemptions, from subsection (1). Ordinance (2007:484).

Section 29

(1) The Swedish Board of Agriculture may issue regulations prohibiting or laying down conditions for breeding that is planned in such a way that it may affect animals' natural behaviour.

(2) Breeding that is planned in such a way that it may entail suffering for the animals shall be prohibited. Detailed regulations concerning this prohibition shall be issued by the Swedish Board of Agriculture. Ordinance (2007:484).

Slaughter etc.

Section 30

(1) Animals shall be stunned prior to slaughter in such a way as to cause rapid unconsciousness. They must not regain consciousness.

(2) The Swedish Board of Agriculture may issue regulations concerning methods of anaesthesia. Ordinance (2007:484).

Section 31

The Swedish Board of Agriculture may issue regulations providing for, or may in individual cases grant, exemptions from the requirement for anaesthesia referred to in section 14, subsection (1), of the Animal Welfare Act (1988:534) in the case of poultry and rabbits. Ordinance (2007:484).

Section 32

The Swedish Board of Agriculture may issue further regulations concerning the slaughter and killing of animals in other cases. Ordinance (2007:484).

Section 32 a

(1) If an animal is subjected to or it may be presumed that it will be subjected to unnecessary suffering at a slaughterhouse, the official veterinarian shall prohibit slaughter, order the animal to be killed immediately or take other measures that are required immediately from an animal welfare perspective.
(2) The Swedish Board of Agriculture may issue additional regulations concerning the duties of an official veterinarian from an animal welfare perspective. Ordinance (2007:484).

Mandatory permits for certain types of livestock holding

Section 32 b

(1) Applications for permits under section 16 of the Animal Welfare Act (1988:534) shall be considered by the county administrative board that, under section 59, is the competent authority to exercise official control of activities for which a permit is required.
(2) The Swedish Board of Agriculture may issue regulations concerning the
1. criteria for regarding a business under section 16, subsection (1), of the Animal Welfare Act (1988:534) as operating on a substantial scale; and
2. exemptions from the permit requirement under section 16, subsection (1), of the same Act. Ordinance (2008:1051).

Section 32 c

Repealed by Ordinance (2008:1051).

Sporting events and exhibitions involving animals

Section 33

(1) A veterinarian appointed by the Swedish Board of Agriculture or, if the Swedish Board of Agriculture so decides, by the county administrative board, shall be present at public sporting events involving animals. Before the event the veterinarian shall inspect the competition arena or racetrack and the animals taking part. If any animal is subjected or liable to be subjected to injury or other suffering the veterinarian shall immediately cancel the event, wholly or in part, or the participation therein of a particular animal.
(2) The Swedish Board of Agriculture may issue further regulations concerning the veterinarian.
(3) The Swedish Board of Agriculture shall fix the veterinarian's fee. The fee shall be paid by the organizer of the event.

(4) Where special reasons exist, the Swedish Board of Agriculture may prescribe, or in individual cases grant, exemptions from the first and second sentences of subsection (1). Ordinance (2007:484).

Section 34

The Swedish Board of Agriculture may issue further regulations concerning the training of animals and their use in sporting events and other activities referred to in section 17 of the Animal Welfare Act (1988:534) and concerning the organization of such events and activities. Ordinance (2007:484).

Section 35

(1) Animals must not be taken from place to place and exhibited to the public in menageries.
(2) Monkeys, predators, with the exception of domesticated dogs and cats, pinnipeds with the exception of sea-lions, rhinoceroses, hippopotamuses, deer, with the exception of reindeer, giraffes, kangaroos, birds of prey, ratite birds and crocodilians must not be taken from place to place and exhibited to the public in other circumstances either.
(3) The animals referred to in subsection (2) must not be exhibited to the public in performances or otherwise at circuses, variety shows or similar entertainments. Ordinance (1993:1485).

Section 36

Animals other than those referred to in section 35, subsection (2) may only be exhibited to the public in performances at circuses, variety shows or similar entertainments and, provided that they have been exhibited in such performances, in livestock buildings and other holding rooms for animals. The young of such animals may also be exhibited in such buildings or rooms even if they have not been exhibited in such performances. The same shall apply to individual animals that accompany a circus in order to be trained for exhibition. Ordinance (2001:284).

Section 36 a

(1) A circus that exhibits animals to the public shall be controlled once a year by the county administrative board in the county where the circus is domiciled, enters the country or gives its first performance. The control shall be made before the circus's first performance of the year in the country. A control shall also be made in the event of any change in the collection of animals or equipment that is of significant relevance to animal welfare or animal health. The Swedish Board of Agriculture may issue more detailed regulations concerning inspections.
(2) The Swedish Board of Agriculture may issue regulations making it compulsory for persons who exhibit animals at a circus to: 1. keep records of

these activities and of the animals used; and 2. supply information about the activities. Ordinance (2007:484).

Section 37

If a zoological garden, zoological park or similar facility is established, it must not be used for the public exhibition of animals until it has been approved by the county administrative board. The same shall also apply when such animals are moved and following the construction of new buildings, extensions and conversions of any significance. Ordinance (2003:105).

Section 38

The measures covered by the provisions concerning doping etc. in section 18 of the Animal Welfare Act (1988:534) shall be specified in regulations issued by the Swedish Board of Agriculture. Ordinance (2003:1124).

Section 39

The cost of control of compliance with the prohibition of doping etc. in section 18 of the Animal Welfare Act (1988:534) shall, if such control takes place at a sporting event, be paid by the organizer of the event and, if it takes place in connection with training, by the animal's owner.

Animal Experiments

Section 40

(1) A permit under section 19 a of the Animal Welfare Act (1988:534) is required for animal experiments using animals in the following animal classes: mammals, birds, reptiles, amphibians, fish and cyclostomes.
(2) Permit matters are examined by the Swedish Board of Agriculture. Ordinance (2007:484).

Section 40 a

The Swedish Board of Agriculture may issue regulations laying down conditions for or prohibiting the breeding, keeping, supply or use of laboratory animals. Ordinance (2007:484).

Section 41

(1) Ethical approvals pursuant to section 21, subsection (1) of the Animal Welfare Act (1988:534) is required for animal experiments using animals in the following animal classes: mammals, birds, reptiles, amphibians, fish and cyclostomes.
(2) For purposes of ethical approval, there are ethical committees on animal experiments. Ordinance (2006:186).

Section 42

The number of ethical committees on animal experiments shall be decided by the Swedish Board of Agriculture; however, it shall be not less than six. The committees shall be distributed throughout the country in the places decided by the Swedish Board of Agriculture. Ordinance (2007:484).

Section 43

(1) Each committee shall have a chairman and one or more vice-chairman and include laypeople, research workers and representatives of the personnel who handle laboratory animals.
(2) The Swedish Board of Agriculture shall appoint the chairman and the vice-chairman, who shall be impartial and shall preferably have legal training and experience as judges.
(3) Half of the other members of the committee shall be lay members. The number of lay members representing animal welfare organizations shall be less than half of the total number of lay members of the committee. Ordinance (2007:484).

Section 44

(1) The number of members of the ethical committees on animal experiments shall be decided by the Swedish Board of Agriculture. However, the number must not exceed 14. If the committee is divided into more than one division, however, the number of members in each division must not exceed 14.
(2) The members shall be appointed by the Swedish Board of Agriculture for not more than four years at a time. Ordinance (2007:484).

Section 45

To constitute a quorum, a committee shall consist of the chairman or a vice-chairman and the number of other members stipulated by the Swedish Board of Agriculture. Half of these other members shall be lay members. The chairman and the vice-chairman must not both simultaneously take part in a decision of the committee. Ordinance (2007:484).

Section 46

A committee may assign the task of preparing matters to one or more of its members.

Section 47

Detailed regulations concerning the organization of the committees and the procedure for decisions on matters brought before them shall be issued by the Swedish Board of Agriculture. Ordinance (2007:484).

Section 48

(1) The ethical committees on animal experiments shall assist those responsible for conducting animal experiments by giving advice.
(2) Ethical reviews of the use of the animals shall be carried out every three years. Ordinance (1998:57).

Section 49

Repealed by Ordinance (2006:186).

Section 49 a

(1) The committee may approve use of laboratory animals that entails a departure from the provisions in sections 1 b, 2, 3, 9, 10, 11, 14, 15, 16, 28 or 29 or provisions adopted pursuant to this Ordinance. However, no departure may be made from provisions specially regulating the treatment of laboratory animals.
(2) The Swedish Board of Agriculture may issue regulations on the formulation of applications for exemptions and decisions on approval referred to in subsection (1).
(3) The committee shall report all decisions on exemptions from sections 9, 10, 11, 14, 15, subsection (1) or 16 to the Swedish Board of Agriculture. (Ordinance 2007:484).

Section 50

The Swedish Board of Agriculture may issue regulations providing for exemptions from: the requirement that 1. no animals other than those bred for the purpose are used in animal experiments; and 2. the requirement for permission to breed, keep, supply or use laboratory animals. Ordinance (2007:484).

Section 50 a

(1) The Swedish Board of Agriculture may issue regulations, or take decisions in individual cases, concerning the duties of supervisors and veterinarians in connection with the breeding, keeping, supply or use of laboratory animals.
(2) The Swedish Board of Agriculture may also issue regulations, or take decisions in individual cases, concerning the training or skills that the personnel should have in connection with the breeding, keeping or supply of laboratory animals. Ordinance (2007:484).

Section 51

The Swedish Board of Agriculture may issue regulations on the educationand skills required of someone who:

1. uses laboratory animals;
2. participates in the use of laboratory animals; or

3. looks after laboratory animals at the facility where the animals are used. Ordinance (2007:484).

Section 52

The Swedish Board of Agriculture may issue regulations providing for exemptions from the requirement for ethical approvals pursuant to section 21 of the Animal Welfare Act (1988:534) if the laboratory animals are not subjected to surgical procedures, injections, bleeding or other suffering. Ordinance (2007:484).

Section 53

Before an animal that is a member of one of the animal classes mammals, birds, reptiles, amphibians, fish and cyclostomes is used in an animal experiment, the animal shall, if the use may involve physical or mental suffering, be stunned. However, if it is necessary in view of the purpose of the use, or if the anaesthetic would cause more suffering than the use in itself, the procedure may take place under partial anaesthesia or without an anaesthetic. Where possible, an analgesic or tranquilizer shall be used in such cases in order to alleviate the animal's suffering, in order to ensure that the animal is not subjected to severe pain, severe anxiety or any other severe suffering. Ordinance (2006:186).

Section 54

The Swedish Board of Agriculture may issue regulations on the obligation for a person using laboratory animals to submit information on the number of animals and type of animal being used. Ordinance (2007:484).

Section 54 a

The Swedish Board of Agriculture may issue regulations on the obligation for a person breeding, keeping, supplying or using laboratory animals to

1. mark the animals;
2. issue instructions concerning the care of the animals and concerning other information that is relevant in the context of animal welfare;
3. keep records of the activity and the animals; and
4. submit information about the activity. Ordinance (2007:484).

Section 55

(1) Facilities and other holding rooms for laboratory animals must not be built, extended or altered without prior approval by the Swedish Board of Agriculture with reference to animal health and welfare. The same shall apply when facilities or holding spaces are modified in such a way as to have significant effects on animal health and welfare or when a facility or holding room which was previously used for other purposes is put to use or equipped as a facility or holding space for laboratory animals.

(2) Facilities and holding spaces shall be inspected before being used or, if more appropriate, as soon as possible afterwards.
(3) Detailed regulations relating to facilities or other holding spaces for laboratory animals and to inspections shall be issued by the Swedish Board of Agriculture. Ordinance (2003:1124).

Section 55 a

Repealed by Ordinance (2006:818).

Section 56

(1) If a person carries out a measure referred to in section 55 without the prior approval of the Swedish Board of Agriculture, the Board shall order payment of the special charge mentioned in section 3 a, subsection (2) of the Animal Welfare Act (1988:534).
(2) The special charge shall be as follows for new buildings, alterations or extensions in the cases specified: in the case of a relatively 1. small number of spaces for few and common species of animals, using well-tried technology: SEK 10 000; 2. in the case of a relatively large number of spaces for few and common species of animals, using well-tried technology: SEK 15 000; 3. in the case of a relatively small or relatively large number of spaces for few species of animals, where either the species of animals are common or the technology used is well-tried: SEK 15 000; 4. in the case of a relatively small or relatively large number of spaces for many species of animals, where either the species of animals are common or the technology used is well-tried: SEK 20 000; 5. in the case of a relatively small or relatively large number of spaces, where the species of animals are relatively uncommon and where the technology used is not well-tried: SEK 20 000; 6. in the case of a very large number of spaces that otherwise satisfy the requirements in points 1, 2, 3 or 4: SEK 20 000; 7. in the case of a relatively large number of spaces, using many species of animals that are relatively uncommon and where the technology used is not well-tried: SEK 40 000; and 8. in the case of a very large number of spaces, using species of animals that are relatively uncommon and where the technology used is not well-tried: SEK 40 000.
(3) If the matter has not been taken up by the Swedish Board of Agriculture within five years of the date when the measure was taken, no special charge may be collected. Ordinance (2007:1395).

Section 56 a

Repealed by Ordinance (2006:818).

Section 57

If a measure concerning a facility or other holding space where laboratory animals are kept that requires prior approval under section 55 has been taken without such approval, the Swedish Board of Agriculture shall take a decision as referred to in section 3 b of the Animal Welfare Act (1988:534). Ordinance (2007:1395).

Section 57 a

Repealed by Ordinance (2006:818).

Competent authority

Section 58

Unless otherwise indicated by sections 59 or 62 or the Government decides otherwise, the Swedish Board of Agriculture shall perform the tasks that are incumbent on a competent authority under the EC provisions that are supplemented by the Animal Welfare Act (1988:534). Ordinance (2007:484).

Control authorities

Section 59

(1) The county administrative boards are competent authorities to exercise official control.
(2) The county administrative boards may agree to transfer official control of certain activities between themselves. Ordinance (2008:1051).

Section 60

Official control of transport of animals by sea between different counties shall be exercised by the county from which the transport by sea originates. Ordinance (2008:1051).

Section 61

The National Food Administration, acting through the official veterinarians and official auxiliaries at slaughterhouses, shall exercise the animal welfare controls that are the duty of official veterinarians and official auxiliaries under Regulation (EC) No 854/2004 of the European Parliament and of the Council of 29 April 2004 laying down specific rules for the organisation of official controls on products of animal origin intended for human consumption.
Ordinance (2006:818).

Section 62

Repealed by Ordinance (2008:1051).

Section 63

The Swedish Board of Agriculture shall exercise official control by coordinating the other control authorities and giving them support, advice and guidance. Ordinance (2007:484).

Official control of non-food-producing animals

Section 64

(1) In performing official controls of animal keepers other than those who keep food-producing animals, the following provisions of Regulation (EC) No 882/2004 of the European Parliament and of the Council of 29 April 2004 on official controls performed to ensure the verification of compliance with feed and food law, animal health and animal welfare rules shall apply:
- Article 3;
- Article 4.2 a–d and 4.3–4.6;
- Article 5.1–3;
- Article 6;
- Article 7;
- Article 8.1 and 8.3;
- Article 9;
- Article 10.1;
- Article 28; and
- Article 54.1, 54.2 a, e, f, h and 54.3–54.5.

(2) What is stated in these Articles concerning feed and food business operators and business operators shall also apply, where relevant, to other animal keepers. Ordinance (2008:1051).

Regulations concerning official control

Section 65

The Swedish Board of Agriculture may issue regulations concerning:

1. how official control shall be conducted;
2. cooperation between control authorities; and
3. the obligation of a control authority or a control body engaged in official control to provide information to the Swedish Board of Agriculture concerning the control activities conducted. Ordinance (2008:1051).

Section 66

Repealed by Ordinance (2008:1051).

Fees

Section 67

The Swedish Board of Agriculture may issue regulations prescribing that a fee shall be paid in connection with matters relating to:

1. approval of new technologies;
2. registration of animal carriers and exemptions from the requirement for lying areas for animals kept outdoors;

3. permission under section 19 a of the Animal Welfare Act (1988:534);
4. approval under section 20 of the Animal Welfare Act and section 37 of this Ordinance;
5. exemptions under section 13 a of this Ordinance; and
6. appointment of a veterinarian under section 33 of this Ordinance.

Ordinance (2007:1395).

Section 68

The Swedish Board of Agriculture may issue regulations concerning the charge to be paid for additional controls under Article 28 of Regulation (EC) No 882/2004 of the European Parliament and of the Council and section 64 of this Ordinance. Ordinance (2008:1051).

Section 69

The National Food Administration may issue regulations prescribing that a fee shall be paid for the animal welfare controls carried out by official veterinarians and official auxiliaries at slaughterhouses. Ordinance (2006:818).

Section 70

Repealed by Ordinance (2008:1051).

Prohibition against keeping animals, taking charge of animals

Section 71

(1) If the police authority finds that there are grounds for prohibiting a person from having animals in his care pursuant to section 29 of the Animal Welfare Act (1988:534), the authority shall notify the county administrative board of this without delay. Such notification shall contain an account of the relevant circumstances.

(2) The same shall apply if there are grounds for taking charge of animals under section 31 of the Animal Welfare Act. Ordinance (2008:1051).

Section 72

Detailed regulations concerning the procedure for taking animals in charge pursuant to sections 31 and 32 of the Animal Welfare Act (1988:534) may be issued by the Swedish Board of Agriculture. Ordinance (2007:484).

Appeals etc.

Section 73

Section 38 of the Animal Welfare Act (1988:534) contains provisions on appeals. Ordinance (2006:818).

Section 74

(1) Decisions referred to in sections 29, 31, 32 and 34 of the Animal Welfare Act (1988:534) and in articles 23, 26.4 b- c, 26.5 and 26.6 of Council Regulation (EC) No 1/2005 of 22 December 2004 on the protection of animals during transport and related operations and amending Directives 64/432/EEC and 93/119/EC and Regulation (EC) nr 1255/97shall have immediate effect unless the authority making the decision determines otherwise.

(2) In other cases an authority may determine that its decision shall have immediate effect even if an appeal is lodged against it. Ordinance (2007:484).

Appendix V

New Zealand

Animal Welfare

(Rodeos)

Code of Welfare 2003*

A code of welfare issued under the Animal Welfare Act 1999

Code of Welfare No.2

ISBN 0 - 478 - 07793 - 9

ISSN 1176 - 2942

1 January 2004

National Animal Welfare Advisory Committee

C/- *MAF*

POBox 2526

Wellington

NEW ZEALAND

Preface

The Animal Welfare Act 1999 came into force on 1 January 2000. It establishes the fundamental obligations relating to the care of animals. These obligations are written in general terms however. The detail is found in codes of welfare. Codes set out minimum standards and recommendations relating to all aspects of the care of animals. They are developed following an extensive process of public consultation and reviewed every 10 years, or sooner if necessary.

I recommend that all those who care for animals become familiar with the relevant codes. This is important because failure to meet a minimum standard in a code could lead to legal action being taken.

I issue codes on the recommendation of the National Animal Welfare Advisory Committee. The members of this committee collectively possess knowledge and experience in veterinary science; agricultural science; animal science; the commercial use of animals; the care, breeding, and management of companion animals; ethical standards and conduct in respect of animals; animal welfare advocacy; the public interest in respect of animals: and environmental and conservation management.

---

* *Source:* <www.biosecurity.govt.nz/files/regs/animal-welfare/req/codes/rodeo-events/rodeo-events.pdf>.

The Animal Welfare (Rodeos) Code of Welfare 2003 is issued by me, by a notice published in the Gazette on 4 December 2003, under section 75 of the Animal Welfare Act 1999. This code comes into force on 1 January 2004.

This code is deemed to be a regulation for the purposes of the Regulations (Disallowance) Act 1989 and is subject to the scrutiny of Parliament's Regulations Review Committee.

Hon Dr Michael Cullen
Acting Minister of Agriculture

1. Introduction, Purpose and Interpretation of Code

1.1 History

The original codes of recommendations and minimum standards for the welfare of animals were prepared by the Animal Welfare Advisory Committee (AWAC), which was established in 1989 by the Minister of Agriculture to advise him on matters concerning animal welfare. The codes were of a voluntary nature and had no legal standing under the Animals Protection Act 1960.

The Animal Welfare Act 1999 established the National Animal Welfare Advisory Committee (NAWAC), which replaced AWAC, and provided for the issue of codes of welfare with legal effect. One of the responsibilities of NAWAC is to advise the Minister on the content of codes of welfare following a process of public consultation.

1.2 Legal Status of Codes of Welfare

Codes of welfare are deemed to be regulations for the purposes of the Regulations (Disallowance) Act 1969. As such they are subject to the scrutiny of the Regulations Review Committee of Parliament.

Codes of welfare contain minimum standards and may also contain recommended practice and recommended best practice. Only minimum standards have legal effect and in two possible ways:

- evidence of a failure to meet a relevant minimum standard may be used to support a prosecution for an offence under the Act (see Appendix I)
- a person who is charged with an offence against the Act can defend himself/herself by showing that he/she has equalled or exceeded the minimum standards (see Appendix I).

Recommendations for ideal husbandry practice under New Zealand conditions set out standards of care and conduct over and above the minimum required to meet the obligations in the Act. They are included for educational and information purposes.

Any person or organisation aggrieved at the operation of a code of welfare has a right to make a complaint to the Regulations Review Committee, Parliament Buildings, Wellington.

This is a Parliamentary select committee charged with examining regulations against a set of criteria and drawing to the attention of the House of Representatives any regulation that does not meet the criteria. Grounds for reporting to the House include:

- the regulation trespasses unduly on personal rights and freedoms
- the regulation is not made in accordance with the general objects and intentions of the statutes under which it is made, or
- it was not made in compliance with the particular notice and consultation procedures prescribed by statute.

1.3 Process for Code Development

A draft code may be developed by anyone including NAWAC or the Minister. It is then submitted to NAWAC. Provided the draft meets criteria in the Act for clarity, compliance with the purposes of the Act, and representatives of persons likely to be affected by the code have been adequately consulted, NAWAC publicly notifies the code and calls for submissions. NAWAC is then responsible for recommending the form and content of the code to the Minister after having regard to the submissions received, good practice and scientific knowledge, available technology and any other relevant matters.

NAWAC may recommend draft standards that do not fully meet the obligations in the Act if certain criteria specified in the Act are met.

The Minister issues the code by notice in the *Gazette.*

1.4 Scope

This code is intended for all persons responsible for the welfare of animals used in rodeos including training and rodeo schools.

The use of animals for rodeos, if it is to be done well, requires both experience and the observance of high standards. Unless that work is done well, the welfare of the animals cannot be adequately protected. This code is intended to encourage all those responsible for its implementation to adopt the highest standard of husbandry, care and handling, and to equal or exceed the minimum standards.

Under the Animal Welfare Act 1999 the "owner" of an animal and the"person in charge" is responsible for meeting the legal obligations for animal welfare. In the case of rodeo animals the owner of the animals will place the animals in the care of others for the purposes of competition.

Responsibility for meeting minimum standards will lie with the owner or person in charge of the rodeo animals.

Advice is given throughout the code designed to encourage owners/operators to strive for a higher level of welfare. Explanatory material is provided where appropriate.

Responsibility for meeting minimum standards during the operation of particular tasks will lie with the person responsible for carrying out that particular task. That person is in charge of the animals at that particular point in time. Generally, a stockhandler is the person in charge of the animals in that stockhandler's care. In practice, the identification of the person in charge will depend on the minimum standard in question.

This code provides for the general principles of the care and use of animals used in rodeos but is dependent on each organisation implementing its own quality assurance programme that incorporates the recommendations and minimum standards of this code *(see section 5-Quality Assurance System).*

Other codes that are relevant, and that are either being produced for the first time, or are in the process of being reviewed. include codes concerned with the transport of animals, emergency slaughter, and the species specific codes. Where relevant these other codes should be consulted (see Appendix II).

This draft was developed by NAWAC. Industry representatives and other interest groups were consulted. As required by the Animal Welfare Act 1999, NAWAC publicly notified the draft code of welfare on 13 December 2001.

1.5 Contents of this Code

Section 69 of the Animal Welfare Act I999 provides that a code of welfare may relate to one or more of the following—

- a species of animal
- animals used for purposes specified in the code
- animal establishments of a kind specified in the code
- types of entertainment specified in the code (being types of entertainment in which animals are used)
- the transport of animals
- the procedures and equipment used in the management, care, or killing of animals or in the carrying out of surgical procedures on animals.

In deciding to issue a code of welfare, the Minister must be satisfied as to the following matters set out in section 73(1) of the Animal Welfare Act—

- that the proposed standards are the minimum necessary to ensure that the purposes of the Animal Welfare Act 1999 will be met; and
- that the recommendations for best practice (if any) are appropriate.

Despite the provisions of section 73(1), section 73(3) of the Animal Welfare Act allows NAWAC. in exceptional circumstances, to recommend minimum standards and recommendations for best practice that do not fully meet the obligations of—

- sections 10 and 11—obligations in relation to physical, health and behavioural needs of animals
- section *12(c)*—killing an animal
- section 21 (1)(b)—restriction on performance of surgical procedures
- section 22(2)—providing comfortable and secure accommodation for the transport of animals

- sections 23(1) and 23(2)—transport of animals
- section 29(a)—ill-treating an animal.

In making a recommendation under section 73(3), section 73(4) requires NAWAC to have regard to—

- the feasibility and practicality of effecting a transition from current practices to new practices and any adverse effects that *may* result from such a transition
- the requirements of religious practices or cultural practices or both
- the economic effects of any transition from current practices to new practices.

This code provides for the physical, health, and behavioural needs of animals. These needs include—

- proper and sufficient food and water
- adequate shelter
- opportunity to display normal patterns of behaviour
- physical handling in a manner which minimises the likelihood of unreasonable or unnecessary pain or distress
- protection from, and rapid diagnosis of, any significant injury or disease being a need, which, in each case is appropriate to the species, environment, and circumstances of the animal- *section* 4 *Animal Welfare Act 1999.*

This code also takes account of—

- good practice
- scientific knowledge
- available technology.

Good practice is taken to mean the carrying out of a customary or expected procedure in a manner which meets the required purpose, is sound and thorough, and which is recognised by others carrying out the practice. In addition good practice meets the legal obligations of the Act, and failure to comply could result in a prosecution.

1.6 Preparation and Revision of the Code

This code is based on the knowledge and technology available at the lime of publication, and may be varied in the light of future advances and knowledge.

Consequently, NAWAC will review this code when deemed necessary. In any event this code will be reviewed no later than 4 December 2013 (being 10 years from the date on which this code was issued by the Minister).

Comments on this code are always welcome and should be addressed to:
The Secretary
National Animal Welfare Advisory Committee
PO Box 2526
Wellington.
Further information can be obtained from the MAF website -
http://www.maf.goVl.nz/biosecurity/animal·welfare/index.htm

1.7 Deemed Codes of Welfare and Codes of Recommendations and Minimum Standards

Deemed codes of welfare, and codes of recommendations and minimum standards and guidelines that were endorsed by AWAC prior to the commencement of the Animal Welfare Act 1999, are listed in Appendix II of this code. The deemed codes of welfare are valid until 31 December 2003 unless revoked prior to that date.

On 19 December 2002 the Animal Welfare Amendment Act 2002 amended the Animal Welfare Act 1999 to deem the regulations and circular listed in Appendix II to be a code of welfare known as the Animal Welfare (Commercial Slaughter) Code of Welfare 2002.

The Code of Recommendations and Minimum Standards for the Welfare of Animals Used in Rodeo Events was revoked under section 191(1) and 76(1) (a) of the Act, by a notice published in the *Gazette* on 4 December 2003.

1.8 Interpretation and Definitions

Minimum Standards

Minimum standards are identified in the text by a heading and use the word "must" or similar words. They are highlighted in boxes within the text.

Recommended Best Practice

The Act provides that codes of welfare may contain recommendations for best practice.

Recommended best practice is taken to mean:

The best practice agreed at a particular time, following consideration of scientific information and accumulated experience and public opinion. It is usually a higher standard of practice than the minimum standard, except where the minimum standard is best practice, It is a practice that can be varied as new information comes to light.

Recommendations for best practice will be particularly appropriate where it is desirable to promote or encourage better care for animals than is provided as a minimum standard.

Recommended best practices are identified by a heading and, generally, use the term ·should".

"**Animal**"—This code applies to animals as defined in the Animal Welfare Act 1999.

"Animal"—

(a) Means any live member of the animal kingdom that is

(i) A mammal; or
(ii) A bird; or
(iii) A reptile: or
(iv) An amphibian; or
(v) A fish (bony or carlilaginous): or

(vi) Any octopus, squid, crab, lobster, or crayfish (including freshwater crayfish): or

(vii) Any other member of the animal kingdom which is declared from time to time by the Governor-General, by Order in Council, to be an animal for the purposes of this Act; and

(b) Includes any mammalian foetus, or any avian or reptilian pre-hatched young, that is in the last half of its period of gestation or development; and

(c) Includes any marsupial pouch young; but

(d) Does not include-

(i) A human being; or

(ii) Except as provided in paragraph (b) or paragraph (c) of this definition, any animal in the pre-natal, pre-hatched, larval, or other such developmental stage,

—section 2 *Animal Welfare Act 1999*

Note: The terms 'stock' and 'animals' are used interchangeably in this code.

1.9 Glossary

Animal Welfare Officer	an official appointed by the rodeo organiser(s) to be responsible for overseeing animal welfare at a rodeo in conjunction with the veterinarian .
Bareback Bronc Riding	riding a horse using rigging and no saddle.
Barrel Racing	a limed event in which an individual horse and rider complete a clover-leaf pattern around three barrels.
Bull or Steer Riding	riding a bull or steer using a girth rope.
Busted	Throwing a calf so that it rotates 180°, landing on the broad of its back.
Chute	a stockade from which animals are released into the arena.
Chute Fighters	animals that regularly resist being held in the chutes.
Chute-Stalled Stock	animals that refuse to leave the chute when the gate is open.
Cinch	a device (usually a strap or buckle) that connects the saddle or bareback rigging to the girth.
Contract Stock	stock maintained for use in rodeo events.
Flagged	when the flag judge drops his/her flag to signify the end of the event.
Flank Strap/Rope	a rope or strap that is tied over the lower back and around the flanks of a horse or bull.

Gullet	The underside of the front of the saddle.
Hazer	a rider who keeps the steer running in a straight line.
Judge	a judge who has been appointed by a rodeo association to officiate at a rodeo.
Non· contract Stock	stock not regularly used in rodeo events, (also called club stock) and which are only used once at a particular rodeo.
Rigging	a girth strap and handle used in bareback riding.
Rodeo	any event that is open to the public and which may include: • bareback bronc riding • barrel racing • bull or steer riding • calf riding • rope and lie • saddle bronc riding • steer wrestling • team roping and includes any rodeo school in which animals and riders are trained 10 compete in rodeos.
Rodeo Organiser	an official of the organising association, and who is responsible for the running of the rodeo.
Rodeo School	an officially organised event for the purpose of instructing students in correct techniques of various rodeo disciplines, training of time event horses and for teaching trainee judges.
Rope and Tie	catching by lasso, throwing and tying a calf by the legs (previously known as calf roping).
Roping Event	a calf roping or team roping event.
Rough Stock	animals used for bareback, saddle bronc and bull riding events.
Rowel	a spoked revolving disk at the end of a spur.
Saddle Bronc Riding	riding a horse that bucks, using a saddle.
Steer Wrestling	catching and throwing a homed steer by one rider with the use of a hazer (also may be known as bull dogging).

Stock	Animals used in rodeo events including rough stock, time event cattle and calves.
Stock Contractor	a person who provides stock for rodeo events.
Team Roping	a steer roping event involving two horse riders, one acting as a header (the person who ropes the horns or head) and the other as a heeler (who rides in and ropes the steer around the back legs) which results in the steer being brought to a standstlll between the two riders.

2. Obligations of Owners and Persons in Charge of Animals

Introduction

The owner or person in charge of an animal has overall responsibility for the welfare of the animal in his or her care. The legal obligations set out below are not an exhaustive list of the obligations in the Act.

(1) The owner or person in charge of animal must—
  (a) ensure that the physical. health, and behavioural needs of the animals are met in a manner that is in accordance with both good practice and scientific knowledge
  (b) ensure that an animal that is ill or injured receives treatment that will alleviate any unreasonable or unnecessary pain or distress being suffered by the animal or that it is killed humanely.

(2) The owner or person in charge of an animal must not without reasonable excuse
  (a) keep an animal alive when it is in such a condition that it is suffering unreasonable or unnecessary pain or distress
  (b) sell, attempt to sell, or offer for sale, otherwise than for the express purpose of it being killed, an animal, when it is suffering unreasonable or unnecessary pain or distress
  (c) desert an animal in circumstances in which no provision is made to meet its physical, health and behavioural needs,

(3) No person may—
  (a) ill-treat an animal
  (b) release an animal that has been kept in captivity, in circumstances which the animal is likely to suffer unreasonable or unnecessary pain or distress
  (c) perfonn any significant surgical procedure on an animal unless that person is a veterinarian
  (d) perform on an animal a surgical procedure that is not significant in such a manner that the animal suffers unreasonable or unnecessary pain or distress,

Defences are set out in Appendix I, The Animal Welfare Act 1999 contains specific procedural requirements before these defences can be relied on, and these requirements are described in Appendix I.

3. Stockmanship

Introduction

The care of rodeo animals requires both experience and the observance of high standards.

Under the Animal Welfare Act 1999 the ·owner" of an animal and the "person in charge" is responsible for meeting the legal obligations to animal welfare. In the case of rodeos the owner or person in charge will place those animals in the care of others for the purpose of competition. During competition the contestant is considered to be the person in charge.

This code establishes minimum standards of care for rodeo animals, and is intended to encourage all owners and persons in charge of rodeo animals to adopt the highest standard of husbandry, care and handling, based on the recommended best practices. While this code is based on current knowledge and technology available at the time of issue, it does not replace the need for experience and common sense in the handling of rodeo animals.

The importance of good stockmanship cannot be over-emphasised. Those responsible for the care of rodeo animals should be competent and well trained. Personnel should be appropriately instructed in the care and maintenance of rodeo animals and how their actions may affect the animals' welfare. Knowledge of the normal appearance and behaviour of animals being used is essential for their health and welfare. It is important that those in charge of the rodeo animals should be able to recognise injuries or early signs of distress so that prompt action is taken or advice sought.

Owners and persons in charge of rodeo animals should ensure that their personnel have either the relevant knowledge and training or appropriate supervision to ensure that the health and welfare needs of the animals in their care are met. Personnel should undergo training either formally or on the job by experienced supervisors. Handling techniques should be included as written procedures in a quality assurance system, which should be easily accessible to all personnel.

Any contract or temporary staff should be trained and competent in the relevant activity.

Quality assurance programmes should emphasise the importance of training of personnel.

The New Zealand Rodeo Cowboys Association holds a number of training days for new contestants.

Minimum Standard No. 1—Stockmanship
Rodeo animals or stock must be cared for by a sufficient number of personnel who possess the appropriate ability, knowledge and professional competence to maintain the health and welfare of the stock or animals in accordance with the minimum standards listed in this code.

4. Responsibilities of Rodeo Personnel

4.1 Rodeo Organiser

Introduction

The rodeo organiser is the person who is responsible for the running of the rodeo.

The organiser has overall responsibility for the welfare of the animals. Whilst all duties are not necessarily performed directly by the organiser, the organizer needs to ensure that the rodeo staff and stockhandlers are adequately performing their responsibilities. The organiser should therefore employ stockhandlers experienced with the animals they are to handle or should arrange sufficient training with experienced handlers to enable each animal's requirements to be recognised and met.

Adequate precautions should be made for ensuring animal safety and public safety.

Minimum Standard No.2—Rodeo Organiser

(a) The rodeo organiser must be competent to handle and care for the all species of animals held in the rodeo or must employ stockhandlers who are competent to handle and care for those animals.

(b) The rodeo organiser must ensure that—

- (i) All contestants and staff are aware of the requirements of this code,
- (ii) No undue or injurious force is used to encourage any animal to participate in a rodeo event,
- (iii) The arena is examined to ensure that it is free of holes, rocks, obstacles and any other hazards that may injure animals,
- (iv) The surface is suitable for the rodeo events,
- (v) Appropriate and well-maintained humane destruction equipment is on site before and during any rodeo,

(vi)	A veterinarian is contracted to provide veterinary services throughout the rodeo,
(vii)	The veterinarian inspects all animals used in competition prior to the start of the rodeo, and any animals that are lame, sick or injured are removed from the draw and are treated If appropriate,
(viii)	All animals used meet the requirements of this code,
(ix)	All equipment is Inspected and compiles with this code,
(x)	The use of all equipment complies with this code,
(xi)	The yards and chutes ara inspected prior to the start of the rodeo and compty with this code, and
(xii)	A conveyance is available to remove a seriously injured animal to a suitable place for further examination and treatment.

Recommended Best Practice

The rodeo organiser should ensure that-

- no person participating in rodeo events is under the influence of alcohol or other drugs
- a report is completed on each occasion in which any animal is injured or any contestant fails to comply with this code, and is to be forwarded to the official body e.g. New Zealand Rodeo Cowboys Association.

4.2 Animal Welfare Officer

Introduction

An animal welfare officer must be appointed to each rodeo by the official body e.g. New Zealand Rodeo Cowboys Association which must specify in writing his or her responsibilities. The animal welfare officer is not to be confused with auxiliary officers who are appointed under the Animal Welfare Act 1999.

The animal welfare officer has direct responsibility for the welfare of the animals and will work in liaison with the rodeo organiser and the veterinarian. The animal welfare officer's role is to liaise with clubs, promoters, stock contractors, contestants and the veterinarian to co-ordinate and evaluate all steps taken to ensure the welfare of the animals.

Despite the appointment of an animal welfare officer, each contestant, being the person in charge of an animal, is still personally responsible for the animal the contestant uses.

Minimum Standard No. 3—Animal Welfare Officer
(a) An animal welfare officer must be appointed and be present at each rodeo.
(b) The animal welfare officer must be competent to assess the welfare of animals competing in the rodeo.

4.3 Contestant

Introduction

All contestants should be aware of the requirements of this code.

Each contestant is responsible for the animals he or she uses during an event, and during that period of use is considered to be the person in charge.

Minimum Standard No. 4—Contestant
(a) Each contestant must comply with all relevant sections of this
(b) Contestants must not intentionally treat animals in a way that causes injury or harm.

4.4 Veterinarian

Introduction

The veterinarian is responsible for providing expert advice on the health, injury or disease status of an animal and its suitability for competition. Veterinarians need to check for lame, sick and injured animals, or animals with defective eyesight and to assess body condition.

Minimum Standard No. 5—Veterinarian
(a) A veterinarian must be In attendance throughout the rodeo, unless called away to an emergency.
(b) All rodeo animals must be examined by the veterinarian prior to the start and In the case of multiple events, also at the end of each day, to determine If they are fit to compete (see Minimum Standard 9).
(c) The veterinarian must be the final arbiter on whether an animal is fit for competition.

Recommended Best Practice

Arrangements should be made so that a veterinarian is present at all times.

The veterinarian should be experienced in treating all species of animals used in the rodeo.

The veterinarian should complete a record of injuries and other defects, which should be included as part of the incident report (see section 4.1).

4.5 Stock Contractor

Introduction

The rodeo organiser(s) should select the stock contractor supplying animals for rodeo events well in advance of the date of the rodeo. The rodeo organiser(s) should aim to use contract stock only. The approved stock contractor must be familiar with this code.

The stock contractor or the owners of non-contract stock (when used) are responsible for the appropriate husbandry and handling of their rodeo stock.

Minimum Standard No.6—Stock Contractor
The stock contractor or the owners of non-contract stock (when used) must ensure that: (i) stock provided by them are in good health and are suitable for the purpose for which they are intended, (ii) all stock provided by them receive due care at all times, including adequate food , water and shelter and that yards, chutes and equipment comply with the requirements of the appropriate part of this code, (iii) unsuitable stock are withdrawn from competition, (iv) all instructions of the veterinarian and animal welfare officer are Implemented, (v) cattle and horses are penned separately in the yards and during transport, (vi) aggressive stock are separated from other stock, (vii) injured stock are treated appropriately end isolated (if necessary), end (viii) animals with young at foot are not yarded or used in any rodeo event.

4.6 Care and Treatment of Animals at Rodeo Events

Introduction

Rodeos involve situations where animals may be subjected to a risk of injuries and distress. Proper consideration must be given to the health and welfare of animals used in rodeos. Events and procedures in rodeos should be specifically designed to prevent any suffering and minimise the impacts on the welfare of animals used. People who have responsibilities in the organisation and running of rodeos must have appropriate training to ensure that the animal welfare needs are met.

In order that the welfare of animals used in rodeo events is safeguarded, rodeo organisers, contractors, stock owners and contestants should clearl y understand and accept their responsibilities. All people involved with and parl icipaling in rodeo events should be familiar with this code.

The judges and the animal welfare officer should be empowered to disqualify any official or contestant who compromises the welfare of an animal.

Minimum Standard No.7—Care of Rodeo Animals
(a) Only experienced stock handlers must undertake the preparation of animals for rodeo events.
(b) Mature stock must be fed and watered at least every 12 hours. Horses and young stock must be fed and watered at least every 8 hours.
(c) Stimulants, sedatives and hypnotic drugs must not be given to any animal used in rodeo events, unless administered by a veterinarian.
(d) Stock must not be exposed to fireworks that are likely to cause them fear or distress.

Recommended Best Practice

Water should be provided ad lib in the holding pens, especially in hot weather.

Stock should be removed from the arena immediately after completion of an event.

Animals (such as pets) that could cause disturbance to stock should not be allowed in the arena or in the line of sight of stock.

Minimum Standard No.8—Injured Animals
(a) Injured animals must be attended to as soon as possible with veterinary attention being sought where appropriate.
(b) Where an animal is injured in the arena and is unable to move on its own accord, it must be removed from the arena by a conveyance, for treatment or destruction.
(e) An injured animal requiring euthanasia must be humanely destroyed as soon as possible.
(d) Any animal that becomes excessively excited, goes down in a chute, or attempts to jump out of the chute in a manner that may cause It to injure itself must be released immediately.

4.7 Selection of Rodeo Animals

Introduction

The selection of animals for use in a rodeo is crucial to ensuring that they are fit for use. Animals that are not lit: for use should not be transported to the rodeo site.

Minimum Standard No. 9—Selection of Rodeo Animals
(a) All animals to be used must be inspected by the veterinarian prior to the commencement of the rodeo.
(b) In multiple day rodeos, an inspection must be made at the end of each day by the veterinarian to ensure that the animals are suitable for use on ensuing days.
(c) Animals unfit to compete must be withdrawn.
(d) Horses used in rodeo events must be sound, in good condition and mature.
(e) Horses must be at least 4 years of age.
(f) Horses used for bucking events must not be used more than 3 times on any one day.
(g) The same cattle must not be used for both steer wrestling and roping events on anyone day.
(h) Cattle must not be used for any event more than 3 times on any one day. (i) Cattle with horns that are likely to cause injury to other animals must have had the tips (the outer 2.5cm) removed.

<table>
<tr><td colspan="2">(i) Cattle or horses that are overweight, obviously pregnant or lactating must not be used.

(j) Chute fighters must not be used.

(k) Rodeo animals must meet the minimum weights in the following table.</td></tr>
<tr><td>Calves (for rope and tie)</td><td>100 kg</td></tr>
<tr><td>Calves (for calf riding)</td><td>150kg</td></tr>
<tr><td>Rough stock (bulls, horses)</td><td>350 kg</td></tr>
<tr><td>Time event cattle (steer wrestling, team roping)</td><td>200 kg</td></tr>
<tr><td>Sheep</td><td>65kg</td></tr>
</table>

Recommended Best Practice

Only horses, cattle (including calves) and sheep should be used in rodeo events.

4.8 Arena and Gear

Introduction

The size of the arena and the condition of gear used are critical in protecting stock from injury. Careful planning and construction of arenas will make the handling and removal of stock from the arenas easier and will increase stock and contestant safety, Arenas which are too small create a potential danger to stock, contestants and spectators.

In general, the standard arena should have a suitable, soil based surface, rotary hoed or softened to a depth of approximately 8·10 cm. Other surfaces may be used provided that they are well drained, provide a secure footing and be at least as safe for the animals as an appropriate soil based surface.

Minimum Standard No. 10—The Arena
(a) The arena must be of a size suitable for the events to take place and to minimise the likelihood of injurious contact with the perimeter fence. (b) The construction height and appearance of arena fencing should discourage stock from attempting to push through the fence or jump over It. (c) Arena fences must be clearly visible and not appear open to the stock. (d) There must be no protrusions on fences, gateways or chutes that are likely to cause Injury to stock.

(e) The arena surface must provide traction and safety for stock.

(f) The arena must be free of holes, rocks, obstacles and any other hazards that may injure stock.

Recommended Best Practice

Where it is thought that stock will pressure certain points of an arena more than others, care should be taken to ensure that the fencing is suitable.

Minimum Standard No. 11—Gear

(a) Before the rodeo commences the rodeo organiser or the animal welfare officer must be satisfied that all gear and equipment to be used In a rodeo has been adequately inspected to ensure that it meets all requirements of this standard.

(b) Fully locked rowels or rowels that are capable of being fully locked must not be used in saddle bronc and bareback riding.

(c) Spurs and equipment must not be used in a way that injures the animal.

(d) The rowel must be dulled and not less than 3 mm in width at its narrowest part and there must be a minimum diameter of 2 cm to the point of the rowel.

(e) Sharp and cutting objects, and any object that may protrude into the skin of an animal, must not be permitted in the cinch, saddle, flank strap, bareback rigging, head-rein (plaited rein attached to the head-stall) or head-stall (halter).

(f) Pads must be used under bareback rigging and must be of adequate thickness to prevent rubbing or chafing.

(g) Rank straps/ropes must be of the quick release type and must be correctly applied and must have linings that are supple and in good condition.

(h) Rank straps/ropes must be placed on the animal in such a way that the lined portion evenly overlies both flanks and the abdomen.

(i) Care must be taken to ensure that sand, grit and other abrasives do not accumulate in the lining of the flank strap.

(j) For cattle used in team roping, the horns must be wrapped with protective material (e.g. horn wraps) to protect the ears and base of the horns from rope burns.

Minimum Standard No. 12—Electric Prods
(a) Electric prods must be— (i) of the standard used generally for the handling, yarding and transport of stock, (ii) used with restraint and only as an aid for loading and handling stock, and (iii) used only when necessary on chute-stalled stock, and then only instantaneously on the shoulder or rump of an animal to clear it from the chute on opening of the gate. (b) Electric prods must not be- (i) used if an animal is loaded and standing in a closed chute, (ii) used on animals in the arena while performing, and (iii) used simply to harass an animal. (c) Casual or inexperienced animal handlers must not use electric prods.

4.9 Specific Rodeo Events

Minimum Standard No. 13—Saddle Bronc Riding
(a) The saddle must be correctly placed and fitted in order to avoid injury. (b) There must be a sufficient clearance under the gullet of the saddle to prevent rubbing or Injury to the wither. (c) The front cinch of the saddle must be of sufficient width to prevent cutting or chafing of the girth. (d) The back cinch must not be so tight as to cause the horse to fall down.

Minimum Standard No. 14—Bareback Bronc Riding
(a) Suitable pads must be placed under the rigging and must extend a sufficient distance past the back of the rigging to protect the horse's back. (b) Contestants must only use pads that have been approved by the judges and the animal welfare officer. (c) The girth on the bareback rigging must be wide enough to prevent chafing or cunning of the girth.

Minimum Standard No. 15—Bull and Steer Riding
Equipment used for bull riding must be fitted so as to fall off the bull once the rider falls or dismounts, to prevent possible injury to bulls.

Recommended Best Practice

The equipment used should be a loose rope with or without a handhold.

There should be no knots or hitches preventing the rope from falling from the animal after the contestant has been thrown or dismounted.

A contestant should not re-set and re-pull the rope more than twice if the bull is standing quietly in the chute.

Minimum Standard No. 16—Rope and Tie
(a) All reasonable precautions must be taken to ensure that calves are not busted during calf roping.
(b) The contestant must adjust the rope and reins in a manner that will prevent the horse from dragging the calf.
(c) After the tie is completed and has been signalled, the roper must immediately mount the horse and ride it forward to loosen the catch rope.
(d) A neck rope must be fined to horses used for roping and tying, through which the catch rope must pass before it is tied to the saddle horn.
(e) Ropes must be removed from the calf immediately after the tie is flagged.
(f) On each day, contract calves must not be used on more than 3 occasions and non-contract calves on no more than 2 occasions.

Recommended Best Practice

All calves should be habituated by being walked or run through the arena from the release chute to the exhaust pen, and being held by a neck rope, thrown and tied. prior to the event.

A contestant should be disqualified from the event if an animal is busted, whether intended or not, or if the rope horse drags the animal after it is roped and thrown.

Calves should be closely monitored following their use in training or by novice contestants.

Minimum Standard No. 17—Steer Wrestling
The steer must not be knocked down or thrown before it is brought to a stop and the catch is made.

Minimum Standard No. 18—Calf and Sheep Riding
(a) In calf riding the calf must be 150 kg or more and the rider must weigh no more than 40 kg.
(b) In sheep riding the sheep must be 65 kg or more and the rider no more than 20 kg.
(c) Sheep and calves must only be ridden once on anyone day.

General Information

Child contestants should be supervised at all times when competing or around the animals to ensure the welfare of the animals is not compromised.

4.10 Transport, Yarding and Handling of Rodeo Animals

Animals should be transported in accordance with the code of welfare for transport of animals.

5. Quality Assurance System

Recommended Best Practice

To ensure that standards of animal welfare and husbandry are maintained the organiser of each event or series of events should implement a quality assurance system that provides for written procedures. The adoption of a generic (e.g. New Zealand Rodeo Cowboys Association) quality assurance programme will meet this recommendation.

The elements of the quality assurance system should provide for the minimum standards and recommendation of best practice of this code.

While the quality system should be based on the general principles of Standard AS/NZ 9002 or a similar quality system it is not essential that the quality system be certified.

A quality assurance system, which can be part of the rules of the rodeo, should provide for—

- the means of evaluating animal welfare within a rodeo
- the provision of proper and sufficient food. water and shelter
- adequate facilities and equipment within each type of animal holding facility
- holding, training and handling practices that are humane, safe for the animals and safe for the handlers and public.

Appendix I: Defences

Introduction

Strict Liability

In the prosecution of certain offences under the Animal Welfare Act 1999 committed after 19 December 2002, evidence that a relevant code of welfare was in existence at the time of the alleged offence and that a relevant minimum standard established by that code was not complied with is rebuttable evidence that the person charged with the offence failed to comply with, or contravened, the provision of the Animal Welfare Act to which the offence relates. [See sections 13(lA), 24(1) and 30(lA) of the Animal Welfare Act 1999, as amended by the Animal Welfare Amendment Act 2002].

Defences

II is a defence in the prosecution of certain offences under the Animal Welfare Act 1999 If the defendant proves that there was in existence at the time of the alleged offence a relevant code of welfare and the minimum standards established by the code of welfare were in all respects equalled or exceeded.—[Sections *13(2)(c),* 24(2)(b) and 30(2)(c)].

If a defendant in a prosecution intends to rely on the defence under sections 13(2)(c) or 3O(2)(c), the defendant must, within seven days after the service of the summons, or within such further time as the Court may allow, deliver to the prosecutor a written notice, The notice must state that the defendant intends to rely on section t3(2) or 30(2) as the case may be, and must specify the relevant code of welfare that was in existence at the time of the alleged offence, and the facts that show that the minimum standards established by that code of welfare were in all respects equalled or exceeded. This notice may be dispensed with if the Court gives leave. [See sections 13(3) and 30(3)].

The strict liability provisions and the defence of equalling or exceeding the minimum standards established in a code of welfare apply to the following offences—

Failing to provide

Section 12 (a) A person commits an oHence who, being the owner of, or person in charge of, an animal, fails to comply, in relation to the animal, with section 10 (which provides that the owner of an animal, and every person in charge of an animal, must ensure that the physical, health, and behavioural needs of the animal are met in a manner that is in accordance with both good practice and scientific knowledge).

Suffering animals

Section 12(b) A person commits an offence who. being the owner of, or person in charge of, an animal fails, in the case of an animal that is ill or injured, to comply, in relation to the animal, with section 11 (which provides that the owner of an animal that is ill or injured, and every person in charge of such an animal, must, where practicable, ensure that the animal receives treatment that will alleviate any unreasonable or unnecessary pain or distress being suffered by the animal).

Section 12(c) A person commits an offence who, being the owner of, or person in charge of, an animal kills the animal in such a manner that the animal suffers unreasonable or unnecessary pain or distress.

Surgical procedures

Section 21 (1)(b)(I) A person commits an offence who, without reasonable excuse, acts in contravention of or fails 10 comply with section 15(4) (which provides that no person may, in performing on an animal a surgical procedure that is not a significant surgical procedure, perform that surgical procedure in such a manner that the animal suffers unreasonable or unnecessary pain or distress.

Transport

Section 22(2) A person commits an offence who fails, without reasonable excuse, to comply with any provision of subsection (1) (which provides that every person in charge of a ship. vehicle or aircraft, and the master of, or if there is no master, the person in charge of, a ship being a vehicle, aircraft or ship in or on which an animal is being transported, must ensure that the welfare of the animal is properly attended to, and that, in particular, the animal is provided with reasonably comfortable and secure accommodation and is supplied with proper and sufficient food and water.)

Section 23(1) A person commits an offence who, without reasonable excuse, confines or transports an animal in a manner or position that causes the animal unreasonable or unnecessary pain or distress.

Section 23(2) A person commits an offence who, being the owner of, or the person in charge of, an animal, permits that animal, without reasonable excuse, to be driven or led on a road, or to be ridden, or to be transported in or on a vehicle, aircraft or a ship while the condition or health of the animal is such as to render it unfit to be so driven, led, ridden or transported.

III-treatment

Section 29(a) A person commits an offence who ill-treats an animal.

Inspection of Premises

Inspectors appointed under the Animal Welfare Act 1999 have the power to enter any land or premises (with the exceptions of dwellings and marae), or any vehicle, aircraft or vessel, at any reasonable time, for the purpose of inspecting any animal-Section 127 (1).

Inspectors include officers of MAF Special Investigation Group, inspectors from approved organisations appointed by the Minister, and the Police.

Appendix II: Codes of Welfare

Codes of Welfare

Animal Welfare (Broiler Chickens: Fully Housed) Code of Welfare 2003
Animal Welfare (Rodeos) Code of Welfare 2003

Codes of Welfare (given transitional status)

- Code of Recommendations for the Welfare of Circus Animals and Information for Circus Operators
- Code of Recommendations and Minimum Standards for the Welfare of Exhibit Animals and Information for Exhibit Animals Operators
- Code of Recommendations and Minimum Standards for the Welfare of Pigs
- Code of Recommendations and Minimum Standards for the Welfare of Layer Hens

List of Regulations and Circular Deemed to be the Animal Welfare (Commercial Slaughter) Code of Welfare 2002

- Clauses 1 (a) and 2, and the heading preceding clause 2, of Part 7 of the Schedule 1 of the Fish Export Processing Regulations 1995 (SR 1995/54):
- Regulation 80(1) of the Game Regulations 1975 (SR 1975/174):
- Regulation 76 of the Meat Regulations 1969 (SR *1969/192):*
- The Slaughter of Stock, Game, and Poultry Regulations 1969 (SR *1969/194):*
- New Zealand Fishing Industry Agreed Implementation Standards 003.4 live Eels and Rock Lobsters Circular 1995.

Published Codes of Recommendations and Minimum Standards

- Code of Recommendations and Minimum Standards for the Sea Transport of Sheep from New Zealand, September 1991 Code No.2
- Code of Recommendations and Minimum Standards for the Welfare of Sheep, July 1996 Code No.3
- Code of Recommendations and Minimum Standards for the Welfare of Dairy Cattle, June 1992 Code No.4
- Code of Recommendations and Minimum Standards for the Welfare of Deer During the Removal of Antlers, July 1992 Code No.5, Amendments August 1994, August 1997
- Code of Recommendations and Minimum Standards for the Welfare of Horses. February 1993 Code No.7
- Code of Recommendations and Minimum Standards for the Welfare of Bobby Calves, July 1997 Code No.8
- Code of Recommendations and Minimum Standards for the Care of Animals in Boarding Establishments, August 1990 Code No.9
- Code of Recommendations and Minimum Standards for the Welfare of Animals at the Time of Slaughter at Licensed and Approved Premises, July 1996 Code No.10

- Code of Recommendations and Minimum Standards for the Sale of Companion Animals, April 1994 Code No.11
- The Animals Protection Act and Its Implications for Those Responsible for Farm Animals, February 1994 Code No.12
- Code of Recommendations and Minimum Standards for the Welfare of Animals Transported within New Zealand. November 1994 Code No.1S, Amendments June 1996, August 1998
- Code of Recommendations and Minimum Standards for the Welfare of Animals at Saleyards, May 1995 Code No.16
- Code of Recommendations and Minimum Standards for the Emergency Slaughter of Farm Stock, December 1996 Code No.19
- Code of Recommendations and Minimum Standards for the Welfare of Dogs, May 1998 Code No.20
- Code of Recommendations and Minimum Standards for the Welfare of Ostrich and Emu. September 1999 Code No.2

Published Guidelines

- Guidelines for the Welfare of Stock from which Blood is Harvested for Commercial and Research Purposes, April 1996
- Guidelines for the Welfare of Yearling Fallow Deer During the Use of Rubber Rings to Prevent Antler/Pedicle Growth, September 1997
- Guidelines for the Welfare of Red and Wapiti Yearling Stags During the Use of Rubber Rings to Induce Analgesia for the Removal of Spiker Velvet, September 1998.

Codes and Guidelines *may* be obtained from:	or can be inspected at
Executive Co-ordinator	ASB House
Animal Welfare	Reception
MAF Biosecurity Authority	Level 3
Ministry of Agriculture and Forestry	101-103TheTerrace
PO Box 2526	WELLINGTON
WELLINGTON	
Tel: 04 474 4129	
E-mail: animalwelfare@maf.govt.nz	

Codes and Guidelines are available on MAF's website. The web page address is: http//www.maf.govl.nzlbiosecurity/animal-welfare

Appendix VI

CITES Secretariat, Convention on International Trade in Endangered Species of Wild Fauna and Flora (last visited Oct 8, 2010).*

Convention on International Trade in Endangered Species

of Wild Fauna and Flora

Signed at Washington, D.C., on 3 March 1973

Amended at Bonn, on 22 June 1979

The Contracting States,

Recognizing that wild fauna and flora in their many beautiful and varied forms are an irreplaceable part of the natural systems of the earth which must be protected for this and the generations to come;

Conscious of the ever-growing value of wild fauna and flora from aesthetic, scientific, cultural, recreational and economic points of view;

Recognizing that peoples and States are and should be the best protectors of their own wild fauna and flora;

Recognizing, in addition, that international co-operation is essential for the protection of certain species of wild fauna and flora against over-exploitation through international trade;

Convinced of the urgency of taking appropriate measures to this end; *Have agreed* as follows:

Article I
Definitions

For the purpose of the present Convention, unless the context otherwise requires:

(a) "Species" means any species, subspecies, or geographically separate population thereof;

(b) "Specimen" means:

(i) any animal or plant, whether alive or dead;

(ii) in the case of an animal: for species included in Appendices I and II, any readily recognizable part or derivative thereof; and for species included in Appendix III, any readily recognizable part or derivative thereof specified in Appendix III in relation to the species; and

* *Source*: <www.cites.org/eng/disc/text.shtml>.

(iii) in the case of a plant: for species included in Appendix I, any readily recognizable part or derivative thereof; and for species included in Appendices II and III, any readily recognizable part or derivative thereof specified in Appendices II and III in relation to the species;

(c) "Trade" means export, re-export, import and introduction from the sea;

(d) "Re-export" means export of any specimen that has previously been imported;

(e) "Introduction from the sea" means transportation into a State of specimens of any species which were taken in the marine environment not under the jurisdiction of any State;

(f) "Scientific Authority" means a national scientific authority designated in accordance with Article IX;

(g) "Management Authority" means a national management authority designated in accordance with Article IX;

(h) "Party" means a State for which the present Convention has entered into force.

Article II
Fundamental Principles

1. Appendix I shall include all species threatened with extinction which are or may be affected by trade. Trade in specimens of these species must be subject to particularly strict regulation in order not to endanger further their survival and must only be authorized in exceptional circumstances.

2. Appendix II shall include:

(a) all species which although not necessarily now threatened with extinction may become so unless trade in specimens of such species is subject to strict regulation in order to avoid utilization incompatible with their survival; and

(b) other species which must be subject to regulation in order that trade in specimens of certain species referred to in sub-paragraph (a) of this paragraph may be brought under effective control.

3. Appendix III shall include all species which any Party identifies as being subject to regulation within its jurisdiction for the purpose of preventing or restricting exploitation, and as needing the co-operation of other Parties in the control of trade.

4. The Parties shall not allow trade in specimens of species included in Appendices I, II and III except in accordance with the provisions of the present Convention.

Article III
Regulation of Trade in Specimens of Species Included in Appendix I

1. All trade in specimens of species included in Appendix I shall be in accordance with the provisions of this Article.

2. The export of any specimen of a species included in Appendix I shall require the prior grant and presentation of an export permit. An export permit shall only be granted when the following conditions have been met:

(a) a Scientific Authority of the State of export has advised that such export will not be detrimental to the survival of that species;
(b) a Management Authority of the State of export is satisfied that the specimen was not obtained in contravention of the laws of that State for the protection of fauna and flora;
(c) a Management Authority of the State of export is satisfied that any living specimen will be so prepared and shipped as to minimize the risk of injury, damage to health or cruel treatment; and
(d) a Management Authority of the State of export is satisfied that an import permit has been granted for the specimen.

3. The import of any specimen of a species included in Appendix I shall require the prior grant and presentation of an import permit and either an export permit or a re-export certificate. An import permit shall only be granted when the following conditions have been met:

(a) a Scientific Authority of the State of import has advised that the import will be for purposes which are not detrimental to the survival of the species involved;
(b) a Scientific Authority of the State of import is satisfied that the proposed recipient of a living specimen is suitably equipped to house and care for it; and
(c) a Management Authority of the State of import is satisfied that the specimen is not to be used for primarily commercial purposes.

4. The re-export of any specimen of a species included in Appendix I shall require the prior grant and presentation of a re-export certificate. A re-export certificate shall only be granted when the following conditions have been met:

(a) a Management Authority of the State of re-export is satisfied that the specimen was imported into that State in accordance with the provisions of the present Convention;
(b) a Management Authority of the State of re-export is satisfied that any living specimen will be so prepared and shipped as to minimize the risk of injury, damage to health or cruel treatment; and
(c) a Management Authority of the State of re-export is satisfied that an import permit has been granted for any living specimen.

5. The introduction from the sea of any specimen of a species included in Appendix I shall require the prior grant of a certificate from a Management Authority of the State of introduction. A certificate shall only be granted when the following conditions have been met:

(a) a Scientific Authority of the State of introduction advises that the introduction will not be detrimental to the survival of the species involved;

(b) a Management Authority of the State of introduction is satisfied that the proposed recipient of a living specimen is suitably equipped to house and care for it; and
(c) a Management Authority of the State of introduction is satisfied that the specimen is not to be used for primarily commercial purposes.

Article IV
Regulation of Trade in Specimens of Species Included in Appendix II

1. All trade in specimens of species included in Appendix II shall be in accordance with the provisions of this Article.

2. The export of any specimen of a species included in Appendix II shall require the prior grant and presentation of an export permit. An export permit shall only be granted when the following conditions have been met:

(a) a Scientific Authority of the State of export has advised that such export will not be detrimental to the survival of that species;
(b) a Management Authority of the State of export is satisfied that the specimen was not obtained in contravention of the laws of that State for the protection of fauna and flora; and
(c) a Management Authority of the State of export is satisfied that any living specimen will be so prepared and shipped as to minimize the risk of injury, damage to health or cruel treatment.

3. A Scientific Authority in each Party shall monitor both the export permits granted by that State for specimens of species included in Appendix II and the actual exports of such specimens. Whenever a Scientific Authority determines that the export of specimens of any such species should be limited in order to maintain that species throughout its range at a level consistent with its role in the ecosystems in which it occurs and well above the level at which that species might become eligible for inclusion in Appendix I, the Scientific Authority shall advise the appropriate Management Authority of suitable measures to be taken to limit the grant of export permits for specimens of that species.

4. The import of any specimen of a species included in Appendix II shall require the prior presentation of either an export permit or a re-export certificate.

5. The re-export of any specimen of a species included in Appendix II shall require the prior grant and presentation of a re-export certificate. A re-export certificate shall only be granted when the following conditions have been met:

(a) a Management Authority of the State of re-export is satisfied that the specimen was imported into that State in accordance with the provisions of the present Convention; and
(b) a Management Authority of the State of re-export is satisfied that any living specimen will be so prepared and shipped as to minimize the risk of injury, damage to health or cruel treatment.

6. The introduction from the sea of any specimen of a species included in Appendix II shall require the prior grant of a certificate from a Management Authority of the State of introduction. A certificate shall only be granted when the following conditions have been met:

(a) a Scientific Authority of the State of introduction advises that the introduction will not be detrimental to the survival of the species involved; and
(b) a Management Authority of the State of introduction is satisfied that any living specimen will be so handled as to minimize the risk of injury, damage to health or cruel treatment.

7. Certificates referred to in paragraph 6 of this Article may be granted on the advice of a Scientific Authority, in consultation with other national scientific authorities or, when appropriate, international scientific authorities, in respect of periods not exceeding one year for total numbers of specimens to be introduced in such periods.

Article V
Regulation of Trade in Specimens of Species Included in Appendix III

1. All trade in specimens of species included in Appendix III shall be in accordance with the provisions of this Article.

2. The export of any specimen of a species included in Appendix III from any State which has included that species in Appendix III shall require the prior grant and presentation of an export permit. An export permit shall only be granted when the following conditions have been met:

(a) a Management Authority of the State of export is satisfied that the specimen was not obtained in contravention of the laws of that State for the protection of fauna and flora; and
(b) a Management Authority of the State of export is satisfied that any living specimen will be so prepared and shipped as to minimize the risk of injury, damage to health or cruel treatment.

3. The import of any specimen of a species included in Appendix III shall require, except in circumstances to which paragraph 4 of this Article applies, the prior presentation of a certificate of origin and, where the import is from a State which has included that species in Appendix III, an export permit.

4. In the case of re-export, a certificate granted by the Management Authority of the State of re-export that the specimen was processed in that State or is being re-exported shall be accepted by the State of import as evidence that the provisions of the present Convention have been complied with in respect of the specimen concerned.

Article VI
Permits and Certificates

1. Permits and certificates granted under the provisions of Articles III, IV, and V shall be in accordance with the provisions of this Article.

2. An export permit shall contain the information specified in the model set forth in Appendix IV, and may only be used for export within a period of six months from the date on which it was granted.

3. Each permit or certificate shall contain the title of the present Convention, the name and any identifying stamp of the Management Authority granting it and a control number assigned by the Management Authority.

4. Any copies of a permit or certificate issued by a Management Authority shall be clearly marked as copies only and no such copy may be used in place of the original, except to the extent endorsed thereon.

5. A separate permit or certificate shall be required for each consignment of specimens.

6. A Management Authority of the State of import of any specimen shall cancel and retain the export permit or re-export certificate and any corresponding import permit presented in respect of the import of that specimen.

7. Where appropriate and feasible a Management Authority may affix a mark upon any specimen to assist in identifying the specimen. For these purposes "mark" means any indelible imprint, lead seal or other suitable means of identifying a specimen, designed in such a way as to render its imitation by unauthorized persons as difficult as possible.

Article VII
Exemptions and Other Special Provisions Relating to Trade

1. The provisions of Articles III, IV and V shall not apply to the transit or transhipment of specimens through or in the territory of a Party while the specimens remain in Customs control.

2. Where a Management Authority of the State of export or re-export is satisfied that a specimen was acquired before the provisions of the present Convention applied to that specimen, the provisions of Articles III, IV and V shall not apply to that specimen where the Management Authority issues a certificate to that effect.

3. The provisions of Articles III, IV and V shall not apply to specimens that are personal or household effects. This exemption shall not apply where:

(a) in the case of specimens of a species included in Appendix I, they were acquired by the owner outside his State of usual residence, and are being imported into that State; or

(b) in the case of specimens of species included in Appendix II:
   (i) they were acquired by the owner outside his State of usual residence and in a State where removal from the wild occurred;
   (ii) they are being imported into the owner's State of usual residence; and
   (iii) the State where removal from the wild occurred requires the prior grant of export permits before any export of such specimens; unless a Management Authority is satisfied that the specimens were acquired before the provisions of the present Convention applied to such specimens.

4. Specimens of an animal species included in Appendix I bred in captivity for commercial purposes, or of a plant species included in Appendix I artificially propagated for commercial purposes, shall be deemed to be specimens of species included in Appendix II.

5. Where a Management Authority of the State of export is satisfied that any specimen of an animal species was bred in captivity or any specimen of a plant species was artificially propagated, or is a part of such an animal or plant or was derived therefrom, a certificate by that Management Authority to that effect shall be accepted in lieu of any of the permits or certificates required under the provisions of Article III, IV or V.

6. The provisions of Articles III, IV and V shall not apply to the non-commercial loan, donation or exchange between scientists or scientific institutions registered by a Management Authority of their State, of herbarium specimens, other preserved, dried or embedded museum specimens, and live plant material which carry a label issued or approved by a Management Authority.

7. A Management Authority of any State may waive the requirements of Articles III, IV and V and allow the movement without permits or certificates of specimens which form part of a travelling zoo, circus, menagerie, plant exhibition or other travelling exhibition provided that:

(a) the exporter or importer registers full details of such specimens with that Management Authority;
(b) the specimens are in either of the categories specified in paragraph 2 or 5 of this Article; and
(c) the Management Authority is satisfied that any living specimen will be so transported and cared for as to minimize the risk of injury, damage to health or cruel treatment.

Article VIII
Measures to Be Taken by the Parties

1. The Parties shall take appropriate measures to enforce the provisions of the present Convention and to prohibit trade in specimens in violation thereof. These shall include measures:

(a) to penalize trade in, or possession of, such specimens, or both; and
(b) to provide for the confiscation or return to the State of export of such specimens.

2. In addition to the measures taken under paragraph 1 of this Article, a Party may, when it deems it necessary, provide for any method of internal reimbursement for expenses incurred as a result of the confiscation of a specimen traded in violation of the measures taken in the application of the provisions of the present Convention.

3. As far as possible, the Parties shall ensure that specimens shall pass through any formalities required for trade with a minimum of delay. To facilitate such passage, a Party may designate ports of exit and ports of entry at which specimens must be presented for clearance. The Parties shall ensure further that all living specimens, during any period of transit, holding or shipment, are properly cared for so as to minimize the risk of injury, damage to health or cruel treatment.

4. Where a living specimen is confiscated as a result of measures referred to in paragraph 1 of this Article:

(a) the specimen shall be entrusted to a Management Authority of the State of confiscation;
(b) the Management Authority shall, after consultation with the State of export, return the specimen to that State at the expense of that State, or to a rescue centre or such other place as the Management Authority deems appropriate and consistent with the purposes of the present Convention; and
(c) the Management Authority may obtain the advice of a Scientific Authority, or may, whenever it considers it desirable, consult the Secretariat in order to facilitate the decision under sub-paragraph (b) of this paragraph, including the choice of a rescue centre or other place.

5. A rescue centre as referred to in paragraph 4 of this Article means an institution designated by a Management Authority to look after the welfare of living specimens, particularly those that have been confiscated.

6. Each Party shall maintain records of trade in specimens of species included in Appendices I, II and III which shall cover:

(a) the names and addresses of exporters and importers; and
(b) the number and type of permits and certificates granted; the States with which such trade occurred; the numbers or quantities and types of specimens, names

of species as included in Appendices I, II and III and, where applicable, the size and sex of the specimens in question.

7. Each Party shall prepare periodic reports on its implementation of the present Convention and shall transmit to the Secretariat:

(a) an annual report containing a summary of the information specified in sub-paragraph (b) of paragraph 6 of this Article; and
(b) a biennial report on legislative, regulatory and administrative measures taken to enforce the provisions of the present Convention.

8. The information referred to in paragraph 7 of this Article shall be available to the public where this is not inconsistent with the law of the Party concerned.

Article IX
Management and Scientific Authorities

1. Each Party shall designate for the purposes of the present Convention:

(a) one or more Management Authorities competent to grant permits or certificates on behalf of that Party; and
(b) one or more Scientific Authorities.

2. A State depositing an instrument of ratification, acceptance, approval or accession shall at that time inform the Depositary Government of the name and address of the Management Authority authorized to communicate with other Parties and with the Secretariat.

3. Any changes in the designations or authorizations under the provisions of this Article shall be communicated by the Party concerned to the Secretariat for transmission to all other Parties.

4. Any Management Authority referred to in paragraph 2 of this Article shall, if so requested by the Secretariat or the Management Authority of another Party, communicate to it impression of stamps, seals or other devices used to authenticate permits or certificates.

Article X
Trade with States not Party to the Convention

Where export or re-export is to, or import is from, a State not a Party to the present Convention, comparable documentation issued by the competent authorities in that State which substantially conforms with the requirements of the present Convention for permits and certificates may be accepted in lieu thereof by any Party.

Article XI
Conference of the Parties

1. The Secretariat shall call a meeting of the Conference of the Parties not later than two years after the entry into force of the present Convention.

2. Thereafter the Secretariat shall convene regular meetings at least once every two years, unless the Conference decides otherwise, and extraordinary meetings at any time on the written request of at least one-third of the Parties.

3. At meetings, whether regular or extraordinary, the Parties shall review the implementation of the present Convention and may:

(a) make such provision as may be necessary to enable the Secretariat to carry out its duties, and adopt financial provisions;
(b) consider and adopt amendments to Appendices I and II in accordance with Article XV;
(c) review the progress made towards the restoration and conservation of the species included in Appendices I, II and III;
(d) receive and consider any reports presented by the Secretariat or by any Party; and
(e) where appropriate, make recommendations for improving the effectiveness of the present Convention.

4. At each regular meeting, the Parties may determine the time and venue of the next regular meeting to be held in accordance with the provisions of paragraph 2 of this Article.

5. At any meeting, the Parties may determine and adopt rules of procedure for the meeting.

6. The United Nations, its Specialized Agencies and the International Atomic Energy Agency, as well as any State not a Party to the present Convention, may be represented at meetings of the Conference by observers, who shall have the right to participate but not to vote.

7. Any body or agency technically qualified in protection, conservation or management of wild fauna and flora, in the following categories, which has informed the Secretariat of its desire to be represented at meetings of the Conference by observers, shall be admitted unless at least one-third of the Parties present object:

(a) international agencies or bodies, either governmental or non-governmental, and national governmental agencies and bodies; and
(b) national non-governmental agencies or bodies which have been approved for this purpose by the State in which they are located. Once admitted, these observers shall have the right to participate but not to vote.

Article XII
The Secretariat

1. Upon entry into force of the present Convention, a Secretariat shall be provided by the Executive Director of the United Nations Environment Programme. To the extent and in the manner he considers appropriate, he may be assisted by suitable inter-governmental or non-governmental international or national agencies and bodies technically qualified in protection, conservation and management of wild fauna and flora.

2. The functions of the Secretariat shall be:

(a) to arrange for and service meetings of the Parties;
(b) to perform the functions entrusted to it under the provisions of Articles XV and XVI of the present Convention;
(c) to undertake scientific and technical studies in accordance with programmes authorized by the Conference of the Parties as will contribute to the implementation of the present Convention, including studies concerning standards for appropriate preparation and shipment of living specimens and the means of identifying specimens;
(d) to study the reports of Parties and to request from Parties such further information with respect thereto as it deems necessary to ensure implementation of the present Convention;
(e) to invite the attention of the Parties to any matter pertaining to the aims of the present Convention;
(f) to publish periodically and distribute to the Parties current editions of Appendices I, II and III together with any information which will facilitate identification of specimens of species included in those Appendices;
(g) to prepare annual reports to the Parties on its work and on the implementation of the present Convention and such other reports as meetings of the Parties may request;
(h) to make recommendations for the implementation of the aims and provisions of the present Convention, including the exchange of information of a scientific or technical nature;
(i) to perform any other function as may be entrusted to it by the Parties.

Article XIII
International Measures

1. When the Secretariat in the light of information received is satisfied that any species included in Appendix I or II is being affected adversely by trade in specimens of that species or that the provisions of the present Convention are not being effectively implemented, it shall communicate such information to the authorized Management Authority of the Party or Parties concerned.

2. When any Party receives a communication as indicated in paragraph 1 of this Article, it shall, as soon as possible, inform the Secretariat of any relevant facts insofar as its laws permit and, where appropriate, propose remedial action. Where the Party considers that an inquiry is desirable, such inquiry may be carried out by one or more persons expressly authorized by the Party.

3. The information provided by the Party or resulting from any inquiry as specified in paragraph 2 of this Article shall be reviewed by the next Conference of the Parties which may make whatever recommendations it deems appropriate.

Article XIV
Effect on Domestic Legislation and International Conventions

1. The provisions of the present Convention shall in no way affect the right of Parties to adopt:

(a) stricter domestic measures regarding the conditions for trade, taking, possession or transport of specimens of species included in Appendices I, II and III, or the complete prohibition thereof; or
(b) domestic measures restricting or prohibiting trade, taking, possession or transport of species not included in Appendix I, II or III.

2. The provisions of the present Convention shall in no way affect the provisions of any domestic measures or the obligations of Parties deriving from any treaty, convention, or international agreement relating to other aspects of trade, taking, possession or transport of specimens which is in force or subsequently may enter into force for any Party including any measure pertaining to the Customs, public health, veterinary or plant quarantine fields.

3. The provisions of the present Convention shall in no way affect the provisions of, or the obligations deriving from, any treaty, convention or international agreement concluded or which may be concluded between States creating a union or regional trade agreement establishing or maintaining a common external Customs control and removing Customs control between the parties thereto insofar as they relate to trade among the States members of that union or agreement.

4. A State party to the present Convention, which is also a party to any other treaty, convention or international agreement which is in force at the time of the coming into force of the present Convention and under the provisions of which protection is afforded to marine species included in Appendix II, shall be relieved of the obligations imposed on it under the provisions of the present Convention with respect to trade in specimens of species included in Appendix II that are taken by ships registered in that State and in accordance with the provisions of such other treaty, convention or international agreement.

5. Notwithstanding the provisions of Articles III, IV and V, any export of a specimen taken in accordance with paragraph 4 of this Article shall only require a certificate from a Management Authority of the State of introduction to the effect

that the specimen was taken in accordance with the provisions of the other treaty, convention or international agreement in question.

6. Nothing in the present Convention shall prejudice the codification and development of the law of the sea by the United Nations Conference on the Law of the Sea convened pursuant to Resolution 2750 C (XXV) of the General Assembly of the United Nations nor the present or future claims and legal views of any State concerning the law of the sea and the nature and extent of coastal and flag State jurisdiction.

Article XV
Amendments to Appendices I and II

1. The following provisions shall apply in relation to amendments to Appendices I and II at meetings of the Conference of the Parties:

(a) Any Party may propose an amendment to Appendix I or II for consideration at the next meeting. The text of the proposed amendment shall be communicated to the Secretariat at least 150 days before the meeting. The Secretariat shall consult the other Parties and interested bodies on the amendment in accordance with the provisions of sub-paragraphs (b) and (c) of paragraph 2 of this Article and shall communicate the response to all Parties not later than 30 days before the meeting.
(b) Amendments shall be adopted by a two-thirds majority of Parties present and voting. For these purposes "Parties present and voting" means Parties present and casting an affirmative or negative vote. Parties abstaining from voting shall not be counted among the two-thirds required for adopting an amendment.
(c) Amendments adopted at a meeting shall enter into force 90 days after that meeting for all Parties except those which make a reservation in accordance with paragraph 3 of this Article.

2. The following provisions shall apply in relation to amendments to Appendices I and II between meetings of the Conference of the Parties:

(a) Any Party may propose an amendment to Appendix I or II for consideration between meetings by the postal procedures set forth in this paragraph.
(b) For marine species, the Secretariat shall, upon receiving the text of the proposed amendment, immediately communicate it to the Parties. It shall also consult inter-governmental bodies having a function in relation to those species especially with a view to obtaining scientific data these bodies may be able to provide and to ensuring co-ordination with any conservation measures enforced by such bodies. The Secretariat shall communicate the views expressed and data provided by these bodies and its own findings and recommendations to the Parties as soon as possible.

(c) For species other than marine species, the Secretariat shall, upon receiving the text of the proposed amendment, immediately communicate it to the Parties, and, as soon as possible thereafter, its own recommendations.
(d) Any Party may, within 60 days of the date on which the Secretariat communicated its recommendations to the Parties under sub-paragraph (b) or (c) of this paragraph, transmit to the Secretariat any comments on the proposed amendment together with any relevant scientific data and information.
(e) The Secretariat shall communicate the replies received together with its own recommendations to the Parties as soon as possible. (f) If no objection to the proposed amendment is received by the Secretariat within 30 days of the date the replies and recommendations were communicated under the provisions of sub-paragraph (e) of this paragraph, the amendment shall enter into force 90 days later for all Parties except those which make a reservation in accordance with paragraph 3 of this Article.
(g) If an objection by any Party is received by the Secretariat, the proposed amendment shall be submitted to a postal vote in accordance with the provisions of sub-paragraphs (h) , (i) and (j) of this paragraph.
(h) The Secretariat shall notify the Parties that notification of objection has been received.
(i) Unless the Secretariat receives the votes for, against or in abstention from at least one-half of the Parties within 60 days of the date of notification under sub-paragraph (h) of this paragraph, the proposed amendment shall be referred to the next meeting of the Conference for further consideration.
(j) Provided that votes are received from one-half of the Parties, the amendment shall be adopted by a two-thirds majority of Parties casting an affirmative or negative vote.
(k) The Secretariat shall notify all Parties of the result of the vote.
(l) If the proposed amendment is adopted it shall enter into force 90 days after the date of the notification by the Secretariat of its acceptance for all Parties except those which make a reservation in accordance with paragraph 3 of this Article.

3. During the period of 90 days provided for by sub-paragraph (c) of paragraph 1 or sub-paragraph (l) of paragraph 2 of this Article any Party may by notification in writing to the Depositary Government make a reservation with respect to the amendment. Until such reservation is withdrawn the Party shall be treated as a State not a Party to the present Convention with respect to trade in the species concerned.

Article XVI
Appendix III and Amendments thereto

1. Any Party may at any time submit to the Secretariat a list of species which it identifies as being subject to regulation within its jurisdiction for the purpose mentioned in paragraph 3 of Article II. Appendix III shall include the names of the

Parties submitting the species for inclusion therein, the scientific names of the species so submitted, and any parts or derivatives of the animals or plants concerned that are specified in relation to the species for the purposes of sub-paragraph (b) of Article I.

2. Each list submitted under the provisions of paragraph 1 of this Article shall be communicated to the Parties by the Secretariat as soon as possible after receiving it. The list shall take effect as part of Appendix III 90 days after the date of such communication. At any time after the communication of such list, any Party may by notification in writing to the Depositary Government enter a reservation with respect to any species or any parts or derivatives, and until such reservation is withdrawn, the State shall be treated as a State not a Party to the present Convention with respect to trade in the species or part or derivative concerned.

3. A Party which has submitted a species for inclusion in Appendix III may withdraw it at any time by notification to the Secretariat which shall communicate the withdrawal to all Parties. The withdrawal shall take effect 30 days after the date of such communication.

4. Any Party submitting a list under the provisions of paragraph 1 of this Article shall submit to the Secretariat a copy of all domestic laws and regulations applicable to the protection of such species, together with any interpretations which the Party may deem appropriate or the Secretariat may request. The Party shall, for as long as the species in question is included in Appendix III, submit any amendments of such laws and regulations or any interpretations as they are adopted.

Article XVII
Amendment of the Convention

1. An extraordinary meeting of the Conference of the Parties shall be convened by the Secretariat on the written request of at least one-third of the Parties to consider and adopt amendments to the present Convention. Such amendments shall be adopted by a two-thirds majority of Parties present and voting. For these purposes "Parties present and voting" means Parties present and casting an affirmative or negative vote. Parties abstaining from voting shall not be counted among the two-thirds required for adopting an amendment.

2. The text of any proposed amendment shall be communicated by the Secretariat to all Parties at least 90 days before the meeting.

3. An amendment shall enter into force for the Parties which have accepted it 60 days after two-thirds of the Parties have deposited an instrument of acceptance of the amendment with the Depositary Government. Thereafter, the amendment shall enter into force for any other Party 60 days after that Party deposits its instrument of acceptance of the amendment.

Article XVIII
Resolution of Disputes

1. Any dispute which may arise between two or more Parties with respect to the interpretation or application of the provisions of the present Convention shall be subject to negotiation between the Parties involved in the dispute.

2. If the dispute can not be resolved in accordance with paragraph 1 of this Article, the Parties may, by mutual consent, submit the dispute to arbitration, in particular that of the Permanent Court of Arbitration at The Hague, and the Parties submitting the dispute shall be bound by the arbitral decision.

Article XIX
Signature

The present Convention shall be open for signature at Washington until 30th April 1973 and thereafter at Berne until 31st December 1974.

Article XX
Ratification, Acceptance, Approval

The present Convention shall be subject to ratification, acceptance or approval. Instruments of ratification, acceptance or approval shall be deposited with the Government of the Swiss Confederation which shall be the Depositary Government.

Article XXI
Accession

The present Convention shall be open indefinitely for accession. Instruments of accession shall be deposited with the Depositary Government.

Article XXII
Entry into Force

1. The present Convention shall enter into force 90 days after the date of deposit of the tenth instrument of ratification, acceptance, approval or accession, with the Depositary Government.

2. For each State which ratifies, accepts or approves the present Convention or accedes thereto after the deposit of the tenth instrument of ratification, acceptance, approval or accession, the present Convention shall enter into force 90 days after the deposit by such State of its instrument of ratification, acceptance, approval or accession.

Article XXIII
Reservations

1. The provisions of the present Convention shall not be subject to general reservations. Specific reservations may be entered in accordance with the provisions of this Article and Articles XV and XVI.

2. Any State may, on depositing its instrument of ratification, acceptance, approval or accession, enter a specific reservation with regard to:

(a) any species included in Appendix I, II or III; or
(b) any parts or derivatives specified in relation to a species included in Appendix III.

3. Until a Party withdraws its reservation entered under the provisions of this Article, it shall be treated as a State not a Party to the present Convention with respect to trade in the particular species or parts or derivatives specified in such reservation.

Article XXIV
Denunciation

Any Party may denounce the present Convention by written notification to the Depositary Government at any time. The denunciation shall take effect twelve months after the Depositary Government has received the notification.

Article XXV
Depositary

1. The original of the present Convention, in the Chinese, English, French, Russian and Spanish languages, each version being equally authentic, shall be deposited with the Depositary Government, which shall transmit certified copies thereof to all States that have signed it or deposited instruments of accession to it.

2. The Depositary Government shall inform all signatory and acceding States and the Secretariat of signatures, deposit of instruments of ratification, acceptance, approval or accession, entry into force of the present Convention, amendments thereto, entry and withdrawal of reservations and notifications of denunciation.

3. As soon as the present Convention enters into force, a certified copy thereof shall be transmitted by the Depositary Government to the Secretariat of the United Nations for registration and publication in accordance with Article 102 of the Charter of the United Nations.

In witness whereof the undersigned Plenipotentiaries, being duly authorized to that effect, have signed the present Convention.

Done at Washington this third day of March, One Thousand Nine Hundred and Seventy-three.

Appendix VII

World Trade Organization, General Agreement on Tariffs and Trade, Articles I, III, IX, X, XI and XX (last visited Oct. 8, 2010).*

THE GENERAL AGREEMENT ON TARIFFS AND TRADE

(GATT 1947)

THE GENERAL AGREEMENT ON TARIFFS AND TRADE

The Governments of the Commonwealth of Australia, the Kingdom of Belgium, the United States of Brazil, Burma, Canada, Ceylon, the Republic of Chile, the Republic of China, the Republic of Cuba, the Czechoslovak Republic, the French Republic, India, Lebanon, the Grand-Duchy of Luxemburg, the Kingdom of the Netherlands, New Zealand, the Kingdom of Norway, Pakistan, Southern Rhodesia, Syria, the Union of South Africa, the United Kingdom of Great Britain and Northern Ireland, and the United States of America:

Recognizing that their relations in the field of trade and economic endeavour should be conducted with a view to raising standards of living, ensuring full employment and a large and steadily growing volume of real income and effective demand, developing the full use of the resources of the world and expanding the production and exchange of goods,

Being desirous of contributing to these objectives by entering into reciprocal and mutually advantageous arrangements directed to the substantial reduction of tariffs and other barriers to trade and to the elimination of discriminatory treatment in international commerce,

Have through their Representatives agreed as follows:

PART I

Article I
General Most-Favoured-Nation Treatment

1. With respect to customs duties and charges of any kind imposed on or in connection with importation or exportation or imposed on the international transfer of payments for imports or exports, and with respect to the method of levying such duties and charges, and with respect to all rules and formalities in connection with importation and exportation, and with respect to all matters referred to in paragraphs 2 and 4 of Article III,* any advantage, favour, privilege or immunity granted by any contracting party to any product originating in or destined for any

---

* *Source*: World Trade Organization at <www.wto.org/english/docs_e/legal_e/gatt47_e.pdf>.

other country shall be accorded immediately and unconditionally to the like product originating in or destined for the territories of all other contracting parties.

2. The provisions of paragraph 1 of this Article shall not require the elimination of any preferences in respect of import duties or charges which do not exceed the levels provided for in paragraph 4 of this Article and which fall within the following descriptions:

(*a*) Preferences in force exclusively between two or more of the territories listed in Annex A, subject to the conditions set forth therein;
(*b*) Preferences in force exclusively between two or more territories which on July 1, 1939, were connected by common sovereignty or relations of protection or suzerainty and which are listed in Annexes B, C and D, subject to the conditions set forth therein;
(*c*) Preferences in force exclusively between the United States of America and the Republic of Cuba;
(*d*) Preferences in force exclusively between neighbouring countries listed in Annexes E and F.

3. The provisions of paragraph 1 shall not apply to preferences between the countries formerly a part of the Ottoman Empire and detached from it on July 24, 1923, provided such preferences are approved under paragraph 5[1] of Article XXV which shall be applied in this respect in the light of paragraph 1 of Article XXIX.

4. The margin of preference* on any product in respect of which a preference is permitted under paragraph 2 of this Article but is not specifically set forth as a maximum margin of preference in the appropriate Schedule annexed to this Agreement shall not exceed:

(*a*) in respect of duties or charges on any product described in such Schedule, the difference between the most-favoured-nation and preferential rates provided for therein; if no preferential rate is provided for, the preferential rate shall for the purposes of this paragraph be taken to be that in force on April 10, 1947, and, if no most-favoured-nation rate is provided for, the margin shall not exceed the difference between the most-favoured-nation and preferential rates existing on April 10, 1947;
(*b*) in respect of duties or charges on any product not described in the appropriate Schedule, the difference between the most-favoured-nation and preferential rates existing on April 10, 1947.

In the case of the contracting parties named in Annex G, the date of April 10, 1947, referred to in subparagraph (*a*) and (*b*) of this paragraph shall be replaced by the respective dates set forth in that Annex.

1. The authentic text erroneously reads "subparagraph 5 (a)",.

PART II

Article III*
National Treatment on Internal Taxation and Regulation

1. The contracting parties recognize that internal taxes and other internal charges, and laws, regulations and requirements affecting the internal sale, offering for sale, purchase, transportation, distribution or use of products, and internal quantitative regulations requiring the mixture, processing or use of products in specified amounts or proportions, should not be applied to imported or domestic products so as to afford protection to domestic production.*

2. The products of the territory of any contracting party imported into the territory of any other contracting party shall not be subject, directly or indirectly, to internal taxes or other internal charges of any kind in excess of those applied, directly or indirectly, to like domestic products. Moreover, no contracting party shall otherwise apply internal taxes or other internal charges to imported or domestic products in a manner contrary to the principles set forth in paragraph 1.*

3. With respect to any existing internal tax which is inconsistent with the provisions of paragraph 2, but which is specifically authorized under a trade agreement, in force on April 10, 1947, in which the import duty on the taxed product is bound against increase, the contracting party imposing the tax shall be free to postpone the application of the provisions of paragraph 2 to such tax until such time as it can obtain release from the obligations of such trade agreement in order to permit the increase of such duty to the extent necessary to compensate for the elimination of the protective element of the tax.

4. The products of the territory of any contracting party imported into the territory of any other contracting party shall be accorded treatment no less favourable than that accorded to like products of national origin in respect of all laws, regulations and requirements affecting their internal sale, offering for sale, purchase, transportation, distribution or use. The provisions of this paragraph shall not prevent the application of differential internal transportation charges which are based exclusively on the economic operation of the means of transport and not on the nationality of the product.

5. No contracting party shall establish or maintain any internal quantitative regulation relating to the mixture, processing or use of products in specified amounts or proportions which requires, directly or indirectly, that any specified amount or proportion of any product which is the subject of the regulation must be supplied from domestic sources. Moreover, no contracting party shall otherwise apply internal quantitative regulations in a manner contrary to the principles set forth in paragraph 1.*

6. The provisions of paragraph 5 shall not apply to any internal quantitative regulation in force in the territory of any contracting party on July 1, 1939, April 10,

1947, or March 24, 1948, at the option of that contracting party; *Provided* that any such regulation which is contrary to the provisions of paragraph 5 shall not be modified to the detriment of imports and shall be treated as a customs duty for the purpose of negotiation.

7. No internal quantitative regulation relating to the mixture, processing or use of products in specified amounts or proportions shall be applied in such a manner as to allocate any such amount or proportion among external sources of supply.

8. (*a*) The provisions of this Article shall not apply to laws, regulations or requirements governing the procurement by governmental agencies of products purchased for governmental purposes and not with a view to commercial resale or with a view to use in the production of goods for commercial sale.
   (*b*) The provisions of this Article shall not prevent the payment of subsidies exclusively to domestic producers, including payments to domestic producers derived from the proceeds of internal taxes or charges applied consistently with the provisions of this Article and subsidies effected through governmental purchases of domestic products.

9. The contracting parties recognize that internal maximum price control measures, even though conforming to the other provisions of this Article, can have effects prejudicial to the interests of contracting parties supplying imported products. Accordingly, contracting parties applying such measures shall take account of the interests of exporting contracting parties with a view to avoiding to the fullest practicable extent such prejudicial effects.

10. The provisions of this Article shall not prevent any contracting party from establishing or maintaining internal quantitative regulations relating to exposed cinematograph films and meeting the requirements of Article IV.

Article IX
Marks of Origin

1. Each contracting party shall accord to the products of the territories of other contracting parties treatment with regard to marking requirements no less favourable than the treatment accorded to like products of any third country.

2. The contracting parties recognize that, in adopting and enforcing laws and regulations relating to marks of origin, the difficulties and inconveniences which such measures may cause to the commerce and industry of exporting countries should be reduced to a minimum, due regard being had to the necessity of protecting consumers against fraudulent or misleading indications.

3. Whenever it is administratively practicable to do so, contracting parties should permit required marks of origin to be affixed at the time of importation.

4. The laws and regulations of contracting parties relating to the marking of imported products shall be such as to permit compliance without seriously damaging the products, or materially reducing their value, or unreasonably increasing their cost.

5. As a general rule, no special duty or penalty should be imposed by any contracting party for failure to comply with marking requirements prior to importation unless corrective marking is unreasonably delayed or deceptive marks have been affixed or the required marking has been intentionally omitted.

6. The contracting parties shall co-operate with each other with a view to preventing the use of trade names in such manner as to misrepresent the true origin of a product, to the detriment of such distinctive regional or geographical names of products of the territory of a contracting party as are protected by its legislation. Each contracting party shall accord full and sympathetic consideration to such requests or representations as may be made by any other contracting party regarding the application of the undertaking set forth in the preceding sentence to names of products which have been communicated to it by the other contracting party.

Article X
Publication and Administration of Trade Regulations

1. Laws, regulations, judicial decisions and administrative rulings of general application, made effective by any contracting party, pertaining to the classification or the valuation of products for customs purposes, or to rates of duty, taxes or other charges, or to requirements, restrictions or prohibitions on imports or exports or on the transfer of payments therefor, or affecting their sale, distribution, transportation, insurance, warehousing inspection, exhibition, processing, mixing or other use, shall be published promptly in such a manner as to enable governments and traders to become acquainted with them. Agreements affecting international trade policy which are in force between the government or a governmental agency of any contracting party and the government or governmental agency of any other contracting party shall also be published. The provisions of this paragraph shall not require any contracting party to disclose confidential information which would impede law enforcement or otherwise be contrary to the public interest or would prejudice the legitimate commercial interests of particular enterprises, public or private.

2. No measure of general application taken by any contracting party effecting an advance in a rate of duty or other charge on imports under an established and uniform practice, or imposing a new or more burdensome requirement, restriction or prohibition on imports, or on the transfer of payments therefor, shall be enforced before such measure has been officially published.

3. (*a*) Each contracting party shall administer in a uniform, impartial and reasonable manner all its laws, regulations, decisions and rulings of the kind described in paragraph 1 of this Article.

(*b*) Each contracting party shall maintain, or institute as soon as practicable, judicial, arbitral or administrative tribunals or procedures for the purpose, *inter alia* , of the prompt review and correction of administrative action relating to customs matters. Such tribunals or procedures shall be independent of the agencies entrusted with administrative enforcement and their decisions shall be implemented by, and shall govern the practice of, such agencies unless an appeal is lodged with a court or tribunal of superior jurisdiction within the time prescribed for appeals to be lodged by importers; *Provided* that the central administration of such agency may take steps to obtain a review of the matter in another proceeding if there is good cause to believe that the decision is inconsistent with established principles of law or the actual facts.

(*c*) The provisions of subparagraph (*b*) of this paragraph shall not require the elimination or substitution of procedures in force in the territory of a contracting party on the date of this Agreement which in fact provide for an objective and impartial review of administrative action even though such procedures are not fully or formally independent of the agencies entrusted with administrative enforcement. Any contracting party employing such procedures shall, upon request, furnish the CONTRACTING PARTIES with full information thereon in order that they may determine whether such procedures conform to the requirements of this subparagraph.

Article XI*
General Elimination of Quantitative Restrictions

1. No prohibitions or restrictions other than duties, taxes or other charges, whether made effective through quotas, import or export licences or other measures, shall be instituted or maintained by any contracting party on the importation of any product of the territory of any other contracting party or on the exportation or sale for export of any product destined for the territory of any other contracting party.

2. The provisions of paragraph 1 of this Article shall not extend to the following:

(*a*) Export prohibitions or restrictions temporarily applied to prevent or relieve critical shortages of foodstuffs or other products essential to the exporting contracting party;

(*b*) Import and export prohibitions or restrictions necessary to the application of standards or regulations for the classification, grading or marketing of commodities in international trade;

(*c*) Import restrictions on any agricultural or fisheries product, imported in any form,* necessary to the enforcement of governmental measures which operate:

(i) to restrict the quantities of the like domestic product permitted to be marketed or produced, or, if there is no substantial domestic production of the like product, of a domestic product for which the imported product can be directly substituted; or

(ii) to remove a temporary surplus of the like domestic product, or, if there is no substantial domestic production of the like product, of a domestic product for which the imported product can be directly substituted, by making the surplus available to certain groups of domestic consumers free of charge or at prices below the current market level; or

(iii) to restrict the quantities permitted to be produced of any animal product the production of which is directly dependent, wholly or mainly, on the imported commodity, if the domestic production of that commodity is relatively negligible.

Any contracting party applying restrictions on the importation of any product pursuant to subparagraph (*c*) of this paragraph shall give public notice of the total quantity or value of the product permitted to be imported during a specified future period and of any change in such quantity or value. Moreover, any restrictions applied under (i) above shall not be such as will reduce the total of imports relative to the total of domestic production, as compared with the proportion which might reasonably be expected to rule between the two in the absence of restrictions. In determining this proportion, the contracting party shall pay due regard to the proportion prevailing during a previous representative period and to any special factors* which may have affected or may be affecting the trade in the product concerned.

Article XX
General Exceptions

Subject to the requirement that such measures are not applied in a manner which would constitute a means of arbitrary or unjustifiable discrimination between countries where the same conditions prevail, or a disguised restriction on international trade, nothing in this Agreement shall be construed to prevent the adoption or enforcement by any contracting party of measures:

(*a*) necessary to protect public morals;
(*b*) necessary to protect human, animal or plant life or health;
(*c*) relating to the importations or exportations of gold or silver;
(*d*) necessary to secure compliance with laws or regulations which are not inconsistent with the provisions of this Agreement, including those relating to customs enforcement, the enforcement of monopolies operated under paragraph 4 of Article II and Article XVII, the protection of patents, trade marks and copyrights, and the prevention of deceptive practices;
(*e*) relating to the products of prison labour;
(*f*) imposed for the protection of national treasures of artistic, historic or archaeological value;

(*g*) relating to the conservation of exhaustible natural resources if such measures are made effective in conjunction with restrictions on domestic production or consumption;

(*h*) undertaken in pursuance of obligations under any intergovernmental commodity agreement which conforms to criteria submitted to the CONTRACTING PARTIES and not disapproved by them or which is itself so submitted and not so disapproved;*

(*i*) involving restrictions on exports of domestic materials necessary to ensure essential quantities of such materials to a domestic processing industry during periods when the domestic price of such materials is held below the world price as part of a governmental stabilization plan; *Provided* that such restrictions shall not operate to increase the exports of or the protection afforded to such domestic industry, and shall not depart from the provisions of this Agreement relating to non-discrimination;

(*j*) essential to the acquisition or distribution of products in general or local short supply; *Provided* that any such measures shall be consistent with the principle that all contracting parties are entitled to an equitable share of the international supply of such products, and that any such measures, which are inconsistent with the other provisions of the Agreement shall be discontinued as soon as the conditions giving rise to them have ceased to exist. The CONTRACTING PARTIES shall review the need for this sub-paragraph not later than 30 June 1960.

Bibliography

Abbott, A. "European Research Animal Use Holds Steady." www.nature.com/news/2010/101007/full/news.2010.524.html.

About Animal Testing. "Rap Information Sharing to Reduce Animal Tests." www.aboutanimaltesting.co.uk/rap-information-sharing-reduce-animal-tests.html.

Act Now.com.au. "No, This Is Not An Issue Page About Peter Rabbit Doing His Final Modern History Exam." www.actnow.com.au/Issues/Animal_testing.aspx.

Aiyar, P. "Help!." *Business Standard*, February 13, 2010, 1. Available at Westlaw: 2010 WLNR 3026572.

Alcock, J. "The Evolution of the Use of Tools by Feeding Animals." *Evolution* 26, no. 3 (1972): 464–73.

The Alex Foundation. "Alex the African Grey Parrot and Subject of Landmark Studies of Bird Intelligence Dies at 31." www.alexfoundation.org/press_release.html.

Allen, G.D. "Pythagoras and the Pythagoreans." www.math.tamu.edu/~don.allen/masters/Greek/pythag.pdf, 1999.

"Animal Cruelty Points to Potential Violence Against Humans." www.sniksnak.com/ac/connection.html.

Animal Defenders International. "Worldwide Circus Bans." www.ad-international.org/animals_in_entertainment/go.php?=281&si=1&ssi=10.

Animal Ethics Infolink. "Other Australian Legislation." http://www.animalethics.org.au/legislation/other-australian-legislation.

Animal Research Review Panel & Industry & Investment New South Wales—Animal Welfare Branch. Other Australian Legislation. www.animalethics.org.au/legislation/other-australian-legislation.

Animal Visuals. "Fact Sheet: Battery Cages." www.animalvisuals.org/empathy/virtualbatterycage/.

Animal Welfare Institute. "Astrid Lindgren Establishes Foundation for Farm Animals." *AWI Quarterly* 48, no. 2 (2009): 7 www.awionline.org/ht/d/ContentDetails/i/1515.

Animals Scientific Procedures Division of the Home Office Science and Research Group. "Animals (Scientific Procedures) Act of 1986: Use, Continued Use and Reuse of Animals (2008)." www.homeoffice.gov.uk/publications/science/769901/licences/project-licences/use-of-animals?view=Binary, 2008.

"Ape Genius." PBS television broadcast. February 19, 2008. Transcript available at www.pbs.org/wgbh/nova/transcripts/3504_apegeniu.html.

Aristotle. "On the Soul." In *Introduction to Aristotle*, edited by R. McKeon. Translated by J.A. Smith. Modern Library, 1992.

Aristotle. *The Pocket Aristotle*, edited by J.D. Kaplan. Translated by W.D. Ross. Washington Square Press, 1958.

Associated Press. "2 Lab Monkeys Killed After Top Court Acts." *New York Times*, April 14, 1991.

Association for Psychological Science. "William James Fellow Award 1997. 'Edward Taub.'" www.psychologicalscience.org/awards/james/citations/taub.cfm. astridlindgren.se. "FAQ—Frequently Asked Questions." www.astrlindgren.com/en/faq.

"Austria Pushes Europe towards a Firm Stance for Animal Rights." *Grand Raps Press*, May 30, 2004, section A14.

Baggot, M. "Swiss Grant Rights to Animals, Consider the Same for Plants—Liberalize Abortion Laws." www.lifesitenews.com/ldn/2008/apr/08042808.html.

Barnard, N.D., et al. "NIH Research Protocol for Silver Spring Monkeys: A Case of Scientific Misconduct (pts.I-II)." *Perspectives on Medical Research Americans for Medical Advancement* 2 (1990). Available at http://www.curedisease.net/reports/Perspectives/vol_2_1990/SilverSprings1.html; www.curedisease.com/Perspectives/vol_2_1990/SilverSprings1.html.

"The Battle in Seattle is the Largest Since the Rallies Against the Vietnam War." http://oikos.org/ecology/wtocan.htm.

Beauty Without Cruelty. "Battery Farming and Chickens." www.bwcsa.co.za/index.php/issues/animals-as-food/chickens.

Bekoff, M. *Animals Matter*. Shambhala Publications, Incorporated, 2007.

Bekoff, M. *Minding Animals*. Oxford University Press, 2002.

Bekoff, M. & J. Pierce. *Wild Justice*. University of Chicago Press, 2009.

Bekoff, M. & P.W. Sherman. "Reflections on Animal Selves." In *Animal Passions and Beastly Virtues*, edited by M. Bekoff. Temple University Press, 2006.

Bekoff, M. "Beastly Passions." In *Animal Passions and Beastly Virtues*, edited by M. Bekoff. Temple University Press, 2006.

Bentham, J. *An Introduction to the Principles of Morals and Legislation*. Oxford Press, 1907.

Benton, T. "Animal Rights: An Eco-Socialist View." In *Animal Rights*, edited by R. Garner. Macmillan, 1996.

Berg, C. & Hammarstrom, M. "The Process of Building a New Governmental Authority Based on Public Demands for Improved Animal Welfare." *Livestock Science* 103, no. 3 (2006): 297–302.

Bergman, O. “Swedish Law Requires Ethical Review of All Animal Experiments.” www.djurforsok.info/english/home/regulations/swedishlawrequiresethicalreviewofallanimalexperiments.4.1c39844f11d7804ba518000170.html.

Berman, H.J. “Toward an Integrative Jurisprudence: Politics, Morality, History.” *California Law Review* 76 (1988): 779–801.

Bernard, E. “A Short Guide to the WTO, the Millennium Round and the Rumble in Seattle.” *Global Policy Forum*, November 29, 1999.

Bhala, R. *Modern GATT Law*. Thomson Sweet and Maxwell, 2005.

Bickhard, M.H. “Consciousness and Reflective Consciousness.” *Philosophy Psychology* 18 (2005): 205–18.

Black's Law Dictionary. 9th edn. West, 2009.

“The Blackstone Group.” www.blackstone.com/cps/rde/xchg/bxcom/hs/Home.htm.

The Blackstone Group. “Anheuser-Busch InBev and Blackstone Announce Completion of Sale of Busch Entertainment Corporation.” www.blackstone.com/cps/rde/xchg/bxcom/hs/news_pressrelease_6207.htm.

Blancou, J. & I. Parsonson. “Historical Perspectives on Long Distance Transport of Animals.” *Veterinaria Italina* 44, no. 1 (2008): 19–30.

Boland, J. “Four Legged Heroes; the Purina Animal Hall of Fame Ceremony Honours 4 Deserving Doggies.” *The Toronto Sun*, April 25, 2006, section 7.

“Bolivia Bans All Circus Animals.” *Associated Press*, September 3, 2009.

Brannon, E.M. & H.S. Terrace. “The Evolution and Ontogeny of Ordinal Numerical Ability.” In *The Cognitive Animal*, edited by M. Bekoff. MIT Press, 2002.

“Briefing Note on the European Labeling System.” Royal Society for the Prevention of Cruelty to Animals, 2010.

British Free Range Egg Producers Associations. “EU Denies Egg Labelling Claims.” www.theranger.co.uk/?show=newsArticle&=21360.

Brown, S.L., et al. “Review of Interspecies Risk Comparisons.” *Regulatory Toxicology & Pharmacology* 8 (1988): 191–206.

Brunton, G.W. “Pythagoras: The First Philosopher and Discoverer of the Forty Seventh Problem of Euclid.” http://www.mastermason.com/Millennium382/Papers/Pythagoras.pdf, 2005.

Budiansky, S. *If a Lion Could Talk*. The Free Press, 1998.

Budkie, M.A. “The Animal Experimentation Scandal: An Audit of the National Institutes of Health Funding of Animal Experimentation.” www.all-creatures.org/wlalw/report-anexp-audit.html.

Bugnyar, T., et al. “The Ontogeny of Caching in Ravens, Corvus Corax.” *Animal Behaviour* 74 (2007): 757–67.

Burnett, T. “Dogs of War.” *The Ottawa Sun*, February 2, 2010.

Callicott, J.B. “Multicultural Environmental Ethics.” *Daedalus* 130, no. 4 (2001): 77–97.

Callicott, J.B. “Review of Tom Regan, *The Case for Animal Rights (1985)*.” In *Law and the Environment*, edited by R.V. Percival et al. Temple University, 1997.

Calloway, C.G. *One Vast Winter Count*. University of Nebraska Press, 2003.

Canadian Council on Animal Care. "History and Funding." http://www.ccac.ca/en_/about/history_funding.

Canadian Council on Animal Care. *Guide to the Care and Use of Experimental Animals Vol. 1*, edited by E.D. Olfert. www.ccac.ca/en/CCAC_Programs/Guelines_Policies/PDFs/ExperimentalAnimals_GDL.pdf, 1993.

Canadian Council on Animal Care. "Legislation in Canada Related to Experimental Animals." www.ccac.ca/en/CCAC_Programs/ETCC/Module01/11.html.

Canadian Council on Animal Care. "List of CCAC Guidelines." www.ccac.ca/en/CCAC_Programs/Guelines_Policies/GDLINES/Guelis.htm.

Canadian Council on Animal Care. "Terms of Reference for Animal Care Committees." www.ccac.ca/en/CCAC_Programs/Guelines_Policies/PDFs/TOR_2006_en.pdf, 2006.

Canadian Council on Animal Care. "Ethics of Animal Investigation (1989)." www.ccac.ca/en/CCAC_Programs/Guelines_Policies/POLICIES/ETHICS.HTM.

Canadian Council on Animal Care. "Annual Surreys of Animal Use." http://www.ccac.ca/en_/publications/audf/stats-aud.

Canadian Federation of Humane Societies. "Who's Watching?." http://cfhs.ca/research/who_s_watching/, 2009.

Carbone, L. *What Animals Want*. Oxford University Press, 2004.

Carroll, A., et al. "Sexual Reproduction of Acropora Reef Corals at Moorea, French Polynesia." *Coral Reefs* 25 (2006): 93–97.

Chandola, M.V. "Dissecting American Animal Protection Law: Healing the Wounds with Animal Rights and Eastern Enlightenment." *Wisconsin Environmental Law Journal* 8 (2002): 3–30.

Charnovitz, S. "The Law of Environmental 'PPMS' in the WTO: Debunking the Myth of Illegality." *Yale Journal International Law* 27 (2002): 59–110.

Charnovitz, S. "The Moral Exception in Trade Policy." *Virginia Journal of International Law* 38 (1998): 689–745.

Chomsky, N. *Reflections on Language*. Pantheon Books, 1975.

Clark, N. "Little Celebration as CITES Ends." http://english.aljazeera.net/focus/wildlifesos/2010/03/2010325185143794333.html.

The Classical Psychologists, edited by B. Rand. University of Michigan Library, 1912.

Clayton, L.A. "Overview of Brazil's Legal Structure for Animal Issues." Animal Legal Historical Center. www.animallaw.info/nonus/articles/ovbrazil.htm, 2003.

Clutton-Brock, J. *A Natural History of Domesticated Mammals*. 2nd edn. Cambridge University Press, 1999.

CNN.com. "Curfew in Effect as Seattle Struggles to Control WTO Protests: WTO Says Violence Did Not Stop Negotiations." www.cnn.com/US/9911/30/wto.04/index.html.

Coolidge, F.L. & Thomas Wynn. *The Rise of Homo Sapiens*. Wiley-Blackwell, 2009.

Commission of the European Communities. "Fifth Report on the Statistics on the Number of Animals Used for Experimental and Other Scientific Purposes in the Member States of the European Union." 2007.

Commission of the European Communities. "Proposal for a Council Regulation on the Protection of Animals at the Time of Killing 'Explanatory Memorandum.'" 2008.

Commission to the European Parliament and Council. "Report on the Development, Validation and Legal Acceptance of Alternative Methods to Animal Tests in the Field of Cosmetics (2008)." COM(2010)480 final (2010).

"Communication from the Commission to the European Parliament and the Council on a Community Action Plan on the Protection and Welfare of Animals 2006–2010." 2006.

"Communication from the Commission to the Council and the European Parliament on Animal Welfare Legislation on Farmed Animals in Third Countries and the Implications for the EU." COM(2002)626 (2002).

Compassion in World Farming. "One Billion Eggs Now From Cage-Free Hens as Leading UK Companies Win 2009 Good Egg Awards." www.ciwf.org.uk/includes/documents/cm_docs/2009/n/nr4708.pdf, 2009.

Compassion in World Farming. "EU Egg Labelling Law Under Threat." www.ciwf.org.uk/news/laying_hens/eu_egg_labelling_law_under_threat.aspx.

Confédération Suisse. "La Nouvelle Législation Sur la Protection des Animaux." www.bvet.admin.ch/themen/tierschutz/02443/index.html?lang=fr.

Conley, M.K. "Caring for Dolphins, Otters, and Octopuses: Speciesism in the Regulation of Zoos." *Animal Law* 15 (2009): 237–64.

Convention on International Trade in Endangered Species of Wild Fauna and Flora. "Member Countries." www.cites.org/eng/disc/parties/index.shtml.

Convention on International Trade in Endangered Species of Wild Fauna and Flora. "Resolution Conf. 9.24 (Rev. CoP14)." www.cites.org/eng/res/09/09-24R14.shtml.

Convention on International Trade in Endangered Species Conf. 9.5 (Rev. CoP14). "Trade with States Not Party to the Convention." www.cites.org/eng/res/all/09/E09-05R14.pdf, 2007.

Convention on International Trade in Endangered Species. "Countries Currently Subject to a Recommendation to Suspend Trade." www.cites.org/eng/news/sundry/trade_suspension.shtml.

Convention on International Trade in Endangered Species. "Notification to the Parties No. 2008/027" (2008).

Cook, R.G. "Same-Different Concept Formation in Pigeons." In *The Cognitive Animal*, edited by M. Bekoff. MIT Press, 2002.

Cook, R. "Report: Michael Vick Got 'Adrenaline' Rush While Killing Dogs." www.ajc.com/sports/atlanta-falcons/report-michael-vick-got-271212.html.

Cook, R.G. & E.A. Wasserman. "Relational Discrimination Learning in Pigeons." In *Comparative Cognition*, edited by E.A. Wasserman et al. Oxford University Press, USA, 2009.

Commission to the European Parliament and Council. "Report on the Development, Validation and Legal Acceptance of Alternative Methods to Animal Tests in the Field of Cosmetics (2008)." COM(2010)480 final (2010).

Compassion in World Farming. "EU Egg Labeling Law under Threat." www.ciwf.org.uk/news/laying_hens/eu_egg_labelling_law_under_threat.aspx.

Cooper, R.N. *Environment and Resource Policies for the World Economy*. Brookings Institution Press, 1994.

Cottingham, J. "A Brute to the Brutes? Descartes' Treatment of Animals." *Philosophy* 53, no. 206 (1978): 551–59.

Council of Europe. "Joint Declaration on Co-operation on Animal Welfare between the Council of Europe, the European Union and the Regional Commission for Europe of the World Organisation for Animal Health (OIE)." http://ec.europa.eu/environment/chemicals/lab_animals/pdf/061124_declaration.pdf.

Council of Europe. "Council of Europe in Brief." www.coe.int/ aboutCoe/default.asp.

"Council of Europe." www.echr.coe.int/ECHR/EN/Header/Basic+Texts/The+Convention+and+additional+protocols/The+European+Convention+on+Human+Rights/.

Council of Europe. "European Convention on the Protection of Animals Kept for Farming Purposes. 'Explanatory Report.'" http://conventions.coe.int/Treaty/EN/Reports/Html/087.htm.

Council of Europe. "Biological Safety—Use of Animals By Humans." www.coe.int/t/e/legal_affairs/legal_co-operation/biological_safety,_use_of_animals/.

Court of Justice for the European Union. "General Court." http://curia.europa.eu/jcms/jcms/Jo2_7033/presentation.

Court, A. *Wild Circus Animals*. Burke, 1954.

Cox, E. *Psychology for a Level*. Oxford University Press, 2001.

Couwels, J. & B. Todd. "SeaWorld Trainer Killed By Killer Whale." www.cnn.com/2010/US/02/24/killer.whale.trainer.death/index.html.

Crawford, R.L. "A Review of the Animal Welfare Enforcement Report Data 1973 through 1995." *Animal Welfare Information Center Newsletter* 7, no. 2 (1996).

Croce, P. *Vivisection or Science*. Zed Books, 1999.

"Cruelty Connections." www.pet-abuse.com/pages/abuse_connection.php.

Curnutt, J. *Animals and the Law*. ABC-CLIO, 2001.

Dalal, M. "Tiger, Tiger, Flickering Light." *Boston College International & Comparative Law Review* 31 (2008): 103–19.

Darwin, C. *The Descent of Man and Selection in Relation to Sex*. 2nd edn. D. Appleton & Company, 1909.

Davis, K. "The Battery Hen: Her Life is Not for the Birds." www.all-creatures.org/articles/egg-battery.html.

Davidson, M.G. "Protecting Coral Reefs: The Principal National and International Legal Instruments." *Harvard Environmental Law Review* 26 (2002): 499–546.

Deckha, M. "The Salience of Species Difference for Feminist Theory." *Hastings Women's Law Journal* 17 (2006): 1–38.

DeGrazia, D. & A. Rowan. "Pain, Suffering and Anxiety in Animals and Humans." *Theoretical Medicine & Bioethics* 12 (1991): 193–211.

Delius, J.D. & J.M. Delius. "Intelligences and Brains: An Evolutionary Bird's Eye View." In *Comparative Cognition*, edited by E.A. Wasserman et al. Oxford University Press, USA, 2009.

Department of the Interior, Office of the Secretary. "U.S. Leads Effort to Protect Wild Tigers from Poaching, Successfully Rallies Support for Resolution on Tiger Farms." June 13, 2007, 2007 WL 1700894.

Descartes, R. *A Discourse on Method and Selected Writings*. Translated by John Veitch. American ed. Dutton, 1951.

DeSombre, E.R. *Global Environmental Institutions*. Routledge, 2006.

Dickinson, E. "Not in Vain." In *One Hundred and One Famous Poems*, edited by Roy Cook. Barnes & Noble Books, 1993.

Dictionary.com, "Ethology." http://dictionary.reference.com/browse/ethology.

Djurförsök.info. "Facts and Numbers." www.djurforsok.info/english/home/facts andnumbers.4.1c39844f11d7804ba518000450.html.

Donovan, J. "Animal Rights and Feminist Theory." In *The Feminist Care Tradition in Animal Ethics*, edited by J. Donovan & C.J. Adams. Columbia University Press, 2007.

Draeger, A.B. "More Than Property: An Argument for Adoption of the Universal Declaration on Animal Welfare." *Drake Journal Agricultural Law* 12 (2007): 277–89.

Druker, P.F. "The Global Economy and the Nation State." *Foreign Affairs* 76, no. 5 (1997): 159–71.

Dudzinski, K.M., et al. "A Comparison of Pectoral Fin Contact between Two Different Wild Dolphin Populations." *Behavioural Processes* 80 (2009): 182–90.

Easton, V.J. & McColl, J. "Statistics Glossary." http://www.stats.gla.ac.uk/steps/glossary/alphabet.html.

Eilperin, J. "Nations Reject Coral Protections at Wildlife Conservation Conference." *Washington Post*, March 22, 2010, http://www.washingtonpost.com/wpdyn/content/article/2010/03/21/AR2010032101204.html www.washingtonpost.com/wpdyn/content/article/2010/03/21/AR2010032101204.html?wpisrc=nl_headline.

El-Ali, J., et al. "Cells on Chips." *Nature* 442 (2006): 403–11.

Elsberry, W.R. "Punctuated Equilibria." www.talkorigins.org/faqs/punc-eq.html.

Encarta World English Dictionary. "Unnecessary." http://encarta.msn.com/encnet/features/dictionary/DictionaryResults.aspx?ref=1861708239.

Encyclopedia Britannica's Advocacy for Animals. "Highways to Hell: The Long-Distance Transport of Farmed Animal." http://advocacy.britannica.com/blog/advocacy/2008/06/highways-to-hell-the-long-distance-transport-of-farmed-animals/, 2008.

ENDCAP. "Circuses." www.endcaptivity.org/index.php?option=content&task=view&=20.

ENDCAP. "Portugal Bans the Keeping of Certain Wild Animals." www.endcaptivity.org/index.php?option=content&task=view&=30.

Engelsman, S.J. " 'World Leader'—At What Price? A Look at Lagging American Animal Protection Laws." *Pace Environmental Law Review* 22 (2005): 329–69.

Ernst, S. "Animal Use and Abuse Statistics: The Shocking Numbers." http://animals.change.org/blog/view/animal_use_and_abuse_statistics_the_shocking_numbers.

"EU Commission Staff Working Paper." SEC(2008)2411/2 (2008).

"Europa." http://europa.eu/index_en.htm.

Europa. "The Council of the European Union." http://europa.eu/institutions/inst/council/index_en.htm.

Europa. "The European Council—An Official Institution of the EU." http://www.european-council.europa.eu/the-institution.aspx.

Europa. "Memorandum 10/398 on Questions and Answers on the New Directive for the Protection of Animals Used for Scientific Purposes." September 9, 2010. Available at http://europa.eu/rapid/pressReleasesAction.do?reference=MEMO/10/398&format=HTML&aged=0&language=EN&guiLanguage=en.

Europa. "Press Release. EU Revises Laws To Better Protect Animals Used in Scientific Experiments." http://europa.eu/rapid/pressReleasesAction.do?reference=IP/10/1105&format=HTML&aged=0&language=EN&guiLanguage=en.

Europa. "Press Release. New EU Labelling Rules Including New EU Organic Logo Come Into Force on 1 July." http://europa.eu/rapid/pressReleasesAction.do?reference=IP/10/861&format=HTML&aged=1&language=EN&guiLanguage=en.

Europa. "Treaties and Law." http://europa.eu/abc/treaties/index_en.htm.

Europa. "How Does the EU Work?." http://europa.eu/abc/12lessons/lesson_4/index_en.htm.

Europa. "The European Commission." http://europa.eu/institutions/inst/comm/index_en.htm.

Europa. "Europe in 12 Lessons." http://europa.eu/abc/12lessons/lesson_4/index_en.htm.

Europa. "The European Parliament." http://europa.eu/institutions/inst/parliament/index_en.htm.

Europa. "EU Institutions and Other Bodies." http://europa.eu/institutions/index_en.htm.

Europa. "Decision Making in the European Union." http://europa.eu/institutions/decision-making/index_en.htm.

European Center for the Validation of Alternative Methods. "About ECVAM." http://ecvam.jrc.it/.

PR Newswire. "European Circus Association Challenges Performing Animal Bans." http://www.prnewswire.com/news-releases/european-circus-association-challenges-performing-animal-bans-62319582.html.

European Commission. "Environment: Laboratory Animals." http://ec.europa.eu/environment/chemicals/lab_animals/home_en.htm.

European Commission. "What are EU Directives?." http://ec.europa.eu/community_law/introduction/what_directive_en.htm.

European Commission. "What are EU Regulations?." http://ec.europa.eu/community_law/introduction/what_regulation_en.htm.

European Commission. "Opinion of The Commission on the European Ombudsman's Draft Recommendation-Complaint by the European Circus Association (ECA), ref. 3307/2006/(PB)JMA." www.vierpfoten.at/website/uploads/090918_CommissionReplytoOmbudsman.pdf.

European Commission. "Implementation of Humane Trapping Standard in the EU." http://ec.europa.eu/environment/biodiversity/animal_welfare/hts/index_en.htm.

European Economic and Social Committee. "Opinion on the Proposal for a Directive of the European Parliament and of the Council on the Protection of Animals Used for Scientific Purposes." NAT/422 (2009).

The European Ombudsman. "Commission Has to Properly Examine Austrian Ban on Wild Animals in Circuses Press Release no. 14-2009." www.ombudsman.europa.eu/press/release.faces/en/4135/html.bookmark.

The European Ombudsman. "The European Ombudsman—At a Glance." www.ombudsman.europa.eu/atyourservice/ataglance.faces.

The European Ombudsman, Diamandouros, P.N. "Draft Recommendation of the European Ombudsman in His Inquiry into Complaint 3307/2006/(PB)JMA against the European Commission." www.ombudsman.europa.eu/cases/draftrecommendation.faces/en/4068/html.bookmark.

"European Parliament Legislative Resolution of May 5, 2009 on the Proposal for a Directive of the European Parliament and of the Council on the Protection of Animals Used for Scientific Purposes." European Parliament Document P6_TA (2009) 0343 (2009).

European Parliament. "Procedure File." www.europarl.europa._eu/oeil/FindByProcnum.do?lang=2&procnum=cod/2008/211.

Evans, C.S. "Cracking the Code: Communication and Cognition in Birds." In *The Cognitive Animal*, edited by M. Bekoff. MIT Press, 2002.

"Expert Working Group on Severity Classifications of Scientific Procedures Performed on Animals, Final Report" (2009).

"Explanatory Memorandum, Proposal for a Directive of the European Parliament and of the Council on the Protection of Animals Used for Scientific Purposes." COM(2008)543 final (2008).

Fairlie, S. "A Load of Hot Air?." *Guardian*, January 30, 2008, http://www.sustdev.org/index.php?option=com_content&task=view&id=2412&Itemid=34.

Farm Sanctuary. "Access Farm Sanctuary Research Report: The Welfare of Hens in Battery Cages." www.farmsanctuary.org/ issues/factoryfarming/eggs.

Favre, D. "Integrating Animal Interests into Our Legal System." *Animal Law* 10 (2004): 87–97.

Fenwick, N., et al. "The Welfare of Animals Used in Science: How the "Three Rs" Ethic Guides Improvements." *Canadian Veterinary Journal* 50 (2009): 523–30.

Fernandez, J.L. "State Constitutions, Environmental Rights Provisions, and the Doctrine of Self-Execution: A Political Question?." *Harvard Environmental Law Review* 17 (1993): 333–87.

Fichtelberg, A. "Liberal Values in International Criminal Law: A Critique of Erdemovic." *Journal International Criminal Justice* 6 (2008): 1–5.

Flombaum, J.I. & L.R. Santos. "Rhesus Monkeys Attribute Perceptions to Others." *Current Biology* 15 (2005): 447–52.

Foer, J.S. *Eating Animals*. Back Bay Books, 2009.

Food & Agriculture Organization of the United Nations. "FAOSTAT." http://faostat.fao.org/.

Food & Agriculture Organization for the United Nations Regional Office for the Near East. "Iran … Iran's egg industry safe: IEC Chief." *Tehran Times*, November 10, 2005, http://agriculturenews.net/index.aspx?Type=Briefnews &=1853.

Fouts, R.S. "Apes, Darwinian Continuity, and the Law." *Animal Law* 10 (2004): 99–124.

Fouts, R.S. et al. "Chimpanzee Signing: Darwinian Realities and Cartesian Delusions." In *The Cognitive Animal*, edited by M. Bekoff. MIT Press, 2002.

Fox41.com. "Trial Underway for Accused Dogfighter." www.fox41.com/Global/story.asp?S=12353272.

Francione, G.L. *Animals, Property and the Law*. Temple University Press, 1995.

Francione, G.L. "Animals, Property and Legal Welfarism: 'Unnecessary' Suffering and the 'Humane' Treatment of Animals." *Rutgers Law Review* 46 (1994): 721–70.

Francione, G.L. "Animal Rights and Animal Welfare." *Rutgers Law Review* 48 (1996): 397–469.

Francione, G.L. "Animal Rights Theory and Utilitarianism: Relative Normative Guidance." *Animal Law* 3 (1997): 75–101.

Francione, G.L. "Reflections on Animals, Property and the Law and Rain without Thunder." *Law & Contemporary Problems* 70 (2007): 9–56.

Franklin, J.H. *Animal Rights and Moral Philosophy*. Columbia University Press, 2005.

FreeBetty.com. "The Real Cost of Caged Eggs." www.freebetty.com/cage_eggs.php.

Fuchs, C. "Convention on International Trade in Endangered Species of Wild Fauna and Flora (CITES)—Conservation Efforts Undermine the Legality Principle." *German Law Journal* 9 (2008): 1565–96.

Gallup, G.G. "Do Minds Exist in Species Other Than Our Own?." *Neuroscience & Biobehavioural Reviews* 9 (1985): 631–41.

Gaukroger, S. *Descartes*. Oxford University Press, USA, 1995.

Gentner, T.Q. "Neural Systems for Individual Song Recognition in Adult Birds." *Annals of the New York Academy of Science* 1016 (2004): 282–302.

Gerber, P. "Scientific Experimentation on Animals: Are Australia and New Zealand Implementing the 3Rs?." In *Animal Law in Australasia*, edited by P.J. Sankoff & S. White. Federation Press, 2009.

Gibson, H. "Dog Fighting Detailed Discussion. Michigan State University College of Law." www.animallaw.info/articles/ddusdogfighting.htm, 2005.

Gierczyk, Y.N. "The Evolution of the European Legal System: The European Court of Justice's Role in the Harmonization of Laws." *ISLA Journal International & Comparative Law* 12 (2005): 153–81.

Global Action Network. "Fur Trade." www.gan.ca/campaigns/fur+trade/factsheets/index.en.html.

Gómez, J.C. "Embodying Meaning: Insights from Primates, Autism and Brentano." *Neural Networks* 22 (2009): 190–96.

Goodall, J. *Harvest for Hope*. Warner Wellness, 2005.

Gorant, J. "What Happened to Michael Vick's Dogs ... ." http://sportsillustrated.cnn.com/2008/magazine/12/22/vick.dogs/index.html.

Gould, J.L. "Can Honey Bees Create Cognitive Maps?". In *The Cognitive Animal*, edited by M. Bekoff. MIT Press, 2002.

Gould, J.L. & C.G. Gould, "The Animal Mind." www.pigeon.psy.tufts.edu/psych26/kohler.htm.

Grandin, T. *Livestock Handling and Transport*. CABI, 2007.

Grant, P.R. & B.R. Grant. "Evolution of Character Displacement in Darwin's Finches." *Science* 313 (2006): 224–26.

Gruber, T.M., et al. "Variation in Stereotypic Behavior Related to Restraint in Circus Elephants." *Zoo Biology* 19 (2000): 209–21.

Gruen, L. "The Morals of Animal Minds." In *The Cognitive Animal*, edited by M. Bekoff. MIT Press, 2002.

Guest, J. "How Reefs Respond to Mass Coral Spawning." *Science* 320 (2008): 621–23.

Güzeldere, G., et al. "Darwin's Continuum and the Building Blocks of Deception." In *The Cognitive Animal*, edited by M. Bekoff. MIT Press, 2002.

Halweil, B. "Meat Production Continues to Rise." www.worldwatch.org/node/5443.

Hart, B.L. "Large Brains and Cognition: Where do Elephants Fit In?." *Neuroscience and Biobehavioral Review* 32 (2008): 86–98.

Haun, D.B. & J. Call. "Great Apes' Capacities to Recognize Relational Similarity." *Cognition* 110 (2009): 147–59.

Haupt, C.E. "Free Exercise of Religion and Animal Protection: A Comparative Perspective on Ritual Slaughter." *George Washington International Law Review* 39 (2007): 839–86.

Haupt, C.E. "The Nature and Effects of Constitutional State Objectives: Assessing the German Basic Law's Animal Protection Clause." *Animal Law* 16 (2010): 213–57.

Hayden, T. "The Battle in Seattle: What Was That All About?." *Washington Post*, December 5, 1999, section B09.

"Health Benefits of Vegetarian Diets." www.vegetarian-nutrition.info/updates/vegetarian_diets_health_benefits.php.

"57 Health Benefits of Going Vegan." www.nursingdegree.net/blog/19/57-health-benefits-of-going-vegan/.

Heinrich, B. "Raven Consciousness." In *The Cognitive Animal*, edited by M. Bekoff. MIT Press, 2002.

Helping Animals. "Deadly Destinations." www.helpinganimals.com/travel_feat_deadlydest.asp.

Hemley, G. (ed.). *International Wildlife Trade*. Island Press, 1994.

Herman, L.M. "Exploring the Cognitive World of the Bottlenosed Dolphin." In *The Cognitive Animal*, edited by M. Bekoff. MIT Press, 2002.

Hilts, P.J. "Use of Research Animals Falls 50% Since 1968." *New York Times*, March 3, 1994, section A18.

Home Office. "Statistics of Scientific Procedures on Living Animals Great Britain 2008." Stationary Office, 2009.

Hovenkamp, H. "Positivism in Law & Economics." *California Law Review* 78 (1990): 815–52.

House, R. "The Appellate Body Rulings in the Shrimp/Turtle Case: A New Legal Baseline for the Trade and Environment Debate." *Columbia Journal of Environmental Law* 27 (2002): 491–521.

Hubrecht, R. & J. Kirkwood (eds.). *The UFAW Handbook on the Care and Management of Laboratory and Other Research Animals*. 8th edn. Wiley-Blackwell, 2010.

Huebscher, D. "Animal Cruelty a Touchy Issue for High Court." *The Leader-Telegram. Eau Claire, Wisconsin*, 13 October 2009.

Humane Society of the United States. "The Humane Society Cage-Free vs. Battery-Cage Eggs: Comparison of Animal Welfare in Both Methods." www.humanesociety.org/issues/confinement_farm/facts/cage-free_vs_battery-cage.html.

Humane Society of the United States. "SeaWorld Attack Reaffirms Whale of a Truth: Captive Orcas Can Be Dangerous." http://www.freerepublic.com/focus/f-chat/2458732/posts.

Humane Society International, *News About CITES 2010,* http://www.hsi.org/news/news/2010/02/.

Hume, D. *A Treatise of Human Nature*. Oxford, 1978.

Hurel Corporation. "Technology: Overview." www.hurelcorp.com/overview.php.

Iamblichus' Life of Pythagoras, or Pythagoric Life. Translated by T. Taylor. Kessinger Publishing, 2003.

Ibrahim, D.M. "Reduce, Refine, Replace: The Failure of the Three R's and the Future of Animal Experimentation." *University Chicago Legal Journal* (2006): 195–229.

Ideland, M. "In the Name of Science? How Members of Animal Ethics Committees Talk about Ethics." http://dspace.mah.se/bitstream/2043/4524/1/In_the_name_of_Science.muep.pdf, 2007.

In Defense of Animals. "Rodeo Facts." www.ausa.org/facts/rodeos.html.

International Committee of the OIE. "Resolution No. XIV Animal Welfare Mandate of the OIE." 2002.

Jacobs, A. "Tiger Farms in China Feed Thirst for Parts." *Deseret News*, February 14, 2010, section A18.

Jamieson, D. *Morality's Progress*. Oxford University Press, USA, 2002.

Jendral, M., et al. "Alternative Layer Hen Housing Systems in Europe." www.afac.ab.ca/reports/reporthenhousing.pdf, 2005.

Jones, R. "Exposed Dark Secret of the Tiger Farm." *Mail on Sunday*, February 21, 2010, 2010 WLNR 3667741.

Johnson, P.E. "Some Thoughts about Natural Law." *California Law Review* 75 (1987): 217–26.

Johnston, D.S. "The Native American Plight: Protection and Preservation of Sacred Sites." *Widener Law Symposium Journal* 8 (2002): 443–61.

Jordbruksverket. "Definition of Animal Experiments and Laboratory Animals." http://www.sjv.se/swedishboardofagriculture/engelskasidor/animals/laboratoryanimals/definitions.4.6621c2fb1231eb917e680002832.html.

Kane, L., et al. "Best Practices by the Coalition for Captive Elephant Well-Being." 2005.

Kane, L., et al. "Optimal Conditions for Captive Elephants: A Report by the Coalition for Captive Elephant Well-Being." 2005.

Kant, I. *The Metaphysics of Morals*. Cambridge University Press, 1991.

Katzung & Trevor's Pharmacology, edited by A.J. Trevor et al. 8th edn. McGraw-Hill Medical, 2007.

Kelch, T.G. "The Role of the Rational and the Emotive in a Theory of Animal Rights." *Boston College Environmental Affairs Law Review* 27 (1999): 1–46.

Kelch, T.G. "Toward a Non-property Status for Animals." *New York University Environmental Law Journal* 6 (1998): 531–85.

Kerra, I. "The Birds and the B's: Challenging Chomsky, Starlings Learn 'Human Only' Syntax Patterns." *University California San Diego News*, April 26, 2006, http://ucsdnews.ucsd.edu/newsrel/soc/gentner_starling06.asp.

Kheel, M. "The Liberation of Nature: A Circular Affair." In *Beyond Animal Rights*, edited by J. Donovan & C.J. Adam. Continuum International Publishing Group, 1996.

Kheel, M. "Nature and Feminist Sensitivity." In *Animal Rights and Human Obligations*, edited by Tom Regan. Prentice Hall, 1989.

Kirby, D. *Animal Factory*. St. Martin's Press, 2010.

Kluger, J. "Inside the Minds of Animals." *Time*, August 16, 2010, 36.

Knight, A. "127 Million Non-Human Vertebrates Used Worldwide for Scientific Purposes in 2005." *Alternative to Laboratory Animals* 36 (2008): 494.

Knowles, J. "Revised Protection for Animals for Scientific Purposes." EVERSHEDS. www.eversheds.com/uk/Home/Articles/index1.page?ArticleID=templatedata Eversheds\articles\data\en\Healthcare\Revised_protection_for_animals_used_for_scientific_purposes.

Krishnan, A. "China Considers Legalising Tiger Trade to Curb Poaching." *Hindu*, February 14, 2010, section 16.

Kuczaj II, S.A. & R.T. Walker. "How Do Dolphins Solve Problems?." In *Comparative Cognition*, edited by E.A. Wasserman & T.R. Zentall. Oxford University Press, 2006.

Krützen, M., et al. "Cultural Transmission of Tool Use in Bottlenose Dolphins." *Procedure of the National Academy of Science, USA* 102, No. 25 (2005) 8939–43.

Lakshiminarayanan, V.R. & L.R. Santos. "Capuchin Monkeys Are Sensitive to Others' Welfare." *Current Biology* 18, no. 21 (2008): R999–R1000.

Landau, E. "Biologists: Killer Whales 'Neurotic' in Captivity." www.cnn.com/2010/US/02/25/whales.seaworld.death/index.html.

Lavery, D. Review of *Cogito, Ergo Sum* by Richard Watson. *The Georgia Review* 437 (1989).

Leopold, A. *A Sand County Almanac*. Oxford University Press, 1966.

Letter from Joyce Poole, Director of Research & Conservation. "Elephant Voices, to Los Angeles City Counsel." www.elephantvoices.org/multimedia-resources/document-download-center/cat_view/71-statements-a-testimonies-.html

Leybold-Johnson, I. "Lawyer Lends His Voice to the Animals." www.swissinfo.ch/eng/Lawyerlendshisvoicetotheanimals.html?cid=979670.

Lind, M. "Hume and Moral Emotions." In *Identity, Character and Morality*, edited by O. Flanagan & A.O. Rorty. MIT Press, 1990.

Lindgren, A. *The Adventures of Pippi Longstocking*. Viking, 1997.

Lonsdorf, E.V., et al. "An Experimental, Comparative Investigation of Tool Use in Chimpanzees and Gorillas." *Animal Behaviour* 77 (2009) 1119–26.

Lovejoy, A.O. *The Great Chain of Being*. Illustrated ed. Harvard University Press, 1964.

Lyons, D.E., et al. "Reflections of Other Minds: How Primate Social Cognition Can Inform the Function of Mirror Neurons." *Current Opinion in Neurobiology* 16 (2006): 230–34.

MacFarlane, S. "Unique Program Saves Michael Vick's Fighting Dogs; Tortured Animals Successfully Underwent Rehab." www.ktvu.com/news/17382977/detail.html#.

MacRae, F. "The Chimps That Beat Humans in a Memory Test." http://www.dailymail.co.uk/news/article-499432/The-chimps-beat-humans-memory-test.html.

Magnotti, L. "Pawing Open the Courthouse Door: Why Animals' Interests Should Matter When Courts Grant Standing." *St. John's Law Review* 80 (2006): 445–95.

Mansfield, A. "India's Legal Doolittle." www.voiceless.org.au/About_Us/Voiceless_in_Print_2008/India_s_Legal_Doolittle.htm.

Marzluff, J.M. & T. Angell. *In the Company of Crows and Ravens*. Yale University Press, 2007.

Masserman, J.H., et al. "Altruistic Behavior in Rhesus Monkeys." *The American Journal of Psychiatry* 121 (1964): 584–85.

Mathijsen, P.S.R.F. *A Guide to European Union Law*. 9th edn. Sweet & Maxwell, 2007.

Matsuzawa, T. "Chimpanzee Ai and Her Son Ayumu: An Episode of Education by Master-Apprenticeship." In *The Cognitive Animal*, edited by M. Bekoff. MIT Press, 2002.

Mavroidis, P.C. *The General Agreement on Tariffs and Trade*. Oxford University Press, USA, 2005.

May, J.R. "Constituting Fundamental Environmental Rights Worldwide." *Pace Environmental Law Review* 23 (2006): 113–82.

McKeon, R. "Introduction." In *Introduction to Aristotle*, edited by R. McKeon. Translated by J.A. Smith. Modern Library, 1992.

McOmber, E.M. "Problems in Enforcement of the Convention on International Trade in Endangered Species." *Brook Journal International Law* 27 (2002): 673–701.

Merriam-Webster's Online Dictionary. "Ethology." www.merriam-webster.com/dictionary/ethology.

Mirza, F. "Helping Animals Speak Up: Switzerland Was the First Country to Give Constitutional Rights to Animals, and So It Seems Fitting that it is Home to the World's One and Only Animal Lawyer." *Swiss News*. http://www.thefreelibrary.com/Helping+animals+speak+up%3A+Switzerland+was+the+first+country+to+give…-a0187622149.

Mitchell, R.W. "Kinesthetic-Visual Matching, Imitation, and Self Recognition." In *The Cognitive Animal*, edited by M. Bekoff. MIT Press, 2002.

Moran, K. "This Dog Proves to be One Man's Best Friend with Act of Heroism." *The Houston Chronicle*, October 2, 1997, section A26.

Morant, B.D. "The Teachings of Dr. Martin Luther King, Jr. and Contract Theory: An Intriguing Comparison." *Alabama Law Review* 50 (1998): 63–113.

Mott, M. "US Dog Fighting Rings Stealing Pets for 'Bait.'" *National Geographic News*. http://news.nationalgeographic.com/news/2004/02/0218_040218_dogfighting.html.

Mulhall, M. "Saving the Rainforests of the Sea: An Analysis of International Efforts to Conserve Coral Reefs." *Duke Environmental Law & Policy Forum* 19 (2009): 321–51.

Murphy, K. "WTO Summit: Protest in Seattle; 400 Jailed as Police Occupy Seattle Streets." *Los Angeles Times*, December 2, 1999, section A1.

Nattrass, K.M. "'...Und Die Tiere' Constitutional Protection for Germany's Animals." *Animal Law* 10 (2004): 283–312.

NECSI. "Gradualism and Punctuated Equilibrium." http://necsi.org/projects/evolution/evolution/grad+punct/evolution_grad+punct.html.

Neill, J. "Meta-Analysis: Research Methodology." http://wilderdom.com/research/meta-analysis.html.

New South Wales Department of Primary Industries. "The Australian Code of Practice for the Care and Use of Animals for Scientific Purposes (Factsheet 8)." www.dpi.nsw.gov.au/agriculture/livestock/animal-welfare/research-teaching/factsheets/awfact08, 2005.

New Zealand Rodeo Cowboys Association. www.rodeonz.co.nz/.

Oliver, M. "Astrid Lindgren, 94; Creator of Pippi Longstocking Adventures." *Los Angeles Times*, January 29, 2009, section B10.

Orca. "Free, How They Live." http://orcafree.org/how.html.

The Organic Trust. "New Regulations Governing the Organic Sector." www.organic-trust.org/news/detail/new_regulations_governing_the_organic_sector.

Ovid. *Metamorphoses*. Translated by Frank Justus Miller. 2nd edn. Harvard University Press, 1984.

Pacheco, A. & A. Francione. "The Silver Spring Monkeys." In *In Defence of Animals*, edited by Peter Singer. Basil Blackwell, 1985.

Page, T. *Vivisection Unveiled*. Jon Carpenter Publishing, 1997.

Palagi, E. "Sharing the Motivation to Play: The Use of Signals in Adult Bonobos." *Animal Behaviour* 75 (2007): 887–96.

Pancevski, B. "New Swiss Law Protects Rights of 'Social' Animals." *Timesonline*, www.timesonline.co.uk/tol/news/world/europe/article3818457.ece.

Panger, M.A. "Object-Use in Free-Ranging White-Faced Capuchins (Celus capucinus) in Costa Rica." *America Journal of Physical Anthropology* 106 (1998) 311–21.

PBS Frontline. "Interview with Michael Pollan." www.pbs.org/wgbh/pages/frontline/shows/meat/interviews/pollan.html.

Pepperberg, I.M. *Alex & Me*. Collins, 2008.

Pepperberg, I.M. "Cognitive and Communicative Abilities of Grey Parrots." In *The Cognitive Animal*, edited by M. Bekoff. MIT Press, 2002.

People for the Ethical Treatment of Animals. "Veal: A Byproduct of the Cruel Dairy Industry." www.peta.org/factsheet/files/FactsheetDisplay.asp?=102.

People for the Ethical Treatment of Animals. "Elephant Incidents in the United States." www.circuses.com/pdfs/Elephant_Incent_List-US.pdf, 2009.

Perel, P., et al. "Comparison of Treatment Effects between Animal Experiments and Clinical Trials: Systematic Review." BMJ, doi:10.1136/bmj.39048.407928.BE (2006).

Perez, K. "Vicktory for Michael Vick Pitbull Ray." http://dogspired.com/awareness/7927/.

Peterson, J. "WTO Summit in Seattle; Activists Bring Turtles' Cause to WTO Fishbowl." *Los Angeles Times*, December 3, 1999, section A1.

Pet-Abuse.com. "Severely Injured Dog Left in Trash Bin." www.petabuse.com/cases/7414/AL/US/.

PETA Media Center. "Government Required Animal Testing: Overview." www.peta.org/mc/factsheet_display.asp?=125.

Pew Commission on Industrial Farm Animal Production. "Putting Meat on the Table: Industrial Farm Animal Production in America" (2008).

Physicians Committee for Responsible Medicine. "Animal Care and Use Committees: Structural Problems Impair Usefulness." www.pcrm.org/resch/anexp/IACUC.html.

Pierce, J. "Mice in the Sink: On the Expression of Empathy in Animals." *Journal of Environmental Philosophy* 5, no. 1 (2008): 75.

Pilkington, E. "Killer Whale Tilikum [sic] to Be Spared After Drowning Trainer by Ponytail." www.guardian.co.uk/world/2010/feb/25/killer-whale-tilikum-drowned-trainer-hair.

Plotnik, J.M., et al. "Self-Recognition in an Asian Elephant." *Procedure of National Academic Science* 103, no. 45 (2006): 17053–57.

Pojeta Jr., J. & D.A. Springer. "Evolution and the Fossil Record." *The American Geological Institute & the Paleontology Society*. www.agiweb.org/news/evolution/, 2001.

Pound, P., et al. "Where Is the Evidence That Animal Research Benefits Humans?." BMJ 328 (2004): 514.

Prelex. "COM(2008) 543, 2008/0211/COD." http://ec.europa.eu/prelex/detail_dossier_real.cfm/CL=en&Dos=195784.

Prior, H., et al. "Mirror-Induced Behavior in the Magpie (Pica pica): Evidence of Self-Recognition." *Public Library Science Biology* 6, no. 8 (2008): 0001–0009.

Professional Rodeo Cowboy Association. www.prorodeo.com/animal_welfare.aspx?xu=3.

Purina Animal Hall of Fame. "Please Welcome Our 2008 Inductees." www.purina.ca/about/halloffame/2008.aspx.

Queensland Government Department of Primary Industries, "Monitoring Program for the Scientific Use Code". http://www.dpi.qld.gov.au/documents/AnimalIndustries_AnimalWelfareAndEthics/MonitoringProgram-ForTheScientific-UseCode.pdf.

Queensland Government, Department of Employment, Economic Development & Innovation, "Animal Ethics and Using Animals for Scientific Purposes" http://www.dpi.qld.gov.au/27_9907.htm.

Queensland Government Department of Primary Industries. "Monitoring Program for the Scientific Use Code." wwwz.dpi.qld.gov.au/extra/pdf/aniimalwelfare/monitoring_program.pdf.

Raffaele, P. "Speaking Bonobo." *Smithsonian Magazine*, November 2006, www.smithsonianmag.com/science-nature/speakingbonobo.html.

Regan, T. *The Case for Animal Rights*. University California Press, 2004.

Reeve, R. *Policing International Trade in Endangered Species*. Royal Institute of International Affairs, 2002.

Reif, T.M. & J. Eckert. "Courage You Can't Understand: How to Achieve the Right Balance Between Shaping and Policing Commerce in Disputes before the World Trade Organization." *Columbia Journal of Transnational Law* 42, no. 3 (2004): 657–714.

Reilly, R. "Mike Vick Went Bankrupt Sitting in Prison, How Did That Happen?." http://sports.espn.go.com/espnmag/story?section=magazine&id=3726426.

Reinhold, R. "Fate of Monkeys, Deformed for Science, Causes Human Hurt After Six Years." *New York Times*, May 23, 1987, section 18.

"Response by Compassion in World Farming to DG Sanco Consultative Document on Labeling: Competitiveness, Consumer Information and Better Regulation for the EU." http://ec.europa.eu/food/food/labellingnutrition/betterregulation/docs/58.pdf, 2006.

Riley, M. "Evolution." www.blackwellpublishing.com/rley/a-z, 2003.

Roberts, I., et al. "Does Animal Experimentation Inform Human Healthcare? Observations from a Systematic Review of International Animal Experiments on Fluid Resuscitation." BMJ 324 (2002): 474–76.

Roman Coliseum. "Tourist Guide to the Roman Coliseum." www.roman-colosseum.info/colosseum/tourist-gue-roman-colosseum.htm.

Ruesch, H. *Slaughter of the Innocent*. Civitas Publications, 1978.

Santagelo, J. "Evading Extinction: A 21st Century Survey of the Legal Challenges to Wild Siberian Tiger Conservation." *Journal Animal Law* 1 (2005): 109–24.

de Santana Gordilho, H.J. "Wildlife and the Brazilian Abolitionist Movement." *Animal Law Journal* 5 (2009): 71–89.

Santos, L.R., et al. "Domain-Specific Knowledge in Human Children and Nonhuman Primates: Artifacts and Foods." In *The Cognitive Animal*, edited by M. Bekoff. MIT Press, 2002.

Santos, L.R., et al. "Rhesus Monkeys, Macaca Mulatta, Know What Others Can and Cannot Hear." *Animal Behaviour* 71 (2006): 1175–81.

Satz, A.B. "Would Rosa Parks Wear Fur? Toward a Nondiscrimination Approach to Animal Welfare." *Journal Animal Law & Ethics* 1 (2006): 139–59.

Schauer, F. "Constitutional Positivism." *Connecticut Law Review* 25 (1993): 797–829.

Schlosser, E. "Fast Food Nation: Meat and Potatoes." *Rolling Stone Magazine*, September 3, 1998, www.ericsecho.org/investigation2.htm.

Schmitz, S. "How Dare They? European Merger Control and the European Commission's Blocking of the Electric/Honeywell Merger." *University Pennsylvania Journal of International Economic Law* 23 (2002): 325–83.

Schulte, B. "Once Groomed for Fighting, Vick's Dogs Find New Lives." *The Virginian-Pilot*, July 8, 2008, section A1.

Schusterman, R.J., et al. "The Cognitive Sea Lion: Meaning & Memory in the Laboratory and in Nature." In *The Cognitive Animal*, edited by M. Bekoff. MIT Press, 2002.

Schwartz, J.M. & S. Begley. *The Mind and the Brain*. Harper Perennial, 2002.

"Seattle P.D. After Action Report World Trade Organization Ministerial Conference Seattle Washington." November, 29—December 3, 1999 (2000).

Shanks, N., et al. "Are Animal Models Predictive for Humans?." *Philosophy, Ethics, and Humanity in Medicine* 4 (2009).

Simpson, C.J. "Mass Spawning of Scleractinian Corals in the Dampier Archipelago and the Implications for Management of Coral Reefs in Western Australia Bulletin 244." Department Conservation & Environment, Perth, Western Australia, 1985.

Singer, P. *Practical Ethics*. 2nd edn. Cambridge University Press (USA), 1993.

Singer, P. "Free Tilly and Other Circus Animals." *The Japan Times Online*, March 11, 2010, http://search.japantimes.co.jp/cgi-bin/eo20100311a1.html.

Singer, P. "All Animals Are Equal." In *Animal Rights and Human Obligations*, edited by Tom Regan Prentice Hall, 1989.

Singer, P. *Animal Liberation*. Harper Perennial Modern Classics, 1990.

Singer, P. "Experiments on Animals." *British Medical Journal* 299 (1989): 1238–39.

Smith, R.K.M. *International Human Rights*. 3rd edn. Oxford University Press (USA), 2007.

Smith, W.J. "When Animals Sue." *National Review Online*, March 3, 2010, http://article.nationalreview.com/426742/when-animals-sue/wesley-j-smith.

SPCA New Zealand. "Battery Cages—Statistics." http://rnzspca. org.nz/battery-cages-statistics-2.

Soper, P. "Judge White and the Exercise of Judicial Power: Why Theories of Law Have Little or Nothing to Do with Judicial Restraint." *University Colorado Law Review* 74 (2003): 1379–88.

Stahle, G. "Swedes Do It Better." www.opendemocracy.net/ecology-foodwithout-frontiers/article_428.jsp.

The Statesman. "Indian Tigers Face Poaching Threat from China." *Statesman*, February 25, 2010, 2010 WLNR 4008891.

Steele, M.A., et al. "Cache Protection Strategies of a Scatter-Hoardimg Rodent: Do Tree Squirrels Engage in Behavioural Deception?." *Animal Behaviour* 75 (2007): 705–14.

Steene, B. "Astrid Lindgren's Legacy." www.opendemocracy.net/article/arts_culture/astr_lindgren_legacy.

Stephens, A. "Animal Rights Slam EU Testing Ban." http://edition.cnn.com/2002/WORLD/europe/11/07/eu.cosmetics/.

Stevenson, P. "The World Trade Organization Rules: A Legal Analysis of Their Adverse Impact on Animal Welfare." *Animal Law* 8 (2002): 107–41.

Strickland, R. "Implementing the National Policy of Understanding, Preserving, and Safeguarding the Heritage of Indian Peoples and Native Hawaiians: Human Rights, Sacred Objects, and Cultural Patrimony." *Arizona State Law Journal* 24 (1992): 175–91.

Sutton, J. "Orca Kills Trainer at Flora's SeaWorld." www.reuters.com/article/USTRE61N6GS20100225.

Sztybel, D. "The Canadian Council on Animal Care's Code of Ethics: A Critical Evaluation. Medical Research Modernization Committee." http://www.mrmcmed.org/DavidSztybel.html.Taylor, K., et al. "Estimates for Worldwide Laboratory Animal Use in 2005." *Alternatives to Laboratory Animals* 36 (2008): 327–42.

ThePoultrySite. "International Egg and Poultry Review." www.thepoultrysite.com/poultrynews/17039/international-egg-and-poultry-review.

Thomas, E.M. "Playing Chicken at the WTO: Defending an Animal Welfare-Based Trade Restriction under GATT's Moral Exception." *Boston College Environmental Affairs Law Review* 34 (2007): 605–37.

Uncaged. "Animal Experimentation—The Facts." www.uncaged.co.uk/vivisect.htm.

United Kingdom Parliament, Select Committee on the European Union. "10th Report of Session 2007–08: The Treaty of Lisbon: An Impact Assessment Vols I–II." www.publications.parliament.uk/pa/ld200708/ldselect/ldeucom/62/62ii.pdf, 2008.

United Kingdom Secretary of State. "Guidance on the Operation of the Animals (Scientific Procedures) Act 1986" (2000).

University of Alabama, Birmingham, Department of Psychology. "Dr. Edward Taub." www.psy.uab.edu/taub.htm.

U.S. Congress. "Office of Technology Assessment, Alternatives to Animal Use in Research, Testing, and Education." http://govinfo.library.unt.edu/ota/Ota_3/DATA/1986/8601.PDF, 1986.

United States Department of Agriculture Economic Research Service. "Livestock, Dairy, and Poultry Outlook: Tables." http://www.ers.usda.gov/publications/ldp/LDPTables.htm.

United States Department of Agriculture. "Animal Care Annual Report of Activities Fiscal Year 2007" (2008).

United States Department of Agriculture Foreign Agricultural Service. "Animal Welfare Labeling—European Commission Report No. E49084" (2009).

United States Department of Agriculture Foreign Agricultural Service. "Italy Food and Agricultural Import Regulations and Standards Country Report No. IT4014" (2004).

United States Department of Agriculture Office of Inspector General-Investigations. "Bad Newz Kennels Smithfield, Virginia. File number: HY-3330-0018." August 28, 2008.

"USDA: Vick Found Dogfighting 'Funny to Watch.'" http://nbcsports.msnbc.com//27850103/.

US Fish &Wildlife Service. "International Protocols, Treaties and Conventions." www.fws.gov/policy/530fw2.pdf, 2009.

US Foreign Policy Encyclopedia. "Treaties." www.answers.com/topic/treaty.

The Valentine Cookbook. "Gram's Soltz (Sultz) and Liver Dumplings." www.valentine-design.com/cookbook/2007/08/grams-soltz-sultz-and-liver-dumplings.html.

Vauclair, J. "Categorization and Conceptual Behavior in Nonhuman Primates." In *The Cognitive Animal*, edited by M. Bekoff. MIT Press, 2002.

V.I.N. "Does Animal Testing Help Human Medicine? 33 Facts to be Considered." *VIN Newsletter* no. 4.

Visalberghi, E. "Insight from Capuchin Monkey Studies: Ingredients of, Recipes for, and Flaws in Capuchins' Success." In *The Cognitive Animal*, edited by M. Bekoff. MIT Press, 2002.

Wabnitz, C., et al. "From Ocean to Aquarium: The Global Trade in Marine Ornamental Species." UNEP World Conservation Monitoring Centre, 2003.

Walker, M. "Killer Whales: What to do with Captive Orcas?." http://news.bbc.co.uk/earth/hi/earth_news/newsid_8536000/8536184.stm.

Wasserman, H.A. "General Signs." In *The Cognitive Animal*, edited by M. Bekoff. MIT Press, 2002.

Watson, R. *Cogito, Ergo Sum*. David R. Godine, 2002.

Webster's Universal Encyclopedic Dictionary. "Cognition." Barnes & Noble Books, 2002.

Weir, A.A.S., et al. "Shaping of Hooks in New Caledonian Crows." *Science* 297, no. 5583 (2002): 981.

Whiten, A. "From the Field to the Laboratory and Back Again: Culture and 'Social Mind' in Primates." In *The Cognitive Animal*, edited by M. Bekoff. MIT Press, 2002.

Wijgerde, T. "Coral Reproduction—Part I: Biology." *Coral Science* (2009).
Wilford, J.N. "The Transforming Leap, from Four Legs to Two." In *The Science Times Book of Fossils and Evolution*, edited by Nicholas Wade. The Lyons Press, 1998.
Winslow, A.P. "Sacred Standards: Honoring the Establishment Clause in Protecting Native American Sacred Sites." *Arizona Law Review* 38 (1996): 1291–1343.
Wise, S.M. *Rattling the Cage*. Perseus Publishing, 2001.
World Radio Switzerland. "Voters Reject Pension Cuts, Animal Lawyers." http://worldradio.ch/wrs/news/switzerland/sunday-march-7-vote-results.shtml?18205.
Organisation for Animal Health OIE, *International Standards*, *http://www.oie.int/international-standard-setting/overview/.*
World Organisation for Animal Health (OIE). "The OIE's Objectives and Achievements in Animal Welfare." www.oie.int/eng/bien_etre/en_introduction.htm.
World Organisation for Animal Health (OIE). "Terrestrial Animal Health Code 2009" (2009).
World Trade Organization. "WTO Disputes Reach 400 Mark." November 6, 2009.
World Trade Organization Secretariat. *Guide to the Uruguay Round Agreements*. Kluwer Law International, 1999.
"240 WTO Protest Cases are Dropped." *Los Angeles Times*, January 5, 2000, section A4.
Wyler, L.S. & P.A. Sheikh. "Report for Congress: Illegal Trade in Wildlife: Threats and U.S. Policy. Congressional Research Service" (2008).
Yarri, D. *The Ethics of Animal Experimentation*. An American Academy of Religion Book, 2005.
Young, S. "Contemporary Issues of the Convention on International Trade in Endangered Species of Wild Fauna and Flora (CITES) and the Debate over Sustainable Use." *Colorado Journal International Environmental Law & Policy* 14 (2003): 167–89.
Youth Science Canada. "Use of Animals in Research." www.ysf.ca/files/PDF/governance/policy/en/4.1.2_Animals.pdf.
Zurlo, J., et al. "The Three R's: The Way Forward." *Environmental Health Perspectives* 104, no. 8 (1996): 878–880.

Table of Authorities

Cases

Balakrishnan et al. v. Union of India, No. 155/1999 (Kerala H.C. June 6, 2000) (India), 204
Taub v. State, 463 A.2d 819, 819–22 (Md. 1983) (USA), 118

World Trade Organization Cases

Argentina-Measures Affecting Imports of Footwear, Textiles, Apparel, and Other Items, WT/DS56/R (November 25, 1997) (Panel Report), 242
Canada Foreign Investment Review Act, L/5504-30S/140 (adopted February 7, 1984) (Panel Report), 249
European Communities—Measures Affecting Asbestos and Asbestos-Containing Products, WT/DS135/AB/R (March 12, 2001) (Appellate Body Report), 245
Japan—Taxes on Alcoholic Beverages, WT/DS8/AB/R (October 4, 1996) (Appellate Body Report), 245
Korea—Measures Affecting Imports of Fresh, Chilled and Frozen Beef, WT/DS161/AB/R, WT/DS169/AB/ (December 11, 2000) (Appellate Body Report), 250
United States—Import Prohibition of Certain Shrimp and Shrimp Products, WT/DS58/AB/R (October 12, 1998) (Appellate Body Report), 261
United States—Restrictions on Imports of Tuna, DS29/R (June 16, 1994) (Panel Report), 251
United States—Restrictions on Imports of Tuna, DS21/R—39S/155 (September 3, 1991) (Panel Report), 251
United States—Standards for Reformulated and Conventional Gasoline, WT/DS2/AB/R (May 20, 1996) (Appellate Body Report), 262

Constitutional Provisions

Statutes

Treaties

Government Endorsed Publications

Table of European Union Treaties and Secondary Legislative Acts

Conventions

Decisions

Directives

Regulations

Proposed Legislation

Treaties

Index

F

G

GLOBAL TRADE LAW SERIES

1. Emmanuel T. Laryea, *Paperless Trade: Opportunities, Challenges and Solutions,* 2002 (ISBN 90-411-9897-0).
2. Xiang Gao, *The Fraud Rule in the Law of Letters of Credit: A Comparative Study,* 2002 (ISBN 90-411-9898-9).
3. Yuwa Wei, *Comparative Corporate Governance: A Chinese Perspective,* 2003 (ISBN 90-411-9908-X).
4. Ross P. Buckley (ed.), *The WTO and the Doha Round: The Changing Face of World Trade,* 2003 (ISBN 90-411-9947-0).
5. Bradley J. Condon, Joyce C. Sadka, Tapen Sinha (eds), *Insurance Regulation in North America: Integrating American, Canadian and Mexican Markets,* 2003 (ISBN 90-411-2226-5).
6. Jan Hoogmartens, *EC Trade Law Following China's Accession to the WTO,* 2004 (ISBN 90-411-2301-6).
7. Yang Guohua, Bryan Mercurio, Li Yongjie, *WTO Dispute Settlement Understanding: A Detailed Interpretation,* 2005 (ISBN 90-411-2361-X).
8. Jan Job de Vries Robbe´, Paul U. Ali, *Securitisation of Derivatives and Alternative Asset Classes, Yearbook,* 2005 (ISBN 90-411-2375-X).
9. Markus W. Gehring, Marie-Claire Cordonier Segger, *Sustainable Development in World Trade Law,* 2005 (ISBN 90-411-2366-0).
10. Yann Aubin, Arnaud Idiart. *Export Control Law and Regulations Handbook: A Practical Guide to Military and Dual-Use Goods Trade Restrictions and Compliance,* 2007 (ISBN 90-411-2601-5).
11. Henry Kibet Mutai, *Compliance with International Trade Obligations: The Common Market for Eastern and Southern Africa,* 2007 (ISBN 978-90-411-2664-1).
12. Yong-Shik Lee, *Economic Development through World Trade: A Developing World Perspective,* 2007 (ISBN 978-90-411-2681-8).
13. Yanning Yu, *Circumvention and Anti-Circumvention Measures: The Impact on Anti-Dumping Practice in International Trade,* 2007 (ISBN 978-90-411-2686-3).
14. Ross Buckley, Vai Io Lo, Laurence Boulle, *Challenges to Multilateral Trade: The Impact of Bilateral, Preferential and Regional Agreements,* 2008 (ISBN 978-90-411-2711-2).
15. K.D. Raju, *World Trade Organization Agreement on Anti-dumping: A GATT/WTO and Indian Jurisprudence,* 2008 (ISBN 978-90-411-2780-8).
16. Xiaochen Wu, *Anti-dumping Law and Practice in China,* 2008 (ISBN 978-90-411-2790-7).
17. Amin Alavi, *Legalization of Development in the WTO: Between Law and Politics,* 2008 (ISBN 978-90-411-2795-2).
18. Henrik Andersen, *EU Dumping Determinations and WTO Law,* 2009 (ISBN 978-90-411-2827-0).

19. Sherzod Shadikhodjaev, *Retaliation in the WTO Dispute Settlement System,* 2009 (ISBN 978-90-411-2811-9).
20. Yi Shin Tang, *The International Trade Policy for Technology Transfers: Legal and Economic Dilemmas on Multilateralism versus Bilateralism,* 2009 (ISBN 978-90-411-2825-6).
21. Reem Anwar Ahmed Raslan, *Antidumping: A Developing Country Perspective,* 2009 (ISBN 978-90-411-3128-7).
22. Pietro Poretti, *The Regulation of Subsidies within the General Agreement on Trade in Services of the WTO: Problems and Prospects,* 2009 (ISBN 978-90-411-3162-1).
23. Esther Lam, *China and the WTO: A Long March towards the Rule of Law,* 2009 (ISBN 978-90-411-3144-7).
24. Jorge Alberto Huerta Goldman, *Mexico in the WTO and NAFTA: Litigating International Trade Disputes,* 2009 (ISBN 978-90-411-3169-0).
25. Laurence Boulle, *The Law of Globalization: An Introduction,* 2009 (ISBN 978-90-411-2828-7).
26. Daniel Lovric, *Deference to the Legislature in WTO Challenges to Legislation,* 2010 (ISBN 978-90-411-3145-4).
27. Gregory W. Bowman, Nick Covelli, David A. Gantz, Ihn Ho Uhm, *Trade Remedies in North America,* 2010 (ISBN 978-90-411-2840-9).
28. Madalina Diaconu, *International Trade in Gambling Services,* 2010 (ISBN 978-90-411-3248-2).
29. Mohamed Ramadan Hassanien, *United States Bilateral Free Trade Agreements: Consistencies or Conflicts with Norms in the Middle East?,* 2010 (ISBN 978-90-411-3281-9).
30. Markus W Gehring, Marie-Claire Cordonier Segger, Andrew Newcombe, *Sustainable Development in World Investment Law,* 2010 (ISBN 978-90-411-3166-9).
31. Nellie Munin, *Legal Guide to GATS,* 2010 (ISBN 978-90-411-2824-9).
32. Thomas G. Kelch, *Globalization and Animal Law: Comparative Law, International Law and International Trade,* 2011 (ISBN 978-90-411-3338-0).